INTERNATIONAL POLITICS

Seventh Edition

INTERNATIONAL POLITICS
A Framework for Analysis

K. J. Holsti
University of British Columbia

PRENTICE HALL, Englewood Cliffs, New Jersey 07632

Library of Congress Cataloging-in-Publication Data

HOLSTI, K. J. (KALEVI JAAKKO)
    International politics: a framework for analysis / K. J. Holsti.—
7th ed.
        p.   cm.
    Includes bibliographical references and index.
    ISBN   0-13-097775-6
    1. International relations.   I. Title.
JX1305.H6 1995
327—dc20   94-6777
                    CIP

Editorial/production supervision
    and interior design: **Joan E. Foley**
Assistant editor: **Jennie Katsaros**
Editorial assistant: **Nicole Signoretti**
Copy editor: **Nancy Savio-Marcello**
Cover designer: **Wendy Alling Judy**
Buyer: **Bob Anderson**

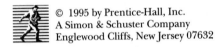 © 1995 by Prentice-Hall, Inc.
A Simon & Schuster Company
Englewood Cliffs, New Jersey 07632

Printed in the United States of America
10   9   8   7   6   5   4   3

ISBN   0-13-097775-6

Prentice-Hall International (UK) Limited, *London*
Prentice-Hall of Australia Pty. Limited, *Sydney*
Prentice-Hall Canada Inc., *Toronto*
Prentice-Hall Hispanoamericana, S.A., *Mexico*
Prentice-Hall of India Private Limited, *New Delhi*
Prentice-Hall of Japan, Inc., *Tokyo*
Simon & Schuster Asia Pte. Ltd., *Singapore*
Editora Prentice-Hall do Brasil, Ltda., *Rio de Janeiro*

CONTENTS

PART IV
EXPLAINING FOREIGN POLICIES

---

11   Explanations of Foreign Policy   250

12   Law and World Opinion in Explanations of Foreign Policy   289

13   Ethics in Explanations of Foreign Policy   309

PART V
MAJOR FORMS OF INTERACTION BETWEEN STATES

Preface

Momentous events occurred in 1989 when the Communist regimes of east Europe collapsed, and the Soviet government under Mikhail Gorbachev instituted major domestic and foreign policy reforms. Many predicted that with the end of the Cold War, the world was entering a new era of a new order. Many of the tension-producing policies of the United States and the Soviet Union were being changed. Rivalry in the Third World diminished, significant arms-control agreements were signed, and conflicts that had dragged on for years were suddenly resolved.

But within months the heady expectations became muted, as Iraq invaded Kuwait on August 2, 1990. The months of 1991 saw yet more war—in Iraq, the former Yugoslavia, and in some of the former republics of the Soviet Union. If we have indeed entered a new era, it is not one in which international conflict will be absent. Nor will there be an absence of significant collaboration between governments. In short, many of the patterns of the past will continue into the future.

This study does not describe current affairs. Rather, it examines the recurrent activities and processes that characterize international politics in the twentieth and early twenty-first centuries. We are not concerned with who said what to whom during a particular state visit, but what government leaders *typically* do in their foreign relations. To the extent that current problems are discussed, they serve as examples and illustrations of broader generalizations.

The study poses three main—and enduring—questions about the activities of states in the international environment: (1) What are the contexts in which states operate, and how do those contexts constrain and influence the choices and policies of government? (2) What do states typically seek to achieve through relations with others, and how do they go about it? (3) How do we explain policies; that is, what factors or considerations underlie choices? The outcomes of those choices, when aggregated, produce *patterns* of relationships. The two most common are conflict and cooperation. (4) In what ways do we describe the main characteristics of those patterns? The book is thus divided, following an introductory chapter, into four main parts: contexts, policies, explanations, and patterns of interaction.

If the book succeeds in doing what it intends, the reader will have a framework within which to place individual events as they unfold and are reported in the media. While those events may have unique characteristics, many will demonstrate the recurring aspects of international politics. The daily fare of the media will then be seen as examples of more general processes that typically take place in the world. For example, we can compare the actions of the United Nations in dealing with Iraq's aggression against Kuwait with the methods it employed in previous international crises. Or we can learn how governments came together to fashion standards for reducing the emission of carbon dioxide, not as a single tale, but as an example of the more general forces that are compelling governments to cooperate in order to deal with environmental problems. In brief, we are concerned with classes of phenomena, recurrences, patterns, and typical behavior. These represent the forests of international politics. For descriptions of the individual trees, the reader must go no further than the daily newspaper or the evening news on radio and television.

The seventh edition has undergone substantial rewriting. The alterations reflect less the events of the last few years than the changing ways we look at international politics. Theoretical work, rather than the reporting of daily events, increases understanding. It also brings some order (and sometimes distortions) to a messy world. This study is a representation of certain aspects of reality; it is not to be confused with the reality itself. No single volume can hope to describe and explain all we want to know about international politics. This study raises as many questions as it seeks to answer. It is designed to encourage readers to think about processes and issues, not just to memorize facts.

The sections toward the end of each chapter, "Questions for Study, Analysis, and Discussion," bring out the main points in the preceding pages. They also raise issues for which there are no answers in the text, but which pose important intellectual, ethical, and policy problems. Readers are invited to think about them and, if possible, to use them as a basis of group discussions.

The bibliographies at the end of each chapter list current and classic works that relate to the main topics. They are designed for those who wish to do further research or reading in any of the areas covered. These bibliographies necessarily have to be selective, but I have included a few sources in languages other than English.

I am grateful to the reviewers of the seventh edition: Joseph Lepgold, Georgetown University; Stafford T. Thomas, California State University, Chico; Herbert K. Tillema, University of Missouri—Columbia; Nikolaos A. Stravrou, Howard University. They made many important criticisms and suggestions, many of which are incorporated in the new text.

K. J. Holsti
Vancouver, British Columbia

INTERNATIONAL POLITICS

Chapter

1

Approaches to the Study of International Politics

After the armies of Imperial Germany invaded Belgium in August 1914, launching one of the most destructive and futile armed conflicts in history, Prince von Bülow asked the German chancellor why all the diplomatic steps taken to avoid the war had failed. "At last I (Bülow) said to him: 'Well, tell me, at least, how it all happened.' He raised his long, thin arms to heaven and answered in a dull, exhausted voice: 'Oh—if I only knew.'"[1] On December 8, 1941, Prince Konoe, a former prime minister of Japan, heard on the radio of the attack on Pearl Harbor. While most Japanese were revelling in the news of the successful attack, Konoe was despondent. A colleague reports that when he met Konoe, the latter's voice was filled with dread and sadness. "It is a terrible thing that has happened. I know that a tragic defeat awaits us at the end. I can feel it. Our luck will not last more than two or three months at best."[2]

Although those events were separated by time and location, the behavior of the two statesmen was similar. Both men had been involved in international crises, and both lamented the outcome, which was war.

Taking a longer-range perspective, other historical parallels that transcend time, place, and personalities can be noted. In the eighth century B.C., the princes of newly formed states in China successfully challenged the power and authority

---

[1]Prince Bernhard von Bülow, *Memoirs of Prince von Bülow* (Boston: Little, Brown, 1932), Vol. 3, p. 166.
[2]Yoshitake Oka, *Konoe Fumimaro: A Political Biography,* trans. Shumpei Okamoto and Patricia Murray (Tokyo: University of Tokyo Press, 1983), p. 161.

of the Chinese emperor, thereby putting an end to the Chinese feudal order. Similarly, in 1648, European diplomats and princes congregated in Westphalia to sign a peace treaty ending the Thirty Years' War. They also declared that henceforth the leader of the Holy Roman Empire could no longer extend its dominion into the territories of princes and sovereigns and that the latter were in no way obliged to respond to the directives of the emperor. This act symbolized the emergence of the modern European state system, replacing the feudal political order that, as in China, had at least theoretically placed an emperor as head, with power radiating down through such lesser political entities as free cities, duchies, and developing dynastic territories.

Every historical occurrence is, of course, unique; the situations in which statesmen construct alliances, decide to go to war, declare independence, or make peace all are different. Yet, when historical phenomena are analyzed from a certain level of abstraction—not just as facts for their own sake—these situations have many common properties. The events the student of international politics attempts to understand may be unique, but, as the cases cited above suggest, they are also comparable. The German chancellor and Konoe had to make many of the same kinds of calculations before acting, and both acted knowing that their decisions could easily lead to disaster. Both the Chinese princes and the European sovereigns 2,000 years later were determined to put an end to political orders in which emperors could intervene in subordinates' affairs and territories. Regardless of historical and geographical context, policy makers for different types of political units, whether tribes, city-states, empires, or modern states, have attempted to achieve objectives or defend their interests by fundamentally similar techniques, of which the use of force and the construction of alliances are only the most obvious examples.

If Thucydides, Frederick the Great, or Louis XIV were to return to life at the end of the twentieth century, they would no doubt be astounded by the immense changes in technology, culture, and the lives of average citizens. They would not be familiar with such international institutions as the United Nations, the International Court of Justice, or multinational corporations; nor would they understand immediately the great ideological conflicts of the twentieth century or comprehend the destructive capacity of nuclear weapons. But they would recognize the types of threats and rewards modern governments make in attempting to achieve their objectives, the techniques of diplomatic bargaining, and the concern governments have for their international prestige. Certainly they would find little new in the attempts of some states to conclude mutually satisfying military alliances or to remain uninvolved in the quarrels of the great powers.

While newspaper accounts of current affairs might leave the impression that events are essentially chaotic, unprecedented, and incomparable, the mind seeks recurrence, patterns, and comparisons, the bases of understanding. The reader is wading through these pages presumably because he or she is not satisfied that reading newspaper headlines, even on a regular basis, "explains" adequately what is going on in the world today. To learn means to go beyond the obvious, to move from knowledge of the discrete to knowledge of the general, to make connections, and to understand concepts. But the very act of understanding requires us to simplify realities and to reduce complexities.

Let us use an analogy from baseball. If I know nothing about the rules and rituals of the game, I would see it as a collection of men or women running around, some throwing a ball, others swinging a stick. I could describe the game in great detail: how the uniforms looked, the different kinds of mitts, which players ran the fastest, and who hit the ball the longest. I would have great detail, but I would not really understand what all the detail amounted to.

Armed with appropriate intellectual tools—knowledge of the rules, purposes, and procedures of the game—I would have much greater understanding; the whole enterprise would "make sense" to me, and I could convey that sense to anyone else with whom I could converse in a common language. But is it sufficient to have knowledge of a single game? It might be more important to understand the game, or to give it meaning, within a larger context. What consequences did the outcome of the game have on a pennant race? What did the game tell me about the fortunes of key players? How did the performance of the teams match those of other teams I have seen?

Others might ask even broader questions. What role does baseball play in North American or Japanese culture? Is the game a form of entertainment, or is it a sport? Has the game deteriorated or improved over the years? Answers would require generalizations based on knowledge of not just a single game, but of many games played over the years. And so it is with the student of international politics. He or she is not interested in lengthy descriptions of individual acts or events. We need to embed those events in a larger context of questions and problems. It is fine to have knowledge of the battles and campaigns of a war. But of more significance are questions about the "meaning" of that war for international relations in general. We might thus see the war as an *example* of broader or more general phenomena. We could ask, for example, why deterrence failed to prevent the war; are the issues over which the war was fought typical of many international conflicts, or are they unique and new? What perceptions and misperceptions helped drive the spiral of conflict acts to the point that one of the parties decided to use force? Does the war indicate anything about trends in the incidence of war in the international system?

It is thus a bias of social scientists to assume the existence of regular patterns of behavior, to explain these in terms of specified variables,[3] and to use historical data

---

[3]A *variable* can be defined as any phenomenon or condition, a change in which produces a change in another phenomenon or condition. In the physical realm, for example, variations in temperature cause changes in the properties of water. We know from observation that when the temperature goes below a certain point, all other conditions being held constant, water freezes. There is an obvious functional relationship between the two variables, temperature and the state of the water. In the social sciences, relationships between variables may be much more difficult to identify and measure because (1) many variables inducing change may be involved simultaneously; and (2) it may be impossible to hold all other conditions constant while observation or experimentation is taking place. For example, we may wish to examine the conditions associated with outbreak of war. We could see if there is some type of relationship between the incidence of war and spending on armaments. If through a perusal of historical data we found a high correlation between variations in expenditures on armaments (independent variable) and incidence of war (dependent variable), we could say that the two variables are somehow associated. It would still remain for us to define the exact nature of the relationship and investigate other types of variables, such as perceptions of threat or degree of commitment to objectives, that may be involved in the outbreak of war. We can say with confidence that a lowering of temperature causes a change in the state of water, but we could not claim with certainty that rising armaments budgets cause wars, since so many other factors may be involved.

primarily to elucidate or illustrate the generalizations they are attempting to make. Students of international politics try to understand and explain the causes and nature of war, imperialism, escalation, crisis, or alliance without having to describe every war, imperialist, escalation, crisis, or alliance in history. A valid generalization is one that can be used to describe all events of a given class. Any general statement about these phenomena must be based, of course, on accurate historical observation; but the social scientist is still concerned primarily with classes or types of phenomena rather than with the particular details of each illustration. He or she is interested in the German chancellor in 1914 and the former Japanese prime minister as examples of decision making in crisis situations. The historian is interested in them as individuals.

What sorts of questions would the examples of Prince von Bülow and Prince Konoe suggest? What *general* problems of international politics might a study of their behavior illuminate? A number come to mind. How are foreign policy decisions in crisis situations arrived at? How do "images," stereotypes, and ideologies affect policy makers' perceptions of reality and, consequently, their choices among alternative courses of action? How do policy makers typically act and react in periods of great stress, in crisis situations? How do trust and suspicion affect the propensity of governments to enter into cooperative ventures? How does one construct an effective deterrent, one that prevents rather than encourages war? How do the personal ethical values of policy makers enter into the development of bargaining strategies or decisions to use armed force?

Researchers have been exploring these and many other kinds of generic problems in international politics. They seek to discover the general sources of classes of behavior or events. In some cases, results have been impressive. For example, psychological experiments and historical case studies suggest that in times of crisis and high tension, policy makers tend to perceive and consider fewer alternative courses of action than when they are not under stress. On a broader scale, we can predict that alliances tend to disintegrate if their members cease to perceive a common adversary. And recent research has found that the initiator of a serious international dispute has about a 60 percent probability of winning the conflict; even minor powers have a better than even chance of prevailing.

Notice that these statements are not laws; they do not state that in the next international crisis, Prime Minister X will perceive only one course of action open to him, that NATO will dissolve next year, or that the next international conflict will be won by the initiator. They are, rather, *probability* or *tendency* statements about *classes* of events. Exceptions can and will occur, but the research has established that, in probability terms, the dependent variable (perception of fewer alternatives, disintegration of alliances, or outcome of conflict) can be predicted from knowledge of the state of the independent variable (level of tension or stress, degree of perception of a common enemy, or type of conflict initiator).

The Use of Organizing Devices

Historians use the organizing devices of time, place, and subject mater (for instance, American policies during the Bosnian crisis, 1991 to 1994) as a means of helping them select relevant data, interrelate the data, and determine the boundaries of their topic. The narrative is usually organized in terms of time sequences.

Social scientists use more abstract organizing devices because they are interested in generic phenomena and processes that transcend time, place, and personality. To capture the essential characteristics of an entire international system, for example, requires a great deal of abstraction. When we view the world, we are looking through different sets of lenses. The lenses are the organizing concepts. If we think international politics are characterized essentially by power, conflict, and war, we are led to examine certain phenomena such as security, deterrence, aggression, ideology, and the like. If, in contrast, we think the world is essentially a benign place, then we are likely to look for evidence of international cooperation, humanitarian good works, the significance of international law, and so forth. We acknowledge that wars take place, but we think these are deviations from the norm of general harmony between societies and states.

To illustrate the importance of organizing devices, we can outline five different "models" of the contemporary international system. Notice that no single one of them is "real" while the others are false. What they demonstrate, rather, is the different perspectives of the observer—the different theoretical lenses through which they observe the world, and the different facts and data they use to describe that world. Which model do you believe best represents the world as you know it today? Or do all the models contain important truths? If we have to choose between them, what kinds of evidence would be necessary to make one of them more persuasive?

Realism

The realist tradition goes back many centuries. It has been the predominant way of characterizing international politics throughout most of the eighteenth, nineteenth, and twentieth centuries. Political thinkers who tried to generalize about the relations between states include such notables as Thucydides, Machiavelli, Hobbes, Rousseau, and, more recently, Hans J. Morgenthau.

Realists start with the critical proposition that the world is made up of states that exist in an environment of anarchy. Anarchy is not to be confused with chaos; quite the contrary. Anarchy may be consistent with order, stability, and regulated forms of interaction between independent units. For international relationships, anarchy means that ultimately states can rely only upon themselves for their security and other purposes. There is no superordinate authority that can manage the relations between sovereigns.

In international relations, however, anarchy is often equated with insecurity, fear, and war. Why? According to Rousseau, states must arm themselves to prepare for the contingency that some neighbor someday may harbor aggressive designs and attack. But in the process of a state accumulating arms for its insurance, other states will interpret these actions as potential threats to their own security. This process of action and reaction is called the *security dilemma*: the means by which one state provides for its security creates insecurity for others.

But why not cooperate instead of compete? Rousseau answers this question with a parable. Seven primitive men, armed with spears, decide that they would have a better chance of catching a stag were they to encircle the animal. They make the rational calculation that if they cooperate, they have an 80 percent chance of killing the animal, although they would then have to divide it among themselves, getting about a 15 percent share each. This is a better situation than if each hunter acts independently. Acting on his own, a hunter would have perhaps only a 5 percent chance of killing the stag, although were he to succeed, he would keep 100 percent of the game.

Through this scenario, Rousseau shows why it is rational to collaborate. Everyone gains. But why does the system fall apart? Because in the hunting situation, a hare comes within easy range of one of the hunters. He calculates that he has about a perfect chance of spearing the hare. In so doing, however, the noise he makes will drive off the stag, and the other hunters will go home hungry. Our lone hunter makes the swift calculation that he would rather have the absolute certainty of the hare than an 80 percent chance of getting 15 percent of a stag. Here, Rousseau shows that in fact it is rational to go for the short-term reward. In the hunting situation, all the participants know that at any time any one of them may defect for a hare or some other animal. For this reason, there is mistrust and the collaborative enterprise falls apart.

And so it is in international relationships. All states stand to gain—to maximize rewards—through collaboration. But since the system of anarchy compels each prince (the hunter) to choose short-term gains, the foundations of collaboration are destroyed, and the potential rewards of joint action are replaced by mistrust, defection, and war.

For the realist, then, the great issues of international politics have to do with questions of security, war, and peace. The reality of diplomacy is that the gains of one state are at the expense of others, and no state can afford to rely on others for its security and welfare. There may be international laws and institutions, but in the crunch, every state will look out for itself. States compete with each other for limited goods: territory, status, prestige, access to raw materials and markets, and control over strategic points, to mention a few. Bonds of sympathy or ideological affinity will not overcome the necessity of seeking advantages against others, and the possibility of having to rely on force to attain or defend them—just as the hunter chose to kill the hare for his own short-run advantage.

Is this pessimistic view of international politics merely a theoretical construct? The history of international relations since the days of the Westphalia treaties would provide overwhelming evidence that it is a reasonably accurate depiction of the dynamics of relations between states in an environment of anarchy. Since 1648 there have been nearly 200 wars, countless crises, and several attempts to create universal empires and hegemonic systems. The Cold War and the present situation in Bosnia and Croatia provide more contemporary evidence. These relations are characterized by substantial insecurity, the perceived need to build up arms for purposes of deterrence, the primacy of security issues in mutual relations, and the assumption that all the adversary's moves are taken for malevolent purposes. While alliances may increase security, ultimately one has to have sufficient armed forces to act alone if necessary. As for the adversary's actions, any gain for it represents a net loss to one's own national security. The reader will have no difficulty finding numerous illustrations that confirm the realists' view of international relations.

A Society of States

Hugo Grotius was an early seventeenth-century jurist who wrote about the early forms of international law. While states were at that time in the formative stages, he made an analogy between the position and conditions of states among one another, and those of individuals within a society. There is, to be sure, international anarchy, but there are also all sorts of bonds and institutions between individual states. There is, in fact, a "society of states," a group of similar actors who regulate their mutual relations through institutions such as diplomacy and trade, and who understand that armed force should be used only for purposes of self-defense, righting an injury, or for upholding the fundamental contours of the states system and its norms and laws.

One traditional mechanism for sustaining the society of states is the balance of power. As a guide to policy, the balance is simply a mechanism by which states collaborate to maintain their independence against threats by those who would seek hegemony or the creation of a world empire. Thus in the early 1700s, the states of Europe collaborated in a war against Louis XIV, who was commonly thought to have designs to create a super-Bourbon state encompassing Spain and France and their extensive overseas empires. Similarly, in 1813 the states of Europe formed the grand coalition that defeated Napoleon, whose plans were to replace the states system with a Paris-centered empire. And again in 1939, the free states of Europe, plus the Commonwealth countries and the United States, joined forces to defeat Hitler's great project for a "Thousand-Year Reich" that would form the center of a German-dominated "New Order." These were all examples of the balance of power in operation. The balance is not intended to prevent war; its purpose is to safeguard the sovereignty and independence of states—the society of states—that are threatened by those who wish to destroy the states system and put some other form of centralized, imperial control in its place.

In addition to the use of force for the community interest, there are many elements of order in the society of states. These include international law, diplomacy, and numerous "rules of the game" that help to provide the states with the flavor of a club. The club of states has admission rules (the rules governing the recognition of states or their admission to international organizations), rules of proper conduct (as, for example, those in the United Nations charter specifying under what circumstances armed force can be used), and rules and procedures for handling international conflicts. There is, then, governance without government, order in a system of anarchy, and regularized procedures for handling various problems. War occurs because of the varying appetites of individual rulers and their states, but the members of the society will always come together to protect their independence and autonomy.

As with the realists, evidence to support this depiction of the essential characteristics of international politics is not difficult to locate. We do have international organizations that set standards and norms of conduct, and provide a variety of services and procedures for handling international conflicts. Since 1648, there have been at least three and perhaps more successful operations of the balance of power against those who sought to destroy the states system. States that refuse to conduct their relations with at least a modest recognition of the rules of the game are excluded from the club. Until the 1970s, for example, the United States insisted that the Communist mainland could not take the seat of China in the United Nations because it was an aggressor state. The United States orchestrated the international ostracism of a government that publicly denounced all the rules of the "bourgeois" states system. The reaction had been the same during the early years of the Bolshevik regime in Russia, and was repeated in the case of South Africa. There are "pariah" states, countries represented by regimes that do not accept some of the fundamental rules of the game. More recently we have seen the Ayatollah Khomeini's Iran and Colonel Khadaffi's Libya ostracized by a number of states for conduct considered inappropriate. All members of the United Nations voted to condemn the Iranian revolutionary government when it did nothing to prevent the holding hostage of the American embassy staff in Teheran. This was a fundamental violation of the elementary rules of diplomatic immunity, and all governments, regardless of their ideological and other differences, joined together to uphold the sanctity of the rule.

The Pluralist-Interdependence Model

The two previous models of international politics focus upon the activities of states. They also agree that the main problems confronting states are security, peace, and order. International politics constitutes a distinct realm of activity, largely divorced from processes such as trade and other forms of communication between societies. The pluralist-interdependence model, in contrast, embeds political problems in the larger social—and particularly economic—setting in which they take place. That model's proponents would deny that the analyst can abstract from a complex web of interrelationships between societies only their political-security aspects. In the modern global system, all policy sectors are intertwined and affect each other.

Who are the main actors in this perspective? States are important, for they set the rules of the economic, communications, technology, and other games that occur simultaneously. But by themselves, they do not set the international agenda, nor can they make decisions as if removed from the interests, values, and aspirations of millions of business firms, banks, shipping companies, political parties, citizens' groups, and the like. It is these nonstate actors that initially raise items to the agenda. These nonstate actors create all sorts of transnational coalitions that circumvent the policies of any individual state. They act as international pressure groups, they publicize problems, and they propose solutions to them. The power of publicity and scientific, technical, economic knowledge largely replace the power of guns and armies. Even in major international forums, such as the United Nations, nongovernmental groups have access to delegates, provide all sorts of information, and lobby for their preferred solutions to a variety of international problems, ranging from the saving of threatened animal species to the treatment of refugees in individual countries.

Policy, then, is not made by a few politicians and bureaucrats inhabiting executive and diplomatic positions. Policy emerges from a lengthy process of interaction and consultation between private transnational groups, politicians, bureaucrats, and many others: hence the term *pluralist*. In many countries policy emerges from a very complex process of bargaining, logrolling, consultation, and sometimes coercion, between a variety of national and transnational groups on the one hand, and officials on the other.

The main characteristic of the contemporary global system is its interdependence. The common sense meaning of this term is that events, trends, and decisions that happen in one place are likely to have an impact elsewhere. An election in Great Britain will have some impact on stock market prices in Tokyo, for example. But the concept is somewhat more complicated. Interdependence suggests mutual dependence: the need of two or more actors to provide goods and services for each other. It suggests that *a* cannot meet its needs—for security, economic welfare, raw materials, food, and the like—without the cooperation of *b*, and perhaps others. It also implies a reciprocal ability of the two or more partners to harm each other, in particular by not fulfilling the need. How much harm? It depends upon the availability of alternate sources of supply or markets. Interdependence can thus be measured by the "costs" *a* incurs to meet a need in the event that *b* decides not to provide it.[4]

As an illustration, suppose that for reasons of war or catastrophe or economic sanctions, the supply of Middle East oil to Europe was shut off. What would be the costs of finding alternative energy sources? In this hypothetical case, they would be very high for the Europeans. But the loss of oil markets for the supplying states would also wreak havoc on the Middle East countries' economies. Both consumers and suppliers would suffer. They are mutually dependent, or interdependent.

In the pluralist-interdependent model, the growing interconnectedness of national economies has significantly increased the vulnerabilities of all states. And as a result, many new types of issues appear on the international agenda. Questions of war and peace no longer predominate. Governments and a bevy of transnational, national, and subnational groups act to raise many economic and technical problems for policy coordination or resolution. Who should deal with the international debt problem, and how? How do governments and firms expand multilateral trade in the face of protectionist pressures? How should governments coordinate national policies to reduce global inflationary pressures? Or how should a variety of actors collaborate to stop the killing of elephants in order to save what remains of the species?

On these kinds of issues—and there are more of them appearing all the time—national power measured in terms of military strength is largely irrelevant. Issues are decided on the basis of scientific evidence, mastery of various negotiating techniques, leadership, the ability to forge coalitions, and many other skills and assets. Leverage does not come solely from possessing armies and navies.

But interdependence may have even more significant consequences than just altering the nature of power, influence, and leverage in international politics. Some have argued that since the bases of national wealth and welfare are no longer founded upon territory, the use of armed force as an instrument of foreign policy is becoming obsolete. We can raise this question: In the perennial trade conflicts between

---

[4]A full discussion of the concept of interdependence in international politics is developed in Robert O. Keohane and Joseph S. Nye, Jr., *Power and Interdependence*, 2nd ed. (Boston: Little, Brown, 1989).

Washington and Tokyo, why hasn't the United States contemplated using military force to coerce Japan into adopting more American-style economic practices? Why don't "trade wars" turn into shooting wars? Why has there been no armed conflict between two liberal-industrial states since the mid-nineteenth century?

The answer, some suggest, is that mutual dependence has significantly raised the costs of war, not just because of destruction but also in terms of the long-run economic costs. In fact, the modern bases of power are science, technology, and knowledge in general, not territory. In such conditions, there are few potential gains to be made from the employment of armed force. In many ways, interdependence in a high technology age is tending to render war obsolete. Purposes are fulfilled through many other means, such as maximizing free trade; enhancing the free flow of communications, ideas, and knowledge between societies; building coalitions of like-minded partners; and promoting the globalization of the transnational, liberal-capitalist ethos and business system that characterize the economic relations of the industrial countries. The gradual envelopment of the post-Communist countries of Eastern Europe into the capitalist order, and the partial opening of China and Russia to Western-oriented business practices and opportunities, show that the capitalist system is becoming truly global. The more it becomes integrated, the less likely are wars among its members.

The View from the South: The Dependency Model

The idea of interdependence implies equality and symmetry between societies. From the perspective of many developing countries, in contrast, asymmetries and inequalities are the most salient characteristics of contemporary international relations. Dependency analysts vigorously contest the characterization of the world contained in the pluralist-interdependence model. That model may be a reasonable rendering of the dynamics of relations between the advanced capitalist states, but it cloaks the exploitative realities of the poor countries' situation with an egalitarian vocabulary.

The picture of relations between societies in the dependency model is hierarchical, unequal, and exploitative. Why? Because the world capitalist system really began to develop in the fifteenth century, as Europe's explorers and later their commercial agents and slavers expanded the continental commercial system to all corners of the world. The conquest of Latin America, Africa, Asia, and the Middle East was hardly undertaken for the benefit of the local populations—quite the contrary. It was done for the commercial gain, through plunder, monopolies, and slavery, of Europe. European (and later American) imperialists exploited the natural resources of what is today called the Third World, paying little or nothing for the benefits. They substituted plantation agriculture—toiled by slaves—for the local subsistence farming, expropriated the best lands, and in many cases massacred or reduced to slavery the indigenous populations.

Over the centuries, the economies of those areas were structured to fit the needs of the European colonizers, and not the long-run economic prospects of the locals. The colonial authorities deliberately prevented local industrialization, for example, in order to prevent competition against the industries at home. Land laws were arranged to favor plantation owners and colonial resource extractors. Colonies could not compete in the international trade system; their markets were tied exclusively to the mother country.

The whole pattern of culture and communications between the colonies was—and remains—hierarchical. If an East African wanted to go to West Africa, he or she usually had to travel through London or Paris. Local colonial newspapers did not cover "news" in other colonies, but dealt only with local issues or matters in the colonial center. The political and educational institutions of the colonies were transplants of British, French, Dutch, American, German, and Spanish institutions. These institutions were created with little regard for the needs of the indigenous population. Of what use, for example, would an Oxford type of degree in modern (English) literature be for a farmer in Kenya?

Once the hierarchical structure of colonialism had been built, it did not require much effort to keep it in place. Formal independence for the colonies did not change much. The personnel changed, but the superior-subordinate economic, communications, and cultural structures remained. This situation is termed *neo-colonialism,* or dependency. Why couldn't the post-independence élites replace colonial structures? In part because those very élites who had agitated for independence were also the ones who benefited from neo-colonial relationships. They were the traders, small manufacturers, and parts suppliers for the economies that had been designed to serve the rich industrial countries. They remain a "comprador bourgeoisie," that class of indigenous capitalists that sustains the strong trade and investment links between the center (the industrial countries) and the peripheries (the former colonies).

In this hierarchical economic structure, the center drains economic surplus (capital) from the poor countries. This is in the form of profits that are remitted, royalties, transfer payments, licensing fees, the sale of technology, and the like. The net effect is that the poor countries are constantly decapitalized, and their economies remain largely dependent upon decisions made in New York, London, Paris, and other metropolitan centers.

The edifice of exploitation is held together by a variety of paternalistic leverages, which take the form of foreign aid; grants of military assistance; training of officers and troops; cultural "exchange" programs (where the flow is from north to south, not vice versa); invasion of the developing countries through the center's media (films, television programming, and the like); advertising; and many other forms of indirect control and influence. Whenever indigenous radical movements try to gain control over the levers of economic power, to attain genuine autonomy and independence, the governments of the center countries cry "communism" and, as a last resort, intervene militarily. The outcome of the use of force in Vietnam, El Salvador, Grenada, Nicaragua, and others was not the victory of American strategic priorities in a global competition with the Soviet Union, but the attempt by the United States to coerce all societies to adopt the American way of doing business and to perpetuate the hierarchical world capitalist system that so much benefits the centers at the expense of the peripheries.

The dynamics of international relations, then, are driven by the world capitalist system, by the overwhelming and predominant needs of the advanced industrial countries to have unfettered access to the raw materials and resources of the developing nations, and to create new markets for their products and surplus capital. As in the pluralist-interdependence model, the ties between economics and politics are inseparable. The function of the state is to serve the interests of international capital, which it does through the various mechanisms mentioned above: foreign aid, military assistance and training, communications and propaganda, and on occasion the use of force. Either through coercion or through the overwhelming might of the modern capitalist consumer advertising ethos, the economies of the poor countries remain geared to others' needs and, therefore, will never become strong, vibrant, technologically innovative, and self-sufficient. At best, they are becoming pale imitations of the economies of the center; at worst, they are being systematically exploited. In the world capitalist system, as it has been structured over the last 500 years, the gains of the center are at the expense of the peripheries.

The focus of this model is on the question of equity and equality, rather than on war and peace. It has a large component of economic determinism, deriving from its Marxist background. Politics is depicted as a game whose rules, players, and outcomes are predetermined by the owners of capital. National power, measured in military terms, is much less significant than the ownership of capital, the ability to innovate technologically, and the capacity to continue extracting economic surplus from the poor countries. To understand international relationships, then, one has to start with an understanding of the origins, structure, and dynamics of the world capitalist system. In this view, the demise of socialism in Russia and Eastern Europe in 1989, and its drastic reformulation in China means the end of some alternative form of socioeconomic organization. These developments represent the ultimate global victory of the capitalist system. In this situation, the long-range outlook for many poor countries is not favorable. The economic coercive power of the great industrial giants, led by the United States, is now so great that even those poor countries that have managed to save vestiges of local autonomy, economic self-sufficiency, and local economic priorities face complete absorption into a global system that is designed to perpetuate inequities.

Evidence to support the main propositions of the dependency model is readily available. In terms of the structural characteristics of the system, the patterns are indeed hierarchical. Trade flows, for example, are predominantly between the industrial countries, and between them and the poor nations. The center exports manufactured and high technology goods to the poor countries, and receives in return raw materials and semi-processed goods. There is little trade among Third World countries, and communications facilities between them are rudimentary. Most developing countries export only several commodities, and often to a single market. This makes them particularly vulnerable to trade sanctions. Price volatility for raw materials is also much greater than for manufactured goods, so the developing countries are subject to wide price fluctuations, frequent depressed prices, and no capacity to regulate them. Poor countries are at the mercy of decisions made elsewhere, primarily among consumers in the industrial countries. Moreover, the trend over the years has been for the *terms of trade* to worsen. This further condemns the poor countries to low economic growth, chronic balance of payments deficits, and huge external debts. The terms of trade concept relates the price of raw materials and semi-processed goods to the long-run price trends of manufactured goods. To take one hypothetical example, in the 1950s Zambia had to export five tons of copper ore to earn the money to import one tractor. By 1990, ten tons were required. The developing countries as a whole have to export more of their products in order to purchase less.

Not only are the economies of the poor countries very vulnerable to economic fluctuations and political pressures, but they have few prospects for diversification. They must import most of the modern technology they use, for they have few resources available for research and development. Where they do enjoy advantages, such as relatively low labor wages, the products they manufacture face all sorts of trade barriers in the industrial countries.

The overall economic picture is one of pronounced dependency, not interdependence. The industrial countries, through their economic policies, have a great capacity to harm and coerce the developing countries. With the exception of the oil-exporting countries, most developing countries have no similar leverage. But it is not just a question of economic dependency. The hierarchical structure is composed of other dimensions as well. Most developing countries receive foreign aid; most must buy their military hardware from the industrial countries, or obtain it through grants. Communications flows go from north to south, and not vice versa. African students flock to Paris, London, the United States, Japan, and elsewhere to obtain higher education. There is no similar flow from the industrial countries to the developing nations. Those in the developing countries who want to get ahead must learn English; very few North Americans can speak any foreign language, and even fewer can speak the major African or Asian tongues.

In terms of the dynamics of the system, there is perhaps less compelling evidence. For one thing, there seems to be little agreement regarding the nature of exploitation. For some proponents of the dependency model, economic transactions between the center and the peripheries are a zero-sum game. As the rich extract economic surplus from the poor, the poor become worse off than they would otherwise be. To put it bluntly, the rich nations have achieved their wealth by impoverishing the Third World. Underdevelopment is the creation or result of development. Other versions of dependency theory insist that it is a question of *relative* gains. There is the phenomenon of dependent development, where the peripheries do make some strides in terms of increased per capita incomes, and where participation in the world economy through trade and investment does bring benefits. But those benefits are not equally distributed, so the gap between the rich and the poor continues to widen. Those benefits also sustain the dependency structures, so there is no possibility for the development of an autonomous economy that is designed to meet local rather than export needs.

The evidence about the question of exploitation and the dynamics of development can be read in different ways. In a typical year American, Japanese, and European investors withdraw more capital from Latin America, in the form of repatriated profits, royalties, licensing fees, and the like, than they put into it. Latin America's economic surplus ends up mostly in the accounts of American, Japanese, and European stockholders, or as repayments of staggering debts incurred during the 1970s when banks from the industrial countries were encouraging Latin Americans and others to take out loans. The terms of trade have significantly worsened for many poor countries, and there is no indication that the trend will reverse. The reader can no doubt think of other types of evidence that would support the exploitation thesis.

On the other hand, some developing countries have made great strides over the last three decades, going through forms of industrial revolutions that were much quicker than those in Europe during the nineteenth century. Today, some formerly poor countries have higher per capita incomes than those found in the center. Singapore is wealthier than New Zealand; Taiwan's per capita income exceeds that of Ireland; Thailand's growth rates over the past decade far outpace those of Great Britain; and Malaysia's per capita income will soon surpass that of most Eastern European countries. There has been tremendous movement among national economies during the second half of the twentieth century. Some of the once-mighty have fallen (relatively), while a number of the once-poor have reached levels barely imaginable only a generation ago. In the dependency model, the dynamics—the mechanisms of exchange and growth—suggest that change is not possible, and yet there is a great deal of evidence to the contrary. Where the model does have an important point to make is in challenging the egalitarian assumptions of the pluralist-interdependence model. Many of the developing nations are, and will probably remain for a long time, dependent, vulnerable, lacking in political and economic leverage, and subject to decisions and actions of others over whom they have little or no influence. Their economies are and will be shaped to meet the needs of others, and attempts to form alternative economic structures will meet with resistance and sometimes coercion from the banks, companies, and governments of the center.

World Society Models

Our final model shares some of the features of the pluralist-interdependence and dependency models. It, too, is impressed with the profusion of connections between societies; it also suggests that political and security issues are embedded within larger socioeconomic structures; and it suggests that one has to look at the world globally, and not from the perspective of the state. Where it differs is in its concern with quality of life problems, rather than with war, order, stability, or economic equality.

The main characteristic of the global system is its unity—not political but social. All societies are interconnected, as indicated by all sorts of data, and we are heading toward the formation of a genuine world society. Social patterns (e.g., family structures, consumption habits, lifestyles) are becoming more similar as the significance of political boundaries continues to erode. The world can be portrayed as a great spider's web made up of billions of daily transactions and communications between all points on earth. Today, there is an unprecedented amount of transnational collaboration among groups that are devoted to solving some of the problems that governments and multinational corporations have created. The great issues on the global agenda include saving the environment, ending the exploitation and suppression of women, reducing population growth, dismantling military-industrial complexes, redefining development to make it more consistent with the earth's remaining natural resources and natural habitats, and many other quality of life problems.

Most of the world's institutions cannot resolve these problems; indeed, they are sources of the problems. It is states and their military establishments that threaten nuclear war; it is the giant corporations that pollute the environment and promote mindless consumerism; the world's universities help perform research that sustains these institutions and their practices; organized religions seek to divide believers, not unite them; and so forth.

One of the difficulties with this model is that it is partly descriptive but poorly developed in terms of explanations and dynamics. Whereas the realist and dependency models have clear explanatory variables—anarchy and the security dilemma in the former, and the mechanisms of exploitation in the latter—world society models lack focus. They take some characteristics of the contemporary world, describe them and note some trends, but they do not develop any theory, isolate the dynamics of the system, or specify exactly what it is that needs explanation. Some versions are unabashedly normative; they draw portraits of how the world *should* look rather than explaining how it functions and why. It is thus difficult to specify the kinds of evidence that would be needed to validate the model. Certainly there is plentiful evidence about increasing contacts between societies, the increased homogenization of social patterns and lifestyles, and the growing problems associated with environmental degradation, for example. But it is not clear whether these are causes or effects, or what kinds of causes or effects they are.

These models are major organizing devices of the field. They identify the main question about international politics to be raised (war and security for realists, economic justice for dependency theorists), and they simplify. Each offers a trade-off: Each loses detail for the sake of increased understanding. Each selects from the vast amount of data about the world what they think best describe the essentials. The essentials can be defined as the patterns, trends, and *typical* behaviors one encounters in looking at the contemporary world. But each is only a partial lens: It magnifies or clarifies certain facts, establishes certain connections or causes, but ignores others. For example, the problem of war is not important in dependency theory. It focuses our attention on what the investigator thinks is important. None is comprehensive enough to describe *all* the important trends, patterns, and dynamics.

The framework of this book derives primarily, though not exclusively, from the realist, "society of states," and pluralist-interdependence models. Readers will also note elements of the dependency and world society perspectives in Chapters 3 and 15, which deal, respectively, with essential characteristics of the contemporary international system and with international collaboration on global problems.

The framework for this book is based on several key assumptions about the nature of political life at the international level. First, politics at whatever level—local, regional, national, or international—is *purposeful*. Political leaders seek to defend and/or achieve known (and sometimes unknown private) goals or objectives. At the national level these goals can include such things as greater economic wealth, prestige, less unemployment, more "law and order," secession from the state, and many others. At the international level, government leaders may seek regional hegemony, territorial expansion, the ethnic purity of their state, status, control of the international narcotics trade, an alliance, or a freer international trade system. To study international politics is essentially to examine the ways that the more than 180 governments of our day seek to defend, advance, or achieve their many and often conflicting objectives and purposes.

But policy makers are not entirely free agents. They are often constrained by a number of factors. Some are domestic: They don't have the resources to do what they might like to do. Others are "systemic"; that is, they derive from some characteristics of the international system or the external environment. Poland in the 1950s, for example, could not have complete freedom of choice on foreign policy matters because of Soviet domination. Today, the United States does not have complete freedom of choice on certain domestic economic issues because of the way the global economy functions. The international system, as the "society of states" model suggests, is characterized by a complex set of norms, laws, "rules of the game," and other constraining devices. States may violate them, but they pay a high cost for doing so, particularly if the violations are systematic and persistent.

In order to understand how and why states behave the way they do, then, we need to begin by looking at the context in which they operate, that is, the international system. Chapter 2 provides some historical examples. The purpose of the chapter is not to describe history but to show how international systems emerge, what are their main structural properties and rules of the game, and how they change. Chapter 3 describes the present international milieu, and some of the forces that impinge today upon the main actors of the system.

Part III, Chapters 4 through 10, looks at the behavior of states: what they seek to defend or achieve, and how they go about it. This part deals essentially with ends and means. Part IV offers explanations: These are the factors that go into policy making. Chapter 11 discusses in some detail the complexities of policy making, while Chapters 12 and 13 discuss how legal and ethical considerations affect policy.

Part V focuses on the major forms of *interaction* between states, namely conflict and cooperation. Chapters 14 and 15 discuss the main properties of these two forms of interaction, how they originate, and how the former can be managed and the latter enhanced.

To summarize, the key organizing devices are the *systems*, or environments, in which state actions occur; the *purposes* of governments; the *means* they employ to achieve, advance or defend those purposes; and, finally, the *forms and types* of *interactions* between states as revealed in conflict and cooperation.

Levels of Analysis

One final problem concerning organizing devices needs to be discussed before the framework of analysis in this book is presented. What should we use as the major unit of analysis in international politics?[5] Should we focus upon the actions and at-

[5]J. David Singer, "The Level-of-Analysis Problem in International Relations," in *The International System: Theoretical Essays*, eds Klaus Knorr and Sidney Verba (Princeton, N.J.: Princeton University Press, 1961), pp. 77–92; Kenneth W. Waltz, *Man, the State, and War* (New York: Columbia University Press, 1959).

titudes of *individual* policy makers? Or might we assume that all policy makers act essentially the same way once confronted with similar situations, and therefore concentrate instead on the behavior of *states*? Could we remove ourselves even further from individuals and examine international politics from the perspective of entire *systems* of states? Or, should we regard the world as a single "global village," composed not of states, but of more than 5 billion individuals organized into different kinds of communities, associations, and transnational networks? Each level of analysis—individual, state, systemic, or global—will make us look at different things, so the student must be aware of the differences among them. For example, if we regard the world from a global perspective, our attention will turn to various kinds of problems caused by population growth and everyday economic activity: resource depletion, destruction of the ozone layer, air and ocean pollution, and the destruction of natural habitats, to mention just a few. These kinds of issues require action at all levels: individual, community, region, state, and beyond. The global environment helps to explain the needs, constraints, and limits to growth and economic development that all communities have to face. Global politics deals with global problems. Most of them have to do with the quality of life, rather than with peace and war or economic equality.

As an example of theory at the level of systems of states, the most common is balance of power. The classical theory of balance of power is an attempt to explain the behavior of many states over a period of time. It proposes that states will form coalitions and countercoalitions to fend off drives for regional or global domination and that a "balancer" will intervene on behalf of the weaker side in order to redress the balance or restore the old equilibrium. The behavior of *individual* political units is thus explained in terms of the state of the whole system (balanced or imbalanced) and the presence or absence of one aggressive state and a balancer. This type of analysis makes no reference to personalities, domestic pressures, or ideologies *within* states. Foreign policy behavior is conceived as a reaction to the external environment, the state of balance or imbalance among *all* the units in the system.

If we look at international politics from the perspective of individual states, rather than from the state of the system in which they exist, quite different questions arise. We can attempt to explain the behavior of states by reference not just to the external environment (the system), but primarily to the domestic conditions that affect policy making. Wars, alliances, imperialism, diplomatic maneuvers, isolation, and the many goals of diplomatic action can be viewed as the results of domestic political pressures, national ideologies, public opinion, or economic and social needs. This level of analysis has much to commend it, for governments do not react just to the external environment or to some balance or imbalance. Their actions also express the needs and values of their own populations and political leaders.

Finally, we may study international politics and foreign policy by concentrating on the actions and behavior of individual statesmen. This is the usual approach of diplomatic historians, based on the sound point that when we say that "states" behave, we really mean that policy makers are defining purposes, choosing among courses of action, and utilizing national capabilities to achieve objectives in the name of the state.

This level of analysis focuses upon the ideologies, motivations, ideals, perceptions, values, or idiosyncrasies of those who are empowered to make decisions for the state.

Which level of analysis gives us the most useful perspective from which to explain or understand politics among nations? Each makes a contribution, but each fails to account for certain aspects of reality that must be considered. We cannot understand Russian foreign policy adequately by studying only the attitudes and values of its foreign minister, nor is it sufficient to analyze Russian social and economic needs. We must have some knowledge, as well, of its domestic politics, of the policies of other major powers, and of transnational problems such as the rise of Muslim fundamentalism and the hyper-nationalism commonly found in the former Soviet republics and in the Balkans. The main characteristics of the external environment are no less important than those of the state's internal environment. Therefore, all four levels of analysis will be employed at different times, depending upon the type of problem to be analyzed. The perspective of international systems is very broad, although not comprehensive, and provides the best approach for delineating the *main* features and characteristics of international political processes over a relatively long period of time. One can describe the essence of the types of relations among Greek city-states without examining the character of each city-state or the motives, ideals, and goals of each statesman in each city-state. Today, the structure of alliances, power, domination, dependence, and interdependence in the world sets limits upon the actions of states and policy makers, no matter what their ideological persuasion or individual ideals are, and no matter what the state of domestic opinion is. The next two chapters will concentrate on the description of international systems, with a view to illustrating the general nature of relationships among their component political units. At the same time, the analysis will illustrate how the main characteristics of an international system affect the behavior of individual states. The system is thus only one variable used to explain how and why states act and interact. Subsequently, the focus will shift to an explanation of foreign policy behavior primarily by reference to domestic national needs and values and to individual variables.

International Politics, Foreign Policy, and International Relations

At what point does foreign policy become international politics? Distinction between the terms may be more academic than real, but it is roughly the difference between the *objectives* and *actions* (decisions and policies) of a state or states and the *interactions* between two or more states. The student who analyzes the actions of a state toward external environment and the conditions—usually domestic—under which those actions are formulated is concerned essentially with foreign policy; the person who conceives of those actions as only one aspect of a pattern of actions by one state and reactions or responses by others is looking at international politics, or the processes of interaction between two or more states. The distinction is illustrated in the figure shown on the following page.

This book will apply both perspectives, depending upon the problem under analysis. A discussion of state objectives, variables affecting their choice, and some

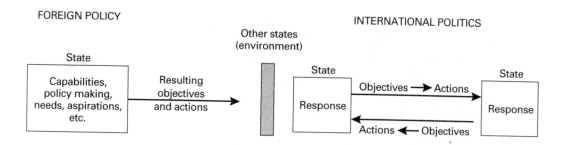

techniques employed to achieve them is related closely to the study of foreign policy, while consideration of international systems, deterrence, and behavior in conflict situations comes closer to the idea of interactions between states.

As distinct from international politics and foreign policy, the term *international relations* may refer to *all* forms of interaction between the members of separate societies, whether government-sponsored or not. The study of international relations includes the analysis of foreign policies or political processes between states; however, with its interest in *all* facets of relations between distinct societies, it would include as well studies of international trade unions, the International Red Cross, tourism, international trade, transportation, communication, and the development of international values and ethics. The student of international politics is not concerned with these types of relationships or phenomena, *except where they impinge upon official government objectives or where they are employed by governments as instruments of inducement to achieve military or political objectives.* An international ice-hockey tournament is an international or transnational relationship. So is a world congress of the International Political Science Association. But the student of international politics is interested in these events only if they have some reasonably immediate impact on intergovernmental relations. Where to draw the line is never entirely clear; "ping-pong diplomacy" interests us because it was a novel vehicle used by the Chinese government to establish more important diplomatic links with the United States, while a more ordinary table-tennis match between Australia and New Zealand would not be noteworthy. Similarly, the student of international relations is interested in all aspects of international trade. In international politics, we are concerned with international trade only to the extent that governments may employ economic threats, rewards, or punishments for political purposes, as when they promise to lower tariffs vis-à-vis another country in return for the right to establish a military base in that country.

Description, Explanation, and Prescription

The purpose of this book is to help the reader understand the diverse phenomena of international politics and, in so doing, to think critically and analytically about the world. Now, of course, the term *understand* has different connotations. I will take it to mean that the reader will (1) obtain a few new facts; but more important, he or she will (2) see the similarity of processes in international politics and foreign policy, even when events are separated by decades; (3) be able to place facts in some sort of framework so that they connect better with each other; and (4) learn to appreciate the difficulties involved in explanations of foreign policies and international politics. This should result in a healthy skepticism toward those plans and ideas that will purportedly solve all the world's problems or those theories that, in a few pages, supposedly explain something as complicated as the motives of Chinese, American, Russian, or Indonesian foreign policies.

Most of the book is descriptive; it seeks to show *how* states act and interact. In places, particularly Chapters 11 through 15, the analysis is more formally *explanatory*; it tries to identify those conditions within and between states that are likely to *cause* certain consequences we call foreign policy, international conflict, or cooperation. In scientific terms, the discussion is not elegant, since we cannot say that factors *a*, *c*, *g*, and *z* inevitably cause certain results in foreign policy or interaction between states. But we can demonstrate how and under what conditions public opinion, ethics, or international law, for example, are *likely* to be related (or unrelated) to certain foreign policies.

Unlike many of the treatises on international politics prior to World War II, this book contains very little prescription. It does not purport to solve the most pressing problems of the age; nor does it constitute a handbook for diplomats. From its pages the foreign minister of a country could not find recipes on how to solve that nation's foreign trade problems (although he or she might learn something about diplomatic bargaining tactics or how to maximize rational behavior in a crisis situation). The reasons that applied knowledge has been omitted are many, but perhaps the main one is the author's belief that before one can intelligently prescribe solutions to problems, it is best to begin by understanding the fundamental conditions and processes of international politics—how people and governments behave in their external relations.

Questions for Study, Analysis, and Discussion

1. What are some distinctions between historical and social scientific approaches to the study of international politics?
2. Why are organizing devices necessary for studying international politics?
3. What is the organizing device for this book?
4. In what ways do our implicit and explicit models of international politics affect the way we "see" the world?
5. What do the five "models" of the international system emphasize? What are the main points of disagreement? What does each leave out?
6. What are the different "levels of analysis"? Why are they important in explaining international politics?
7. What are the main differences between the concepts of foreign policy, international relations, and international politics?
8. What is the difference between description, explanation, and prescription? In what ways are these distinctions revealed in the five models of international politics?

Selected Bibliography

Aron, Raymond, Peace and War. Garden City, N.Y.: Doubleday, 1966.
Ashley, Richard, and R. B. J. Walker, "Reading Dissidence/Writing the Discipline: Crisis and the Question of Sovereignty in International Studies," *International Studies Quarterly,* 34 (September 1990), 367–416.

Barber, Arthur, "The Citizen, the Scholar, and the Policymaker," *Background,* 8 (1964), 79–86.

Der Derian, James, "Introducing Philosophical Traditions in International Relations," *Millenium,* 17 (2) (1988), 189–94.

———, *and Michael Shaprio, Eds., International Intertextual Relations: The Boundaries of Knowledge and Practice in World Politics.* Lexington, Mass.: Lexington Books, 1989.

De Senarclens, Pierre, La Politique Internationale. Paris: Armand Colin, 1992.

Donelan, Michael, Elements of International Political Theory. New York: Oxford University Press, 1990.

Dyer, Hugh C., and Leon Mangasarian, The Study of International Relations: The State of the Art. New York: St. Martin's, 1989.

Enloe, Cynthia, Bananas, Beaches & Bases: Making Feminist Sense of International Politics. London: Pandora Press, 1989.

George, Jim, and David Campbell, "Patterns of Dissent and the Celebration of Difference: Critical Social Theory and International Relations," *International Studies Quarterly,* 34 (September 1990), 269–94.

Glaser, William A., "The Types and Uses of Political Theory," *Social Research,* 22 (1955), 275–96.

Gonick, Lev S., and Edward Weisband, Teaching World Politics: Contending Pedagogies for a New World Order. Boulder, Colo.: Westview Press, 1992.

Grant, Rebecca, and Kathleen Newland, Eds., Gender Issues in International Relations. London: Open University Press, 1991.

Haglund, David G., and Michael K. Hawes, Eds., World Politics: Power, Interdependence, and Dependence. Toronto: Harcourt Brace Jovanovich, 1990.

Halliday, Fred, "State and Society in International Relations: A Second Agenda," *Millenium,* 16, 2 (1987), 216–29.

Higgott, Richard, and J. L. Richardson, International Relations: Global and Australian Perspectives on an Evolving Discipline. Canberra: Department of International Relations, the Australian National University Press, 1991.

Hollis, Martin, and Steve Smith, Explaining and Understanding International Relations. Oxford: Clarendon Press, 1991.

Holsti, K. J., The Dividing Discipline: Hegemony and Pluralism in International Theory. London: Allen & Unwin, 1985.

Holsti, Ole R., "The Citizen, the Scholar, and the Policymaker: Some Dissenting Views," *Background,* 8 (1964), 93–100.

Keohane, Robert O., Neorealism and Its Critics. New York: Columbia University Press, 1986.

Kruzel, Joseph, and James N. Rosenau, Eds., Journeys Through World Politics: Autobiographical Reflections of Thirty-four Academic Travellers. Lexington, Mass.: Lexington Books, 1989.

Lapid, Yosef, "The Third Debate: On the Prospects of International Theory in a Post-Positivist Era," *International Studies Quarterly,* 33 (1989), 235–54.

Linklater, A., "Realism, Marxism and Critical Theory," *Review of International Studies,* 12 (1986), 301–12.

Lyons, Gene M., "The Study of International Relations in Great Britain," *World Politics,* 38 (1986), 626–45.

Merle, Marcel, "La 'problematique' de l'étude des relations internationales en France," *Revue Française de Science Politique,* 3 (juin 1983).

Morgan, Patrick M., Theories and Approaches to International Politics. New Brunswick, N.J.: Transaction Books, 1987.

Morgenthau, Hans J., "Common Sense and Theories of International Relations," *Journal of International Affairs,* 21 (1967), 207–14.

Nye, Joseph S., Jr., "Neorealism and Neoliberalism," *World Politics,* 40 (1988), 235–51.

Olson, William C., and A. J. R. Groom, International Relations Then and Now: Origins and Trends in Interpretation. London: HarperCollins Academic, 1991.

Russell, Frank M., Theories of International Relations. New York: Appleton-Century-Crofts, 1936.

Singer, J. David, "The Level-of-Analysis Problem in International Relations," in *The International System: Theoretical Essays,* eds. Klaus Knorr and Sidney Verba. Princeton, N.J.: Princeton University Press, 1961.

———, "The Responsibilities of Competence in a Global Village," *International Studies Quarterly*, 29 (1985), 245–62.

Smith, Steve, "The Development of International Relations as a Social Science," *Millenium*, 16, 2 (1987), 189–206.

Sullivan, Michael P., *International Relations: Theories and Evidence*. Englewood Cliffs, N.J.: Prentice Hall, 1976.

Sylvester, Christine, *Feminist Theory and International Relations in a Post-Modern Era*. Cambridge: Cambridge University Press, 1994.

Tickner, J. Ann, *Gender in International Relations: Feminist Perspectives on Achieving Global Security*. New York: Columbia University Press, 1992.

Viotti, Paul R., and M. V. Kauppi, Eds., *International Relations Theory: Realism, Pluralism, Globalism*, 2nd ed. New York: Macmillan, 1992.

Walker, R. B. J., *One World, Many Worlds: Struggles for a Just World Order*. Boulder, Colo.: Lynn Rienner, 1988.

Waltz, Kenneth N., *Man, the State, and War*. New York: Columbia University Press, 1959.

Wright, Qunicy, *The Study of International Relations*. New York: Appleton-Century-Crofts, 1955.

Chapter

2

Historic
International Systems

We begin with a historical excursion. It is not, however, just for background or archeological reasons. Presumably we can learn a great deal about contemporary international politics without having to dredge up antiques. The purpose of the exercise is more theoretical than historical. We use the past, in other words, to illuminate the present and to allow comparison. This chapter examines three historical international systems, using a common set of categories for analysis. The survey has four purposes: (1) to demonstrate how foreign policy behavior transcends historical contexts; (2) to invite comparison between periods; (3) to show how the structures of international systems influence the behaviors of their constituent units; and (4) to account for changes from one type of system to another.

An international system can be defined as any collection of independent political entities—tribes, city-states, nations, or empires—that interact with considerable frequency and according to regularized processes. The analyst is concerned with describing the typical or characteristic behavior of these political units toward one another and explaining major changes in these patterns of interaction.[1] While ob-

---

[1]The concept of "system" as it has been employed in "general systems analysis" is a formal method of analysis that can be used for studying social systems. We use the term in two ways: (1) as a description of regular or typical patterns of interaction among independent political units; and (2) as one variable that helps explain the behavior of the units comprising the system. For the difference between the usages of the concept, see Jay S. Goodman, "The Concept of System in International Relations Theory," *Background*, 8 (1965), 257–68.

servers of international affairs have traditionally explained the behavior of states in terms of national attributes and needs, or individual characteristics of policy makers, the external environment and particularly the level of technology and structure of power and influence in an international system may have profound effects on the general orientations or objectives of a state toward the rest of the world. Thus, the major characteristics of any international system can be used as one set of variables to help explain the typical objectives, actions, and interactions of that system's component political units. This chapter will focus on international structures and political processes of selected historical civilizations without, however, including lengthy descriptions of individual historical events or personalities, except where these had such a great impact on the system that they changed its major characteristics. Historical detail is sacrificed in order to emphasize typical or recurring patterns of behavior among interacting political units, permit greater understanding of comparative international politics, and assess the effects of structures and processes on the behavior of component political units.

Each historical system will be analyzed from five aspects. First, the *boundaries* of the system—the line between interaction and environment—will be designated. Any international system has identifiable boundaries—geographic, cultural, or issue lines beyond which actions and transactions between the component political units have no effect on environment, and where events or conditions in the environment have no effect on the political units. Although the Chinese states and the Greek city-states existed simultaneously in the fifth century B.C., there was no interaction between them; to the Chinese, the Greek political units were merely part of an unknown environment. Although the Greeks conducted exploration and trade that brought them into contact with many peoples in Eurasia, the political life of these peoples had little effect on Greek politics.

Second, what are the main *characteristics of the political units* whose interactions form an international system? We are concerned with the types of governments and administrations that political units developed, the role of the average citizen or subject in the political unit's external relations, and the methods by which resources of the unit were mobilized to achieve external objectives.

Third, any international system has a definable *structure*, a characteristic configuration of power and influence or persisting forms of dominant and subordinate relationships. Sometimes a system's structure is typified by concentration of power in one state, which then dominates others; in other eras, power may be diffused quite equally among a large number of states so that none is capable of dominating or leading the others for any period of time; or the structure may be polar or multipolar, where two or more antagonistic blocs of states, each led by states of superior strength, array against each other. We also want to identify the "great powers" of each era, analyze how they acquired their position, and describe the situation of the lesser political entities—satellites, neutrals, or reluctant alliance partners. This analysis also requires discussion of the *stratification* within each system and the criteria commonly employed to distinguish between "great powers" and lesser units. Descriptions of the structure of each system also include identification of the major subsystems, such as the most important rivalries, issues, alliances, blocs, or international organizations.

Fourth, each international system will be analyzed in terms of the most common form of *interaction* among the component units—diplomatic contacts, trade, types of rivalries, and organized violence or warfare.

Finally, interactions and processes in most systems are regulated or governed by *explicit or implicit rules or customs*, the major assumptions or values upon which all relations are based. As regulators of each system, the techniques and institutions used to resolve major conflicts between the political units will also be considered.

It would be impossible in two chapters to describe the main characteristics of these five categories for all international systems that have arisen and declined in history. This chapter will concentrate instead on three civilizations for which there is considerable historical evidence on interstate relations: the Chinese state system under the Chou dynasty, the Greek system of city-states, and the international politics of Europe from 1648 to 1814. The succeeding chapter will conclude with a discussion of the more familiar contemporary global system.

The International Politics of the Chou Dynasty, 1122 B.C.–221 B.C.

Even though scholars on the Orient usually classify these nine centuries of Chinese history under the Chou title, there were at least two and possibly three fundamentally different structures in which international political processes took place. One was the feudal order, which lasted from 1122 B.C., with establishment of the dynasty, until approximately 771 B.C., when the central Chou monarchy was defeated by insurgent feudal lords and "barbarians" and was forced to move its capital from Hao (near the present city of Sian) to Loyang, farther east. This feudal epoch has been called the "Western Chou" period. The era from 771 to 483 B.C., known as the "Spring and Autumn" period, developed a system of independent states, sometimes arranged into two antagonistic blocs, replacing the small, hierarchical feudal order of the Western Chou period. The period of the "Warring States" (403 to 221 B.C.) was noted politically for conflict and competition among the larger states, decline of stable alliances and the polar power structure, and eventual destruction of the system itself.

The Boundaries of the Chou System

During the Western Chou (feudal) period, the political influence of the Chou dynasts extended only to the territory of the lower Huang Ho basin, roughly the area between the Huang Ho and Yangtze rivers in central China. There were, of course, inhabitants throughout the territory that comprises modern China, and the Chou authorities had contacts with some of them, even though they were regarded as barbarians (*wu*). Aside from these sporadic involvements with the *wu*, the Chou political units developed in isolation from the rest of the world. As the system of large independent states replaced the feudal structure, contacts were made with people on the Indian subcontinent, but there is no evidence that these interactions had any immediate political significance to the Chinese states. During the Warring States period, the larger political units extended their domain and sinicized many of the areas populated by the *wu*, so that by 221 B.C. parts of present-day Manchuria, the eastern tip of the Shantung Peninsula, and some territory south and east of the Yangtze River were organized politically and became components of the system.

The Characteristics of the Political Units

In the feudal era, the main political unit was the Chou monarchy, which dispensed land, titles, and favors upon its vassals. The bureaucratic organization of the monarchy was already well-developed in this period and differentiated to serve a variety of government functions.

In addition to the central monarchy, which theoretically held title over all the known territory of China, a number of small feudal units, created and sustained by the central monarchy, also played an important political role. The Chou kings donated tracts of land, including towns and villages, to feudal lords and retiring civil servants in return for the payment of taxes. Vassals were also obligated to carry out certain other duties, such as following the king in wars and expeditions against the *wu*, guarding the frontiers of Chou lands, and supplying manpower to the king for his armies. The territorial extent of these feudal units varied considerably. Most consisted of walled cities and surrounding lands, extending over a radius of up to sixty miles;[2] but, in some instances, the monarch would reward a deserving noble with a tract of land the size of New York State. The noble could then subdivide the land into fiefs ranging in size from several fields to several hundred square miles, an area comparable to a large Texas ranch.[3] The literature of the period indicates that there were at least 130 large feudal states subservient to the central monarchy during the Western Chou period, although some authorities mention as many as 1,800.[4]

In theory, nobles and vassals were not allowed to expand their territory at the expense of neighboring feudatories without royal sanction. But even during the height of Chou power, feudal lords maintained some relations with each other (rather than directly through the monarchy) and in some cases fought wars over territorial spoils.

Within their own states, the nobles enjoyed considerable autonomy, appointing their own officials and levying taxes in accordance with their own needs. They maintained their own armies (partly for purposes of internal security) and, if they desired, could split up their land among relatives and subvassals, creating even smaller political units (fiefs). During the early parts of the Spring and Autumn period (771 to 483 B.C.), the strength and independence of feudal lords grew rapidly at the expense of the central Chou authority. Emulating the administrative mechanisms within the Chou domains, the vassals themselves created regular government organizations as state functions expanded and became more pervasive in the lives of ordinary people. Large-

[2]Owen and Eleanor Lattimore, *China: A Short History* (New York: W.W. Norton, 1944), p. 66.
[3]Dun J. Li, *The Ageless Chinese: A History* (New York: Charles Scribner's, 1965), p. 47.
[4]There seems to be little agreement regarding the number of units in the feudal system. Richard L. Walker, in *The Multi-State System of Ancient China* (Hamden, Conn.: Shoe String Press, 1953), mentions that in 722 B.C., when the feudal order was declining rapidly, there were 170 states (p. 20); Edward T. Williams, in *A Short History of China* (New York: Harper & Row, 1928), mentions the existence of about 1,800 states during the height of the Chou dynasty (p. 56); and Friedrich Hirth, in *The Ancient History of China to the End of the Chou Dynasty* (New York: Columbia University Press, 1923), claims that about 130 states were noted in the Chou literature (p. 11).

scale irrigation and construction projects, collection and storage of grains, construction of walled cities, and organization and maintenance of armed forces required the establishment of coherent administrative structures and processes.[5] With the aid of administrative mechanisms that made them independent and self-sufficient, the feudal lords and royal princes were able not only to maintain control over their own expanding territories, but to resist the influence of the central monarchy as well.

Another development that strengthened the independence of the feudal states was the growth of rudimentary forms of nationalism. In the Western Chou period, popular patriotism had been directed toward village chiefs and the "Son of Heaven," the Chou monarch, and only occasionally to the feudal lord. But, after 771 B.C., ordinary people began to recognize and emphasize the differences in dialects, customs, religion, and cults among the states as their contacts with others began to proliferate, and the position of the Chou monarch—the symbol of unity—eroded. Pride in local distinctions and loyalty to the prince of the state became much more pronounced toward the end of the Spring and Autumn period. The significance of this development was that during the period of the Warring States, princes could more easily organize peasant militias and armies to fight their wars for them. In turn, peasants and townsmen believed that they were fighting not just as a duty to a feudal lord but for the independence and honor of their own state.[6]

In addition to the Chou monarchy, the feudal realms of the early Chou period, and the large independent states that developed in the Spring and Autumn period, a fourth type of political unit also existed in the Chinese system. This was the attached state (*fu-yung*), independent only in relation to some purely local affairs. These attached states were mostly holdovers from the feudal era, small bits of territory that had not been conquered and absorbed by the larger feudal rulers as they developed their administrative mechanisms and armed forces. In external relations, the attached states were almost totally dependent upon their neighbors.[7]

The Structure of the Chou System

The center of influence during the Western Chou period resided with the political unit—the central monarchy—which could create or extinguish lesser political entities. The structure of the system in the feudal era was hierarchical. Most feudal lords were dependent upon the Chou monarchy for lands, subsidies, and protection against each other; but because of the difficulty of transportation and communication between units on the territorial fringes of the system, as well as the development of administrative mechanisms within the feudal units, there were different degrees of dependence and subservience between the small political units and the monarchy. The Chou kings ruled directly over extensive tracts of territory near the present city of Sian. Next to this they created a circle of small states, each ruled by a direct relative of the king's family. Because of close family and geographical relationships, these local

[5]Walker, *The Multi-State System of Ancient China*, p. 37.
[6]Ibid., p. 36.
[7]See Derk Bodde, "Feudalism in China," in *Feudalism in History*, ed. Rushton Coulborn (Princeton, N.J.: Princeton University Press, 1956), p. 56.

rulers—usually princes—were in a weak position to increase their authority at the expense of the Chou monarch. Another circle of states farther from the capital was ruled by other nobles who had also received their territory from the king but who were distant members of the ruling house or relatives by marriage. Toward the fringes of the system (called the "region of tranquil tenure") the monarchs created a multitude of small states governed by former military or civil officials, who were awarded territory, villages, and towns in return for services to the Chou kings. The function of these states (termed *kuo*) was to watch over the activities of hostile tribes beyond the borders of the system. For this service, the vassals received special royal subsidies. At the farthest region of the system stood the area of "wild domain": land inhabited by barbarian tribes, Chou vassals whose loyalty was doubtful, and groups that retained sporadic connections with the Chou but were not wholly sinicized.

In part, this feudal structure was held together for several centuries by obligations that the vassals and members of the royal family had to fulfill toward the central monarchy or their immediate superiors. The relationships of dominance and subordination were also sustained by an official mythology, which held the king to be the "Son of Heaven," ruling by divine decree. A challenge to his power could thus be interpreted as a form of sacrilege.

But the Chou dynasts were incapable of preventing the eventual growth of power among the many vassals. The feudal lords through the centuries had consolidated political, military, and administrative power over ever-larger pieces of territory and had succeeded in creating self-sufficient states. By the beginning of the Spring and Autumn period, many of them had acquired or conquered enough territory to make it possible for them not to rely on the royal family for subsidies or grants of land. When ambitious nobles went to war and defeated a neighbor, they no longer turned the conquered rulers into subvassals but incorporated them and their land as integral parts of their own territory.[8] The smaller units were simply swallowed up by the larger.

Moreover, the rulers of these territories increasingly derived their authority from inheritance, rather than from the central monarchy. Regardless of lineage, they called themselves princes, and by the fifth century many were known as kings.[9] By the beginning of the eighth century, successors of the original vassals and princes were already going to battle against each other and even against the Chou monarchy itself. In 707 B.C., a vassal actually defeated the Chou monarch's army[10] and, fifty years later, a group of leaders from the more powerful states determined the succession of the Chou throne.[11] Increasingly, the central monarchy had to rely for its prestige and power on those theoretically subordinate to it. Between the eighth and seventh centuries B.C., therefore, the patterns of dependency had become reversed. Although the monarch retained a certain ceremonial importance, leaders of independent states in no way felt compelled to observe the wishes of the king.

[8]Li, *The Ageless Chinese*, p. 59.
[9]Williams, *A Short History of China*, p. 62.
[10]Li, *The Ageless Chinese*, p. 50.
[11]Walker, *The Multi-State System of Ancient China*, p. 27.

In four centuries, the structure of the Chou system changed from one in which the characteristic relationship was of a feudal type, with clearly established patterns of dominance and subordination, to a system in which a small number of independent states interacted with one another, with no permanent hierarchy of power and influence. The most important conditions that made this development possible were the relative isolation of many of the feudal units from the central authority,[12] their aggrandizement at each other's expense (thereby creating larger territorial units), growth of popular loyalties, and establishment of administrative mechanisms that made the political units more self-sufficient.[13] The number of units in the late Spring and Autumn and Warring States periods varied with each new conquest or absorption but fluctuated normally between ten and fifteen. By 230 B.C., there were only seven major states and three smaller entities remaining as independent units.

The processes by which smaller states were absorbed into larger ones normally involved the use of force. The state of Ch'i, for example, was particularly successful in expanding its territory at the expense of smaller neighbors. Chronicles of the period record that in 664 B.C., Ch'i "brought Chang to terms"; four years later, it "removed" Yang. In 567, Ch'i "extinguished" Lai and T'ang; and in 549, it "seized" Chieh-ken.[14] In other cases, the rulers of small states voluntarily sought the protection of larger units and ended up as protectorates, attached states, or quasi-independent provinces. In 645, the government of the state of Ch'i lost territory when it paid a ransom of eight cities in order to obtain the return of its ruler, who had been seized by the people of Ch'i. In some other cases, states either bartered or sold territory to others.

As unoccupied territory available for absorption declined, states warred increasingly among themselves. One result was a tendency toward the polarization of power between the states of the north, which (for ceremonial purposes only) still identified themselves with the Chou monarchy but were under the effective leadership or domination of Ch'i, and the several states of the south under the domination of Ch'u. These two groupings constituted crude alliance subsystems and were also the instrumentalities of Ch'i and Ch'u, used partly for their own purposes. These two blocs were roughly analogous to the Western and Soviet blocs after World War II, except that they were never very stable. The period of the Warring States, for example, saw members of both blocs fight vigorously against their own allies.

In a system where territorial expansion became a prime objective of state policy and power was distributed among ten or fifteen large states, there was no role for neutrals. Those units that attempted to remain outside the quarrels of other states or alliances ultimately faced extinction, absorption by another state or bloc, or, in the case of the Chou (northern) alliance, a type of quasi independence that allowed for considerable cultural and political autonomy but not military neutrality.[15]

---

[12]Cf. Wolfram Eberhard, *A History of China* (London: Routledge and Kegan Paul, 1950), p. 34.

[13]The economic reasons for the decline of feudalism are discussed in Li, *The Ageless Chinese*, pp. 60–61.

[14]Walker, *The Multi-State System of Ancient China*, p. 29.

[15]Ibid., p. 101.

By the third century, whatever was left of Chinese unity dissipated as all states began to wage war against each other, regardless of alliance commitments or traditional friendships. Wars became great campaigns of massacre and annihilation, with serious consequences to the political and economic stability of both victors and defeated. Between 230 and 221 B.C., the westernmost state of Ch'in, a semibarbarian and partly isolated political unit, conquered Han, Chao, Wei, Ch'u, Yen, and finally Ch'i, bringing to an end the Chou dynasty and the system of independent states. The system was replaced by the Chin empire, ruled by the Han dynasty, which successfully destroyed all symbolic vestiges of feudalism and the political independence of separate territorial units.[16]

The forms and criteria of stratification during the Western Chou period were similar to those in the European medieval order: The status and prestige of each political unit was based upon the personal relationships between the central dynast and his vassals. Thus, each political unit was ranked at diplomatic and ceremonial functions according to the original title conferred on its leader by the monarch, corresponding approximately to the titles of prince, duke, marquis, earl, viscount, and baron. By the Spring and Autumn period, stratification became established upon the visible elements of a state's power and prestige; rulers who attended international conferences in the eighth century B.C. no longer ranked themselves according to the official titles of their feudal ancestors. Prestige and status in the system after 771 B.C. were based primarily upon a state's available military resources and secondarily upon the prestige, wealth, and family connections of its rulers. The number of four-horse military chariots was the most conspicuous indicator of a state's power.[17] Another indicator of a state's prestige and status was the number and quality of allies it could count upon for military assistance.

Since the Chinese were very conscious about their international ranking, they frequently attempted to impress neighbors, allies, and enemies by winning spectacular military victories or, if warfare was wanting, by conducting large military reviews before visiting dignitaries from other states. In 529 B.C., for example, the government of Ch'i organized a military performance in which it displayed more than 4,000 chariots.[18] Since the largest army mobilized for battle during the early Chou dynasty contained only 3,000 chariots,[19] it is clear that this state exhibited almost its entire military capability in an effort to impress others with its might.

Whether measured by available military forces, family connections, wealth, or allies, there was no persistent hierarchy of status or power after the strength of the Chou monarchy had declined to symbolic proportions. Military power and diplomatic status were diffused among a number of relatively large and equal states. These could be considered the great powers of the epoch, states that, although roughly equal with each other, determined the fate of lesser political units either by absorption or through leadership of alliances. During the early part of the Spring and Au-

[16]Li, *The Ageless Chinese*, p. 56.
[17]Cf. Cheng Te-k'un, *Shang China* (Cambridge: W. Heffer and Sons, Ltd., 1960), p. 295. Richard Walker points out that even today, the translation of the term *great power* is commonly rendered in Chinese as a "country of ten thousand four-horse chariots."
[18]Walker, *The Multi-State System of Ancient China*, p. 48.
[19]Cheng, *Shang China*, p. 295.

tumn period, no one state was predominant in the system, as alliance patterns shifted rapidly and leadership passed back and forth among Ch'i, Chin, and Ch'un in the north, and Ch'u, Wu, and Yueh in the south. During the latter portion of this period and throughout the Warring States period, however, power and status gravitated primarily to the leaders of the two main alliance systems, Ch'i and Ch'u, and ultimately to Chin, which conquered all the other states.

Below these great powers were smaller states, political units that maintained all the requisites of independence but, for lack of military capabilities, economic resources, family connections, or defense establishments (such as walled cities), had to rely for their survival upon the great powers and their alliances. A third tier of states included the *fu-yung*, or attached states, and smaller protectorates that owed their independence to the good will of their protectors. These units were seldom over eight square miles in size and, as the lowest units in the political order, did not have direct diplomatic access to the ceremonial center of the system, the Chou monarchy, but had to communicate indirectly through their protectors.[20]

The Forms of Interaction

During the feudal period, levels of political and commercial interaction among the units were low, except when formal diplomatic and ceremonial exchanges were arranged between the dukes, princes, and other nobility and the central Chou monarchy. Interaction and communication followed closely the hierarchical pattern of authority in the system, although feudal units in close proximity naturally had many relations with each other.

In the Spring and Autumn and Warring States periods, each of the independent states conducted its external relations without reference to the official center of the empire. There was a proliferation of contacts between states, not only formal and diplomatic, but trade and commercial as well. The Chinese states never established permanent diplomatic organizations, but recurring occasions for arranging alliances, declaring war, making peace, or maintaining prestige in the system through ceremonial or military displays led to almost constant diplomatic exchanges between the units. Chinese sources of this period list such diplomatic exchanges as *ch'ao*, a court visit paid by one ruler to another; *hui*, meetings between permanent government officials of two or more states; *p'in*, friendly missions of information or inquiry; *shih*, exchange of emissaries; and *shou*, hunting parties where government representatives combined diplomatic affairs with recreation.[21] The ceremonies attending these types of exchanges were so lengthy that many states did have, in effect, permanent diplomatic communication with each other.

These exchanges often had a direct connection with a state's security or expansionist objectives, even when contacts ostensibly had ceremonial purposes. Almost all the major events in the life of a ruling family—assumption of a throne, burial of a former ruler, marriages between families or rulers, or even births of children into a ruler's family—required diplomatic representation from other friendly states,

---

[20]Walker, *The Multi-State System of Ancient China*, p. 38.
[21]Ibid., p. 75.

and these occasions were used for bargaining over state interests.[22] Marriages between ruling families were a means of creating and sustaining alliances, a practice familiar to students of early European diplomatic history.

A unique aspect of transactions within the Chinese system was the extent to which they occurred between states with different religious or cultural traditions. Though Ch'u and Ch'in were not fully sinified states, they were able to interact with the others essentially on a basis of equality. Apparently wars, alliances, and peace were made in the light of a state's immediate objectives and interests, whereas ideological or cultural distinctions remained largely irrelevant to a state's orientation toward others. Hence, if a state found it in its own interest to conclude an alliance with even the most uncultured barbarians at the fringes of the system, it would not hesitate to do so.[23]

Commercial exchange was another form of interaction. Normally this was a private affair of merchants, who were free to travel from state to state and conduct their transactions without administrative interference. However, insofar as grain and other commodities were necessary to feed armies, governments maintained an interest in having sufficient stores to support their forces in times of poor harvest. Since they could not always obtain adequate supplies from their own peasants, occasionally they had to send out economic missions to purchase agricultural products from other states.[24]

War was a frequent form of interaction between states during the Spring and Autumn and Warring States periods. It is recorded, for example, that Duke Huan of Ch'in went to war twenty-eight times in a reign lasting forty-three years.[25] In the feudal order, force (provided partly by the vassals) was used primarily by the Chou dynasts against the *wu* and occasionally against errant nobles whose actions were deemed damaging to the interests of the empire. In the system of independent states, all the units used organized violence as a method of achieving objectives—whether territory, slaves, "honor," or allies. During the feudal era, engagements were seldom fought as battles of annihilation, but more as trials of strength, finesse, and glory.[26] Fairly rigid rules of warfare prevailed (for example, a charioteer could not fight against anyone of lower or higher rank) and helped to moderate the destructiveness of battle. By the period of Warring States, however, wars had become great contests, fought brutally by huge armies numbering in the hundreds of thousands. Mass slaughter replaced dueling by charioteers, and the casualties of battle reached proportions enormous even by contemporary standards. In 274 B.C., a Ch'in general reportedly killed 150,000 enemy soldiers, and the massacre of prisoners of war was a common occurrence.[27]

The Chinese also used various forms of subversion and intervention in other states' internal affairs as methods of achieving their objectives. The number of dynastic quarrels and marriages arranged between families of different states led to sit-

[22]Ibid., p. 78.
[23]Ibid., p. 99.
[24]Ibid., p. 80.
[25]Li, *The Ageless Chinese*, p. 50.
[26]Kenneth S. Latourette, *The Chinese: Their History and Culture* (New York: Macmillan, 1959), p. 61; Marcel Granet, *Chinese Civilization* (New York: Meridian Books, 1951), p. 290.
[27]Cf. Eberhard, *A History of China*, p. 57; Li, *The Ageless China*, p. 56.

uations in which one government could support certain claimants to the throne in a neighboring territory and, if it succeeded in creating disloyal factions or cliques, could then help foment revolutions or *coups d'état* and place a subservient, or at least friendly, ruler on the throne. According to one authority,[28] the Chinese states persistently employed the techniques of subversion to expand their influence into other areas. In the Spring and Autumn period, for example, there were at least thirty-six instances of successful subversion, frequently brought to a conclusion when the intervening state made a show of force at the last moment in order to ensure the victory of rebel elements.

The Rules of the System

In the latter periods of the Chou dynasty, there was considerable discrepancy between the official rules, traditions, and myths that were supposed to govern relations between political units and the actual behavior of independent states. The official mythology and customary rules of behavior, buttressed by the writings of philosophers such as Confucius, emphasized unity, obedience to the "Son of Heaven," harmony among all parts of the political order, and the obligation of all lower entities—whether sons to fathers or vassals to lords—to higher authorities.

But practice during the Spring and Autumn and Warring States periods did not accord with the myths and customs appropriate to the feudal order. In a system of many powerful, ambitious, and independent states, such rules were anachronisms. Instead, the main units developed rules or customs that reflected the major political and military characteristics of the system. The official theories of hierarchy, imperial rule over all subjects, and attending patterns of superior-subordinate relationships were belied by the assumptions of later periods, which recognized that the great powers, at least, were more or less sovereign equals, free from all restraints imposed by the Chou monarchy. Treaties concluded after 771 B.C. were treaties between equals, even where the Chou authorities were involved. Obligations were entered into only by the consent of both parties to the treaty, and no authority had legal or customary rights in another independent state's territories, as they did in the Western Chou era. Even compacts between the Chinese states and various barbarian groups were concluded on a basis of equality. There was, however, no belief in the sanctity of independence; throughout the Spring and Autumn and Warring States periods, the larger units conquered and amalgamated lesser territories, with no intention of returning their independence after a short period of occupation. Conquered territories were simply annexed.

More explicit rules were formulated into treaties, which contained the specific obligations of states toward each other and provided means for enforcement. One guarantee of compliance with treaties was the practice of exchanging hostages. A state would concede several cities or members of the ruling family as hostages, to be kept—or destroyed—by the other treaty partner if the first broke its obligations. Among customary rules were those demanding that states send envoys to each other at frequent intervals, that members of the two main alliance systems send a mini-

---

[28]Walker, *The Multi-State System of Ancient China,* p. 86.

mum of one mission every three years to the court of the league president, and that "summit" meetings be held at least every five years.[29] Other rules prescribed in detail the types of conduct and behavior appropriate in warfare, although toward the end of the system the rules of warfare were systematically violated in great campaigns of annihilation.

Most conflicts during the feudal era were mediated directly by the Chou monarchy—except those on the periphery of the system, where central influence was at a minimum. With the decline of the Chou dynasty's effective position among the newly arising independent states, conflicts had to be resolved directly by those involved. During the early Spring and Autumn period, there were no institutions that could provide mediatory or conciliatory services; but, as the two alliance systems developed, they did establish techniques for resolving conflicts arising *within* the alliance. It was in the interest of the alliance—or at least to the advantage of the predominant powers in each alliance—to maintain peace and collaboration between alliance members. When disputes broke out among them, therefore, other members often found it necessary to intervene, either to secure a mediated resolution or, if that was impossible or improbable, to threaten or force one or both parties to terminate their quarrel. In 546 B.C., moreover, some of the smaller states that had been increasingly victimized by larger neighbors called a conference of states, which successfully drafted a multilateral treaty of nonaggression. This resulted in forty years of relative stability and nonviolence in interstate relations. Whatever techniques were employed by the Chinese states in the Spring and Autumn period were quickly cast aside, however, in the period of Warring States, when conflicts were resolved almost entirely by the use of force.[30]

We can now summarize two points that will be of particular concern to us throughout this book: the sources of change from one system type to another and the influence that the structure of the system has on the foreign policy activities of the individual states. For the first, let us put in chart form those social, political, and economic factors that brought stability or change to the system. By stability, we do not mean the absence of war or conflict, but rather the persistence of *essential characteristics of the system* (boundaries, nature of the units, structure, forms of interaction, and rules). Other developments were occurring, however, that brought about fundamental changes in any one or more of the system's characteristics (see Table 2-1).

How can these three fundamentally different types of Chinese international systems be related to the foreign policies of the typical states making them up? How, in particular, can the structure of the system serve as one variable explaining the foreign policy behavior of the political units?

In the feudal era, the units were weak in relation to the central monarchy and had little freedom to maneuver in their external relations. Bound to the center by traditional mythical and contractual obligations, the lesser units seldom had a choice but to conduct their relations with each other in accordance with the policies and rules set forth by the emperor. In parts of the Spring and Autumn and Warring

[29]Ibid., p. 81.
[30]Li, *The Ageless Chinese*, p. 53; Walker, *The Multi-State System of Ancient China*, p. 88.

TABLE 2-1
Sources of Stability and Change in Ancient Chinese International Systems

PERIOD	SOURCES OF STABILITY	SOURCES OF CHANGE
Western Chou (1122–771 B.C.)	"Son of Heaven" myth Emperor's control over all land Grants of titles Contribution of troops and taxes by units to emperor Emperor's superior military and administrative capacities	Poor communication between outer "states" and central monarchy Developing administrative and military capabilities of states Beginnings of local nationalism Territorial aggrandizement by some states
Spring and Autumn (771–483 B.C.)	Continuing myth of emperor's unity Development of bilateral and customary rules to regulate interaction between states Development of conflict resolution mechanisms (mostly domination of small states by large) Easier communication Rough balance of power between major antagonists	Tendency toward polar power structure Development of increasingly large armies Decline of customary rules of warfare Growth of large states
Warring States (403–221 B.C.)	Weak operation of alliances	No more territory for external expansion Rise and predominance of Ch'in Destruction of blocs and balance between them Wars of annihilation

States periods, however, when military capabilities and diplomatic influence were widely diffused among a number of relatively equal political units and when the blocs were not operating, the structure placed fewer limitations on external actions and objectives. To be sure, the smaller states were virtual satellites or protectorates, but the medium and large states enjoyed considerable freedom of action. They could forge or destroy alliances, seek security through isolation, or attempt, although usually unsuccessfully, to defend themselves by remaining neutral. Unlike the feudal system, wherein objectives and policies were either set by the monarchy or agreed upon through bargaining between the monarch and vassals, the diffuse system involved bargaining directly between competing independent states. The Chinese system during the Spring and Autumn period thus suggests that if power is diffused, the latitude for choice of foreign policy is substantial, but security from outside attack may be low. Strategy, alliance making, war, and rapid shifts in orientation toward neighbors and more distant states are characteristic features of the diffuse system. In the feudal system, on the contrary, most action is confined to court intrigues and secret bargaining, and major objectives are determined for the units by the emperor. Freedom of action is limited, but security from outside attack may be enhanced. In the bloc system of the Warring States period, the latitude of choice of lesser alliance partners was considerably restricted. The goals and diplomacy of all lesser states were made to conform to the interests of the bloc leaders. Generalizations such as these seem to be confirmed from other historical international systems as well.

The International Politics of Greek City-States, 800 B.C.–322 B.C.

The Greek world was geographically more extensive than its Chinese counterpart. While the Chinese remained isolated from most other cultural groups, Greek merchants and travelers found their way to India, the shores of the Baltic, Spain, and the north coast of Africa. Most of the famous city-states were located on the Greek peninsula and on islands of the Aegean Sea, but the Greeks also colonized locations throughout the shores of the Mediterranean, establishing their political organizations and culture in the areas in which the cities of Nice, Marseilles, and Naples are currently found. Since these people maintained commercial and diplomatic relations with the Phoenicians, Persians, Arabs, Indians, and various tribes in Europe and Southern Russia, the geographical boundaries of the system are difficult to establish. Persian expansion in the Aegean was a major threat to the interests of all Greek city-states on the peninsula; although the activities of the Phoenicians had little impact on relations between most Greek city-states, they determined the fate of several Greek colonies on the Italian peninsula. Non-Greek political units thus played an important, though sporadic, role in Greek life. Since the relations among city-states and colonies constituted the majority of interactions and transactions in the system, however, we will describe these rather than emphasize the Greeks' relations with the "barbarians," people of non-Hellenic culture on the fringes of the Greek world.

The Nature of the Political Units

The city-state (*polis*) was the main form of political organization throughout the Greek world from the eighth century B.C. until Philip of Macedonia conquered the peninsula in the late fourth century B.C. Most of these units were comprised of a group of towns or a small city, usually walled, surrounded by relatively small areas of agricultural territory. Attica, for example, was the area occupied by the Athenian people. It included many small agricultural villages, but the city of Athens was the center of political life and administration, and the people throughout Attica were called Athenians. The population of the city-states varied from the largest, such as Syracuse, Acragas, and Athens, with about 25,000 male citizens, to the smallest, such as Siris and Thourioi in Sicily, which contained only several thousand inhabitants. In size, the city-states ranged from several hundred square miles, including outlying agricultural territory, to small towns built on the shores of the Mediterranean Sea comprising only several hundred acres. Most *poleis* were about 100 square miles.

The forms of government in the city-states varied from priest-kings ruling over tribal organizations, small oligarchies of the rich, and military tyrannies to freely elected governments, wherein citizens (omitting women, peasants, merchants, and slaves), whose tenure in office rotated frequently, formulated and administered policies directly.

The city-state cannot be understood adequately when described only in terms of its political institutions, for the Greeks considered the *polis* the *ideal* social organization for liberating an individual from a natural state and for providing justice, promoting fellowship and harmony, and training personal character. Despite the many economic, cultural, and language ties among Greek city-states, there was no struggle to create a common framework for uniting all the Hellenic people into a more viable empire. The Greeks emphasized the virtue of limited political organizations—small enough to allow for the assembly of all free citizens to help make political decisions and small enough for government and administration never to seem impersonal influences over the lives of citizens. The state and society were thus indistinguishable concepts among the Greeks.

Aside from the *poleis*, three other types of political units played roles in the Greek international system. One was the tributary state, a *polis* that came under the hegemony of another city-state but was allowed to maintain some degree of autonomy in internal affairs. During the fifth century, when Athens dominated the Delian League, a number of the smaller members of the alliance became tributary states. Most of these were obliged—ostensibly as alliance partners—to accept Athenian domination over their external relations, contribute to the Athenian treasury (officially, a contribution to the alliance), and make war and peace according to the interests of Athens. Failure to follow Athenian leadership resulted in serious punishment, including occupation of the recalcitrant city-state by Athenian troops and construction of permanent Athenian garrisons.

The third type of political unit was the military colony, *cleruchy*, which some city-states established to guard strategic territories, waterways, and trade routes. The *cleruchy* also served as an outlet for surplus population from the mother city-state, particularly after these cities grew to the point where their own agriculture could not provide adequate food supplies for the population.

Finally, many city-states also established nonmilitary colonies throughout the Aegean and Mediterranean seas. They erected these towns and cities primarily as new sources of food supply and areas for relieving population congestion at home. Many city-states also sent politically unreliable citizens and unwanted aspirants for public office to their colonies, sometimes in exile, sometimes to fill honorific positions. Although the original connection between the city-state and its colonies was one of dependence, after several decades most colonies became independent of their mother city-states and retained only formal religious ties. Otherwise, the colonies organized their own political administration and conducted their own external affairs.[31]

The Structure of the System

As each city developed during its formative years in relative isolation, the system originally displayed a highly diffuse structure of influence and power. Each unit was independent. Although frequent wars over territory, personal rivalries, and frontiers ended in the total destruction of some city-states, there were few permanent hierarchies of dominance-dependence. Some city-states had wider-ranging interests and

---

[31]For description of some of the city-states, see Kathleen Freeman, *Greek City States* (London: Methuen, 1948); for the colonies, Johannes Hasebrook, *Trade and Politics in Ancient Greece* (London: G. Bell, 1933), pp. 106–8.

activities than others, and consequently gained more prestige. By the fifth century, however, the structure of the system became more stratified and rigid, with city-states such as Athens, Sparta, Acragas, Corinth, Argus, and Thebes increasingly dominating the actions and transactions of the smaller units around them. The main sources of change from a diffuse to a "polar" international system, where power and influence coagulated around two blocs of states, were the rapid growth and extension of Athenian naval and commercial strength, and the threat of Persian penetration into the Ionian islands, Thrace, and Macedon.

As a response to this external danger, the Greeks established the Hellenic League as a military alliance and placed it under the leadership of Sparta and Athens. Despite the semblance of Greek unity during the Persian Wars (492–477 B.C.), there were serious conflicts between members of the League, mostly occasioned by the smaller city-states' fear of Athenian imperialism and expansion. Thus, after the Greek victories over the Persians, Athens' competitors, led by Sparta, formed a rival organization, the Peloponnesian League, an intricate alliance and collective security system designed to deter further Athenian expansion and in some cases to "liberate" areas already under Athenian domination. A bitter competition over trade and naval supremacy between Corinth and Athens led ultimately to the Peloponnesian Wars involving the two military alliances.

By the outbreak of these wars in 431 B.C., Athens had already become an empire, ruling directly or indirectly (ostensibly through a new multilateral alliance, the Delian League) over a number of independent and tributary city-states. But this hegemony was not created solely by Athens' commercial superiority or even by the imperialism of Cimon and Pericles. Many city-states voluntarily accepted Athenian laws, courts, and currency simply because these Athenian institutions were more admirable than their own arrangements.[32] Athens also provided many services for other city-states, such as leading the alliance against Persia, clearing the seas of pirates, and organizing trade connections with non-Hellenic peoples.

By 431 B.C., then, the Greek city-state system had become partly polarized into two large blocs. The Athenian empire led one bloc and was followed by its voluntary or tributary allies, including the prominent city-states of Rhodes, Miletus, Corcyra (a formidable naval power), as well as other units located in the eastern Aegean and northern and western Greece. Sparta led the Peloponnesian League, with Ellis, Arcadia, and Corinth as its most important allies. Unlike the Chinese system, wherein neutral status was not condoned, many city-states and colonies on the Greek peninsula and throughout the shores of the Mediterranean Sea remained free from direct involvement in the Peloponnesian Wars. The system was not, therefore, organized completely around the two blocs.

By the middle of the fifth century, an identifiable order of stratification had replaced the more diffuse, egalitarian distribution of power, status, and prestige found in the era when the city-states were relatively isolated from one another. The criteria according to which states were ranked during and after the fifth century were pri-

---

[32]Adda B. Bozeman, *Politics and Culture in International History* (Princeton, N.J.: Princeton University Press, 1960), p. 86.

marily military, commercial, and cultural. Sparta and Athens assumed leadership of the two blocs because of their military or commercial capabilities. Sparta gained respect and prestige from the fighting efficiency, bravery, and loyalty of its soldiers. Even those who abhorred Sparta's authoritarian political and social institutions admired the greatness of its armies.[33] Athens, on the other hand, wielded considerable influence over the other city-states by virtue of its citizens' aggressive commercial practices. When it had achieved a position of trading predominance, it could easily reduce smaller states to subservience by applying boycotts and embargoes on their trade. Other states moved voluntarily toward Athens, expecting profitable trade relations and protection of commercial routes by the Athenian fleet. Sparta, which possessed only one colony and few commercial connections, had to rely essentially on military force to achieve its objectives.

Also contributing to Athens' prestige and status were the cultural and political contributions of its citizens. Many city-states accepted direct Athenian rule or political leadership in external affairs in order to obtain the advantages of Athenian political institutions, laws, culture, and commercial practices. Above all, perhaps, cultural excellence was a criterion of greatness. Athens was to the Greeks what Paris was to Europe in the eighteenth century, the cultural center of the system—in Pericles' words, "the educator of Hellas."[34]

The Forms of Interaction Among the City-States

Prior to the fifth century, the city-states conducted little trade among themselves, as each unit was virtually self-sufficient in the few necessities of life and the commodities needed to sustain a fairly simple technology. Governments generally took no part in trading activities (except in some cases, to obtain revenues), and merchants faced numerous obstacles to successful transactions, including land and sea pirates, nonconvertible monies, and nonenforcement of debts among citizens of different city-states.[35] By the fifth century, however, the growth of population and merchant classes and the need to obtain military supplies prompted rapid development in commercial activity among the units. Commercial transactions aided the city-states in their internal development but also led to important rivalries. By the time of the Peloponnesian Wars, private merchants no longer operated on their own, but relied extensively on governments to provide protection and open new sources of raw materials and markets. Simultaneously, many governments used trade to build up military resources and employed their merchants as agents through which they could place diplomatic pressure by threatening boycotts and embargoes on other city-states. The tradespeople of Athens, backed by the powerful Athenian fleet, were particularly aggressive in developing markets abroad, and the Athenian government occasionally helped them exclude the trade of rival city-states, such as Corinth, from sources of supply. By the time Athens dominated large parts of the Aegean Sea and the Gulf of Corinth, no city-state could conduct extensive overseas trade without the tacit approval of Athenian authorities.

[33]H. D. F. Kitto, *The Greeks* (Edinburgh: R. Clark, 1951), p. 94.
[34]Ibid., p. 76.
[35]Hasebrook, *Trade and Politics in Ancient Greece,* p. 85.

One form of interaction that prevailed even in the early period of the city-states was the meetings of Greeks at religious festivals and councils. The Greeks observed one basic religious form and created a number of institutions (called *amphictyonies*) to maintain the purity of the religion and provide means for organizing common festivals and sacrifices. The shrines at Olympia and Delphi offered centers for inter-action of all Greeks. Religion, then, was one of the unifying elements in the system (truces were always declared during the Olympic Games) and helped the Greeks ap-preciate their common inheritance and distinguish themselves from the "barbar-ians" with whom they had developed many contacts. The religion did not, however, lead to any political unification among the many units; indeed, as each city-state had its own deities, religious symbols were often the basis for violence and conflict, not political cooperation. One of the major problems of the system was that despite the Greeks' propensity to fraternize with each other in social, religious, recreational, in-tellectual, and aesthetic matters, they were unable to carry these forms of coopera-tive behavior into political and military relationships.

If the political units could cooperate in some questions of common concern, generally their interests conflicted and their governments resorted to the use of force to resolve those conflicts. War was a recurrent phenomenon of the system, and most peace treaties were drafted to remain in effect for only a specified time. Part of the explanation for the frequency of violence lies in the coupling of religious and polit-ical symbolism within the city-states. In the early period of the Greek system, wars arising over territorial quarrels often developed into ideological crusades involving the honor and glory not only of the city-state but also of its particular deities. For this reason, many wars were fought with terrible brutality. The victors typically demol-ished the city-state, put the adult male population "to the sword," and took the re-maining inhabitants as slaves.

The sources of war varied. In the early period, wars over religious issues were numerous; one example was the conflict between Athens and Crissa, which erupted into armed violence after the Crissans destroyed Apollo's temple at Delphi. Border conflicts frequently led to warfare, and conflicts arising out of internal revolts and civil wars, in which outside city-states intervened, were not uncommon after the fifth century. War was also used to obtain control over strategic waterways and mountain passes. Athens used force several times to punish recalcitrant allies or city-states that had attempted to defect from the empire or Delian League to join the league of states led by Sparta. Finally, the search for booty and commercial advantage were important sources of military violence. Throughout the period, economic interac-tion became more prominent but did not always lead to cooperative forms of be-havior. On the contrary, wars, conflicts, and rivalries tended to become more in-tense as the economic stakes involved in a quarrel increased. However, not every divisive issue could become a cause for a contest of arms, since wars were costly, de-structive, and often indecisive. Other means of wielding influence had to be em-ployed as well.

Among these was the practice of diplomacy, formal efforts by the government of one city-state to induce another city-state, through oral persuasion, to act in the interests of the first. Diplomacy was conducted through the medium of the ambassador, usually an honored citizen with oratorical skills, who was sent to persuade governing officials of another city-state to make formal decisions by concluding treaties of friendship, alliance, or commerce. In wartime, ambassadors—including those sent by the "barbarians"—normally enjoyed diplomatic immunities and were used primarily at the end of hostilities to negotiate the terms of peace, deliver prisoners, and make arrangements for burial of war victims.

The Major Rules of the Greek System

The Greeks developed a number of rules, observed in treaties or custom, that regulated diplomatic relations and the conduct of warfare. These gave recognition to the independence and equality of the units and defined the limits of immunities for both diplomats and religious shrines in time of war; other rules pronounced standard procedures for declaring war, providing asylum, and conferring citizenship.[36] Since wars were often costly and indecisive, the Greeks also developed procedures for resolving conflicts short of force. Arbitration and conciliation, two procedures for interjecting third parties into diplomatic bargaining situations, were among the important contributions the Greeks made to subsequent diplomatic practices.[37] They occasionally employed these procedures for handling recurring boundary disputes, conflicts involving public debts, and quarrels arising from differing interpretations of treaties.[38] Normally, parties to a dispute honored the decision of arbitrators, particularly since the arbitrators enjoyed great public prestige. Despite arbitral procedures, war and violence continued to be employed as means of settling conflicts, leading ultimately to the exhaustion of the most important city-states.

The fate of the Greek system was analogous to that of the Chinese: Both succumbed, after a long period of bitter strife between two major blocs, to a superior force that, although part of the system, was considered to be "barbarian" and alien. For the Chinese states, Ch'in was the danger lurking behind the Wei River; for the Greeks, Macedonia was the external threat.

It could be argued that the development outside Greece of much larger territorial and administrative units commanding extensive military power made the Greek city-states obsolete, just as developing dynastic states in sixteenth- and seventeenth-century Europe superseded the small independent walled cities of medieval Europe. By the third century B.C., no system based on such small units as the city-states could remain isolated from the new giants. Larger political units— first the Persians, succeeded by the Macedonians and ultimately the Romans— made the city-states appear weak and paltry in comparison. Either the Greeks would have had to unite into one large territorial empire, participating as just one

[36]Arthur Nussbaum, *A Concise History of the Law of Nations* (New York: Macmillan, 1961); Coleman Phillipson, *The International Law and Custom of Ancient Greece and Rome* (London: Macmillan, 1911).

[37]The Greeks did not invent these procedures. Many primitive tribes and more extensive empires had developed procedures and institutions by which disinterested third parties attempted to reconcile two feuding families, tribes, or nations. The Europeans, however, developed the practice during the eighteenth and nineteenth centuries, using the Greek experience as a model.

[38]Marcus N. Tod, *International Arbitration Amongst the Greeks* (Oxford: The Clarendon Press, 1913). For further discussion of arbitral procedures, see Chapter 14.

of several larger entities in the politics of the Mediterranean area, or they would be engulfed, as they were, by new states that had previously been merely peripheral actors in Greek life. The small republics and city-states of Renaissance Italy were similarly engulfed by the larger dynastic states of Europe in the fifteenth and sixteenth centuries.

The Inter-State System of Europe, 1648–1814

Our last historical states system developed and functioned throughout the European continent in the years between the Treaty of Westphalia that terminated the Thirty Years' War (1618–1648) and the end of the Napoleonic wars. Why was this a distinct international system? Primarily because the nature of the units and their common forms of interaction prior to and after the Thirty Years' War were substantially different, but also because the essential rules of the system, many of which are still with us, were developed and articulated in the Treaty of Westphalia. Finally, the wars of the French Revolution and Napoleon introduced some essentially new characteristics to international politics, particularly in the nature of warfare and the mobilization of publics for foreign policy purposes. The period from 1648 to 1814 was relatively homogeneous in the sense that the inter-dynastic politics retained their essential characteristics for almost one and one-half centuries.

Before examining the five characteristics of this system, we should say a word about the cultural context of Europe during this period. Although the continent was carved up into a number of dynastic states and lesser entities, there was a sense of European cultural unity. Writers and politicians of the day often spoke of "Christendom," referring to the religion that united the Europeans and set them apart from the Ottoman "heathens" and the "barbarians" inhabiting lands overseas. French was commonly spoken by members of the aristocracy throughout Europe; France (or more distinctly, the French court) set the cultural standards for the continent in many ways; and the kings, queens, dukes, and even lesser nobility were thoroughly European in their selection of husbands and wives. The modern concept of nationality was not yet fully developed. A cultural cosmopolitanism pervaded the continent, and even in politics, identifications were personal rather than national. Loyalties extended to a court, a king, a queen, or a lesser noble rather than to a nation. Thus, it was common for French nobles to work in the diplomatic service of the Prussian king, for British-born generals to direct the armies of the Russian czar, and for Italian artists to work in the pay of the king of Spain. Authors wrote their works for European, not national, audiences; musicians gravitated to the centers of excellence and financial support, no matter what their nationality. We thus have the anomaly of a *culturally united* Europe—particularly after the great schism between Protestants and Catholics had been resolved through war in the 1630s and 1640s—but a Europe that was *politically divided*. There are some parallels to the late twentieth century, where we see an increasingly interdependent world economy, but where politically mankind remains fragmented into more than 180 separate states.

The Boundaries of the System

The boundaries of the states system for the period from 1648 to 1814 were essentially religious. Europe was defined in terms of Christianity, and the predominant relationships were between the "princes of Christendom." These princes (the kings) had regular contacts with the Ottoman Empire, and many of the European states had established colonies in North America, the Caribbean, Latin America, India, and the East Indies. The system was on the verge of becoming global in terms of trade and travel. With the exception of the heart of Africa, most of the areas of the world were at least known, and many had been deeply penetrated or colonized by European settlers, traders, and military garrisons. But insofar as membership in the system was concerned, it was strictly a European affair. The great variety of political units in Asia, Africa, and elsewhere—kingdoms, sultanates, chiefdoms, free cities, and the like—were not members of the European diplomatic club. Europeans' diplomatic exchanges with them were sporadic, and not based on concepts of equality and reciprocity. The rules that guided relations between the European dynasts were seldom observed in relations with peoples generally considered to be "barbarians," heathens, or other types of inferiors. When we speak of the European states system of the period from 1648 to 1814, therefore, we include mostly the complicated mutual relations of the European dynasts. Even Peter the Great, who turned Russia into a large replica of other European states in the late seventeenth and early eighteenth centuries, was regarded in other European courts as something of a curiosity, and not quite fit to become a member of the club of European dynasts.

The Nature of the Political Units

We call the units *states* because for several centuries the medieval European order of free cities, church properties, private holdings, and local warlords had given way to centralized political units conceived in territorial terms and subject to no superior authority. The young Louis XIV faced serious insurrection against central rule in France in the mid-seventeenth century, but by the time of his death in 1715, France had become a unified, centrally controlled and administered state. The long process of state creation had taken place earlier in Great Britain, and was to occur much later in Prussia and Italy. In the eighteenth century Austria was made up of a collection of lands held together by ties of loyalty rather than by central administrative mechanisms and a sense of nationality; Russia was in a similar situation.

   The politics of the times were dynastic, but they also involved critical questions of state building. The main issues revolved around dynastic claims and succession crises (who was the rightful heir to a throne). But the dynasts also concentrated efforts on restricting the powers of powerful nobles, for example by removing the nobles' taxing powers and ancient rights to raise armies. State creation and consolidation meant primarily developing bureaucratic mechanisms to administer the monarchs' realms, instituting national taxation systems, and organizing armed forces under central command. Dynastic concerns extended into foreign policy as well. Monarchs frequently went to war to assert their hereditary claims in foreign jurisdictions, and dynastic marriages were commonly arranged as means of buttressing military alliances.

The common person—about 90 percent of the population, mostly made up of the peasantry—played little or no role in these politics. Many of the monarchs considered their realms as their private domains. There was no assumption that the inhabitants of those domains had any right to participate in the formulation of the monarch's decisions. Loyalties were personal and reciprocal: A duke or a count owed allegiance to the crown and offered his services to it in return for certain royally granted privileges and status. The peasants received more or less effective protection against marauders, highwaymen, and pirates. In return, they paid taxes to the monarch's treasury, often at near-ruinous levels.

The System Structure

Power among the dynastic states was diffused. For most of the period, there were eight "powers," and many lesser states. It was primarily the decisions made in Vienna, Paris, London, Stockholm, Petersburg, Berlin, Madrid, and Constantinople that determined whether there would be peace or war. No single power dominated the system, although the proposed unification of the French and Spanish crowns in the early 1700s would have led to French hegemony on the continent. The other powers joined together to prevent this eventuality, and ultimately went to war against France (the War of the Spanish Succession). The Treaty of Utrecht that terminated that war reconfirmed the principle of the sovereign independence of the dynastic states, and underlined the importance of the balance of power as a mechanism for maintaining states' independence.

One consequence of power diffusion among the eight great powers was constantly shifting alliances throughout the period. The dynasts were free to choose their diplomatic strategies and tactics; none accepted any form of subordination, and although most owed some theoretical allegiance to the Holy Roman Emperor, this was a symbolic allegiance at best. But the dynasts paid a price for their autonomy: insecurity. Today's friend often became tomorrow's enemy. The princes frequently plotted to "downsize" or destroy each other. In the case of Poland, they succeeded: Poland was carved up three times, with the spoils going to Prussia, Russia, and Austria. In 1795, Poland ceased to exist. But for some lucky turn of events, Austria and Russia would have reduced Prussia to its original shape in the form of seventeenth-century Brandenburg. And Bavaria laid claim to most of Austria. There was, in brief, a good deal of international predation. Thus, the absolute freedom of choice, established through the doctrine of sovereignty and the destruction of the hierarchical residues of medievalism, had as its counterpart substantial insecurity. Unlike the early Chou system, where the central authorities could provide some security for the subordinate units, the dynastic states of eighteenth-century Europe could gain security only by their own wits and by alliances. But an alliance was no guarantee against possible treachery.

The Forms of Interaction

By contemporary standards, the forms and density of interaction between the princes of Christendom were limited. Communications were slow and unreliable, and trade between the states, as we will see, often assumed the form of economic warfare. The

Europeans did, however, develop one of the enduring institutions of international relations: a professional diplomatic corps stationed permanently abroad. These agents were sent for the traditional purposes of negotiation, reporting, and intelligence work. They reported regularly to their home court, so the dynasts were informed of all the latest developments—including court intrigues—abroad. In this period, the early predecessors of bureaucratized foreign ministries began to emerge. All of this meant that governments were constantly in touch with each other. One consequence was that the element of surprise was reduced. Any particular court knew pretty well what its counterparts were up to and could prepare for any eventuality.

During most of the eighteenth century, foreign trade was commonly regarded as a zero-sum game: The gains of one were at the expense of the other. Governments generally tried to create monopolies: The Spaniards would not allow others to conduct trade with their holdings in the West Indies; they also tried to corner the market on the slave trade. The Dutch held a monopoly on shipping in the Baltic; and the French and the British constantly warred against each other in order to establish exclusive trade arrangements in North America.

The search for monopoly and commercial exclusivity had a power-politics motive and was guided by doctrines of mercantilism that were widely popular in eighteenth-century Europe. Under this doctrine, the state should be deeply involved in commercial activity, including foreign trade. The purpose was not only to promote economic well-being but also to amass resources necessary to build and sustain military establishments. Until ideas about free trade began to become more fashionable toward the end of the century, governments viewed commerce in the context of state diplomatic goals, and not as an activity that directly benefits private subjects.

The consequence was that international trade as a form of interaction generally fostered conflict rather than cooperation and mutual gain. Commercial rivalry and attempts to create or sustain monopoly positions in trade and shipping contributed to more than one third of the wars between 1648 and 1814. Three wars between Great Britain and Holland in the 1650s and 1660s derived almost exclusively from trade and navigation issues.[39]

War was a frequent form of interstate contact. Between the Treaty of Westphalia and the final defeat of Napoleon in 1814, there were fifty-eight wars in Europe, or one every 2.9 years. Most were of relatively short duration (the typical war lasted an average of less than two years), but this figure is not entirely indicative of the prevalence of interstate violence. Many wars had more than two combatants, and the War of the Spanish Succession (1700–1713), as well as the Seven Years' War (1756–1763), were world wars, fought not only on the continent but also in the new colonial areas of North America, the Caribbean, the Indian Ocean, and the East Indies.

Yet, by contemporary standards, the wars were not highly destructive. This was not only because of the relatively crude military technology of the age, but also because armed forces were manned primarily by mercenaries. Armies and navies were costly, and the dynasts and their military leaders adhered to strategies that called for

---

[39]Data are from K. J. Holsti, *Peace and War: Armed Conflicts and International Order, 1648–1989* (Cambridge: Cambridge University Press, 1991), chapters 3 and 5.

outmaneuvering the opponent rather than annihilating him. To engage in open battle was to risk losing a heavy investment. An army depleted by battle casualties, disease, and desertion was not easy to replace.

War in the eighteenth century was highly institutionalized. It was recognized as a legitimate form of statecraft, to be used upon the decision of the dynast and his or her advisers, to advance state interests, including the honor and prestige of the monarch. Many of the monarchs of the seventeenth century were themselves leading warriors (such as Louis XIV), and even as late as the mid-eighteenth century a good king was defined partly in terms of his prowess on the battlefield. Charles XII of Sweden and Frederick the Great of Prussia were among the great military commanders and leaders of the era.

War was also institutionalized in the sense that it was surrounded by ceremony and etiquette. Most armed conflicts began with formal declarations of war. Battle formations had to be designed according to certain pre-established patterns, and maneuvers followed, almost ritually, detailed specifications. Sieges were also directed according to set procedures, and surrenders were accompanied by great formalities. There were considerable efforts made to protect civilian lives (commanders of towns or garrisons could honorably surrender once a breach of a wall had been achieved by the sieging party) and to care for wounded soldiers. Massacres of civilians and combatants were rare, and the object of considerable scorn among the royal entourages. To lose a battle or war was less onerous than to compromise honor by breaking the conventions and etiquette of the day.

The Rules of the System

The Treaty of Westphalia (in fact, it was two separate treaties signed, respectively, by the Protestant leaders in Osnabrück, and their Catholic counterparts in Münster, about 50 kilometers distant) formally acknowledged the basic principles upon which the states system has operated for more than 340 years. These documents stated that no supranational authority, such as the Pope or the Holy Roman Emperor, had any legal jurisdiction within the realms of the dynasts. This is the principle of sovereignty, the principle that underlies the relations between all states to this day. The principle of sovereignty is relatively simple: Within a specified territory, no external power—whether the Pope, the Holy Roman Emperor, or any other body—has the right to exercise legal jurisdiction or political authority. This establishes the exclusive domestic authority of a government. That authority is based on a monopoly over the legitimate use of force. Put in the simplest way, the government of Switzerland, for example, cannot extend its laws and police powers into the territory of Italy. This may seem perfectly obvious to us, but it was a radical idea at the time of the Thirty Years' War. Until then, both the Catholic Church and the Holy Roman Emperor had claimed ecclesiastical and political rights to intervene within the domains of a dynast.

A corollary of the sovereignty principle was that subnational units—duchies, free cities, or baronies, for example—have no legal standing abroad. They could no longer make treaties with dukes or cities of neighboring territorial jurisdictions, and they had none of the rights of states under international law. They could no longer, for example, go to war, obtain benefits from the laws of neutrality, and the like.

A second corollary of sovereignty is that no state has the right to interfere in the domestic affairs of another state. This prohibitive injunction has been breached frequently, but it is assumed and observed most of the time by most states. The world might look very different in its absence, and there is considerable evidence that new formulations are coming into being. We will say more on this in the next chapter.

The doctrine of sovereignty means, finally, that all states are *legally* equal. Regardless of size, age, type of government, natural resources and all the other things that distinguish states from each other, all states are equally sovereign and enjoy equally the benefits deriving from treaties, customs, and other sources of law.

These are the basic propositions upon which inter-dynastic and international relations have been conducted since 1648. That there are violations of the norms does not deny their existence.

But the rules that guided statecraft in the period from 1648 to 1814 went far beyond the formulations of sovereignty. In addition to them were a number of assumptions about what sorts of behavior were tolerable and intolerable. These assumptions were not always recorded in treaties or other international documents. They constituted what is more appropriately thought of as unquestioned customs surrounding relations between states. For the era from 1648 to 1814, the notion of territoriality as the basis of political organization was only beginning to emerge. Dynastic holdings were often noncontiguous (e.g., the king of England, George I, was also the king of Hanover; the king of Spain "owned" numerous holdings in what today is Italy), and the notion of lineal frontiers was only rudimentary. But by the end of the eighteenth century, it was commonly accepted—as it is today—that a state occupies a defined piece of territory, and that its jurisdiction extends only to the extremities of that territory. So sovereignty referred not only to a domination over subjects, but also over real estate. To think otherwise might seem strange to us, but at the time of the Westphalia treaties, the notion of territory rather than people as the basis of political jurisdiction was not well understood or defined.

Another assumption is somewhat more obvious, and it underlies the system of international law that was beginning to develop in the late seventeenth century. This is the notion that treaties are binding (*pacta sunt servanda*). Once a sovereign state freely enters into a treaty relationship, its obligations and responsibilities must be met unless circumstances have changed to such an extent that the original treaty is irrelevant or blatantly harmful to one of the signatories. This is hardly a revolutionary idea, but, by contrast, in certain eras of the ancient Chinese international system, treaties were often seen as temporary stratagems; hence the reliance on the exchange of hostages to make certain that the terms would be honored.

There were other rules that operated to guide the mutual relations of the seventeenth- and eighteenth-century dynasts. Diplomatic immunities (do not harm or kill the messenger) underlay the new system of exchanging professional diplomats. The advantages of clear and open diplomatic communication on a permanent basis far outweighed some of the risks associated with diplomatic espionage. Communications could not take place were ambassadors or other envoys subject to arrest, torture, or execution. Assassination of dynasts to advance state or family interests was not condoned. This was an unstated assumption of the times. To us, it hardly seems revolutionary or even significant. But we should recall that politically motivated assassinations had been practiced fairly routinely in Europe throughout the fifteenth and sixteenth centuries.

The various monarchs of Europe developed few institutions, beyond diplomacy and war, to manage their relations. The Treaty of Westphalia succeeded in creating a type of political order for Europe, although it did not create peace. As we have seen, it established a number of the "rules of the game." These formally established the international system as one based on sovereign independence. Left to their own devices, the dynasts plotted, plundered, and acted in a predatory manner against each other, with war the frequent consequence. There were crises that were handled by diplomats in such a manner as to prevent war, and a number of wars were terminated by the mediation of a third party, usually a neutral monarch. But these mediations were devices to end wars, not to prevent them. Because the dynasts did not typically see war as a great social problem, they did not think it necessary to construct conflict-resolving mechanisms. Thus, they constructed no international organizations, and few monarchs would dare to interject themselves in the quarrels of others merely for the sake of peace. And so wars occurred regularly, alliances shifted frequently, and the dynasts could, often for rather frivolous reasons, take up the sword.

Despite the prevalence of warfare, the formal and informal rules of the system helped to maintain stability; that is, to sustain dynastic political orders, independence, and sovereignty. Few actors were eliminated, as they had been in China during the Spring and Autumn and subsequent periods. Most of literate Europe was appalled at the successive carvings up of Poland. While the fortunes of the powers varied considerably—Prussia grew to be a major power, while Sweden declined to a second-rate power—none was threatened with extinction. If a monarch ruled by divine right, as was the typical justification for dynastic rule and succession, to destroy another monarch would be contrary to God's great plan and will. This religious consideration was as important in moderating international politics as were the rules, treaties, and customs of the time. Finally, the mechanism of the balance of power helped to preserve the independence of states and to sustain the principle of political sovereignty developed at Westphalia. Those who had pretensions to continental hegemony, as Charles V and his Hapsburg successors had in the sixteenth and seventeenth centuries and as Louis XIV entertained during his later years, were successfully stymied by coalitions of dynasts who wanted to retain their autonomy and independence. Hence, for the period until the defeat of Napoleon in 1814, few of the essential characteristics of international politics changed fundamentally.

Conclusion

What generalizations can we make from the review of these three historical international systems? The reader should attempt to make as many comparisons as possible, including comparisons with our contemporary global system. Perhaps the most interesting questions are raised about the changes in the systems. What were the sources of change? Frequently they were technological and administrative. Once-subordinate states created their own administrative systems and effectively challenged universal powers such as the Chou dynasty or the Holy Roman Emperor. Ideologies or religions of universal solidarity, sustained by the church or the universal monarch, were challenged by various forms of sectarianism, leading to political fragmentation. The notion of medieval Christian solidarity, organized under the Pope and the Holy Roman Empire, was successfully challenged by the Protestant heresy. The doctrine of sovereignty became a practical legal instrument for justifying political fragmentation, and for creating and sustaining the autonomy of dynastic rulers. The parallels between the decline of the Chou monarchy and the decline of European imperial and religious unity are striking.

Technology played an important role in causing some critical types of change. The inability of the Greek city-states to survive as independent political entities was partly caused by the development of the torsion catapult and the siege tower, both instruments that allowed the Macedonians, and later the Hellenistic kings and Roman attackers, to bypass or override the walls of the Greek cities. Population distributions also mattered: As noted, most Greek city-states had small populations, and hence small armies. But Alexander the Great, succeeding Hellenistic kingdoms, and the Romans fielded armies in the tens of thousands. The city-states could not effectively defend themselves against superior technology and numbers, and so they passed into history. The Greek system of city- states was succeeded by competing empires.

Another kind of change is in the distribution of power among the units in the system. The structure of power was *diffuse* in the Spring and Autumn periods in China, during the period from 600 to 431 B.C. in the case of Greece, and throughout the period from 1648 to 1814 in Europe. Why did it change, and what were the consequences? In China and Greece, political fragmentation, accompanied by frequent wars and state insecurity, ended with one of the external actors conquering all others and converting them into an empire. This was not the fate of Europe; but had Napoleon won, he would have transformed Europe into a French-centered continental empire. We see, then, certain cyclical patterns: Empires tend to disintegrate into systems of political fragmentation, of diffuse power among several or more great powers, only to be followed again by empire. In the case of Europe, the great efforts by Napoleon, Hitler, and Stalin to create continental empires came to nought, so the pattern has not repeated itself in modern history. But there is a lesson: When a number of independent states exhaust themselves through war, as was the case in China and Greece (and also in fifteenth-century Italy), an outsider may come in to get the spoils and to create a homogeneous political order, usually an empire. In the twentieth century, it was the intervention of the United States in Europe that prevented the "outsider" (first Hitler, then Stalin) from building a European-centered empire. The consequences of the political collapse of Europe after World War I and World War II came close to paralleling the fate of the Chinese states in the face of Ch'in.

In some of the periods, there was also a *polarized* power structure, where two blocs of states vied against each other. This structure of power emerged during the Warring States period in China, and in Greece during the fourth century B.C. with the two great alliances led by Athens and Sparta. The reader will quickly see the parallels with the distribution of power between the socialist and Western blocs following World War II.

Thus, we have three fundamentally different types of international systems, as defined by the structure of power. There is the empire or feudal system, where power is concentrated at the center or core, and where the subservient political units, enjoying only limited autonomy, exchange services (provision of manpower and taxes for the emperor's court and armies) for security. The forces of fragmentation build in strength, however, and imperial unity is threatened. Ultimately, the units attain independence (sustained by legal doctrines such as sovereignty). The configuration of power is diffused among a fairly large number of "great powers." But the drive to establish hegemony motivates some of them, and a polarized, or bloc, system may emerge. In such a system, the lesser states—as was the case in NATO and the Warsaw Pact during the late 1940s and throughout the 1950s—are willing to exchange their freedom of action for the security provided by the predominant powers or, as they are called today, the "superpowers."

The reader will see in this chapter no mention of individual events, or what might be called the headlines of the day in ancient China, Greece, or eighteenth-century Europe. We have moved from description of individual events to the characterizations of *typical* structures and processes that spanned many years, in some cases centuries. We have also provided a basis for comparisons with our own age. Lest we think that every major development of the late twentieth century is unprecedented or historically unique, there are always parallels to be drawn between eras—but watch out for false analogies. The year 1989 brought about fundamental changes in the structure of international power: A polarized system was certainly decaying already in the 1960s and 1970s, but its demise was verified only at the end of the next decade. We appear to be moving toward a system of more diffused power, something that also occurred in ancient China, in fifth-century B.C. Greece, and in Europe after the Treaty of Westphalia. The consequences are problematic. But before we contemplate those, we must outline the major characteristics of our new system. The main question is this: What is new, and what is mainly a continuation of past international practices?

Questions for Study, Analysis, and Discussion

1. What is an international system?
2. What criteria can be used to distinguish different systems from each other? Are there criteria other than those used in the chapter?
3. How does the structure of a system impact on the external policies of its constituent members?
4. What is the significance of the Treaty of Westphalia to historical European and contemporary international politics?
5. What sorts of factors can explain changes from one type of international system to another? Provide examples from the Chinese, Greek, and early modern European systems.
6. How can one define *stability* within an international system?

7. In what ways were Europe's eighteenth-century dynastic states different from states today? In what ways would those differences account for differences in foreign policy behavior in the two eras?

Selected Bibliography

Adcock, Frank, and J. D. Moseley, Diplomacy in Ancient Greece. London: Thames and Hudson, 1975.

Bayley, C. C., War and Society in Renaissance Florence. Toronto: University of Toronto Press, 1961.

Bozeman, Adda B., Politics and Culture in International History. Princeton, N.J.: Princeton University Press, 1960.

Eisenstadt, S. N., The Political Systems of Empires. New York: Free Press, 1963.

Fliess, Peter J., Thucydides and the Politics of Bipolarity. Baton Rouge: Louisiana State University Press, 1966.

Ghoshal, U. N., "The System of Inter-State Relations and Foreign Policy in the Early Arthasastra State," in *India Antigua.* Leiden: Brill, 1947.

Gills, Barry K., and Andre Gunder Frank, "World System Cycles, Crises and Hegemonial Shifts, 1700 B.C. to 1700 A.D." *Review,* 15, 4 (1992), 621–87.

Graham, A. J., Colony and Mother City in Ancient Greece. Manchester: Manchester University Press, 1964.

Hanrieder, Wolfram, "Actor Objectives and International Systems," *Journal of Politics,* 27 (1965), 109–32.

Hasebrook, Johannes, Trade and Politics in Ancient Greece. London: Bell, 1933.

Korff, Baron S. A., "An Introduction to the History of International Law," *American Journal of International Law,* 18 (1924), 246–59.

Larus, Joel, Ed., Comparative World Politics: Readings in Western and Pre-Modern Non-Western International Relations. Belmont, Calif.: Wadsworth, 1964.

Lubasz, Heinz, Ed., The Development of the Modern State. New York: Macmillan, 1964.

Mattingly, Garrett, Renaissance Diplomacy. London: Jonathan Cape, 1955.

McGregor, Malcolm F., The Athenians and Their Empire. Vancouver: University of British Columbia Press, 1987.

Modelski, George, "Agraria and Industria: Two Models of the International System," *World Politics,* 14 (1961), 118–43.

———, "Comparative International Systems," *World Politics,* 14 (1962), 662–74.

———, "Kautilya: Foreign Policy and International System in the Ancient Hindu World," *American Political Science Review,* 58 (1964), 549–60.

Nussbaum, Arthur, A Concise History of the Law of Nations. New York: Macmillan, 1961.

Phillipson, Coleman, The International Law and Custom of Ancient Greece and Rome. London: Macmillan, 1911.

Russell, Frank M., Theories of International Relations. New York: Appleton-Century-Crofts, 1936.

Walker, Richard L., The Multi-State System of Ancient China. Hamden, Conn.: Shoe String Press, 1953.

Watson, Adam, "Systems of States," *Review of International Studies,* 16 (April 1990), 99–110.

———*The Evolution of International Society.* London: Routledge, 1992.

Chapter

3

___

The Contemporary Global System

This chapter will be long for two reasons: (1) The contemporary global system is complex, as the five models introduced in Chapter 1 suggest; and (2) it is necessary to spell out in some detail those characteristics of the system that bring stability (continuity of the systems's main features) and those that are changing it. We begin by examining the five criteria for comparing systems, as introduced in the previous chapter: boundaries, the nature of the units, the structure, major forms of interaction, and the rules that guide or govern those interactions.

The Global System

We say that today we have a global system because all political and social units of the world are interconnected. There is no longer any region that is thoroughly isolated from the rest, and with only some very minor exceptions, all societies in the world have been organized politically into states of one kind or another. And those states and societies all mutually interact, though certainly not in a symmetrical manner. Decisions made in Moscow, Tokyo, and Paris, for example, may have numerous intended and unintended consequences in Addis Ababa, Bangkok, Santiago, and Libreville. Because of the asymmetries in the world, however, events and trends in the latter places, while perhaps newsworthy, are much less likely to have a direct impact on a Russian, Japanese, or French citizen.

All 184 members of the United Nations maintain contacts with one another—at times only sporadic and insignificant, as, let us say, are the bilateral relations between Paraguay and Bhutan, and at others, very deep, persistent, and significant, as they are between Washington and London. All states are members of the society of states (as indicated by United Nations membership) and they commonly accept the elementary norms and rules of membership, as we will describe them below. There are, then, no more boundaries *between* systems in the world. All states and their societies belong to a single entity, what we call the global system.

This system did not emerge spontaneously. Europe was the core throughout the fifteenth to nineteenth centuries. Through various waves of colonialism, the most recent occurring in the last thirty years of the nineteenth century, almost all of Africa and the South Pacific were colonized, and China was thoroughly penetrated by Western economic, military, and diplomatic agents. Only a few societies—Ethiopia and Siam, for example—were left out of the formal political, economic, and military expansion of European society. The remainder either became settler colonies, like the United States, Canada, Australia, and New Zealand, or arenas for Western economic and commercial expansion and exploitation.

The "Westernization" of the world did not involve only the expansion of military power and commercial activity. Ideas and ideologies were also exported. These included Christianity, science and technology, Western concepts of bureaucratic government, and secular ideologies surrounding the production and consumption of wealth. Indigenous traditional social forms and ideas did not die out, but they faced powerful competition. Many of them ultimately succumbed to Western forms.

Among those Western ideas were variants of Marxism, democratic theory and, in particular, the doctrine of national self-determination. Starting in early nineteenth-century Europe, and expanding slowly around the world through the end of World War I, the idea of self-determination served as the source of nationalist uprisings against multi-ethnic empires, such as Austria-Hungary, and against colonialism. In the latter case, the colonial authorities sowed the seeds of their own destruction. We will return in a few moments to the ideological underpinnings of modern states; here it is sufficient to point out that there has been a tremendous explosion of state-making during the past century. On the eve of World War I, there were sixteen states in Europe, and a few entities like Japan and China had become at least provisional members of the states system. World War I and the collapse of the Austrian, Russian, and Ottoman empires created in a historical instant the following new states: Finland, Estonia, Latvia, Lithuania, Poland, Czechoslovakia, Hungary, and Yugoslavia (made up of pre-existing states). A number of states or quasi-states on the peripheries of Europe gained membership to the League of Nations, thus implying their entry into the society of states; among them were Turkey, Persia (Iran), and Abyssinia (Ethiopia).

The process of state-creation gained new vigor as the result of World War II. Whatever their long-range intentions, the colonial powers had neither the will nor the power to maintain control over huge tracts of land and millions of people who had all come to believe in the doctrine of self-determination. The United Nations was created in 1945 by 52 members, mostly from Europe and Latin America. Today, in only a half century, the membership has increased to 184. Put another way, 72 percent of the contemporary states of the world have been born in the last 50 years. Only about a dozen states (e.g., France, Great Britain, Spain, Holland, Sweden, and the like) can claim to have pedigrees that go back more than 200 years.

Our global system is thus a "young" system. Most of its members have not been around for very long, and even a majority have no history as a sovereign state that goes back further than one generation. The ideas and institutions of diplomacy are old, as they were developed in Europe starting in the fourteenth century, but the players of contemporary diplomatic games are for the most part novices.

The Nature of the Units

There are some important differences between the ways states were created in nineteenth- and early twentieth-century Europe, and how they evolved in the colonial world following World War II. It is important to keep these differences in mind, because they have significant consequences on how states conduct their foreign policies, and what kinds of international problems they face.

Throughout the nineteenth century, the sentiments and ideologies of nationalism generally preceded the creation of states. Minority nationalities in multi-national empires such as czarist Russia, Austria-Hungary, and the Ottoman Empire developed feelings of national solidarity and group identity, and ultimately began demanding political independence on the theory that each "nation" (ethnic/language/religious group) should form the basis of separate states. The process started with Greek agitation for independence from the Ottoman Empire. Greek independence was achieved, with the help of the European powers, in 1832. Subsequently, Romanians, Bulgarians, and other Balkan peoples, most of whom were Christian rather than Muslim, fought and gained independence. By the early twentieth century, the multinational empires were doomed, and during World War I they collapsed. The successor states were founded upon the principle of nationality, validated usually by elections or plebiscites. The old idea that a state could be made up of the dynasts' hereditary realms had been replaced with the notion of popular sovereignty and the idea that a political order is legitimate to the extent that it gives expression to distinct ethnic, language, and religious groups. The concept of nationality, previously referring just to a geographic location where distinct groups lived, now became wedded to the concept of the state.

Of course this idea could not be implemented without difficulties because population distributions do not follow neat territorial frontiers. All of the new successor states contained significant minorities—the Slovaks in Czechoslovakia, the Hungarians in Romania, the Germans in Poland, and the like. Should they also not have their own states? Here the question became practical and political. The principle of self-determination can be taken only so far. The intermixture of populations, economic practicalities, and strategic considerations preclude complete adherence to the principle. Some states, it was commonly acknowledged in post–World War I Europe, could not survive except in the multi-ethnic and multi-language format.

The point, then, is that nationalism and the sense of nationhood existed prior to the creation of these new states. The states existed in sentiment, loyalty, identification, and solidarity before they earned or gained formal sovereignty.

The process of state-formation in many of the colonial areas was quite different. In the nineteenth century, the colonial powers drew boundaries, particularly across Africa, to suit their own purposes. Those purposes had little or nothing to do with ethnic, language, and religious population distributions. Frequently, boundaries were nothing but straight lines fashioned in a foreign ministry as part of a deal to carve up a region of Africa or Asia among competing powers. Many of these states were *created* by the colonial powers, and their existence as independent states was validated by the United Nations before a strong sense of nationalism had developed. There is, for example, no single people that corresponds to the territorial boundaries of the Central African Republic, Cameroon, Nigeria, Kenya, and many other new states. These states are made up of multiplicities of ethnic, language, and religious groups. Individuals' loyalties extend primarily to the tribe, clan, region, or other significant reference group, and often only secondarily—if at all—to the state that has been created in their names.

Most of these states, to be sure, had "national liberation movements." Their leaders spoke in the name of the "people," but their political referent was the geographic and often artificial colonial creation, not a distinct and unified society. Their right to rule in the post-independence period was seldom validated by elections or plebiscites. The result has been that many of the new states are "weak"—not weak militarily, but in the sense that significant sectors of the populations do not identify strongly with the ruling groups or the post-colonial state and its symbols. Sentiments of nationalism are not deeply rooted, if they exist at all, and the social fabric of the country is weakened by frequent or incessant communal conflicts between the various groups that make up the population. Secessionist movements abound among minorities seeking to create their own states. The Palestine Liberation Organization is one of the best-known groups attempting to create its own state, but there are dozens of others spread throughout Africa, Asia, and Southeast Asia. In the 1990s, there is even a secessionist movement on the island of Bougainville that wants independence from Papua–New Guinea. In the next chapter we will outline some of the foreign policy consequences of the fact of "weak" states.

Ethnic heterogeneity is not, of course, the only source of state weakness. In Europe, countries such as Switzerland and Finland are multi-ethnic, but they are "strong" states in the sense of commanding loyalties from all segments of the population and maintaining extensive and effective government services throughout the society. How many weak states are there? A 1981 study underlined the extent to which most states are comprised of many different societies or nations. Of the 161 independent states at that time, 12 percent has at least *three* large ethnic groups that made up between 34 and 97 percent of the total; the remainder were distributed between 5 and 19 different minority groups. Thirteen percent of the countries had two major nationalities that comprised between 65 and 95 percent of the population. Ten percent had one group that constituted between 40 and 60 percent of the total, with the remainder distributed between 7 and 25 different groups. Thirty-eight percent of the states had one group that constituted between 60 and 95 percent of the population.[1] And 27 percent of the countries could be considered reasonably homogenous, where just one national group accounted for more than 95 percent of the population. The point is clear: A majority of states have populations divided among two or more—and often many more—distinct ethnic, language, and religious groups. India is a marvel of survival, with 36 major languages, groups professing all of the world's major religions, and literally hundreds of ethnic, communal, and caste groups. It has survived in part because the Indian constitution guarantees equal rights for all and bases citizenship on membership in the community. Many other countries base citizenship on ethnicity, which renders all others automatically into minorities. In country after country, these minorities are victimized, excluded from political influence and office, and sometimes threatened with genocide or expulsion. Rule based on ethnicity rather than citizenship is one of the chief characteristics of weak states.

The second major point about the units of the contemporary international system is that the disparities among their attributes are today more pronounced than ever before. In eighteenth-century Europe, differences between Denmark and France or Saxony and Hesse were marked, but they were a matter of gradations. Today, the differences are so great as to suggest significant qualitative distinctions. The largest country—China—has a population of about 1 billion. In contrast, Nauru's population numbers about 6,000. It would take millions of Singapores to equal the land mass of Russia. The government of Norway rules through democratic consent, and its leaders gain little through holding office except prestige and popularity. In contrast, the governments of Haiti under the Duvaliers, or Nicaragua under the Somozas, were run as personal fiefdoms, without any basis of popular legitimacy. Rule was maintained by coercion, fear, graft, and corruption. The rulers enriched themselves personally, using tax revenues and foreign aid to amass fortunes. The rulers and their friends lived opulently among popular squalor. There are still a few regimes of this type, but their numbers are quite small and probably dwindling. There are also, however, numerous praetorian military regimes that perpetuate themselves through coercion and terror. The major difference from the previous category is that their leaders do a better job of hiding their privileges, and they go to some lengths to manufacture manifestations of popularity. Romania under Nicolae Ceaucescu and North Korea under the venerable Kim Il-Sung are examples.

Finally, the level of technological development, public education, and general well-being among populations varies extensively. In the eighteenth century, a French visitor to newly "discovered" Thailand could report that Thai society was not entirely different from that of his home country. The majority of the population was made up of the peasantry; there was a small commercial class, an aristocracy, and other groups of privilege. The similarities were perhaps as pronounced as were the social differences between the two countries.

---

[1]See Gunnar P. Nielsson, "States and Nation-Groups: A Global Taxonomy," in *New Nationalism of the Developed West*, Edwar A. Tiryakian and Ronald Rogowski, eds. (Boston: Allen and Unwin, 1985), pp. 30–32.

Today, there are much greater disparities between societies. Populations in countries such as Japan have annual per capita incomes of $20,000 or more; there is a high degree of income equality where typically the top 10 percent of income earners do not own more than 25 percent of the national wealth. Literacy rates are over 99 percent. Life expectancy approaches eighty years. Daily calorie and protein consumption are well above minimum requirements. Citizens have full and often free access to medical and dental care. Secondary school participation rates (the proportion of the relevant age group, twelve to seventeen, actually attending school) are usually over 80 percent. These are just some of the indicators of well-being and equality of opportunity.

In contrast, many populations in Africa, South Asia, Central America, and a few other regions demonstrate all the characteristics of widespread poverty, despite some great strides forward compared to several decades earlier. Life expectancies are about thirty years less than those found in the wealthy countries. Literacy rates, although growing rapidly, are well under 50 percent of the population. Calorie and protein intake are insufficient to maintain health and normal growth. Access to medical services is often difficult and services are of generally low quality. Secondary school participation rates are often as low as 20 percent of the relevant age group, while less than 1 percent attend any sort of post-secondary education. Population growth rates remain high, while the amount of land available for cultivation holds steady or shrinks due to desertification, soil erosion, deforestation, and pollution. Mass migrations to the cities create immense housing problems, slums, and unemployment. The processes of development have in many cases worsened many of these problems. Finally, wealth distribution is highly uneven. Typically, the richest 10 percent of the population owns more than 40 percent of the country's wealth, while the poorest 20 percent owns less than 5 percent.

Despite these great disparities between the wealthy industrial countries and the poorest developing countries, it is important to acknowledge great strides made by many developing nations over what is historically a very short time. Table 3-1 lists the growth rates and percentage increases of several "quality of life" indicators among industrial and developing societies. While significant gaps remain in some cases, the "catching up" of some countries is remarkable.

The important point about the great disparities of attributes is that they help create international dependencies. The lack of resources makes many developing states weak in all dimensions. To survive, they need outside sources of economic aid, frequent doses of humanitarian assistance to help cope with natural disasters such as droughts and floods, military aid to build and maintain even rudimentary armed forces (which are often used more for maintaining the regime against its internal critics and secessionist movements than against external attack), and markets for their few exports. We will look in more detail later at the problems of dependency. Here it is adequate to underline that about 50 percent of the states of the contemporary world are weak and yet confront immense problems associated with development.

TABLE 3-1
Quality of Life Indicators, Selected Countries

COUNTRY	LIFE EXPEC- TANCY		PER CAPITA INCOME PERCENT OF U.S. PCI				PERCENTAGE OF AGE GROUP ENROLLED IN SECONDARY SCHOOL		DAILY CALORIE SUPPLY PER CAPITA		
	1977	1991	1977	Percent of U.S.	1991	Percent of U.S.	1976	1990	1965	1988	Percent Change
Ethiopia	39	48	$ 110	1	120	0.5	6	15	1,824	1,658	− 8
Tanzania	51	49	190	2	100	0.4	3	4	1,832	2,151	+20
Ivory Coast	46	57	690	8	690	3.1	17	N/A	2,360	2,365	+ 1
Nigeria	48	49	420	5	340	1.5	10	20	2,185	2,039	− 6
India	51	58	150	2	330	1.5	28	44	2,111	2,104	*
Indonesia	48	59	300	4	610	2.7	20	45	1,800	2,670	+49
Malaysia	67	71	930	11	2,520	11.3	45	56	2,247	2,686	+16
Singapore	70	74	2,880	27	14,210	64	55	69	2,297	2,892	+27
South Korea	63	72	820	10	6,330	29	63	87	2,256	2,878	+28
Brazil	62	66	1,360	16	2,940	13	18	39	2,402	2,709	+12
Venezuela	66	72	2,660	31	2,730	12	38	35	2,321	2,547	+10
Trinidad and Tobago	70	70	2,380	28	3,670	17	36	80	2,497	2,960	+20
Syria	57	66	910	11	1,160	5	9	52	2,195	3,168	+44
Japan	76	79	5,670	67	26,930	121	85	96	2,687	2,848	+ 6
Canada	74	77	8,460	99	20,440	92	82	100	3,212	3,447	+10
Finland	72	75	6,160	72	23,980	108	78	100	3,111	3,170	+ 1
United Kingdom	73	76	4,420	52	16,550	74	56	84	3,353	3,252	− 3
Greece	73	76	2,810	33	6,340	29	22	99	3,049	3,699	+21
Switzerland	74	78	9,970	117	33,610	151	N/A	N/A	3,412	3,547	+ 1
U.S.A.	73	76	8,520	N/A	22,240	—	(est)	92	3,224	3,666	+13

N/A = Data not available. * = Change is negligible.
Source: data are from World Bank, *World Development Report* (New York: Oxford University Press, 1993).

Nations and States

A common error in analyses of international politics is to confuse the terms *state* and *nation*. Technically, inter*national* relations is a misnomer. It really should be something like *interstate relations*. The concept of a nation refers to a community whose members see themselves as distinct from other communities, usually different in terms of history, culture, language, ethnicity, religion, or some combination of them. The idea of nationhood is a variable, not a constant. In mid- nineteenth century Italy, for example, only about 3 percent of Italians could speak the common language; most spoke highly distinct regional dialects, and most identified themselves as Sicilians, Romans, and the like. By the end of World War I, however, most Italian immigrants to North America identified themselves as Italians. The Italian nation had grown or developed within less than seventy-five years. We can also see the collapse of certain community identities, or the overcoming of one identity with another. Many of the elites of Yugoslavia after World War II identified themselves primarily as Yugoslavs. By the 1990s, they had shed themselves of this identity and adopted the narrower identities of Serbs, Croats, Slovenes, Macedonians, and the like. Seventy years of Yugoslav statehood and forty-five years of Communist rule failed to eradicate these more primordial identities.

One of the great sources of international conflict in the twentieth century—a point re-emphasized in Chapter 15—has been the lack of "fit" between the demographic distributions of nationalities and the boundaries of states. As suggested, there are very few states based on a single ethnic community (Japan, Iceland, Denmark are among them). The multi-ethnic character of most states has led to countless conflicts and wars. Usually, this is where the population of one community seeks to extend protection or aid to its kin in a neighboring state. Or, even more likely, a minority within one state seeks secession in order to unite with its ethnic kin in a neighboring state. This is the phenomenon of *irredentism*, and it is a common source of conflict. Consider, for example, the case of the Albanians. Over 50 percent of the Albanians live outside Albania; most are in the Kosovo region of Serbia and in neighboring Macedonia. Predictably, there is a movement among Kosovo's Albanians to unite with their brethren in Albania proper, rather than to remain, as they consider it, second-class citizens deprived of many rights in the Serbian region called Kosovo. This leads to tensions between Albania and Serbia (Yugoslavia); some observers fear ultimate armed conflict between Serbia and Albania, triggered by the Kosovo Albanians' search to "liberate" themselves from Serbia and to unite with Albania. This scenario is repeated in many areas of Africa, South Asia, the Balkans, and in regions of the former Soviet Union. Wherever one finds a national community distributed between two or more states, irredentism is likely to lead to international conflict.

In addition to having more than one nation within a state, there is also the problem of stateless nations. The Palestinians are a prime example, as are the Kurds, whose population concentrations straddle four different countries—Iraq, Iran, Syria, and Turkey. As could be expected, many Kurds wish to create their own state. As a minority, particularly in Turkey and Iraq, they are oppressed in many ways and believe that they cannot sustain their unique identity and culture unless they have the protection that can be afforded by their own state. The Kurdish problem has been a constant source of tension between the countries where they are located.

We thus have nation-states, where the national community and the state largely coincide, nations without states, and multinational states. There are, finally, a few states without nations. The Vatican has many of the attributes of a state (a territorial base, a bureaucracy, a diplomatic corps, and the like), but it has no underlying community based on ethnicity or language. Its relevant community is spread throughout the world as, namely, the community of believers. But this is not a nation.

Nationalism is not necessarily a force leading to international conflict (it should not be confused with patriotism, which is a sense of pride in a nation's or state's achievement). It is a set of ideas that helps to distinguish peoples from one another; it is also a form of ideology that can be used to mobilize communities to seek statehood. This search has historically led to war. Most states, including the United States, have been born through wars, both civil and international. Since 1945, many engaged in wars of "national [sic] liberation," not unlike the American war of independence. The goal is statehood. It was true for American colonials in the 1770s; for the Greeks, Bulgars, Romanians, Serbs, and other Balkan peoples in the nineteenth century; and since 1945, for the numerous colonial peoples of the Southern Hemisphere. In some cases, nations coexist reasonably well within a single state (Switzerland and India, for example), but where some communities face oppression, exclusion from political power, or persecution ranging from genocide to disenfranchisement, they are likely to take up arms to gain independence, that is, sovereign statehood. This search for statehood is one of the predominant historical trends of the last two hundred years, and it continues unabated.

The Collapse of States

If the flowering of statehood has been one of the hallmarks of the modern international system, it does not mean that all states endure. Many, as suggested, suffer from debilitating weaknesses. Some continue to exist primarily through the support of external friends who provide critical financial, material, and personnel assistance. It is unlikely, for example, that Jordan could have survived as a state without critical assistance from Great Britain from the 1920s until the 1970s. Some states fail; they collapse. They remain sovereign entities in name only but otherwise have few of the hallmarks of sovereignty, in particular, a monopoly over the legitimate instruments of order and coercion. They cannot provide minimal security, law and order, nor functioning economic and communications infrastructures. Contemporary Lebanon is run less by the official government than by local militias, warlords, Palestinian refugees, the Israeli military (in the extreme south), the Syrian military (in the Bekaa Valley), and diverse religious movements. There is an official government, but it does not rule. Popular loyalties are split among the diverse groups, and as most are heavily armed, the central government has no way to make its authority effective. In 1990 to 1991, the government of Somalia fled into exile, and diverse warlords filled the vacuum. None could provide the essential services of a state, and when mass starvation developed, largely as a result of the multi-faced civil war, no authority could provide necessary assistance. The United Nations eventually intervened to provide minimum food but soon became involved in the local warlords' feuds.

The Somali case is not just a civil war between two factions attempting to gain control of the state. It is a case of the absolute collapse of statehood, leading to social catastrophe. Even in the bitter war in Bosnia, governments began or continued to function behind the lines. In Somalia and Lebanon, governance gives way to large-scale chaos.

Nonstate Actors

Compared to the dozens of micro-states and weak states, there are a number of nonstate actors that have a great deal more influence developing and promoting issues on the international agenda. Although there are great varieties of nonstate actors functioning today, we will consider only those that have the most important impact on international politics. These would include (1) territorial nonstate actors, such as national liberation movements; (2) nonterritorial transnational organizations, such as multinational corporations; and (3) intergovernmental organizations, such as NATO or the Organization for Economic Cooperation and Development (OECD).

The politically most important territorial nonstate actors are the various national liberation movements and secessionist groups. Their activities may be conducted throughout the world, but they are territorial because the purpose of their actions is to create states. The most famous of these organizations is the Palestine Liberation Organization. Its activities are conducted throughout the world. Even though it is not a state, it maintains "diplomatic" relations with a number of governments and less formal contacts with militant groups in many countries. It has observer status at the United Nations, it commands military strength, and it has determined what sort of peace arrangements are being made in the Middle East. Through its propaganda and, in the past, terrorist activities, it underlined the plight of the Palestinian population to the point where it became one of the most significant and enduring problems on the international agenda. Compared with many weak states, the decisions and activities of the PLO have had greater impact on world issues and on the foreign policy attention of the major powers.

Nonterritorial transnational organizations are characterized by (1) organized activities occurring simultaneously in a number of countries; (2) objectives that do not relate to interests within any given territory; and (3) component parts that are essentially nonpolitical. The Catholic Church is perhaps the oldest organization with these characteristics. Although it has an administrative center in Rome, its activities occur in virtually every country in the world. Like all nonterritorial transnational organizations, its livelihood depends upon unfettered access to people living in all countries. Its activities are also transnational in the sense that if one component unit gets into difficulties, it can draw upon the financial, administrative, personnel, and spiritual capabilities of other units or of the entire organization. The Church, of course, has only a very indirect and intermittent impact on international politics, but occasionally its involvement becomes more apparent. The Pope has made pronouncements on a variety of international issues, including economic development, arms control, and the nature of political regimes. To the extent that these pronouncements influence public attitudes or the views of foreign policy makers, the impact may be direct.

A newer type of nonterritorial transnational organization is the multinational corporation (MNC). Like the Church, its operations depend upon access to a number of societies. Also like the Church, its activities are primarily nonpolitical. The Church exists to save souls and to cultivate the spiritual life of people no matter where or how they live. The multinational corporation exists to make profits for shareholders and to expand markets. The component units of the multinational corporation are independent, yet tied together by financial and personnel bonds. If one unit gets into financial difficulties, it can be rescued by the headquarters or some other unit. If one of the units is no longer profitable, it can be closed down and reestablished somewhere else.

Most authorities on the multinational firm distinguish between nationally based firms that conduct some operations abroad and true multinationals. To be classified in the latter group, a firm must have some minimum number of foreign subsidiaries operating in various countries. A minimum of six countries is often used as the cutoff point. Others have listed as MNCs only those corporations whose assets, sales, earnings, production, and employment come significantly (perhaps 25 percent) from abroad.

Multinational corporations reflect the increasing globalization of the world economy. Just as in Europe and America, where most firms began with local markets and ultimately spread their activities to regions and then the entire nation, since World War II many industrial giants have continued expanding their productive and marketing activities to other regions of the world. Until the late 1960s, most MNCs were American- or European-based, but over the last two decades, Japanese firms have become prominent as economic actors in many regions of the world. Most recently, we have witnessed the appearance of MNCs whose home is a developing country (LDC). Korean-based Hyundai operates a variety of enterprises throughout the world; Indian companies have projects in African countries such as Zambia, Somalia, and Tanzania; a number of Brazilian-based companies have built plants throughout Latin America and in several African countries. Many of these LDC-based MNCs specialize in technologies and products particularly appropriate for developing nations. Whatever the advantages and disadvantages of MNCs, they are becoming an increasingly visible form of economic organization, one which is no longer confined to the major industrial nations of the West.

By their size in physical and financial assets, we would assume that multinational corporations have a great impact on the contemporary global system. The assets of some of the largest MNCs, such as Unilever, IBM, General Motors, British Petroleum, and Mitsubishi, far outstrip the economic capabilities of small states. How can we measure the *political* impact of such immense concentrations of wealth and centers of control over economic resources? By allocating factors of production and controlling investment flows, no doubt the activities of MNCs seriously influence the character of economic development. Payment of royalties and taxes, establishment of new plants or closing down of old ones, decisions on where to locate plants, and advertising—these and many other decisions can crucially affect a developing country's economic structure, tax revenues, level of employment, and consumption patterns. It can be argued, for example, that by fostering consumerism through advertising, MNCs seriously distort development patterns in poor countries. Rather than promoting rural development, public transportation, or communal enterprise, MNCs try to create markets for middle-class needs and aspirations. By helping to destroy or alter indigenous cultural and economic patterns, moreover, the MNC may, at least indirectly, foster social strains and ultimately radical political movements. Several important guerrilla groups in Latin America, for example, claim that MNCs lead not only to direct political imperialism but also to a more subtle form of cultural pollution. Whatever the indirect impact, it is hard to identify and measure. No doubt it is greater among small, weak countries than in the industrial countries, where a majority of the activities of MNCs are already located.

The direct *political* impact of the MNC is perhaps easier to deal with. While it is more intermittent, it is also more obvious. For example, MNCs have occasionally played an important role in the domestic policies of host states. The United Fruit Company's record of activities in the "banana republics" of Central America is well known: It primarily involved attempts to keep governments in power that would allow the company to operate unfettered by regulations and excessive taxes. When a government hostile to its interests came to power in Guatemala in 1952, the company apparently assisted in helping the American government, through exiles in Honduras and Nicaragua, to overthrow the Arbenz regime. In 1970, the International Telephone and Telegraph Company promoted a scheme for toppling the Allende government in Chile. Nothing came of the matter, as U.S. government officials had already undertaken their own program to oust Allende (see Chapter 9).

Despite such examples of direct involvement in host-country politics, studies show that such episodes are exceptional. William Thompson studied 274 successful and unsuccessful military coups in the period from 1946 to 1969 and found very little evidence of direct involvement by MNCs.[2] Likewise, there is little evidence that MNCs have been a significant factor either as causes of, or participants in, international wars. There are, however a number of cases where the interest of an MNC and a home government coincided, so that the intervention of the home government against the host country served the interests of the MNC. Such was the case of the American government's involvement in the overthrow of the Mossadegh regime in Iran in 1953, after which American oil companies obtained new operating privileges in that country; the European oil companies' strong support of the French-British-Israeli invasion of the Suez Canal in 1956; the direct role of the Union Miniére Company in the Belgian government's support of the Katanga secession from the Congo in the early 1960s; and the pressure that American oil companies put on Washington to "do something" about Fidel Castro's nationalization of their assets in Cuba, so that the interests of the oil companies were probably one factor, among many, taken into consideration in planning the abortive Bay of Pigs invasion of 1961. Again, however, the evidence indicates that these are exceptional cases; although MNCs constantly seek, through persuasion of various sorts, to have the host governments treat their operations with a minimum of interference, or without high taxation, the occasions where such activity has included subversion are few. When a company prevails upon the home government to take up its case, if it feels it is being dealt with unfairly by the host government, there are regular and legitimate procedures provided under international law. It should be acknowledged, too, that often host governments have nationalized the assets of MNCs or instituted extremely high taxation rates, and that these steps were taken without the threat or commission of retaliation either by the MNCs or the home government. An increasing trend for hosts to expropriate MNC assets suggests that impact does not flow in only one direction.

Intergovernmental organizations (IGOs) are also nonstate actors that often have important influences on international politics and the domestic orders of states. Most IGOs reflect the interests of their members, but, occasionally, it makes sense to talk of the European Community's "policy," the "action" of the United Nations, or the "reaction" of NATO. These organizations often develop a common "external" policy that has behind it all the forces of persuasion the organization can muster. And sometimes the policy may contravene the interests of any single member's state.

---

[2] Cited in George Modelski, "Multinational Business: A Global Perspective," *International Studies Quarterly,* 16 (December 1972), 10–17.

Thus, the United Nations was instrumental in creating the Congo Republic and in reducing the possibilities of intervention into the Congo crisis by the United States and the Soviet Union. The European Community has a single external tariff and, on many occasions, bargains as a single political actor in its relations with nonmembers. The Food and Agriculture Organization can be expected in the coming decades to play an important role in helping to set up food reserves; in some cases, its activities could spell the difference between mass starvation and life in some of the LDCs.

As the web of international relationships has become more dense because of growing commercial, social, and communications transactions, the need for collaboration and coordination between governments has grown as well. Today there are more than 344 formal intergovernmental organizations (IGOs). And if the offshoots of these groupings, as well as some organizations blending inter-governmental and transnational characteristics, are included, the number is more than 1,100. Their growth in recent years has been prodigious. More than 94 percent of them have appeared since 1940, meaning that in a typical postwar year, more intergovernmental organizations were created than in the entire nineteenth century. The pace of growth, moreover, seems to be accelerating, as fully 70 percent of the IGOs have been established since 1960.[3] A large proportion of the IGOs deal with economic issues, and the densest web of memberships is in Western Europe where, for example, many countries belong simultaneously to such important organizations as NATO, the European Community, the Nordic Council, Euratom, and hundreds of more specialized intergovernmental agencies. Denmark, with 164 memberships in IGOs, leads the world. The United States in the early 1980s belonged to 122, while Canada had 110 memberships. While the industrial states of the West tend to have the most memberships, joining IGOs is among the first actions taken by states that have just achieved independence. The motivations for all states are essentially the same: the expectation of economic benefits and efficiencies, and, in other cases, increments of security and protection. It is not possible to measure the impact of such a great variety of organizations, but the dynamic growth in their numbers suggests that many of them provide substantial benefits to their members.

The global political system is thus inhabited by a variety of actors and agents, in addition to modern states, developing countries, and many micro-states. Some have considerable impact on selected global issues; others operate across national boundaries to achieve specific objectives, but without translating their concerns into major diplomatic issues. In general, nonstate actors can play several roles in international politics: (1) introduce an issue onto the international diplomatic agenda; (2) publicize and raise citizen consciousness regarding certain global or regional problems; (3) lobby national governments and international organizations to make decisions favorable to their cause; and (4) seek an outcome through direct action, sometimes (though relatively rarely) involving the threat or use of force.

---

[3]Harold K. Jacobson, William M. Reisinger, and Todd Mathers, "National Entanglements in International Governmental Organizations," *The Americal Political Science Review*, 80 (December 1986), 141–59.

A good illustration of these four types of activities is provided by the Greenpeace movement, a transnational organization with headquarters in London, but with national and regional organizations located throughout the world. In areas such as depletion of whale populations by the major whaling nations, French testing of nuclear weapons in the South Pacific, and the culling of seal pups on the ice floes off of Atlantic Canada, Greenpeace has been instrumental in bringing to an end certain activities (with the exception of the French nuclear tests). This has been done by a combination of publicity, carefully staged encounters with those whose activities they challenge—usually dramatic David-versus-Goliath confrontations—dissemination of scientific research results to international organizations and citizens' groups, lobbying national governments and organizations such as the International Whaling Commission, and mounting protests. Overall, Greenpeace has been highly successful in all of its roles and has used its transnational contacts to challenge governments and industries with resources far more extensive than its own.

Most nonstate actors, however, seek to achieve or defend very specific interests, few of which have a direct relationship to critical issues leading to war and peace. Governments are the arbiters of these ultimate questions. The state remains the critical actor of international politics, because (1) only it commands the allegiance of peoples occupying a defined territory; (2) only it possesses the capabilities to employ the ultimate threat (war); (3) governments, unlike most transnational organizations, are concerned with the full range of welfare and security issues of a population; and (4) only governments enjoy sovereignty. All other types of actors exist and operate only with the consent of governments. The example of the PLO supports the generalization: It has many of the characteristics of a government and on several occasions has been a major determinant of crisis and war. But it has these characteristics precisely because its objective is to create a Palestinian state; that is, to join the international society of states as a sovereign, legally equal, and territorially based political order. Amnesty International, multinational corporations, the International Red Cross, and the International Ice Hockey Federation seek none of these goals and are not, therefore, the critical actors of international politics.

While the state thus remains the most important actor in world politics, the argument has been made that its importance is declining and the political significance of nonstate actors has increased. States are no longer able to control transnational movements and influences from abroad. Populations are becoming increasingly sophisticated and competent, and their loyalties to the state, even when surrounded by iron curtains, can no longer be assumed. Armed with modern communications and transportation, regional or worldwide contacts, and the ability to learn what is going on outside their country, they can fatefully support, oppose, or even topple their governments. We have had many illustrations of the seeming decline of government control in the face of grass-roots transnational movements and the growing competence of publics. Several come to mind.

In 1987, the Russian nuclear reactor in Chernobyl broke down and caused a major leak of radioactive material. In the past, it had been the practice of the Soviet government not to publicize disasters within the USSR. But in this case, after several days of silence the authorities had to concede that a major catastrophe had occurred.

Radiation levels throughout Scandinavia and other parts of Europe jumped dangerously. American spy satellites took photographs of the flaming reactor and Russian officials' attempts to evacuate the immediate area. The event could not be kept from international examination. Through various forms of international communication, Soviet citizens soon learned of the disaster—long before Soviet authorities and national media acknowledged that it had taken place.

The wave of revolutions in the world throughout the latter part of the 1980s had great demonstration effects. Corazon Aquino's "yellow power" revolution in the Philippines toppled the Marcos regime in 1986 and set the example for South Koreans, whose massive demonstrations (and riots) ultimately forced the government to promise fair elections and to end military rule. The Korean democrats' success was conveyed through the media to the Burmese, who organized protests demanding the democratization of the country and the end of military rule.

The demonstration effect of democratic opposition to Communist rule in Eastern Europe was perhaps even more dramatic. It took the Solidarity movement almost ten years to achieve the capitulation of Communist rule and the creation of genuine pluralist political institutions in Poland. Taking heart from the Poles, the Hungarians achieved roughly the same results in about ten months. Thousands of East Germans then used Hungary as the escape route to West Germany, causing a massive population hemorrhage, vast demonstrations in East German cities, and the ultimate collapse of the Communist regime. The entire process took about one month. Shortly after, the demonstrations began in Prague, and in ten days the Communist authorities capitulated. It took only a few days of demonstrations, riots, and finally the execution of Nicolae Ceaucescu, to bring down the Communist government in Romania in December 1989. The process passed on to Bulgaria. What had begun as a meeting of shipyard workers in Gdansk, Poland, in 1979 ended ten years later with the collapse of communism in Eastern Europe. Despite the Communist regimes' monopoly of power, and their command of the media, the courts, the secret police, and the military, they stood defenseless against the spontaneous forces of opposition. Success in one country immediately brought emulation in another.

International demonstration effects and loss of government control are not confined to political developments. Private investors and speculators can shift billions of dollars or other currencies within a matter of moments. As the world economy becomes increasingly integrated, major events in one country can have immediate impact abroad. The stock market crash of October 1987 occurred almost simultaneously in Auckland, Tokyo, Toronto, Hong Kong, Amsterdam, New York and elsewhere. Interest rates in one country can have impacts on unemployment levels, tax policies, and interest rates in many others. Fads, fashions, and drug trade cannot be confined to single countries. In short, states have become increasingly porous to outside influences and transactions.

In the face of these integrating forces, is the state declining? One of the paradoxes of the contemporary global system is that despite all the technologies that shrink distances and help create millions of contacts between individuals of different societies, the forces of political fragmentation, separateness, and local loyalties are also strong and even increasing. Dozens of movements in both industrial and developing countries seek not integration but separation. The ultimate goal of much political activity in the contemporary world is the creation of more states. Autonomy and independence remain potent values, and they are buttressed by the nineteenth-century doctrine of self-determination, which is invoked by countless ethnic, language, and religious groups to justify their search for a separate state. The list of secessionist or independence movements is lengthy and continues to grow: the Tibetans in China; the Sikhs in the Punjab; the Kashmiris; the Tamils in Sri Lanka; the Shans, among others, in Myanmar (Burma); the Palestinians; the southern Sudanese; the Muslims in the Philippines; and the Kanakas in New Caledonia, just to mention a few. The phenomenon is not confined to the weak states of the developing world. There have been separatist movements in Spain (the Basques), France (the Corsicans), Italy (the Tyroleans), and Canada (the Quebecois).

To argue, then, that the state as the premier unit in international relations is fading away ignores a great deal of evidence to the contrary. That the state can no longer control *all* the activities of its citizens, or keep out all unwanted external influences, is correct, but this does not mean that the state as the premier form of political organization—a unit that provides a full range of services for its citizens—is becoming obsolete. As we will see in the next chapter, the state remains the only organization that can provide the two essential services that allow a society to survive and grow: security and welfare, broadly conceived. No other organization can provide these simultaneously. This is not to argue that all states provide them well, efficiently, justly, or fairly. But then most other kinds of organizations cannot provide them at all.

Political fragmentation is also sustained by the sentiment of nationalism, a crucial ingredient in personal identity. Individuals, according to William Bloom, seek to identify "in order to achieve psychological security."[4] Such security is necessary for personality stability and emotional well-being. National identity, he suggests, "describes that condition in which a mass of people have made the same identification with national symbols . . . so that they may act as one psychological group when there is a threat to, or the possibility of enhancement of, these symbols of national identity." It is precisely because many of the new states are artificial constructs that nationalism in them is so weak. In the new states, the symbols and affinities remain directed toward the ethnic group, tribe, region, or some other social subunit of the state. But elsewhere identifications are strongly established with the state, its symbols, and with fellow nationals. One has only to note the attention and adulation accorded to one's athletes in international sports contests to see evidence of the continuing significance of nationalism. American television during the Olympic Games focuses almost solely on the performance of American athletes, and generally ignores that of others. Fans attending World Cup soccer matches every four years emblazon themselves with national symbols: flags, the national colors painted on their faces and worn on their clothes. An unhappy outcome to a match has on occasion caused riots and deaths. Travelers abroad often seek out the company of their fellow nationals rather than that of the locals. The examples could be multiplied easily. They all constitute evidence of

[4]In *Personal Identity, National Identity and International Relations* (Cambridge: Cambridge University Press, 1990) 52–53.

the continuing force of nationalism in a world that is in many ways shrinking. One can be a good European, or even a "world citizen," but one remains foremost a Scot, a Swiss, an Austrian, or a Pole. A Latin American shares a language, religion, and history with many others on the continent. But he or she will still identify the self primarily as a Peruvian, a Colombian, or an Argentinian. In many cases, the profusion of the means of communication helps to sustain, and even create, national identities more than a sense of international or global solidarity.

Thus, while it is important to identify when, how, and under what circumstances nonstate actors have an impact on the international agenda, the proliferation of such actors and the greater ease of communication between societies has not appreciably diminished the activities of states. The decisions and actions of their governments and their interrelations remain the focus of inquiry.

The Structure of the System

Most analysts agree that the structure of power and influence in the world between the onset of the Cold War and some point in the 1970s was polar. Only the United States and the Soviet Union had the capacity to destroy each other. To fashion a solution on any number of conflicts in the world required the tacit or formal approval of one or (often) both. As the greatest donors of foreign aid and the most significant sources of modern weaponry, they could greatly influence, and in some cases command, lesser states' foreign policies. The combined Israeli-French-British invasion of the Suez Canal region in 1956 had to be terminated because of Soviet protests and lack of American support. Wars in Afghanistan, Angola, the Ogaden, and between Iraq and Iran came to an end when the Soviets decided to stop supplying their clients.

The two superpowers were not, of course, omnipotent. But they were the only countries that defined their interests in global terms and that had the military capabilities (in the case of the Soviet Union, only by the late 1970s) to defend or expand those interests. By contrast, even the second tier of states, including Great Britain, France, and China, had mostly regional interests and did not have the capacity to extend military power beyond those regions.

The world was polarized, if we measure polarity using military indicators. On questions of peace and war, the fate of many nations lay in decisions made in Moscow and Washington. But in other issue areas, the structure of power and influence looked significantly different. On matters of international trade and finance, for example, the Soviet Union and China were not even in the game. Japan, militarily weak, was and remains a major actor. Decisions made in Tokyo, not Moscow or Beijing, have the greatest impact on world financial institutions and trade practices. When we talk about a world power structure, then, we may have to specify what kinds of issues are in contention.

If there was a consensus about polarity during the height of the Cold War, there is little agreement about trends since the 1970s. Has there been a vast decline in American power? Are we entering a new structure of multipolarity, perhaps a configuration something akin to that of the mid-nineteenth century in Europe? Here the problem is that one can make a pretty convincing case in support of different positions. It all depends upon the evidence that one uses to measure power. The reader may have his or her own favorite evidence, but even if we agree on the figures, we may not agree on the inferences to be made from them.

Consider economics. All the figures point to a *relative* decline of the United States during the past two decades. American gross national product used to make up about 35 percent of the world total in the 1950s. Today it constitutes about 20 percent. At the height of the Cold War, Americans were indisputably better off than the citizens of any other country. Today, compared with Americans, the citizens of several countries, including Switzerland and Japan, on average are wealthier, live longer, have easier and cheaper access to health care, and are less frequently victims of violent crime, alcoholism, road accidents, and the like. In the 1950s, the United States was the most important trading nation in the world, and Americans had more money invested abroad than any other nationality. Today, the Japanese have either surpassed or are close to approximating American economic activities abroad. In 1989, for example, Japan became the world's largest overseas investor on an annual basis. In the first two decades after World War II, American scientists won almost all the Nobel prizes. They still maintain a commanding position, but increasingly non-Americans are earning those laurels. One also reads almost daily about the leading position of Japan in certain high-tech industries, about the threat to American industrial predominance by Japan or by the integrating European economy. There is, in brief, no lack of data to substantiate the case of America's relative decline in the world.

But here we need to introduce more content to the notion of structure. The question about dominance is not which country possesses the most guns, or which has the largest foreign currency holdings, or whose athletes win the most medals in international competitions. By structural power, we mean the authority and capacity to set the rules of the game and to determine how the others will play the game (further discussion is in Chapter 5). Those who attempt to play other games can be persuaded or coerced to conform only by those with superior structural power.

Looked at this way, the argument about the decline of the United States is less compelling. On most security and commercial issues, the United States has the capacity to lead, coerce, and persuade. An arms-control agreement without American participation would mean little. The United States has over the years coerced and cajoled the Japanese to open up markets to American goods. It is unlikely that the Japanese could marshall similar coercive ability against the United States.

But there is more than coercive capacity involved. Structural power includes unstated assumptions about standards and rules: who should conform to what and how. One illustration will make the point.

In the 1980s the American trade authorities, at the prompting of the lumber industry, charged that Canadian provinces were subsidizing their own wood industries by charging unreasonably low rents for cutting rights. In the United States, lumber companies bid competitively for cutting rights in federal forests; many others themselves own forests. In Canada, in contrast, the provinces "own" almost all the forest resources and charge a fee (stumpage rate) for cutting rights. There is no competitive bidding for stands of timber, as there is in the United States. In other words, the ways that the American and Canadian wood companies gain access to the resource differ significantly. American trade authorities threatened that if the Canadian provinces did not begin charging higher stumpage fees, the United States would impose punitive tariffs on all Canadian lumber entering America. The assumption underlying the negotiation of a final solution to the problem was that the American method of providing access to wood resources was the "normal" way of doing things, and that Canadian methods had to be adjusted. No one imagined, or proposed, that perhaps the Americans should reorganize *their* lumber industry to conform to the Canadian model.

In many of the debates about world trade, there has been an assumption that the American definition of a "level playing field" is the only definition; all other countries must play according to that definition or face economic retaliation. It seldom occurs to Americans that the way they do business, as, for example in maintaining the archaic British system of weights and measures, constitutes a barrier to trade, and that it is the United States that is out of tune with the rest of the world. No other economy has the capacity, single-handedly, to coerce the United States to change.

There is much evidence, then, that in terms of structural power, the United States maintains a position of global predominance and has the capacity to maintain it in the foreseeable future. The supports of the position remain basically intact: The United States maintains a leading position in world manufacturing; in high-tech production; in ownership and control of world communications facilities; in databanks; in the production of computers; and in the fast-growing new technologies of artificial intelligence, space exploration, microelectronics, biotechnology, and the like. The position is likely to endure for some time because the United States has by far the largest number of research-oriented universities, and because spending on national defense research—a vast system of state-subsidized research with huge commercial benefits—remains the highest in the world by far. The dollar remains the world's most important currency, and the United States provides the world's most extensive credit facilities. Combined, the predominance of military power, along with significantly leading positions in knowledge, finance, and production, guarantee America's leading position.[5]

Others, like Japan and a uniting Europe, will gain increasing leverage in some issue sectors. The reforming and restructuring of Eastern Europe will be undertaken primarily under the auspices of Western European leadership. The United States appears to play only a secondary role there. On the critical questions of peace and war, the shape of the global economy, and the fashioning of settlements to prolonged conflicts such as the Middle East situation, the United States will remain the critical actor. In the newer issue areas of global pollution and atmospheric degradation, American leadership is essential because the United States contributes approximately 25 percent of the total atmospheric polluting agents. This is not to say that the United States has, or will, provide that leadership.

[5]The thesis and supporting evidence is spelled out in Susan Strange, "The Future of the American Empire," *Journal of International Affairs*, 42 (1988), 1–17. See also Joseph S. Nye, Jr., *Bound to Lead: The Changing Nature of American Power*, (New York: Basic Books, 1990).

The structure of the international system in some sense looks more multipolar. Certainly with the collapse of the Communist systems in Eastern Europe and the Soviet Union, and the daily revelations of Russian economic weakness, it is hard to consider Russia as approximate to the United States. Russia retains the second most powerful military arsenal, but intercontinental missiles and tanks will not buy diplomatic influence on a broad range of contemporary issues. The general conclusion is that in terms of structural power, the United States remains predominant, but increasingly it is having to coordinate its policies with other important industrial countries. We may be entering an era of less polarity and more collective hegemony represented by the great coalition of industrial societies centered in Europe, North America, and Japan.

The Forms of Interaction

Interactions between societies have grown at an unprecedented pace. Whether measured in terms of the total volume of world trade, mail flows, tourism and travel, telephone calls, foreign investment, international conferences of scientists and other academics, or international sports competitions, the figures all show precipitous increases. They are matched by contacts between governments. More governments have more embassies and consulates abroad now than at any previous time. There has been a vast growth in the numbers of intergovernmental organizations, ad hoc conferences, and summit meetings. We need not spell out these developments in statistics. The trends are clear and well-known; what their consequences are remains more problematic.

What may be more significant than the aggregate growth rates of transactions between individuals, societies, and governments is their patterns. Recall the dependency model of international relations outlined in Chapter 1. That "image" of the world is based in part on the highly skewed patterns of global transactions. Most trade is *between* industrial countries, as are tourism, mail flows and other forms of communication, foreign investment, interactions between transnational organizations, sports contacts, and formal diplomatic communications. There is a significant north-south trade pattern, but it is skewed in its makeup: The north exports high technology and manufactured goods, while the south continues—though less so than previously—to export primary products and manufactured goods of a lower technological grade. South-south trade, investment, tourism, and other forms of communication, are only in an infant stage. You will see evidence of this on your own campus: There are significant numbers of students from Third World countries in most major Western universities. But you will find almost no Westerners enrolled in the University of Lusaka, Universiti Sains Malaysia, or the University of Calcutta and their many counterparts in other Third World countries. The Western tutelary position in formal scientific knowledge is reproduced in the world's media patterns: Because information and news tend to flow from north to south, people in the industrial countries would know little about other regions of the world, while literate populations in the Third World and the former Soviet Union know considerably more about the West. The concentration of global-reaching media resources in a few conglomerates like CNN ensures that the manufacturing of news will continue to have a strongly Western bias.

One trend that is not so obvious is war. Because we have so many forms of warfare today, ranging from various forms of terrorism and "low intensity conflict" to more conventional operations, it is difficult to identify all wars, or to determine when they began and ended. Nevertheless, victims of war have numbered well over 20 million since 1945, and the number of wars has not declined from previous eras despite numerous international organizations whose major task is to prevent them.

Of course, war has not occurred randomly among the states in the system. The great powers traditionally have employed force more frequently than have lesser states. What is striking about the post-1945 figures is that all the wars and armed interventions—with the exception of the Soviet invasions of Hungary in 1956 and Czechoslovakia in 1968, the Bosnian war of the 1990s, and local wars in some former Soviet republics—have occurred in the Third World. One reason is that many of the struggles for independence or national unity were waged through armed combat. In fact, most post-1945 wars have had to do with the creation and unification of states. There have been relatively few classic state-versus-state wars, except in the Middle East. Elsewhere, most wars have been of the "national liberation" or national unification type.

War, then, remains an important form of interaction between states and would-be states. Many wars began as domestic rebellions and ultimately became internationalized. While the number of wars adjusted for the number of states has decreased, all the forces that help bring the world together have not significantly altered the security and insecurity problems of many states. Increased communications have not necessarily increased understanding, and certainly not mutual sympathies. Frequent recourse to arms indicates that many changes and adjustments are not being achieved through peaceful means of interaction, such as trade and diplomacy.

The Major Rules of the System

The rules and principles articulated in the Westphalia treaties and developed through the eighteenth century continue to serve as the foundation of contemporary international relationships. States formally remain sovereign, they are legally equal regardless of the differences in their attributes, and they are enjoined not to interfere in each others' internal affairs. These rules are sustained by ideologies of self-determination, by nationalism, and by the international legitimacy accorded to the state. It is still only states that can join international organizations like the United Nations; only states can enter into treaty relations; states cannot legislate for, or administer their own rules on, other states' territories; and blatant interference in the domestic political processes of foreign countries usually brings strong protests. Rules still protect the immunity of diplomats, and most states remain legally equal in the sense that they commonly share rights and responsibilities.

There have been significant changes in interpretation regarding these fundamentals of the states system. While the rule of noninterference persists, it is broken with such regularity that it may not survive as a fundamental norm. In Washington,

D.C., there are thousands of lobbyists in the pay of foreign governments. Some make contributions to the political campaign funds of congressional and presidential candidates. Others offer access to decision-making centers. Similar forms of persuasion take place in many other national capitals. But because local rules allow these activities, they are not considered illegitimate even if technically they obviously influence domestic politics.

In the area of human rights, an even more significant revolution has taken place. For years a variety of governments claimed that their internal governing arrangements could not become a matter of negotiation with foreigners. The South African regime protested for decades that other countries' involvement in the matter of race relations constituted gross interference in South Africa's internal affairs. Similarly, even after the Helsinki Final Act of 1975 had spelled out a number of norms relating to human rights (the freedoms of speech, religion, and assembly, for example), the Communist signatories claimed repeatedly that no foreign country had the right to discuss or criticize how they dealt with their own citizens. But this was to no avail. Over the years, a consensus seems to be emerging among many governments that gross violations of human rights are everybody's business, and that foreign governments have the right and even a duty to do something about injustices. There are now enough precedents to suggest that this may become a norm of the system, although many states continue to reject its application. In the field of human rights, the principle of noninterference has become contested.

Norms relating to the use of force in foreign policy have also changed. The Westphalian rules assumed that a sovereign had the right to formulate his or her realm's foreign policies free of restraints from supranational authorities such as the Pope or the Holy Roman Emperor. Among those prerogatives was the use of armed force. There was a tradition associated with doctrines of just war, but most of these had gone into abeyance during the eighteenth century. In general, until the late nineteenth century armed force was considered to be one of several instruments of statecraft, and an essential attribute or corollary of sovereignty.

The two great world wars of the twentieth century and the development of weapons of mass destruction have changed attitudes toward the use of force. First in the League of Nations Covenant, and later in the charter of the United Nations, norms regulating the use of force were spelled out in detail. At present force can be used in only two circumstances: (1) in self-defense, individually or collectively; and (2) as coercive sanctions approved by the Security Council of the United Nations, or some other international organizations. In the latter case, a state can use military means on behalf of *community* objectives. While these rules might seem to rule out Hitler-style aggressions, they are by no means without controversy. In almost any circumstance, a government can say that it employed force for defense purposes.

Whatever the loopholes, the important point, in contrast to practices in earlier centuries, is that today there is a presumption *against* the use of force. To have any justification, it must be used as a last resort and only in cases of extreme provocation or danger. But an additional problem has appeared in post-1945 uses of force. As we have seen, most involved the armed struggles of national liberation movements to end colonialism. There is no norm that rules out force when it is used against colonialism; at least this is the position taken by the governments of many new countries. The whole issue of the use of force, including various forms of low-intensity conflict, by nonstate actors—primarily secessionist groups—has become murky.

The Sources of Stability in the System

Recall that by the word *stability*, we do not necessarily mean peace and harmony. Stability refers to the persistence of the main characteristics of the international system, as defined by its geographic scope, the nature of the units (actors), system structure, major forms of interaction, and the rules and norms that underlie it.

The geographic scope of the system cannot change. It is already global and virtually all peoples are organized into the predominant form of political organization, the state. There are, of course, no other systems, barring the discovery of extraterrestrial life.

The prevalence of nationalism has consequences for both stability and change. As suggested, the days of the state do not seem to be numbered, even though the ability of states to control transnational interactions has declined substantially in recent years. The aspiration for statehood remains the primary goal of many communities. With the collapse of the Soviet Union and Yugoslavia, we have witnessed the birth of at least nineteen new states since 1989, and the process of fragmentation in that area has not yet run its course. If the dozens of "national liberation" movements active in the Third World today achieve their goals, we can expect another dozen or so new members of the United Nations by the end of the millenium. The days of the multinational empire have now passed, and we are perhaps seeing only the beginning of an era when most communities will be organized on the basis of the state principle.

Westphalian principles of sovereignty, legal equality, and noninterference also help sustain the states system. While many decry the "costs" of sovereignty—in particular the difficulties of getting international agreement on regulating many of the destructive consequences of modern industrial life—the sovereignty principle provides important forms of protection, particularly for weak states. Iraq's conquest and annexation of Kuwait in the summer of 1990, followed by the United Nations coalition's military reversal of that conquest, demonstrates the continued vibrancy of the sovereignty concept. The forcible annexation of another state is what the United Nations was designed to prevent. In that sense, the United Nations is a conservative organization. Like the balance of power in the eighteenth and nineteenth centuries, it was designed to protect the independence of its members.

The collapse of communism as an ideology also helps sustain the system. The original Leninist and Maoist purpose of communism was to promote world revolution and to organize the world on the basis of class interests, rather than states. This dream of a world transcending states ultimately developed into a Russian-dominated regional empire clothed under Leninist rhetoric. Since the death of Mao Tse-tung in 1976 and the ideological innovations of Mikhail Gorbachev in the late 1980s, the idea of organizing the world on a basis other than statehood remains alive only among some Muslim fundamentalists. They define the world in terms of spiritual communities and regard states as Western inventions that do not accord with God's plan of human organization. State boundaries, in this view, are artificial and are used by Western-oriented leaders to perpetuate their rule. Ethnicity and/or language are no basis for political organization. Religious belief is the critical criterion of community.

While this world view appeals to some, the attraction of nationalism—which sustains the states system—appears today much stronger than religious belief.

Many argue that the triumph of liberalism also helps to sustain the system. Unlike the clash of ideologies that produced World War II and the Cold War, the growing world consensus around liberalism is destined to make the world a safer place. Wars between the states of Western Europe are hard to imagine, and the hope is that ultimately there will be a great "zone of peace" stretching from Vancouver to Vladivostok. Whether this is wishful thinking remains to be seen, but all the post–Cold War leaders of the West have expressed the hope that the elements of the former Soviet Union, and ultimately China, will become carbon copies of Western liberal democracies. The expectation is that the more political communities come to resemble each other, the less likely there will be drives for hegemony, conquest, ideological warfare, and ultimately, world war. The "Vancouver to Vladivostok" scheme is clearly based on the principles of economic liberalism (free markets) and political democracy.

The reader may wish to speculate on other sources of stability. Are there other items in the realm of ideas, actions, and technology that help perpetuate the states system?

The Sources of Change in the System

Nationalism has many consequences. It helps sustain the idea of statehood as the primary form of political organization for communities. But the drive for statehood may also have de-stabilizing consequences for the system. The pressures of political fragmentation are acute in many areas of the world, and they are helping to bring about the birth of new states. But many of the new states (and some older ones as well) will be barely (or not at all) viable if the hope is to make them ethnically "pure." Can tiny (in terms of population, not necessarily territory) states, each with its own minorities, survive as economic entities? What will be the fate of Bosnia's "ethnically pure" mini-states (or Bantustans, if you prefer)? If such creations are fundamentally weak, will they tempt outsiders? If the goal of all communities is to have their own state, can this be done without war and bloodshed? What about the remaining minorities? If they are persecuted or oppressed, they will turn to armed struggle. The idea that every state must be founded on a single ethnic group can lead only to an infinite regress of "wars of national liberation." To take the most extreme example, Africa is populated by more than 3,000 distinct ethnic/language/tribal groups. What is the consequence of a vision which argues that every group must have its own state?

The only antidote to the explosion—mostly by violence—of statehood, is the alternative concept of the *citizen*. The political community is composed of citizens, regardless of their ethnic origins, preferred religion, or other attributes. Most Western states are based on the concept of citizenship, not ethnicity. The result is that, because they enjoy equal rights, most "minorities" (a minority is an invented concept, not a fact of life) do not seek separate statehood.

The ideology of nationalism, when the "nation" is defined by ethnicity, thus may have some long-run consequences for the character of the international system. It might help contribute to more war; it might increase the numbers of states in international organizations to the point where those organizations find it difficult to operate effectively (a majority of states today do not pay their dues to the United Nations); and it might help increase the growing gap between the rich and poor of the world. There is plenty of room for speculation about the long-range consequences of nationalism.

Technology may significantly alter the main characteristics of international systems. We have already noted how improvements in military technology helped to end the reign of Greek city-states in the three centuries before Christ. The application of Chinese chemistry to cannons through the medium of gunpowder similarly rendered the European medieval walled city obsolete, and thus proved an important factor in helping monarchs centralize power and develop the modern state.

In our era, the development of weapons of mass destruction has fundamentally altered calculations about the costs and advantages of war. Throughout modern European history, and indeed in most historic civilizations, war was commonly regarded as just one of many means of defending and achieving the objectives of political communities. In an era when war can lead to mutual suicide, as was the case of Cold War relations, the rationality of armed combat begins to erode. Even the use of limited force over a marginal issue runs the risk of escalation and nuclear exchanges. Nuclear weapons have been, then, instruments not only of deterrence against an adversary but also of self-deterrence. Unfortunately, the greater costs and risks of war do not render it obsolete, but it is significant that since 1945 there has not been a major power war (Korea was a marginal exception), whereas prior to World War II, such wars were a regular feature of the European landscape.

Technology may have a more subtle affect on war as a major occurrence between states. Throughout history, political units, whether empires, city-states, or nomadic tribes, have expanded territorially. They have done so for a variety of reasons, but paramount among these was the search for an increased tax base. A larger population and resource base can be exploited for revenues to pay administrative and military costs—and often the opulence—of central governments. Some territory also held important strategic value: mountain passes, naval straits, river valleys, and the like.

As we will see in the next chapter, today the bases of national strength, wealth, and prestige reside less in territory than in science and technology. Wealth comes more from brainpower than from land. Territory in itself means little, except where it continues to maintain strategic significance. We see many states that are richly endowed with territory (Central African Republic, Chad, Sudan) but are in no sense wealthy, strong, or prestigious. In contrast, Japan, with only the territorial dimensions of California, has the world's highest living standards. These were achieved through education, science, technology, and trade, and not through territorial expansion. Thus, one of the oldest causes of war—the control over territory—has altered significantly during the past century or so. One of the classical features of the European-

based international system dating from the mid-seventeenth century, namely war between its members, has drastically changed. Among the industrial states, we can no
longer argue that war is one of its characteristic forms of interaction. Rousseau's security dilemma is rarely to be seen in Western Europe, North America, and perhaps
in some other regions of the world, including South America and Southeast Asia.

Technology has also aided in the growth and proliferation of nonstate actors
and their capabilities. This may be an important source of change for states and their
interactions. For example, today a variety of nonstate actors have access to modern
communications and weapons technology, thus providing them with considerable
political leverage. Drug cartels, transnational "liberation" movements, and crime organizations can effectively challenge governments and other nonstate actors. The
drug cartels in Colombia, for example, have seriously corroded that country's government's ability to maintain law and order and provide security for citizens and
politicians alike. Criminal organizations run massive transnational economic enterprises, launder the profits of criminal activities, and move their operations from country to country as constraints and opportunities arise. Their ability to protect and expand turf is intimately linked to access to modern weapons and communications
facilities. Some organizations constitute essentially a "state within a state," and it is
not inconceivable that eventually some formal sovereign states will be little more
than the "front" for highly organized criminal groups.

The globalization of the world's economy is another development that is likely
to have significant changes in the structure and processes of the international system
over coming years. We have already noted how transnational processes weaken or reduce the authority of modern governments. Because capital, talent, and resources can
move almost instantaneously to wherever there are opportunities, state decision makers are less able to control their own economies. How does this affect international relationships? For one thing, it forces governments to collaborate whereas they might
prefer to "go it alone." The American government cannot reduce interest rates as a
means of stimulating domestic investment if other important industrial countries maintain higher rates. Think of yourself as an investor. If you own $10,000 worth of Amer-
ican government bonds paying annual interest of 5 percent, while similar bonds in
Germany are paying 8 percent, you would cash in your American bonds and purchase
their counterparts in Germany. Now if several million people did that simultaneously,
it would create problems in the United States in the form of lowering the value of the
currency and increasing the U.S. national debt, among other things. So these mutually dependent governments are forced to cajole, compromise, bargain, and coerce
until their main domestic economic policies are more or less synchronized.

What the effects of economic globalization are on international politics remains a matter of some debate, however. Some argue that the interconnectedness
of economies mutes conflict, and certainly diminishes the risk of war. One reason
that the United States, for example, has not exercised more coercion against Japan
is the fear that if diplomatic tensions increase too much, thousands of Japanese investors in the United States would pull out, thus causing serious economic disloca-
tion, including unemployment, in America. Following the thought of nineteenth-
century liberals, many observers today are convinced that increased trade and the

globalization of the economy are "mighty engines of peace," to quote British Prime Minister John Major. Others argue with equal conviction that economic interconnectedness increases conflicts between governments and societies, particularly during eras of economic downturn or stagnation. They quarrel over trade, they resort to overt or hidden protectionism, and occasionally they adopt competitive practices that verge on trade wars.

James N. Rosenau[6] has argued that _mass education_ has also had profound effects on the nature of international politics. Citizens around the world are becoming increasingly competent as literacy rates rise, and as communications facilities reach to the world's backwaters. Informed citizens cannot be fooled by self-serving elites and despots. Societies can no longer be sealed off by walls, barbed-wire fences, or radio jamming. More people today know more about the outside world than ever before. And as they increase their knowledge, they also increase their political skills. These can be used to constrain governments from totalitarian practices, from undertaking foreign adventures (or at least from sustaining them over long periods), and from systematically distorting the truth. Liberal theory has long held that the ordinary people of the world generally want peace; it is governments that lead nations to war. In an age of universal literacy—another fifty years should achieve that goal—and increased popular activism, dictators, despots, and international predators will pay a high price for unpopular policies.

Whether or not one agrees with this analysis depends on one's view of human nature. Perverted forms of nationalism are not held only by governments. The practices of "ethnic cleansing" remind us that under certain circumstances people are quite happy to kill their neighbors. Wars are not just launched by top officials. There are, for better or worse, plenty of "popular" wars remaining with us, and many of them are organized, aided, led, and fought by ordinary people.

Although we could expand the list of factors that are changing some of the main characteristics of the contemporary international system, it is better for the reader to propose his or her own candidates. There is, however, one final candidate. It is the change in our conceptions of sovereignty.

In discussing nationalism, we suggested that the drive for statehood among diverse communities (mostly ethnic) was helping to proliferate the number of state and nonstate actors in the international system. The forces of political fragmentation are powerful. Yet, once statehood has been achieved, it is becoming increasingly permeable. Once a society could hide behind the legal shield of sovereignty and the physical seals of frontiers and iron curtains. How a government dealt with its population was not a matter that could be easily monitored or changed by other governments. To insist otherwise was to bring forth the charge of interference in the internal affairs of the state, another important Westphalian concept.

But as norms governing human rights become internationalized, there is the slowly evolving view that the internal affairs of a state, if the abuses are too systematic and widespread, may become the legitimate concern of other states. Sovereignty, in other words, is conditional upon meeting minimal standards of human rights observations. Hence, few denounced the United Nations–United States efforts to pro-

[6]In _Turbulence in World Politics: A Theory of Change and Continuity_ (Princeton, N.J.: Princeton University Press, 1990).

tect Kurds and Shiites against Saddam Hussein's army by imposing "no-fly" zones in the north and south of Iraq. Iraqis claimed this was a major violation of the principle of sovereignty, and indeed it was. Similarly, many countries imposed economic sanctions against South Africa on the grounds that *apartheid* constituted a fundamental denial of human rights. South Africa protested, using the noninterference rule (which is also enshrined in the United Nations charter), yet to no avail.

But a few instances of international action to protect populations at risk (usually minorities) in violation of the sovereignty doctrine do not yet add up to common practice. In many instances of systematic abuse of citizens by governments (Idi Amin's Uganda in the 1970s, Pol Pot's massacres in Kampuchea in the late 1970s, and the like) the world community did almost nothing. Individual governments did take some actions, but there was no general consensus among them to take effective measures on the behalf of victims. It is too early to say, then, that a definite trend in the erosion of the sovereignty concept has developed yet. The direction is there, but not always the political consensus or will to act.

Readers will note throughout the discussion oblique references to the five models of international politics introduced in the first chapter. Our contemporary international system contains many of the elements of the realist vision (formal anarchy among sovereign states, the persistence of war and security dilemmas in some areas of the world); the society of states view (many "rules of the game," the club-like features, including mechanisms for ostracizing those who do not follow the rules, and the many bonds that tie societies together); pluralist-interdependence models (the significance of nonstate actors, economic mutual dependence); dependency models (the growing gap between living conditions in the north and south, the persistence of asymmetrical economic ties); and world society models (increasing similarities of lifestyles thanks to global communications, the erosion of the sovereignty principle). Our world is made up of many complex patterns of interaction, and trends with contradictory or mixed consequences. Communications, for example, may enhance mutual understanding, but they can also whip up frenzies of nationalist fears or hatreds for "others." Nationalism, in so far as it helps communities seek statehood, perpetuates the Westphalian system but when it takes the form of secession or persecution of minorities, it invites foreign intervention and thus erodes the principle of sovereignty, one of the cornerstones of that system.

This chapter has sought to be suggestive, not definitive. Readers should try their hand at adding other factors of stability and change, or teasing out some of the further implications of the trends discussed above.

By now it should be clear that the international system, which is an imagined concept (you cannot see it or touch it), does have an impact on the way states behave toward each other. The concept of sovereignty, for example, presupposes that most countries most of the time will tolerate the existence of their neighbors and others. If countries wish to trade, allow their citizens to travel, exchange diplomats, and join international organizations, they have to accept many rules of the game and custom established over past centuries. In a system dominated by two contending military alliances, smaller states enjoy little latitude of choice; if they challenge the hegemons, as did the Hungarians in 1956 or the Nicaraguans in the 1980s, they will pay a high price. Globalized economic activity has a deep impact on all countries, most particularly on the weak and less developed. The international context does not determine what states seek to do, but it has a profound impact on the ways and means they defend and achieve their purposes. We turn, then, to the question of state purposes.

Questions for Study, Analysis, and Discussion

1. What are some of the distinctions between strong and weak states? What are their consequences for international relations?
2. What would the world look like if self-determination were extended to all peoples?
3. What is the difference between states based on concepts of citizenship and those based on ethnicity?
4. Does the evidence in Table 3-1 suggest that the "gap" between rich societies and poor societies is narrowing or widening?
5. Aside from those listed in the chapter, provide some examples of significant non-territorial transnational actors. In what ways do they affect international politics?
6. What sorts of evidence would you need to support or challenge the view that multinational corporations are a major positive factor in the development of most Third World countries?
7. How would you characterize the contemporary international system in terms of the distribution of power and influence? Multipolar, unipolar, or what?
8. Has the *density* of transactions in the world reached such proportions that we could argue the contemporary international system is fundamentally different from its nineteenth-century predecessor?
9. What do you think are the main indicators of the persistence of the Westphalian states system?
10. What are the main indicators of significant change away from the Westphalian system? Do we have a "new" system?

Selected Bibliography

Anderson, Benedict, Imagined Communities: Reflections on the Origins and Spread of Nationalism. London: Verso, 1983.

Andreff, Wladimir, Les Multinationales. Paris: Éditions la Découverte, 1987.

Armstrong, David, Revolution and World Order: The Revolutionary State in International Society. Oxford: Clarendon Press, 1993.

Aron, Raymond, The Century of Total War. Garden City, N.Y.: Doubleday, 1954.

Becker, David G., Jeff Frieden, Sayre Schatz, and Richard Sklar, Postimperialism: International Capitalism and Development in the Late Twentieth Century. Boulder, Colo.: Lynn Rienner, 1987.

Birch, Anthony, Nationalism and National Integration. London: Unwin Hyman, 1989.

Bloom, William, Personal Identity, National Identity and International Relations. Cambridge: Cambridge University Press, 1990.

Braillard, Philippe, and Mohammad-Reza Djalili, Tiers Monde et Relations Internationales. Paris: Masson, 1984.

Brass, Paul, Ethnicity and Nationalism. Newbury Park, Calif.: Sage, 1992.

Bull, Hedley, The Anarchical Society. New York: Columbia University Press, 1977.

———, *and Adam Watson, Eds., The Expansion of International Society.* Oxford: Clarendon Press, 1984.

Caporaso, James, Ed., Dependence and Dependency in the Global System, special issue of *International Organization,* 32 (Winter 1978).

Carlsson, Jerker, and Timothy M. Shaw, Eds., Newly Industrializing Countries and the Political Economy of South-South Relations. London: Macmillan, 1988.

Chazan, Naomi, Ed., Irredentism and International Politics. Boulder, Colo.: Lynn Rienner, 1990.

Clark, Ian, The Hierarchy of States: Reform and Resistance in the International Order. Cambridge: Cambridge University Press, 1989.

Connor, Walker, "When Is a Nation?" Ethnic and Racial Studies, 13, 1 (January 1990), 92–104.

Cox, Robert W., Production, Power and World Order: Social Forces in the Making of History. New York: Columbia University Press, 1987.

Davidson, Basil, The Black Man's Burden: Africa and the Curse of the Nation-State. London: James Currey, 1992.

Elkins, Paul, A New World Order: Grassroots Movements for Global Change. London: Routledge, 1991.

Emerson, Rupert, From Empire to Nation. Cambridge, Mass.: Harvard University Press, 1960.

Feld, Werner J., Nongovernmental Forces and World Politics: A Study of Business, Labor, and Political Groups. New York: Praeger, 1972.

Forsythe, David P., The Internationalization of Human Rights. Lexington, Mass.: Lexington Books, 1991.

Fukuyama, Francis, The End of History and the Last Man. New York: Avon Books, 1992.

Galtung, Johan, "A Structural Theory of Imperialism," Journal of Peace Research, 8 (1971), 81–117.

Gasiorowski, Mark J., "The Structure of Third World Economic Interdependence," International Organization, 39 (Spring 1985), 331–42.

Gilpin, Robert, War and Change in World Politics. Cambridge: Cambridge University Press, 1981.

Gross, Leo, "The Peace of Westphalia, 1648–1948," American Journal of International Law, 42 (1948), 20–41.

Hall, John A., "Nationalisms: Classified and Explained," Daedalus, 122, 3 (Summer 1993), 1–28.

Heraclides, Alexis, The Self-Determination of Minorities in International Politics. London: Frank Cass, 1991.

Holsti, Ole R., Randolph Siverson, and Alexander George, Eds., Change in the International System. Boulder, Colo.: Westview Press, 1981.

Huntington, Samuel P., "Transnational Organizations in World Politics," World Politics, 25 (April 1973), 333–68.

Jackson, Robert H., Quasi-states: Sovereignty, International Relations, and the Third World. Cambridge: Cambridge University Press, 1990.

Jervis, Robert, "The Future of World Politics: Will It Resemble the Past?" International Security, 16 (1992), 39–73.

Kennedy, Paul, The Rise and Fall of the Great Powers: Economic Change and Military Conflict from 1500 to 2000. London: Unwin Hyman, 1988.

———, *Preparing for the Twenty-First Century.* New York: Random House, 1993.

Keohane, Robert O., and Joseph S. Nye, Power and Interdependence: World Politics in Transition, 2nd ed. Boston: Little, Brown, 1989.

Krasner, Stephen D., Structural Conflict: The Third World Against Global Liberalism. Berkeley: University of California Press, 1985.

Lall, Sanjaya, and Paul Streeten, Foreign Investment, Transnationals and Developing Countries. London: Macmillan, 1977.

Lapidoth, Ruth, "Sovereignty in Transition," Journal of International Affairs, 45, 2 (Winter 1992), 325–45.

Leonard, H. Jeffrey, "Multinational Corporations and Politics in Developing Countries," World Politics, 33 (April 1980), 454–83.

Livernash, Robert, and Mary Paden, "Nongovernmental Organizations: A Growing Influence in the Developing World," in Resources Institute, World Resources 1992–1993. New York: Oxford University Press, 1992, pp. 215–34.

Luard, Evan, The Globalization of Politics. London: Macmillan, 1990.

Mayall, James, Nationalism and International Society. Cambridge: Cambridge University Press, 1990.

Mearsheimer, John J., "Back to the Future: Instability in Europe after the Cold War," *International Security,* 15, 1 (1990), 5–56.

Merle, Marcel, Les Acteurs dans les Relations Internationales. Paris: Economica, 1986.

———, *and Christine de Montclos, L'église Catholique et les Relations Internationales.* Paris: Éditions du Centaurion, 1988.

Michelman, Hans J., and Payanotis Soldatos, eds., Federalism and International Relations: The Role of Subnational Units. London: Oxford University Press, 1990.

Miller, J. D. B., The World of States. London: Croom Helm, 1981.

Milner, Helen, "The Assumption of Anarchy in International Relations Theory: A Critique," *Review of International Studies,* 17, 1 (1991) , 67–86.

Morse, Edward, Modernization and the Transformation of International Relations. New York: Free Press, 1976.

Moynihan, Daniel P., Pandemonium: Ethnicity in International Politics. Oxford: Oxford University Press, 1993.

Northrop, F. S. C., The Taming of the Nations. New York: Macmillan, 1952.

Nye, Joseph S., "Multinational Corporations and World Politics," *Foreign Affairs,* 53 (1974), 153–75.

Onuf, Nicholas G., World of Our Making: Rules and Rule in Social Theory and Internatinal Relations. Columbia, S.C.: University of South Carolina Press, 1989.

Plishke, Elmer, Microstates in World Affairs: Policy Problems and Options. Washington, D.C.: American Enterprise Institute, 1978.

Rejai, Mostafa, and Cynthia H. Enloe, "Nation-States and State-Nations," *International Studies Quarterly,* 13 (1969), 140–57.

Rosencrance, Richard, The Rise of the Trading State: Commerce and Conquest in the Modern World. New York: Basic Books, 1985.

Rosenau, James N., Turbulence in World Politics: A Theory of Change and Continuity. Princeton, N.J.: Princeton University Press, 1990.

Rothstein, Robert L., The Weak in the World of the Strong. New York: Columbia University Press, 1977.

Ruggie, John Gerard, "Territoriality and Beyond: Problematizing Modernity in International Relations," *International Organization,* 47, 1 (Winter 1993), 139–74.

Russett, Bruce, "The Mysterious Case of Vanishing Hegemony: Or Is Mark Twain Really Dead," *International Organization,* 39 (Spring 1985), 207–31.

Ryan, Stephen, Ethnic Conflict and International Relation. Aldershot, Hants.: Dartmouth, 1990.

Scott, Andrew M., The Dynamics of Interdependence. Chapel Hill: University of North Carolina Press, 1982.

Singer, Max, and Aaron Wildavsky, The Real World Order: Zones of Peace/Zones of Turmoil. Chatham, N.J.: Chatham House Publishers, 1993.

Smith, Anthony, State and Nation in the Third World. Aldershot, Hants.: Wheatsheaf Books, 1983.

———, "Chosen Peoples: Why Ethnic Groups Survive," *Ethnic and Racial Studies,* 15 (July 1992), 436–56.

Strange, Susan, "The Persisting Myth of Lost Hegemony," *International Organization,* 41 (1987), 551–74.

Taylor, Philip, Nonstate Actors in International Politics. Boulder, Colo.: Westview Press, 1984.

Vincent, John R., Human Riguts and International Relations. Cambridge: Cambridge University Press, 1986.

Vital, David, The Inequality of States. New York: Oxford University Press, 1967.

Wight, Martin, Systems of States. Leicester: Leicester University Press, 1977.

Woods, Lawrence T., "Nongovernmental Organizations and the United Nations System: Reflecting Upon the Earth Summit Experience," *International Studies Notes,* 18, 1 (Winter 1993), 9–15.

Zacher, Mark, "The Decaying Pillars of the Westphalian Temple: Implications for International Order and Governance," in *Governance Without Government.* James N. Rosenau, ed., Cambridge: Cambridge University Press, 1991.

Zartman, I. William, Ed., Collapsed States: The Disintegration and Restoration of Legitmate Authority. Boulder, Colo.: Lynne Rienner, 1994.

Chapter

4

The Purposes of States: Foreign Policy Goals and Strategies

The international or global system constitutes the environment in which the units of international politics operate. Their goals, aspirations, needs, attitudes, latitude of choice, and actions are significantly influenced by the overall distribution or structure of power in the system, and by its rules, habitual modes of conducting relations between states, and by transnational values (such as self-determination, autonomy, wealth). This section will shift the analysis from systems to the units that constitute them—in this case, mostly sovereign states. In order to explain what conditions make states (and sometimes other actors) behave as they do, we need first to describe what, typically, they do. Using the state-as-actor approach for the time being, our concern will be to explore the components of foreign policy.

What is foreign policy? How do we make sense of all the phenomena that transcend national borders—sending a diplomatic note, attending a summit meeting, enunciating a doctrine, making an alliance, or formulating long-range, but vague, objectives such as "peace with freedom" or a "new world order." They are all aspects of foreign policy: ideas or actions designed by policy makers to solve a problem or promote some change in the policies, attitudes, or actions of another state or states, in nonstate actors (e.g., terrorist groups), in the international economy, or in the physical environment of the world. But there is a vast difference in scope between sending a single diplomatic note to a friendly state (a specific action) and defining what a government will seek throughout the world in the long run. In the succeeding chapters of this section, we will look at individual actions: things governments do to sustain or change others' behavior. This chapter, in contrast, defines what governments seek to do in general: the purposes and goals states have, and the strategies they employ to achieve or defend them. Thus, Chapter 4 emphasizes needs, ideas, and aspirations.

This is a rational view of the world of states: that governments carefully identify their purposes and then organize the means of attaining them. It is a model or characterization of behavior, not a precise description of all governments at all times. Some governments appear to do little but muddle along; they have no clear ideas or goals. Some regimes seem to have little purpose except to maintain office for as long as possible. Others take few initiatives abroad: They mostly just respond to the problems that others pose for them. There are plenty of examples of what appears to be mindless drifting. But even habitual actions may be goal-oriented. For whether they have clearly articulated plans, priorities, and purposes, or they appear to be aimlessly drifting, most governments most of the time are trying to maximize certain values or, as we would say, seeking to achieve or defend known purposes.

What purposes do all governments have in common? These, of course, have changed over the years. In eighteenth-century Europe, expansion of the royal realms, conquering colonial territories, and securing a succession to a crown were important priorities. Obviously those are no longer vital issues today. In their place we have at least four purposes that are common to all contemporary states: (1) security; (2) autonomy; (3) welfare, broadly conceived; and (4) status and prestige. Not all states place the same priority on those purposes at any given time. Those who make foreign policy may wish in an ideal world to maximize all of them, but in the real world to maximize one may be at the cost of another. We often hear of the competing priorities of "guns versus butter." This is just another way of saying that if you want effective armaments for deterrence, you may have to sacrifice some units of welfare—by imposing higher taxes, for example. Or, policy makers may find that their strategy of promoting economic growth through the creation of a regional free trade arrangement actually reduces their political autonomy. The making of foreign policy involves, among other things, deciding what sorts of priorities among these common values one wants to emphasize, and how one is going to pay for them.

Does this list of foreign policy purposes exhaust the possibilities? While these are what governments are commonly concerned with, some governments, on the other hand, pursue other types of purposes. We will deal with other purposes in the last section of this chapter. First, let us offer definitions of security, autonomy, welfare, and status or prestige, and list some of the strategies that governments typically employ to achieve or defend those purposes.

Security

Probably few concepts employed in statecraft and in the study of international politics have as vague referents as do *security* or *national security*. The terms have been used and abused by many governments to justify external aggression and the stifling of internal opposition. Robespierre, Napoleon, Kaiser Wilhelm, Joseph Stalin, and

Senator Joseph McCarthy and some of his colleagues, to mention just a few, have justified purges; restraints on the freedoms of speech, press, and assembly; character assassination; and even mass murder in the name of "national security." Most governments that have launched wars of aggression or significant military interventions abroad have similarly claimed that their policies were designed to defend or preserve national security. This was a rationale both for American intervention against Nicaragua in the 1980s and Iraq's attack on Kuwait in 1990. But in most instances, the search for security involves more benign attitudes and actions.

One reason we can claim that the search for security is universal is that all states, with only some exceptions (Costa Rica and Iceland) maintain military forces. All commit a significant (1 to 30 percent) proportion of their total economic output (GNP) for arms dedicated to maintaining internal and external security. These expenses may be used to deter or to cope with crime, rebellion, secession, revolutions, and *coups d'etat*. Governments also maintain armed forces to deal with the eventuality that at some time in the future, some other state—or a nonstate actor such as a terrorist group—will present a threat. That threat can be directed against the lives of citizens or their private activities, against territorial integrity, against a country's "way of life," or against the independence of the state and its institutions.

What kinds of threats are likely to evoke a military response? Barry Buzan makes the important distinction between *threats* and *vulnerabilities*.[1] Vulnerabilities derive largely but not entirely from geographic characteristics: They are potential avenues for military invasion or economic coercion—mountain passes, narrow waterways, major transportation corridors, and the like. The Turkish straits create certain vulnerabilities for Turkey: Great powers have had a traditional interest in gaining control over them in order to gain access to the Mediterranean (Russia) or to the Black Sea (Great Britain or France in the nineteenth century). As a flat land with no natural barriers, Poland has traditionally been vulnerable to invasion from the east and the west. Turkey and Poland have deployed military forces in such a manner as to reduce those vulnerabilities. Until the twentieth century, Great Britain enjoyed relative safety—low vulnerability to direct attack—because of the channel separating it from the continent. Yet it maintained a large navy to provide protection for shipping, because it was vulnerable to a cut-off of supplies needed to sustain an industrial economy. During the same time, North Americans were literally invulnerable to attack from any quarter, and thus maintained only small armed forces.

Threats are those more immediate capabilities in the hands of adversaries that may be used to exploit vulnerabilities. Throughout the Cold War, we heard of the "Soviet threat," not so much in terms of known Soviet intentions to attack, but in the inference that if the Soviets had immense military capabilities, they might at any time be tempted to exploit vulnerabilities. Soviet citizens were sent the same message regarding NATO's military strength: The Soviet leadership did not have to produce incontrovertible proof of the imperialists' intention to attack to create a sense of vulnerability and fear.

---

[1]In *People, States and Fear: An Agenda for International Security Studies in the Post-Cold War Era* (London: Harvester Wheatsheaf, 1991), 112.

Threats are not always explicit and self-evident, nor is there universal agreement that any particular vulnerability will be exploited by others in a threatening manner. The "threat" may well be contested. Many in the West during the 1970s and 1980s were not convinced that the USSR did in fact pose a threat. Government officials, however, are likely to err on the side of caution. The threat may have receded, or perhaps even disappeared, but one never knows about the future. As long as vulnerabilities remain, some particular mixture of military forces will be necessary as a form of insurance against the future.

What is being threatened? Except for the short period of Hitler's conquests and more recently Iraq's annexation of Kuwait, few states have been obliterated, so physical survival is not one of the most common threats. Threats may take the form of a demand or claim to territory, armed incursions into a neighbor, or control over strategic territorial assets. This is a claim against the physical base of a state, or actions in violation of sovereignty. If the state is weak, in the sense we used the term in the previous chapter, it is also vulnerable to domestic rebellion and secession, in which case the threat to the state is primarily internal. But because outside powers frequently become involved in the domestic politics of their neighbors (particularly where ideological or ethnic contests are going on), internal turmoil can escalate into the threat of external intervention. The armed intervention of the United States in Grenada in 1983 and in Nicaragua (via the *Contras*) during the 1980s demonstrates the linkage. The threat here is not so much to the state or its physical basis as it is to a particular regime. The beleaguered regime will obviously claim that "national security" is being threatened even though it is its tenure in power that is at stake.

Threats may also be directed against ideas and ideologies. The Soviet threat throughout the Cold War was often portrayed as an assault on traditional Western liberal values, or to the "American way of life." Finally, a threat, or taking advantage of certain vulnerabilities, may be defined in terms of the deprivation of economic assets or national wealth. Certain states or regimes may be vulnerable to blockade, sanctions, or the cut-off of critical energy supplies; or (for a weak economy) to subversive efforts by multinational corporations (see the discussion in Chapter 9 of the role of one corporation in the subversion of Chile in the early 1970s), or to drastic declines in the world price of its major export commodity. The reader can no doubt list other kinds of vulnerabilities and threats.

We also need to mention new kinds of threats. Traditionally, governments have chosen to go to war to protect certain values, however they are defined. A vulnerability that is exploited or even challenged by an adversary's military forces has usually been a sufficient cause for responding with force. But in a nuclear era, the most overwhelming threat may be war itself. In a condition of nuclear war, all the values—territory, population, regime, ideologies, and economies—can be destroyed in a matter of days or even hours. For those who possess nuclear weapons, then, the main task of national security policy is less to cope with a specific, identifiable threat than it is to prevent war.

In addition to military threats, many argue today that whole societies face threats that migrate easily across state frontiers. These constitute threats not against the security of the state or regime, or to a state's territorial integrity, but rather to the society at large. These would include massive refugee movements (a fear commonly held in Western Europe after the Soviet Union collapsed), the spread of AIDS, various forms of transborder pollution, and the international narcotics trade. If these are indeed threats, we would have to broaden significantly the notion of "national security." The classical means of coping with vulnerabilities and threats—by manipulating the size, quality, and deployment of armed forces—are of course irrelevant to these new kinds of threats.

Governments can enhance their security by decreasing vulnerabilities and/or by diminishing the perceived threat from one or more perceived adversaries.[2] How this is done involves a mixture of military deployments (reducing vulnerabilities) and particular policies toward other states (reducing threats). Following are some common security policies that emphasize threat reduction.

Isolation

One way to avoid threats may be to remain uninvolved in the affairs of others and, in particular, to avoid military commitments to others. Noninvolvement makes one less likely to be used as a pawn, particularly by the great powers. But there is another sense of the word *isolation*; that is, to make oneself sufficiently unattractive as not to invite the attention of others. Reclusiveness preempts other actors' interests in you.

In previous international systems, geographic remoteness and certain physical features helped sustain strategies of isolation. Broad seas, high mountains, and extensive deserts made the costs of penetration or invasion too great to be worth the trouble. Bhutan closed itself off and existed as an isolated society, almost totally secure in its Himalayan redoubt, for almost 1,000 years until the late 1950s, when India began to take an interest in Bhutan's affairs because of its proximity to China (Tibet), which was then India's primary adversary. Japan practiced a strict isolationism from the time of its first contacts with the Dutch and Portuguese in the sixteenth century, until 1854, when the United States coerced Japan to open itself up for commercial and missionary activities.

The United States adopted a military isolationist strategy in relation to Europe throughout the nineteenth century; not failing, however, to practice imperialism, territorial expansion, and systematic intervention into the affairs of Caribbean and Central American states. More recently, Burma and Albania sustained policies of rigorous isolation by expelling foreigners; prohibiting foreign investments; allowing only very limited and highly controlled forms of foreign aid; discouraging all forms of external penetration, including tourism; avoiding all forms of military entanglements; and generally sealing off their societies from various forms of external contact. This strategy allowed those countries considerable autonomy in terms of their domestic policies, and kept externally derived threats to a minimum. The costs in terms of economic progress, however, were great. In both cases, the main threats to the regime were internal (secession of minorities in Burma, popular uprising in Albania), not external.

[2]Ibid.

Why did these strategies apparently work? In none of the cases was the isolated state a supplier of needed goods or resources to others. None provided access to or control over areas or points of strategic significance to neighboring great powers (Bhutan became a virtual dependency of India only when Chinese-Indian relations deteriorated in the late 1950s). In brief, the isolationist states offered little of what others wanted or needed, and they were sufficiently strong to close off their societies from normal contacts with the outside world. They did not need large military forces to act as deterrents against outside threats. Their energies were directed, rather, toward developing internal security agencies (and, in Burma, the army) to suppress any threats against the regime.

Self-Reliance

A variation on the theme of isolation is self-reliance. It has in common with isolation the unwillingness to make military commitments to others or to accept their "assistance." It differs in the means of reducing threats: In isolation, it is done by making oneself unattractive and by rigid exclusion of foreign presences. In self-reliance, it is done essentially by deterrence: Build up military capabilities to keep all adversaries at bay. One still hears occasionally the pronouncement of those who would like the United States to adopt a "fortress America" security strategy. That would mean terminating membership in all alliances (on the grounds that allies are unreliable and do not pay an adequate share of the costs of defense) and concentrating all military capabilities on the home base. American commitments abroad would be significantly scaled back, on the assumption that wars and instabilities in other regions of the world would not have direct security consequences for the United States. During the early 1960s, China practiced such a policy. It effectively terminated its alliance with the Soviet Union, refused to redefine its relationships with Western countries, and loudly proclaimed its determination to protect both the "revolution" and China by its own means.

Neutrality and Nonalignment

States that face pronounced vulnerabilities—often because of geographic location—and potential threats may form their security strategy by obtaining formal recognition of their wishes to remain uninvolved in the conflicts of their neighbors. In exchange they promise not to make military alliances with others, or to allow their territory to be used in a manner prejudicial to the interests of a neighbor or other power.

The term *neutrality* needs some clarification. In contemporary usage, it has several formats. Technically, neutrality refers to the legal status of a state during armed hostilities. Under the international laws of neutrality, a nonbelligerent in wartime has certain rights and obligations not extended to the belligerents. These rules state, for example, that a neutral may not permit use of its territory as a base for military operations by one of the belligerents; may not furnish military assistance to the belligerents; and may enjoy freedom of passage of its nonmilitary goods and passengers on the open seas and, under certain conditions, through belligerent blockades. But in common parlance today, a neutral state has a special status during peacetime as well. Its hallmarks are noninvolvement in others' conflicts, avoidance of all military alliances, and prohibiting the use of its territory by others for military purposes.

In the case of most neutrals, the policy is developed unilaterally, or through various bilateral or multilateral instruments. In other instances, it is the great powers that, to resolve a conflict, decide to neutralize a state. The European powers neutralized Switzerland in 1815, Belgium in 1831, and Luxembourg in 1867. More recently, the recipe for restoring sovereignty to Austria in 1955 was its neutralization by the occupying powers. Laos was neutralized by the major Western governments and the Soviet Union in 1962. The terms of neutralization are basically the same as those of neutrality: The state in question binds itself not to allow foreign troops or military installations on its territory, and pledges not to enter into any agreements constituting a form of military alliance.

What is nonalignment? It has been used to describe the policies of the new states, mostly of the Third World, as distinct from the European neutrals (Finland, Sweden, Switzerland, Ireland, Austria). The nonaligned movement encompasses a variety of states with different kinds of security problems. Many, in fact, make military agreements with each other, or belong to multilateral organizations that are in effect military alliances (for example, the [Persian] Gulf Cooperation Council). They are therefore not true neutrals. Their neutrality was limited to pledges not to join either of the two Cold War treaty organizations, NATO and the Warsaw Pact. But even here, the term *nonaligned* has been stretched to fit almost any security policy. India had a security treaty with the Soviet Union, and Cuba was a major military and economic client of Moscow. Unlike the European neutrals, nonaligned countries have no pledges to remain uninvolved in great power conflicts; this would hardly be possible, in any case, because many of those conflicts have been fought on the territories of nonaligned states. Nonalignment in fact refers to a very loose coalition of states that agree, in principle if not often in fact, that they should avoid making military commitments to serve the interests of the great powers, and that share many of the attributes of underdevelopment and therefore have some common concerns on international economic issues. Most nonaligned states are certainly not self-reliant in either military or economic dimensions. In general, nonalignment is not a very useful analytical term because it seems to cover so many different kinds of behavior. States that are neutral or neutralized limit their freedom of choice (avoid alliances and other military arrangements) in order to reduce vulnerabilities and threats. Nonaligned states, as seen in the security policies of many developing countries over the last four decades, do not so restrict themselves. While perhaps not joining NATO or WTO, they have adopted all sorts of security strategies, ranging from isolation and self-reliance to joining or forming regional alliances.

Alliance Strategies

Perhaps the most common strategy for reducing vulnerabilities or diminishing threats is to augment military power, not just by building up one's own capabilities, but by enlisting the aid of others. As Thucydides observed 2,500 years ago, and as modern experimental and historical studies have substantiated, mutual fear is the most solid basis upon which to organize an alliance.[3] When two or more parties perceive a common threat, they are likely to engage in various types of military collaboration, which can range from the informal provision of technical advisers, granting of arms, or exchange of information, to its most concrete form: a formal alliance.

There are a variety of alliance forms. The distinctions between them are important, because they have significant effects on military planning and deployments. Some, for example, provide only for the augmentation of a country's military forces through foreign assistance; others imply much greater commitments. Military alliances can be classified and compared according to four main criteria: (1) the nature of the *casus foederis* (the situation in which mutual commitments are to become operational); (2) the type of commitments undertaken by the alliance partners; (3) the degree of military integration of the military forces of the alliance partners; and (4) the geographic scope of the treaty.

The Casus Foederis.   Although partners to an alliance have similar or overlapping foreign policy objectives, negotiators of the treaty are usually very cautious in defining the *casus foederis*. Some treaties, particularly those in recent years that have been used for offensive purposes, contain a very vague definition of the situation that will bring the alliance into operation. Because of universal condemnation of outright aggressive military alliances, offensive treaties seldom express their real purpose. The 1939 German-Italian "Pact of Steel," for example, provided: "If it should happen, against the wishes and hopes of the contrasting parties, that one of them should become involved in warlike complications . . . the other contracting party will come to its aid as an ally and will support it with all its military forces." The term *warlike complications* is so vague that it could (and did) commit Italy to assist Hitler in almost any situation. Soviet mutual-assistance treaties with Bulgaria and Romania (1948) also had such obscure definitions of the *casus foederis* ("drawn into military activities" was the phrase used) that it was difficult to predict when and under what exact circumstances the Soviet, Romanian, and Bulgarian armies would begin military operations. In contrast to the vague *casus foederis* are those that contain a very precise definition of the situation in which the alliance is to be put into effect militarily. The NATO treaty, in Article 5, states that military measures can be taken only in response to an actual *armed attack* on one of the signatories.

Commitments Undertaken.   Alliance treaties also differ according to the type of responses and responsibilities required once the situation calling for action develops. The Soviet-Bulgarian treaty of 1948 unequivocally provided that if one of the parties is "drawn into military activities," the other will *"immediately* give . . . military and other help by all means at its disposal." This type of commitment is called a "hair-trigger" clause, because it automatically commits the signatories to military action if the *casus foederis* occurs. A similar clause is found in the Brussels pact among Great Britain, France, Belgium, the Netherlands, and Luxembourg. Since the clause establishes automatic commitments, it leaves little leeway for decision makers and diplomats to decide what to do once the *casus foederis* arises.

[3]Thucydides, *A History of the Peloponnesian War,* trans. Benjamin Jowett (Oxford: Ashendene Press, 1930), Book III, Par. 11; Ole R. Holsti, Terrence Hopmann, and John D. Sullivan, *Unity and Disintegration in International Alliances: Comparative Studies* (New York: John Wiley, 1973).

In contrast, some treaties only vaguely spell out the type of responses the treaty partners will make. The ANZUS treaty, which ties Australia, New Zealand, and the United States into a defensive alliance system, provides that each party will "act to meet the danger . . . in accordance with its constitutional processes." This treaty contains no precise military commitments, nor does it prescribe any course of action to which the parties commit themselves if one of them is attacked. Similarly, the renewed Japanese-American security treaty of 1960 provides only for "consultations" between the parties if Japan is attacked.

Alliance responsibilities may be mutual or one-sided. Mutual-defense treaties theoretically require all the signatories to assume equal commitments toward each other. According to the principles in the NATO and Warsaw treaties, an attack on any one of the signatories is to be considered an attack on all, requiring every signatory to come to the aid of the victim of aggression or armed attack. Other alliance treaties impose unequal burdens on the signatories. After "consultations," the United States may become obligated to defend Japan against external attack, but the Japanese are *not* obligated under the 1960 security treaty to assist in the defense of North America if war or invasion should occur there.

A variation of the unequal-burden treaty is the *guarantee* treaty, whereby one or more states receive guarantees for their security from a third party or parties, while the guaranteeing power or powers receive nothing in return except perhaps the possibility of enhancing stability and peace. Guarantee treaties of this variety were popular in the 1920s; one prominent example was the Locarno treaty of 1925, in which Great Britain and Italy undertook to come to the assistance of France, Belgium, or Germany, depending on which was attacked or was the target of a violation of the Franco-Belgian-German frontiers. For guaranteeing these frontiers, Italy and Great Britain received in return no tangible commitments from the beneficiaries.

Integration of Forces.   Alliances may also be distinguished according to the degree of integration of military forces. Alliance treaties in historic international systems seldom provided for more than casual coordination of military planning, while national forces remained organizationally and administratively distinct. European alliances in the eighteenth century typically required signatories to provide a specified number of men and/or funds for the common effort, but otherwise set forth no plans for coordinated military operations or integrating forces or commands. Any coordination that did take place was the result of ad hoc decisions made after hostilities began. In one of the most enduring alliances of the nineteenth century, the Austro-German Dual Alliance of 1879, rudimentary military coordination was carried out only through the services of military attachés in Vienna and Berlin; and when the alliance was put to the test in 1914, German military and political leaders knew very little about Austria's mobilization plans.

Since World War II, the major leaders of both coalitions sought to increase military integration to the extent that allied forces would operate, if war came, almost as one unified armed force. Integration may be accomplished by establishing a supreme commander of all allied forces (such as the Supreme Allied Commander, Europe, in NATO); standardizing weapons systems for all national forces (barely begun in NATO); integrating military personnel of different countries into one command structure (as proposed in the ill-fated European Defense Community); or permitting one of the major alliance partners to organize, draft, and direct all strategic and tactical war plans for the other partners. Major alliances today also have permanent headquarters, continuous political and military consultations, innumerable meetings of technical experts, and a continuing avalanche of memoranda and staff studies.

Geographical Scope.   Finally, alliances differ with respect to the scope of their coverage. Soviet mutual-aid treaties were designed to cover only the territory of the state that is attacked or "drawn into military activities," but one of the major problems in drafting and interpreting the NATO treaty concerned whether the signatories could be committed to defend the overseas colonies or territories of France or Great Britain. The French and British governments insisted that NATO obligations extend to at least some of their overseas territories; so Article 5 of the treaty was drafted to read: ". . . an armed attack on one or more of the Parties is deemed to include an attack on the territory of any of the Parties . . . , on the Algerian department of France, on the occupation forces of any Party in Europe, on the islands under jurisdiction of any Party in the North Atlantic area north of the Tropic of Cancer, or on the vessels or aircraft in this area of any of the Parties." In 1965, coverage of the treaty was extended to Malta, which had received protection under Article 5 by virtue of being "an island under the jurisdiction of" Great Britain, but which received its independence in 1964.

Although these distinctions relating to the forms and types of alliances may seem quite technical, they are important because precise definitions of scope, *casus foederis,* and obligations lend predictability to the responses alliance partners will make in crisis situations. Predictability is an important element in international stability and may become crucial in crisis situations. One of the main objections against secret treaties and alliances is that decision makers cannot plan actions and predict responses of both friends and potential enemies if they are not familiar with treaty commitments and obligations. However, it must be acknowledged that treaties do not provide complete predictability, and the circumstances of the moment will largely determine the responses alliance partners make in critical times. The NATO treaty, for example, stipulates that the parties will decide how to commit themselves only at the time an "armed attack" takes place against one of the signatories. Yet, if the Soviets had launched a massive invasion of Western Europe, there is little doubt that previously drafted retaliatory plans of the NATO bureaucracy would have come into effect almost instantaneously, with slight latitude for negotiations and discussions among the treaty partners. In such a situation, even when alliance commitments are common knowledge, do alliance strategies succeed?

No generalizations can be offered as to whether defensive alliances successfully deter aggression or provide stability for the international system. Presumably, a potential aggressor faced with an overwhelming coalition against it will not risk destruction of its society when it possesses foreknowledge of certain defeat. Yet decision makers do not always behave rationally in crisis situations, and there are enough examples (discussed in more detail in Chapter 10) of their going to war knowing that the probability of success was low to disprove this presumption. All we can say is that alliances probably inject a factor of caution among decision makers with aggressive designs; defensive alliances increase greatly the risks and costs to the aggressor, but do not necessarily prevent organized violence. We can only speculate on the wars that did not begin because alliances effectively performed the deterrence function; but both past and present reveal occasions when defensive alliances failed to deter, lower tensions, or promote stability in the system.

Strains in Alliances

Aside from poor military coordination or planning, one reason that alliances may fail to deter potential aggressors is that they lack political cohesiveness or are riven by quarrels and political disagreements. Presumably, any military coalition will be more effective to the extent that its members agree on the major objectives to be achieved, help each other diplomatically, and trust that once the *casus foederis* arises, the partners will in fact meet their commitments. In any international system comprised of independent and sovereign states, however, there is no automatic guarantee that even the most solemn undertakings will be fulfilled if those commitments are in conflict with the prevailing interests of different governments. Several situations can cause strains in alliances, impairing their effectiveness both as deterrents and as fighting organizations.

The first is when the objectives of two or more parties begin to diverge. If all partners of a defensive military coalition perceive a common enemy or threat, the alliance is likely to withstand strains caused by ideological incompatibilities or distrust arising from personality differences between political leaders. But if the objectives become incongruent, or the potential enemy of one alliance partner is not the enemy of the other, serious problems of cooperation and coordination arise and make the alliance more formal than real.

The American-Pakistani alliance during the Cold War was more a means through which Pakistan received arms than a coalition leading to meaningful diplomatic cooperation. When the United States induced Pakistan to join SEATO in 1954, it regarded the Moslem country as a bulwark against communism. The purpose of the alliance, as seen from Washington, was to prevent the USSR or Communist China from moving into South Asia. Pakistan, however, concluded the alliance primarily to obtain American arms and diplomatic support against India, its traditional enemy. Diplomatic relations between the United States and Pakistan reached a low point in the 1960s when Pakistan criticized the United States for failure to lend it support on the Kashmir issue and, as the Pakistan government saw it, for giving comfort to the Indians. Left virtually isolated on the Kashmir problem, Pakistan turned increasingly to Communist China, which was also embroiled in a border conflict with India. The American response to Pakistan's flirtation with China was manifested in reduction of economic and military aid. American diplomats desperately tried to induce the government of Pakistan to reiterate that the "common enemy" was China, a view the Pakistanis could not easily accept as long as their only diplomatic support against India came from Beijing.[4]

[4]See Mohammed Ayub Khan, "The Pakistan-American Alliance: Stresses and Strains," *Foreign Affairs,* 24 (1964), 195–209.

Alliance cohesion is also apt to be strained if a threat arises against only one or a few of the alliance partners, so that other members do not perceive the same threat.[5] The Cyprus issue has long divided Greece and Turkey and created strains between each of them and other NATO members. Planning to fight an unlikely war against the Soviet Union seemed less important to them than the emotion-laden ethnic issues surrounding the Cyprus conflict. Indeed, in this case, the alliance has functioned more as an arena for prosecuting an intra-alliance conflict than as an organization for collective security.

A third factor that may lead to strains in military alliances is incompatibility of the major social and political values of allying states. By themselves, ideological incompatibilities seldom prevent formation of military coalitions as long as the parties face a common enemy. The study by Ole R. Holsti and his colleagues of 130 alliances, nonaggression pacts, and ententes reveals that ideology is not an important factor in creating alliances, although ideologically homogeneous partners are more likely to create alliances of high commitment (such as military undertakings rather than ententes).[6] We would hypothesize that in a condition of high threat, alliances of ideologically heterogeneous partners might cohere; but, given lack of a common enemy, or even a low level of threat perception, ideological factors would operate to reduce alliance cohesion. Certainly there are recent illustrations that would lend some support to the hypothesis. Ideologically mixed alliances may be confronted with misunderstandings and suspicion, usually expressed in unwillingness to share military secrets or coordinate military programs and campaigns, and a decided feeling that the other alliance partner is failing to live up to its commitments. During World War II, the Soviet Union, which for two decades had urged and worked for the overthrow of "decadent" bourgeois regimes in Western Europe, eagerly formed an alliance with these regimes once it was attacked by Germany. The threat posed by Nazi Germany to the rest of the world was so apparent that even Western liberal democrats and conservatives supported the alliance with the Communists. On the other hand, the wartime alliance operated with many irritations because of deep-seated attitudes of distrust and ideological differences. Stalin feared that the Western Allies would make a separate peace with Germany, leaving the Nazis free to crush his regime; alternately, he interpreted the failure of the Allies to invade France before 1944 as evidence of their intention to let the Nazis and Communists bleed each other to death so that the capitalists could come in later to pick up the pieces. Even at the administrative level, distrust was reflected in Stalin's refusal to allow British and American military officials to observe Soviet operations in the field, let the Western Allies establish air bases on Soviet territory, or permit Lend-Lease officers to investigate Soviet military and matériel requirements. The allied wartime coalition was only a temporary marriage of convenience. On the other hand, the Anglo-American alliance is strong and withstands frequent disagreements between the two partners, not just because the overall interests of the two countries coincide but also because the two countries represent similar cultural, political, and social traditions.

[5]Holsti et al., *Unity and Disintegration in International Alliances*, p. 98.
[6]See Ibid., 66–68.

Finally, development of nuclear weapons may have divisive effects on modern alliances.[7] In the post–World War II period, most states of Western Europe were eager to receive the protection of the American "nuclear umbrella." Militarily weak, they had no capacity to deter a possible Soviet invasion carried out by the massive Red Army in Eastern Europe and had to allocate their scarce resources for rebuilding their war-torn economies. By the 1960s, the situation had changed. Europe was recovered economically and entering a period of unprecedented prosperity. The Russians no longer possessed a military manpower advantage as compared to NATO. Most important, the nuclear monopoly held by the United States in the late 1940s and early 1950s had come to an end. Washington, New York, and Houston were as vulnerable to Soviet nuclear attack as Leningrad, Moscow, and Baku were to an American nuclear salvo. In a system of Soviet-American *mutual* deterrence, some observers—particularly French military officials—questioned whether the United States would be willing to destroy itself in order to protect Western Europe from the Soviet Union.

Is a deterrent really credible if the guaranteeing power knows beforehand that it must destroy itself to save others? Contemporary critics of American-European relations have argued that even though they find no fault with American intentions to defend Europe, they are not convinced that in all possible crisis situations, the Americans could be expected to live up to their commitments. This is not a uniquely American weakness, they emphasize. It is a fact of international life that no state is apt to invite its own destruction in order to defend others. In this kind of nuclear statement situation, the "others" must be armed with nuclear weapons so that if the "nuclear umbrella" fails to operate, smaller allies would still have independent means of deterring possible moves against their vital interests.

Contracting Out

Most states ultimately rely on themselves for security, and do so by deploying various types of armed forces. But occasionally, some states are incapable of sustaining the costs of maintaining such forces. In these circumstances, they "contract out" to others to provide for their protection. In the nineteenth century, there were a number of "protectorates" attached to the British Empire. These were proto-states that had full internal autonomy, but were not sovereign. The imperial power provided military forces for the protectorate, usually in exchange for economic privileges. Today, there are few states that rely completely upon others for their protection. Iceland has no military forces but allows the United States to maintain a military base on the island. In the event of a military threat to the country, it would have to rely upon American troops. This would be done under the auspices of NATO. In the 1980s the government of Sri Lanka asked India to send a force to help it cope with an armed secessionist movement. This was a case of "contracting out" for purposes of internal security.

---

[7]For experimental evidence on the divisive effects of the spread of nuclear weapons technology, see Richard A. Brody, "Some Systematic Effects of the Spread of Nuclear Weapons Technology: A Study Through Simulation of a Multi-Nuclear Future," *Journal of Conflict Resolution,* 7 (1963), 663–753.

All of these strategies, ranging from isolationism to binding alliances, are the most common observed in the practices of independent states in all kinds of international systems. They were as common in the Chinese states system of the Spring and Autumn period, and in eighteenth-century Europe, as they have been in the twentieth-century global system. Why individual states select a particular strategy depends upon a number of considerations, such as geographic location, ideological affinity, the availability or unavailability of locally produced military capabilities, the nature of the perceived or anticipated threat, and the like. We will consider some of them in Chapter 10. Here, we can mention at least one significant factor: the success or failure of past security strategies. One learns lessons from them. Sweden adhered to a strategy of self-reliant neutrality for almost 200 years: It had not been directly involved in a war since 1809. It was a very successful strategy that is being abandoned now only because Sweden is joining the European Community. In contrast, Belgium's declaration of neutrality in 1936 failed to deter Hitler from invading the country on his way to the conquest of France in 1940. That disaster proved to the Belgians that their country's security in the future must lie in alliances. Belgium's vulnerability (it is the invasion route to France from the east) could not be altered singlehandedly by a buildup of Belgian military forces, and both in 1914 and 1940, Belgium's attempts to diminish the threat by constant reiteration of its neutral status brought no results.

Autonomy

Autonomy is the ability to formulate and carry out domestic and external policies in terms of a government's own priorities, whatever those might be. It is the capacity to withstand influence, coercion, or rule by others. You and I are autonomous to the extent that we can define our own interests, goals, and actions. If you choose to major in music, philosophy, or engineering because those fields are of greatest interest to you, or because they offer long-range opportunities, or because they allow you best to develop and exercise your talents, you are acting autonomously. If, on the other hand, you choose a field because your parents insist upon it, to the exclusion of your own wishes, you are not acting autonomously. Autonomy does not preclude obligations and various forms of self-limitation, provided they are undertaken voluntarily. Any treaty, for example, implies obligations and thus limits complete freedom of choice. But so long as a government is not coerced into signing a treaty against its will, it is acting autonomously.

The doctrine of sovereignty provides the legal basis for autonomy. But it does not prevent coercion or reduce the constraints that operate through various forms of dependency or asymmetrical vulnerabilities. One of the charges made by developing countries is that although they have formal sovereignty, they enjoy little autonomy: The international economic system is structured in such a manner that they have little latitude of choice. Weak, dependent states are subject to the whims of the international marketplace or to the various forms of economic pressure the industrial countries can apply. If a developing country wishes to obtain a loan from the

World Bank, for example, it may have to adopt austerity policies (e.g., reduction of state subsidies, curtailment of social services, increased taxes, and higher interest rates) that can lead to popular discontent and the electoral defeat (or *coup*) of the government. The conditionality of the loans seriously erodes the capacity of recipients to fashion their domestic economic policies in terms of their own political and economic priorities. Rather than lose autonomy, some governments have refused loans or, having received them, have reneged on the austerity measures that in some cases led to severe social privation.

But virtually all states in our interdependent world are faced with the problem of erosion of autonomy. In order to secure or maximize other purposes such as security, welfare, and status, they are compelled to limit their freedom of choice and action. As we have seen, alliance commitments involve obligations, as do declarations of neutrality. Yet, to the extent that these undertakings are entered into voluntarily, autonomy has not been reduced. There is, at least theoretically, still the choice available of withdrawing from the alliance, or changing from neutrality to a coalition strategy, or refusing a loan from the World Bank.

Autonomy can be maintained, or its erosion reduced, by building up military, scientific, and economic strength, or by reducing reliance upon external sources, particularly where that reliance is asymmetrical. Strategies of economic diversification—locating new markets for exports and obtaining multiple sources of needed imports—also enhance autonomy, increasing the latitude of choice and reducing the price of sudden unavailability of markets and supplies.

The long-range trend in the global system, however, is in the direction of autonomy erosion. The costs of unilateral actions, whether military or economic appear to be increasing. But most important, it appears that other values—and particularly welfare—cannot be maximized or achieved except by voluntarily relinquishing complete freedom of action.

Welfare

In the twentieth century, it has become an article of public faith and a widespread expectation that in addition to security, governments' main tasks are to provide their citizens with social services and promote economic growth and efficiency; these tasks generally enhance or sustain public welfare. This is a relatively new idea. In ancient times and even in Europe until the late eighteenth century, the "good" state was most commonly defined in terms of its capacity to provide justice and public order. There was no well-developed idea that the state also had an obligation to deliver a variety of services, ranging from fire protection to pensions for the elderly.

Today, we have the concept of the welfare state, which goes far beyond the idea that the government must provide for those who cannot provide for themselves. It also means that the state has a direct responsibility for maximizing economic growth, for minimizing unemployment, and for providing a variety of services that enhance the quality of life and the economic and personal opportunities of all citizens. Most of us take for granted that through our taxes, governments will provide free or cheap education at least through the secondary level, housing for those who cannot otherwise afford it, minimal health services, fire protection, unemployment insurance, disaster relief, and many other things.

The range of publicly funded services varies from society to society. One of the main claims of socialist societies was that, unlike their capitalist counterparts, they provided a comprehensive set of social services at minimal user cost, to the point where no member of the society ever had to suffer economic insecurity. In contrast, among many of the newer states governments have neither the tax resources nor the administrative capacity to provide more than rudimentary services for most of the population. Traditional family networks and organizations such as churches and charities must take care of providing basic needs for those whose economic or health prospects are absent or limited.

In liberal democracies, governments often get elected or defeated on the basis of their performance in delivering a broad range of services, and in their capacity to manage and strengthen the national economy. Welfare has typically been identified by various indicators of economic growth. While this may seem obvious, it is definitely a cultural artifact. In other civilizations, and in some regions of the contemporary world, welfare (aside from some basic economic needs) is defined in terms of criteria such as religious piety, moral character, family cohesion, and leading a life of virtue. In the industrial countries today, moreover, there is evidence of change in our conceptions of welfare. It is no longer defined solely in terms of economic growth, but to it are added considerations of environmental standards. According to contemporary jargon, governments should seek to maximize "sustainable development" rather than just to amass more wealth for their citizens.

To increase wealth and economic efficiency—the bases of social welfare—societies must trade. This is the rule deriving from the principle of *comparative advantage*. This principle is simple; its practical application, and its consequences, are much more problematic. The idea is that those countries that enjoy particular advantages of resources, climate, geography, knowledge, and the like, should specialize in producing those things that they can make cheapest. Greenlanders could produce bananas, but the cost to do so, when compared to the cost of buying them from Ecuador, would make little sense. Everyone benefits if Greenlanders exchange tinned fish, for example, for Ecuadorian bananas. This simple principle underlies the idea of free trade. But it gets more complicated when we get into commodities based on more sophisticated technologies.

Manufactured goods have greater economic "spinoffs" than do primary commodities like bananas or fish: They create more wealth. A computer, for example, has literally thousands of applications, each of which can help produce something else, or help produce it more efficiently. In contrast, bananas and fish have few applications. Those economies, then, that produce a variety of manufactured and high technology goods will end up significantly more wealthy than those that produce only primary commodities or raw materials. According to the principle of comparative advantage, computer producers should exchange their products for bananas or fish. The problem is that over the long run, free trade in such an exchange relationship will result in unequal benefits. If banana-producing economies wish to advance, thereby producing more wealth, they will have to take measures to industrialize as well.

Exactly how a government will try to maximize wealth is a matter of choice. Just as in the search for security, there are options and strategies. In commercial relations, however, because there are so many commodities, products, and services involved, governments may pursue mixed strategies, promoting free trade in agricultural commodities, for example, while vigorously subsidizing and protecting the high technology sector. Many of the economic conflicts in the world today arise from countries' different approaches to wealth maximization, for to gain an advantage in economic production and trade often comes at the expense of the position of another economy. Following are some of the main foreign trade strategies.

Autarky

Autarky, or economic self-sufficiency, was the condition of many political units in the pre-industrial age. Since recorded history, most societies survived through the development of their own resources, but there has always been some trade in staples and luxuries. Typically, if rulers lacked sufficient resources for amassing wealth, they would go to war to obtain them. In earlier centuries, plunder and occupation were more common strategies for increasing wealth than was trade.

Today, for the purpose of maximizing wealth, following the principle of comparative advantage would seem attractive to many. But the result is sometimes the creation of external dependencies, and for some states, security considerations loom more important than marginal gains through trade. The state therefore undertakes a variety of policies to become economically self-sufficient. If it succeeds in doing so, it is less likely to become a hostage to others' leverage and, particularly in wartime, a self-sufficient state can prosecute its military campaigns without fear of trade disruption through naval or air interdiction.

Nazi Germany is a good example of a state practicing a strategy of autarky. During the 1930s, the German government used a variety of means to attain economic self-sufficiency, including developing substitutes for ordinary imports (e.g., coffee and synthetic rubber), stockpiling, licensing imports, and structuring the economies of neighboring countries to serve German needs. The Germans, for example, cornered the sources of wheat, oil, and other staples in the Balkans by offering their exporters artificially high prices, credits, and guaranteed markets. Soon the Balkan countries had a high export and import concentration with Germany, from which they could escape only at great cost.

Germany of course never reached full autarky, but it had drawn a lesson from the blockade the Allies had imposed on it during World War I. That blockade had effectively destroyed German morale and was a factor in the German decision to accept an armistice in November 1918. Hitler, whose plans for war against Europe were already well developed in the 1920s, wanted to make certain that the Reich's economic dependency on others would be drastically reduced before he launched the Wehrmacht against Poland, France, Russia, and others. He used the state apparatus to organize and control the private economy so as to minimize imports and to build up local industries to replace foreign supplies.

Other examples of the use of autarkic policies include Burma since the early 1960s, China during the late 1960s, and Albania until the 1990s. But most governments have learned that unless there are compelling security reasons for following such a strategy, the economic results are likely to range from very costly to disastrous. In an era of dynamic technological innovation, those who do not trade, exchange information, and become involved in competition are likely to find themselves left behind.

Mercantilism

Mercantilism was the conventional trade doctrine of the European states in the seventeenth and eighteenth centuries. Its basic premise was that trade is a zero-sum game: Any advantage gained by one is at the expense of the other. State apparatuses of France, Great Britain, Holland, Spain, and others were used to develop the national economy. This was done through a variety of public works (e.g., building roads and canals), through attempts to create shipping and trade monopolies in the colonial areas, and occasionally through outright plunder. While economic growth was the value to be maximized, underlying it was the larger purpose of expanding national power for diplomatic purposes.

More modern versions of mercantilist doctrine were outlined in the nineteenth century by Alexander Hamilton, the first American Secretary of the Treasury, and the German historian, Friedrich List. Both argued that national power is based on manufacturing, and that economic values are to be subordinated to the more important task of state-building. In order to promote industrial strength, the state has to organize foreign trade and, in particular, to protect infant industries with tariffs and other exclusionary devices. List charged that the British doctrine of free trade was really a form of imperialism in disguise. There is no immutable division of labor based on the law of comparative advantage. The nineteenth-century division of labor was actually created through economic and political power. Once having achieved a position of industrial and trade predominance through subsidies, war, colonialism, and other means, the British were now—in the nineteenth century—advocating the principles of free trade where, of course, they would enjoy all the fruits of having been the first to industrialize.[8] List and his followers advocated the unification of the German states under Prussian leadership, state-sponsored development of the means of communication, and the use of high tariffs to keep out the flood of cheap English goods while building up German industry, and thus a strong German state.

Virtually all governments have used their resources and a mixture of exclusionist policies to bolster national economies, to increase public wealth, and also to build up the state. Throughout its history, until only recently, the Communist regime of the Soviet Union practiced blends of autarkic and mercantilist policies. Economic considerations were typically subordinated to state interests—usually concerns of "national security"—and the state provided a variety of subsidies and other supports to build up industries where the Soviet Union had no comparative advantage.

[8]Cf. Robert Gilpin, *The Political Economy of International Relations* (Princeton, N.J.: Princeton University Press, 1987), p. 181. Some of the discussion following summarizes further points by Gilpin.

Communist regimes have not been the only practioners of mercantilist poli-cies. Many developing countries have organized their economies and foreign trade to advance the great project of state-building, and many of the Western industrial countries have used a variety of means to protect or advance the interests of partic-ular sectors of the economy. The Japanese government has been instrumental in de-veloping a national industrial strategy, establishing priorities, aiding certain high technology industries, and helping to cushion the impact of "sunset" industries that were no longer competitive in international markets. The United States has used its immense military and space program spending to subsidize research and develop-ment with potential private market applications. The countries of the European com-munity provide subsidies to their agricultural sectors. In trade sectors such as com-munications, robotics, and computer chips, there are national security implications. Those countries that seek or have achieved a leading military position in the world are extremely sensitive about commanding the "leading edge" of high technology.

The instrumentalities of contemporary mercantilism include traditional ex-clusionary devices like tariffs and quotas, but also such policies as currency devalu-ations (thus making one's exports cheaper abroad, and imports more expensive), state subsidies for research and development, direct subsidies to various industries, export subsidies (e.g., withholding taxes on products designed for export), and the provision of credits or free insurance to exporters.

The strategies of autarky and mercantilism, whether national or sectoral, can be implemented unilaterally; and if others do not retaliate, they can be effective means of building up state capacity and military power. The transformation of Ger-many from a land of dozens of small agricultural states in the 1830s into the pre-em-inent military-industrial power of continental Europe by the 1890s would likely have been impossible without mercantilist policies. The same was true for the industrial-ization and modernization of Japan, the Soviet Union, and several other countries.

Free Trade

Despite the popularity of mercantilist policies, the predominant philosophy guiding international trade for the last two centuries has been free trade. The debate be-tween free traders and economic nationalists (mercantilists) has been going on since before the French Revolution, and there is no end in sight because the two parties do not agree on the purposes of trade. For the liberals, the purpose of trade is to in-crease wealth; for nationalists, it is to build up the state and a modern industrial base. The liberals argue that adhering to the principle of comparative advantage assures benefits for all. It makes no economic sense, for example, for a very small tropical country to build refrigerators for a market of 1 million consumers, where the unit cost will be very high. Better to let a foreign, technologically sophisticated industry that services a market of 200 million provide the refrigerators in exchange for trop-ical products. The cost will obviously be much lower. But from the point of view of the mercantilists, *who* produces *what* is of critical importance. What country can af-ford or risk having key industrial suppliers located abroad? Can a state become or remain militarily effective if it has to import all its hardware, communications facilities, data processors, and missiles? The fact is that not all states started from the same base. In the seventeenth and eighteenth centuries, Great Britain used force, coercion, and monopolistic practices to fuel its industrialization. The British created an international division of labor; it did not just happen by accident. Unless a state is content to remain an extractor of raw materials, with a basically agricultural economy, and thus "underdeveloped," it will have to practice mercantilist policies to catch up with the others.

But one of the lessons of the Great Depression and World War II was that competitive mercantilist policies have disastrous results, where in fact everyone ends up worse off. In the 1930s, tariffs and quotas were used to protect national industries, and governments devalued their currencies to try to get an edge on their competitors. International trade withered, industrial output declined, and unemployment hit historically unprecedented heights in most industrial countries. Competitive mercantilism did not create the depression, but it made it more severe and longer in length.

These results convinced the peace planners—and particularly the Americans—that the postwar trade order must be based on liberal principles. The purpose of trade, so apparent in a war-destroyed world, was to maximize wealth. Mercantilism, it was commonly believed, had been a major cause of World War II. As a means of reconstruction or increasing welfare, mercantilism was a totally discredited doctrine in the 1940s. The postwar trade order would be built on the foundations of maximizing free trade through dismantling tariffs, quotas, and other trade-reducing policies; applying reciprocity; and promoting the free flow of investment funds, information, and people. But unlike mercantilist policies, free trade could not be instituted unilaterally. It had to be negotiated among representatives of the leading economies, with the tacit or explicit consent of many others.

The official trade strategy of the United States and other leading industrial powers has been to create a multilateral world trade order based on the idea of letting the market determine the location of economic activities. The primary instrument for creating this multilateral, market-based, liberal trade order has been the General Agreement on Tariffs and Trade (GATT), launched in 1947. GATT is a set of rules and procedures designed to foster reductions of tariffs and other impediments to trade, to develop new trade policies, and to resolve trade disputes. It currently has more than 100 members, which together carry on about 80 percent of the world's trade. With the new membership of the Eastern European countries and Russia, GATT will ostensibly govern the trade practices of all the industrial countries and many developing nations.

Multilateral negotiations, culminating in the 1993 Uruguay Round that reciprocally reduced tariffs by an average of 33 percent, have effectively dismantled the high tariffs erected in the 1920s and 1930s. Through its conflict-resolving activities, GATT has been able to defuse a number of potential trade wars. In 1971 GATT approved a General System of Preferences (GSP), which authorizes the industrial countries to provide preferential tariff treatment to developing countries. There are various escape provisions for economies facing serious adjustment problems resulting from the dismantling of tariffs and other protective devices, and the GATT agreements allow for the creation of regional free trade arrangements, such as the European Common Market and the Canada–Mexico–United States Free Trade Agreement (NAFTA) of 1993.

While the global free trade strategy pursued under the auspices of GATT has dramatically reduced barriers to trade and has developed a set of regulations to guide policy makers, it has been, relatively, a greater success for the industrial countries than for others. Despite the GSP, many developing countries still view GATT as a "rich man's club," and have not joined it. They claim that many barriers to their exports still exist among the industrial countries, and that most of the agreements negotiated in the Uruguay Round involved commodities traded primarily among the industrial countries. Today, the GATT system is under severe challenge by a variety of protectionist and mercantilist practices among all states. That it has vitally helped to create the huge growth of world trade since World War II is beyond dispute. But for a variety of reasons related to the fundamental changes occurring in the world economy, many governments have relied on strategies other than global multilateralism to advance their welfare and security goals.

Economic Coalitions

Developing countries have argued over the years that the international trade and investment system is designed to protect the privileged position of the industrial countries, and that in the operation of the world market system, poor states do not share in an equitable distribution of benefits. Like the nineteenth-century German economic nationalists, they argue that the advantages gained by early development—largely aided through the exploitation of colonialism—have enabled the industrial countries to practice the "imperialism of free trade." The principle of comparative advantage may result in an equitable increase of mutual wealth when one is exchanging, for example, fruits for lumber. But in a system where the exchanges involve primary commodities for high technology items, the benefits of trade will go disproportionately to those who command modern technology. Based on various data, economists from the developing countries can make a good case that the terms of trade have steadily worsened and that there is little hope of catching up under the system of free trade, as it has been defined and institutionalized by the industrial countries.

Under these circumstances, many developing countries have pursued, mixed with other policies, a strategy of forming a grand diplomatic coalition to seek fundamental reforms and restructuring of the world trade system. It began initially under the name of the "Group of 77," organized as a caucus of developing countries attending the 1964 United Nations Conference on Trade and Development. It has maintained its pressure as an active lobby within UNCTAD and in the UN General Assembly, promoting the concept of a New International Economic Order (NIEO). Although the Group of 77 succeeded in getting the industrial countries to engage in a variety of "North-South" dialogues in the 1970s, and in passing a General Assembly proclamation called the Charter of Economic Rights and Duties of States, it has achieved only a few modest successes, primarily in obtaining greater pledges of industrial country contributions to the Special United Nations Fund for Economic

Development, and formulating regulations for trade in commodities. Overall, the grand coalition strategy has brought few fundamental changes in the world trade order, and as the individual developing countries have better identified their own particular needs, they share a diminishing base of common purposes. At the rhetorical level, Malaysia and Botswana might share general attitudes, but when it comes to defining their concrete interests, they face fundamentally different problems. Today, there is substantially less talk about a New International Economic Order, and more emphasis on following regional and bilateral strategies.

Cartels

A more effective multilateral strategy involves the formation of cartels; that is, collective monopolies of producers. The most famous and significant is undoubtedly the Organization of Petroleum Exporting Countries (OPEC) that groups thirteen oil exporting nations. OPEC regulates the production of each member—a matter of intense bargaining and occasional defection—so as to maintain high world prices.

OPEC has been eminently successful from the point of view of the producers. Through the dramatic oil price increases from 1973 to 1975, they were able to effect a vast shift of financial resources from the industrial countries to themselves. The total sum for the decade was in the order of one-half trillion dollars—the greatest transfer of wealth in world history, even superseding the plundering of Latin America's and Mexico's silver and gold by the Spaniards during the sixteenth and seventeenth centuries.

The magnitude of economic disruption brought through the sudden manipulation of oil trade was startling. Non–oil producing developing countries were hit the hardest. Their energy costs multiplied by factors of five to ten, leading many to acquire huge debts which today dramatically hinder their economic growth prospects. The industrial countries have promoted conservation; developed alternative energy sources; stored stockpiles (to avert catastrophe should there be a reduction or shutoff of oil, particularly from the Middle East); located new sources of oil; and made purchases from other quarters, including Russia. The consumption of oil has remained fairly static, and oil prices during the 1990s declined to about one half of their peak of $35 in the 1970s. Even so, the Third World oil-producing countries have amassed funds and diplomatic influence that could scarcely have been imagined in the 1950s. The cartel strategy brought rewards that no United Nations declarations or North-South negotiations could have produced.

But cartels are not for everybody. They require a certain set of conditions, most of which are not reproducible for other commodities. Ask yourself how you would get along without oil: It would mean no access to cars (that great symbol of individual freedom), airplanes, and ships. Transportation systems would collapse. And consider the thousands of products that we use daily that are based on petroleum: plastics, fertilizers, paints, cosmetics, and the like. The point is obvious: Control over oil resources provides a unique form of international leverage. Are there other commodities that the developing countries can control in a similar fashion? If tropical fruits, copper, coffee, hardwood, tin, and tea were cartelized (as some already are), what would be the consequences of a threatened or actual shutoff? At a relatively low cost, consumers would either forgo the commodity, use an alternative, or develop a synthetic. Few of us would have difficulty getting along without pineapples. Thus, while the producers of these commodities are in a position to create a cartel (where none already exists), they cannot translate their control over production and prices into significant diplomatic and commercial leverage.

Regional Free Trade Agreements

It is difficult to negotiate free trade arrangements on a global basis. The interests of more than 180 countries are not easy to reconcile, even were there intellectual agreement that a free world market maximizes wealth for all. There is no such agreement, and the characteristics of the various national economies diverge in so many ways that few would be convinced that any single recipe could bring the desired results equitably to all.

An alternative to global free trade is to negotiate arrangements with groups of partners who share economic philosophies and whose economies would stand to gain by maximizing the free exchange of goods, investment funds, ideas, and people between them. The best-known arrangement is the European Union, which since its inception in 1957 has systematically abolished tariff and other barriers between its members. The Union has also standardized or harmonized many industrial products (e.g., agreement on types and quality of safety devices on automobiles, or testing standards for pharmaceuticals), and constructed a common set of tariffs against nonmembers (a customs union). The long-run purpose is not just free trade between national economies, but full economic integration where ultimately there will be a single production unit, a single unified market, totally free movement of commodities and capital between all regions, a common currency, and freedom of movement in the labor market (where, for example, a Danish worker could move to Spain without having to immigrate).

But most countries are not willing to go so far. Their purpose, rather, is to maximize free trade, but without giving up national control over economic policies and policies over trade with third-party countries. The NAFTA is one example. Under its terms, the parties are committed to removing tariffs and other trade barriers on a specified list of commodities over a defined term—in this case, ten years for most goods. The parties agree that their citizens may freely invest in each other's country, subject to the usual regulations (some exclusions are listed). But toward third countries, Mexico, the United States, and Canada will develop their own trade policies, there will be no formal standardization or harmonization of products (although pressures for Canadians and Mexicans to conform to American standards will be great), and there is no conversion to a single currency. Unlike the European Union which seeks to integrate economies, the NAFTA has no other purpose than to enhance trade and investment between three separate economies.

The New Protectionism

While most of the governments of industrial countries and some leading developing nations are committed to strategies of bilateral and multilateral free trade as the means of enhancing national welfare, in practice they have also employed a variety of mercantilist devices (1) to protect local industries against foreign competition; or (2) to create or take advantage of export opportunities abroad. Rather than relying on tariffs, which are highly visible and thus subject to domestic and foreign criticism, those governments employ subsidies and tax concessions to exporters, or use health regulations, administrative red tape, and other devices to keep out foreign goods and services. While Japan has perhaps the most notorious and comprehensive ways of preventing external penetration of its markets, virtually all governments employ one or more of them. The United States and the Europeans, for example, have coerced Japan, Korea, and other leading export nations into signing "orderly marketing agreements" and "voluntary export restraints" to limit their exports of specific commodities.

The United States has even moved from a position of equal opportunity as envisaged in GATT (where all states are encouraged to grant equal access to markets) to equality of outcome, where fair trade is defined in terms of whether or not an economy has a negative or positive trade balance with any other country. During the Bush and Clinton administrations, for example, the United States has insisted that there must be "balanced" trade with Japan, and under Section 301 of the Trade Act of 1974, may itself determine what is "balanced" and "fair" trade. Estimates suggest that even if Japanese markets were freely available to all American exports, the American trade deficit with Japan would decline by no more than 10 percent. The problem is that Japan has a distinct business culture and a population with unique purchasing demands. American "crowbar" diplomacy to "open" Japanese markets is not likely to achieve much, particularly since Japanese violations of GATT rules (it has few quotas and in general its tariffs are low) are infrequent except for a few commodities such as rice. In 1993, the United States even proposed that Japan accept limits for *all* exports to America, an idea that could set a dangerous precedent for others to follow. The trend line is thus in the direction of increasing qualifications to and deviations from GATT rules. While free trade arrangements are proliferating at the regional level, at the global level the exceptions are becoming increasingly conspicuous.

What is involved in the new protectionism is an attempt by governments to *create* comparative advantage in internationally competitive industries, particularly those at the "high value-added" end of the industrial spectrum; that is, the industries of high technology. The devices are also part of a general policy of economic development through exports (or, to use the economists' vocabulary, "export-led growth"). States are attempting to jump over their competitors into ever higher levels of industrial technology. The overall pattern is for industry-government collaboration to slow down the international diffusion of states' domestic technologies while forcing other economies to share theirs. Other forms of state interventionism include subsidies for industrial research and development, funding state enterprises, organizing joint business-government ventures, and the like.

The practice of strategic bargaining to regulate trade and investment and the development of a variety of forms of government intervention into trade matters have led to an erosion of liberal principles and practices regarding international trade. The new forms of protectionism, economic regionalism, and state intervention to promote the fortunes of high technology industries for export have led to increasingly complex forms of competition. For the industrial countries, at least, welfare is increasingly defined not only in terms of economic growth, low levels of unemployment, and the like, but also in terms of leadership and command of the "leading edges" of technology. In this area, welfare and prestige or status values become joined.

Status and Prestige

From ancient times, political units have not been concerned only with providing for security and welfare, and protecting or enhancing autonomy. Another value that seems to permeate all political associations, whether tribes, city-states, states, or empires, is status or prestige. There is no precise meaning to these terms as applied to the relations between states, but let us simply use them in a common sense way: Political associations seek to generate deference, respect, and sometimes awe among others. How have they done this? Many foreign policies reflect or incorporate these values.

Traditionally prestige and status were earned primarily through military prowess and might. In Chapter 2 we referred to the great displays of four-horse chariots put on by the Chinese states in front of visitors. The modern counterparts are the great military parades in Moscow, Paris, and elsewhere during national or "revolutionary day" festivities. Displays of military strength in this fashion have little purpose other than to demonstrate to those at home and abroad that the country is mighty and prepared to meet any challenges from others. Today, it is not just the display, but what is being displayed. One, though certainly not the only, motivation for developing nuclear weapons is to achieve the status of a "nuclear power." In the 1950s, Mao Tse-tung claimed that the Chinese would go without pants if that was what was required to develop a nuclear capability. The French in the 1950s and 1960s developed their nuclear weapons as much for reasons of prestige as for any serious deterrent effect. As General de Gaulle made it clear on numerous occasions, France could never retain the status of a great power—its traditional status going back at least to the seventeenth century—without nuclear weapons. The explicit or implicit hierarchy of states in our minds—how we rank states in various ways—remains to a large extent based on the military might and potential of each country. Most political leaders are well aware of this and act accordingly.

Military displays and demonstrations of the use of force are not, of course, the only bases of status. International leadership can rarely be sustained solely by the symbols and use of force. Athens was the greatest power of the Hellenic world of the fifth century **B.C.** by virtue of its domestic political practices and its citizens' leadership in the arts and letters; thus Athens was the center of Hellenic culture. France—or more distinctly, Paris—played a similar role in the eighteenth and early nineteenth centuries. All of Europe's aristocrats and royal families took their fashion and artistic cues from developments in the French capital, French was spoken by all educated people from Moscow to London and from Stockholm to Naples, and France provided the leading figures of literature and the arts in general.

In our age, leadership in science and technology has largely replaced the arts and letters as an important basis of national status and prestige. This is just one of the reasons why the "new protectionism" has become so important in the policies of many states. While most governments support the arts and literature in one way or another, the amounts spent on these activities compared to science and technology is minuscule. In the scheme of national values, space exploration has a commanding lead over, let us say, ballet. The national psychic gratification of landing people on distant planets—an event which is probably watched by a world television audience of billions—is far greater than the rave reviews a touring symphony orchestra might receive abroad.

For many developing countries, visible symbols of industrialization are important sources of status and prestige. These would include ostentatious steel mills that constitute a drain on national resources rather than a source of new wealth; inefficient national airlines; gaudy superstructural facilities, such as freeways and fancy airports that are used only by a tiny fraction of the population; and again, the ubiquitous displays of advanced military hardware.

Sports have also become a major indicator of national status and prestige. It is for this reason, among others, that they have become highly subsidized and organized by governments. The Olympic Games and World Cup soccer are great festivals of nationalism, where countries' medal standings are almost as important as the individual performances of athletes. International sports contests also offer opportunities for countries in the lower areas of the hierarchy of states to have their moment of glory. A gold medal in a major event by an athlete from a small country may create more publicity abroad for that country than all of its foreign policy actions combined that year. More people know Kenya for the excellence of its long-distance runners than for anything its government has done in international relations, and who can forget the Jamaican bobsled team? The state-sponsored use of steroids and other drugs by some Communist countries' athletes was related as much or more to concerns of national prestige than to the aspirations of the athletes themselves.

The reader can no doubt identify other sources of international prestige and status. We can conclude by suggesting that the search for these values is universal, but governments spend greatly varying amounts of national resources for their promotion. Under Communist leadership, the Soviet Union appeared to have inexhaustible funds for self-promotion through propaganda, weapons displays, well-publicized space programs, funding of athletes and artists and their tours abroad, and other means. The North American and British governments devote substantially fewer resources, allowing private activities of a world-class character to speak for themselves. But, compared to many smaller countries, their expenditure of public funds for status-related activities remains comparatively large.

Other Purposes and Goals

All states seek security, autonomy, welfare, and prestige, arranging them in different sets of priorities depending upon a variety of external circumstances and domestic pressures. But beyond these universals, there are substantial differences in the ambitions, aspirations, and interests of governments. They range from the immediate and concrete (expanding territory) to the abstract and long-term (creating a new world order). The following list is only suggestive of the great variety of things states seek.

Protection of Ethnic, Ideological, or Religious Colleagues

When politics are conceived as a hardhearted game of power, we assume that there is little role for sentiment. This is not the case. Governments, representing broad public attitudes, frequently offer aid, support, or protection to ethnic kin or to populations with similar political, social, and religious beliefs who are reputedly suffering at the hands of a foreign government. Ethnic affinities are particularly strong. If ethnic kin in a neighboring state are believed to be persecuted or oppressed, a government will often seek to protect or relieve them. That is the basis of Arab support of the Palestinian cause, Pakistan's periodic involvement on behalf of the Muslims in India's Kashmir state, Hungary's concern with the treatment of the Magyar minority in Romania, and many other contemporary cases. Not infrequently, the feelings of sentiment are so strong that a government will intervene militarily on behalf of the oppressed, or will seek to annex the territory containing them. Many of the wars of the nineteenth and twentieth centuries have arisen from these "sympathy" issues. Where countries have been divided, then the foreign policy objective becomes national unification. For this and other reasons, the Vietnamese and Koreans, among others, have gone to war.

Sympathies need not be limited to ethnic kin. For ideological and human rights reasons many governments and private bodies have provided moral, financial, and in a few cases, armed support for the anti-*apartheid* movement in South Africa. Throughout the period of de-colonization, the socialist countries and a few Western countries (e.g., Sweden) provided moral and material support for a variety of "national liberation" movements in the Third World. The Soviet Union and to a lesser extent China made anti-imperialism a main theme of their foreign policies and devoted considerable resources for the purpose.

More recently, the cause of protecting human rights has become a part of some governments' foreign policies. Although there is little consistency in the policies— Western countries have been less concerned about human rights abuses among their friends and allies than among their Communist adversaries, for example—there is a presumption that how governments treat their citizens can become a matter of legitimate concern and assistance from other governments.

Dreams of World Reorganization

Some governments and their leaders have had ambitions stretching far beyond the immediate security, welfare, prestige, or sympathy concerns of their state. We are referring here to those great dreams of global empire, the efforts to reorganize the world or vast regions of it along new power, territorial, or ideological lines. These aspirations, when sought through military conquest, subversion, and revolutionary activity, have caused the great wars of the states system, because the dreams were fundamentally incompatible with the basic principles of that system; namely sovereignty, independence, autonomy, and noninterference in internal affairs.

Napoleon sought to create a French-centered European empire, and almost succeeded. Hitler wanted to create a "new order" for Europe; it was to be based on race. The German people would conquer Eastern Europe and the Soviet Union, turning their populations into sources of cheap labor. The "thousand year Reich" would then dominate the rest of the continent, turning the remaining states into satrapies and satellites, all organized economically to fulfill the needs of the German economy. There would not be a hierarchy of states, but a hierarchy of races, with the Germanic peoples at the top, dominating all others, and the Slavs at the bottom. Jews, Gypsies, and other groups were to be annihilated through policies of genocide. National frontiers would be replaced by racial frontiers. As the German "race" expanded, so would the frontiers of the German state. This dream, to which Hitler was willing to devote all of Germany's resources and German lives, was obviously incompatible with a system of sovereign states, whose territorial borders were created historically through wars, negotiations, peace treaties, and other means. The fight against Hitler was not just to maintain a balance of power on the continent, but to preserve the states system as it has existed for three centuries.

Antedating Hitler's grandiose plans for reorganizing the world was the Bolsheviks' long-range goal of promoting world revolution. This was a fundamental tenet of the Soviet government, and although it was abandoned by Mikhail Gorbachev in the 1980s, it remained an aspiration, if not a clear-cut foreign policy program, for more than seventy years.

What did "world revolution" mean to the Soviets for so many years? It constituted a long-range goal of promoting, assisting, and supporting socialist revolutions anywhere in the world, leading ultimately to the creation of a single world socialist system. What would this system look like? Soviet pronouncements on the "new" world were often contradictory and never became authoritatively articulated. Some versions had a continuation of the states system, but each separate state would have a socialist economy and a Soviet-style government. Others argued that ultimately all states would disappear and a genuine world state, organized economically on socialist principles, would evolve. Still others, learning from practical experience, thought in terms of a "commonwealth" of socialist states, all accepting the leadership of the Soviet Union. There was little difference between this vision and a Moscow-centered world or regional empire. The way that the Soviet Union established its relations with other "fraternal" countries after 1945 made it clear that coercion, force, and the imposition of Soviet economic, social, and political institutions would hold the "commonwealth" together.

The early Bolsheviks assumed that the world revolution would be completed within a few years after the end of World War I. Stalin spoke in terms of a generation or more. Khrushchev predicted that capitalism and imperialism would collapse during the time of his generation's grandchildren; that is, sometime between 1985 and 2020. Leonid Brezhnev, who died in 1982, alluded to the post-capitalist world as monolithically united under the ideology of socialism, but somewhat fragmented in the sense that sovereign states would remain. He depicted the existing socialist states as a "well-knit family of nations, building and defending the new society together, and . . . enriching each other with experience and knowledge." This family would be "strong and united" and the "people of the world would regard it as the prototype of the future world community of free nations."[9] Among the last explicit statements on the shape of the new world, this comment showed a moderating stance toward world revolution compared with activist and aggressive statements of the early 1920s. During Brezhnev's reign, the official view was that there were now two systems of states, the socialist and the capitalist. By providing evidence of its superior capacity to provide welfare and artistic and human growth, the socialist system would expand and ultimately become a world system—naturally rather than by force. The collapse of communism between 1989 and 1991 put an end to this vision of world order.

Both Nazism and communism offered visions of world order fundamentally different from Westphalian principles that emphasize the territorial exclusiveness, sovereignty, and independence of *separate* states. Nazism proposed to organize the world on the principle of race; Marxism-Leninism proposed to organize it on the principle of class. The most recent vision of a different type of world organization has been articulated by the Ayatollah Khomeini and some of his successors.

The Ayatollah also rejected the concept of the state as the basic unit of human political organization. The only genuine community is the community of *believers,* the *umma.* All secular governments based on nationality or on the results of imperialism are illegitimate. Those that oppress are the worst. The political organization of Islam must be based on religion, not on secular principles, for the task of governance is not just to provide order and justice, but to make "man into what he should be. . . . In the prophet's view, the world is merely a means, a path by which to achieve a noble aim that man is himself unaware of but that is known to the prophets."[10] The sole "identity" of Muslims is their membership in the community of believers. The ultimate fate of this community is to become politically organized under the imams, the line of male descendants of Muhammad's cousin Ali. But until the twelfth imam reappears, all secular governments are temporary, and most of them are illegitimate. The only legitimate governments are those ruled by the "trustees of Islam," those who have mastered Islamic law. It is the primary task of such authorities to liberate all oppressed peoples from their oppressors (imperialists, nationalists, and Zionists). The struggle for Islamic rule is thus also a struggle for justice.[11]

What does this mean in practical terms? First, it suggests that the imam's regime in Iran is just a base for leading the fight for liberation of the oppressed. The primary step is to unify the Islamic world. The Islamic Republic's (Iran's) constitution states: "According to the Koran all Muslims are of the same and one single religious community, and the Islamic Republic of Iran is bound to base its general policies on the coalition and unity of Islamic nations, and it should exert continuous efforts to realize the political, economic, and cultural unity of the Islamic World."

---

[9]*Documents of the 24th Congress of the Communist Party of the Soviet Union* (Moscow: Novosti Press Agency, 1971), 19.

[10]Quoted in *Islam and Revolution: Writings and Declarations of Imam Khomeini,* trans. Hamid Algar (Berkeley, Calif.: University of California Press, 1981), 31–33.

[11]For further discussion, see David Armstrong, *Revolution and World Order: The Revolutionary State in International Society* (Oxford: Clarendon Press, 1993), 188–97.

Promoting the Islamic "revolution," then, is the main task of the Republic. In its relations with others, the Republic must be guided by Islamic principles. With other Muslims, this means emphasis on unity, and opposition to all illegitimate so-called Muslim regimes that place national needs above needs of the *umma*. As for the institutions of the society of states, Khomeini saw them primarily as instruments of oppression. No United Nations charter or Western international law can supersede Islamic law.

To the consternation of many of Iran's neighbors, Khomeini, somewhat in the fashion of Lenin and Trotsky, repeatedly emphasized the importance of "exporting" the Islamic revolution, not just to extend God's message, but also to "liberate" oppressed peoples. "An Islamic movement . . . cannot limit itself to any particular country, nor even to the Islamic countries; it is the continuation of the revolution by the prophets."[12]

The Ayatollah's visions and pronouncements have been translated into distinct actions by the Islamic Republic. These include the following: spiritual guidance and financial support for Shi'ite movements outside of Iran; the attempt to overthrow the Sunni-dominated regime of Saddam Hussein in neighboring Iraq; involvement in various revolutionary networks in the Middle East, particularly its links with the Hizbollah (Party of God), which has often used terrorist tactics in Lebanon; extensive propaganda programs; establishment of "training camps" for fellow believers; and vigorous opposition to the Israel-PLO mutual recognition and peace plan of 1993.

Whatever the ultimate fate of the Ayatollah's vision, since his death Iran has had to reconcile itself to the fact that it is a state in a community of states. Khomeini's successors have had to restore friendlier relations with the Gulf and other Arab states, most of which saw Khomeini's plans and programs as a threat to their survival. During the long and costly war with Iraq (1980–1988), Iran had to rely on others for military assistance and diplomatic support. Iran remains a member of the United Nations, and while the present leadership continues to give expression to the Ayatollah's ideas at least at the rhetorical level, its foreign policy appears to be guided by more conventional concerns of security, wealth, and prestige. The Ayatollah's vision has had only limited appeal outside of Iran. The forces of secularism and nationalism which predominate in the contemporary global system have not been receptive to the idea that the world should be based on fundamentally different principles.

Concluding Reminders

The foregoing discussion has listed several universal values, purposes that all states pursue or protect. How they do so remains a matter of choice. Governments have different priorities, and even among those priorities there are many elements of choice and political debate. How, for example, should a nuclear weapons–owning state deploy them to maximize deterrent effect? Should a government build up its

---

[12]Quoted in F. Rajaee, *Islamic Values and World View* (Lanham, Md.: University Press of America, 1983), 82.

nuclear arsenal to maximize deterrence, or would welfare values (e.g., lower taxes and more private consumption) be assisted by a strategy of arms-control and disarmament negotiations? Should a medium-sized power have nuclear weapons at all? Should a small state maintain an army of three or four divisions, and how should they be deployed? The answers depend on the kinds of threats and vulnerabilities, real and potential, that a country faces, and on the weight of other government priorities. A particularly interesting example of the playing out among competing priorities is now offered by NATO countries. If the Cold War is over, then how much national wealth should be devoted to the military? In the United States, there are strong demands for dramatic decreases in military spending. But some Americans, perhaps less to cope with immediate threats or vulnerabilities than to maximize American status and prestige (to remain "No. 1"), insist that the country should remain armed at a high level.

As for other values and purposes, they are as many as human beings can contrive or care about. We have listed some of the common ones, and the less common ambitions of creating new world orders. But how one goes about such grandiose tasks involves many choices. Even the Bolsheviks in the 1920s, who thought that the victory of socialism was inevitable because of the inherent contradictions in capitalism, debated at great length whether the Soviet republic should expend its resources on promoting revolution abroad or use those resources to build up the Soviet society. Once in power, Stalin chose the latter priority, although he never abandoned fully the world revolutionary dream, and in later years he committed vast sums of money and other resources for foreign propaganda, subversion, and subsidies to foreign Communist parties.

Choices are thus made not only in terms of priorities but also in the selection of means (policies and actions) to give them effect. To close our discussion and to demonstrate the connection between values or purposes and policies, we can outline, as an illustration, the salient points of Colonel Khadaffi's foreign policies for Libya. Table 4-1 lists various Libyan values and the policies that have been used to maximize, defend, or achieve them. Under the Policies/Actions column, the incompatibility of values is noted by parentheses. This indicates where the commitment to one policy benefits (plus sign) or is incompatible with (minus sign) another value.

Some actions contribute to more than one value. Libya's termination of air base agreements with the United States and Great Britain shortly after Khadaffi overthrew the traditional monarchy in 1969 significantly reduced Libya's military vulnerability. Those air bases could have been used as staging depots for American or British intervention against the Libyan government. The move also substantially increased Libya's autonomy, but because Libya lost the revenues from the base leases, there was a net decrease in welfare value. From the perspective of a radical nationalist, however, the security and autonomy gains were well worth the loss of revenue. The reader can make a similar list for the foreign policy priorities and actions of any other country, including his or her own.

We turn in the next chapters to the various means and actions governments typically employ to achieve or defend their purposes, and to maximize the priorities and values they have chosen. We will begin in Chapter 5 with the analysis of influ-

TABLE 4-1
Purposes and Actions in Libyan Foreign Policy

VALUE/PURPOSE	POLICIES/ACTIONS
Security	1. Terminate U.S. and British air base agreement (+ autonomy)
	2. Diversify weapons sources (+ autonomy)
	3. Build up armed forces (– welfare)
Autonomy	1. Nationalize foreign-owned oil companies (+ welfare)
	2. Terminate U.S. and British air base agreements (– welfare, + prestige)
	3. Establish diplomatic relations with socialist states (+ security, prestige)
Welfare	1. Nationalize foreign-owned oil industry (+ autonomy)
	2. Invade Chad, gain control over resources of contested Aouzou strip
Prestige/status	1. Frequent military displays
	2. Anti-imperialist rhetoric
Other purposes	
1. Support ethnic/ ideological kin	1. Contribute troops to 1973 Egypt-Israel War
	2. Host, arm, train "liberation" units for PLO radical factions
	3. Terrorist activities against "Zionist" and "imperialist" targets.
2. Promote Arab/Muslim unity	1. Constitutional mergers with Tunisia and Syria (– autonomy)
	2. Attempted *coups* against "reactionary" regimes in Egypt and Sudan
	3. Diplomatic and financial support for Muslim groups in Philippines
	4. Financial support for Pakistan's nuclear energy program (– welfare)
	5. Intervene militarily on behalf of pro-Muslim faction in Chad civil war (– welfare)

ence techniques in general, and then in the succeeding chapters, we will examine more specific methods of moving toward goals and priorities.

Questions for Study, Analysis, and Discussion

1. Are there important goals that most states seek to achieve or defend in addition to security, autonomy, welfare, and status?
2. In your country, which of the four common goals take priority? What sorts of debates are there about the appropriate priorities?
3. Should the concept of "national security" refer to non-military threats such as AIDS, transborder pollution, the narcotics trade, and population migration?
4. How would you define the concepts of *division of labor, comparative advantage*, and *mercantilism*? What forms of protectionism/mercantilism does your government practice today?
5. In what ways does your government seek to enhance its international reputation, status, and prestige?
6. Should your government spend taxpayers' money to assist foreign victims of human rights abuses or war, when the national interest is not directly involved?
7. Does the United States have a historic "mission" to bring to other peoples the advantages of democracy and the principles of the private market? Should any other country have a similar "mission"? Why or why not?
8. Have alliances been rendered obsolete by the end of the Cold War?

Selected Bibliography

Anabtawai, Samir N., "Neutralists and Neutralism," *Journal of Politics,* 27 (1965), 351–61.
Armstrong, David, Revolution and World Order: The Revolutionary State in International Society. Oxford: Clarendon Press, 1993.

Banerjee, Malabika, The Nonaligned Movement. Calcutta: KLM Private Ltd., 1982.

Beard, Charles A., The Idea of National Interest. Chicago: University of Chicago Press, 1966.

Buzan, Barry, People, States and Fear: An Agenda for International Security Studies in the Post–Cold War Era. Boulder, Colo.: Lynne Rienner, 1991.

Deudney, Daniel, "Environmental Degradation and National Security," *Millenium,* 19, 3 (1990), 461–76.

Dominguez, Jorge I., To Make a World Safe for Revolution: Cuba's Foreign Policy. Cambridge, Mass.: Harvard University Press, 1989.

Frankel, Joseph, National Interest. London: Macmillan, 1970.

Frieden, Jeffry A., and David A. Lake, International Political Economy: Perspectives on Global Power and Wealth, 2nd ed. New York: St. Martin's Press, 1991.

Friedman, Julian R., Christopher Bladen, and Stephen Rosen, Eds., Alliances in International Politics. Boston: Allyn & Bacon, 1970.

Gill, Stephen, and David Law, The Global Political Economy: Perspectives, Problems, and Policies. Baltimore: Johns Hopkins University Press, 1988.

Gilpin, Robert, The Political Economy of International Relations. Princeton, N.J.: Princeton University Press, 1987.

Goodman, Elliot, The Soviet Design for a World State. New York: Columbia University Press, 1960.

Hettne, Björn, "Neo-Mercantilism: The Pursuit of Regionesse," *Cooperation and Conflict,* 28 (September 1993), 211–32.

Holsti, K. J., et al., Why Nations Realign: Foreign Policy Restructuring Since World War II. London: Allen & Unwin, 1982.

Holsti, Ole R., P. Terrence Hopmann, and John D. Sullivan, Unity and Disintegration in International Alliances: Comparative Studies. New York: John Wiley, 1973.

Homer-Dixon, Thomas F., "On the Threshold: Environmental Changes as Cause of Acute Conflict," *International Security,* 16 (Fall 1991), 76–116.

Isaac, Robert A., Intenational Political Economy: Managing World Economic Change. Englewood Cliffs, N.J.: Prentice-Hall, 1991.

Jackson, John H., The World Trading System: Law and Policy of International Economic Relations. Cambridge, Mass.: M.I.T. Press, 1989.

Job, Brian, Ed., The Insecurity Dilemma: National Security of Third World States. Boulder, Colo.: Lynne Rienner, 1991.

Kapstein, Ethan Barnaby, The Political Economy of National Security: A Global Perspective. New York: McGraw-Hill, 1992.

Keohane, Robert O., "The Big Influence of Small Allies," *Foreign Policy,* 2 (Spring 1971), 161–82.

Lyon, Peter, Neutralism. Leicester: Leicester University Press, 1964.

Matthews, Jessica Tuchman, "Redefining Security," *Foreign Affairs,* 68, 2 (1989), 162–77.

Misra, K. P., Ed., Nonalignment: Frontiers and Dynamics. New Delhi: Vikas, 1982.

Morse, Edward L., Modernization and the Transformation of Intenational Relations. New York: Free Press, 1976.

Osgood, Robert E., Ideals and Self-Interest in American Foreign Relations. Chicago: University of Chicago Press, 1953.

Ramazani, R. K., Revolutionary Iran: Challenge and Response in the Middle East. Baltimore and London: Johns Hopkins University Press, 1986.

Russett, Bruce M., "An Empirical Typology of International Military Alliances," *Midwest Journal of Political Science,* 15 (1971).

Singer, J. David, and Melvin Small, "Formal Alliances, 1815–1939," *Journal of Peace Research,* 1 (1966), 1–32.

Sorensen, Theodore C., "Rethinking National Security," *Foreign Affairs,* 69 (Summer 1990), 1–18.

Spero, Joan, The Politics of International Economic Relations. New York: St. Martin's Press, 1990.

Stubbs, Richard, and Geoffrey Underhill, Eds., Political Economy and the Changing Global Order. Markham, Ont.: McClelland & Stewart, 1994.

Thomas, Caroline, In Search of Security: The Third World in International Relations. Boulder, Colo.: Lynne Rienner, 1987.

Tow, William T., Subregional Security Cooperation in the Third World. Boulder, Colo.: Lynne Rienner, 1991.

Tussie, Diana, and David Glover, Eds., The Developing Countries in World Trade: Policies and Bargaining Strategies. Boulder, Colo.: Lynne Rienner, 1993.

Walker, Stephen, Ed., Role Theory and Foreign Policy Analysis. Durham, N.C.: Duke University Press, 1987.

Willetts, Peter, The Non-Aligned Movement. New York: Nichols, 1979.

Chapter
5

Foreign Policy Actions: Power, Capabilities, and Influence

States have a variety of purposes: Many are common to all, and some are unique to each. Many purposes or goals can be achieved primarily through domestic policies. Public welfare, for example, is promoted by tax and monetary policies, social welfare programs, steps to limit unemployment, and the like. Security can be enhanced by certain kinds of military deployments and by various national means of reducing vulnerabilities (e.g., stockpiling, or beefing up military controls over strategic routes such as mountain passes or waterways). But in an age where societies are closely connected through transnational associations and networks of dependency, many purposes can only be achieved or defended by manipulating, sustaining, or altering conditions in other countries. Aside from purposes, foreign policy also includes the *actions*—the things governments do to others—in order to defend or achieve the kinds of purposes outlined in the previous chapter.

An act is basically a form of communication intended to change or sustain the attitudes and behavior of those upon whom the acting government is dependent for achieving its own goals. It can also be viewed as a "signal" sent by one actor to influence the receiver's image of the sender.[1] In international politics, acts and signals take many different forms. The promise of granting foreign aid is an act, as are propaganda appeals, displays of military strength, wielding a veto in the UN Security Coun-

---

[1]A comprehensive treatment of how governments "signal" each other is in Robert Jervis, *The Logic of Images in International Relations* (Princeton, N.J.: Princeton University Press, 1970).

cil, walking out of a conference, organizing a conference, issuing a warning in a diplomatic note, sending arms and money to a liberation movement, instituting a boycott on the goods of another state, or declaring war. These types of acts and signals, and the circumstances in which they are likely to succeed, will be discussed in this and the following five chapters. Our organizing principle will be the amount of threat involved in the various techniques of influence. Diplomatic persuasion seemingly involves the least amount of threat; economic pressures, subversion, intervention, and various forms of warfare involve increasingly greater amounts of threat and punishment.

The international political process commences when any state—let us say state A—seeks through various acts or signals to change or sustain the behavior (for instance, the acts, images, and policies) of other states. Power can thus be defined as the general capacity of a state to control the behavior of others. This definition can be illustrated as follows, where the solid line represents various acts:

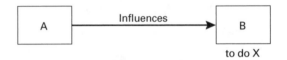

A seeks to influence B because A has established certain objectives that cannot be achieved (it is perceived) unless B (and perhaps many other states as well) does X. If this is the basis of all international political processes, the capacity to control behavior can be viewed in several different ways:

1. Influence (an aspect of power) is essentially a *means* to an end. Some governments or leaders may seek influence for its own sake, but for most it is instrumental, just like money. States use influence primarily for achieving or defending other goals, which may include prestige, territory, souls, raw materials, security, or alliances.
2. State A, in its acts toward state B, uses or mobilizes certain *resources*. A resource is any physical or mental object or quality available as an instrument of inducement to persuade, reward, threaten, or punish. The concept of resource may be illustrated in the following example. Suppose an unarmed robber walks into a bank and asks the teller to give up money. The teller observes clearly that the robber has no weapon and refuses to comply with the order. The robber has sought to influence the behavior of the teller but has failed. The next time, however, the robber walks in armed with a pistol and threatens to shoot if the teller does not give up the money. This time, the teller complies. In this instance, the robber has mobilized certain resources or capabilities (the gun) and succeeds in influencing the teller to comply. But other less tangible resources may be involved as well. The appearance of the robber, particularly facial expression, may convey determination, threat, or weakness, all of which may subtly influence the behavior of the teller. In international politics, the diplomatic gestures and words accompanying actions may be as important as the acts themselves. A government that places troops on alert but insists that it is doing so for domestic reasons will have an impact abroad quite different from the government that organizes a similar alert but accompanies it with threats to go to war. "Signals" or diplomatic "body language" may be as important as dramatic actions such as alerts and mobilizations.
3. The act of influencing B obviously involves a *relationship* between A and B, although, as will be seen later, the relationship may not even involve overt communication. If the relationship covers any period of time, we can also say that it is a *process*.

4. If A can get B to do something, but B cannot get A to do a similar thing, then we can say that A has more power than B regarding that particular issue. Power, therefore, can also be viewed as a *quantity*, but as a quantity it is only meaningful when compared to the power of others. Power is therefore relative.

To summarize, power may be viewed from several aspects: It is a means; it is based on resources; it is a relationship and a process; and it can be measured, at least crudely.

We can break down the concept of power into three distinct analytic elements: Power comprises (1) the *acts* (process, relationship) of influencing other states; (2) the *resources* or *leverage* used to make the wielding of influence successful; and (3) the *responses* to the acts. The three elements must be kept distinct. Since this definition may seem too abstract, we can define the concept in the more operational terms of policy makers. In formulating policy and the strategy to achieve certain goals, they would explicitly or implicitly ask the following five questions:

1. Given our goals, what do we wish B to do or not to do? (X)
2. How shall we get B to do or not to do X? (implies a relationship and process)
3. What resources are at our disposal so that we can induce B to do or not to do X?
4. What is B's probable response to our attempts to influence its behavior?
5. What are the *costs* of taking actions 1, 2, or 3—as opposed to other alternatives?

Acts

Before discussing the problem of resources and responses, we have to fill out our model of the influence act to account for the many types of acts that may be involved in an international relationship. First, the exercise of influence implies more than merely A's ability to *change* the behavior of B. Influence may also be seen when A attempts to get B to *continue* a course of action or policy that is useful to, or in the interests of, A.[2] The exercise of influence does not always cease, therefore, after B does X. It is often a continuing process of reinforcing B's behavior.

Second, it is almost impossible to find a situation where B does not also have some influence over A. Our model has suggested that influence is exercised in only one direction, by A over B. In reality, influence is multilateral. State A, for example, would seldom seek a particular goal unless it has been influenced in a particular direction by the actions of other states in the system. At a minimum, there is the problem of feedback in any relationship. If B complies with A's wishes and does X, that behavior may subsequently prompt A to change its own behavior, perhaps in the interest of B. The phenomenon of feedback may be illustrated as follows:

[2]J. David Singer, "Inter-Nation Influence: A Formal Model," *American Political Science Review*, 57 (1963), 420–30. State A might also wish state B to do W, Y, and Z, which may be incompatible with the achievement of X.

Third, there is the type of relationship that includes "anticipated reaction."[3] This is the situation where B, anticipating rewards or punishments from A, changes its behavior, perhaps even before A makes any "signals" about possible action. Deterrence theory clearly assumes that B—the potential aggressor against A—will not attack (where it might, were there no deterrent), knowing that an unacceptable level of punishment would surely result. A similar situation, but in reverse, is also common in international politics. This is where A might wish B to do X, but does not try to influence B for fear that B will do Y instead, which is an unfavorable response from A's point of view.

Fourth, power and influence may be measured by scholars, but what is important in international politics is the *perceptions* of influence and capabilities held by policy makers and the way they interpret another government's signals. The reason that governments invest millions of dollars for gathering intelligence is to develop a reasonably accurate picture of other states' capabilities and intentions. Where there is a great discrepancy between perceptions and reality, the results to a country's foreign policy may be disastrous. To take our example of the bank robber again, suppose that the person held a harmless toy pistol and threatened the teller. The teller perceived the gun to be real and deduced the robber's intention to use it. As a result, the teller complied with the demand. In this case, the robber's influence was far greater than the "objective" character of the robber's capabilities and intentions; and distorted perception by the teller led to an act that was unfavorable to the bank.

Finally, as our original model suggests, A may try to influence B *not to do* X. Sometimes this is called negative power, or deterrence, where A acts in a manner to *prevent* a certain action it deems undesirable to its interests. This is a typical relationship in international politics. By signing the 1938 Munich treaty, the British and French governments hoped to prevent Germany from invading Czechoslovakia; Israeli attacks on PLO facilities in Lebanon were designed to demonstrate that PLO guerilla operations against Israel would be met by vast punishments, the costs of which to the PLO would far outweigh the gains of the terrorist acts. Such a cost-benefit analysis, the Israelis hope, would deter the PLO from undertaking further operations. The reader should keep in mind the distinction between compellance and deterrence.

Resources

The second element of the concept of power consists of those resources that are mobilized in support of the acts taken to influence state B's behavior. It is difficult to assess the general capacity of a state to control the actions and policies of others unless we also have some knowledge of the capabilities involved.[4] Nevertheless, it should be acknowledged that social scientists do not understand all the reasons why some

---

[3]Herbert A. Simon, "Notes on the Observation and Measurement of Political Power," *Journal of Politics*, 15 (1953), 500–16. For further analysis, see David A. Baldwin, "Inter-Nation Influence Revisited," *Journal of Conflict Resolution*, 15 (December 1971), 478–79.

[4]We might assess influence for historical situations solely on the basis of whether A got B to do X, without our having knowledge of either A's or B's capabilities.

actors—whether people, groups, or governments—wield influence successfully, while others do not.

It is clear that, in political relationships, not everyone possesses equal influence. In domestic politics, it is possible to construct a lengthy list of capabilities and attributes that seemingly permit some to wield influence over large numbers of people and important public decisions. Robert Dahl lists such tangibles as money, wealth, information, time, political allies, official position, and control over jobs, and such intangibles as personality and leadership qualities.[5] But not everyone who possesses these capabilities can command the obedience of other people. What is crucial in relating resources to influence, according to Dahl, is that one *mobilize them for one's political purposes* and possess the skill to mobilize them. One who uses wealth, time, information, friends, and personality for political purposes will probably be able to influence others on public issues. A person, on the other hand, who possesses the same capabilities but uses them to invent a new mousetrap is not apt to be important in politics. The same propositions also hold true in international politics. The amount of influence a state wields over others can be related to the capabilities *mobilized* in support of *specific* foreign policy objectives. To put this proposition in another way, we can argue that resources do not determine the uses to which they will be put. Nuclear power can be used to provide electricity or to deter and perhaps destroy other nations. The use of resources depends less on their quality and quantity than on the external objectives a government formulates for itself.

The *variety* of foreign policy instruments available to a nation for influencing others is partly a function of the quantity and quality of capabilities. What a government seeks to do—the type of objectives it formulates—and how it attempts to do it will depend at least partially on the resources it finds available. A country such as Fiji which possesses relatively few resources, cannot, even if it would desire, construct intercontinental ballistic missiles with which to intimidate others, establish a worldwide propaganda network, or dispense several billion dollars annually of foreign aid to try to influence other countries. We can conclude, therefore, that how states *use* their resources depends on their external objectives, but the choice of objectives and the instruments to achieve those objectives are limited or influenced by the quality and quantity of available resources.

Many contemporary international relationships reveal how often the "strong" states do not achieve their objectives—even when attempting to influence the behavior of "weak" states. How, for instance, did Marshal Tito's Yugoslavia effectively resist all sorts of pressures and threats by the powerful Soviet Union after it was expelled from the Communist bloc in the late 1940s? Why, despite its overwhelming superiority in capabilities, was the United States unable in the 1960s to achieve its major objectives against a weak Cuba and North Vietnam? How have "small" states gained trading privileges and all sorts of diplomatic concessions from those nations with great economic wealth and military power? The ability of state A to change the behavior of state B is, we would assume, enhanced if it possesses physical resources to use in the influence act; but B is by no means defenseless or vulnerable to diplo-

---

[5]Robert A. Dahl, *Who Governs?* (New Haven, Conn.: Yale University Press, 1961).

matic, economic, or military pressures because it fails to own a large modern army, raw materials, and money for foreign aid. The successful exercise of influence is also dependent upon such factors as personality, perceptions, friendships, and traditions, and, not being easy to measure, these factors have a way of rendering power calculations and equations difficult. Aside from these situational factors, we may specify certain other conditions that help determine, regardless of military and economic capabilities, whether acts of influencing will succeed. These conditions, or variables, also help explain why states with very weak capabilities are often able to resist the demands of the strong and sometimes achieve their own demands at the expense of the interests of major powers.

Responses

Our last concept is the *responses* to various sets of influence. The target, our state B, has numerous options. Among the most likely are (1) to accommodate (that is, to do or not do X); (2) to ignore—to pretend the message or signal has not been received; (3) to procrastinate; (4) to bargain, by seeking to change A's objectives; and (5) to resist, usually by following a tit-for-tat strategy of matching A's offers or threats or possibly escalating. In most historical cases, the higher the stakes involved in the *issue* that divides A and B, the greater the possibility that B will choose to resist—even if it knows its resources do not match those of A. Studies of crises between nations show that threats are least likely to succeed—that is, B will successfully resist or war will ensue—when the clashing objectives involve questions of sovereignty and prestige; threats are most likely to succeed when economic issues are involved.[6] This is another way of saying that governments value political autonomy, prestige, and other core values, such as territory, more than economic welfare, and that when the former are in contention, resistance, whether by tit-for-tat or escalation strategies, is a more likely response than accommodation, procrastination, or bargaining through discussion and counteroffers. The other side of the proposition would be that B is most likely to be accommodating when A uses persuasion and rewards on issues of less value or concern to B. Degree of commitment to objectives and values remains a crucial determinant of acts of influence, one that is more significant than the comparative resources of the parties in the influence relationship.

Variables Affecting the Exercise of Influence

One reason that gross quantities of resources cannot be equated with effective influence relates to the distinction between a state's overall capabilities and the *relevance* of resources to a particular diplomatic situation. A nuclear force, for example, is often thought to increase the diplomatic influence of those who possess it. No doubt nuclear weaponry is an important element in a state's general prestige abroad and may be an effective deterrent against a strategic attack on its homeland or "core"

---

[6]Peter Karsten, Peter D. Howell, and A. F. Allen, *Military Threats: A Systematic Historical Analysis of the Determinants of Success* (Westport, Conn.: Greenwood Press, 1984), 65–67.

interests. Yet the most important aspect of a nuclear capability—or any military capability—is not its possession, but its relevance and the ability to signal one's determination to use it. Other governments must know that the capability is not of mere symbolic significance. The government of North Vietnam possessed a particular advantage over the United States (hence, influence) because it knew that in almost no circumstances would the American government use strategic nuclear weapons against its country. It therefore effectively broke through the significance of the American nuclear capability as far as the Vietnam War was concerned. A resource is useless unless it is both mobilized in support of foreign policy objectives and made credible. Likewise, nuclear weapons would be irrelevant in negotiations on cultural exchanges, just as the Arab countries' vast oil resources could not be effectively mobilized to influence the outcome of international negotiations on satellite communications. Influence is always specific to a particular issue, and resources must be relevant to that issue.

A second variable that determines the success or failure of acts of influence is the extent to which there are *needs* between the two countries in any influence relationship. In general, a country that needs something from another is vulnerable to its acts of influence. This is the primary reason that states deficient in many capabilities can nevertheless obtain concessions from stronger countries. Consider the case of France and Germany and some of the small states in the Middle East. Both European countries are highly dependent upon Arab lands for oil supplies. They have an important need which only the Arab countries can satisfy at a reasonable cost. On the other hand, the Middle Eastern countries that control these oil resources may not be so dependent upon Germany and France, particularly if they can sell their oil easily elsewhere. Because, in this situation, needs are not equal on both sides, the independent states (in terms of needs) can make demands (or resist demands made against them) on the dependent great powers and obtain important concessions. The German and French governments know that if they do not make these concessions or if they press their own demands too hard, the Arab states can threaten to cut off oil supplies. Their dependence thus makes them vulnerable to the demands and influence acts of what would otherwise be considered second-rank states. To the Arab states, oil is much more important as a capability than is military force—at least in their relations with major powers. In the form of a general hypothesis, we can suggest that, regardless of the quantity, quality, and credibility of a state's capabilities, the more state B needs, or is dependent upon, state A, the more likely that state A's acts—threats, promises, rewards, or punishments—will succeed in changing or sustaining B's behavior.

A third variable that has assumed increasing importance in the past several decades, and one that can be considered an important resource, is level of technical expertise. An increasing number of issues on the international and foreign policy agendas are highly technical in nature: law of the sea, satellite broadcasting, international monetary matters, and the like. Many of these issues are discussed in international forums, where leadership often depends more on knowledge of the technical issues than on other types of resources. Those governments that come armed with technical studies, have a full command of the nature of the problem, and are prepared to put forth realistic solutions are more likely to wield influence than are governments that have only rudimentary knowledge of the problem and no scientific studies to back their national positions. A number of recent case studies have demonstrated conclusively that the outcomes of negotiations on technical questions cannot be predicted from the gross power of the participants and that knowledge, among other factors, accounts for more than raw capabilities.[7]

Understanding the dynamics of power relationships at the international level would be relatively easy if resource relevance, credibility, need, and knowledge were the only variables involved. Unfortunately, political actions do not always conform to simple hypotheses, because human characteristics of pride, stubbornness, prestige, and friendship enter into all acts of influence as well. A government may be highly dependent upon some other state and still resist its demands; it may be willing to suffer all sorts of privations, and even physical destruction and loss of independence, simply for the sake of pride. The government of North Vietnam was willing to accept a very high level of destruction of lives and productive facilities by American bombers rather than make diplomatic or military concessions to the United States. The same could be said about Iraq in its confrontation with the United Nations coalition in 1990 and 1991.

After relevant resources, need, and knowledge, the fourth variable that determines the effectiveness of influence is the ephemeral quality of responsiveness.[8] Responsiveness can be seen as a disposition to receive another's requests with sympathy, even to the point where a government is willing to sacrifice some of its own values and interests in order to fulfill those requests; responsiveness is the willingness to be influenced. In one study, it was shown that members of the State Department in the United States may take considerable pains to promote the requests and interests of other governments among their superiors and in other government agencies, provided that the requesting government feels that the issue is important or that the need must be fulfilled.[9]

One final variable involving costs and commitments should be identified. Success in the wielding of influence seems to be related also to the extent to which the objectives of the states are compatible or the degree of commitment each government has toward those objectives. If I am strongly committed to attending a poker game Friday night and you ask me to go to a football game, no matter what sorts of arguments you make, I will not go. The costs of breaking the commitment—displeasure of friends and possible dismissal from the poker group—would far outweigh the possible advantages of seeing a ball game. But where no significant costs are associated with not

[7]See, for example, the case studies in Robert O. Keohane and Joseph S. Nye, *Power and Interdependence: World Politics in Transition,* 2nd ed. (Boston: Little, Brown, 1989). See also David Baldwin's strong emphasis on the relevance of resources to particular situations in "Power Analysis and World Politics: New Trends versus Old Tendencies," *World Politics,* 31 (January 1979), 161–94.

[8]The concept of responsiveness is introduced by Karl W. Deutsch et al., *Political Community and the North Atlantic Area* (Princeton, N.J.: Princeton University Press, 1957); developed by Dean G. Pruitt, "National Power and International Responsiveness," *Background,* 7 (1964), 165–78. See also Dean G. Pruitt, "Definition of the Situation as a Determinant of International Action," in *International Behavior: A Social-Psychological Analysis,* ed. Herbert C. Kelman (New York: Holt, Rinehart & Winston, 1965), 393–432.

[9]Pruitt, "National Power," 175–76.

going to the poker game—perhaps there are already too many players—then I might well be persuaded to see some football instead. My interests are not well defined, I have no firm commitment to one course of action; hence, I will be more open to persuasion, provided that you have relevant resources (your offer to pay my way) and I recognize that you would rather not go to the game by yourself (responsiveness).

How Influence Is Exercised

Social scientists have noted several fundamental techniques that individuals and groups use to influence each other. In a political system that contains no one legitimate center of authority that can command the members of the group or society, bargaining has to be used among the sovereign entities to achieve or defend their objectives. Recalling that A seeks one of three courses of conduct from B (B to do X in the future, B not to do X in the future, or B to continue doing X), it may use six different tactics, involving acts of:

1. Persuasion. By persuasion we mean simply initiating or discussing a proposal with another and eliciting a favorable response without explicitly holding out the possibility of punishments. We cannot assume that the exercise of influence is always *against* the wishes of others and that there are only two possible outcomes of the act, one favoring A, the other favoring B. For example, state A asks B to support it at a coming international conference on the control of narcotics. State B might not originally have any particular interest in the conference or its outcome; but it decides, on the basis of A's initiative, that something positive might be gained, not only by supporting A's proposals, but also by attending the conference. In this case, B might also expect to gain some type of reward in the future, although not necessarily from A. Persuasion would also include protests and denials that do not involve obvious threats.

2. The Offer of Rewards. This is the situation where A promises to do something favorable to B if B complies with the wishes of A. Rewards may be of almost any type in international politics. To gain the diplomatic support of B at the narcotics conference, A may offer to increase foreign-aid payments, lower tariffs on goods imported from B, support B at a later conference on communications facilities, or promise to remove a previous punishment. The last tactic is used often by negotiators. After having created an unfavorable situation, they promise to remove it in return for some concessions by their opponents.

3. The Granting of Rewards. In some instances, the credibility of a government is not very high, and state B, before complying with A's wishes, may insist that A actually give the reward in advance. Frequently, in armistice negotiations, neither side will unilaterally take steps to demilitarize an area or demobilize troops until the other shows evidence of complying with the agreements. One of the clichés of diplomacy holds that deeds, not words, are required for the granting of rewards and concessions.

4. The Threat of Punishment. Threats of punishment may be further subdivided into two types: (a) positive threats, where, for example, state A threatens to increase tariffs, institute a boycott or embargo against trade with B, or use force; and (b) threats of deprivation, where A threatens to withdraw foreign aid or in other ways withhold rewards or other advantages that it already grants to B.

5. The Infliction of Nonviolent Punishment.   In this situation, threats are carried out in the hope of altering B's behavior, which, in most cases, could not be altered by other means. The problem with this tactic is that it often results in reciprocal measures by the other side, thus inflicting damage on both and not necessarily bringing about a desired state of affairs. If, for example, A threatens to increase its military capabilities if B does X and then proceeds to implement the threat, it is not often that B will comply with A's wishes, because it, too, can increase its military capabilities. In this type of situation, both sides indulge in the application of punishments that may escalate into more serious forms unless the conflict is resolved. Typical acts of nonviolent punishment include breaking diplomatic relations, raising tariffs, instituting boycotts and embargoes, holding hostages, organizing blockades, closing frontiers, or walking out of a diplomatic conference.

6. Force.   In previous eras, when governments did not possess the variety of foreign policy instruments available today, they frequently had to rely upon the use of force in the bargaining process. Force and violence were not only the most efficient tactics, but in many cases the only means possible for influencing. Today, the situation is different. As technological levels rise and dependencies develop, other means of inducement become available and can serve as substitutes for force.[10]

Relational and Structural Power

To this point, we have looked at power and influence in the sense of two or more parties bargaining with each other to achieve or defend certain purposes or goals. We have assumed that both parties are more or less independent entities and that there is nothing in the context in which they are bargaining that establishes advantages. But in social relationships of all kinds, bargaining takes place within a particular context of position, authority, and tradition. In a family, for example, children may bargain with their parents to allow them to watch a television program that is broadcast after the normal bedtime. In this relationship, however, the parents have the presumed authority to grant or withhold permission. Children, in contrast, do not have the authority to "permit" their parents to go to a movie. The presumption of authority is just one indication of what we have called "structural power." As in

[10]François de Callières, a renowned French diplomat of the eighteenth century, also suggested the utility of these techniques when he wrote, "Every Christian prince must take as his chief maxim not to employ arms to support or vindicate his rights until he has employed and exhausted the way of reason and persuasion. It is to his interest, also, to add to reason and persuasion the influence of benefits conferred, which indeed is one of the surest ways to make his own power secure, and to increase it." *On the Manner of Negotiating with Princes*, trans. A. F. Whyte (Boston: Houghton Mifflin, 1919) 7. In a treatise on foreign policy written in approximately 300 B.C., Kautilya noted four fundamental techniques for obtaining the desired results from other Indian states: conciliation (*sama*), gifts (*dana*), dissension (*bheda*), and punishment (*danda*). See George Modelski, "Kautilya: Foreign Policy and International System in the Ancient Hindu World," *American Political Science Review*, 58 (1964), 553. Chapter 14 of this text includes further analysis of bargaining strategies in conflict situations.

families, it exists—though often more subtly—in international relationships. We can illustrate the concept with a hypothetical example.

Imagine that you are the king or queen of a small island state in the middle of an ocean. You rule over a traditional society that has had few contacts with the outside world. The economy of your realm is based on subsistence agriculture and fishing. Your society has a variety of unique traditions, including language, a system of weights and measures, political institutions based on hereditary royalty principles, and religion.

Contact with the outside world has been limited primarily to exchange of agricultural commodities for things such as medicines and some low technology items, and the visits of a few intrepid tourists. With the import of modern medicines, however, the local population has begun to increase rapidly as life expectancy expands, and the infant mortality rate declines. Your society now suffers from a serious overpopulation problem. The land and fisheries can no longer sustain minimal nutrition and housing standards. Violence increases as conflicts over land tenure and unemployment escalate. Some locals are calling for your head and demanding a new system of land ownership.

You understand that in the long run, the economy of your realm will have to change. You will have to begin a program of industrialization. That will provide employment for many, while easing pressure on the scarce land resources. But in order to launch these industries, you will have to enter into vastly expanded commercial and diplomatic contacts with foreigners. Only they can provide the technologies, equipment, and knowledge to launch the program. But how can your people interact with others when they have no common language? How can plants be built when foreign specifications employ an entirely different set of weights and measures?

You soon learn that if you want those things that foreigners can provide, you are going to have to alter your institutions and traditions, and harmonize many of your economic practices with the ways of the foreigners. Soon you will have to spend scarce resources on teaching the foreigners' languages. You will have to learn a whole new set of weights and measures—and probably abandon your own. You will probably need to build a modern airport and shipping facilities, raising taxes to develop these important components of an industrial infrastructure. Someone will have to build hotels to house the foreigners, and they will require all sorts of amenities that are unknown to your society. Eventually, bureaucracies will have to be developed, and your people will have to learn a whole new way of doing things. The foreigners, thinking that your system of government is undemocratic, will no doubt agitate for reforms. In brief, the more you wish to obtain from abroad, the more you will have to conform to their standards, values, and ways of doing things. You may be able to get some good bargains through astute negotiations, but in the long run, you will have to conform to foreigners, and not vice versa. They have set the rules of the game, very likely they will decide where and when to play, and in case of a dispute, they will probably provide the referee. The contracts that will form the basis of the relationship will incorporate the foreigners' legal standards (e.g., the law of treaties), and if there is a disagreement on interpretation, you will have to go to their judges (e.g., the International Court of Justice) for a resolution of the conflict. Whether you wish it or not, the pressures on your society for conformity to others' rules, values, and ways of doing things will be intense.

This may seem an extreme example, but it is hardly unique. The processes of standardization and economic homogenization may not involve formal coercion and violence (although during the heyday of imperialism they did); but the room for unique social, economic, and political institutions is diminishing in the contemporary world.

Who has structural power? Today, it is perhaps less any particular state than it is the hegemony of Western industrial civilization. As we have seen in the previous chapter, the predominant politico-economic ideologies of our age are free market capitalism and democracy. These ideas now have wide support throughout the industrial world, but they have been at the core of American foreign policy for many decades. Certainly the United States since the end of World War II has sought to define universal rules for trade, investment, political legitimacy, and many other activities. Where these rules have not prevailed because of their general effectiveness in raising welfare (wealth) standards, they have been promoted by persuasion, coercion, and occasional violence. In recent years, for example, the United States, often supported by Europe, has coerced (through threats of trade protectionism) Japan to alter a number of traditional business practices and social institutions. Many of these customs have roots that go back centuries, and although their effect is to limit foreign access to Japanese markets, that was not their original intention. As some American trade negotiators have acknowledged, the whole thrust of United States trade policy in relation to Japan is to "make them become more like us." What it means for the Japanese is that they must harmonize, adjust, and innovate according to American standards, and not vice versa.

In the case of the Sandinista government in Nicaragua, its deviation from American norms in its domestic and foreign policies brought an economic boycott and embargo, and the American-funded *contras* as a response.

This is not to judge the long-run costs and rewards of the exercise of structural power. But it shows that power in international relations is not confined to the bargaining that goes on over individual issues. When you are looking for the effects of structural power, ask some of the following questions: Whose agenda is being discussed? Whose rules are being debated? Who established those rules? Who determines whether the "playing field" is even? Who provides the referees? Whose standards are prevailing? Whose language do we use when debating and bargaining? In the long run, the answers to these questions may tell us more about power and influence in international relations than the outcomes of bargaining over specific issues.

Questions for Study, Analysis, and Discussion

1. Is leadership in world affairs still based primarily on military capabilities?
2. What are the main differences between relational and structural concepts of power?
3. Examine a recent instance where your government attempted to influence the policies of other states. What techniques did it use? Were they successful? Why or why not?

4. Why are perceptions of capabilities or resources important in the exercise of influence?
5. What is the difference between compellance and deterrrence
6. Between two governments, is it possible to have "friendly" relations on one issue, where diplomatic persuasion is the norm for wielding influence, while having hostile relations in another issue, where threats are the predominant means of wielding influence?
7. Who are the "influentials" in world politics today? On what is their influence based?

Selected Bibliography

Bachrach, Peter, and Morton S. Baratz, "The Two Faces of Power," *American Political Science Review,* 56 (1962), 947–52.

Baldwin, David A., "The Power of Positive Sanctions," *World Politics,* 24 (October 1971), 19–38.

———, "Inter-Nation Influence Revisited," *Journal of Conflict Resolution,* 15 (December 1971), 471–86.

———, "Power Analysis and World Politics: New Trends versus Old Tendencies," *World Politics,* 31 (January 1979), 161–94.

———, "Interdependence and Power: A Conceptual Analysis," *International Organization,* 34 (Autumn 1980), 471–506.

———, *Paradoxes of Power.* London: Basil Blackwell, 1989.

Cox, Robert, and Harold K. Jacobsen, The Anatomy of Influence. New Haven, Conn.: Yale University Press, 1973.

Ferris, Wayne H., The Power Capabilities of Nation-States. Lexington, Mass.: D.C. Heath, 1973.

Goldmann, Kjell, and Gunnar Sjöstedt, Power, Capabilities, Interdependence. Beverly Hills, Calif.: Sage, 1979.

Gourevitch, Peter, "States in the International System: Changing Relationships and the Role of Middle Powers," in *International Relations: Global and Australian Perspectives on an Evolving Discipline,* eds. Richard Higgott and J. L. Richardson. Canberra: Department of International Relations, The Australian National University, 1991, 228–40.

Gross, Ernest A., "Moral Power in International Relations," *Journal of International Affairs,* 12 (1958), 132–37.

Haskel, Barbara G., "Access to Society: A Neglected Dimension of Power," *International Organization,* 34 (Winter 1980), 89–120.

Keohane, Robert O., and Joseph S. Nye, Power and Interdependence: World Politics in Transition, 2nd ed. Boston: Little, Brown, 1989.

Knorr, Klaus, Military Power and Potential. Lexington, Mass.: Raytheon/Heath Co., 1970.

———, *The Power of Nations: The Political Economy of International Relations.* New York: Basic Books, 1975.

Leng, Russell J., "Influence Technique Among Nations," in *Behavior, Society, and International Conflict,* Vol. III, eds. Philip E. Tetlock et al. New York and Oxford: Oxford University Press, 1993, 71–125.

Mack, Andrew J. R., "Why Big Nations Lose Small Wars: The Politics of Asymmetric Conflict," *World Politics,* 27 (January 1975), 175–200.

Peterson, Walter J., "Deterrence and Compellence: A Critical Assessment of Conventional Wisdom," *International Studies Quarterly,* 30 (September 1986), 269–94.

Stoll, Richard, and Michael D. Ward, Power in World Politics. Boulder, Colo.: Lynn Rienner, 1988.

Thakur, Ramesh, "The Elusive Essence of Size: Australia, New Zealand, and Small States in International Politics," in *International Relations: Global and Australian Perspectives on an Evolving Discipline,* eds. Richard Higgott and J. L. Richardson. Canberra: Department of International Relations, The Australian National University, 1991, 241–87.

Chapter

6

The Instruments of Policy: Diplomatic Bargaining

In seeking to achieve objectives, realize values, or defend interests, governments must communicate with those whose ideas, actions, and behavior they wish to deter, alter, or reinforce. Today there are many occasions and media of communication that may be employed for conveying hopes, wishes, or threats to others. At a press conference, a political rally, or a banquet, government officials make statements directed not just to domestic audiences but to foreign governments and peoples as well. Nevertheless, most official attempts to wield influence abroad are carried out through formal diplomatic channels or by direct communication between foreign ministers and heads of state.

The subjects of interstate communication include definitions of a government's objectives, rationalizations for them, threats, promises, and the holding out of possibilities for concluding agreements on contentious issues. Diplomats are partially successful when they can get the government to which they are accredited to see a particular situation as their own government perceives it; they are totally successful when they are able to alter or maintain the actions of a foreign government in a manner favorable to the interests of their own government. Normally during the process of communication, those who formulate policy will reassess their objectives in the light of changing circumstances and varying foreign responses. Diplomats then convey the modified objectives to foreign governments; and the whole routine continues until consensus is reached through bargaining, until it is imposed by the use of force, or until one government abandons or withdraws from its objectives if they meet resistance abroad.

But before there can be negotiations or even more casual exchanges of information or views, states, through their governments, must recognize each other. This is a formal way of expressing entry into the club of states. Without formal recognition, political entities enjoy none of the rights and protections afforded under international law.

Diplomatic Recognition

Traditionally extending recognition to new states was done almost automatically once a political unit fulfilled the following conditions: a defined territory, a permanent population, and governmental capacity to enter into diplomatic and treaty relations. Among the consequences of formal recognition is that states can exchange ambassadors and other diplomats. Communication is thus formally sanctioned.

In the twentieth century, the practice of recognition has changed in some important ways. It has become more controversial and political, and less automatic. Diplomatic recognition provides the political unit a form of external legitimacy and support. Should states grant recognition to a province, or any other section of a country that has seceded through violence, but which otherwise meets the conditions of statehood? To recognize the breakaway unit would be a hostile act against the "parent" state. This situation confronted governments in 1990 after Lithuania declared its independence from the Soviet Union. In the reverse case, governments may refuse to grant recognition to a new state even if it has met the minimal conditions. This is tantamount to excluding it from the international community, and perhaps a calculated step to try to bring its downfall. With the exception of Egypt, none of the Arab states recognized Israel until 1994, although its capacities as a state were not in doubt since about 1949. Many countries did not recognize the Soviet Union's annexation of the Baltic states in the early 1940s.

In the case of some new states, recognition has been granted even before the minimal requirements were met. In this manner, the international community, usually through the United Nations, has itself *created* states which, without such external support, would probably not be viable. The principles of self-determination and freedom from colonialism have overridden the traditional bases of statehood.

In addition to recognition of statehood, there is the problem of recognizing the new head of government of an existing state. Where governments come and go through regularized procedures, as in parliamentary and presidential elections, recognition is granted automatically. But where a government comes to power through revolution, *coup d'état*, or assassination, the decision to extend or withhold recognition becomes a matter of diplomatic and strategic policy. Until the 1970s, the United States maintained that the government in Taiwan was the sole legitimate ruling authority of all China. Withholding recognition of the Communist government on the mainland was just one of many pressures the United States placed on its adversary. Without recognition, formal diplomatic communications were difficult, if not impossible; at the 1954 Geneva Conference to settle the fate of Indochina, John Foster Dulles, the American secretary of state, did everything possible to avoid direct contact with his Chinese counterpart, Chou En-lai. This refusal of recognition extended to the ceremonial conclusion of a treaty, after which Dulles refused to shake the hand of his Chinese counterpart. Nonrecognition is a clear sign of disapproval, and if enough governments withhold recognition, the target may find it difficult to carry on the normal business of diplomatic and commercial relations with other states.

If diplomatic relations are formally established through recognition policies, they can also be disrupted. This is just one of many forms of diplomatic pressure designed to alter the behavior of the target or to express disapproval. In 1967, the Soviet Union broke diplomatic relations with Israel to signal support for the Arabs in the Six Day war. After the diplomatic hostage-taking incident of 1979 and 1980, Iran and the United States broke off diplomatic relations. The United States has had no formal diplomatic relations with Cuba since shortly after Fidel Castro took power in 1959. Where two states have disrupted the formal channels of communication by breaking diplomatic relations, they may request a third country to use its offices to maintain minimal links between the two countries. The Swiss embassy in Havana, for example, looks after the few remaining American interests in Cuba. A variation of the theme is to downgrade relations. In 1982, for example, the Chinese government asked the Dutch ambassador to leave as a form of protest for the Netherlands' sale of submarines to Taiwan. Relations between the two governments were henceforth conducted at the level of *chargés d'affairs*. Finally, a government may call home its ambassador "for consultations" of indeterminate length. This is a way of signaling displeasure, thereby downgrading the level of communications between the two governments in question. In June 1989, after the massacre of students in Tiananmen Square in Beijing, the Canadian government called home its ambassador and suspended several technical aid programs to symbolize its hostility toward the Chinese authorities' actions against their own citizens.

These different ways of manipulating diplomatic practices, including recognition, are means of conducting conflict and attempting to wield influence over other governments. But most of the time, once recognition has been granted, the advantages of maintaining full diplomatic relations outweigh the often symbolic results of cutting off or downgrading communications.

The Institutions, Rules, and Personnel of Diplomacy

The emissary is among the first of the distinct political roles established in human society. Between primitive tribes, whether friendly or antagonistic, communication was necessary; and special personnel, with certain religious, bargaining, or language skills, were appointed to conduct discussions on a variety of issues. Emissaries bargained over the allocation of hunting territory, settling of family or clan disputes, or planning of an intertribal marriage. Today, diplomats seek to extend national interests in foreign territories, protect the national society from a perceived threat, increase the volume of trade, resolve a conflict over contested territory, or regulate traffic in drugs.

It was not until the fifteenth century that the concept of a permanent mission, or legation, was instituted in Europe. Italian city-states during the late Renaissance period first developed a diplomatic service and recognized the need for establishing a corps of professional diplomats. The functions of these early diplomats included obtaining information, safeguarding political and military interests, and expanding commerce. Indeed, organized diplomacy may have owed as much for its origins to the development of extensive trade networks in Europe and the Middle East as to political and military matters. The Venetian diplomatic service, for example, was originally a commercial organization. The new dynastic regimes emerging in Europe later emulated the diplomatic institutions established on the Italian peninsula; and by the eighteenth century, diplomacy was recognized as an important and honorable profession, even if its methods were not always so reputable.

Classical diplomacy operated among few political units: In 1648, for example, there were only twelve well-defined sovereign states in Europe, and the affairs of one did not frequently impinge on the interests of the other. In the present international system, not only are there more than 180 sovereign states, but their economic, political, and military interdependence means that almost any major domestic or foreign policy decision in one will have repercussions on the interests of many others. In this setting, the problem of achieving mutually acceptable solutions to all issues is difficult and usually cannot be resolved through the relatively slow and cumbersome procedures of bilateral negotiations. The bilateral patterns of diplomatic communication of the eighteenth century gave way first to ad hoc multilateral conferences and, more recently, to permanent multilateral diplomatic and technical organizations.

Until the latter part of the nineteenth century, most multilateral conferences dealt with the terms of peace following major European wars; but after the Franco-Prussian war from 1870 to 1871, governments began to send delegates to conferences dealing with the codification of international law (The Hague Conferences of 1899 and 1906) and with the more technical economic problems that European governments commonly faced.[1] In 1875, a group of governments established the Universal Postal Union, the first permanent international machinery involving the membership of most of the states in the world.

Today, the concept of multilateral conference diplomacy is institutionalized in the United Nations and its specialized agencies. These organizations are widely known, but multilateral diplomacy also occurs constantly in thousands of ad hoc conferences and less formal meetings between diplomats or government officials. During the nineteenth century, for example, the American government sent diplomatic representatives to 100 conferences, or an average of one per year; in the period from 1956 to 1958, American diplomats, specialists, and politicians attended 1,027 international conferences, an average of one per day.[2]

---

[1]These conferences considered such subjects as agriculture, regulation and production of sugar, international standards of sanitation, tariffs, international telegraphy, navigation on the Danube, the prime meridian, liquor traffic, statistics, maritime signaling, and weights and measures.

[2]Elmer Plischke, *The Conduct of American Diplomacy*, 2nd ed. (New York: Van Nostrand Reinhold, 1961), p. 474.

Another development of significance in diplomatic procedures has been the rapid increase in direct communication between heads of state. As modes of transportation have made travel a simple affair, high-ranking officials and policy makers can bypass the traditional diplomatic intermediary and maintain direct communication among themselves. Telephone conversations and fact-to-face meetings between government leaders have become commonplace. Former U.S. President George Bush personally knew a great number of his foreign colleagues and thus conducted a significant amount of consultation, bargaining, and arm-twisting by late-night telephone calls. Such casual diplomacy was almost unknown between Soviet and American leaders during the Cold War but has become commonplace in the post–Cold War era. Similar personal fraternization takes place among the leaders of the European Union and more broadly, between government officials of the leading industrial countries. In June and July 1990, for example, heads of such governments met personally three times in four weeks at top-level gatherings of the European Union, NATO, and the G-7 (leading industrial countries).

A final notable development in diplomatic method has been the inclusion of ordinary citizens in diplomatic delegations. We might call this trend the "democratization of diplomacy." Most of the Great multilateral conferences of our era include important sideshows: the meetings of nongovernmental organizations that do their own bargaining and pass their own resolutions. These are then conveyed to the official diplomats. At the Earth Summit conference in Rio de Janeiro in June 1992, for example, there were far more delegates of international nongovernmental organizations present than regular diplomats. Although the diplomats convened separately and ultimately negotiated the final documents and treaties, nongovernmental groups constantly lobbied delegations. The most dramatic alteration of diplomatic method in this regard has been to include civilians in the actual formal state-to-state negotiations. In recent discussions and negotiations concerning human rights under the auspices of the Conference on Security and Cooperation in Europe (CSCE), some representatives of nongovernmental organizations have been included in various national delegations. While this degree of public penetration of diplomacy is relatively rare, it is nevertheless an important trend.

Whether conducted through trained diplomats or by heads of state, communication between governments representing widely diverse social, economic, and political systems is naturally vulnerable to all sorts of distortion owing to cultural differences, ideological cleavages, and plain misunderstandings. Since permanent diplomatic institutions were established in Italy during the fifteenth century, governments have commonly recognized that it is to their mutual advantage to observe certain rules of procedure that help make communication easier to conduct and less liable to distortion. Diplomatic bargaining processes become impaired if no one agrees as to who is entitled to represent a state or if diplomatic envoys are subject to harassment or intimidation by those to whom they are accredited. Three sets of rules concerning protocol, immunities, and noninterference have therefore been developed in Western international law and custom to facilitate communication between states.

Protocol

Diplomatic protocol is of considerable importance in assisting diplomats to pursue their tasks in an effective manner. Although the rituals of protocol may seem merely ceremonial leftovers of a previous era, they have a definite function even today. Rank, for example, constantly added irritants to international relations in the eighteenth century, and solution of the problem at the Congress of Vienna in 1815 has helped in many ways to reduce little frictions that may have led to poor relations and communication between governments. In the early years of modern diplomacy, the Pope claimed the right to decide the ceremonial order of the various dynasts' representatives; but, as the influence of the church in secular affairs declined, diplomats and their governments were left to their own devices—sometimes with disastrous results. Rank, protocol, and precedence had great symbolic significance; ambassadors and envoys frequently received orders not to permit other courts' envoys to precede them in ceremonial processions, for such acts could reflect adversely on the prestige and honor of their own dynast. In formal processions, for example, diplomats would plan strategies enabling them to gain favorable positions in the line. Several incidents have been recorded wherein coachmen were killed attempting to gain advantages over their rivals. It was not uncommon, moreover, for ambassadors to engage in duels to vindicate their honor or prestige when it was questioned by another envoy. In such circumstances, the candor and friendly personal relations necessary to successful diplomacy were not always easy to display.[3]

In 1815, four diplomatic ranks were established and universally adopted by European courts and foreign offices. The highest rank was assigned to ambassadors and papal nuncios, followed by envoys extraordinary and ministers plenipotentiary, ministers resident, and *chargés d'affaires*. These titles are still in use today and determine the ranking of diplomatic officials at ceremonial and political functions. The question of precedence was not, however, completely solved by agreement on the question of rank. Therefore, the delegates to the Congress of Aix-la-Chapelle in 1818 agreed that among members of the same rank, precedence should be established no longer on the prestige or power of the diplomat's government, but solely on the length of time the diplomat had served as ambassador in one country. Thus, if the ambassador of Luxembourg to the United States has served in Washington, D.C., longer than the British ambassador, he or she always precedes the British ambassador. Diplomats who have served the longest period in a foreign capital are normally referred to as the *doyens*, or deans, of the diplomatic corps and on ceremonial occasions always precede other ambassadors.

Immunities

If governments are to seek to influence each other's policies and actions through effective communication, they must assume that their diplomatic agents abroad will not be abused or placed under conditions that would prevent them from engaging

[3]See Hans Morgenthau, *Politics Among Nations*, 4th ed. (New York: Knopf, 1968).

freely in bargaining and persuasion. Even among primitive people, envoys or messengers were usually regarded as sacrosanct and enjoyed special privileges and immunities. Communication would have been impossible if emissaries had been treated as "heathen," burned, tortured, or eaten before delivering their messages. In ancient China, Greece, and India, as well as in the Ottoman Empire, diplomatic immunities were regularly accorded to envoys and messengers from "barbarian" communities. On occasion, ambassadors were imprisoned or slain because they were suspected of trickery; but in most cases (as indicated in the ancient Indian *Mahabharata*, "The King who slays an envoy sinks into hell with all his ministers"), there were strong ethical sanctions and reasons of self-interest against violating diplomatic immunities.[4]

It is still the general rule of international law that diplomats and their embassies are to be treated as if they were on their native soil. They are immune from prosecution under the laws, customs, rules, or regulations of the government to which they are accredited. Those who enjoy diplomatic status (usually all the full-time foreign staff of the embassy) may not be arrested by national police officials, nor may the premises of an embassy be visited by local law enforcement agents without the invitation of the embassy staff. If a French official enjoying diplomatic status parks his or her auto in a restricted zone in Stockholm, for instance, the official is not liable to fine, trial, or imprisonment by Swedish officials. However, if diplomatic officials commit serious crimes abroad, the host government may either demand that they be recalled or request that their immunities be lifted so that they can be indicted and tried in the receiving country's courts of law. A Central American diplomat was arrested upon his arrival in New York when police apprehended him attempting to smuggle a large amount of heroin into the United States. The State Department requested the foreign government to strip the official of his diplomatic status, which it consented to do; and he was eventually tried, convicted, and imprisoned according to American legal procedures.

If in this case the Central American government had refused to recall the ambassador or lift his diplomatic status, the United States could have declared him *persona non grata*, thus forcing the Central American government to recall him. In most cases, governments do recall their diplomats when requested to do so, and designating a diplomat *persona non grata* usually results from a diplomat's political actions, not from breaking a local law. Ambassadors and other diplomatic officials are usually declared *persona non grata* only when their efficiency has been impaired by indiscreet political statements, interference in internal affairs of the host country, or taking advantage of their status to indulge in espionage activities. During the Cold War, there was a rather rapid turnover of diplomatic personnel in the Western embassies in Moscow and the Soviet embassies in Western capitals, as numerous diplomats were apprehended while conducting illegal intelligence activities (many were

[4]See Frank M. Russell, *Theories of International Relations* (New York: Appleton-Century-Crofts, 1936), p. 42. In several instances, the Soviet government promised immunity and safety to emissaries and delegations, only to imprison or execute them upon arrival. The cases in question involved a group representing the Polish underground in 1945 and the military and political leaders of the Hungarian revolution in 1956. The universal condemnation of the Iranian authorities' imprisoning fifty American diplomats for use as hostages from 1979 to 1981 derived from the recognition that a fundamental norm protecting interstate communication had been violated. If many governments acted similarly, international chaos could result.

intelligence agents posing as diplomats). Retaliation also became an accepted practice; for example, if a British diplomat was expelled from the Soviet Union, the British government normally requested the immediate recall of a Soviet diplomat in London. Although the activities of diplomats during the Cold War taxed the laws and customs of immunity, they were still recognized as essential to effective diplomacy, and there was surprisingly little discussion over the merits of either abandoning or proscribing them.

Noninterference

If diplomatic officials ordinarily enjoy immunities from the laws of the country to which they are accredited, other customs have developed that limit the types of actions they can undertake in attempting to influence the policies of foreign governments. Chief among these is the stricture that they cannot in any way interfere in the internal political processes of another country. Normally, they are expected to confine official discussions to government personnel. Certainly they may defend their own government's policies to the foreign public by addressing private groups; but they must not make appeals to these people asking them to put pressures on their own government; nor can they provide funds to political parties, or provide leadership or other services to insurgents, political factions, or economic organizations.

These rules of noninterference are well established in law and customary practice, but as the domestic affairs of countries have increasingly important foreign policy implications, the rules are in many cases circumvented. In 1919, President Wilson toured Italy exhorting the Italian people to press their government to make concessions at the Paris Peace Conference; foreign aid and technical personnel frequently "suggest" how foreign governments should reform their economy, organize a military force, or put down civil rebellion. As will be discussed in Chapter 9, diplomats have amassed an impressive record of intervention in other countries' internal affairs by fomenting civil disorders, subsidizing subversive political factions, disseminating covert propaganda, or training security forces (and sometimes torturers) to suppress citizens' dissent.

The Functions of Diplomats

Aside from the main role of diplomats in bargaining and communicating information between governments, they perform several other duties that should be mentioned briefly.

Protection of Nationals

Protection of nationals, which involves protecting the lives and promoting the interests of nationals residing or traveling abroad, is a routine task, although during catastrophes or civil disorders, the role of diplomats in this capacity may become very important. Nationals have to be protected or evacuated if necessary, they must be represented by legal counsel if jailed, and their property or other interests abroad must be protected if the local government does not provide such service. It is the general practice among major powers to assign consular agents rather than embassy personnel to perform these duties. Consulates, which may be established in many cities in a country, are diplomatic substations that serve travelers to and from the host country with regard to visas and other information, protect the interests of their own citizens when on foreign soil, and assist in commercial transactions. Consular agents occasionally perform the other three major functions of diplomats, but only when normal diplomatic communication has been disrupted.

Symbolic Representation

In their role as symbolic representatives, diplomats of other eras seldom did more than attend court ceremonies; today, however, ambassadors, in addition to attending ceremonial and social occasions, must address foreign groups and be present at all events with which their country is somehow connected, no matter how remotely. If a Russian ballet group visits Paris, the Russian ambassador is expected to be on hand for the opening performance; if the United States constructs a medical center for children in some developing country, the American ambassador must not only attend its opening but also display a continuing interest in its activities. Whether in agriculture, medicine, music, physics, or military policies, if their government has some stake in a project, diplomats must symbolize that stake by their physical presence and continuing concern. In their symbolic capacity, ambassadors are concerned with the totality of relations—whether political or not—between their own country and the one to which they have been sent.

Obtaining Information

Because information and data are the raw materials of foreign policy, the gathering of information—by official acts, at cocktail parties, or by covert means—is the most important task of the diplomat, aside from his or her bargaining activities. Precise information must be made available to those who formulate policy if there is to be a minimum discrepancy between the objective environment and the image of the environment held by policy makers. Data concerning military potential, personalities, and economic trends or problems may be supplied by intelligence units abroad; but intelligence experts work under limitations when it comes to assessment of trends, intentions, responses, attitudes, and motivations. Although diplomats may also provide a large quantity of raw data in their reports, their main role in providing information is to use their skill and familiarity with the foreign society to interpret the data and make reliable assessments and forecasts of responses of the receiving government toward their own government's policies. They might be asked to predict answers to some of the following questions: What are the implications for the host government's foreign policy if a new party is elected to power or a military junta gains control through a *coup d'état?* What is the influence of a certain columnist or radio commentator upon official policy and public opinion? What tactics are likely to be adopted by the foreign government in forthcoming negotiations over the allocation of foreign-aid grants? How would the foreign government react to a major diplomatic maneuver by the diplomat's government in another area of the world? What position might the foreign government take in a future international conference on tariffs, on the regulation of narcotics, or on an issue before the General Assembly of the United Nations?

The success of diplomats in answering and assessing such questions will depend upon the scope and variety of sources of information they are able to cultivate among party leaders, government officials, trade unions, the press, and the military.

How do diplomatic officials obtain vital information? Most comes from reading and examining reports, debates, and newspaper articles published in the country where they are stationed. Since the volume of information in these sources is normally beyond the capacity of any one individual to assess, ambassadors rely on extensive staff assistance and full-time specialists concerned with a particular range of problems. Commercial attachés not only negotiate trade agreements and promote trade relations but also have the responsibility for knowing in detail the development, structure, problems, and leaders of the foreign country's economy. Cultural, agricultural, labor, scientific, and military attachés perform the same duties within their respective areas of competence, while intelligence officials attached to the embassy have the responsibility for obtaining more covert information.

Information is also obtained through informal means. "Entertainment," one diplomat claimed, "oils the hinges of man's office door." Although legislators and taxpayers frequently disparage diplomats for the time and money they spend on cocktail parties and dinners, there are definite advantages to these informal occasions. In a social setting it is often easier to persuade and to obtain vital information. The strain of rigid protocol is removed and unofficial views can be exchanged, while the element of personal acquaintance—and sometimes plentiful quantities of liquor—may increase confidence and trust. Rumors can be assessed and verified, personal reactions elicited, and all types of interesting information obtained more easily at social functions than during official calls and in official communications.

The Purposes of Diplomatic Communication

In most cases, the purpose of negotiation between two or more governments is to change or sustain each other's objectives and policies to reach agreement over some contentious issue. However, such negotiations may have other purposes or side effects as well. Before analyzing the techniques diplomats employ in bargaining and securing agreements, those other objectives should be noted.

First, a large amount of diplomatic communication between governments is undertaken primarily for exchanging views, probing intentions, and attempting to convince other governments that certain actions, such as attending a conference, lowering tariffs, or proffering diplomatic support on a particular international issue, would be in their interest. Here there is no hard bargaining, and diplomats or government officials do not ordinarily employ threats or offer rewards. The majority of routine diplomatic contracts between governments are of this nature, and almost all visits by heads of states are undertaken not for bargaining, but simply for "exchanging views" and "consulting."

Second, bilateral diplomatic meetings or multilateral conferences may be arranged for the purpose of stalling or creating the illusion that a government is seriously interested in bargaining, even though it really desires no agreement. During the conduct of warfare, one state may agree to armistice negotiations to assuage public opinion, while it simultaneously steps up its military campaigns. By agreeing to negotiate, it may be able to draw attention away from its other activities. During the Bosnian war, several sides signed numerous cease-fires primarily as a means of preventing possible NATO intervention into the conflict. Few of these actually terminated the fighting.

Third, a government may enter into diplomatic negotiations primarily for the purpose of making propaganda; it uses a conference not so much to reach agreement over a limited range of issues as to make broad appeals to the outside public, partly to undermine the bargaining position of its opponents. In an age when "secret diplomacy" is viewed with suspicion and many diplomatic negotiations are open both to the press and the public, a conference that is certain to receive extensive publicity around the world offers an excellent forum for influencing public attitudes. Soviet negotiators earned a reputation for employing some international conferences for propaganda purposes, but any time two or more governments cannot agree—or do not wish to agree—upon the issues under consideration and yet desire to gain some advantages from their efforts, they are likely to use the proceedings primarily to embarrass their opponents and extol their own actions and attitudes. The open forum of the General Assembly offers one important arena for attempting to influence nondiplomatic opinion. Indeed, many observers of United Nations affairs note that most speeches made in that body are designed primarily for public domestic and international consumption, not for the information of other delegates.

Diplomacy, however, is used primarily to reach agreements, compromises, and settlements where government objectives conflict. It involves, whether in private meetings or publicized conferences, the attempt to change the policies, actions, objectives, and attitudes of other governments and their diplomats by persuasion, offering rewards, exchanging concessions, or making threats.

In an age where technological innovation creates all sorts of problems that transcend national borders, however, diplomacy also has the major task of arranging collaborative arrangements to manage such problems as pollution of the seas, the proliferation of nuclear weapons, the price of coffee and wheat, and various arms races, just to mention a few. Although involving the modification of behavior through persuasion, diplomacy in many instances today takes on the aura of a highly technical, bureaucratized mutual learning experience in which governments attempt to construct rules and formulas for allocating costs that will provide stability, predictability, and lower costs and risks to a variety of international "problems." Diplomacy in such contexts is much more than the mere trading of concessions until some mutually acceptable bargain can be fashioned. It also involves mutual learning about important problems, and developing general principles around which specific agreements can be formulated. Diplomacy, as this and many other examples suggest, is concerned ultimately not only with persuasion but also with creating and systematizing new knowledge, enunciating general principles, and "educating" those who do not have all the relevant knowledge surrounding a problem. It is for this reason that many delegations to multilateral conferences are staffed by technical experts and even nongovernmental scientists, as well as by career diplomats.

The Negotiating Process: Preliminaries

Bargaining over contentious issues may begin through a series of signals by the parties to the effect that they wish to enter into formal discussions. As the long history of "peace feelers" during the Vietnam war reveals, it may take a great deal of time, and military successes or failures, before both sides are convinced that formal bargaining is a better (or supplementary) means of pursuing objectives. But even once the parties have agreed to enter into negotiations, a number of preliminary points have to be resolved before any substantive discussion can take place.

Table 6-1 lists some of the preliminary issues involved in the negotiating process. The location of the talks is usually decided first. If the negotiations are between adversaries, then the customary rule during the past two decades has been to select the city of a "neutral" state. Geneva has been the most popular location for multilateral conferences involving Cold-War issues and disarmament, and Vienna and Helsinki have been used to discuss limitations on strategic armaments, troop reductions in Europe, and overall European security. If, on the other hand, the negotiations are between states that normally maintain friendly relations, they will usually take place in the capital of one of the parties.

TABLE 6-1
Formal Negotiating Process

SETTING	PROCESS	OUTCOMES
1. Open vs. closed meetings	1. Preparation of rules of the game (talks about talks)	
2. Bilateral vs. multilateral meetings	a. Place (city)	
3. Stress or crisis situation, or more normal circumstances	b. Parties and size of delegations	
	c. Languages, seating	
4. Time available (open or closed; e.g., ultimatum)	d. Press coverage, etc.	
	2. Substantive bargaining	
5. A mediator role? Or only direct participants	a. Presentation of positions ←	Original objectives of parties
	b. Presentation of demands or conditions	
	c. Symbolic acts or signals →	New alternatives created or
	d. Persuasian ←	maximum and minimum
	e. Promises	conditions revised
	f. Threats	
	g. Commitments	
	h. Concessions	→ Possible outcomes:
		a. Treaty or "understanding"
		b. Postponement of negotiations
		c. Ending negotiations and leaving problem unresolved

The parties to be represented at the negotiations often raise problems. The usual criterion is, Who is involved in an issue area? Those who have some stake in the outcome are normally invited. But often there is the problem of parties with no formal diplomatic status. The early stages of the Paris negotiations over Vietnam, starting in 1968, involved lengthy discussions about whether or not the Viet Cong could have representation separate from the delegation of North Vietnam. This complicated question then brought up a related issue: What should be the shape of the table around which discussions would take place? Negotiations about this problem went on for several weeks, until eventually the United States accepted the Viet Cong as a distinct party to the negotiations. Finally, agreements have to be made on the problems of translation, publication of documents, the role of advisers, and, most important, whether the meetings will be open to the press.

All these matters may occupy a great deal of time. We may not be impressed with all the quibbling that goes on over matters that appear trivial. But many of these preliminaries are seen by the delegations or governments as reflecting upon questions of fundamental importance, including their bargaining strength and prestige. The implications of each minor procedural decision may be great. For example, the United States delegation initially opposed the seating of the Viet Cong as a separate party in the Paris discussions. It had to adopt this position because in previous public statements the American government had taken the position that the Viet Cong were organized and directed by Hanoi. To agree to the seating of the Viet Cong separately implied that the American view of the situation in Vietnam had been incorrect and that the Viet Cong did indeed represent a political movement indigenous to the Republic of Vietnam, quite separate from the government and Communist party of North Vietnam.

A number of conditions, or the "setting," surrounding the process may vitally affect the outcome. These are listed in Table 6-1. Are the meetings to be open or closed to the press? Are the meetings between two parties, or more? Is the situation perceived as critical by all the parties? If so, we could expect discussions to last only a short time. Closely related is the time that is perceived as available. If the parties see the situation as running out of hand, requiring *some* solution, then there will be great pressure to focus on immediate issues and reduce the amount of careful probing of intentions and evaluation of each of the opponent's statements. There may be a feeling that *any* solution is better than letting "events take their course" or permitting oneself the luxury of time to think matters over.[5]

Finally, the negotiations may be expected to take on particular characteristics if at least one of the parties plays the role of an official or unofficial mediator. Mediation will be discussed in Chapter 14; suffice it to say here that the bargaining process becomes more complicated, but favorable solutions are more likely if one

---

[5]Hitler often tried to create an atmosphere of crisis when he confronted foreign diplomats. In discussions with Chamberlain, Daladier, and others on the Czech issue, he made it clear that if some solution were not devised quickly, the Reichswehr would march. The unfortunate diplomats always negotiated in an atmosphere of crisis and in a time setting that Hitler had manufactured. The outcomes of these negotiations might have differed if the foreign diplomats, not Hitler, had defined this important part of the setting.

party can propose sets of alternatives different from those put forth by the main protagonists, or can make certain that communication between the adversaries does not break down.

The Negotiating Process: Inducing Agreement

The choice of techniques and tactics to employ in diplomatic negotiation depends generally upon the degree of incompatibility between two or more nations' objectives and interests, the extent to which the nations are committed to those interests, and the degree to which the parties want to reach agreement. Diplomatic negotiations between friends and allies seldom display the same characteristics as those between hostile governments. Where there is already considerable agreement about the principles of an issue, negotiation may involve only working out the details or deducing the consequences from the principles. When governments are responsive to each other's interests, moreover, they have a good basis for arranging compromises and exchanging concessions. In negotiations within the European Union, for instance, the parties agree widely on the objectives of the organization and have intimate knowledge of each other's economic needs and interests. To a large extent, they can negotiate over essentially technical matters and do not have to worry about reconciling great principles. A common desire to reach agreement may also induce the bargaining agents to make concessions. The alternative is to adhere inflexibly to a position, prevent agreement, and accept the adverse publicity for adopting such a position.

Where objectives are fundamentally incompatible and both sides maintain strong commitments to their respective positions, the problem of influencing behavior, actions, and objectives through diplomatic bargaining becomes much more complex. Two stages toward reaching a settlement in such conditions are involved. First, one party must get the other to *want* an agreement of some sort; it must somehow make the other realize that any agreement or settlement is preferable to the status quo of incompatible positions or nonagreement or, conversely, that the consequences of nonagreement are more unfavorable to it than the consequences of agreement. Second, once the stage of "agreeing to an agreement" has been reached, the two parties must still bargain over the specific terms of the final agreement.

Of the two steps, the first is probably more difficult to achieve when commitments to incompatible objectives are strong; as long as one or both parties believe they can achieve their objectives through actions other than negotiations, diplomatic bargaining cannot lead to settlement. Although the PLO in 1988 implicitly acknowledged the right of Israel to exist as an independent state, it was not until 1993 that its leadership was willing to make some sort of formal recognition of that fact. Similarly, the government of Israel repeatedly asserted that it would never negotiate with the PLO, a "terrorist organization," which meant, in effect, that it did not wish to make an agreement that would alter the status quo, with Israel continuing its occupation of the West Bank and Gaza. It was not until the Norwegian foreign minister helped arrange secret negotiations in Oslo in 1993 that a formula for mutual recognition and a peace agenda were finally negotiated. It tells us something about the advantages of secret diplomacy that this arrangement was worked out while there were formal, official negotiations between the Middle East's main players taking place in Washington.

If both sides have made the prior decision that agreement is more desirable than nonagreement or maintenance of the status quo, it remains for them to bargain over the specific details of settlement. Diplomats can employ a great variety of bargaining techniques. Basically, they present their conditions, define their own objectives, and use persuasion by making arguments or presenting data to illustrate the correctness of their views or the degree of their needs. In essence, they engage in a debate. Occasionally they can use threats and offers of rewards to try to obtain acceptance of their proposals and, if this fails, reassess their original positions in terms of possible concessions that they hope will elicit agreement or a change in the objectives of the other side. All the time, they must simultaneously reveal their *commitment* to their bargaining positions, lest the other party assume that they do not feel very strongly about their conditions and would be willing to compromise them without significant compensations.

Promise of a reward offers some future advantage in return for agreement on a specific point under contention. This may range from promises of "soft" peace terms, monetary loans, or diplomatic support at some future conference to such symbolic acts as unilaterally releasing prisoners of war or suspending hostilities.

The effectiveness of threatening actions depends above all on their *credibility*. State B has to believe that the threat will be carried out if it does not meet state A's demands. Credibility would seem to be established when B realizes that A can fulfill the threat and thereby damage B, without seriously harming its own interests. If, for instance, state A's diplomats threaten to walk out of a conference, and B knows that such action would seriously jeopardize the chances of obtaining an agreement it wants, it might very well be willing to make last-minute concessions to prevent a breakdown of negotiations.

To be credible, threats must also appear to be one-sided. State A has to make it clear that if the threat is fulfilled, it will not damage its own interests—in other words, the costs to the target of the threat will be much greater than to the party that makes the threat. If A threatens to walk out of a conference (usually after some signal, such as sending home the chief negotiator for "consultations"), but B knows that A would suffer serious public condemnation for "wrecking" the conference, the threat is not very credible. Indeed, B might be seriously tempted to call A's bluff, in which case A would be placed in a most difficult position.

In some instances, those who make threats may also have to take certain actions that demonstrate that they have the *capacity* to fulfill them. This might involve mobilizing troops, cutting off foreign aid or trade for a short period, ordering a reduction in embassy personnel, or staging a short walkout from a conference—all actions designed to indicate that the "real thing" can be done if necessary.

Finally, it may be advantageous to make deliberately vague threats or, as some might put it, ominous warnings. Although these may not be entirely credible, they have the advantage of giving the threatening side many alternative forms of punishing actions—or inaction—if the other side does not take heed. The common diplomatic phrases "we will not stand (or sit) idly by" while state B does something, or state B "must bear complete responsibility for the consequences of its actions" are threats of this kind. They do not commit the threatener to specific actions, but indicate that state B's actions are perceived as dangerous and *could* lead to counteraction or reprisal. The vague threat avoids placing A in a position where it cannot maneuver. As Jervis points out, there is an inherent conflict between the desire to make a credible threat and the desire to preserve freedom of action.[6]

The problem with making threats in diplomatic negotiations is that even if they are reasonably credible, the other side might test them. In this case, the threatener has to act and perhaps damage its own interests or back down and earn the reputation of being a bluffer. In other words, if the threat is actually challenged, it has failed its purpose.

In addition to exchanging concessions—even if highly asymmetrical—negotiators often have to enunciate terms that are relatively free of the risk of defection or agreement breaking in the future. Most agreements include the notions of exchange and reciprocity; but there has to be some reasonable confidence that the do's, don'ts, and exchanges inherent in the agreements will actually be carried out, or if they are not, that there will be some mechanism for resolving disputes or providing sanctions. We can see particularly in the history of arms-control negotiations that parties have often turned down proposals on the grounds that they did not include verifiable means for detecting violations. Over the years, governments have used all sorts of devices to manage risks. These have included exchanging hostages (holding them until all terms of the agreement have been implemented), obtaining guarantees from third parties (the United States commitment to assist Israel in the event that the Israel-Egypt Peace Treaty of 1979 was violated), the provision of automatic sanctions, and in many other ways making nonperformance costly for the potential defector.[7]

Persuasion through argument and presentation of information, offering rewards, making threats, establishing commitments, and managing risk are thus the major techniques employed in the process of diplomatic bargaining between nations. Some of the problems common to these techniques are listed above, but each bargaining situation is unique, and no one can predict with certainty which methods of inducement will work. We can only suggest the conditions under which they would be more likely to succeed.

So far, the discussion might imply that all negotiations involve solely the statement of maximum positions which, after the employment of various tactics, are whittled down through compromises and concessions to some reasonably equitable distribution of advantages between the bargaining parties. This is indeed a common pattern, but there are other possibilities. In a situation of extreme power asymmetry, one party may be in a position to make a virtual *diktat*. It offers *its* terms on a take-it-or-leave-it basis. Some compromises may be made on matters of details, but the basic pattern is one where the weaker party is compelled to give legal sanction to a

[6]Robert Jervis, *The Logic of Images in International Relations* (Princeton, N.J.: Princeton University Press, 1970), p. 90.

[7]For a detailed treatment of this problem, see Richard B. Bilder, *Managing the Risks of International Agreement* (Madison: University of Wisconsin Press, 1981).

capitulation. This form of negotiation was common in Hitler's treatment of weak or defeated opponents and was attempted initially by the North Vietnamese in the Paris negotiations. Another type of negotiation involves the search for a general *formula* or set of principles acceptable to both sides. There is little bargaining involved in the sense of using threats or rewards; rather, one or both parties (often a mediator) searches for alternative solutions which are presented for consideration as a package. Once a formula is accepted, then bargaining begins in order to fill out the details. This type of bargaining was prominent in negotiating the Israel-PLO mutual recognition and peace agenda agreements in Oslo in 1993.[8]

The Negotiating Process: Problem Solving

Most of the tactics just described are used primarily in situations where one government attempts to change the actions and policies of others—that is, to persuade them to do what they would not otherwise do. Problem solving, in contrast, is a process where two or more parties attempt to develop rules to handle some problem arising in the physical or diplomatic environment. Whereas in bargaining situations, a zero-sum condition prevails—the gain of one side is seen as a loss for the other—in problem solving, the parties generally see that common study of a problem, pooling of resources, and general cooperation may result in mutual advantage and that no major values will have to be sacrificed to obtain an agreement. Differences may arise over the exact specification of rights, duties, and costs, but these are primarily matters of detail that lie above an underlying consensus on objectives.

The thousands of scientific, cultural, technical, economic, and communications treaties and institutions are the result of parties' getting together to resolve some problem common to them, where they recognize that unilateral action would be fruitless. Examples include agreements and institutions to regulate fisheries (where, despite attempts to maximize catches, governments share a common interest in preventing the depletion of stock), mail, telephonic communications, the narcotics trade, international police work, and the like.

Negotiators in problem-solving situations usually begin by presenting data and technical studies of a problem. These form the basis of proposals put forth as draft treaties or constitutions for a new international organization. Often the technical research, analysis, and interpretation of the data are conducted by specialists from more than one government, working together. Although some of the more punitive diplomatic techniques discussed earlier are used occasionally, problem solving normally stresses the gains to be achieved through mutual concessions; and the diplomacy emphasizes that it is basically in the national interest to make short-term sacrifices for greater long-term gains. The point to emphasize is that, of all diplomatic contacts between governments, and between governments and international organizations, problem solving predominates. We are less aware of it because it is seldom

---

[8]For the distinction between concession-type negotiations and searching for alternative formulas, see I. William Zartman, "Negotiation as a Joint Decision-making Process," in *The Negotiation Process: Theories and Applications,* ed. Zartman (Beverly Hills, Calif.: Sage, 1978), 67–86.

newsworthy; it is certainly less dramatic than a great peace conference or summit meeting, and hence only infrequently makes the headlines. But beneath the issues of war and peace and the diplomatic interchanges that deal with these problems lies a vast network of contacts between governments, concerned primarily with coordinating and putting into treaty form those solutions through quiet problem-solving procedures.

To this point, we have portrayed negotiations as taking place only between two or more governments, usually in an adversarial situation. But in complex negotiations, such as those of the Law of the Sea that lasted almost a decade, there is another game being played as well: the negotiations that take place *between* different government departments, and even the debates *within* large diplomatic delegations. The process of hammering out a national position may take as long as the negotiations with other delegations. On the Law of the Sea, for example, ministries dealing with fisheries, defense, the environment, and foreign affairs had to enter lengthy negotiations to hammer out a unified position. But once that was achieved, it frequently threatened to become unraveled during the negotiations, as each delegation had to respond to the proposals of others. In some negotiations, moreover, delegations can become so split among themselves that no unified position can be sustained, and personnel have to be changed to obtain a consensus. Diplomats have also been known to resign rather than to carry out instructions with which they cannot personally agree. Diplomacy, then, is often a multi-layered bargaining exercise, and not just the trading of concessions between adversaries.

Informal Bargaining: Diplomatic "Body Language"

Diplomatic processes and bargaining are subject to a variety of ploys, gambits, and symbolic actions that not only serve as barometers of the friendship or hostility of two or more governments but also may be used to create atmosphere for the more formal aspects of negotiations.

Anyone who watches television or reads newspaper accounts will be familiar with some diplomatic tactics. Using the metaphor of the theater, Raymond Cohen has chronicled a variety of "staging effects" that government leaders frequently use as signaling devices and prestige-raising artifacts.[9] Meetings of heads of state, for example, are carefully choreographed to create maximum impression on television viewers. President de Gaulle of France, a master of diplomatic theater, always arranged his press conferences and visits of other heads of state in milieus that emphasized France's ancient glories, its status as a great power, and its great contributions to civilization. The messages were designed to be lost neither on the president's guest nor on the watching television audience. On one of his visits to Ottawa, Richard Nixon's aides proposed that one of the rooms where Canadian Prime Minister Trudeau was to receive the president should be refurbished and painted blue, because Nixon's television image would look more impressive in that environment.

[9]In *Theatre of Power: The Art of Diplomatic Signalling* (London and New York: Longman, 1987).

Receiving ceremonies for visiting heads of state or governments also act as a good barometer of diplomatic relations, and the amount of public exposure via the media is carefully crafted to make diplomatic points. Red carpet treatment, twenty-one-gun salutes, reception lines at the airport, flags along the highways from the airport, and the luxury of the visitor's accommodations all convey more than courtesy; they indicate status and degrees of good will and hostility. Cohen cites, as an example, Egyptian leader Abdel Nasser's return to Cairo from an Afro-Asian conference in 1955. At this time the Americans and British maintained an attitude of distrust and hostility toward Nasser's Middle East policies, as well as toward the increasing indications of Afro-Asian solidarity. The American, British, and French ambassadors were instructed not to go to the airport to receive the returning statesman. When he stepped off the airplane, the only great power representative was the Soviet ambassador. Reportedly, Nasser was furious and humiliated at the intended snub.[10]

The elements of theater apply not only to staging and protocol. Costume and gestures are also designed to convey images, messages, and signals. President de Gaulle carefully chose his wardrobe to symbolize the politics of the occasion. When addressing his generals or commemorating wartime experiences, he donned the uniform he wore during his leadership of the French resistance while in London during World War II. On other occasions, conservative but elegant wardrobe was more appropriate.

When PLO leader Yassir Arafat was invited to address the United Nations General Assembly in 1974, he had to draft a careful speech, weaving his way from the expectations of those who might grant him international respectability by emphasizing the value of peace with Israel, while not alienating his activist supporters who wanted to continue the violent war of Palestine liberation. Dressed in his warrior attire—*kaffiyah,*unshaven face, tinted glasses, windbreaker—he offered the olive branch and asked Israel and its supporters not to let it fall from his hand. Acknowledging the prolonged applause, he raised his hand in salute, exposing under his windbreaker the outlines of a revolver holster. Many speeches about the possibility of having to return to armed combat would not have made the point better. Here was the peace-seeker, but also the freedom fighter.

Nineteen years later, at the signing ceremonies of the Israel-PLO mutual recognition agreement in front of the White House, Arafat appeared in the uniform of a high-level military commander (not guerrilla fatigues); and no weapon was to be seen. President Bill Clinton heightened the dramatic effect of the signing by coaxing Prime Minister Yitzhak Rabin and Arafat—mortal enemies in fact and in popular perceptions—to shake hands in front of a vast global television audience.

Not to be outdone by Arafat's sartorial ingenuity, Colonel Khaddafi presented himself in Beijing dressed in a white and gold uniform, dark glasses, and stylish hairdo, surrounded by women guards dressed in battle fatigues.[11] When it is to his advantage to create another image, he is televised dressed in Bedouin garb, sitting in a tent in the desert. In each case, the wardrobe is carefully tailored to the substance of the diplomatic messages intended to be conveyed.

[10]Ibid., p. 99.
[11]Ibid., pp. 40, 77.

Facial and other gestures may also be plotted to convey impressions and signals. Among fraternal Communists from different parties and countries, rigorous protocol scenarios were designed to convey degrees of warmth and coolness with the leading party leaders, those of the Soviet Union. A great deal could be inferred about the state of relations by watching facial gestures upon arrival or departure from Moscow, noting whether the visitor was greeted with a bear hug or a handshake, or in what order the guests were received at receptions. Smiles and expressions of emotion were used to express exceptional friendship, while dourness, disinterest or, during meetings of the world's Communist parties, failure to applaud a speech on cue, indicated different degrees of hostility.

Perhaps we should not overemphasize the importance of the theatrical in diplomacy; it is the substance of discussions and negotiations that matter. Yet, as political leaders are exceptionally sensitive to slights, slipups, and displays that reflect upon their personal prestige, as well as that of their country, the general tone established through ceremonies and hospitality may have a strong bearing on substantive discussions. On more than one occasion, talks have been broken off because a leader felt slighted by his or her host.

The art of diplomatic theater was not invented with the coming of television. Ceremonial and formal diplomatic exchanges of the eighteenth century were no less contrived than they are today. At those times, they were intended to impress—or send signals to—court officials and professional diplomats. Today, the audiences are much broader, and to the extent that those audiences play a role in the formulation and implementation of foreign policy, their attitudes and opinions may be vitally affected by the theatrical aspects of diplomacy. This is the realm of propaganda.

Questions for Study, Analysis, and Discussion

1. What are the advantages and disadvantages of secret diplomacy?
2. What are the major functions of diplomats?
3. In what ways can procedural questions significantly affect substantive negotiations?
4. With instantaneous communications available between most capitals, are professional diplomats still needed?
5. What are some of the major negotiating ploys frequently used by diplomats? Can you think of others? Under what circumstances would they be most likely to succeed?
6. What ploys do you use in bargaining with friends, parents, or companions/spouses? In what ways do these mirror diplomatic negotiations? In what ways do they differ?
7. Describe the theatrical elements of a recent set of negotiations or meeting between heads of government. What purposes do such arrangements serve?

Selected Bibliography

Barston, Ronald P., Modern Diplomacy. Essex, U.K.: Longman, 1988.
Blaker, Michael, Japanese International Negotiating Style. New York: Columbia University Press, 1977.
Cohen, Raymond, Culture and Conflict in Egyptian-Israeli Relations: A Dialogue of the Deaf. Bloomington and Indianapolis: University of Indiana Press, 1990.

————, *Theatre of Power: The Art of Diplomatic Signalling.* London and New York: Longman, 1987.
Craig, Gordon A., "On the Diplomatic Revolution of Our Times," The Haynes Foundation Lectures, University of California, Riverside, April 1961.
————, "Totalitarian Approaches to Diplomatic Negotiations," in *Studies in Diplomatic History and Historiography in Honour of G.P. Gooch,* ed. A. O. Sarkissian. London: Longmans, Green, 1961.
Habeeb, W. M., Power and Tactics in International Negotiations: How Weak Nations Bargain with Strong Nations. Baltimore and London: Johns Hopkins University Press, 1988.
Iklé, Fred C., How Nations Negotiate. New York: Harper & Row, 1964.
Jönsson, Christer, Soviet Bargaining Behavior: The Nuclear Test Ban Case. New York: Columbia University Press, 1979.
Kremenyuk, Victor A., International Negotiation: Analysis, Approaches, Issues. San Francisco: Jossey-Bass publishers, 1991.
Lall, Arthur S., Modern International Negotiation: Principles and Practice. New York: Columbia University Press, 1966.
————, *Ed., Multilateral Negotiation and Mediation: Instruments and Methods.* Elmsford, N.Y.: Pergamon, 1985.
Lockhart, Charles, Bargaining in International Conflict. New York: Columbia University Press, 1979.
McClanahan, Grant V., Diplomatic Immunity: Principles, Practices, Problems. New York: St. Martin's Press, 1989.
Miller, Robert Hopkins, et al., Inside an Embassy: The Political Role of Diplomats Abroad. Washington, D.C.: Congressional Quarterly Books, 1992.
Newsom, David D., Ed., Diplomacy Under a Foreign Flag: When Nations Break Relations. New York: St. Martin's Press, 1990.
Nicolson, Sir Harold George, Diplomacy, 3rd ed. London, New York: Oxford University Press.
————, "Diplomacy Then and Now," *Foreign Affairs,* 40 (1961), 39–49.
Nogee, Joseph L., "Propaganda and Negotiation: The Case of the Ten-Nation Disarmament Committee," *Journal of Conflict Resolution,* 7 (1963), 510–21.
Putnam, Robert D., "Diplomacy and Domestic politics: The Logic of Two-Level Games," *International Organization,* 42, 3 (Summer 1988), 427–60.
Sawyer, Jack, and Harold Guetkow, "Bargaining and Negotiation in International Relations," in *International Behavior: A Social-Psychological Analysis,* ed. Herbert C. Kelman. New York: Holt, Rinehart & Winston, 1965.
Sebenius, James K., Negotiating the Law of the Sea. Cambridge, Mass.: Harvard University Press, 1984.
Strang, William, The Diplomatic Career. London: A. Deutsch, 1962.
Watson, Adam, Diplomacy: The Dialogue Between States. London: Eyre Methuen, 1982.
Winham, Gilbert, "International Negotiation in an Age of Transition," *International Journal* (Winter 1979–1980), 1–20.
————, "Negotiation as a Management Process," *World Politics,* 30 (October 1977), 1–20.
Wood, John R., and Jean Serrs, Diplomatic Ceremonial and Protocol. New York: Columbia University Press, 1970.
Zartman, I. William, "Common Elements in the Analysis of the Negotiation Process," *Negotiation Journal,* 4, 1 (January 1988), 31–43.

7

The Instruments of Policy: Propaganda

International political relationships have traditionally been conducted by government officials. Prior to the development of political democracy and modern totalitarianism, the conduct of foreign affairs was the exclusive province of royal emissaries and professional diplomats. Louis XIV's famous phrase, *"l'état, c'est moi,"* may seem strange to those who think of government in impersonal terms; but until the nineteenth century, the interests of any political unit were usually closely related to the personal and dynastic interests of its rulers. The wielding of influence was limited to direct contacts between those who made policy for the state. Diplomats bargained and court officials made policy decisions, but all were relatively indifferent to the public response abroad, if any, to their actions. They had to impress their foreign counterparts, not foreign populations.

Communications across the boundaries of political units were in any case sporadic. Travel was limited and few people had any firsthand knowledge even of their own countrymen. In most societies, nonaristocratic people were illiterate, unknowledgeable about affairs outside their town or valley, and generally apathetic toward any political issue that did not directly concern their everyday life. The instruments of communication were so crude as to permit only a small quantity and languorous flow of information from abroad. Populations were isolated from outside influences; if a diplomat could not achieve his or her government's designs through straightforward bargaining, it would be to no avail to appeal to the foreign population, which had no decisive influence in policy making.

With the development of mass politics—widespread involvement of the average citizen or subject in political affairs—and a widening scope of private contacts between people of different nationalities, the psychological and public opinion dimensions of foreign policy have become increasingly important. Insofar as people, combined into various social classes, movements, and interest groups, play a role in the determining of policy objectives and the means used to achieve or defend them, they themselves become a target of persuasion. Governments no longer make promises of rewards or threats of punishment just to foreign diplomats and foreign office officials; they make them to entire societies. One of the unique aspects of modern international political relationships is the deliberate attempt by governments, through diplomats and propagandists, to influence the attitudes and behavior of foreign populations, or of specific ethnic, class, religious, economic, or language groups within those populations. Officials hope that these foreign groups or the entire population will in turn influence the attitudes and actions of their own government. To cite one illustration: During 1974, the military junta in Chile hired an American public relations firm in New York to frame programs for altering Americans' highly unfavorable "image" of that government. This action was by no means untypical; today there are more than 400 active agencies in the United States doing public relations work on behalf of a foreign government.[1] Most of the agencies are concerned with promoting tourism and trade, but others have a distinctly political mission: Their task is to influence certain segments of a population in hopes that these will, in turn, affect government programs. The propagandist's model of the influence process appears in the accompanying figure.

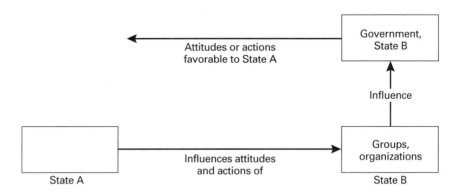

Virtually all governments conduct external information programs. All the major powers have large bureaucracies at home and officials abroad whose task it is to create favorable attitudes abroad for their own government's policies. Even the smallest states have press attachés and public relations people attached to their embassies in major countries. Their function is to make contacts with press officials, to send out bulletins and news sheets to all sorts of organizations and individuals that

[1]W. Phillips Davison, "Some Trends in International Propaganda," in *Propaganda in International Affairs* L. John Martin, ed. (Philadelphia: Annals of the American Academy of Political and Social Science, Vol. 398, 1971), p. 12.

might be interested in events and conditions in the small country, and to answer myriads of questions submitted to them by prospective tourists and schoolchildren—in short, their function is to create a favorable "image" of their country abroad.

In view of the extensive networks of nongovernment transactions in the world, propaganda is also conducted at unofficial levels, where a group or movement in one state seeks to alter or reinforce attitudes in another. For example, various spokesmen of black groups in South Africa toured many countries, telling audiences of the conditions of their people under the government's apartheid policies. They hoped these audiences would influence their own governments to change their policies toward South Africa and thereby promote a change in that government's policies toward its black population. This is the case where a nonstate actor seeks to improve its condition or achieve its domestic objectives by making linkages with foreign groups or audiences. The model would appear as follows:

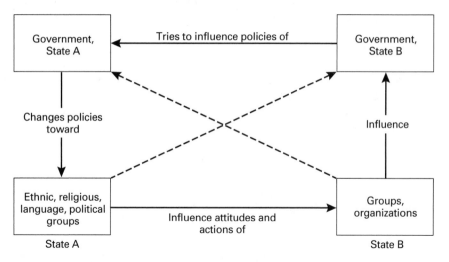

The flow of communication may become even more complex if groups within a society attempt to alter directly attitudes and policies of a foreign government. This is indicated by the broken lines. Consumers' boycotts of South African products are one example. Such "unofficial" lines of persuasion are extensive in the world today, particularly as the importance of nonstate actors increases in international politics. Multinational corporations not only disseminate commercial advertising but work on governments and publics, through public relations campaigns, to try to create a better "climate" for investment and operation. Transnational voluntary associations frequently employ information officers and staff to "tell their story" to audiences around the world. And terrorist groups and individuals have resorted to skyjacking, kidnapping, and seemingly senseless killings as means of publicizing their grievances throughout the world. A sudden, dramatic act can have a much greater political impact than the standard propaganda program disseminated through print or broadcasting. Although the subsequent discussion focuses on government propaganda, we should remember that a variety of nonstate actors and transnational organizations can conduct their tasks successfully only to the extent that they are able to create or sustain favorable public attitudes in many countries. International propaganda is not a monopoly of government information ministries.

During the post–World War II period, we have observed growing numbers of transnational coalitions that operate to bring items to the international agenda, raise funds for their multifarious activities, publicize issues and causes, and alter governments' and each other's behavior. These coalitions themselves are workable because of innovations in communications technology. Today they can communicate instantaneously through telephonic, facsimile, and other means, in some cases making face-to-face meetings unnecessary. They can reach audiences of millions through low-cost desktop publications, or through the production of video clips and full-length films. In Chapter 3 we mentioned such transnational coalitions as Greenpeace. To that we could add peace groups, business associations, environmental groups, and the like. All of them employ the variety of modern media to further their causes. While we may not think that their "publicity" is propaganda, the methods of persuasion such groups employ are not fundamentally different from those used by governments.

Since propaganda involves essentially a process of persuasion, it cannot be equated with scientific efforts to arrive at some truth. It is not logical discourse or dialectical investigation. It relies more on selection of facts, partial explanations, and predetermined answers. The content of propaganda is therefore seldom completely "true," but neither is it wholly false, as is so often assumed. The propagandist is concerned with maximizing persuasiveness, not with adhering to some standard of scholarship or uncovering some new fact.

Selecting the Target: Whose Attitudes Can Be Changed?

Despite rapid development of communication media in the past century, only a relatively small number of people in any given society are likely targets of foreign-oriented information. Various studies consistently reveal that even in industrialized societies with high literacy rates and mass consumption of news, only a small percentage are interested or involved in international affairs. In many developing countries, the average person's "world" remains confined to a small region or province. Unless a foreign-originated communication has some direct relevance to his or her everyday life, it is unlikely to reach that person or make any impact.[2] In a 1975 study, researchers discovered significant differences in levels of knowledge about the United Nations in different regions of the world. While about 90 percent of the respondents in industrialized countries had heard of the UN, the figure was 40 percent for Latin America, about 30 percent for Africa, and 10 percent in India. Yet, while having heard of the UN, only 29 percent of the American respondents could name one or more UN agencies or programs, compared to a figure of almost 50 percent for Western

[2]For a review of studies on the limited size of targets, see W. Phillips Davison, *International Political Communication* (New York: Praeger, 1965), Chapter 3.

Europeans.[3] Among those who are potential targets, how effective are communications, and what personal and social characteristics predispose people to react favorably to foreign-sponsored messages?

Some psychologists and sociologists make a distinction between the "nuclear" personality and the "social" personality. The former includes basic attitudes toward objects, ideas, and people, which are usually formed in infancy and reinforced during childhood. These attitudes may or may not relate to political phenomena. In some families, politics are not a matter of general discussion, so the child is left in later years to form his or her own opinions, based on his or her own experiences and social relationships outside the family. Still, any child develops general liberal or authoritarian attitudes, whether they have a political content or not. In other families, fundamental political attitudes—in addition to liberal or authoritarian predispositions—are instilled in the child to the extent that no amount of propaganda, or even experience, is likely to change them. Children born and raised in homes where the parents are vocally prejudiced against specific minorities normally grow up with the same prejudices and do not alter them until or unless they move to a different environment. Some attitudes are so deeply ingrained that even a new environment will not prompt an examination of them. The "nuclear" personality and the attitudes central to that personality, thus, are not amenable to change simply by being subjected to propaganda.

Following the early childhood years, as individuals become a part of larger associations, they form attitudes on new ideas, objects, and people; often, these conform to the prevailing attitudes of peer groups. The strength of these group-established attitudes and opinions can be seen in experiments that failed to modify attitudes of individuals contrary to predominating views within the groups to which those individuals belonged. The significance of the "social" personality is that one's political attitudes tend to be functional to the groups to which one belongs. Or, as one of the consistent findings of voting-behavior studies indicates, an individual's political preferences are likely to be similar to those of his or her closest associates.

These findings suggest that it is easier to change the attitudes of small associational groups such as environmental associations, which already share similar attitudes, than of an entire national population, which does not constitute a likely target unless all the members of the national society are united strongly on some value, such as the maintenance of national prestige or independence. It is the propagandist's job to find the key groups in society and determine what kinds of appeal will arouse the desired response in the selected targets.

The next question is, How do individuals handle information and experience that directly contradict their established attitudes? People are resourceful in resisting information that does not fit their own pictures of reality. Voting-behavior studies in the United States indicate that the more partisan voters are before the election, the less likely they are to subject themselves to the campaign appeals of the party for which they will not vote. Those who do subject themselves to information that

---

[3]Cited in Klaus Hufner and Jens Nauman, "Are the Moral and Value Foundations of Multilateralism Changing?" *International Political Science Review*, 11 (July 1990), 328–29.

contradicts their views may lose confidence in their opinions but will frequently go out of their way to seek any information that substantiates their original position. Others, when exposed to "unfriendly" information, may reject it or perhaps distort its meaning and significance. Or they might question the credibility of the information or its source and pass it off as mere "propaganda." Certainly, one's initial attitude toward the communicator will have an important bearing on one's reception of the information.[4]

Propaganda is apt to be effective when directed toward people who share at least partially the attitudes of the communicator. It is more successful in strengthening *existing* attitudes or crystallizing predispositions than in converting those already hostile. Thus, one of the standard ploys of propagandists sending messages to a hostile audience is not to reveal their own identity. Nazi propagandists frequently used this "black" propaganda, either by failing to mention the source altogether, or by creating some fictitious cover name that would seem legitimate to the audience. The United States International Communications Agency spends more time and money trying to reinforce the pro-American attitudes of selected elites in friendly countries than attempting to convert those whose political leanings go in other directions. The External Service of the BBC takes a slightly different approach. Regardless of its targets' political affiliations, it attempts to maximize impact by creating a reputation for impartiality. Whereas most governments' foreign information programs have an identifiable "slant," the BBC presents mostly factual news accounts and critiques of British policies at home and abroad. The purpose is to establish *credibility* for the information source while simultaneously providing a service for those who are regularly subjected to only official government news sources.

Finally, propaganda seems to be most effective when directed toward crowds. We have already suggested that attitudes and beliefs are mechanisms that satisfy social adjustment. Individuals are not likely propaganda targets if the content of the propaganda conflicts strongly with the values and opinions that circulate among their closest social connections. We are all wary of adopting and articulating unpopular views—not just because they are unusual, but because we might face social ostracism for expressing them. Crowds, on the other hand, do not necessarily contain an effective network of personal contacts. They are particularly susceptible to propaganda appeals but, only if there is already some shared attitude between propagandist and the target.

> The study of crowd psychology . . . has shown that, although people do many things whilst in a crowd that they might not otherwise, . . . new attitudes spring . . . from the individual members of the crowd and not, as was formerly thought, from a mysterious entity described as the "crowd" mind. Because of . . . intensification of emotion [in crowds] it is possible to cause disorganized masses of people to behave in other than their everyday manner, to stimulate and lead them more easily than an organized public which is prepared to listen to reason and discuss a problem. But it is not possible to make them do anything. Negro-lynching crowds exist because anti-Negro feelings already exist: the crowd intensifies the feeling to the point of action but does not create it.[5]

[4]Percy H. Tannenbaum, "Initial Attitude Toward Source and Content as Factors in Attitude Change Through Communications," *Public Opinion Quarterly*, 20 (1956), 414.

[5]J. A. C. Brown, *Techniques of Persuasion: From Propaganda to Brainwashing* (Middlesex: Penguin, 1963), p. 68.

It is not clear why people are more suggestible in the crowd, but many observers have noted that individual credulity tends to fall to a low level when emotions are raised in a large gathering. In their domestic propaganda, the Nazis were well aware of this characteristic and put on fantastic parades and party rallies to impress the people. There is some evidence that the arousal of any strong emotion may make the individual in the crowd more suggestible, sometimes even when that emotion is directed initially *against* the leader of the crowd.

Creating Impact

After the selection of appropriate targets, the second task of propagandists is to catch the attention of those to whom they will direct their message. Attention-getting may be difficult, particularly among people apathetic or hostile to the communicator. Therefore, the devices used by propagandists tend to be spectacular, colorful, or unusual and may not be related to the substance of the message. When attention is elicited, propagandists then attempt to evoke and play on emotions. They cannot do this, obviously, by presenting a calm catalogue of facts (except where the facts "speak for themselves"). Rather, symbols are used to bring about an emotional response, from anxiety and guilt to hatred, which is probably the most potent of all unifying emotions. The common conception that propaganda is synonymous with lying probably arose from efforts of the Allies and Germans during World War I to create hatred toward the enemy by fabricating stories about atrocities and inhumane behavior. Propagandists frequently appeal to hatreds or try to create them, during times of great international tension and in the actual conduct of war, when a maximum number of people and allies have to be mobilized to support a government. In these circumstances, hatred of a national enemy becomes a virtue, while the emotions of love, anxiety, and guilt are seldom included in the various propaganda themes.

The adage "actions speak louder than words" undoubtedly applies in international propaganda efforts. The images that foreign populations possess of other countries are usually based on news reports, movies, and cultural events rather than on direct experience. Since most people are uninformed about foreign affairs, their conceptions and attitudes toward foreign countries are seldom detailed. Spectacular, newsmaking foreign policy actions will be noticed by a relatively broad cross section of a foreign population, whereas regular government information programs abroad will reach a much smaller audience. In short, people are apt to be more impressed with what governments do than with what propagandists say they do. Where a great discrepancy between the words and actions of a government exists, either people abroad become disillusioned or the credibility of the propagandist is compromised, thus making the target populations wary of incoming information. The credibility of North Korean propaganda that claimed that the United States had used germ warfare during the Korean War was reduced (except among those who really *wanted* to believe the charges) after the Communists refused to admit an impartial Red Cross investigation. In these instances, all the emotions and expectations that had been raised and attitudes that had been crystallized through verbal and pictorial messages were compromised by the self-defeating actions of the governments that sent the propaganda.

The main strategy of foreign information programs is to sustain or alter the attitudes and behaviors of politically relevant groups within a society. The purpose is to build support or "understanding" for the emitting government's policies. One example is the considerable lengths to which the Chinese government went during the early 1990s to explain abroad its policies of denying certain rights to its own citizens. This strategy reached a particularly high point when the Chinese sought to obtain the right to host the Olympic Games at the end of the millennium. Another strategy is to alter target groups' loyalties toward their own government. This is a classic format for subversion. The United States, through "Radio Marti" beamed at Cuba, has formulated programs clearly designed to undermine Cubans' support for Fidel Castro. This type of propaganda has been coordinated with the American economic boycott of the island. We will discuss briefly some other examples of subversive propaganda in Chapter 9.

Propaganda Techniques

Having established a target and an appropriate strategy, propagandists then may use a variety of specific techniques in delivering the messages. Among the more prominent are:

1. Name-Calling. The propagandist attaches an emotion-laden symbol to a person or country. Targets are expected to respond favorably, from the propagandist's point of view, to the label without examining any evidence. Propagandists relate their appeals to stereotypes that already exist in the audience. Thus, Communists become "Reds," labor leaders become "union bosses," and constitutional governments become "capitalist cliques."

2. Glittering Generality. This is similar to the preceding technique but is used to describe an idea or policy rather than individuals. The term *free world* was a favorite generality of Western propagandists. "Socialist solidarity" was used in the Communist world to describe the complex relations among Communist states and parties, and "the African soul" is supposed to create a similar image of strength and unity.

3. Transfer. The propagandist attempts to identify one idea, person, country, or policy with another to make the target approve or disapprove it. One way to evoke a particularly hostile attitude among religious people against communism is to equate it with atheism. Communists regularly equated capitalism with decadence, and anti-Semites hope to create public support for their bigotry by associating Jews with Communists.

4. "Plain Folks." Propagandists are aware that their problems are compounded if they appear to the audience as "foreigners" or strangers. They seek, therefore, to identify as closely as possible with the values and style of life of the targets by using local slang, accent, and idiom.

5. Testimonial. Here, the propagandist uses an esteemed person or institution to endorse or criticize an idea or a political entity. A variation of this is the "appeal to authority," where the target is asked to believe something simply because some "authority" says it is true.

6. Selection.   Almost all propaganda, even when it uses the other techniques discussed above, relies on the selection of facts, although it is seldom very specific in its factual content. When a detailed presentation is given, the propagandist uses only those facts required to "prove" predetermined objectives.

7. Bandwagon.   This technique plays on the audience's desire to "belong" or be in accord with the crowd. It is similar to the testimonial, except that a mass of people, rather than a single esteemed person or institution, serves as the attraction. The messages of Communist propagandists frequently used such phrases as "the whole world knows that . . . ," "all peace-loving people recognize that . . . ," or "all progressive people demand that . . . ." This technique implies that the target is in a minority—if he or she opposes the substance of the message—and should join the majority. Or, if the target is sympathetic to the propagandist, this technique will reinforce one's attitudes by demonstrating that one is on the "right" side, along with everyone else.

8. Frustration Scapegoat.   One easy way to create hatred and relieve frustrations is to create a scapegoat. Revolutionary regimes faced with complex internal economic and social disorders and popular frustrations frequently create an internal or external "spook" to account for the people's miseries. The most famous example was the myth created by Hitler that Germany's internal and foreign problems were created by "the Jews"—who were often equated with Communists.

9. Fear.   Consciousness can be raised, and attitudes changed, when audiences are made aware of an impending or imminent threat to their lives and welfare. In times of international crisis, governments are as active in mobilizing their own populations for expressions of solidarity as they are in coping with their adversary. Transnational coalitions and some governments have used, among other themes, the fear of nuclear war to promote arms-control and disarmament measures, and the fear of ecological degradation to raise awareness of environmental issues.

The reader will have noticed that these techniques are used not only in foreign propaganda but in all organized efforts to persuade, including political campaigns, and particularly in commercial advertising. Several of these techniques may be used simultaneously to create the maximum effect.

The Media of Foreign Information and Propaganda Programs

Almost all governments try to influence attitudes and actions of foreign populations. For most, the purpose may be only commercial: inviting foreigners as tourists, investors, and developers. Posters, films, newspaper advertisements, magazine layouts, and radio or television commercials may be the main media for transmission of ideas, symbols, and images. A somewhat smaller range of governments actively support traveling troupes, sports teams, and various cultural exhibitions, usually with a general purpose of having one's "presence" known. The content of these forms of communication is seldom explicitly political; it concerns status and prestige, a type of low-keyed flag showing.

Print media offer a variety of flexible alternatives for propaganda. They can be easily targeted toward specific audiences; they are relatively cheap; and they can have sufficient length to make a case reasonably convincing by providing extensive facts, figures, illustrations, and the like.

But the print media have their limitations. Some governments refuse entry to foreign-published propaganda materials. Societies with high illiteracy rates are not particularly choice targets. Many audiences prefer entertainment to long political tracts. Some governments that quickly change their foreign policy lines may find it embarrassing that there are written records of positions they once held but no longer promote. And in some societies, it is a crime to possess foreign propaganda materials.

Radio suffers from few of these limitations. For this reason, it is probably the most broadly used medium for disseminating information abroad. The radio is cheap; the potential pool of targets is very large, as almost all people in the world have access to receivers; it is relatively expensive for governments to control broadcasts from abroad by "jamming" and other means; radio leaves no written record; and it is versatile. Programs can easily join explicit political messages with light entertainment. In countries where the press is controlled, tuning in on foreign broadcasts is one way of finding out about world events and even about events at home that are not publicized by the ruling party. Most Poles learned about events during the Solidarity uprising in the early 1980s from BBC radio broadcasts, the Voice of America, and Radio Free Europe; and as soon as American satellite photos had confirmed the Chernobyl nuclear accident in 1986, this information was broadcast immediately to the Soviet Union, where the government had made no announcements concerning the disaster to its own people.

The Voice of America broadcasts about 1,000 hours per week in 42 languages. Radio Free Europe and Radio Liberty, once under the administration of the CIA but now under the auspices of the Board of International Broadcasting, beam programs to five Eastern European countries and to Russia and some of the former Soviet republics. China has extensive foreign radio programs, broadcasting about 1,400 hours per week in 43 languages. Taiwan, Egypt, Germany, England, North Korea, South Korea, Cuba, India, Israel, and Australia follow in hours per week of broadcasting and in the number of languages.

Examples of content and style: The BBC, after chiming the tones of Big Ben, delivers a rather dry, unembellished, but impeccably accurate and nonpoliticized rendition of the daily news. The North Koreans beam "commentaries" southward, characterizing South Korea as a country run by a fascist dictatorship propped up by American imperialists, contrasting their own situation, where the all-seeing Kim Il-Sung has shown the way for progress, democracy, and eternal bountifulness. During the 1980s, clandestine stations under the auspices of the KGB or CIA urged rebels in El Salvador or Afghanistan to press their fight to a victorious finish. More broadly, the Voice of America broadcasts a serious debate about American environmental problems, the cost of the space program, or the problems of reforming health programs.

Television is playing an increasingly significant role in government information programs. The medium is to a certain extent limited because its signals cannot be broadcast as far as those of radio, and because all signals have to be received by a local station. In these circumstances, governments can easily control incoming broadcasts. In more open societies, however, the availability of satellites can help disseminate government-sponsored news quickly. For example, after the United States' bombing attack on Libya in 1986, foreign reporters were invited to United States embassies abroad to direct questions, via satellite, of Secretary of State George Shultz and Defense Secretary Caspar Weinberger. This was done on the United States Information Agency "Worldnet" program, which is available to any foreign station that cares to play it. A similar hookup in 1983, where the leaders of the small Eastern Caribbean countries were interviewed and confirmed that they had asked the United States to intervene in Grenada, was apparently instrumental in changing opinions that had been initially hostile to the American intervention.[6]

The previous chapter introduced the metaphor of the theater in discussing diplomacy and diplomatic signaling. Television has increased the opportunities for creating images and sending messages to broad audiences. There is no medium so well adapted to raising diplomatic processes to the level of a "media event." At least in the industrialized countries, television is ever-present in dens, living rooms, salons, and bedrooms. In 1983, there were 437 sets per 1,000 population in industrialized countries (but only 26 per thousand, or one for every 38 citizens, in the developing countries).[7] A major world sporting event, such as the Olympic Games, the Super Bowl, or the World Cup soccer final, can have an audience of almost one half of mankind: about 2.5 billion.

There are few diplomatic events that would attract such broad and diverse audiences. But a major summit meeting, a royal wedding, the opening salvos of a war, major terrorist incidents, and the conclusion of a peace treaty can have audiences in the hundreds of millions. The signing of the Israel-PLO mutual recognition document in front of the White House in September 1993 was estimated to have been watched live by almost 2 billion viewers. If properly staged, such televised events can have considerable impact to undifferentiated audiences; if not always altering attitudes or bringing about desired actions, then at least raising awareness of problems, friendships, and hostilities.

In closed societies, leaders can mobilize or order the television cameras to record only what they want. Before an event is broadcast for public consumption, the films are carefully edited to show the leaders in the best light. In societies where the media are not under direct government control, there are still ways of ensuring that embarrassments will not reach the television screen. Presidents and prime ministers can give preferential treatment to reporters who do not try to embarrass them; they can deny answering questions, or even access to certain events, to those whose work has portrayed the leader unfavorably. Both Lyndon Johnson and Richard Nixon went even further in placing political pressure on the television networks to stop showing films of the Vietnam War that portrayed the United States in a bad light.

The potential for televised propaganda programs will expand considerably as direct satellite broadcasting becomes increasingly available—that is, when receivers

---

[6]*The New York Times*, May 8, 1986, p. A-10.

[7]Communications figures from various sources are summarized in Alex Inkeles, "Linking the Whole Human Race: The World as a Communications System," in *Business in the Contemporary World*, Herbert L. Sawyer, ed., (Lanham, N.Y., and London: University Press of America, 1988), pp. 135–74.

can get signals (through dishes) directly from the satellite without an intervening receiving station. Government controls over foreign emissions will then be considerably reduced unless new jamming technologies can be developed. Assuming that the capacity to penetrate societies will outstrip the capacity of regulatory devices, the "war of words" that is carried on mainly by means of radio today may be substantially changed into propaganda competition of voice and picture. Governments will have a substantially enhanced capacity to construct for their viewers the "reality" they want to project abroad. The advantages of radio will remain substantial, since in many developing countries the cost of television receivers remains prohibitively expensive, but among industrial countries, the days of societies relatively closed off from each other are fast waning. As in other realms of international relations, the availability of new technologies will greatly change *how* policies are pursued and implemented.

The Impact of Propaganda in International Politics

It is difficult to generalize about the conditions under which propaganda appeals will succeed and about the extent to which the hundreds of millions of dollars spent each year by the major powers on foreign information programs result in desired attitudes and actions by various "targets." Surveys and studies by propaganda agencies are often unreliable, because administrators have to prove that the resources spent bring desired results. And although it is relatively easy to measure the number of listeners to radio programs or attendance at cultural-exchange events, it is virtually impossible to identify the impact these media have on attitudes and actions.

The extent to which governments, wealthy and poor, large and small, engage in foreign-directed information programs suggests that at least they are convinced that the commitment of funds and manpower to persuade others brings some benefits. For most, those benefits are little more than attaining some international visibility, a "presence" abroad. In some particular instances, as the case of the American intervention in Grenada suggests, testimonials can bring attitude changes, particularly regarding policies or topics about which targets have little previous information or no set attitudes. Opinions can be created, but where they are already set, disconfirming information seldom makes a significant impact.

While technologies for disseminating information are expanding rapidly, there is no evidence that the listening, reading, or viewing publics are growing dramatically. American estimates indicated that during the Cold War less than 15 percent of the adult Soviet population listened even occasionally to the Voice of America (audience figures for Eastern Europe were much higher).[8] Because Radio Moscow beams only on shortwave to North America, its audience is minuscule. Due to its reliability and reputation for objective presentations, the BBC probably has among the world's largest audiences. Even so, objective information does not necessarily lead to any political action; forming or changing attitudes is at best a difficult task. To motivate listeners to political action is even more difficult.

[8]*The New York Times*, November 25, 1985; Kay Bartlett, "Battles of the Airwaves: Nation Speaks to Nation in All Sorts of Languages," *The Vancouver Sun*, January 15, 1985, p. B8.

There are also great differences in the availability of communications facilities and technologies between different regions of the world. If there is interest, it is relatively easy to make points or raise issues in populations that are flooded with newspapers, magazines, radios, televisions, and video recorders. This is the case in the industrial countries, but we must not assume that what exists in those areas is global. While transistor radios have become commonly available throughout the world, the number of transmitting stations is highly skewed. There is a total of about 30,000, of which only 8,000 are located in what we call the Third World. Put in other terms, the developing countries have about 20 percent of the transmitters broadcasting to 75 percent of the world's population.[9] There is an even more pronounced difference in the distribution of television transmitters. Even though the total number of transmitters doubled in the 1970s, most of the growth was in the industrial countries. In 1983, forty-five political units (including dependent states, small islands, and the like) had no access to television at all. The potential viewing audience in the developing world is huge, but it remains today a fraction of the numbers in the industrial countries. We can estimate that a major international event such as a summit meeting is in fact viewed by a small fraction of the world's population.

For many, then, although information about the outside world is available, the village, the valley, or the small island remain the meaningful environments for day-to-day life. In any one of the half million villages in India, for example, it is unlikely that more than 5 percent of the population would even know the name of the British prime minister, the American president, or the Russian leader, much less have watched any of them perform their diplomatic theatrics. The situation is changing, to be sure, but we are a long way from having a global communications community.

There are, as well, asymmetries in communications patterns, which have been documented and verified through numerous studies. As in the dependency characterization of the world (outlined in Chapter 1) the messages of private and public communication go predominantly between the industrial countries, and in a southerly direction from them to the Third World. News about the Third World available through the media dominated by corporations from the industrial countries is slanted heavily toward riots, rebellions, and natural disasters. Films, news service products, and television programs from the industrial countries flood the Third World, but there is little reciprocity. One anomaly is that Americans, who have led the "communications revolution," are also among the most parochial populations. Compared with other countries, Americans' share of foreign news is less. Only 2 percent of American television programs are of foreign origins, while for the rest of the world the figure stands at about 30 percent, and reaches as high as 70 percent in some countries.[10] American news programs seldom cover diplomatic events unless there is some direct American involvement in them. The summit meetings of Central American presidents that led eventually to peace in Nicaragua were not even mentioned in most American news broadcasts; meetings of Arab leaders, while sometimes mentioned or covered very briefly, receive little attention compared with an American secretary of state's visit to Cairo or Jerusalem.

[9]Inkeles, "Linking the Whole Human Race," p. 150.
[10]Ibid., p. 152.

Such examples are numerous. The point is that the *opportunities* for disseminating persuasive political messages are highly skewed in the world. The governments of the major industrial countries have an immense advantage of access to global media. A few prominent Third World leaders, such as Nelson Mandela, have received great opportunities as well, and they have used the media to good political effect. But they are the exception rather than the rule. There are dozens of "liberation" leaders who remain totally unknown outside of their own countries. For a variety of reasons, including the structure of world communications, they have little impact abroad.

In the long run, most propaganda clearly does not create new attitudes or lead to any particular actions. Indeed, most of it is "facilitative communication," the main purpose of which is simply to keep in contact with foreign audiences and to maintain an awareness of the general foreign policy goals or social characteristics of a state. Awareness in itself often creates positive attitudes over a period of time, if not political action.[11] In the short run and in highly favorable circumstances of political turmoil, revolution, war, or general fear, however, propaganda can be used very effectively—that is, to the point where "targets" can be motivated to undertake actions desired by the communicator. As Chapter 9 reveals, propaganda has been used particularly effectively in attempts at subversion where a "revolutionary" situation already prevails in the target state.

Questions for Study, Analysis, and Discussion

1. What types and/or groups of people are particularly open to persuasion?
2. What are some of the main themes and tactics governments and other political groups use for persuading audiences?
3. Describe a recent effort by a foreign government to alter or sustain your beliefs or attitudes toward it or its policies. What themes were used? What was your response?
4. If available in your library, look up an issue of *Soviet Life* published during the Brezhnev era. Examine its contents and try to determine in what ways, if any, the publication was designed to alter attitudes toward the Soviet Union. What themes, styles of presentation, or messages made an impact on you?
5. The next time you watch a major diplomatic event on television, identify its "theatrical" elements and the impressions they make on you.
6. Propaganda becomes particularly obvious during times of crisis or war. In what ways is the adversary typically portrayed by government officials? Good examples of government characterization and stereotyping of the opponent include the American response to Iraq's invasions of Kuwait in 1990, Margaret Thatcher's portrayal of the Argentine government during the Malvinas war, and, at the popular level, recent characterizations of Japan and the Japanese in American novels and films.

Selected Bibliography

Abelson, H. J., *Persuasion: How Opinions and Attitudes Are Changed.* New York: Springer, 1959.
Biryukov, N., "Broadcasting and Diplomacy," *International Affairs* (Moscow) 10 (1964), 63–68.

[11]L. John Martin, "Effectiveness of International Propaganda," in *Propaganda in International Affairs*, ed. Martin, pp. 62–70.

Bogart, Leo, Premises for Propaganda. New York: Free Press, 1976.

Brown, Donald R., International Radio Broadcasting. New York: Praeger, 1982.

Brown, J. A. C., Techniques of Persuasion: From Propaganda to Brainwashing. Middlesex: Penguin, 1963.

Davison, W. Phillips, International Political Communication. New York: Praeger, 1965.

Deutsch, Karl W., and Richard L. Merritt, "Effects of Events on National and International Images," in *International Behavior: A Social-Psychological Analysis,* ed. Herbert C. Kelman. New York: Holt, Rinehart & Winston, 1965.

Doob, Leonard W., Public Opinion and Propaganda, 2nd ed. Hamden, Conn.: Archon, 1966.

Haigh, Robert W., George Berbner, and Richard B. Byrne, eds., Communications in the Twenty-First Century. New York: John Wiley, 1981.

Head, Sydney W., World Broadcasting Systems: A Comparative Analysis. Belmont, Calif.: Wadsworth, 1985.

Janis, Irving L., and M. Brewster Smith, "Effects of Education and Persuasion on National and International Images," in *International Behavior: A Social-Psychological Analysis,* ed. Herbert C. Kelman. New York: Holt, Rinehart & Winston, 1965.

Lasswell, Harold D., Daniel Lerner, and Hans Speier, eds., Propaganda and Communication in World History. Honolulu: University of Hawaii Press, 1979.

Lee, John, ed., Diplomatic Persuaders. New York: John Wiley, 1968.

Martin, L. John, Propaganda in International Affairs. Philadelphia: Annals of the American Academy of Political and Social Science, Vol. 398, 1971.

Merrill, John C., ed., Global Journalism: A Survey of the World's Mass Media. New York: Longman, 1983.

Mitchell, J. M., International Cultural Relations. London: Allen & Unwin, 1986.

Ross, Clive, The Soviet Propaganda Network. London: Pinter, 1988.

Smith, Anthony, The Geopolitics of Information: How Western Culture Dominates the World. London: Faber & Faber, 1980.

Sorenson, Thomas C., The Word War: The Story of American Propaganda. New York: Harper & Row, 1968.

Tuch, Hans N., Communicating with the World:U.S. Public Diplomacy Overseas. New York: St. Martins Press, 1990.

Varis, Tapio, "The International Flow of Television Programs," *Journal of Communication,* 34,1 (1984), 143–52.

Vermaat, J. A. Emerson, "Moscow Fronts and the European Peace Movement," *Problems of Communism* (November–December 1982), pp. 43–56.

Chapter

8

The Instruments of Policy: Economic Rewards and Coercion

Chapter 4 emphasized that welfare goals, broadly conceived, constitute a major objective of most governments. In addition to security, prestige, and autonomy, governments seek access to markets and sources of supply to enhance their domestic economic growth. For a large number, commercial opportunities abroad constitute a fundamental basis for domestic economic well-being. Only a few states are endowed sufficiently with the full range of natural resources, foods, and energy to sustain modern or modernizing economic establishments. For others, trade, financial flows (foreign investment), and sometimes foreign aid are critical for survival and economic progress. The farmers of England or Japan could, by themselves, grow only enough food to sustain approximately one quarter of their countries' populations; without access to oil, a majority of the economies in the world would revert to preindustrial forms; of forty-one countries in sub-Sahara Africa, nineteen earn more than 10 percent of their gross national product (GNP) from aid transfers from the industrial countries;[1] and for a large number of countries, both industrial and developing, trade constitutes more than one quarter of their GNP. In short, international economic transactions have become critical components of modern life and of the welfare goals of governments.

Economic opportunities and transactions also create vulnerabilities. Disruptions of transaction flows can in some cases cripple economies and, in most, at least

---

[1]Organization for Economic Cooperation and Development (OECD), *Twenty-Five Years of Development Cooperation: A Review* (Paris: OECD, 1985), p. 128.

invoke serious costs. Countries that export only a few commodities (the profile of many developing nations), that send those exports to only one or a few markets (trade concentration), or that rely heavily upon single countries for sources of supply are particularly vulnerable. The United States and Russia are better protected against attempts at economic coercion because trade constitutes a relatively small proportion of total economic activity (less than 20 percent), they are reasonably self-sufficient in a broad range of commodities and resources, their sources of imports are diversified among many suppliers, and they have the modern technology to fashion alternatives if materials cannot be obtained from abroad.

In general, the structure of economic relations in the contemporary world is such that vulnerabilities are distributed more heavily among the developing countries than the industrial nations. Countries such as Japan, Great Britain, and Canada are highly reliant upon trade, but at least they have trade profiles characterized by a wide range of imports and exports, reasonably diversified markets and sources of supply (except Canada, 75 percent of whose trade is with the United States), and diplomatic influence. In contrast, many of the poor countries export only a few commodities and are almost totally dependent upon others for their sources of energy, machines, spare parts, and the like. It is not surprising, therefore, that a large proportion of the use of economic instruments of policy, either as rewards or punishments, have been directed by industrial countries against developing nations.

The manipulation of economic transaction flows can be organized for all sorts of political purposes. As in all international relationships, the government that manipulates these flows is seeking to change the attitudes and behaviors, whether domestic or foreign, of a target government. Many governments, spurred by human rights and other organizations, applied economic sanctions against the South African government until 1993 as a means of coercing it to abandon *apartheid* policies. The United States imposed economic sanctions against Nicaragua in 1985 as just one of the means of trying to coerce the Sandinista regime to restore forms of political pluralism in that country, and acted similarly against Libya to try to compel the Khadaffi regime to cease support for terrorist activities. In the 1960s, the Soviet Union dramatically curtailed trade with China and withdrew its technicians and aid officials from Beijing in an effort to coerce (or persuade) the Chinese Communist authorities to change their attitudes on key ideological issues and on some critical questions of foreign policy. In these and many other cases, the economic instruments of policy are wielded to change attitudes and behavior on both the target's domestic *and* foreign policies, and the objectives sought may be reasonably clear (e.g., the dismantling of apartheid). In other instances, the government that orders various forms of economic sanctions may have little chance of success, particularly where the target is not vulnerable. In these cases, the objectives may be more symbolic, to demonstrate commitment, to show resolve, or to protest visibly.

Economic instruments can also be used for *rewarding* or *supporting* the behavior of governments. Disbursements of foreign aid, in addition to the economic contribution they make, demonstrate degrees of sympathy between governments. Granting favorable tariff rates or expanding quotas on specific imports are forms of rewards. And in recent years, transferring military hardware, spare parts, and services related to military capabilities, often at subsidized prices or as outright gifts, has become an important way of rewarding friends and visibly demonstrating support for the domestic and/or foreign policies of the recipients.

Most recent cases of economic coercion have featured a single state, or a small group of states, attempting to coerce a single target. But as we pointed out in Chapter 1, the contemporary states system can also be conceived as a society of states, with fundamental rules, norms, and values that serve the interests of all. We thus have the notion of "outlaw" states, actors that violate the norms and expectations of a large number of the members of the states society. International organizations, to the extent that their charters and covenants reflect fundamental norms and rules, may also organize a *community* effort to coerce. The League of Nations on three occasions organized international sanctions (in 1921, 1934, and 1936); and, from 1966 to 1979, the United Nations applied sanctions against the Rhodesian government which had unilaterally declared its independence from Great Britain in an attempt to maintain a white supremacist government under Ian Smith. In 1990 the UN imposed comprehensive and mandatory economic sanctions on Iraq for that government's violation of the norm against aggression—in this case, against Kuwait. And in 1992, the UN ordered member states to cut all trade relations with Serbia so that it would cease supporting Bosnian Serbs' "ethnic cleansing" policies in the Bosnian civil war.

Techniques of Economic Coercion and Reward

Because of the complexity of commercial transactions between societies, governments, in seeking to change or sustain the behavior of others, have a broad range of instrumentalities. In all cases, governments for a variety of non-commercial purposes manipulate the flow of goods, capital, and technology to grant rewards or to raise costs. The following list is not exhaustive, but includes the most frequently used techniques.

1. Tariffs.   Almost all foreign-made products coming into a country are taxed for the purpose of raising revenues and protecting domestic producers from foreign competition, or for other domestic economic reasons. The tariff structure can be used effectively as a foreign policy inducement or punishment when a target country stands to gain or lose important markets for its products by its upward or downward manipulation. During the Cold War the U.S. government extended preferential tariff treatment to those members of the Warsaw Pact whose foreign or domestic foreign policies showed some independence from Moscow. Yugoslavia, Romania, and Poland received most-favored-nation treatment (the same tariff rates as those extended to the most favored nation; that is, accorded the lowest rates), but in the wake of the imposition of martial law in 1981, President Reagan withdrew that status from Poland. Since 1989, the U.S. has made the grant of most-favored-nation status conditional upon the institution of democratic processes and free market economies in Eastern Europe and the Soviet Union.

2. Quotas.   To control imports of some commodities, governments may establish quotas rather than tariffs (tariffs may, of course, be applied to the items that enter under quotas). Under such arrangements, the supplier usually sends goods into the country at a favorable price but is allowed to sell only a certain amount in a given time period. The U.S. government maintains quotas on the import of sugar from the Philippines, the Dominican Republic, and other sugar-producing nations. Since these countries sell a large portion of sugar (their major export crop) to the United States, any shift in the size of the quotas can either assist or severely damage their economies.

3. Boycott. A trade boycott organized by a government eliminates the import of either a specific commodity or the total range of export products sold by the country against which the boycott is organized. Governments that do not engage in state trading normally enforce boycotts by requiring private importers to secure licenses to purchase any commodities from the boycotted country. If importers do not comply with this requirement, any goods purchased abroad can be confiscated and the importers can be prosecuted.

4. Embargo. A government that seeks to *deprive* another country of goods prohibits its own businesses from concluding any transactions with commercial organizations in the country against which the embargo is organized. An embargo may be enforced either on a specific category of goods, such as strategic materials, or on the total range of goods that private businesses normally send to the country being punished.

5. Loans, Credits, and Currency Manipulations. Rewards may include favorable tariff rates and quotas, granting loans (a favorite reward offered by the major powers today to developing countries), or extending credits. The manipulation of currency rates is also used to create more or less favorable terms of trade between countries.

6. Blacklists. Governments use blacklists to identify firms that are doing business with the target country. Most Arab governments have maintained blacklists against foreign firms doing business with Israel. Those firms are then officially precluded from conducting commercial operations or arranging deals with the firms or governments of the Arab countries in question.

7. Licensing. Export and import licenses can be granted or denied. This is a particularly effective way of controlling exchanges of particular types of goods—a selective reward or coercion—without undertaking the risks and costs of general boycotts and embargoes. Most industrial states maintain licensing to prevent or control trade in nuclear fuels.

8. Freezing Assets. In a relatively open world economy, companies, governments, and individuals often maintain assets abroad, in the form of investments, bank accounts, and real estate. If sufficiently large, such assets can become hostages. In 1979, the United States froze the assets of Iran, amounting to almost $12 billion, in retaliation for the invasion of the U.S. embassy in Teheran. The promise to unfreeze the assets was an important component of the settlement the United States and Iran finally reached to end the diplomatic hostage-taking incident.[2] The U.S. and Great Britain froze the assets of Iraq when it invaded Kuwait in 1990, and in 1993 several governments applied the same pressure against the military government of Haiti.

[2]For details, see M. S. Daoudi and M. S. Dajani, *Economic Sanctions: Ideals and Experience* (London: Routledge & Kegan Paul, 1983); David Baldwin, *Economic Statecraft* (Princeton, N.J.: Princeton University Press, 1985).

9. Granting or Suspending Aid, Including Military Sales or Grants. Flows of finance, technical know-how, technology, services, and military *matériel* have become important components of international relationships. Donors can manipulate the quantities and types of foreign aid for political purposes, and the granting of military capabilities, or their withdrawal, can have critical impact on target states' ability to defend themselves or to prosecute other aspects of foreign policy.

10. Expropriation. Governments may seize ownership of assets belonging to companies of the target state. Usually this is done for economic purposes, but on occasion, expropriation—or its threat—has been used as leverage in attempting to change the domestic and/or foreign policies of the target state.

11. Withholding Dues to an International Organization. Some governments seek to influence the actions and practices of international organizations, as well as other states. When those organizations take votes or actions that challenge the interests of some of their members, those who object can threaten to or actually withhold financial support from the organization. Until 1988, the Soviet Union refused to contribute to the financial support of various UN peacekeeping operations, and the United States in recent years has withheld or reduced the size of its dues to the United Nations, the International Labor Organization, and the United Nations Educational, Scientific, and Cultural Organization (UNESCO).

Governments choose among the various repertoires according to the goals being pursued, the types of economic vulnerabilities faced by the target state or organization, the comparative costs and risks of various techniques, and, since dependence is often a bilateral proposition, assessment of the possibility of countermeasures. Purely symbolic acts may be good for feelings of rectitude or for propaganda, but when sanctions such as boycotts or embargoes will lead to massive unemployment at home, or where the target can easily obtain alternative sources of supply, the decision becomes difficult. In a number of cases, the short-term costs will outweigh the unpredictable long-range benefits. As we will see below, estimating the costs and possible successes or failures of economic coercion is no simple matter. We should consider, as well, that economic techniques of influence are usually employed as just one of many instrumentalities organized to achieve certain objectives. These would include diplomacy, propaganda, and—as in the case of American support for the anti-Sandinista *Contras* in Nicaragua—covert, interventionist, and military techniques.

Economic Rewards and Coercion in Operation

The postwar history of Soviet-Yugoslav relations provides one example of how economic instruments, along with propaganda, military threats, and diplomacy, played an important role in Soviet attempts to influence developments in Yugoslav foreign and domestic policies. Shortly after World War II, the Soviet Union began to assist the new Communist regime in Yugoslavia by enlarging trade and providing small amounts of economic assistance. In 1948, however, Tito was expelled from the Communist bloc because of his unorthodox domestic policies and unwillingness to submit to Soviet domination in ideological and political matters. The Yugoslav heresy resulted in threats of military action by Hungary, Romania, and Bulgaria; vituperation in Communist propaganda organs; and excommunication of the Yugoslav Communist party from the Cominform. The Soviet Union also organized a Communist bloc embargo and boycott against Yugoslavia. The embargo was potentially an effective technique of punishment because in 1948 Yugoslavia sold over 50 percent of its exports to the bloc and received 95 percent of its imports from the same source.[3] The unfavorable economic impact of the embargo and boycott on Yugoslavia was short-lived, however, because Tito was able to turn to Italy and Great Britain for compensating trade agreements and to the International Bank for Reconstruction and Development for development loans.

After Stalin's death, Soviet-Yugoslav relations intermittently deteriorated and improved. In 1955, the Soviet government signed a barter pact for the exchange of commodities worth over $79 million annually. In the same year, the USSR canceled a $90 million Yugoslav debt and attempted to get other Eastern European countries to expand trade with the former heretic. Between 1955 and 1958, the bloc countries committed themselves to loans of nearly $500 million in attempting to win back Tito's loyalty and subservience to Moscow on ideological matters. Tito continued to vacillate, however, and each time in 1957 and 1958 that he emphasized his independent Communist line, the Soviet government either threatened to cut off assistance or conveniently "delayed" granting new loans. In May 1958, Premier Khrushchev suspended negotiations on loans that amounted to nearly $300 million. By 1963, Tito had mended relations with the Soviet Union—without compromising his independence—and was amply rewarded through new trade agreements and increased Soviet loans.[4]

Considering Yugoslavia's economic dependence on the Soviet bloc, Communist economic punishments and rewards should have succeeded; they failed simply because Yugoslavia turned to the West and found alternative supply and market sources.

A case where alternatives were not available and economic sanctions succeeded occurred in the relations between Finland and the Soviet Union in 1958. After parliamentary elections in 1958, in which Finnish Communists won over one quarter of the seats, a coalition government headed by a Social Democrat was formed. This government did not include among its ministers any Communists, however. The Soviet government held a traditional enmity against all Finnish Socialists, and the Soviet premier wasted no time in announcing his displeasure and distrust of the new Finnish prime minister. The Soviet government also objected to inclusion of Conservatives in the new cabinet. Various articles in the Soviet press pointed to the "rightist" government as symptomatic of a general resurgence of "reactionary" forces in Finland and criticized these "rightists" for attempting to destroy friendly Soviet-Finnish relations and planning to increase Finnish trade with the West at the expense of Soviet-

---

[3]Harold J. Berman, "The Legal Framework of Trade Between Planned and Market Economies: The Soviet-American Example," *Law and Contemporary Problems*, 24 (1959), 504.

[4]Figures are provided in Berman, "The Legal Framework of Trade," and in Robert Loring Allen, *Soviet Economic Warfare* (Washington, D.C.: Public Affairs Press, 1960), pp. 16, 41.

Finnish trade. To indicate that it would not tolerate such political leadership in a neighboring country, the Soviet government began to apply a number of diplomatic and economic pressures:

1. The Soviet ambassador in Helsinki returned to Moscow and was not replaced. The ambassador left without paying the usual courtesy farewell visit to the Finnish president.
2. The Communist Chinese ambassador left Helsinki for Peking for "consultations."
3. The Soviet government refused on "technical grounds" to sign an agreement with Finland covering fishing rights in the Gulf of Finland.
4. Talks that had proceeded smoothly on the Finnish lease of a Soviet canal (in former Finnish territory) for shipping logs to the Gulf of Finland were suspended.
5. A Finnish trade delegation scheduled to travel to Moscow to negotiate the 1959 trade agreement was left waiting without a Soviet invitation.
6. In November 1958, the Soviet government abruptly halted all trade with Finland, including goods that had already been ordered. This action had the most serious effect, since many Finnish metal and machinery products sold in the Soviet Union could not be sold in Western markets because their prices were not competitive. In other words, since no alternative markets existed, the Soviet cancellation of trade threw many Finnish workers out of jobs, adding to an already severe winter unemployment problem.

Recognizing that such economic pressures could seriously damage the Finnish economy and worsen an already serious unemployment problem, several members of the cabinet resigned; and a new government more to the liking of the Kremlin was eventually formed. The Soviet economic pressures in this case worked very efficiently.[5]

That power and influence do not flow only from the major powers or those who possess military might is illustrated in the oil embargo imposed by the Arab countries against Western Europe, Japan, and the United States in 1973. During two previous Arab-Israeli wars, the Arabs had attempted to use oil as a means of reducing Western support for Israel. These efforts did not succeed, however, because the Arab governments were divided among themselves on whether to apply an embargo and because the United States, a surplus oil producer until the late 1960s, was willing to share oil purchases from Venezuela with the Europeans. By 1973, in contrast, all the industrial countries were highly dependent upon Arab oil, and the Arab governments presented a united front against all governments that had publicly sympathized with Israel's diplomacy or war-making efforts. The Arab governments, once the October War started, cut back production by 5 percent each month and placed a complete embargo against the United States and the Netherlands. The purpose was clear: to place the industrial countries into a severe energy shortage that could be avoided or overcome only if the targets changed their policies toward Israel. It was hoped, too, that the most vulnerable countries, such as Japan and Great Britain, would urge Washington to reduce its commitment to Israel and take a more sympathetic stand toward the Arabs' claims for land lost to Israel in the 1967 war and for

---

[5]K. J. Holsti, "Strategy and Techniques of Influence in Soviet-Finnish Relations," *The Western Political Quarterly,* 17 (1964), 63–84.

the plight of the Palestinian refugees. Japan complied first and publicly disclaimed its policy of diplomatic support for Israel. The European governments, through a series of individual symbolic and policy actions, eventually induced the Arabs to lift the embargo against them. The American position on the Middle East also changed, if very quietly. While military support for Israel did not end, Secretary of State Henry Kissinger began to urge the Israelis to make concessions on key territorial issues. As the American commitment to "peace" through concessions by both sides developed, the oil began to flow again—although at vastly increased prices. Arab solidarity, the extensive dependence of the industrial countries on Arab oil supplies, and lack of stockpiles were the conditions that enabled the "weak" successfully to confront the "strong."

Cuban-American relations during the period of the Castro regime provide many examples of American efforts to use economic instruments of policy for foreign policy objectives. President Eisenhower's decision in March 1960 to organize an emigré force to overthrow Castro gave the Cuban leader, who had learned of the decision several months later, justification for arranging what had not been possible earlier—namely, switching his army's dependence from Western to Communist sources and undertaking major programs of expropriation of American assets in Cuba. Cuba was also dependent upon Western sources and facilities for oil until the American secretary of the treasury persuaded American and British companies to refuse Castro's request for refining Soviet oil. Castro thereupon obtained a commitment from the Communist countries to supply all of Cuba's oil, confiscated American and British refineries, and refused to pay the $50 million owed for earlier deliveries. When Castro began to expropriate other American-owned property in Cuba, the State Department and Congress retaliated by ordering reduction of quotas on the import of Cuban sugar. This hardly subtle measure of punishment failed to deter the Cuban government from adopting an increasingly anti-American foreign policy. Since American officials feared that Castro might also seek to spread revolution beyond the island, they took measures to isolate the regime diplomatically and economically from the rest of the Caribbean and Central America. This involved an American embargo on the sale of weapons to Cuba; the State Department simultaneously implored other Western governments to control shipments of military goods to the Castro regime. Later, when the Cubans had made explicit their association with the Communist bloc, the American government instituted a complete economic and travel boycott of Cuba. Since the United States had traditionally purchased a majority of Cuba's exports, this punishment seriously crippled the Cuban economy until the Cubans found alternate markets for their products (mainly sugar) in the Soviet Union, Eastern Europe, and Communist China. Although American measures helped to isolate Cuba, they did not bring down the Castro regime, so more pressures were applied. First, the United States imposed an almost complete embargo on exports to Cuba, excluding only food and medicines. Next, American diplomatic officials continued to urge other governments to reduce their exports to the island. To help enforce this policy, the State Department prohibited all foreign vessels carrying goods to Cuba from stopping in American ports to pick up new cargoes on their return voyage. This policy was not received with enthusiasm among foreign shipping companies but did reduce further trade between Europe and Cuba. As a final measure, the American government in 1964 imposed controls even on the export of food and medicine to the island.

How effective was the application of these economic punishments? Cuba briefly became economically isolated from its traditional trading partners, and its economy suffered seriously. Spare parts for automobiles, trucks, boats, and industrial plants became unavailable, and most economic indicators (except unemployment) moved steadily downward. Food rationing was also imposed. Combined with several poor sugar harvests, the punishments created almost disastrous effects on the Cuban economy.

But, as in the case of Yugoslavia, the Cubans were eventually able to find alternative markets for their exports and some sources of supply to keep the economy running. By granting large loans and providing shipping facilities, the Communist-bloc countries prevented the total collapse of Cuba's economy. At times, Castro might have wondered whether he could keep his regime in power, but the punishments did not modify his aggressively anti-American behavior. The economic isolation of Cuba from the West might have succeeded in one respect, however. Since the Cuban government had to allocate so many resources and so much human energy into keeping the economy from collapsing, it may not have had either the time or resources to undertake major programs of external expansion, revolutionary agitation, or subversion in Latin America.

Another problem with the policy of punishment was that it failed to get total support from European countries. As with many international embargoes and boycotts, unless all the participating countries perceive the target as a threat to their own security or economic interests, they are not likely to sympathize completely with policies that deprive their business community of economic opportunities. In the case of the embargo on Cuba, many NATO allies and nonaligned governments thought that the United States was too sensitive to Castro's presence in Cuba. They did not greet the embargo with much enthusiasm; and when, for example, British and French companies made major sales to Cuba, their governments made no attempts to prevent the fulfillment of the trade contracts. With the collapse of communism, Cuba's sources of supply and markets diminished dramatically. Since 1990 it has suffered serious economic difficulties, and the United States has insisted that the tight economic blockade of the island will stay in place until President Castro dismantles Cuba's socialist economy and removes himself from office.

In 1966, the United Nations, acting under its authority to impose economic sanctions in the event of a threat to peace, breach of the peace, or act of aggression, voted to require member states to desist from trade of certain types of commodities with Rhodesia. The purpose of the sanctions was to force the white supremacist government of the colony (which had declared independence from Great Britain without British consent) to arrange for a transition to independence in which all citizens, not just whites, would vote for a government. The practical effect of the objective was to require a minority white government to disband itself, in order for the vast black majority of Rhodesia to take political power. Degrees of compliance with the sanctions order varied greatly from country to country and, as is often the case of trade prohibitions against market economies, traders quickly found ways to obtain needed goods through third parties. South Africa provided considerable assistance and various forms of black market activities dampened the immediate impact of trade cut-offs. In the short run, the sanctions appeared unproductive, particularly since their immediate effect was to create a "rally-round-the-flag" frame of mind among many of the whites, as well as blacks. In the long run, however, the boycotts and embargoes contributed significantly to an unemployment problem in Rhodesia—particularly among blacks—that encouraged enrollment in the black guerrilla forces. The guerrilla war forced the Smith regime eventually to relinquish power to the black majority. The sanctions, in short, were effective in symbolizing the illegitimacy of the Smith regime and in helping to create conditions for a politically effective guerrilla movement.[6]

Does the systematic application of economic pressures to achieve political objectives normally succeed? These cases would indicate that results may be as unfavorable to the state employing the pressures as to the target of the punishments. Soviet pressures forced Yugoslavia to become more reliant upon the West, a turn of events hardly in keeping with Soviet interests; later offers of rewards were undoubtedly instrumental in obtaining Yugoslav support for selected Soviet foreign policy proposals. The case of Finland and the Soviet Union illustrates the effective use of economic and other pressures to bring about changes in the internal politics of the target country. In the cases of the oil embargo and Cuba, the results were mixed. Although Cuba may have had to concentrate on problems of survival as opposed to revolutionary activity abroad, there is little doubt that American pressures literally forced Cuba to become dependent upon the Soviet bloc. And in the short run, the oil embargo forced some Western governments to change policies toward the Middle East conflict. But in the long run, the dramatic Arab action alerted the major oil-consuming countries to their highly dependent condition. Multibillion-dollar programs to develop alternative sources of supply, as well as emergency oil-sharing schemes, have resulted, so that presumably, in future cases of embargo, the importers of oil will be less vulnerable.

In the case of economic pressures by the major powers against each other, the record indicates a fairly high probability of failure. In the late 1960s the Soviet government attempted to "punish" West Germany for the latter's attempts to play off one Warsaw Treaty Organization member against the other through lucrative trade arrangements. Soviet efforts, primarily through the manipulation of promised gas deliveries, proved useless. The Jackson-Vanik amendment to the United States foreign trade bill of 1974 made extension of most-favored-nation treatment to the Soviet Union conditional upon significant liberalization of the Soviet authorities' policies on Jewish emigration. The Soviet response to this tactic was to toughen emigration policies substantially, leading to a significant decline in Jewish emigration. This effort to link trade "carrots" with Soviet domestic policies was also a notable failure. In 1980, the United States imposed a number of economic sanctions against the Soviet Union for the latter's invasion of Afghanistan in December 1979. These measures included a partial grain embargo, halting the delivery of high tech-

[6]Baldwin, *Economic Statecraft*, p. 199.

nology items such as oil drilling equipment, and, most dramatically, boycotting the 1980 Olympic Games in Moscow. The costs to the Soviet Union were not negligible. The grain embargo was predicted to reduce meat supplies, as the Russians had to divert more of their wheat to immediate necessities such as bread and away from feeding cattle. Oil drilling equipment was important to a Soviet industry that was facing declining production rates. And the American Olympic boycott, supported by some key countries such as West Germany, Japan, Canada, and Kenya, reduced the significance of Soviet gold medals. But in terms of bringing about a change in Soviet policy in Afghanistan, the economic pressures must be judged as a failure. To the USSR, the costs of pulling out of Afghanistan and seeing the collapse of its client government in that country far outweighed the costs of the American embargoes and boycotts. As a symbolic action, a form of protest, and a warning, the U.S. economic coercion had better results, however. It could help deter Afghanistan-style interventions in the future, and it was probably the best option, compared to doing nothing or taking military action.

What of various forms of economic pressures that are more subtle and directed against regimes that are highly dependent? Richard S. Olson studied such techniques, as they have been applied by major powers against developing countries.[7] A prime example would be the "silent blockade" imposed by the United States against Chile after the election of the Marxist president, Salvadore Allende, in 1970. Details of this case are outlined in the next chapter. Here, it is only important to acknowledge that a variety of "quiet" economic pressures had serious economic consequences in Chile, without engendering a nationalist, anti-American response.

Olson outlines a variety of steps that can be taken that are far less dramatic than embargoes and boycotts but which nevertheless can have significant negative consequences for a developing economy. These include (1) declines in foreign investment; (2) delays in delivery of spare parts; (3) snags in licensing or other technology transfers; (4) shutting off or reducing bilateral and multilateral loans and credits (as the United States did in Chile); and (5) refusal to refinance existing debts. Although not a direct cause, "quiet" economic coercion, according to Olson's studies, can lead to economic decline, and such decline, where dependency and social conflicts are already notable, can result in change of regime and ultimate compliance with the major power's economic objectives. Cases where such cause-effect relationships seem impressive include Ghana, 1969 to 1972; Brazil, 1962 to 1964; Peru, 1965 to 1968; and Chile, 1970 to 1973. In all but the Ghanaian case, the United States was the source of the "invisible blockade." And in each of the South American cases, the regime which resulted from internal turmoil was more amenable to American economic policies in the region.

These examples illustrate some of the failures and successes of economic coercion in recent international relationships. But in order to make generalizations, we have to rely on more than selected examples. In a major study of economic sanctions between 1914 and 1984, Gary Hufbauer and Jeffrey Schott catalogued a total

---

[7]For details, see Richard Stuart Olson, "Economic Coercion in World Politics: With a Focus on North-South Relations," *World Politics*, 31 (July 1979), 471–94.

of 103 cases, including community sanctions organized under the auspices of the League of Nations or the United Nations.[8] They defined sanctions as deliberate, government-inspired threats or withdrawals of "customary" trade or financial relations. The measures were specifically aimed at altering the foreign or domestic policies of the targets. Among the most common purposes or objectives of economic sanctions were (1) to end or deter military adventures by the target (e.g., American pressure on Egypt in the early 1960s to remove its interventionary force from Yemen); (2) to weaken the economic capacity of the target, and thereby its ability to sustain a large military program (e.g., NATO's embargo of strategic goods and technology applied against the Soviet Union and China during the Cold War); (3) to destabilize a foreign government (e.g., the United States attempts to overturn the Sandinista regime in Nicaragua from 1985 to 1990); (4) to achieve a host of more specific goals such as the promotion of human rights or preventing the spread of nuclear weapons (e.g., Canadian economic sanctions against South Africa from 1986 to 1993, and cessation of the supply of nuclear fuels to India and Pakistan from 1974 to 1976); and (5) to obtain compensation in cases of the target's expropriation of foreigners' property.

As we would expect, the great powers have largely monopolized the use of economic means of coercion. Of the 103 cases, the United States, alone or with its allies, applied them 68 times. Great Britain employed them twenty-one times, the Soviet Union ten times, and among the smaller states, the members of the Arab League used them four times in the last two decades.

Hufbauer and Schott's analysis was largely animated by the question whether or not economic sanctions work. It is difficult to assess the overall record because such an evaluation must be considered in the context of the probable costs and outcomes of alternative techniques of influence. From the point of view of stated primary objectives—and we must remember that often multiple objectives are involved—economic sanctions have had at best a mixed record, especially when applied against great powers. But, as Baldwin reminds us, *all* foreign policy objectives are seldom achieved fully.[9] Politics is as much a search for approximations as absolutes, and when secondary objectives are achieved, at least not all is lost. But the main problem is one of comparative costs; that is, the costs and benefits of sanctions versus other courses of action, including doing nothing. Given the American objective of isolating, weakening, and bringing down the Castro government, were there less costly and more effective alternatives to the embargoes and boycotts? What would have been the costs and anticipated consequences of an American invasion of the island? Or of doing nothing? Could Stalin have bought the ideological orthodoxy and national subservience of Yugoslavia in 1948 by offering greater economic rewards, enhanced propaganda programs, or diplomatic persuasion? Keeping in mind these caveats and recognizing that sanctions are usually employed together with other means of reward or coercion, Hufbauer and Schott concluded that economic sanctions helped bring about a desired change in the target's domestic or foreign poli-

---

[8]In *Economic Sanctions Reconsidered: History and Current Policy* (Washington, D.C.: Institute for International Economics, 1985).

[9]Baldwin, *Economic Statecraft*, pp. 122–30.

cies in 36 percent of the 103 cases. They were most effective (53 percent) when used to destabilize a government, and least effective (20 percent) in demonstrably weakening the military capacity of an adversary.[10] One of the most interesting findings was that economic coercion is significantly more effective when applied against friends, strong trade partners, and allies than against hostile adversaries. Another finding was that since 1973, sanctions have had lower rates of success than earlier. Finally, they have been significantly more effective when applied against countries with weak, unstable economies.

Economic coercion is most likely to be effective when the following conditions are met:

1. The economic relationship between the coercer and the target is highly asymmetrical in terms of vulnerabilities.
2. Alternative sources of supply or markets are not readily available to the target.
3. The target does not have the technology or resources to fashion substitutes for those items it can no longer import from the coercer.
4. The target country contains a large disaffected population (e.g., blacks in South Africa) that can increase its political leverage due to the economic costs of the boycotts and embargoes.
5. The costs of applying the sanctions to the coercer are significantly less than those suffered by the target.
6. There is little international sympathy for the government of the target.
7. The attempts at economic coercion are coupled with other techniques of statecraft.
8. The economy of the target is already weak, characterized by high unemployment, low investment, severe inflation, and the like.

Economic Warfare

Economic warfare refers to those economic policies used as an adjunct to military operations during wartime. The objective is either to hold or conquer strategic resources, so that military forces can operate at maximum strength, or to deprive the enemies of these resources, so that their capacity to fight will be weakened. Economic warfare was used extensively by all the major combatants in both world wars, as none of the belligerents except the United States could raise and sustain a modern army and feed a civilian population by relying solely on its own resources. Mutual dependence thus becomes even more crucial during wartime. Using examples primarily from World War II, one can summarize the techniques that have been used as follows:

1. Blockade.   In both wars, the Allies established blockades around Germany in an attempt to "starve" it of materials necessary to prosecute the war. Although rules of international law specifically prescribe the nature and extent of legitimate blockades, the Allies frequently disregarded these rules and blockaded even neutral vessels carrying nonmilitary goods to Germany. In World War II, the Allied blockade was applied at first only to Germany; but as the European neutrals—Sweden, Switzerland, Portugal, Turkey, and Spain—were able to sell and ship valuable raw materials and manufactured goods to the Third Reich, the blockade authorities also threat-

---

[10]Hufbauer and Schott, *Economic Sanctions Reconsidered,* p. 80.

ened to impose strict controls over them. Two American economic warfare officials have described the function and problems of blockades as follows:

> It was theoretically possible for us to cut off all imports from overseas [to the neutrals] in order to force a neutral country to cease its trade with Germany, or to use our blockade controls as a club to compel a neutral citizen to follow a pro-Ally line. In practice, however, the situation was seldom so simple, and open pressure of this sort was rare. Some of the reasons for Allied hesitation . . . involved complex considerations of international law, political and diplomatic expediency, and military strategy, as well as economic warfare pure and simple.
>
> The possibility of such sanctions was always there, however, implicit in all our relations with the neutrals. It was our major source of bargaining power, and in the later stages of the war, as our military and diplomatic position became stronger, it was used more and more effectively to curb neutral aid to our enemies. We prevented Spain from importing essential petroleum products until the Franco government curbed exports of tungsten to the Axis and made other concessions. We employed similar pressure less dramatically against Sweden and Switzerland, to force cuts in their economic aid to Germany.[11]

2. Blacklist.   Since much of the trade between the neutrals and Germany was conducted by private firms, Allied pressures were exerted directly on them. One device that has been used effectively by governments (sometimes in peacetime as well) against private traders is the blacklist. During World War II, these lists, drafted by British and American economic warfare authorities, included the names of Axis nationals or agents located outside enemy territory, as well as neutral or even Allied citizens who were conducting trade with the Axis states. Persons on the list were considered enemies of the United States or Great Britain; their property was subject to seizure; no American or Briton could deal commercially with them in any way; and they could not travel or ship any of their commodities to occupied Europe through any routes or facilities under Allied control. These people could carry on trade with the Axis only if they were prepared to lose all markets in the Allied countries and face the confiscation of their goods during shipment to Europe.

3. Preemptive Buying.   Most of the Allied program was concentrated on trying to outbid German agents for materials that the neutrals were willing to export to either side. Where the blacklist was not feasible, the Allies paid greatly inflated prices for commodities in order to keep the Germans from purchasing them. With combined American and British financial resources, the Germans were hard-pressed to match the exorbitant prices the Allies were willing to pay. But preemption did not always take the form of legal market operations. Sometimes it involved smuggling, hijacking, flooding mines, tying up transportation, sabotage, or any other means that would deprive the Axis of needed supplies.

4. Rewards.   Economic warfare during World War II used rewards as well as threats and punishments, although it was normally a combination of the two. Sweden, for example, was promised access to Allied oil and other products, which its armed forces desperately needed, when it agreed to reduce the export of bearings

---

[11]David L. Gordon and Royden Dangerfield, *The Hidden Weapon: The Story of Economic Warfare* (New York: Harper & Row, 1947), p. 13.

to Germany. By selling Spain the materials it needed to maintain its economy, the Allies succeeded at least partially in reducing Spanish economic dependence upon Germany.

The success of economic warfare, according to Gordon and Dangerfield, has been difficult to assess. Certainly the German armies did not collapse as a result of shortages created by Allied preemptive buying and the blockade. But the Germans did have to pay high prices for some needed items, and they had to invest other material and human resources in creating substitutes. Had the materials been readily available, the Germans could have freed thousands of people and millions of dollars for other purposes.

Economic Rewards in Foreign Policy

Most of the economic techniques of statecraft discussed in the previous pages have been used in a coercive fashion, as forms of punishment to increase costs for target states, or to deprive military opponents access to sources of supply during wartime. Some of the techniques, particularly those involving uses of tariffs, quotas, and licenses, can also be employed as rewards by granting greater access to markets. These are relatively unimportant forms of rewards, since they cannot often be manipulated with ease. Tariff structures, for example, are often set through multilateral negotiations, and the General Agreement on Tariffs and Trade includes fairly restrictive conditions under which nations can raise or lower them. The most important forms of economic rewards are foreign aid and military assistance.

Foreign aid—the transfer of money, goods, technology or technical advice from a donor to a recipient—is an instrument of policy that has been used in foreign relations for centuries. In the past it was used primarily for short-run political advantages rather than for humanitarian purposes or long-range economic development. In the eighteenth century, statesmen regularly offered their foreign counterparts "pensions" or bribes of cash for the performance of certain services. Governments also used military aid in the form of subsidies and donations of men and equipment.

The British were the first to formulate aid policies designed primarily to foster long-range economic development. Through the Colonial Development and Welfare programs beginning in the 1930s, they sought to diversify the economies of their colonies and prepare them for both political and economic independence. After World War II, the United States displaced Britain as the main dispenser of foreign aid, first to help reconstruct war-damaged European economies—for which the Americans spent $12 billion in the European Recovery Program—and later to assist the developing countries in creating modern military forces and begin the long road to economic viability and industrialization. After Stalin's death in 1953, the Soviet Union joined the expanding group of states donating funds and technological advice to Asia, Africa, and Latin America. Today, almost all industrialized states and oil-producing countries contribute at least some of their wealth and skills. Most of the programs are bilateral undertakings negotiated directly between donors and recipients; there are also multilateral aid organizations and programs, such as the International Bank for Reconstruction and Development and the United Nations Technical Assistance Program, through which industrialized members of the organization make available personnel with special skills to the developing members. Although these multilateral programs have grown rapidly during the last decade, their value still constitutes less than 25 percent of the aid that flows from industrialized countries to the Third World.

The amount of aid disbursed through bilateral and multilateral aid programs continues to grow. In the 1990s, total volumes surpass $60 billion annually, with about 80 percent of this figure donated by the Western industrial countries. The Arab oil-producing states have also been major but declining aid donors. Members of the former Soviet bloc provide about 10 percent, but during the economic and political turmoil of the 1990s, they have become net importers of capital and technical assistance. China remains a minor aid donor, most of it channeled to Africa and a few neighbors.

The figures in Table 8-1 underline several long-range trends in aid donorship. In 1980, the United States was the largest single donor, but it was surpassed in 1992 by Japan. The American proportion of total aid has also declined steadily. France and Germany combined, for example, provide more aid than the United States. The amount of aid from the Arab oil producers has also declined, although Saudi Arabia continues to provide more than some industrial countries. OPEC's Arab members have created their own multilateral aid agency (Arab Fund for Economic and Social Development), with Egypt and Turkey as major recipients of assistance.

One measure of largesse is the amount that economic assistance programs represent as a portion of a country's total economic production. The figures show that Saudi Arabia contributes far more of its wealth to other countries than do any other

TABLE 8-1

Official Development Assistance, Selected OECD and OPEC Donors ($ billion U.S.)

COUNTRY	1980	% GNP	% TOTAL AID	1991	% GNP	% TOTAL AID
United States	7.1	0.27	26	11.4	0.20	20.5
Japan	3.4	0.32	12.4	11.0	0.32	19.7
France	4.2	0.63	15.4	7.5	0.62	13.5
West Germany	3.6	0.44	13.2	6.9	0.41	12.4
Great Britain	1.9	0.35	7.0	2.5	0.32	4.5
Netherlands	1.6	0.97	5.9	3.3	0.88	6.0
Sweden	1.0	0.78	3.7	2.1	0.92	3.8
Canada	1.0	0.43	3.7	2.6	0.45	4.7
Australia	0.7	0.48	2.6	1.0	0.38	1.9
Total OECD	27.3			55.5		
In 1980 $	27.3			35.2		
Saudi Arabia	3.9	5.16	53.7	1.7	1.44	64.0
Kuwait	1.0	3.52	10.4	.4	N/A	14.4
United Arab Emirates	1.0	5.08	10.4	.6	1.66	21.0
Libya	0.2	0.60	2.1	.1	0.09	0.9
Algeria	0.3	0.90	3.1	.05	0.01	0.2
Total OPEC	9.6			2.9		
In 1980 $	9.6			1.7		

N/A = Data not available.

Source: World Bank, *World Development Report* (New York: Oxford University Press, 1993).

governments. Among the industrial countries, the Netherlands and Sweden are significantly above average, devoting almost 1 percent of their GNPs to aid programs. By contrast Japan, a wealthy society, contributes only about one third of a percent. The United States has the lowest figure.

The political/strategic motivations of many donors are apparent from distribution figures (not reported in Table 8-1). Most American economic assistance is directed to a few key allies and clients such as Israel, Egypt, Turkey, and Pakistan. World Bank figures show, in fact, that less than 20 percent of American aid goes to the lowest income economies. The same pattern held for the Soviet Union when it was a major aid donor: Most went to allies and clients such as Cuba, Vietnam, Afghanistan, and Ethiopia. India is one of the few nonaligned states that receives significant sums from all the largest donors.

Finally, there is an ever-increasing number of donor countries. Until the 1970s, most donors were the great powers, a few wealthy members of the British Commonwealth, and several smaller European countries. Today, all of the members of the OECD, a significant proportion of OPEC, and some of the emerging industrial nations such as Korea, Brazil, and Singapore constitute the aid donor community. The result is that recipients have an increasing variety of sources of supply and skills, thus reducing their dependency and vulnerability.

From the perspective of recipients, there are other significant trends. The total amount of aid transfers in 1991 amounted to $7.20 per capita among the recipients. Yet there are immense variations from country to country. In the same year, the figure for Zambia was $63; for Indonesia it was $9.30. Some countries, such as Mozambique and Somalia, get 50 percent or more of their GNP from aid transfers. Economic collapse would be likely without them. Most countries in Africa, in fact, rely heavily on external sources of capital and technical assistance.

Spread among all recipients, however, the total amount of aid represents only about 5 percent of capital needs. Except for the highly dependent countries, most developing nations rely on their own resources for economic progress. The combination of a larger number of donors, the generally low proportion of GNP represented by aid, and some significant growth rates among many recipients suggests the conclusion that the manipulation of aid programs for political purposes will be generally less effective in the future than it has been in the past. Those who remain tied to a single, significant donor retain substantial vulnerability; those who have diversified their aid contacts are in a stronger bargaining position.

Types of Foreign Aid

There are four major types of bilateral aid programs: (1) technical assistance; (2) grants and commodity import programs; (3) development loans; and (4) emergency humanitarian assistance. Technical assistance, the least costly of all types of aid programs, is designed to disseminate knowledge and skills. Personnel with special qualifications from industrialized countries go abroad to advise on a wide variety of projects. Some famous American programs and organizations such as "Point Four" and the Peace Corps have been associated with projects such as malaria control, land reclamation, road construction, and development of medical, water, and educational facilities. Some programs have also emphasized public administration—developing managerial and organizational skills—and law enforcement capabilities. The impact of these programs can be very great within specified areas, while the costs are relatively modest. Significant advances in agricultural output, such as the effects of the "Green Revolution" in India, and in the development of fisheries (thus increasing protein consumption) have been notable successes in recent decades.

Grants and commodity import programs were the preferred methods of transferring capital and goods until the late 1950s. These were outright gifts for which no economic repayment was expected. This was the form in which most American funds for the European Recovery Program (Marshall Plan) and the Mutual Security Program were dispensed. Under Public Law 480, also known as the "Food for Peace" program, the United States annually distributed abroad millions of tons of surplus food for which the recipients paid low prices in their own currencies rather than in dollars. The payments were usually kept in special funds that were lent back to the receiving country for economic development projects. These transactions constitute at once grants, subsidies, and loans.

Except for military hardware and emergency aid, most donors no longer provide outright grants. The largest component of bilateral aid programs, as well as the development programs of the World Bank and International Monetary Fund, is loans. Technically, this is not aid at all, since repayment is expected. Loans constitute essentially a commercial transaction, particularly insofar as most donors insist that goods and services made available through the loans be purchased from them. This is the meaning of the term *tied aid*; it is a requirement that fosters business and future commercial relations between donor and recipient, and thus serves the economic interests of the donor. The "tie" may even include a requirement that the recipient use only the shipping services of the donor for its purchases. The premium of the loan thus constitutes the difference between the prices paid for the goods and services from the donor and the prices the recipient would pay were there competitive international bidding for the goods and services.

Most bilateral loans do constitute aid to the extent that their interest rates and other terms of repayment are more liberal than those available through normal commercial banking institutions. Many donors provide one-, five-, even ten-year grace periods with no repayment, concessional interest rates, and generous opportunities for rescheduling payments. In some instances, donors have simply written off loans for countries facing severe debt burdens.

Most governments have special funds available for emergency humanitarian relief programs. These are designed to provide assistance in the event of natural calamities such as earthquakes, floods, and volcanic eruptions. Official government assistance is frequently complemented by donations of funds and labor by voluntary organizations, such as the International Red Cross, and broad public appeals. During the famine in Ethiopia and Sudan from 1984 to 1986, and in civil war–torn Somalia in 1992, people in many countries, including some in the Third World, provided hundreds of millions of dollars of relief supplies and logistical support through their donations.

Objectives of Foreign Aid Programs

Official foreign aid programs, like many foreign policy undertakings, have multiple objectives. Their long-range and general purpose is to assist developing countries to mobilize their economies for sustained economic growth, to help alleviate the worst manifestations of poverty, malnutrition, and lack of social opportunities, and, as a strategic payoff, to bring about political stability—meaning decrease in civil strife and international conflict. The hypothesized cause-effect relationships do not have much empirical support (for example, the incidence of internal violence is most probable when countries are developing rapidly, not when they are poorest), but they constitute part of the mythology surrounding most aid programs.[12]

Whatever general long-range goals underlie aid programs, the major donors usually have more immediate concerns. This is indicated by the patterns of aid distribution. Most Soviet aid went to its allies and clients in the Third World; most OPEC assistance goes to Muslim countries; and a large proportion of American assistance is directed to key allies or friends such as Israel (not a developing country), Egypt, and Turkey. Statistics on aid distributions reveal clearly that *need* as a criterion of aid ranks significantly behind political and strategic considerations; at least this is the case for the major powers' aid program. Smaller donors, such as Sweden, Canada, and the Netherlands, distribute a higher percentage of their aid programs to low-income countries than do the major powers; their political motivations are less evident.

Overall, donors use aid primarily to demonstrate sympathies for recipients' domestic or foreign policies, to symbolize alliance relationships, and to support friendly regimes that face difficult times, either economically or from local oppositions. Byproducts of aid relationships include political influence and possible leverage (the threat to reduce or terminate aid programs), developing future commercial opportunities with the recipient, and, finally, the satisfaction of seeing aid projects being immediate social and economic improvements at the grass-roots level.

Whatever the short- and long-run objectives of aid donors, recipients are sovereign states with their own priorities and purposes. Donors cannot dictate exactly how their loans or grants will be used, and the needs perceived by the recipients may not always coincide with the expectations of donors. This is the reason why we are often reminded of the waste involved in aid programs, corruption, and the prevalence of huge projects that appear to have little long-range economic payoff. Considerations of prestige and visibility may loom much higher in the minds of some recipient governments than in the hopes of the donors. Gaudy projects spread around the country illustrate to the local people that their government is pursuing modernization and is capable of possessing the symbols of an industrialized, powerful nation. In Hans Morgenthau's words:

> Prestige aid has in common with modern bribes the fact that its true purpose, too, is concealed by the ostensible purpose of economic development or military aid. The unprofitable or idle steel mill, the highway without traffic and leading nowhere, the airline operating with foreign personnel and at a loss but under the flag of the recipient

[12]See Hans J. Morgenthau, "A Political Theory of Foreign Aid," *The American Political Science Review,* 56 (1962), 301–9.

country—all ostensibly serve the purpose of economic development and under different circumstances might do so. Actually, however, they perform no positive economic function. They owe their existence to the penchant, prevalent in many underdeveloped nations, for what might be called conspicuous industrialization, spectacular symbols of, and monuments to, industrial advancement rather than investments satisfying any objective economic needs of the country. . . . They perform a function similar to that which the cathedral performed for the medieval city and the feudal castle or the monarch's palace for the absolute state.[13]

Some regimes are so weak and the nations they attempt to govern so internally divided that they must be propped up by the contributions of foreign governments. This subsistence aid, both economic and military, is designed to provide the basic minimal services that keep a political order intact. Even India, which does not possess many spare resources, distributes economic and military aid to Nepal and Bhutan for the purpose of helping local governments cope with the elementary needs of modernization. An important byproduct for India is maintaining diplomatic influence in these small neighboring countries, which act as a buffer between India and China. Perhaps helping a regime to remain in power is the ultimate reward in foreign policy.

Aid donors frequently attach conditions to their programs. Many deal with the *domestic* policies of recipients. Some conditions are economic: The recipient is expected to adopt certain fiscal, tax, subsidy, or other measures in order to increase national economic performance or open up the economy for foreign investors. Other conditions are more obviously political; their purpose is to help sustain regimes in power or to help remove them. In recent years, the human rights records of recipients have also come under donor scrutiny. For example, the Development Assistance Committee of the OECD (representing twenty-one industrial countries) in 1991 specified that foreign aid should encourage democratization and respect for human rights, and that grants should be targeted to reduce corruption and wasteful military expenditures among recipients. In 1993 the Canadian government explicitly adopted a policy that all foreign aid distributions would take into consideration the human rights record of recipients. Those countries with a record of systematic human rights abuses would be denied certain types of assistance.

The European Community, Japan, the United States, and Canada have also become major donors of assistance to the former socialist states. While most of this aid has been in the form of loans to purchase donors' goods and services—in other words, a form of subsidy for, let us say, American farmers—the assistance has been conditional upon the recipients' commitment to democratic reforms and the institutionalization of private market economies. Those governments considered to lag behind in such political and economic transformations have had aid commitments reduced or held up pending better performance. In all of these examples, the purpose of aid has been to assist recipients, but always in the expectation that they will alter their domestic policies in some way consistent with the interests and values of donors. During the Cold War, the usual criterion was the degree to which the re-

[13]Ibid., pp. 303, 304.

cipient was "soft" on communism. In the 1990s, the criteria are mostly economic and/or improvement in the quality of governance of the recipient.

Examples of the manipulation of aid to sustain or alter recipients' *foreign policies* are equally plentiful. During the Sino-Soviet conflict in the 1960s, the Soviet Union withdrew aid personnel and terminated extensive aid programs to China because of the latter's stand on certain ideological issues, as well as their border disputes. In 1993 the United States threatened to "review" its aid programs to Russia unless the Russians agreed to stop selling certain kinds of military hardware to countries such as Iran.

Foreign aid can also be used to *reward* parties for their domestic or foreign policy behavior. A recent example is the formation of a group of donors to supply assistance to the Palestinians who in 1993 signed a mutual recognition and peace plan with Israel. Donors recognized that the prospects for successful implementation of the peace plan would increase to the extent that the Palestinians in Gaza and the West Bank saw some tangible economic rewards. The rejectionists' local support would, in contrast, diminish. All the rejectionists could offer was further bloodshed and sacrifice. Behind the offer of large amounts of aid to the PLO, however, lurked the possibility of aid cut-off if the Palestinians did not meet their commitments under the agreement. This is just one of many ways that leverage is created in international politics.

Table 8-2 summarizes the multiple objectives of the various kinds of bilateral aid programs. Because aid programs have such diverse motives and expectations, it is difficult to evaluate their effectiveness. We will make some tentative observations at the conclusion of this chapter. Here it is enough to reemphasize that aid as an in-

TABLE 8-2
Donor Objectives of Bilateral Economic Aid Programs

TIME FRAME	PRIMARY OBJECTIVES	EXPECTED BYPRODUCTS	TYPES OF DONORS
Long-range	1. Economic development; reduce poverty	1. Political Stability	1. Western
	2. Eventual self-sufficiency of recipient	2. Democratization	2. Western
		3. Speed up historical trend toward socialism	3. Soviet Union
		4. Arab/Muslim solidarity	4. Arab (OPEC)
Medium-range	1. Maintain diplomatic presence in recipient	1. Commercial, trade opportunities	1. All donors
	2. Symbolize friendships and commitments to, and support for, recipients	2. Enrich bilateral relations	2. All donors
	3. Maintain access to, and influence over, recipients' domestic and foreign policies		3. Great powers
Immediate	1. Change recipient's current domestic or foreign policies	1. Obtain support for donor's foreign policies	1. Great powers
	2. Sustain a recipient's regime in power	2. Protect donor's core objectives	2. Great powers
	3. Humanitarian emergency relief	3. Possible future good will	3. All donors

strument of policy has many purposes, most of which can be seen as long-range rewards that help the development programs of the recipients. But with the exception of emergency humanitarian assistance, aid programs are also designed to support the short-run political objectives of donors, as well as those of recipients. These may be only symbolic or various ways of "showing the flag" abroad, but in all instances, expected byproducts, at least of the bilateral programs, serve either or both the commercial and diplomatic interests of donors. As suggested, the distribution of aid in the world today demonstrates that political and security considerations underlie a large portion of the aid programs, particularly those of the great powers.

Military Sales and Transfers

Long before technical assistance and foreign aid programs came into fashion after World War II, governments had assisted friends and allies with the provision of military aid—*matériel,* training facilities, and officers—or with subsidies and loans with which to purchase military goods and services. Today, many states, including all the major powers, transfer arms and spare components or provide training facilities for a variety of recipients. Aside from the former Soviet Union and the United States, which have traditionally maintained the largest military aid programs, countries such as Syria and Libya funded programs for arming and training military groups of the Palestine Liberation Organization; Cuba provided similar assistance for Sandinista Nicaragua, Angola and Mozambique; India supports minor programs for the armed forces of Nepal and Bhutan; and a number of countries in the 1960s provided *matériel* and training facilities for the fledgling armed forces of Tanzania.

The United States launched the largest military assistance programs in 1949 through the Military Defense Assistance Act (1949). The Military Assistance Program (MAP) provided loans or grants of military equipment, spare parts, and mechanical training to the governments of over fifty countries. Under the program's auspices, more than 500,000 officers and enlisted personnel from approximately 100 countries have come to the United States for training, or have received instructions in their home countries.[14] The aggregate for sales or grants of weapons, economic support, training, and provision of spare parts reached the sum of almost $8 billion annually under the Reagan administration (from a figure of $3.8 billion in 1977). Most of the increase was for military sales credits. The largest recipients of this assistance have included Israel, Egypt, Greece, Turkey, Spain, Pakistan, South Korea, and Saudi Arabia.

The Soviet Union maintains similar programs, averaging about $3.5 billion during the 1970s and 1980s.[15] The Soviet Union's major recipients included Libya, Algeria, Iraq, Ethiopia, Angola, and Syria.

The international demand for arms has not been met solely by grants, gifts, and free training programs. There is an immense global arms market, supported and

[14]Data and details in Ernest Graves and Stephen A. Hildreth, Eds., *U.S. Security Assistance* (Lexington, Mass.: Lexington Books, 1985), Chap. 1.

[15]John F. Cooper and Daniel Papp, eds., *Communist Nations' Military Assistance* (Boulder, Colo.: Westview Press, 1983), p. 44.

fueled by regional conflicts such as those in the Middle East, and by the birth of new states which, upon becoming independent, had little more than local police forces to maintain security. As relatively nonindustrialized countries, most have had to purchase their military hardware from major suppliers abroad.

The international arms trade is large, but it has been decreasing as a result of the end of the Cold War as well as the settlement of some very costly local wars. In the 1990s, the arms bazaar racked up volumes worth in excess of $50 billion annually, with about 60 percent of the sales going to developing countries. The Soviet Union, the United States, France, China, Great Britain, and Germany were the primary sources of supply. In the 1990s, the volume has decreased by almost 50 percent, but sales to volatile regions such as the Middle East and the Aegean (Greece and Turkey) continue at high levels. In 1991, the main sellers were the United States ($11.2 billion), Russia ($3.9 billion), Germany ($2 billion), and China ($1.1 billion).[16] Other significant sellers were Brazil, the former Yugoslavia, Great Britain, and France. Major importers were India ($2 billion), Turkey ($1.6 billion), Israel ($1.6 billion), Greece ($1.1 billion), Saudi Arabia ($1.1 billion), and Thailand ($1.1 billion). In the aftermath of the 1991 war against Iraq, the Gulf States purchased new arms amounting to several billion dollars, mostly from the United States. While developing countries continue to purchase arms, often at the expense of critical domestic requirements, most of the sales are registered in the Middle East, and between Pakistan and India. Elsewhere, arms sales have been declining significantly from the exceptionally high levels of the 1980s.

There are multiple purposes for these arms sales, but the most prominent seems to be for the suppliers to create local balances of power and, it is hoped, decrease the probabilities of war in those regions. Whether or not these purposes are achieved is a matter of considerable debate. Those identified with increased sales argue that "stability" is reached through balancing. Others argue that such sales only exacerbate tensions and, if war should break out, make it more destructive. There is unfortunately little empirical evidence on either side of the argument, since we cannot know of wars that did not occur because of arms sales, and of those that did occur, it is difficult to establish that arms sales were a contributing factor. Whatever the case, certainly one of the lessons of the 1991 Gulf War was that its cost was immeasurably increased because of Soviet, British, German, and American arms sales to Iraq in the 1970s and 1980s. One of the observations among critics was that the competitive arms sales to Saddam Hussein had created a Frankenstein which ultimately led to the Gulf War. That war cost in excess of $50 billion, a sum much greater than all the profits reaped through arms sales to Iraq during the preceding decades.

Although most arms transactions are nominally commercial, suppliers' governments anticipate a number of benefits from selling military hardware. Some are purely economic, such as improving balance of payments situations, reducing the costs per unit of producing arms for oneself, maintaining employment in the domestic arms industry, and stimulating research and development with potential in-

---

[16]Figures are from Stockholm International Peace Research Institute, *Yearbook*. New York: Oxford University Press, 1992.

dustrial benefits. From the point of view of international politics, however, there are more important strategic-diplomatic rewards potentially available. These include gaining access to a country for building military bases or gaining transit, refueling, and other privileges; helping to sustain friends and allies against domestic and external threats; visibly making a commitment to one's clients; preempting opponents' penetration of the market; possibly increasing diplomatic influence; creating regional balances of power; and the like.[17]

Just as in economic assistance, military aid provides donors with often overt and sometimes more subtle forms of control over the recipients. Arms by themselves are seldom sufficient for deterrent or offensive purposes. They require spare parts and maintenance; if conflicts between recipients and donors develop, the latter can cut off the supply of parts, as the United States threatened to do against Pakistan during its war against India in 1965. Military assistance provides the donor with leverage of various forms. For this reason a growing number of recipients have sought to diversify their source of supply. For example, India, which was a major beneficiary of Soviet military assistance programs, in recent years has been purchasing weapons from a variety of sources, thus helping to ensure that replacements and spare parts would be available during times of crisis. It has also developed a significant arms industry of its own. From the recipients' point of view, reliability of supply is a major consideration. The donor, in contrast, has a major interest in restricting the competition.

Conclusion

Economic techniques of persuasion, whether as rewards and supports, or as potential or actual deprivations, have advantages and disadvantages. Compared with the use of force, they are probably much cheaper for the donors, even if their results are less immediate. Economic rewards are undoubtedly necessary in an era when many regimes are constructed on shaky foundations, and when numerous states are torn by secessionist and other disaffected movements. Many developing states, in brief, could not survive without external assistance, both economic and military. Economic rewards and military assistance have become standard techniques of symbolizing donors' support for recipients and have not infrequently constituted the difference between the demise and survival of regimes. Rewards, of course, have their costs, namely the dependence that develops between recipients and donors. Enhanced leverage for donors is the consequence.

These forms of dependence have declined over the years, however, as more and more players enter the economic and military aid game. Recipients have been able to locate an ever-greater number of potential donors and, where necessary, have obtained arms on the open market. Middle-ranked countries with few concrete security interests in the Third World make up an increasingly significant part of the sources of foreign aid. Very few recipients in the Third World remain dependent upon a single source, for either economic or military support.

---

[17]Keith Krause, "International Trade in Arms," *Background Paper #28,* Canadian Institute for International Peace and Security (Ottawa, March 1989), p. 4.

Questions for Study, Analysis, and Discussion

1. What conditions are necessary to increase the probabilities that economic sanctions will achieve their objectives?
2. Other than changing the domestic and/or foreign policies of targets, what other goals can be achieved by economic sanctions?
3. Draft the profile of a country that would be particularly vulnerable to economic sanctions.
4. Should aid donors require recipients to adhere to certain human rights standards in their domestic politics and policies? If so, what does this mean for the concept of sovereignty?
5. Most of the sales or grants of arms are justified on the grounds that they enhance "national security." In what ways is this the case? Are some arms sales likely to decrease national security?
6. In your view, what sorts of "strings" or conditions should be attached to foreign aid programs?
7. Is most foreign aid motivated primarily by charitable or humanitarian concerns? What sort of evidence do you need to establish the main purposes of aid?
8. In what ways do foreign aid programs promote the interests of donors rather than recipients?

Selected Bibliography

Adler-Karlsson, Gunnar, *Western Economic Warfare, 1947–1967: A Case Study of Foreign Economic Policy*. Stockholm: Almqvist & Wiksell, 1978.

Baldwin, David A., *Economic Statecraft*. Princeton, N.J.: Princeton University Press, 1985.

Bobiash, Donald, *South-South Aid: How Developing Countries Help Each Other*. New York: St. Martin's Press, 1992.

Cassen, Robert, *Does Aid Work? Report to an Intergovernmental Task Force*. New York: Oxford University Press, 1986.

Daoudi, M. S., and M. S. Dajani, *Economic Sanctions: Ideals and Experience*. London: Routledge & Kegan Paul, 1983.

Doxey, Margaret, "International Sanctions," in *World Politics: Power, Independence, and Dependence*, eds. David G. Haglund and Michael K. Hawes. Toronto: Harcourt Brace Jovanovich, 1990, pp. 242–61.

———, "Sanctions in an Unstable International Environment: Lessons from the Gulf Conflict," *Diplomacy and Statecraft*, 2, (1991), 208–225.

Graves, Ernest, and Stephen A. Hildreth, eds., *U.S. Security Assistance*. Lexington, Mass.: Lexington Books, 1985.

Hirschman, Albert O., *National Power and the Structure of Foreign Trade*. Berkeley: University of California Press, 1945, Chap. 2.

Hoadley, J. Stephen, "Small States as Aid Donors," *International Organization*, 34 (Winter 1980), 121–38.

Hufbauer, Gary Clyde, Jeffrey J. Schott, and Kimberly A. Elliott, *Economic Sanctions Reconsidered: History and Current Policy*, 2nd ed. Washington, D.C.: Institute for International Economics, 1990.

Huntington, Samuel P., "Foreign Aid for What and for Whom," *Foreign Policy*, 1 (Winter 1970–1971), 161–89.

Kapstein, Ethan Barnaby, ed., *Global Arms Production: Policy Dilemmas for the 1990s*. Lanham, Md.: University Press of America, 1992.

Krause, Keith, Weapons Between States: The Arms Trade in Global Politics. Cambridge: Cambridge University Press, 1991.

Leyton-Brown, David, ed., The Utility of International Economic Sanctions. New York: St. Martin's Press, 1987.

Looney, Robert E., and Craig Knouse, "Predicting the Success of Economic Sanctions," *Jerusalem Journal of International Relations,* 13 (1991), 40–65.

Lumsdaine, David H., Moral Vision and International Politics: The Foreign Aid Regime. Princeton: Princeton University Press, 1993.

Martin, Lisa, Coercive Cooperation: Explaining Multilateral Economic Sanctions. Princeton, N.J.: Princeton University Press, 1992.

McKinlay, Robert, and Anthony Mugham, Aid and Arms to the Third World: An Analysis of the Distribution and Impact of U.S. Official Transfers. London: Pinter, 1984.

Miller, Robert, ed., Aid as Peacemaker: Canadian Development Assistance and Third World Conflict. Ottawa: Carleton University Press, 1992.

Nincic, Miroslav, and Peter Wallensteen, Dilemmas of Economic Coercion: Sanctions in World Politics. New York: Praeger, 1984.

Olson, Richard S., "Economic Coercion in World Politics: With a Focus on North-South Relations," World Politics, 31 (July 1979), 471–94.

Organization for Economic Cooperation and Development (Oecd), Twenty-Five Years of Development Cooperation: A Review. Paris: OECD, 1985.

Sewell, John W., "Foreign Aid for a New World Order," *Washington Quarterly,* 14 (Summer 1991), 35–45.

Zimmerman, Robert F., Dollars, Diplomacy, and Dependency: Dilemmas of U.S. Economic Aid. Boulder, Colo: Lynne Rienner, 1993.

Chapter
9

Clandestine Actions and Military Intervention

It was a theme of Chapter 3 that social and technological changes in the political units that make up any international system may have important consequences for the processes that occur within that system. Development of sovereign states and simultaneous decline of other forms of political organization—such as city-states—brought forth new techniques, institutions, and norms of statecraft in the seventeenth and eighteenth centuries. Just as gunpowder helped destroy the foundations of the feudal order, and the growth of dynastic absolutism reduced the international political influence of the Catholic Church, mass media of communication, rapid transportation, a complex and interdependent international economy, weapons technology, and mass politics have helped to diminish the "impermeability" of the territorial state. The possibility of obtaining informal or nonofficial access to foreign societies has grown as the size of government missions abroad—once confined to a few diplomats and consular agents—has increased. Short of building walls or iron curtains, most states have relatively few effective means of preventing outside infiltration or the movement of funds, propaganda, or military *matériel* from abroad. States with lengthy frontiers passing through forests, jungles, deserts, or mountains are often incapable of preventing outside penetration.

To achieve objectives, defend interests, or promote social values abroad, governments may—instead of sending diplomatic notes or making military threats—infiltrate foreign voluntary organizations, sponsor strikes and riots, create political scandals, attempt a *coup d'état;* or, on their own territory, organize, train, and arm a group of foreign dissidents and then send them home to conduct guerrilla warfare or subversion. States that are relatively weak in conventional military capabilities are able to mount campaigns of external subversion and infiltration at little cost, either in funds and *matériel* or in the risks of military retaliation by the target country. In our era, the capacity to penetrate politically and quasi-militarily into foreign societies may be as important as a capability to make military threats, impose naval blockades, or carry out conventional military assaults. In particular, weak states (militarily speaking) with revolutionary or expansionist objectives may attain objectives by conducting clandestine actions abroad. Certainly a state is no longer powerful *only* if it possesses a vast conventional or nuclear military establishment.

Clandestine activities are not, of course, entirely a product of the modern age. They were organized as well in China during the Chou dynasty, in ancient Greece, and particularly in fifteenth-century Italy. In the dynastic international system of the eighteenth century, intervention for ideological principles seldom occurred, and monarchs were not generally concerned with the domestic policies of their brethren.[1] Louis XIV occasionally conspired to interfere in British constitutional issues, but the main concern over other states' internal political life was with questions of inheritance and royal affairs. Dynasts concluded military alliances, as in the Triple Alliance of 1717, to place certain candidates on foreign thrones, and indulged in all sorts of court intrigues for the same purposes. But there were no attempts to subvert foreign societies in the name of ideological principles, and governments had not yet developed the techniques of mass persuasion, terrorism, or guerrilla warfare commonly observed today in international politics. States were, on the whole, "impermeable" to outside influences.

Intervention became more common in the nineteenth century, particularly as a method of promoting or putting down revolutions inspired by liberal and nationalist movements. The wars of the French Revolution were revolutionary wars, often different in objectives and techniques from the wars in the preceding century. Conservative regimes, following their victories over Napoleon, assigned themselves the obligation to intervene militarily against societies that were experiencing domestic liberal revolutions. Later in the same century, the United States frequently sent contingents of marines to Latin American and Caribbean states to influence the course of local politics and revolutions. In general, however, the principle of nonintervention in other states' internal affairs was observed with considerable regularity.

The record of the twentieth century is a contrast. In 200 revolutions that occurred during the first half of the century, some form of foreign intervention took place in almost one half; in approximately 50 of these revolutions, *more than one* outside power intervened. Soviet Russia, Nazi Germany, and Fascist Italy interfered in their neighbors' domestic political life with unprecedented regularity. Since the end of World War II, the record has not improved. Most international crises of the period have started basically as *internal revolutions* or civil disturbances, in which one or more external states eventually became involved. This list would include Greece,

---

[1]See Edward V. Gulick, *Europe's Classical Balance of Power* (Ithaca, N.Y.: Cornell University Press, 1955), pp. 62–65.

China, Algeria, Laos, Lebanon, Jordan, Iraq, Kuwait, Yemen, the Congo, Vietnam, the Dominican Republic, Czechoslovakia, Cambodia, Ethiopia, Angola, Sri Lanka, Afghanistan, Nicaragua, and Panama. Istvan Kende, in one study of revolution, war, and intervention, records sixty-seven "internal regime" wars between 1945 and 1970.[2] Outside intervention by one or more powers occurred in fifty-two (77 percent) of these civil disruptions.

In a more recent study of twelve civil wars during the 1970s, Duner counted acts of intervention by fifty different countries.[3] These ranged from outright invasion to financial support and military training for either the government forces or the rebels. Of the sample of civil wars, only one was carried out completely free from military intrusion by outsiders.

The major powers have the longest history of military intervention abroad. Using rigorous criteria to define military intervention, Tillema and Van Wingen have identified seventy-one military interventions by the United States, the Soviet Union, France, and Great Britain between 1946 and 1980. To these data we would add the United States' intervention in Grenada (1982), Nicaragua (1982 to 1990), and Panama (1989), and the French intervention in Chad during the early 1980s. Of the seventy-one, Britain undertook thirty-seven (mostly in colonial territories or dependencies), France seventeen, the United States ten, and the Soviet Union seven. More than 80 percent of these interventions were preceded by civil or foreign-directed violence within the target country; over 80 percent were also great-power responses to requests by the target governments to intervene on their behalf. Since they were requested by established governments, they were legal in the strict sense; about two thirds of all great power interventions in the postwar period were so defined. If we count all military interventions, including United Nations peacekeeping efforts, there were 269 between 1945 and 1989. The use of armed forces, for a wide variety of purposes is a common form of interstate influence.[4]

While historically the great powers have been the most active interventionary states, with some dramatic military actions that lengthened into protracted wars, the newer countries have not refrained from this type of activity to achieve or defend their objectives and interests. In Duner's study of twelve civil wars, for example, thirty-four out of the fifty countries that intervened in one fashion or another were developing nations. The list of interventionary activity in which the major powers have not been the primary actors is long and growing. In the Middle East, Libya has been active in various subversive and terrorist measures and interventions, with an attempt to overthrow the government of Sudan in 1976 and the military intervention in Chad in the 1980s as prime examples. Egypt was involved militarily in the Yemen civil war in the 1960s, while Algeria, until the mid-1960s, served as perhaps the most well-organized and widespread center in Africa for financing, organizing, and training for-

[2]Istvan Kende, "Twenty-Five Years of Local Wars," *Journal of Peace Research*, 8 (1971), 5–22.

[3]Bertil Duner, *Military Intervention in Civil Wars: The 1970s* (Aldershot, Hampshire: Gower, 1985), p. 68.

[4]Herbert K. Tillema and John R. Van Wingen, "Law and Power in Military Intervention," *International Studies Quarterly*, 26 (June 1982), 220–50; Tillema, *International Armed Conflicts Since 1945: A Bibliographic Handbook of Wars and Military Interventions*. (Boulder, Colo.: Westview Press, 1991).

eign nationals in the techniques of clandestine political action, subversion, and guerrilla warfare. Syria today maintains a large contingent of troops in Lebanon, and Saudi Arabia has funded and in other ways supported rebels in Afghanistan, and helped bankroll Iraq's war against Iran in the 1980s.

In sub-Saharan Africa, various forms of subversion and intervention have been commonplace. Until President Nkrumah was ousted in a *coup d'état* in 1966, Ghana had both party and government organizations charged with ideological and military training of opposition groups from Nigeria, Togo, and the Ivory Coast. Ghana was seriously implicated in subversive attempts in both the Ivory Coast and Nigeria in the early 1960s. In a popular move, Tanzanian troops invaded Uganda in 1979 to help terminate the tyranny of Idi Amin. South Africa frequently resorted to military forays into neighboring states for a variety of purposes. Cuba intervened to support the Angolan government (previously the M.P.L.A. faction of a coalition government) and Ethiopia with thousands of troops.

All of these examples illustrate the extent to which foreign and domestic politics are linked. The various forms of interventionary activity we are about to describe are symptomatic of the permeability and fragility of states, particularly of the newer states which rest on weak foundations of legitimacy and political capability.

Although major military interventions and systematic subversion may be easy enough to identify, there are other forms and types of interventionary activities that are less obvious. What do we mean by the term *intervention*? Recall that in a system of sovereign states, a major principle or norm is that each of the units in the system will have *exclusive* authority within its domestic political realm. Each state will develop and apply its own laws, and each will determine who will govern, how they will do it, and for how long. If officials of state A run the internal affairs or choose the political leaders of state B, then B cannot be considered sovereign. An obvious example would be the situation in Eastern Europe until the death of Stalin in 1953. Up to that point, Stalin appointed and removed party and government leaders of the satellite countries much as he selected the personnel and policies of the Soviet Union itself. Indeed, in a few instances he even appointed Russians to top positions in Poland, Czechoslovakia, and Hungary. Although those countries maintained their status as sovereign states, in reality they were modeled upon a colonial pattern.

The concept of intervention is not, however, adequately defined with such examples. What of the case where a government does nothing to affect the fortunes of a civil war abroad, and thereby implicitly assists the rebels? Did not President Bush's decision *not* to intervene on behalf of the Kurd rebels in Iraq in 1991 amount to intervention on behalf of Saddam Hussein? Or when a government trains and arms the police of a foreign country, thereby allowing its rulers to suppress any manifestation of dissidence or political opposition, is this not a form of intervention? The line dividing nonintervention from intervention is never clear and precise.

We will use the term *intervention* to designate any activity that *deliberately seeks to change the political leader(s) or the constitutional structure of a foreign political jurisdiction.*[5]

---

[5]Cf. J. H. Leurdijk, *Intervention in World Politics* (Leeuwarden, the Netherlands: Eisma B. V. Publishers, 1986), p. 114.

An additional component is that the activity is done without the consent or against the wishes of the legally constituted or recognized authorities.

Note that this definition favors the legitimacy of incumbent regimes and authority structures. This reflects the conservative bias of the nonintervention norm, and the general principle that who governs and how they govern is not a question that permits outside meddling. After the Thirty Years' War (1618–1648), which revolved around religious issues, the rulers of the day resolved that each prince would determine the religion of his subjects, and no outside power could reverse that decision. In this way, religion as a source of international conflict was successfully removed. The same idea underlies the norm enunciated in the charter of the United Nations and many other international documents—that governments shall not interfere in each other's internal affairs. Thus, in general, policies designed to support or sustain foreign authority structures are considered legitimate, while those that attempt to subvert them are usually classified as intervention.

Conditions That Encourage Intervention

There are many inconsistencies between national frontiers, on the one hand, and ethnic, religious, or linguistic frontiers, on the other. Many states today have only conditional viability; that is, they can exist only with the minimal support of all groups within their boundaries. If there are deep social cleavages, and some groups within the society feel oppressed, the likelihood of civil disturbances is increased. If these minority groups formulate a strategy that requires highly organized or violent political action, they are apt to need support from the outside. Local Communist parties obtained funds, propaganda, training, and sometimes weapons from the Soviet bloc; Afghan rebels during the 1980s received support from China, Pakistan, Saudi Arabia, Egypt, and the United States. Liberation movements in Rhodesia relied extensively on African governments for sanctuaries, funds, and *matériel*; and cliques of military leaders have sought foreign support and diplomatic recognition before or during their attempts to seize power. However much these connections may seem to promote purely local interests, there is little doubt that some sort of debt is created between the dissidents and the external patron. The patron can intervene on behalf of the group, faction, or clique, and after it gains power, use its influence with the group to secure its own foreign policy interests. Any unstable political order—and there are many in the contemporary world—offers opportunities for external intervention. We can suggest the hypothesis that the greater the ethnic, religious, economic, or ideological conflicts within a society, the greater the probability that an external goverment will intervene to serve its own interests.

Second, political loyalties, which have traditionaly extended to the predominant political institutions and authorities, whether clan, tribe, nation, or empire, are sometimes directed instead to external political entities or ideologies. In the seventeenth century, religious loyalties frequently superseded national or regional sentiments. Similarly, in the late eighteenth century, many European liberals welcomed French "liberation" even if it meant occupation by foreign troops and imposition of alien political institutions. Most people today accept the general proposition of primary loyalty to their own state ("My country right or wrong"), but there are many exceptions among people who do not accept the legitimacy of the order under which they live. The quip that the postwar French Communist party was neither Right nor Left, but East, illustrates the existence of transnational ideologies and loyalties directed essentially toward foreign states. This characteristic of modern politics naturally creates opportunities for foreign states, symbolizing these transnational ideologies, to become involved in other nations' domestic politics.

Third, the nuclear stalemate forced the major antagonists of the Cold War into the sector of irregular warfare and subversion, where the possibility of uncontrolled military escalation is slight. Blatant military aggression to achieve external objectives may face both universal diplomatic condemnation in the United Nations and instant nuclear retaliation, whereas establishment of client regimes and satellite states through subversion and intervention may be sufficient to achieve some objectives at a minimal cost of national capabilities and resources, and with much lower risks.

Fourth, governments with revolutionary external objectives are naturally prone to use for foreign purposes the same kinds of techniques their leaders successfully employed in gaining domestic power. While on one level the French revolutionaries, Soviets, Nazis, and others maintained "correct" diplomatic relations with foreign states, they simultaneously attempted to promote revolutionary activities against the social and political orders of those same states. Using "race" as the basis of political loyalty, Hitler proclaimed that a German's first duty was to the Third Reich, whether he lived in Austria, Czechoslovakia, or the United States. Communist governments also spoke of "normalization of relations," "peaceful coexistence," and noninterference in other people's affairs; but their ideological pronouncements and domestic policy statements clearly revealed that when it was in their interest to do so, they would promote, organize, or support foreign revolutions and rebellious uprisings.

Many governments with revolutionary external objectives or doctrinal commitments have created a variety of extra-diplomatic agencies, whose main functions are to dispense propaganda, organize agitation, train foreign revolutionaries, and direct subversion. Among the more prominent of these external revolutionary organizations were the Comintern, the Cominform, the German Abwehr, and various Soviet and Communist Chinese organizations and institutes that have or had the function of providing revolutionary and ideological training for foreign Communist leaders. Although not concerned with doctrines of revolution, the Central Intelligence Agency of the United States has been heavily involved in subversive activities abroad. These organizations sometimes play a major role in defining the objectives and techniques of states' foreign policies and on occasion literally usurp the functions of more traditional diplomatic institutions. During the early 1920s, when the Soviet government was actively engaged in organizing and supporting revolutionary activities throughout Europe, a number of the most important foreign policy decisions were made within the organization of the Comintern. Soviet diplomats were frequently bypassed as intermediaries between the Soviet government and foreign groups and had to remain content to deal with relatively unimportant aspects of Soviet foreign policy. In any event, the new revolutionary dimensions of foreign relations opened by the Bolsheviks required people with experience and outlook considerably different from those of professional diplomats. The directors of the Comintern and other external revolutionary organizations were primarily revolutionaries and agitators, concerned with the mechanics of organizing violence and political support for doctrinal ends, not people engaged with such mundane matters as trade relations, diplomatic conferences, passports, and territorial treaties.[6]

Finally, intervention is closely linked to hegemonial relationships; that is, the relationships of subordinate states to great powers. Leurdijk's study of military interventions shows clearly that most armed interventions in the twentieth century have been undertaken by the major powers against small states within their sphere of influence.[7] Of the fifty-one total armed interventions, the United States led with seventeen (33 percent), of which all but three took place in Central America and the Caribbean. Similarly, most Soviet armed interventions were directed not at capitalist states, but against contiguous members of the socialist "commonwealth." Intervention of the armed variety is thus characteristic of systems of regional domination. Fully 78 percent of Leurdijk's cases of armed intervention could be classified as hegemonial.

Although the norm of nonintervention remains firmly established as one of the foundations of the modern states system, great powers have frequently developed doctrines to justify their interventionary activities, particularly within areas of regional domination. The Roosevelt Corollary (1904) to the Monroe Doctrine was an explicit statement of intent—and duty—to intervene in Central and Latin America under specified conditions. It read: ". . . Chronic wrongdoing or an impotence which results in the general loosening of the ties of civilized society, may in America, as elsewhere, ultimately require intervention by some civilized nation, and in the Western Hemisphere the adherence of the United States to the Monroe Doctrine may force the United States, however reluctantly, in flagrant cases of such wrongdoing or impotence, to the exercise of an international police power." While subsequently repudiated, this doctrine was refurbished and modernized to justify American armed intervention any time a threat of "international communism" appeared in the region. Similarly, the Brezhnev Doctrine was enunciated in 1968, justifying Soviet armed intervention against any socialist state that was threatened by "international reaction." In 1989, the Soviet government repudiated the Brezhnev Doctrine, adopting instead what might be termed the Sinatra Doctrine, under which the Eastern European countries could all do it "their own way"; that is, select their own political system and leaders free of Soviet intimidation.

In the following pages we will discuss five forms of intervention: (1) various types of clandestine political actions; (2) terrorism; (3) demonstrations of force; (4) subversion; and (5) military intervention. Governments normally use combinations of these techniques simultaneously, but we shall keep them distinct in examining several cases.

---

[6]See Theodore H. Von Laue, "Soviet Diplomacy: G. V. Chicherin, Peoples' Commissar for Foreign Affairs, 1918–1930," in *The Diplomats, 1919–1939*, eds. Gordon A. Craig and Felix Gilbert (Princeton, N.J.: Princeton University Press, 1953), pp. 234–81.

[7]*Intervention in World Politics*, Chap. 7.

Clandestine Political Action

Probably the oldest technique of interference in other countries' internal affairs is the offering of bribes. In the eighteenth century, granting monetary rewards to foreign diplomats and government officials was a typical means of achieving diplomatic objectives. It was the accepted custom (although not publicized) to pay another dynast's foreign minister or diplomats a "pension"—that is, a bribe—for performance of certain services or maintenance of certain attitudes on key issues of the day. Documents from the French court of Louis XV reveal that between 1757 and 1769, France subsidized Austrian statesmen by over 82 million *livres*.[8] American covert political action abroad has included bribery, or at least the subsidy of subversive agents; British and French agents in the nineteenth century frequently gained control of future colonies by bribing native political leaders; and, of course, Nazi and Communist financing of clandestine political action in foreign countries is well documented.

Dissemination of covert propaganda—through unidentified radio transmitters, underground newspapers, or leaflets of unclear origin—can also be classified as clandestine political action that attempts to influence internal political processes in the interests of a foreign government. American propaganda in the crucial Italian provincial elections of 1975, for example, was not always clearly identified, and various other American actions on behalf of the Christian Democratic Party were of a clandestine nature.

Alexandr Kaznacheev, a Soviet diplomat who defected in 1960 in Rangoon, revealed some of the methods his government used to influence domestic political affairs in Burma. In addition to giving directions and helping finance the underground Burmese Communist party, the Soviet embassy in Rangoon would "plant" stories in the Burmese press and sometimes blackmail politicians. One of Kaznacheev's jobs in the Soviet embassay was to translate into English copies of articles he received from Soviet intelligence agencies in Moscow. Some of these articles would describe supposed American complicity in various campaigns of subversion in Asian countries (some were reasonably accurate, others pure fabrication); others contained generally anti-American materials. Soviet intelligence officials in Burma would then arrange through local agents to have the articles published in Burmese newspapers, especially pro-Communist publications. The newspaper would translate the article into the native language and sign it as coming from one of its "special correspondents" abroad. Thus a story conceived in Moscow became publicly identified as the testimony of on-the-spot reporters.[9]

Clandestine political action may also include assassination of government officials, diplomats, party leaders, or economic elites. Even though assassination is not a prevalent form of interfering in a country's affairs, foreign governments

---

[8]Hans Morgenthau, "A Political Theory of Foreign Aid," *The American Political Science Review*, 56 (1962), 302.

[9]Alexandr Kaznacheev, *Inside a Soviet Embassy* (Philadelphia: Lippincott, 1962), p. 172.

occasionally finance or encourage local dissident elements who are willing to do the job.[10]

Terrorism

Forms of terrorism are as varied as definitions. There are all sorts of groups of individuals who have vague revolutionary programs, the achievement of which is thought to require "revolutionary action" against class or ideological "enemies." We can recall the activities of the Red Brigade in Italy, the Bader Meinhoff group in Germany, and their counterparts in Japan and other countries. While many enemies are selected as discrete targets, other terrorist methods, such as detonating explosives in crowded shopping areas, are designed for maximum psychological effect. The victims are anonymous to the groups. The purpose is to demonstrate the state's inability to provide protection, to publicize the group's complaints or political agenda, or simply to create fear. We are less concerned with such groups than with the terrorist activities governments and their agents employ to achieve their purposes.

Proto-state groups including the Palestine Liberation Organization and innumerable secessionist movements (in Sri Lanka, the Punjab, Kashmir, and elsewhere) have used terrorist tactics for many years. Through them they receive notoriety (some praise, more commonly, condemnation), make headlines, and create a variety of propaganda impacts. For most of them, the ultimate purpose is secession and/or the creation of states. They employ terrorist techniques because they are relatively weak and do not have easy access to large supplies of arms or money for raising and training large armies. Terrorism is, in a sense, the strategy of the weak.

Governments such as Libya and Syria have harbored a variety of groups committed to radical solutions for the Middle East problem. They have provided training, funds, safe haven, and other forms of support, all in the cause of the "liberation" of Palestine, or in the service of the Islamic "revolution." State terrorism is used as an adjunct to, or substitute for, other techniques of statecraft. It serves foreign policy purposes and is also used by governments against their own citizens in the name of "national security."

Demonstrations of Force

Demonstrations of force are a form of diplomacy designed usually to coerce, but also to deter, and, in some instances, to show visible support for friends and allies. Unlike wars, demonstrations of force are highly circumscribed and carefully designed

---

[10]It seems to be an unwritten rule of modern international politics—particularly in countries with a Western tradition—that assassination of leaders of hostile states is not an acceptable manner of settling conflicts or achieving objectives. Even Hitler attempted only one assassination (the Austrian chancellor, Dollfuss, in 1934) of a government leader; during World War II, Allied leaders never became enthusiastic supporters of the German underground's plots on Hitler's life. Apparently American officials did organize a plan to assassinate Fidel Castro, but in the 1970s adopted a policy prohibiting assassination of foreign leaders. President Bush ruled out assassination as a means of removing Saddam Hussein during and after the coalition war against Iraq in 1991.

movements of military capabilities, whose effects are more psychological than physical. They are usually of short duration and do not involve continuing contests of violence. Measures such as military alerts, troop movements (usually unanticipated) in sensitive areas, and unusual naval maneuvers all constitute demonstrations of force. The latter, known as "gunboat diplomacy," have been particularly fashionable means of demonstrating resolve and conveying threats. Unlike interventionary activities, where developing countries have become frequent participants, demonstrations of force constitute techniques of influence employed primarily by the great powers. For example, of 133 instances of gunboat diplomacy from 1946 to 1978, 55 were recorded by the United States and the Soviet Union. The world's greatest naval power, the United States, accounts alone for about one third of the total postwar incidents. Indeed, the United States organized a high proportion of all demonstrations of force. Between 1946 and 1975, Americans employed armed forces more than 200 separate times, almost one half of which were various kinds of interventions or demonstrations designed to support or change the political authority structure or personnel of another country.[11] Two examples of demonstrations of force will illustrate the problems and prospects of these forms of support or coercion.

In 1961, a demonstration of force prevented supporters of the deposed Trujillo dictatorship from overturning the newly established provisional regime in the Dominican Republic. Throughout November, rumors had circulated in Santo Domingo that Trujillo's three sons (one of whom was commander-in-chief of the Dominican Forces) were ready to launch an assault on the provisional government, whereupon the United States sent twenty-two warships to patrol off the Dominican shore. The provisional government had not asked for this show of force, but it later acknowledged that the American action had prompted the Trujillos to flee the Dominican Republic and had averted a *coup d'état* and possible civil war. This was a classic case of force demonstration to sustain a regime.

The events in Czechoslovakia in 1968 illustrate force demonstration to alter authority structures. The Dubček government was well aware of Soviet, Polish, and East German antipathy to its reform programs. During the spring of 1968, Warsaw Pact joint maneuvers had taken place in Czechoslovakia, and there were persistent reports that the Soviet contingents were making their withdrawal, after completion of the maneuvers, unduly slow. During the summer, as relations between Prague and Moscow worsened, Soviet troops were mobilized near the Czech frontier and were sent on "maneuvers" for an extended period of time. The meaning of these military steps was of course clear to all the parties concerned: The Soviet Union might intervene militarily if the Dubček government did not abandon some reforms held most distasteful by the Soviet government. The demonstrations of force did not per-

[11]A quantitative analysis of demonstrations of force is in Robert Mandel, "The Effectiveness of Gunboat Diplomacy," *International Studies Quarterly*, 30 (March 1986), 59–76; Barry Blechman and Stephen S. Kaplan, *Force Without War: U.S. Armed Forces as a Political Instrument* (Washington, D.C.: The Brookings Institution, 1978). The types of military activity included establishing a presence ("showing the flag"), visits, patrol, reconnaissance and surveillance, movements of equipment or forces to a target, evacuation, blockade, and the like. Only 14 of the 215 incidents included the use of firepower. See Blechman and Kaplan, p. 54.

suade the Czech authorities to alter their policies, with the result that the Soviet government and four of its Eastern European allies intervened militarily and forced the Czechs to remove Dubček and his associates.

Subversion

The distinguishing feature of subversion is that it is organized, supported, or directed by a foreign power to precipitate a crisis that will lead to a change in the constitutional structure or personnel of the target. Two cases will illustrate the technique.

Nazi Subversion of Czechoslovakia, 1938–1939

The main target of Nazi subversion of Czechoslovakia was the 3.5 million German-speaking Czechs living in the Sudetenland. Shortly after Hitler became the German chancellor, some Sudeten Germans organized a political party (SDP, Sudeten German Party) under the leadership of Konrad Henlein. In his early political career, Henlein professed no desire to turn his party into an agency for carrying out Hitler's plans to take over Czechoslovakia. In a 1935 speech, he specifically declared that the German minority in Czechoslovakia would seek to protect its rights and interests only by cooperating with the Czech government and people. Less than seven years later, Henlein boasted publicly of the role that he and his party had played in subverting Czechoslovakia for Nazi Germany. He pointed out that his party, with the support of many Sudetenland Germans, had so completely destroyed internal stability and created so much confusion throughout Czechoslovakia that the entire country became "ripe for liquidation," according to Hitler's plans. Henlein attributed his success to having turned 3.5 million Sudetenlanders into 3.5 million National Socialists.[12]

Henlein's first step in preparing for eventual Nazi "liquidation" of the Czech nation was to mobilize the Sudeten Germans, many of whom were neither Nazis nor pro-German, to his cause. He accomplished that objective by deliberately provoking incidents with Czech authorities, whose reprisals led the Sudeten Germans to believe that they were being persecuted as a minority. The SDP held mass public meetings, circulated manifestos demanding "rights" for the German minority, and issued false or exaggerated propaganda stories about Czech political outrages against the Sudeten Germans. Once a split within the society was achieved through propaganda, it was exacerbated by giving the militant side a feeling of insecurity—in this case by claiming that the Sudeten Germans had to remain vigilant lest they be completely destroyed as a distinct nationality by the Czechs. Social perceptions of threat rose to such a high level that political compromise became unacceptable and was, of course, discouraged by the subversive party. Moreover, the Henleinists systematically penetrated Sudeten German social and cultural groups and purged their leadership of anti-Nazi or Czech sympathizers. By 1938, an important part of the German community in Czechoslovakia had become not only anti-Czech, but pro-Nazi as well.

---

[12]Vincent Urban, *Hitler's Spearhead* (London: Trinity Press, n.d.), p. 16.

Because some Sudetenlanders, particularly in rural areas, were reluctant to give their support to the SDP, the party also indulged in kidnapping and terrorism. The campaign—which was executed by a corps similar to the German SS, called the Frei-williger Schutzdienst (FS)—was directed against both uncooperative Germans and innocent Czechs. The terror against the Czechs caused reprisals, which permitted the Henleinists to charge the Czechs with further "atrocities" against the Sudeten Germans. While Henlein's party was active in its work of propaganda, infiltration, and terror, its leaders simultaneously wore a mask of political respectability by en-tering into formal negotiations with the Czech government to seek "honorable" guar-antees for the rights of the Sudetenlanders.

By 1938, it was apparent to the Czech government—if not to foreign diplo-mats—that Henlein and the Nazis did not wish any real accommodation, but sought only to create a situation that would warrant German diplomatic and military inter-vention and ultimate cession of the Sudetenland to Germany. On August 6, 1938, Henlein released a fateful order to his followers, inviting them to organize a series of violent acts that would give Nazi Germany an excuse for intervening. His own at-tempt to seize power one month later failed, and he was forced to flee to the Third Reich. Now without leadership in the SDP, German intervention had to proceed openly. As clashes between Czechs and Sudeten Germans increased in violence and frequency, causing repressive action by the Czech army, Hitler began a series of pro-paganda broadcasts throughout Europe, which sought through vitriolic language and gross exaggeration to create the impression that the Sudeten Germans were in-deed the subject of systematic persecution. Using a combination of military invasion threats against Czechoslovakia and reasoned appeals for "peace" against the West-ern governments, Hitler, through the Munich settlement, eventually annexed the Sudetenland to Germany; Czechoslovakia was left a rump state without viable mili-tary defenses.

Although the SDP and its paramilitary FS organized and conducted most of the infiltration, propaganda, and terror, the Nazi government of Germany made the policy decisions on the strategy of subversion. Henlein maintained contact with Himmler's SS through a German liaison officer in Czechoslovakia, and his lieutenants frequently traveled to Germany to attend festivals, fairs, and competitions, where they were exhorted and instructed by Nazi officials in the techniques of subversion.[13] Henlein himself agreed, in March 1938, to coordinate and clear all policy with the German Foreign Office and to submit all public statements (commands to his fol-lowers) to the Germans for approval. The Nazi government also supplied money and weapons to the FS for conducting its campaign of terror and intimidation, and mem-bers of the Gestapo occasionally crossed the frontier into Czechoslovakia to kidnap Czech citizens. Throughout the period, the German government also released an avalanche of propaganda directed at three distinct targets: (1) the Sudeten Germans, to rally them behind the SDP and against the Czechs; (2) the Czechs, to undermine their morale; and (3) other European countries, to create the impression that Ger-

---

[13]U.S. Department of State, Chief Counsel for the Prosecution of Axis Criminality, *Nazi Conspiracy and Aggression,* 1 (Washington, D.C.: Government Printing Office, 1946), pp. 544, 546.

many was intervening only to safeguard the rights of a minority. Finally, the German government took advantage of the violence in Czechoslovakia to threaten military intervention. Czechoslovakia did not collapse, then, solely through Henlein's activities. Subversion was used to create conditions that gave the Germans a pretext for threatening and finally carrying out annexation and military invasion.

American Subversion in Chile, 1970–1973

American use of force abroad to protect commercial interests, maintain "law and order," and prevent inroads by "international communism" has occurred frequently since the declaration of the Monroe Doctrine in 1823. One study lists more than 100 American military interventions in Latin America between 1806 and 1933.[14] Despite the signature of important articles in both the Rio Treaty (1947) and the Bogotá Charter (1948) prohibiting direct or "indirect" interference in Latin American countries' internal affairs, in practice American governments have never admitted that such principles could invalidate the right and responsibility of the United States to intervene, in case of external armed attack, Communist penetration, or even *anticipated* Communist activity, in Latin America's domestic politics. No Latin American government or revolutionary group has been immune from American subversion or intervention if that government or group allowed local Communists to play a prominent role in its activities; and any amount of Soviet, Chinese, or Cuban supply of arms, advisers, or technical assistance was usually defined as evidence of Communist subversion, and hence justification for countersubversion or intervention.[15] In short, American governments have historically reserved for themselves the right to decide what forms of domestic political change in Latin America are legitimate or illegitimate, tolerable or intolerable.

The American invasions of the Dominican Republic in 1965, Grenada (1982), and Panama (1989) are more recent cases of direct use of military force. Subversive techniques have also been used frequently. In the late 1950s, the United States employed a combination of economic and political pressures to help drive General Trujillo out of the Dominican Republic; and in the early 1950s, the United States, by financing and arming a group of Guatemalan emigrés in Honduras, organized the downfall of the Arbenz regime in Guatemala, which had earned Washington's enmity by expropriating idle lands of the United Fruit Company, importing weapons from East Germany, instituting social reforms, and allowing full civil liberties to reign in the country. In the 1980s the United States employed a combination of economic coercion and indirect intervention, via the *Contras*, in an attempt to overturn the Sandinista regime in Nicaragua.

The U.S. government's attempts to influence Chilean political life go back as far as 1964, when through covert means it helped finance the electoral victory of Eduardo Frei Montalva, a Christian Democrat with a reformist program, over the So-

---

[14]Cited in C. Neale Ronning, ed., *Intervention in Latin America* (New York: Alfred A. Knopf, 1970), p. 25.

[15]For quotations and the ideological underpinnings of American responses to Latin American social reform, see Melvin Gurtov, *The United States Against the Third World: Antinationalism and Intervention* (New York: Praeger, 1974), pp. 82–84.

cialist candidate, Salvador Allende. But Frei's victory had been narrow, and Allende's popularity was fully established during the campaign. Since, according to the Chilean constitution, Frei could not run again for the presidency in 1970, Allende was considered by most observers to be the strongest candidate in the elections of that year. The Central Intelligence Agency therefore posted a team in Santiago long before the elections, with instructions to keep the balloting "fair." The CIA operatives interpreted this to mean that they should try to prevent Allende's election. They ultimately spent approximately $3 million to buy votes, organize anti-Allende propaganda, and subsidize conservative Chilean news media, and a further $350,000 to bribe Chilean congressmen, who, under the constitution, had to ratify the results of the election. These efforts, of course, failed to prevent Allende's accession to the presidency.

The American government, fearing that Chile would serve as a base for South American revolutionaries (many activists and agents from China, the Soviet Union, Cuba, and Communist parties throughout Latin America flooded into Chile after the election), then set about to create conditions in Chile that would make it difficult for Allende to administer the country effectively. One American corporation with Chilean investments, ITT, channeled funds to anti-Allende groups, and put pressure on Washington to act directly to bring down the Allende government. Indeed, ITT went so far as to approach the CIA with a plan of its own, which would involve a *coup d'état* by the Chilean military forces. After the Chilean government nationalized American-owned copper mines and refused to pay what the companies demanded in compensation, the pressure by private firms on Washington increased, and the response became increasingly positive.

The means used to help create economic and social turmoil in Chile included economic embargoes and classic subversion. Between November 1970 and early 1972, the United States Export-Import Bank (under the Department of the Treasury), the Inter-American Development Bank, and the World Bank under American influence cut back credits and new loans to Chile. Private American banks quickly followed the lead of these lending institutions. Although European banks did renegotiate Chilean debts, the United States refused to enter into bilateral discussions with Allende's officials to take similar steps. The Allende government was hardly a good credit risk, but the evidence suggests that shutting off the flow of funds necessary to finance Chile's imports was basically a political decision designed to create further instability in Chile. The credit embargo did not have effects as severe as those of the total American embargo against Cuba, but it did create a shortage of spare parts in important sectors of Chile's economy (most of Chile's trucks, cars, and industrial machinery originally came from the United States). We can infer the political objectives underlying the credit embargo by the fact that it was lifted as soon as the military junta had disposed of Allende.

Direct activities by CIA agents in Chile complemented the muted and "low profile" economic pressures. Personally ordered by President Nixon, a secret attempt by CIA agents to organize a Chilean military *coup d'état* to prevent the installation of Allende as president failed.[16] The CIA then turned its attention not so much toward

---

[16]For details, see Thomas Powers, "Inside the Department of Dirty Tricks," *The Atlantic* (August 1979), pp. 45–57; Seymour M. Hersh, "The Price of Power, Kissinger, Nixon, and Chile," *The Atlantic Monthly* (December 1982), pp. 31–58.

removing Allende as supporting opposition groups. It channeled funds to the opposition press in an effort to keep it alive—Allende had steered government advertising to only those newspapers that supported him. Additional funds went to opposition politicians, private firms, and trade unions. The CIA also infiltrated Chilean agents into the upper echelons of Allende's party; and provocateurs were asked to make deliberate mistakes in their government jobs, thus adding to the economic management problems already facing Allende. Finally, CIA agents organized street demonstrations and funded a truckers' strike that had disastrous consequences on the economy. There is no evidence that the CIA organized or directly supported the ensuing military *coup d'état*, but it was clearly trying to create conditions that would drastically increase the probability of a military intervention into Chilean politics.[17]

Military Intervention

A final form of intervention is the sending of large quantities of troops either to stabilize a regime against rebels or to help overthrow an established set of authorities. Massive military intervention may build up over a period of time, as in Vietnam, where the United States started by sending military advisers for training purposes, then had them perform various combat support activities, and finally sent more than a half-million troops to conduct military operations. More often, the intervention is the result of a crisis; troops are then sent in rapidly, often catching the target regime or rebels by surprise.

The classic case of sudden intervention to overthrow a regime is provided by the combined Soviet, East German, Polish, Hungarian, and Bulgarian invasion of Czechoslovakia in August 1968. We have already pointed out how the Soviet government had used demonstrations of force in attempts to alter the Dubček government's policies. In addition, a series of conferences between the Czechs and other Warsaw Treaty governments had failed to convince them that the Dubček regime's policies were not aimed at restoring capitalist and multiparty systems to the country. In particular, Walter Ulbricht of East Germany was afraid that the Czech reforms might lead to civil disturbances in his own country. Indeed, the Soviet and Eastern European governments acted partly on the image of a domino theory: If the reforms in Czechoslovakia were not ended, they might infect the rest of the Communist bloc and seriously threaten the socialist system. The military operations were undertaken with great speed and surprise. After the country was effectively in the hands of the occupation troops, the Soviet government used a combination of kidnappings, threats, and persuasion to have Dubček and his followers deposed from their party and government positions. At the same time, the more orthodox Communists, who had been expelled or demoted from their positions during Dubček's period of reform, reappeared "to restore order." After the Soviet government had achieved its

[17]The facts of the Chilean episode come from Elizabeth Farnsworth, "Chile: What Was the U.S. Role? More Than Admitted," and the rebuttal of her arguments by Paul E. Sigmund, "Less Than Charged," in *Foreign Policy*, 2 (Spring 1974), 127–56; *Time*, September 30, 1974; Hersh, "The Price of Power," *The Atlantic Monthly* (December 1982), pp. 31–58.

objectives, it negotiated a treaty with the new Czech regime for the withdrawal of all Warsaw Treaty troops.

The massive American intervention in Vietnam, starting in the early 1960s, offers a case of a military effort to sustain a friendly regime facing domestic rebellion and external subversion—in this case from North Vietnam. A more recent example is provided by the Indian government's dispatch of a "peacekeeping" force to Sri Lanka in 1988 to assist that government's military efforts against the Tamil minority that had taken up arms to form a secessionist state. The Indian army enjoyed some success in temporarily pacifying Sri Lanka and eventually withdrew to India in 1990.

These are but three of many examples of recent military interventions. In the past, they were used primarily by the individual great powers against small client or dependent states. Today we are seeing more interventions by regional powers such as India, and more collective efforts, usually sanctioned by an international or regional organization.

Collective Intervention

In the old European-centered international system (except the period from 1791 to 1823, approximately), ideological consensus, impermeability of states, crude media of communication, and the doctrine of noninterference helped to preclude one sovereign's attempts to influence the purely domestic affairs of another.[18] Noninterference is still accepted as one of the foundations of international law and one of the norms that governments should faithfully observe in their foreign relations. The charter of the United Nations specifically prohibits member states (and presumably the organization itself, in most circumstances) from interfering in each other's domestic problems. The norm does operate, of course, in most international transactions.

Although actions involving interference in the internal affairs of other states continue to constitute part of the techniques of achieving objectives for many countries, a new set of norms seems to be developing, with less restrictive criteria to indicate when such actions are permissible. Clearly, the old norms of complete noninterference in other states' internal affairs are infringed upon frequently. Although it is premature to speculate on any long-term trend, many governments take the position that in certain instances, intervention and interference in other states' internal affairs may be legitimate if those actions have the prior approval of some collective body or international organization, or if the organization itself assumes such a

---

[18]Under the vague understandings comprising the Quadruple (later Quintuple) Alliance of 1815, the major powers of Europe pledged to intervene on behalf of any European monarch who was threatened by liberal revolution. At the Congress of Troppau (1820), devoted to discussion of the liberal revolution in Naples, the assembled Excellencies, Highnesses, and Majesties solemnly declared that "when political changes, brought about by illegal [without royal approval] means, produce dangers to other countries by reason of proximity, and when the Allied Powers can act effectively as regards these conditions, they shall, in order to bring back those countries to their allegiances, employ, first, amicable means, and then coercion." The Allied Powers subsequently intervened in Naples (1821) and Spain (1823) to restore absolute monarchies.

task. Traditional legal principles prohibiting all forms of external interference are most clearly spelled out in Article 15 of the Charter of Bogotá (1948), in which the Latin American states and the United States solemnly pledged that

> no state or *group* of states has the right to intervene directly or indirectly, for any reason whatever, in the internal or external affairs of any other state. The foregoing principle prohibits not only armed attack but also any other form of interference or attempted threat against the personality of the state or against the political, economic, and cultural elements.

Under Article 16, the signatories further agreed that "no state may use or encourage the use of coercive measures of an economic or political character in order to force the sovereign will of another state or obtain from it advantages of any kind." Similar principles were contained in a 1965 United Nations "Declaration on the Inadmissibility of Intervention in the Domestic Affairs of States and the Protection of Their Independence and Sovereignty."

In contrast to these strict rules, the recent practice of the Organization of American States, and unilaterally the United States, has been quite different. If unilateral intervention has been involved, the acting party has in many cases sought prior approval from the Latin American states, implying that if that approval is forthcoming, the intervention is legitimate. In both the Guatemalan and Cuban episodes, the United States government sought multilateral approval for its actions. Prior to intervening against Grenada in 1982, the United States obtained approval from Grenada's Caribbean neighbors. In the American intervention in the Dominican Republic during 1965, however, the United States took military action *before* it turned to the OAS to seek approval of its policies.

More significant, perhaps, are those occasions when the OAS itself determined to intervene collectively against one or more of its members. In 1960, for instance, the Inter-American Peace Commission of the OAS, in an action hardly compatible with the spirit of the Bogotá charter, condemned the Trujillo regime for "flagrant and widespread" violations of human rights in the Dominican Republic. Later that year, the foreign ministers of the Latin American states publicly condemned Trujillo for plotting against the life of Venezuela's president. The foreign ministers' resolution, which called upon members of the OAS to impose partial economic sanctions on the Trujillo regime, was the first time that truly collective action had been applied in the Western Hemisphere. Again, in 1964, the OAS Council voted almost unanimously to impose economic and diplomatic sanctions against the Castro regime in Cuba.

In 1990, a group of five West African states intervened militarily in the Liberian civil war of 1990. The armed incursion, undertaken in the name of the Economic Community of West African States (ECOWAS), was led by Nigeria. Although each participant had some concrete interests to promote, the purpose of the operation was largely humanitarian, to put an end to a civil war that was ravaging Liberia and causing thousands of refugees to seek shelter in neighboring countries.

Despite the doctrine of noninterference, international organizations have increasingly reflected members' concerns for humanitarian assistance and for protecting the lives and security of ethnic minorities and other groups that are at risk or the objects of systematic persecution. Recent practice reflects growing public sensitivity to victims of human rights abuses and natural calamities. Former Canadian Prime Minister Mulroney explained by analogy the justification for a United Nations–enforced "no-fly zone" to protect the Kurds in Iraq against Saddam Hussein's army: In the old days when a husband beat his wife, it was a private matter. Today, in contrast, there is a widespread sentiment that the community has a right to interfere in a private quarrel to protect the victim of abuse. The society of states has a similar "right" to violate the country's sovereignty in order to protect the populations at severe risk.

As we saw in Chapter 3, one of the hallmarks of weak states is the lack of government legitimacy, and the frequent incidence of suppression of minorities. The big questions is when and whether individual states, or international organizations representing the community of states, should intervene to provide protection. The problem is that while the humanitarian motive may be laudable, no operation fails ultimately to affect the domestic politics of the target. It is therefore a breach of the noninterference norm. The ECOWAS multilateral peacekeeping forces in Liberia ultimately favored one faction and in fact used armed forces against one of the rebel leaders. In the United Nations operation in Somalia—originally undertaken with Somali consent for the purpose of feeding a starving population—the task of trying to rebuild the Somali state after its collapse in 1991 inevitably required taking sides among the many warlords that were competing for power. In Somalia, it was not a case of intervening against or on behalf of a particular public authority, but of trying to *create* a public authority in an environment of chaos.

Conclusion

Diplomatic interference, clandestine political actions, terrorism, subversion, and military intervention will remain important techniques in the relations between some states. Regional hegemons use them to maintain primacy in their backyards, and many developing countries use them to support ethnic, ideological, or religious kin in neighboring states. When weak states are on the verge of collapse or in the throes of systematic human rights abuses, the international community may intervene to prevent or reduce great tragedies. The phenomenon of state weakness that is so prevalent in many areas of the Third World, in the Balkans, and in the former Soviet Republic suggests that these forms of influence-wielding will be a characteristic feature of contemporary international politics for some time to come.

Intervention always generates strong policy debates. Since it violates a fundamental norm of the Westphalian system, and since intervention is seldom applied consistently (the world watched in apathy as the Pol Pot regime systematically liquidated around one million Kampucheans in the 1970s, but applauded when Tanzania intervened in Uganda in 1979 to help bring the downfall of Idi Amin), the charges of hypocrisy and double standards are often heard. Muslim governments made a telling point in the 1990s when they criticized the United States and the Europeans for failing to intervene in Bosnia to halt Serbian "ethnic cleansing" policies, yet those same states went quickly to war against Iraq for conquest and abuse of Kuwait. Oil, it was suggested, was the difference.

Double standards suggest that national interests are in play; there is no such thing as a purely humanitarian intervention. But is this the case? Decisions not to intervene militarily in Bosnia were based on numerous studies that suggested such operations could not succeed and, indeed, might well expand the Bosnian war to encompass all the Balkans. In the Iraq case, the estimation was that a war to liberate Kuwait was feasible in terms of costs. In the case of Somalia, none of the participants in the UN military operation had any stake in the country, one of the poorest on earth. The purposes were primarily humanitarian.

We will not see an end to the various forms of intervention in the post–Cold War environment. The dilemmas faced by weak states, some of which are barely viable, and many of which face various degrees of popular disaffection leading to secessionist movements, mean that civil wars, turmoil, and hyper-nationalism or extreme communalism will continue to be characteristic features of the international landscape. Other states, as well as international organizations, seldom remain indifferent to these trends.

Questions for Study, Analysis, and Discussion

1. Secessionist groups justify terrorism in the name of "national liberation" and self-determination. Do you believe such groups are justified in using terrorism as a means of achieving their objectives? Why or why not?
2. In what ways are weak states particularly vulnerable to outside intervention? Can you provide examples?
3. Is the doctrine of noninterference in the domestic affairs of states (enshrined in the UN charter) becoming obsolete?
4. What are some of the main techniques of subversion?
5. Should the intelligence agencies of democracies attempt to overthrow foreign governments? Under what circumstances? If subversion needs to be secret to succeed, what role should legislatures play?
6. Does the international community have a "right" to intervene to protect minorities at risk in their home country?
7. If you were a policy maker, what criteria would you develop to guide your decisions whether or not to intervene with military force in situations such as Bosnia or Somalia?
8. In what ways does the recent practice of multilateral intervention support the "realist" or Grotian models of the international system?

Selected Bibliography

Blechman, Barry M., and Stephen S. Kaplan, *Force Without War: U.S. Armed Forces as a Political Instrument.* Washington, D.C.: The Brookings Institution, 1978.

Bull, Hedley, ed., *Intervention in World Politics.* Oxford: Clarendon Press, 1984.

Christopher, Andrew, and Oleg Gordievsky, *KGB: The Inside Story.* New York: Harper Collins, 1990.

Crozier, Brian, *The Rebels: A Study of Post-War Insurrections.* Boston: Beacon Press, 1960.

Duner, Bertil, *Military Intervention in Civil Wars: The 1970s.* Aldershot, Hampshire: Gower, 1985.

Feste, Karen A., *Expanding the Frontiers: Superpower Intervention in the Cold War.* New York: Frederick A. Praeger, 1992.

George, Alexander, Forceful Persuasion: Coercive Diplomacy as an Alternative to War. Washington, D.C.: United States Institute of Peace, 1992.

McConnell, James M., and Bradford Dismukes, "Soviet Diplomacy of Force in the Third World," *Problems of Communism* (January–February 1979), pp. 14–27.

MacDonald, Douglas J., Adventures in Chaos: American Intervention for Reform in the Third World. Cambridge, Mass.: Harvard University Press, 1992.

McGowan, Patrick, and Charles W. Kegley, Jr., Threat, Weapons, and Foreign Policy. Beverly Hills, Calif.: Sage, 1980.

Mandel, Robert, "The Effectiveness of Gunboat Diplomacy," *International Studies Quarterly,* 30 (March 1986), 59–76.

Marchetti, Victor, and John D. Marks, The CIA and the Cult of Intelligence. New York: Alfred A. Knopf, 1974.

Rowe, Edward Thomas, "Aid and Coups d'État: Aspects of the Impact of American Military Assistance Programs in the Less Developed Countries," *International Studies Quarterly,* 18 (1974), 239–55.

Schmid, Alex P., Soviet Military Intervention Since 1945. New Brunswick, N.J.: Transaction Books, 1985.

Schraeder, Peter J., ed., Intervention in the 1990s: U.S. Foreign Policy in the Third World. Boulder, Colo.: Lynne Rienner, 1992.

Scott, Andrew M., The Revolution in Statecraft: Informal Penetration. New York: Random House, 1966.

Sommerville, Keith, Foreign Military Intervention in Africa. New York: St. Martin's Press, 1990.

Thakur, Ramesh, "Non-Intervention in International Relations: A Case Study," Political Science, 42 (July 1990), 25–61.

Tillema, Herbert K., "Foreign Overt Military Intervention in the Nuclear Age," *Journal of Peace Research,* 26 (1989), 179–95.

————, *International Armed Conflict Since 1945: A Bibliographic Handbook of Wars and Military Interventions.* Boulder, Colo.: Westview Press, 1991.

United States, Department of State, Patterns of Global Terrorism. Washington, D.C.: U.S. State Department, 1991.

Vincent, R. J., Nonintervention and World Order. Princeton, N.J.: Princeton University Press, 1974.

Chapter
10

Weapons, War, and Political Influence[*]

An overwhelming majority of international transactions are carried on by means of bargaining, persuasion, or reward rather than violence. The routine issues that make up a large proportion of any nation's foreign relations rarely provoke statesmen to use or even threaten to use force. Nevertheless, recourse to violence has been and continues to be an important characteristic of the international system. In his classic study of war, Quincy Wright identified 278 wars occurring between 1480 and 1941.[1] Although the major powers were able to avoid a thermonuclear exchange during the height of the Cold War, international violence has erupted at various levels of intensity in nearly every region since World War II. Even according to a fairly restrictive definition of war—interstate conflict resulting in at least 1,000 battle deaths—there were thirty wars in the three and a half decades after 1945. Moreover, this figure excludes some conflicts (civil wars, insurgencies, and the like) that have had significant international implications.[2] There has been no abatement of international conflict during the years since 1980; and many civil wars, including those in Northern Ireland, Cyprus, Grenada, Nicaragua, Mozambique, Afghanistan, Lebanon, Chad, Angola, Ethiopia, El Salvador, Cambodia, Sri Lanka, Bosnia, Somalia, Georgia, Haiti, Liberia, Zimbabwe, Zaire, and elsewhere, have been marked by intervention of external pow-

*Note: This chapter was written by Professor Ole R. Holsti, Department of Political Science, Duke University.
[1]Quincy Wright, A Study of War, Vol. 1 (Chicago: University of Chicago Press, 1942), p. 650
[2]Melvin Small and J. David Singer, Resort to Arms (Beverly Hills, Calif.: Sage, 1982).

ers. The end of the Cold War has significantly reduced the danger of war between the major powers, but it has not eliminated the use of violence as an instrument of policy. Indeed, the receding influence of the major powers since the late 1980s has been accompanied by ethnic and national conflicts in Africa, Central Europe, successor states of the former Soviet Union, and elsewhere. More than thirty wars were raging in various parts of the world during the early 1990s. The conflicts in Cambodia, Bosnia, and Somalia attracted a good deal of international attention, including interventions under the auspices of the United Nations.

The legitimacy of force as an instrument of foreign policy, although often denounced by philosophers, historians, and reformers, has rarely been questioned by those responsible for foreign policy decisions of their countries. Some states have traditionally maintained orientations of nonalignment or isolation; but no nation is "neutral" with respect to its own security, and neutrality does not imply unconditional renunciation of force. Switzerland, for example, maintains active defense forces; India has tested a nuclear bomb; Sweden had been the scene of an extended debate on the desirability of acquiring nuclear weapons; and some of the staunchest adherents to a posture of nonalignment during the Cold War maintained armed forces proportionately larger than those of the United States, the Soviet Union, or China. Indeed, except in the case of a "puppet regime" established by an outside power, it seems unlikely that any government could long maintain itself in office unless it was committed to the use of all possible means, including force, to preserve the existence of the state and other interests deemed vital.

Some types of countries may be more prone than others to the use of force as an instrument of foreign policy. In the work previously cited, Wright reported that newly established states were more likely to use violence than were older, more mature countries, but that democracies had been involved in war as often as autocracies. Countries with industrial economies were less warlike than those with agricultural economies, and the states with socialist economies have been among the most warlike. On the other hand, some recent studies, based on data since World War II, suggest that democracies are more peaceful than authoritarian nations, and that smaller states tend to engage in more conflictual and high-risk foreign policies.[3]

Although war has existed in virtually all civilizations and epochs, our theories and evidence about it are largely based on the Western state system of the past three centuries. Whether these theories are equally valid for all parts of the international system may be questioned. For example, although the concept of "security dilemma" is generally regarded as an inherent part of an anarchical international system, it does not necessarily take the same form in all areas. Within parts of the Third World, especially in Africa, the threat to the security of many citizens has as often originated in

[3]Wright, *A Study of War*, pp. 828–41; Michael Haas, "Societal Approaches to the Study of War," *Journal of Peace Research*, 4 (1965), 307–23; and Maurice A. East. "Size and Foreign Policy Behavior: A Test of Two Models," *World Politics*, (1973), pp. 556–76. The relationship between democracy and peacefulness is more fully explored in Michael Doyle, "Kant, Liberal Legacies, and Foreign Affairs," *Philosophy and Public Affairs*, 12 (1983), 205–35, 325–53; Doyle, "Liberalism and World Politics," *American Political Science Review*, 80 (1986), 1151–70; and Zeev Moaz and Bruce Russett, "Normative and Structural Causes of Democratic Peace," *American Political Science Review* 87 (1993), 624–38.

the repressive actions of their own governments as from hostile neighbors. A similar observation might be made about other major concepts related to the study of war.[4]

Beyond the generalization that democratic nations have never gone to war against each other, the relationships in these studies are not always strong, and they should not obscure the fact that even states that have consistently denounced violence in international affairs will use force to achieve objectives or defend their interests *as they define them*. India, whose leaders have been outspoken opponents of violence in international relations, has used its military forces to capture the enclave of Goa from Portugal; to prevent Pakistani control over the disputed area of Kashmir; to defend its northern frontiers against border incursions by Chinese forces; to dismember Pakistan by forcing it to grant independence to the area that now constitutes the country of Bangladesh; and to intervene in the civil war in Sri Lanka. Many other examples could be cited. The important point is that the decision to use violence reflects the continuing validity of the dictum of Karl von Clausewitz, a Prussian general and strategist, that war is the continuation of politics by other means. State leaders ultimately make the choice; indeed, the determination of "core interests" and the decision on appropriate means to defend or attain them have traditionally been considered inherent and legitimate attributes of sovereignty. Serious attempts to modify this aspect of sovereignty are largely a twentieth-century phenomenon. But even the United Nations charter permits countries to use force individually and collectively for purposes of self-defense in the event of an armed attack.

Those responsible for national security are rarely willing to rely merely upon the good will or professions of peaceful intent of other countries to ensure their own safety; as a consequence, they are likely to perceive few substitutes for procurement, maintenance, and deployment of military forces. A state that makes no provisions for defending itself, moreover, is unlikely to find others that will take on the task, because such countries are scarcely desirable allies. Thus, while we may be able to attribute a particular war to an aggressive leader and an expansionist social-political system, a more general reason for the use of violence in international relations is the absence of effective systemic constraints on its use.[5]

Weapons as Instruments of Policy

As instruments of national policy, weapons share one important characteristic with all other techniques: Their purpose is to achieve or defend the goals of the state by influencing the orientations, objectives, and actions of other states. As such, weapons are ethically neutral, and we must distinguish between the goals sought through the use of force and the instruments themselves. The same weapons used by the Soviets to defend their homeland against the invading Nazi armies were also used to suppress the Hungarian revolution in 1956, and the liberal Czech regime

---

[4]For further elaboration of this point, see K. J. Holsti, "International Theory and War in the Third World," in *The Insecurity Dilemma; National Security of Third World States*, ed. Brian Job (Boulder, Colo.: Lynne Rienner, 1992), pp. 37–62.

[5]Kenneth Waltz, *Man, the State and War: A Theoretical Analysis* (New York: Columbia University Press, 1959).

in 1968, and to invade Afghanistan in 1979. Thus, it is the goals for which the weapons are used rather than the weapons themselves that can properly by judged by ethical standards.

Except for students of tactics (narrowly defined), the role of weapons must be considered in a political rather than a purely military context. The validity of Clausewitz's strictures against a rigid distinction between politics and military strategy have become more evident as developments in military technology have transformed war from a diversion of monarchs to a potential menace against the continued existence of life on earth. In the nuclear age, it has become more readily apparent than ever that military forces exist not solely for the purpose of inflicting damage upon enemies; they may also be used as a threat to buttress bargaining in diplomacy or as means of communicating one's intentions to potential adversaries. In 1938, Hitler invited the chief of the French air force, General Joseph Vuillemin, to inspect the Luftwaffe and to witness a demonstration of precision bombing by high-altitude dive bombers. The ploy was effective, as Vuillemin, terrified by the impressive display of German air power, became a leading exponent of appeasing German demands against Czechoslovakia.[6] Military "maneuvers" near frontiers, putting military units on "alert" status, and the deployment of forces—even small symbolic units—in a conspicuous manner have frequently been used to add credibility to one's diplomacy. Small countries that are prepared to undertake a policy of "punitive resistance" may cause more powerful ones to leave them alone. During the last stages of World War II, Switzerland possessed a well-trained army of fifty divisions, which made the prospects of an invasion too costly for Germany to consider.[7] These examples and the discussion about threats of intervention in the preceding chapter illustrate a few of the ways in which military power may be used as an instrument of foreign policy without actually resorting to violence.

Even when violence is employed, the scale of intensity is extremely broad, depending on the amount of force, its duration, and the geographical scope within which it is used. At the low end of the scale, we might find actions such as those of infantry troops armed with little more than hand-carried weapons; the brief clashes of Chinese and Soviet troops along the Ussuri River in 1969 and between Ecuador and Peru in 1981 are examples. The high end of the scale is marked by the indiscriminate employment of every available means of destruction, irrespective of costs or consequences. Fortunately, we have had no instance of unlimited violence by the major powers since the advent of nuclear weapons; perhaps actions of this type can best be illustrated by Hitler's desperate efforts to save his Third Reich during its final months, mitigated only by the unwillingness of some German generals to carry out his most demonic orders. Between these extreme examples there are obviously many other possibilities involving the use of force to defend or gain external objectives.

[6]Leonard Mosely, *On Borrowed Time* (New York: Random House, 1969), pp. 25–27. The American aviator Charles Lindbergh, also invited to witness Luftwaffe war games, became a strong opponent of U.S. aid to Britain on the grounds that Germany was certain to defeat the British.

[7]Dean Acheson, *Present at the Creation* (New York: W. W. Norton, 1969), p. 61.

Role of Nuclear Weapons

Force and threats to use force have persistently played a part in international relations, and developments in military technology often have had an important impact on structures and processes of political systems. Thermonuclear weapons and long-range ballistic missile systems are not merely quantitatively different from those that preceded them; they also possess qualitative attributes that have had, and will continue to have, a significant impact on the international system, its member units, and the nature of relations between them. This is not to say that conventional armaments are obsolete; indeed, most military forces are still limited to such weapons, and even the nuclear powers have found it expedient to maintain conventional forces to deal with limited provocations. In most circumstances nuclear power cannot easily be converted into political influence.

The most obvious characteristic of nuclear weapons is their destructive capacity. The bombs that obliterated the Japanese cities of Hiroshima and Nagasaki at the end of World War II had an explosive power of 20 kilotons (20,000 tons of TNT). By recent standards, such weapons are considered almost miniature. In 1961, the Soviet Union tested a bomb rated at 61 megatons (61,000,000 tons of TNT), which exceeded the combined explosive power of all weapons fired during World War II. A single Russian SS-18 or American MX missile is capable of delivering ten multiple independently targetable reentry vehicles (MIRVs) in the megaton range or a single 25-megaton warhead, a distance of 12,000 kilometers, within less than one mile of its target. In mid-1991, the United States and the Soviet Union each possessed about 10,000 strategic nuclear warheads, all with a destructive capacity far greater than those that devastated Hiroshima and Nagasaki in 1945, and the stockpiles of the other nuclear nations added significantly to this total.[8] During the 1960s, the U.S. Defense Department estimated that a general war between the United States and the Soviet Union might kill 149 million Americans and 100 million Soviets—and other estimates have been even more pessimistic. Under these circumstances, it is hardly surprising that some traditional views of the function of military forces have been rendered obsolete, and that nuclear war as an instrument of policy has been deemed irrational but, unfortunately, not impossible. Even before the end of the Cold War, both Soviet and American leaders expressed the view that there are few, if any, goals that can be served by the actual *use* of nuclear weapons ("A nuclear war cannot be won and must never be fought"); thus, the *threat* to use these weapons, rather than their actual use, has become of paramount importance.

It is not only the destructive capacity of thermonuclear weapons that has had an impact on the international system. The development of accurate long-range ballistic missiles has provided the means for their delivery across continents at speeds that have reduced warning time to almost none. Space and time, which once provided protection against devastating surprise attack, have all but lost their defensive

---

[8]As of the early 1990s, informed estimates of strategic nuclear stockpiles were: former republics of the Soviet Union (10,909 warheads, including over 3,000 in the possession of Ukraine, Kazakhstan and Belarus); United States (9,862); France (525); China (415); Great Britain (200); and Israel (50–200). India and Pakistan are also believed to possess or be close to possessing nuclear weapons. *The New York Times*, March 3, 1993.

value in the nuclear-missile age. This development is somewhat analogous to the harnessing of gunpowder in the late Middle Ages, which contributed to the decline of feudalism. With the introduction of the cannon to warfare, the feudal lord was no longer able to ensure the security of his subjects within the walls of his castle or fortified town. Out of the destruction of the feudal system emerged a new unit of security—the nation-state. In a somewhat similar manner, the destructive capacity and range of nuclear missiles lay the territorial state open to total destruction.[9] Before World War I, a nation at war was unable to inflict severe damage on the adversary's territory, industrial capacity, or population without first defeating its armed forces, whereas today it is possible to do so.

The Global Arms Race

Since World War II, the policies of countries armed with nuclear weapons have clearly dominated the international system, but acquisition and deployment of military instruments are by no means limited to the major powers. Nor, despite the huge defense budgets of the five major nuclear powers—the United States, Russia, Great Britain, France, and China—is the expenditure of vast resources for military means restricted to these countries. As a percentage of their gross national products (GNPs) the defense expenditures of the "Big Five" are as follows: United States 5.3 percent; Britain 4.0 percent; France 2.4 percent; Russia 9.9 percent; and China 5.0 percent. Countries diverting more than 10 percent of the GNP to military spending include: Israel 11.1 percent; Jordan 11.2 percent; Iraq 21.1 percent; Oman 17.5 percent; Saudi Arabia 11.8 percent; Kuwait 62.4 percent; North Korea 25.7 percent; Ethiopia 20.1 percent; Vietnam 11.0 percent; Croatia 24.1 percent; Yugoslavia 27.8 percent; Sudan 15.8 percent; and Mozambique 10.2 percent. Some other countries would no doubt join this list were reliable data on their budgets available. At the other end of the spectrum, one major power, Japan, spends about 1 percent of its GNP on military items, and such countries as Costa Rica, Ivory Coast, Mauritius, Estonia, Latvia, Lithuania, Nigeria, Iceland, the Gambia, Ghana, Jamaica, Brazil, and Mexico, have even smaller defense budgets proportionate to national income.

Global military spending has exceeded $1 trillion annually since the late 1980s, four times the 1970 figure, and the end of the Cold War has only marginally reduced total defense spending. The major powers continue to have the largest defense budgets, but the fastest growth in military spending at present is among some of the developing countries. The huge expenditures for armaments by some of the oil-producing countries such as Iraq, Syria, Oman, Kuwait, and Saudi Arabia is impressive evidence of the high priority that even less-developed countries place on acquisition of modern armaments. While defense budgets of the major industrial powers have declined in the post–Cold War era, a regional arms race has been taking place in Asia. During 1991–1992, China's defense spending increased by 50 percent, and it increased by a further 15 percent in 1993. Taiwan, Malaysia, Thailand, and Japan

---

[9]John Herz, "The Rise and Demise of the Territorial State," *World Politics,* 9 (1957), 473–93. However, see also Herz, "The Territorial State Revisited: Reflections on the Future of the Nation-State," *Polity,* 1 (1968), 12–34.

have also increased their defense budgets. Although Russia and the United States have reduced their defense spending, both have been active sellers of weapons to Asian Countries, at least in part to protect jobs in their defense industries. Using another criterion, the percentage of total population in the armed forces, we find that Israel, Jordan, Iraq, Oman, North Korea, Singapore, Kuwait, Syria, and United Arab Emirates have proportionately larger armed forces than any of the major powers.[10]

Thus, although nuclear weapons are of undeniable importance, several important points should be kept in mind: (1) Virtually all countries maintain armed forces; (2) the intensity of violence in military actions may vary across a wide scale, but force is rarely used in an unlimited manner; (3) sources of international instability are by no means confined to the actions and conflicts between nuclear powers; and (4) although nuclear weapons have had a revolutionary impact on some aspects of international relations, many observations about force as an instrument of policy are equally valid for nuclear and for conventional weapons.

The Spread of Nuclear Weapons

Military strength has traditionally been one of the attributes distinguishing the so-called great powers from the small ones. Since World War II, this distinction has tended to give way to that between the nuclear powers and those not so armed. The high cost of developing and procuring nuclear capabilities initially prohibited all but a few industrial countries from developing them. The period of Soviet and American nuclear monopoly immediately after World War II coincided with a tendency of countries within the international system to group themselves into opposing alliances led by the two nuclear powers. Paradoxically, however, in the long run nuclear weapons may have contributed to loosening of the bipolar system. The diffusion of nuclear knowledge, reactors, and materials has dramatically reduced the cost and difficulty of developing nuclear military capabilities. At the same time, as the potential destructiveness of war has risen, junior members of alliances have become more skeptical that other countries will risk devastation to honor treaty commitments. Charles de Gaulle put the question most succinctly: "Will Washington commit suicide to save Paris?" Hence, there is the incentive to develop and rely on one's own nuclear forces.

Less than two decades after the first atomic explosion, it was authoritatively estimated that countries economically and technologically capable of supporting a nuclear military program numbered as high as twenty, including Canada, Japan, West Germany, Sweden, Egypt, Argentina, Brazil, South Africa, and Israel. Israel is widely believed to have nuclear weapons, and the longstanding suspicion that South Africa had joined the nuclear powers was confirmed in 1993, when the Pretoria government announced that it had abandoned its nuclear program and destroyed its arsenal of six atomic bombs. Despite some belated efforts by the United States, Great Britain, and the Soviet Union to delay expansion of the nuclear club—indirectly by the Test Ban Treaty in 1963, and directly by the Non-Proliferation Treaty of 1970— the decision of whether to acquire nuclear weapons now lies beyond the effective

[10]The figures in this and the previous paragraph have been calculated from data in International Institute for Strategic Studies, *The Military Balance, 1993–1994.*

control of leaders in Moscow or Washington; and such decisions are as likely to re-flect regional security problems as they are those of the superpower relations. India's successful nuclear test has increased the motivation for Pakistan to follow suit, and that country may well be the next to join the nuclear club. Acquisition of nuclear weapons by any country would almost certainly trigger a local or regional arms race.

In a world that has faced a growing gap between burgeoning demands for en-ergy and diminishing conventional sources of it, pressures to exploit nuclear energy will increase, and they are likely to do so again before very long. As India's experience has made dramatically evident, a country with the capacity to use nuclear technology for "peaceful" purposes also has within its grasp the ability to produce weapons.

At present, nuclear technology has tended to create two classes of international citizenship. In the long run, however, nuclear capabilities may tend to dilute the im-portance of traditional bases of power—population, territory, industrial capacity, and the like—and, therefore, reduce rather than expand the differential between large and small countries. To be sure, a country with a large population, vast territory, and widely dispersed industrial capacity may be in a better position to survive a nuclear attack—and is thus capable of employing threats more effectively—than one with limited population and territory. In the prenuclear era it was unlikely that a minor power could inflict an unacceptable level of damage on one of its large neighbors, much less threaten its existence; it is not inconceivable, however, that in the not too distant future, a small country armed with nuclear weapons may be in a position to inflict such damage. This is precisely the reasoning that underlies the French nuclear *force de dissuasion.* The ability to "tear off an arm" is assumed to be sufficient to deter even a much more powerful adversary.

However, for most countries nuclear power is currently only indirectly relevant to the conduct of their foreign policies. Although possessing weak and crude mili-tary capability in comparison to those of the nuclear powers, these countries also enjoy the advantage of being unlikely direct targets of any nuclear exchange. It is thus one of many paradoxes of the nuclear age that the threat of destruction hangs most heavily over those states with the greatest military power; in some respects, then, security is inversely rather than directly related to military capabilities.

Deterrence as a Form of Inter-Nation Influence

The awesome destructive capacity of nuclear weapons has rendered the cost of their use prohibitive except in cases of extreme provocation. Because few, if any, political ends can be gained through nuclear war, the primary function of these weapons is that of posing a threat to potential enemies. Deterrence, by which decision makers in one state seek to prevent certain actions by potential adversaries by threatening them with military retaliation, can be considered one of the means by which coun-tries attempt to influence others.

It is important to stress that deterrence is not an invention of the nuclear age, as attempts to influence others through threats of sanctions are as old as diplomacy, and it lies at the center of such domestic institutions as criminal law. By posing a threat to the values of a potential attacker, the defender seeks to preclude certain types of behavior—specifically, unacceptable threats to the status quo. This was President Saddam Hussein's strategy when he tried to deter a U.S.-led attack on Iraq by locating several thousand hostages at or near military targets. Deterrence can also be viewed as a process of communication; decision makers of one nation seek to communicate to their counterparts abroad, "If you undertake activities X, Y, or Z, we shall surely retaliate with actions whose costs to you will outweigh any gains you may achieve." It is generally assumed that the threat of nuclear retaliation is severe enough to deter any country from attempting an all-out attack on the defender. Some deterrence theorists have also suggested that a powerful nuclear capability will suffice to deter aggression at lower levels of violence, such as conventional attacks, guerrilla incursions, and the like. In the colorful words of Sir John Slessor, former British chief of the air staff, "The dog that we keep to take care of the cat can also take care of the kittens." As we shall see later, this view has come under increasing challenge.

The premises underlying strategic deterrence are that: (1) Decisions by both the defender and the challenger will be based on rational calculations of probable costs and gains, accurate evaluations of the situation, and careful assessments of relative capabilities; (2) a high level of threat, such as that posed by nuclear weapons, inhibits rather than provokes aggressive behavior; (3) the value hierarchies of both the defender and the challenger are similar, at least to the point that each places the avoidance of large-scale violence at or near the top; (4) both sides have similar frames of reference so that signals of resolve and reassurance are perceived and interpreted accurately; (5) decisions are not sensitive to such extraneous considerations as domestic political pressures; and (6) both sides maintain tight centralized control over decisions that might involve or provoke the use of strategic weapons. Deterrence thus presupposes rational and predictable decision processes. Put somewhat differently, most deterrence theories assume that the state can be thought of as a unitary rational actor. Later we shall consider whether these premises are valid in all circumstances.

Credibility

One obvious requirement for effective deterrence is possession of sufficient capabilities to carry out the threatened retaliation. But influence over the behavior of others is not merely a function of weapon characteristics, as can be illustrated by the case of the bandit who uses a realistic-looking toy pistol to convince a bank teller to hand over some money. Success should be attributed not to the robber's weapon but, rather, to the teller's perception of it. Communicating to potential adversaries about one's strategic capabilities is usually relatively easy. Because weapons and military personnel are tangible objects and their attributes (speed, range, destructive capacity, numbers, accuracy, and the like) are relatively easy to measure, probabilities of misperception are reduced; and any distortions are likely to be on the side of overestimating rather than underestimating the adversary's capabilities—"just to be on the safe side." Also, there are usually ample opportunities for communicating about military capabilities; for example, the annual May Day parade in Moscow provided

Soviet leaders an opportunity to impress foreigners with the latest weapons in their arsenal.

Objectively speaking, the destructive capacity of modern weapons and the potentially catastrophic costs of general war should ensure sufficient caution in foreign-policy decisions to make their use unnecessary. Certainly this should be true of nuclear weapons. But success in avoiding general war to date should give rise to only cautious optimism; the frequency of war indicates that the threat to use force and even the possession of superior military capabilities have often failed to deter.[11] To explain these failures, as well as to understand the conditions for successful deterrence, we must look beyond the attributes of weapons systems. First, as in many diplomatic bargaining situations, the defender must be able to establish the *credibility* of the threat; that is, potential aggressors must be impressed that in case of provocation, the threatened retaliation will in fact be carried out. Mere possession of powerful weapons, even an overwhelming superiority of capabilities, does not ensure credibility; just as in a series of negotiations, threats need more than merely their enunciation to be made believable. Consider again our example of the bank robber, who in this case enters the bank with a genuine weapon. If, for whatever reason, the teller were convinced that the threat was a bluff, she would not meet the bandit's demands. His failure could not be attributed to characteristics of his weapon—in fact, a more powerful weapon might more readily be seen as a bluff—but rather to the low credibility (as perceived by the teller) of his threat to use it. This simple example illustrates the point that credibility is not inherent in the weapon but is rather a function of the challenger's perception of the defender's weapon and intentions and motivations. That is, A's deterrent effect on B = B's estimate of A's capabilities × B's estimate of A's intent. Although this formula[12] oversimplifies a complex relationship (a point to which we will return later in considering the deterrent effect of "overkill" capacity), it does highlight the key point that if either perceived capability or intent is zero, deterrent effect is also zero.

Because credibility depends upon beliefs and perceptions, a crucial problem is that of communicating intent. Compounding the problem is the very real difficulty of gaining hard and verifiable evidence about such elusive and sometimes mercurial attributes as motivations. History is not barren of instances in which disaster arose from faulty assessments of others' capabilities—witness the American estimates of Japanese and Chinese military strength in 1941 and 1950, respectively—but the decidedly more difficult task of adducing intentions has no doubt created for more problems. George Kennan has observed that

> in everything that can be statistically expressed—expressed, that is, in such a way as not to imply any judgment on our motivation—I believe the Soviet Government to be excellently informed about us. I am sure that their information on the development of

---

[11]Bernard Brodie, "The Anatomy of Deterrence," *World Politics*, 11 (1959), 14–15. Excellent case studies of deterrence failure may be found in Roberta Wohlstetter, *Pearl Harbor: Warning and Decision* (Stanford, Calif.: Stanford University Press, 1962); Alexander L. George and Richard Smoke, *Deterrence in American Foreign Policy: Theory and Practice* (New York: Columbia University Press, 1974); and Robert Jervis, Richard Ned Lebow, and Janice Gross Stein, eds., *Psychology and Deterrence* (Baltimore: Johns Hopkins University Press, 1985).

[12]Adopted in somewhat modified form from J. David Singer, *Deterrence, Arms Control, and Disarmament* (Columbus, Ohio: Ohio State University Press, 1962), p. 162.

our economies, on the state of our military preparations, on our scientific progress, etc., is absolutely first-rate. But when it comes to the analysis of our motives, to the things that make our life tick as it does, I think this whole great system of intelligence-gathering breaks down seriously.[13]

This disability is not, of course, limited to the former Soviet Union, or even to totalitarian countries. The Munich Conference, Pearl Harbor, the Korean invasion, the Suez crisis, the American responses to early intelligence about installation of Soviet missiles in Cuba, the Yom Kippur War, the Argentine invasion of the Falkland Islands, the Vietnam War, and Iraq's invasion of Kuwait are only a few of the more prominent cases in which leaders of democratic governments seriously misread the motivations and determination of their adversaries. In general, the more ambiguous the information, and the more dissimilar the frames of reference of the challenger and the defender, the greater the likelihood of distortion between the intent behind the sender's message and the meaning assigned to it by the intended audience. Thus, it is much easier to impress opponents about tangible objects such as weapons than about one's motivations to use them in various circumstances.

One method of communicating with potential adversaries is through declaratory policy. During the Cold War, American leaders repeatedly asserted that a Soviet attack on Western Europe would evoke the same response as a direct attack on the United States; Soviet leaders made similar proclamations with respect to Eastern Europe. But it is difficult to communicate intent by words only; because actions speak louder than words, visible actions that convey a relatively unambiguous message are usually necessary to buttress policy declarations. During the early 1960s, when Premier Khrushchev was apparently unconvinced of the credibility of certain American defense commitments, President Kennedy is reported to have complained, "That son of a bitch won't pay any attention to words. He has to see you move."[14] Despite repeated American pronouncements concerning the intent to defend West Berlin against Soviet encroachment, the USSR was not deterred from undertaking various efforts to undermine the status of that city. Even such actions as the Berlin airlift of 1948–1949, while adding credibility to the American commitment, did not permanently deter the Soviet Union. On the other hand, repeated failure to carry out a threatened retaliation rapidly erodes credibility. Assertions in 1939 by British and French leaders that they would support Poland in case of Nazi attack had little deterrent effect, in part owing to their previous failure to act against Italian and German aggression in Ethiopia, Albania, Austria, and Czechoslovakia.

In our discussion of diplomatic bargaining, we pointed out that credibility is enhanced if the threat is roughly commensurate with the importance of the issue in contention. Similarly, in the area of deterrence, it is generally recognized today that the threat to unleash a massive thermonuclear response to aggression, even if supported by the necessary capabilities, is not apt to be credible in cases of limited provocation (such as guerrilla raids). But in the years immediately following World War II, it was widely assumed that the threat of nuclear retaliation would automatically deter aggression at any level. This premise underlay the defense policies of the British

---

[13]George Kennan, *Russia, the Atom, and the West* (New York: Harper & Row, 1957), pp. 21–22.
[14]Arthur M. Schlesinger, Jr., *A Thousand Days* (Boston: Houghton Mifflin, 1965), p. 391.

Conservative government on its return to office in 1951. The invasion of Korea, despite American nuclear superiority, and concern for the costs of maintaining large conventional forces, led the Eisenhower administration to adopt a new deterrent posture. In January 1954, Secretary of State John Foster Dulles announced a major change in American defense policy, declaring that henceforth, Soviet-sponsored aggression on the periphery of the free world might be met not in kind (as in the Korean War), but perhaps with "massive retaliatory power" delivered "by means and at places of our own choosing."[15] In other words, limited aggression might be met with direct retaliation against its presumed sponsor—Moscow.

Whatever credibility a policy of massive retaliation might have had during the period of American nuclear monopoly (1945–1949) was drastically reduced after the Soviet Union attained nuclear capabilities. By 1954, both the United States and the Soviet Union could unleash a massive nuclear attack on each other, but neither could escape the frightful costs of a retaliatory attack. Under these circumstances, a threat to respond to any aggressive act with a thermonuclear strike might well be questioned. By 1957, a few months after the successful launching of the Soviet space satellite *Sputnik I*, even Secretary Dulles accepted the view that Western security would rest in part on local defense, although he stressed the use of tactical nuclear weapons rather than conventional means.[16] By 1961, the doctrine of massive retaliation had been abandoned in favor of strategies that were designed to cope better with the full range of challenges by an opponent. It is especially hard to conceive of a credible role for nuclear threats in the kinds of ethnic and tribal conflicts that have marked the post–Cold War era.

Stability

Effective deterrence must be *stable* as well as credible. Adversaries must not only be able to communicate a resolve to carry out a threat if the provocation is severe enough; they must also impress enemy leaders of their intentions without provoking a preventive or preemptive strike out of fear. Stated differently, a deterrence policy must simultaneously be able to convey messages of threat and reassurance. The possible consequences of the "reciprocal fear of surprise attack" can be illustrated by an analogy:

> If I go downstairs to investigate a noise at night, with a gun in my hand, and find myself face to face with a burglar who has a gun in his hand, there is danger of an outcome that neither of us desires. Even if he prefers just to leave quietly, and I wish him to, there is danger that he may *think* I want to shoot, and shoot first. Worse, there is danger that he may think that I think he wants to shoot. Or he may think that I think he thinks I want to shoot. And so on. "Self-defense" is ambiguous, when one is only trying to preclude being shot in self-defense.[17]

---

[15]John Foster Dulles, "The Evolution of Foreign Policy," U.S. Department of State, *Bulletin*, 30 (January 25, 1954), 107–10.

[16]John Foster Dulles, "Challenge and Response in United States Policy," *Foreign Affairs*, 36 (October 1957), 25–43.

[17]Thomas C. Schelling, *The Strategy of Conflict* (Cambridge Mass.: Harvard University Press, 1960), p. 207.

Leaders of two mutually hostile countries, each possessing powerful military forces that might be capable of inflicting a decisive blow with a surprise attack, may find themselves in a similar situation. Each may prefer to back off but may be unable to convince the other of its preference.

In summary, then, a deterrent, whether conventional or nuclear, requires more than merely possession of powerful military forces—even if they include nuclear weapons. Before 1945, the effectiveness of weapons was measured primarily by their performance against those of enemies and only secondarily for their deterrent effects. The contribution of nuclear weapons to national security is assessed less by their capacity to inflict devastating damage on enemies than according to their ability to influence the behavior of potential adversaries so that the occasion for using them will not arise. The outbreak of war, necessitating actual use of military capabilities, represents a failure of deterrence.[18] Thus, an effective deterrent must be both threatening (sufficiently credible that adversaries are not tempted to undertake prohibited actions) and stable (reassuring enough to reduce any incentives to launch a preemptive strike out of fear).

Deterrence in Crisis Situations

Most importantly, deterrence must be stable under conditions of great international tensions, when policy makers may be making important decisions while experiencing severe stress. Yet no system of deterrence can be absolutely stable, if only because all weapons are to some degree provocative, because the capacity of individuals and organizations to deal effectively with complex problems is not unlimited, because leaders may be as sensitive to domestic political considerations as to international ones, and because in any foreseeable international system there will always be countries or subnational groups who are prepared to challenge the status quo with force.

Decision Time

Probably the most pernicious attribute of crisis is time pressure; the aphorism that "haste makes waste" can take on a terrible new meaning in nuclear confrontations. Not only is short decision time likely to constrain full exploration of policy options; it may also materially increase the probabilities of unintended escalation and war. Let's assume that military technology has made nuclear war as an instrument of policy unthinkable because it has become too costly even for the "winner." (A similar argument was, incidentally, also quite popular during the decade before 1914.) We still cannot totally overlook the unintended ways in which war might occur: escalation of limited war into a thermonuclear holocaust; catalytic war, in which major powers are drawn into a conflict initiated by other countries; war arising from an accident or a breakdown in discipline among subordinate military personnel; and a war

---

[18]Glenn H. Snyder and others have pointed out that deterrence may operate *in war* as well as *before war*. This does not negate the point, however, that the outbreak of violence represents a failure of deterrence. Glenn H. Snyder, *Deterrence and Defense: Toward a Theory of National Security* (Princeton, N.J.: Princeton University Press, 1961).

resulting from erroneous intelligence, faulty interpretation of radar images, or other types of communication difficulties.[19]

Most of these occurrences are extremely unlikely, owing to complex devices and procedures designed to circumvent accidents. For example, a number of aircraft armed with nuclear weapons have crashed without a nuclear detonation, owing to safety devices built into the triggering mechanism. The presence of such safeguards does not, however, provide absolute insurance against errors of human perception, judgment, and performance. But in the absence of time pressure, these scenarios can perhaps be dismissed as too improbable for serious concern.

The capacity to respond with weapons of almost incalculable speed of delivery and destructiveness has created one of the crucial paradoxes of the nuclear age: The very decisions that, because of their potentially awesome consequences, should be made with the greatest deliberation may have to be made under the most urgent pressure of time. "He who hesitates is lost" may be a sound rule for card players; we can scarcely afford to have statesmen act on that principle. The most effective deterrence system is thus one that clearly and continually impresses everyone with the fact that striking first is the irrational, not the "safe" choice.

Ample experimental and historical evidence from both the pre-nuclear and nuclear eras indicates that individual and group decision-making processes tend to become less effective with the compression of decision time. Beyond a moderate level, time pressure has an adverse effect on creativity, memory, productivity, accuracy, and other factors crucial to decision making under conditions of uncertainty. When decision time is short, the ability to estimate the probable outcomes—the costs and benefits—of each policy option is likely to be reduced, and concern for short-run consequences of decisions increases. To some extent, then, decisions made under stress may be more apt to violate some of the premises about calculated decision processes that underlie nuclear deterrence: Extreme stress may increase the likelihood of reflexive behavior and concomitantly decrease the probability of cautious and calculated policies. (For further discussion, see Chapter 14.)

The 1914 Crisis

The events leading up to World War I, a classic example of a minor local crisis that escalated rapidly into a global war, can be used to illustrate how weapons, time, and stress can affect decision making.[20] Archduke Francis Ferdinand, heir apparent to the throne of Austria-Hungary, was assassinated June 28, 1914, in Sarajevo by a young Serbian nationalist. Within a week, Germany had promised "blank check" support for Austria's policy of punishing and humiliating Serbia and perhaps even provoking a "local war." On July 23, the Austro-Hungarians presented Serbia with an ultimatum of unprecedented severity, the answer to which was regarded as unsatisfactory. Five days later, Vienna declared war against its southern neighbor. When war between Austria-Hungary and Serbia could no longer be prevented, it also became

[19]Singer, *Deterrence, Arms Control, and Disarmament.*
[20]The following discussion of the 1914 and Cuban missile crises draws upon Ole R. Holsti, *Crisis, Escalation, War* (Montreal and London: McGill-Queen's University Press, 1972).

evident that efforts to localize it might fail. As late as August 1, many European states-men expressed the belief that if time permitted a reconvening of the concert pow-ers, general war might be avoided. But at the same time, attention turned to the risks of being unprepared for the war that might break out.

Here was the dilemma. Time would be required if a general European war was to be averted; above all, a moratorium on military operations was necessary. It was clear that military alerts, mobilizations, and deployment of troops near frontiers could stimulate similar actions by others. But increasingly, these considerations were overshadowed by another: To permit a potential adversary any time advantage in mo-bilizing the military power of the state was *perceived* to be disastrous. On July 28, Nicholas II had warned, "I foresee that I will succumb very soon to the pressure put upon me and will be compelled to take extreme measures which will lead to war." Three days later, in the course of his desperate last-minute correspondence with the kaiser, the tsar asserted, "It is technically impossible to stop our military preparations which were obligatory owing to Austria's mobilization."

The reaction of German officials to the events leading up to mobilization and war was almost identical. On the one hand, they repeatedly asserted that, owing to the pres-sure of time, they had no choice but to take vigorous military measures against the threat to the east. On the other hand, they claimed that only Russia was free to act in order to prevent war. Wilhelm, like the tsar, finally asserted that he had lost control of his own military and that only the actions of the adversary could stop further escalation.

On July 29, Russia had ordered—and then canceled—a general mobilization. Later it was decided in St. Petersburg that the mobilization of the four southern mil-itary districts would deter an Austro-Hungarian attack on Serbia without, it was as-sumed, alarming Germany. But, in part because Russia had no effective plan for a partial mobilization, the tsar was persuaded to reverse his decision once again on July 30 in favor of general mobilization, German warnings notwithstanding.

In response to what was perceived as a mounting threat against its eastern fron-tiers, the German government proclaimed a "state of threatening danger of war" on July 31 and dispatched a twelve-hour ultimatum to Russia demanding a cessation of military preparations. The kaiser then ordered mobilization on August 1. The French government simultaneously ordered general mobilization. Although official British mobilization was delayed until August 2, Winston Churchill, first lord of the Admi-ralty, and many others had advocated such action considerably earlier.

Thus, each mobilization was defended as a necessary action—made more ur-gent by the pressure of time—to a previous decision within the other coalition. A gnawing awareness that the probable responses to one's military measures would be countermeasures by the opponents failed to deter, and assurances of defensive in-tent failed to reassure adversaries sufficiently to cause them to abandon their own military steps. Ten days after the small-scale mobilizations by Serbia and Austria-Hungary on July 25, each of the major participants had ordered a general mobi-lization, a decision commonly regarded in 1914 as an act of war. The armies total-ing fewer than 400,000 troops, called to fight a limited war between two countries, had grown to nearly 12 million men, representing, in addition to Serbia and Austria-Hungary, Montenegro, Russia, France, Germany, Belgium, Turkey, and Great Britain.

Does the outbreak of World War I have any relevance for national security policy during an age in which weapons systems have only the slightest resemblance to those existing in 1914? An analysis of European military technology and doctrines would reveal, for example, that objectively, time was of incalculably less importance than in the 1990s. Yet, any analysis confined to the "objective" situation misses the point that individuals and groups make decisions on the basis of their appraisal of a situation. In the high-stress situation in 1914, European statesmen believed that time was of crucial importance, and they acted on that assumption. During the culminating phases of the crisis, foreign policy officials attributed to potential enemies the ability to deliver a sudden and possibly decisive military blow, even though they knew that their own armed forces lacked such a capability. As a consequence, the costs of delaying immediate military action were perceived as increasingly high and perhaps decisive. Decision makers in each alliance perceived those of the other coalition as able and willing to launch a massive first strike and thus hastened their own preparations.

The Missile Crisis of 1962

The events of October 1962, an intense international crisis that escalated to the brink of war and then de-escalated, can be contrasted with the decision making during the weeks immediately preceding the outbreak of World War I.[21] The first nuclear confrontation in history was precipitated by the establishment of Soviet missile sites in Cuba. For a period of approximately one week, the likelihood of a full-scale nuclear exchange between the United States and the Soviet Union was higher than at any time since World War II.

As in 1914, time pressure was woven inextricably into the entire crisis situation. American policy makers believed that once the Soviet missile sites in Cuba had become operational, the options for dealing with the issue would be drastically reduced. There was also the countervailing force created by the president and his advisers, who sought to minimize the probability that either side would respond by a "spasm reaction."

One important aspect of American policy making during the crisis was a deep concern for adequate information upon which to make decisions. The administration resisted taking action until photographic evidence of the missile sites were available. During the week after discovery of the missiles, a series of alternatives was being considered pending more accurate information; and while the decision to institute a naval blockade of Cuba was being hammered out, open discussion of the alternatives was encouraged.

Groups that achieve early consensus because dissent on matters of policy is subtly or overtly discouraged often produce decisions of low quality;[22] this was true, for

---

[21]The most complete analysis of the missile crisis, based not only on transcripts of the Ex Com meetings in Washington but also on several conferences during the late 1980s involving American and Soviet policy makers of the time, is James G. Blight and David A. Welch, *On the Brink: Americans and Soviets Reexamine the Cuban Missile Crisis* (New York: Hill and Wang, 1989). In recent years, the United States and Russia have continued to release archival evidence on the crisis, adding significant details about the confrontation.

[22]Irving Janis, *Victims of Groupthink: A Psychological Study of Foreign Policy Decisions and Fiascos* (Boston: Houghton Mifflin, 1972); and Ole R. Holsti and Alexander L. George, "Effects of Stress on the Performance of Foreign Policy-Makers," in *Political Science Annual: Individual Decision-Making*, Vol. 6 Cornelius P. Cotter, ed. (Indianapolis, Ind.: Bobbs-Merrill, 1975).

example, of the group in Washington that sanctioned the CIA plan to invade Cuba in 1961. Although many of the same persons were involved in the decisions regarding missiles in Cuba, President Kennedy took various steps to encourage open and sometimes heated debate. As a consequence, at least six significantly different policy options—ranging from doing nothing to launching air strikes and an invasion to dismantle the missiles—were considered and argued in detail. A participant in the decision making at the highest level wrote that President Kennedy, aware that discussions of alternatives in the National Security Council would be franker in his absence, encouraged the group to hold some meetings without him.

It was not until Saturday, October 20, almost a week after the photographic evidence became available, that the consensus developed. The president himself acknowledged that the interim period was crucial to the choice of a policy; he asserted that if the decision had to be made during the first twenty-four hours after verification of missile sites, the government would not have chosen as prudently as it did one week later, when it finally settled on the naval quarantine against introduction of further missiles.

Unlike many decision makers in the 1914 crisis, American leaders also displayed a considerable concern and sensitivity for the manner in which Soviet leaders were apt to interpret American actions. President Kennedy and others were acutely aware of the possibility of misperception by their counterparts in the Kremlin. Only weeks earlier, a serious miscalculation by the president and most of his advisers may have played a major part in the events leading up to the crisis. It was an almost unexamined article of faith in Washington that the Soviets would never place sophisticated weapons in bases so far from Moscow and within reach of a volatile leader such as Fidel Castro. Evidence to the contrary was thus dismissed, all the more easily because it came mostly from Cuban refugee sources which had proved unreliable in the past. The Soviets, for their part, appeared to have misperceived how Washington would react to strategic missiles in Cuba, apparently believing that the president was too weak to act resolutely.

Sensitivity for the position of the adversary manifested itself throughout the crisis. There were attempts to ensure that Chairman Khrushchev and his colleagues not be rushed into an irrevocable decision; it was agreed upon among members of the decision group that escalation of the crisis should be slowed down to give Soviet leaders time to consider their next move. An interesting example of Kennedy's concern emerges from his management of the naval quarantine. The president ordered the Navy to delay intercepting a Soviet ship until the last possible moment, and he sent his order "in the clear" rather than in code. The Soviets, certain to intercept the message, would thus be assured that they had time in which to consider their decisions. There was, in addition, a conscious effort not to reduce the alternatives of *either* side to two—surrender or total war. An air strike on the missile bases or an invasion of the island would have left the Soviets only two alternatives: acquiescence to destruction of the Soviet position in Cuba and heavy casualties, or counterattack. A blockade, on the other hand, would give the Soviet government a choice between turning back the weapons-bearing ships or attempting to run the blockade.

The decision to impose a naval quarantine was based on the reasoning that it would allow further and more massive actions should the Soviet Union fail to withdraw its missiles. The Kremlin leadership was then given both the time and the opportunity to reassess its policy. However, although the quarantine succeeded in preventing further shipments of missiles to Cuba, it did not result in removal of those already deployed there. The threat of an air strike was employed in an ultimatum delivered by Attorney General Robert Kennedy to Soviet Ambassador Dobrynin. Just prior to a White House meeting at which the air-strike option would again be discussed, Chairman Khrushchev accepted the compromise plan calling for Soviet withdrawal of offensive missiles in exchange for an American pledge not to invade Cuba. Recently released evidence indicates that President Kennedy would have exchanged NATO missiles in Turkey for those in Cuba had it been necessary to resolve the crisis.

Comparison of the decision processes in 1914 and 1962 underscores the importance, in a crisis, of the ability to lengthen decision time. Most important, the policy makers were aware not only of the frightful costs of miscalculation, failures in communication, or panic, but also of the consequences of reducing options to war or total surrender. They appear not to have lost sight of the need to consider the consequences of their decisions for the adversary. Yet, the ability of American and Soviet leaders to avoid a nuclear Armageddon in 1962 is no assurance that even great skill in crisis management will always yield a peaceful outcome. Indeed, recently released evidence indicates that the crisis was even more dangerous than originally believed. Khrushchev neither ordered nor authorized the downing of an American U-2 aircraft over Cuba. He may, however, have given local commanders authority to use nuclear weapons to defend Cuba in the case of an American invasion. According to an analyst who has had access to classified files on the crisis, it "was neither a managed nor a manageable crisis. Too many critical elements were not under anyone's control. . . . [It] was both more complex and far more dangerous than anyone at the time could fully appreciate."[23] This is no doubt what Kennedy had in mind when he said some months later, referring to the missile crisis, "You can't have too many of those."

Deterrence Strategies

It is a truism that no strategy or weapon system can ensure that adversaries will abstain from attack either out of aggressive intent or out of fear. This does not mean, however, that all military doctrines and weapons are equally credible and stable and will therefore contribute equally to national security and to the effectiveness of deterrence. Throughout the remainder of this chapter, we will use these two criteria—credibility and stability—to examine a number of issues relating to strategic doctrines and characteristics or weapons systems: capability requirements; limited nuclear war; targeting policy; active defense (anti-ballistic missile system); and arms control and

---

[23]Mary S. McAuliffe, "Return to the Brink: Intelligence Perspectives on the Cuban Missile Crisis," *Society for Historians of American Foreign Relations Newsletter*, 24 (June 1993), 4–18.

disarmament. Because the primary purpose of military policy today is to influence the behavior of potential adversaries, our discussion will focus on weapons and strategies as instruments of influence. We will be less concerned with the problems of fighting a war—the ultimate form of punishment—than with the possible consequences of various strategic doctrines on the behavior of others. In short, our focus will be political rather than purely military.

Capability Requirements

Two related "rules" have generally dominated national security policy: the *para bellum* doctrine—"if you want peace, prepare for war"—and the premise that security is a direct function of military superiority vis-à-vis prospective enemies. Whatever the merits of the *para bellum* doctrine (the frequency of wars both prior to 1945 and since then suggests that it may not be a sufficient guide in all situations), the almost irresistible conventional wisdom that deterrence can be enhanced merely by piling up more and better weapons than the opponent can amass must be qualified in a number of respects.

Invulnerability.   An important element of stable deterrence is a mutual second-strike capacity. The speed, range, and destructive capacity of modern weapons may provide a potential attacker with the opportunity and the temptation to destroy the adversary's retaliatory capacity with a surprise attack. If a country's leaders believe that a surprise attack will permit a quick victory without much likelihood of retaliation because the opponent's weapons can be destroyed before they are used, the latter's deterrent posture is hardly credible. Irrespective of the other attributes, weapons that are a tempting target for a first strike may prove to be no deterrent at all. The concentration of American naval power at Pearl Harbor in 1941 provided Japan with an irresistible temptation to try to gain its objectives with a sudden knockout blow, and the neatly arrayed aircraft on Egyptian airfields gave Israel an opportunity to ensure victory in the Six-Day War of 1967 within the first few hours. Thus, deterrent effect is a function not of *total* destructive capacity, but of reliable *weapons capable of surviving a surprise attack.*

Nor do vulnerable forces satisfy the requirement of stability, because, by failing to provide decision makers with the "capacity to delay response," they require a finger to be kept on the trigger at all times. Fear that the opponent could launch a crippling surprise attack reduces decision time and increases pressure to launch a preemptive strike at the first signal (which may turn out to be false) that such an attack is imminent. When both countries' deterrent forces are vulnerable, the situation is even less stable, as neither side can afford to delay. Each may prefer to back off, but neither can be certain of not having its "rationality" exploited. Conversely, invulnerable strategic forces—those that cannot be eliminated, even by the most severe attack that the enemy can mount—may mitigate some of the more severe time pressures attending a crisis. Knowledge that one's forces are secure should reduce the motive to shoot first and ask questions later. The temptation to launch a first strike should diminish as the certainty and probable costs of devastating retaliation increase. Equally important, when retaliatory systems are invulnerable, the incentive to undertake a preemptive attack in the absence of complete information (as, for example, in case of a nuclear explosion of unknown origin) declines as the ability to delay response increases decision time.

Survival capability of deterrent forces can be enhanced by a number of methods. An *increase in numbers* can, at least temporarily, make it more difficult for the attacker to succeed in a first strike. This method is relatively crude, and it will be effective only if the adversary does not increase its forces proportionately. The search for numerical superiority may decrease vulnerability in the short run, but its long-term consequences are almost certain to be an arms race that leaves neither side more secure. *Dispersal of forces* at home and in overseas bases may also provide some protection, but this alternative becomes less attractive as the political costs of foreign bases increase. "*Hardening*" retaliatory weapons (such as land-based missiles) by placing them in heavily reinforced underground silos, although relatively expensive, can provide adequate protection against all but a direct strike. Assuming a specified probable error in the accuracy of attacking missiles, hardening requires the attacker to expend more weapons on each target, thereby reducing the probability of a crippling first strike. Expectations that missiles in protected silos would prove to be the "ultimate" retaliatory weapons have proven mistaken, however, because reconnaissance satellites can find them and, even more important, because missile guidance systems have become increasingly accurate. Multiple independently targetable reentry vehicles (MIRVs) are so accurate that 50 percent of the warheads can be expected to land within a few hundred meters of the target. Thus, although bigger warheads can threaten the invulnerability of retaliatory forces, the far more salient danger arises from the increasing accuracy of missile systems.[24]

Placing retaliatory sources at the *maximum possible distance* from a potential enemy ensures their survival only as long as the gap in distance is not closed by longer-range delivery systems. A further measure of protection can be provided by *concealment*, but this method is already somewhat vulnerable to advances in the technology of detection. Orbiting "spy" satellites can yield considerable intelligence information without incurring any of the political costs of manned overflights. Finally, a country may seek to protect its retaliatory forces by adopting a *launch-on-warning* policy. For reasons discussed above, however, doing so would create a highly unstable situation.

At present, the most reliable method of decreasing vulnerability is *mobility*. Missile-launching submarines have become major components of American and Russian defense forces, and they are an important element in the British and French nuclear deterrent. Important characteristics of this weapon system are these: (1) It combines high mobility with the capabilities of dispersal, distance, and concealment; (2) unlike missile sites or air bases located near cities, it provides the enemy with no incentive to attack major population centers; (3) it does not require foreign bases; and (4) it may remain beyond striking distance of its targets (communicating reassurance), but it can rapidly be brought into firing position without losing its invulnerability.[25]

---

[24]Because the blast effect increases only as the cube root of the increase in yield, an increase in accuracy will threaten protected targets much more than will an increase in explosive power.

[25]Because submarine-launched ballistic missile forces are the most stable element of deterrence, any technological breakthrough in antisubmarine warfare capabilities that threatens their invulnerability would be highly destabilizing.

One point should be emphasized, however. The ability of the invulnerable deterrent forces to delay response may be a necessary but not a sufficient factor to eliminate the incentives to strike first and to ensure crisis-stable deterrence. None of the countries in the 1914 crisis had the ability to unleash a rapid destructive blow, crippling the retaliatory capabilities of the adversary. But in the tense days preceding the outbreak of general war, decision makers in Berlin, St. Petersburg, Paris, and London increasingly attributed to their potential enemies both the *ability* and the *intent* to do so. The penalties for delay were perceived to be too high. The ability to delay response is therefore not likely to contribute to crisis management unless policy makers perceive that the risks of acting in haste are greater than those of using a strategy of delay and, equally important, unless they are willing to attribute the same preferences to the adversary's leadership.

Force Levels.   The theory of a linear relationship between military capability and deterrent effect has been questioned as nuclear arsenals have reached the "overkill" range. Whether the capacity of nuclear weapons to destroy any existing society has tended to make state leaders more cautious in considering decisions that might precipitate a nuclear war has been neither proved nor disproved, but it is at least plausible; the proposition that the capacity to destroy any potential adversary or coalition of opponents five, ten, or a hundred times over increases caution proportionately seems untenable.[26] Sheer numerical superiority can provide some short-run protection against a crippling and decisive first strike. Expert opinion about the number of warheads needed for minimum deterrence vary widely. At the low end of the range, former U.S. Secretary of Defense Robert McNamara recently proposed reducing nuclear arsenals to 100 to 200 warheads, a number that he felt would be sufficient to deter any efforts at nuclear blackmail.[27]

Flexibility.   Perhaps the most serious limitation to the theory of a linear relationship between destructive capability and deterrent effect lies in the ability to deter aggression at many levels of intensity. One aspect of the issue has been discussed earlier—the credibility of threatening "massive retaliation" to deter limited aggression.

Before 1945, a single weapons system could generally be counted upon to perform multiple tasks. For example, a strong French army could be deployed to defend the eastern frontiers against Germany; the same army could, with little modification, also pacify colonial areas. Similarly, the British Navy could serve as an instrument for multiple goals—a deterrent against attack on the home island, protection of shipping and commerce, or destruction of an enemy fleet in war.

Whether nuclear arsenals are capable of serving multiple defense requirements is more open to question. For example, can the same weapons be used to deter an attack against one's home territory, to dissuade adversaries from launching a limited war, and to prevent or cope with various types of limited threats? During the years immediately after World War II, the deterrent function of nuclear weapons was as-

[26]Although nuclear weapons have vastly increased the dangers arising from war, some analysts have also developed the thesis that it is precisely this quality, by inducing caution, which has accounted for almost half century of peace among the major powers. John Lewis Gaddis, *The Long Peace* (New York: Oxford, 1989).

[27]Robert S. McNamara, "Nobody Needs Nukes," *The New York Times*, February 23, 1993.

sumed to be self-evident. The invasion of South Korea by Communist forces called this premise of the Truman administration into question. The defense policy of the Eisenhower administration placed considerable emphasis on the deterrent effectiveness of strategic weapons across a broad spectrum of situations. This line of reasoning underlay British defense policies of the 1950s, as well as those of France since the 1960s. Rejecting the "massive retaliation" doctrine of the Eisenhower administration in favor of a policy of "flexible response," Presidents Kennedy and Johnson actively sought to restore a balance between nuclear and conventional forces. With very indifferent success, they also attempted to persuade NATO allies in Europe to focus their resources on forces of the latter type. For fiscal and domestic political reasons the Nixon and Ford administrations moved toward a reduction of ground forces and back toward greater reliance on the deterrent effects of strategic weapons. According to the "Nixon Doctrine," local forces were to provide the bulk of ground forces. Following the Iran hostage crisis and the Soviet invasion of Afghanistan, the Carter administration announced plans to enhance conventional forces. The Reagan administration increased conventional forces and pressed NATO allies to follow suit. The political transformation of Eastern Europe and the end of the Cold War have led to major reductions of conventional forces by Russia, the United States, and many other industrial countries.

Defense analysts have generally accepted the need for flexible forces. The credibility of a threatened nuclear response to limited provocation may be quite small and will diminish each time limited aggression goes unchallenged. A commitment to meet *every* provocation automatically with a nuclear response denies one the possibility for recalculating costs and gains with changed circumstances. Moreover, nuclear retaliation is of questionable validity, either militarily or morally as a response to limited aggression.

The threat of strategic retaliation may well prove effective against an unambiguous attack against targets of high value. During the Cold War, Soviet and American strategic forces effectively deterred either country from launching a direct attack on the other (assuming that the motivation to do so may in fact have existed). But even in Europe, an area where American alliance commitments were presumably the most credible, the nuclear forces proved inadequate to deter periodic Soviet attempts to alter the status quo by coercive means—for example, in West Berlin. Nor has a combination of American strategic forces and alliance commitments been sufficient to deter limited probes in other areas or to deal with such issues as the hostages in Iran or the Soviet invasion of Afghanistan, much less to cope with international terrorism or drug trafficking, to restore a legitimate government in Haiti, or to end civil wars in Bosnia or Somalia. Certainly the threat of nuclear retaliation must be regarded as of very limited utility in areas where frontiers are ambiguous; where the credibility of commitments to allies may be suspect; where regimes are unstable; where the difference between genuine domestic revolutionary movements, private armies of dissident domestic factions, and foreign guerrilla forces is often blurred; and where clandestine aid across frontiers is difficult to identify and even harder to prevent.

Another aspect of the relationship between weapons and influence has been identified by Thomas Schelling, who has distinguished between (1) *deterrence,* the ability to prohibit certain policies (negative influence) on the part of enemies; and (2) *compellance* or *coercive diplomacy*, the capacity to persuade the adversary to undertake specified actions (positive influence).[28] American strategic capabilities may have deterred the Soviet Union from overt large-scale aggression in Europe, but attempts to compel North Vietnam to cease supplying its forces in South Vietnam and those of the Viet Cong by bombing transportation routes indicate the difficulty of achieving this type of influence even with conventional weapons. Similarly, Israeli commando raids may deter some types of Arab behavior, but they have not been successful in compelling Arab leaders other than the late Anwar Sadat and Yassir Arafat to negotiate face to face with Tel Aviv, nor even to recognize Israel's right to exist. Chinese and Soviet attacks on each other's frontier positions during the 1970s may have served some deterrent functions, but they were not an effective way of compelling the adversary to renounce ideological "heresies" or to acknowledge the other as the leading Communist nation. Post–Cold War efforts to force warring factions in Angola, Bosnia, and Somalia to sign and adhere to peace agreements have further demonstrated the difficulties of implementing effective compellance policies.

Targeting Policy

Until the Twentieth century, military operations were generally directed at the opponent's military forces. To be sure, vast numbers of civilians were killed in such conflicts as the Thirty Years' War, but they were rarely the primary target. That changed with the ability to deliver weapons by means of aircraft. During World War II, Germany launched air raids against Warsaw, Rotterdam, London, Coventry, and many other cities with the deliberate intention of demoralizing the enemy by terror tactics against civilian populations. The Allies later retaliated with fire-bombing raids against Dresden and other German cities. However, even air attacks on military-industrial complexes inflicted heavy casualties on civilians.

The military effectiveness and morality of such uses of air power has continued to be controversial, especially with the advent of nuclear weapons. The debate has generally centered on the probable effects of threatening military targets (counterforce strategy) or population centers (countercity strategy). In assessing the merits of these doctrines, we can again apply our criteria of effectiveness; that is, what do these targeting strategies contribute to the credibility and stability of strategic deterrence?

The stated intent of counterforce is to impress upon potential adversaries that, in the event of war, (1) their strategic striking forces would be destroyed; (2) they would thus suffer a military defeat; and, while some versions would target the adversary's top leadership, (3) every effort would be made to minimize casualties among noncombatants.[29] Another purpose is to reduce the damage should a nuclear war

---

[28]Thomas C. Schelling, *Arms and Influence* (New Haven, Conn.: Yale University Press, 1966). See also Alexander L. George, and William E. Simons, eds. *The Limits of Coercive Diplomacy*, 2nd ed. Boulder, Colo.: Westview, 1993.

[29]Critics of such "decapitation" targeting strategies point out that eliminating the adversary's leadership vastly complicates the task of negotiating an end to the conflict, especially with a nation in which the rules of leadership succession may be murky; with whom does one then negotiate?

break out. Hence, a counterforce targeting policy is usually associated with the strategic doctrine of "damage limitation." Counterforce strategy, according to its advocates, is a more credible deterrent than a countercity doctrine because an authoritarian regime places a higher value on its military force than on the lives of its citizens. Thus, a threat to destroy its ability or will to wage war will prove more effective than a threat against other types of targets, including urban or industrial centers. Counterforce strategists further assert that should deterrence fail and a war actually break out, striking at the adversary's military targets rather than cities is the least immoral policy, not only because it minimizes the loss of civilian lives in an actual war but also because it is the only policy short of pacifism that is consistent with the "just-war" doctrine that noncombatants must not be held hostage. Such a targeting doctrine also gives the opponent an incentive to avoid cities, thereby potentially reducing loss of life on both sides. And even if the enemy leaders are unwilling to spare population centers, their forces, which will have been reduced by a counterforce retaliation, will possess less capacity to strike at cities.

Critics of counterforce doctrines emphasize that the policy cannot be totally divorced from a number of first-strike implications. For example, a strike at the adversary's strategic weapons will clearly prove more effective if undertaken before those weapons have been launched. Although a decision to strike the enemy's cities may be delayed—as targets, their value does not decrease with time—the value of a strike against the adversary's strategic weapons is highest before the enemy has launched any of its forces, thereby significantly heightening incentives for a first strike.

Counterforce strategy also serves as an impetus to both quantitative and qualitative arms races. The force level necessary for posing a credible threat to targets other than military ones is finite and relatively easy to calculate. As stationary targets incapable of concealment, cities and industrial sites provide the opponent's leaders with little incentive to increase their arms stockpiles indefinitely; nor do such "soft" targets provide much incentive for continually upgrading strategic forces by replacing older weapons with faster, larger, or more accurate ones. Hence, a countercity strategy, associated with a doctrine of "mutual assured destruction," is compatible with finite deterrent capabilities. On the other hand, a nation committed to a counterforce strategy has considerable reason to build up stockpiles; the greater one's strategic superiority, the greater the likelihood of an effective strike against military targets.

An effective counterforce capability against protected strategic systems requires (1) overwhelming strategic superiority; (2) increasingly accurate intelligence and guidance systems to locate and pinpoint strikes against such targets; and (3) command, control, communications, and intelligence (C^3I) capabilities that will survive even in the midst of a nuclear war.[30] Efforts toward achievement of this position will succeed only in the unlikely case that the adversary fails to increase its forces.

If a counterforce strategy is to accomplish its objective of saving the maximum number of lives in case of a failure in deterrence, it is necessary to move the military

---

[30]Submarine-launched ballistic missiles (SLBMs), in many respects the deterrent that comes closest to satisfying our criteria of credibility and stability, are less accurate than ICBMs, and are thus less likely to threaten missiles located in "hardened" underground silos. However, increasingly accurate SLBMs such as the Trident C-4 may ultimately erase this distinction.

targets as far as possible from urban population centers—that is, to take effective steps to deal with the "co-location problem." To assume that, under conditions of a major war, combatants would spare military targets in order to save cities is to attribute to leaders of countries at war a degree of magnanimity rarely encountered even in less deadly circumstances. This requirement is virtually impossible to meet in densely populated areas such as Europe; even within the United States many key military targets are located in or near major urban centers, although, in recent years, public pressures have at times been successful in requiring that military installations be placed away from cities and suburban areas.

During the Cold War arms race, both the United States and the Soviet Union acquired the diversified nuclear arsenal for an "all options" policy that would permit retaliatory strikes against both an adversary's cities and its military targets. It is not unlikely that this state of affairs was brought about less by a calculated assessment of the arguments for and against the two strategic doctrines than by a process of bureaucratic politics in Washington and Moscow. That is, rather than making a hard choice between the counterforce and countercity viewpoints, and thereby risking an aggravation of interservice rivalries, both the United States and the USSR reached a "compromise" by accepting both views—and acquiring the hardware necessary for both.

The debate over targeting doctrines amply illustrates the difficulties of trying to apply ethical criteria to questions of defense policy. Should war break out, any effort to spare lives as envisioned by advocates of counterforce is clearly desirable. But if adherence to such a targeting policy destabilizes deterrence through heightening the reciprocal fear of surprise attack, can claims of greater morality be sustained?[31]

Active Defense (Anti-Ballistic Missile Systems and the Strategic Defense Initiative)

A potentially significant component of deterrent capabilities is the ability to protect targets by destroying attacking airplanes or missiles before they reach their destination. Credibility is enhanced if, owing to an effective active defense system, the deterrence can threaten a potential aggressor with the knowledge that the costs of a counterstrike can be reduced if not eliminated.

Up to and during World War II, active defense could prove effective by inflicting only limited damage to the attacker. During the Battle of Britain in 1940, an attrition rate of 10 percent eventually forced the Luftwaffe to abandon its policy of attempting to bomb England into submission. In heavy Allied raids on Schweinfurt during the summer and autumn of 1943, Germany's ability to down one sixth to one quarter of the attacking aircraft was a major victory for the defense.[32]

Intercontinental ballistic missiles armed with thermonuclear weapons have added substantially to the burdens of defense. Identification and destruction of a

[31]For thoughtful discussions of the relationship of ethics to strategy, see Arthur Lee Burns, *Ethics and Deterrence: A Nuclear Balance without Hostage Cities*, Adelphi Paper No. 69 (London: Institute for Strategic Studies, 1970); and Michael Walzer, *Just and Unjust War* (New York: Basic Books, 1977).

[32]Hans J. Morgenthau, "The Four Paradoxes of Nuclear Strategy," *American Political Science Review*, 58 (1964), 123–35.

missile is a considerably more difficult task than that of downing even a supersonic bomber. A second problem is even more serious. The destructive capabilities of thermonuclear weapons and the size of existing stockpiles are such that even an attrition rate of 90 percent (which is currently regarded as impossible) cannot prevent utter devastation of most targets.

As a consequence, there is little likelihood that any ABM system can provide protection for cities, industrial sites, airfields, or other "soft" targets. The case for ABMs, then, rests on their ability to provide protection for retaliatory forces such as missiles in underground silos. Whereas the ability to destroy, for example, 50 percent of attacking missiles is totally inadequate to protect cities, such an attrition rate might be sufficient to deter a potential attacker from attempting a counterforce strike against retaliatory forces. But even in this more limited role, the case for ABMs is not unambiguous. The history of military technology suggests that advances in defensive weapons are usually superseded by developments in offensive capabilities. The ABM is not an exception. It is susceptible to penetration by means of decoys, multiple-warhead (MIRV) missiles, evasions by maneuverable (MARV) missiles, or nuclear blasts that render its complex radar system ineffective. Finally, as a number of defense analysts have pointed out, ABMs tend to be more useful to the initiator of a nuclear exchange. Thus, their deployment has some first-strike implications that would tend to reinforce the adversary's disbelief about a declaratory second-strike policy.[33]

Vocal debates on the ABM issue abated in 1972 with the SALT I Treaty between the United States and the USSR. That agreement limited each nation first to two ABM sites, and then to just one. Subsequently, the United States chose not even to finish its one site in North Dakota. However, the SALT I Treaty did not end the search for missile defense, as both the Soviet Union and United States pursued extensive research and development efforts. In 1983, President Reagan announced a Strategic Defensive Initiative ("Star Wars") program aimed at making nuclear weapons "impotent and obsolete." SDI was intended to provide several layers of defense, using such advanced technologies as high-energy particle beams to destroy missiles. The program became the most controversial defense issue of the 1980s. Scientists were divided on its practicality. Others, including some in the military, were concerned that its high cost—some have estimated it at up to $1 trillion—would drain away resources from other national security programs. Advocates of arms control feared that it would require abandoning the ABM part of the SALT I Treaty. Even the most ardent supporters of SDI acknowledge that it will not render nuclear weapons obsolete, if only because they can be delivered by means other than ballistic missiles—for example, by low-flying cruise missiles. The successful interception of many Iraqi Scud missiles by Patriot missiles during the Persian Gulf War has been cited by supporters of the SDI program. It should be remembered, however, that the Scuds are relatively crude weapons that posed a far less potent challenge to defensive systems than ICBMs

[33]There are a number of parallels in this respect between ABMs and civil defense programs. That is, both may save some lives in the case of war, but neither is without first-strike implications. Except in periods of intense international crisis, such as during the Berlin crisis of 1961, civil defense programs have received relatively little attention in most countries.

armed with multiple warheads, decoys, and "penetration aids." The SDI program has survived the end of the Cold War, but its mission and funding have been scaled back, and it has been renamed Global Protection Against Limited Strikes (G-PALS).

Does Deterrence Work?

If the yardstick is avoidance of a general nuclear war, then we could conclude that since 1945 deterrence has worked effectively. Despite some periods of great international tensions involving countries armed with nuclear weapons, none has attacked or been attacked. Even threats to do so have been avoided—perhaps the sole exception was the Soviet threat during the Suez crisis of 1956 to unleash an attack on France and Britain if they did not withdraw their forces from Egypt.

For several reasons, however, an unqualified positive judgment on deterrence does not seem warranted. First, although none of the major powers has undertaken an attack on another, we can only speculate about the reasons; we cannot prove conclusively that restraint has been the result of successful policies of strategic deterrence. Although some important Russian and American archives may be opened in the not too distant future, they are unlikely to yield unambiguous evidence on this issue.[34]

Second, the record since World War II demonstrates rather conclusively that efforts to deter probes, limited attacks, or even outright invasion of allies or client countries have often failed. Moreover, as a result of these failures the international system has been wracked periodically by crisis and conflicts—for example, the Korean War, the Cuban missile confrontation of 1962, repeated crises over the status of Berlin, battles along the frontier between China and the Soviet Union, the Falkland Islands war, the long war between Iran and Iraq in the 1980s, the repeated conflicts involving Israel and its neighbors, the 1991 Persian Gulf War arising from Iraq's invasion of Kuwait, and many others. The existence of nuclear weapons may have instilled caution among decision makers by significantly raising the risks of employing highly provocative measures to compel the opponent to retreat or compromise during a crisis, as well as the risks of superpower intervention in conflicts involving other countries. But if a major function of nuclear arms is to prevent those types of moves that *begin* crises, then they can be judged, perhaps, as inadequate.

Finally, it is important to remember that deterrence is not a policy for all seasons. It is but one of many means by which leaders can attempt to cope with the international environment and to influence other countries. Even during the height of the Cold War, when the international system was marked by a tight bipolar configuration, efforts to stretch deterrence into an all-purpose policy were often less

[34]Even analysts who have systematically analyzed international relations during the past century disagree sharply on the extent to which deterrence policies have been successful and the reasons for their success or failure. Among the difficulties is establishing beyond dispute when deterrence has been successful. Is the absence of a challenge evidence of deterrence success or the lack of any intent to undertake a challenge? See Richard Ned Lebow and Janice Gross Stein, "Deterrence: The Elusive Dependent Variable," *World Politics* 42 (1990), 336–69; and Paul Huth and Bruce Russett, "Testing Deterrence Theory; Rigor Makes A Difference," *World Politics* 42 (1990), 446–501.

than successful. As the relatively simple structure of the Cold-War international system has been transformed—as the result of an increase in the number of countries, a breakdown of alliances, the growing importance of various types of non-national actors, diffusion of effective power, the salience of a broader range of issue areas, the disintegration of the Soviet Union and the end of the Cold War—the effectiveness of policies that rely solely on the threat of military retaliation is almost certain to decline. Perhaps, most importantly, the assumptions about rational and predictable decision processes (outlined earlier) have not always proved to be valid. That is not to say that deterrence will cease to be of importance in the relations between states. Nor is it to argue that the ability to maintain "crisis-stable" deterrence has lost its importance; this is at least a necessary if not a sufficient condition for any meaningful steps toward halting or reversing the global arms race. It is only to state that an effective foreign policy will increasingly need to rely upon a creative mix of negative and positive means of influence. Countries that are able to do so not only will be serving better their national interests, they are also more likely to contribute to a more stable international system.

Arms Control and Disarmament

Arms control and disarmament cannot be divorced from considerations of deterrence. Leaders responsible for national security are unlikely to exhibit much interest in the limitation of weapons if the outcome may reduce their deterrence capabilities. Motives not directly related to national security, such as a desire to reduce the burden on national budgets of military spending, have only rarely proved to be a sufficient incentive to produce lasting and effective disarmament measures. The protracted arms races prior to 1914 and 1939 and since 1945, as well as the example of many developing states that spend a vast proportion of their meager resources on military forces, suggest that purely economic motives will not arrest spiralling arms races. On the other hand, the fear of national, if not global, annihilation provides unprecedented incentives to stabilize deterrence by measures to reduce the fear of surprise attack, arrest the diffusion of nuclear weapons, minimize the probabilities and effects of technological breakthroughs, and diminish the likelihood of unintended war through accident or escalation.

Attempts to control or abolish the use of force are nearly as old as war itself, and they have taken the form of trying to limit both the ends sought through war and the instruments of violence. Included in the former category are the medieval concepts of the "just war," which implied that force could be used only for certain legitimate ends; the 1928 Kellogg-Briand Pact, outlawing the use of war; the Nuremberg war-crimes trials, in which the doctrine of "crimes against humanity" was used to punish top-ranking Nazi leaders; and the United Nations charter, in which signatories renounced the use of force except in self-defense.

More modest attempts have been made to limit and control the instruments of violence. During the nineteenth century, a movement to "humanize" the conduct of war led to agreements at the Hague Conference of 1899 outlawing certain weapons, including expanding (dum dum) bullets. The 1925 Geneva Protocol outlawed the use of poison gas; as of 1993, 141 countries have ratified it. Delegates at the Washington Conference of 1922 sought to prevent renewal of a naval arms race by limiting capital ship of the five major naval powers—England, the United States, France, Japan, and Italy—according to the ratio of 5:5:3:1.75:1.75, respectively. Subsequent efforts during the interwar years to limit either naval or land forces were unsuccessful, and even the Washington Naval Convention failed to survive the arms race of the 1930s.

Since World War II, considerable activity on questions of arms control and disarmament has produced a number of multilateral agreements (see the list of arms-control agreements in Chapter 15). For example, the 1987 INF Treaty, the first agreement by which the United States and the Soviet Union eliminated an entire class of weapons—missiles with a range of 300 to 1,500 miles—achieved a breakthrough on the thorny issue of verification by providing for intrusive on-site inspection to ensure that the missiles had actually been destroyed.

The Strategic Arms Reduction Talks (START) initiated by Presidents Reagan and Gorbachev during the 1980s have resulted in two important treaties reducing nuclear warheads and strategic delivery systems. START I, a treaty between the United States and four successor states of the former Soviet Union—Russia, Kazakhstan, Ukraine, and Belarus—was the first agreement that reduced rather than merely placed a ceiling on nuclear warheads and intercontinental strategic delivery systems. By its terms Kazakhstan, Ukraine and Belarus would no longer possess strategic nuclear weapons. START I was ratified in 1992 and 1993 by all of its signatories except Ukraine.

The START II Treaty, signed in the closing days of the Bush administration, is a Russian-American agreement that becomes operative only after START I has been ratified by all five of its signatories. The first phase reduces warheads to 3,800 to 4,250 and places limits on the numbers of multiple warhead (MIRV) missiles, as well as on those that may be launched from submarines (SLBMs). Further reductions to 3,000 Russian and 3,500 U.S. warheads will take place by the year 2003, or possibly three years earlier if the United States assists Russia in dismantling its most powerful MIRV missiles (SS-18 and SS-19). Most significantly, this second phase of START II commits both sides to eliminate all MIRVs. Following the precedent set by the INF Treaty, both START agreements incorporate a stringent regime of data exchanges and twelve types of on-site inspections. The success of these agreements will of course depend on the continuation in power in Moscow and elsewhere of leaders committed to adhering to the treaties.

The record in other areas of arms control has been mixed. More than 120 countries signed an agreement in 1993 to ban the production, stockpiling, and use of chemical weapons, and to destroy existing stockpiles of such weapons within ten years. The treaty, which includes provisions for on-site inspections, becomes operative in 1995 if at least sixty-five signatories have ratified it. Iraq, a country known to possess and have used chemical weapons, is not among the signatories. Important as these achievements are, however, they have at best slowed down rather than reversed the global arms race. Effectiveness of the Partial Test Ban Treaty is diminished by the boycott of two nuclear countries, China and France. Although Paris and Beijing have recently ratified the Nuclear Non-Proliferation Treaty, a number of important regional powers, including Argentina, Brazil, India, Israel and Pakistan, have refused to do so and, as of 1993, several of the former Soviet republics have yet to ratify it. The limits of the non- proliferation regime were revealed by post–Gulf War inspections of weapons programs in Iraq, a signatory of the Non- Proliferation Treaty. By spreading its purchases of "dual-use" technology across scores of suppliers in many countries, Iraq had moved surprisingly close to achieving nuclear status. Finally, North Korea, another NPT signatory, has successfully evaded international efforts to inspect its nuclear facilities.

The tendency to equate arms control with former international agreements may, however, lead to overly pessimistic conclusions about the feasibility of placing limits on the procurement or deployment of arms. Self-imposed limits on violence are sometimes more enduring than those found in treaties and have even survived wars. Whether from fear of reprisal, military impracticality, or unwillingness to bear the onus of initiating its use, neither the Allies nor the Axis powers used poison gas during World War II. During the Korean War, both qualitative and geographical limitations were imposed on American and United Nations armed forces; despite considerable domestic pressure to bomb Manchuria, to unleash Chinese forces on Taiwan, and to use tactical nuclear weapons, these plans were firmly rejected by President Truman. Although the USSR provided North Korean forces with vast quantities of military aid, Soviet land forces were withheld from the war and American supply bases in Japan were not attacked.

Other types of self-imposed arms-control measures that have been practiced by the United States and the Soviet Union, in the absence of any formal agreement to do so, include (1) efforts, even prior to the 1970 treaty, to prevent the diffusion of nuclear weapons, although the cost has been high in alienating such important allies as France and China; (2) moratoria on nuclear tests for limited periods of time; (3) occasional reductions in military budgets; and (4) restraint in deployment of certain types of weapons, such as orbiting thermonuclear bombs. The period of warming relations between Washington and Moscow since the late 1980s has also witnessed a number of unilateral steps by both countries to reduce significantly their armed forces and defense spending. A notable example may be found in Mikhail Gorbachev's UN speech of December 7, 1988, which pledged unilateral withdrawal of troops from Eastern Europe and significant cuts in defense spending. During the early 1990s, Presidents Bush and Gorbachev both initiated a number of arms-control steps, including taking some nuclear forces off alert status. Although such limitations pale in comparison to existing arms stockpiles, they nevertheless illustrate the point that not all efforts to control armaments require formal agreements.

Finally, informal and tacit cooperation on arms-control measures may take place. After an especially harrowing near-accident involving nuclear weapons in early 1961, American scientists developed a sophisticated safety system, the so-called permissive action links. (PALs), which prevents nuclear weapons from being armed without a release from a responsible command center. The Kennedy administration deliberately alerted the Soviets to the concept and importance of the system at an academic arms-control symposium in late 1962, and the information necessary to build the safety devices was passed to Soviet scientists at the 1963 Pugwash Conference.[35]

Given the unquestionable importance of controlling international violence, why have efforts to control arms not yielded much more substantial results? Not the least of the reasons is the lack of agreement even on the roots of the problem: Are armaments the causes or the symptoms of international tension? The answer is elusive, and the relationships of arms races to war can be debated. The arms race during the late nineteenth and early twentieth centuries probably contributed to the outbreak of World War I in 1914, but more vigilant French and British defense politics during the 1930s might have enabled them to deter the aggressive ambitions of German and Italian leaders. Moreover, arms have been and are among the most comprehensible instruments for making threats. In situations where objectives are incompatible and where the two sides are strongly committed to their objectives, they may not be able to influence each other's behavior through diplomatic persuasion or by offering rewards. In the absence of some central authority that can legislate peaceful change, states will always have to contemplate those situations in which intolerable demands are made or actions taken against them, and the only possibility of successful resistance lies in deterrence through the threat to retaliate. If arms are viewed not merely as instruments of destruction but as bargaining capabilities, manipulated in various ways to influence others states' behavior, we can better understand why former Soviet foreign minister Litvinov's admonition. "The only way to disarm is to disarm," appears deceptively simple. Thus, solution of tension-creating political issues might at least create an atmosphere in which weapons are seen as less necessary. But it is usually assumed that one can negotiate tension-reducing agreements only from a position of strength—that, to use Winston Churchill's words, one must "arm to parley." In this sense arms can be viewed as symptoms of deeper tensions.

Even though arms can be used for creating bargaining positions, they can also contribute to international tensions, thereby reducing the possibilities of settling outstanding political issues. Decision makers tend to perceive the intent behind their own weapons programs as purely defensive but to infer aggressive intent from those of the adversary. Doubts about the purpose of the enemy's weapons are apt to be resolved on the "safe" side—that is, by assuming the worst. ("Why else would they maintain such large arsenals?") Thus, in high-tension situations, decision makers are unlikely to settle for mere parity in armaments. We cannot, however, assess the probable consequences of arms races merely by examining gross figures for defense spending. Competition to develop weapons of increasingly greater accuracy and capability for destabilizing deterrence is much more likely to raise international tensions, especially in times of crisis. But arms races that add to the invulnerability of one's own deterrent without threatening those of adversaries will be much less likely to do so.[36]

[35]Edward Klein and Robert Littell, "Shh! Let's Tell the Russians," *Newsweek*, May 5, 1969, pp. 46–47.

[36]For this reason, mathematical studies of arms races based solely on gross expenditures (sometimes called "Richardson processes," after the British meteorologist who pioneered such analyses), however valid they may have been for earlier arms races such as that preceding World War I, may not be especially relevant for explaining or predicting the outbreak of war in the contemporary international system.

Decisions about levels of armaments are based on estimates of the adversary's current and expected future capabilities. These estimates may or may not be accurate; to the degree that they are incorrect, the error is likely to be in the direction of overestimating the capabilities of potential adversaries. Such misperceptions provide substantial fuel for arms races. One study revealed that military leaders invariably overestimated the military capabilities of potential enemies. In 1914, for example, although the French and Germans accurately calculated the capabilities of third powers, the Germans judged the French army to be larger than their own, whereas the French believed that their army was smaller than that of the Germans.[37] The CIA appears to have consistently overestimated economic growth rates in the former Soviet Union and, consequently, the level of its defense spending. On the other hand, during the 1960s Secretary of Defense McNamara predicted that the USSR had "opted out" of the strategic arms race, settling for a position second to the United States, an assessment not borne out by events of the 1970s and 1980s.

Further complicating the problem of arms control is the fact that the impetus for acquiring weapons may arise not only from external sources, such as the policies of adversaries or general international tensions. Technological developments may also create pressures for acquiring new weapons—for example, any scientific breakthrough that opens up possibilities for new applications or even for a change of strategic doctrine that is then used to justify acquisition and deployment of the weapons. And if there is no immediately obvious mission for the new weapons, there is always the clinching argument: "If we don't do it, they (the enemy) may." Thus, threats of a technological breakthrough by potential adversaries is a potent inhibitor of agreements that curtail weapons research and development activities. This fear, particularly important as the time between generations of weapons has become shorter, was cited more often than any other by those opposing the Nuclear Test Ban Treaty of 1963.

In addition, decisions about defense policies are often as heavily influenced by bureaucratic and other internal political considerations as by the state of international politics. Competition between departments and services for a share of the defense budget may be almost as intense as the international rivalries attending an arms race. This point is illustrated by the removal from office of Soviet Premier Nikita Khrushchev in 1964. His refusal to give the armed forces—or as Khrushchev called them, the "metal-eaters"—all the resources they demanded was, according to many informed observers, the main reason for his ouster. In 1967, President Johnson faced various pressures from pro-and anti-ABM forces, as well as the prospect of being vulnerable to charges of permitting an "ABM gap" if he chose to run for reelection the following year. Johnson's decision to deploy a partial ABM system reflected a compromise that was more sensitive to domestic political realities than to the international strategic situation.[38] Consider also the Anglo-German naval rivalry during the

---

[37]S. F. Huntington, "Arms Races," in *Public Policy, Yearbook of the Graduate School of Public Administration, 1958*, eds. Carl Friedrich and Seymour Harris (Cambridge, Mass.: Harvard University Press, 1958). Since the end of the Cold War, another motive has helped to sustain weapons procurement—a reluctance to add to unemployment by closing defense plants.

[38]Morton Halperin, *Bureaucratic Politics and Foreign Policy* (Washington: The Brookings Institute, 1974), Chapters 1 and 16.

early years of the twentieth century. This was a classic example of an arms race, because each country was responding directly to the other's naval strength. But specific budget decisions did not reflect merely the increasing military capabilities of the opponent. Winston Churchill, then first lord of the Admiralty, recalled one instance of bureaucratic disagreement: "In the end a curious and *characteristic* solution was reached. The Admiralty had demanded six ships; the economists offered four; and we finally compromised on eight."[39] No doubt similar episodes occur with regularity in defense ministries everywhere, irrespective of the nation's social, political, or economic system.

Countries may also acquire sophisticated weapons for other reasons, such as "prestige" or to maintain a regime in power. These motives do not, however, preclude the possibility that neighboring countries will then feel the need to follow suit, setting off a regional or local arms race. Nor are leaders of countries that arm themselves for these reasons necessarily more apt to show enthusiasm for arms-control agreements. It is scarcely conceivable that ruling groups in Libya, Serbia, Cuba, Algeria, North Korea, Syria, Iran, Jordan, Iraq, El Salvador, and a great many other countries would welcome the prospect of governing without a powerful military.

Earlier we cited fears of surprise attack, technological breakthroughs, and diffusion of nuclear weapons as the primary incentives for stabilizing deterrence through arms control. Paradoxically, these fears are also among the most formidable barriers to arms-control agreements. Unlike the case with trade agreements—which are self-executing and in which violations are immediately apparent and are not likely to endanger national survival—doubts that the other parties are actually carrying out the agreements in good faith are hard to allay. Especially in a situation with a historical background of distrust and tensions, the tendency to expect the worst of others becomes deeply ingrained in the habits and expectations of decision makers. Even gestures that, if taken at face value, would be regarded as conciliatory tend to evoke suspicions of deceit. "Inherent bad-faith models" of the adversary are hard to erode; and although threats may well be taken at face value, attempts to communicate reassurance, even through unilateral arms reduction, may be discounted. When Secretary of State Dulles was questioned in 1957 about the value for reducing world tensions of a Soviet plan to decrease unilaterally their armed forces by 1,200,000 men, he quickly invoked the theme of the bad faith of the Soviet leadership. He was asked, "Isn't it a fair conclusion from what you have said this morning that you would prefer to have the Soviet Union keep these men in their armed forces?" He replied, "Well, it's a fair conclusion that I would rather have them standing around doing guard duty than making atomic bombs."[40] Similarly, there is little indication that unilateral decisions of the Carter administration to cancel several major weapons programs—for example, the B-1 bomber and the "neutron bomb"—had any influence on Soviet defense policies. Suspicions of bad faith are by no means always unjustified, and each proven violation not only would add to the difficulties of achieving

[39]Winston S. Churchill, *The World Crisis: 1911–1914* (New York: Charles Scribner's, 1928), p. 33. Italics added.

[40]John Foster Dulles, "Transcript of News Conference, May 15, 1956," U.S. Department of State, *Bulletin* 34 (1956), 884–85.

further arms-control agreements; but also would strengthen the hands of those in each country who resist any limitations on weapons.

If a desire to arrest nuclear proliferation is an incentive for significant arms-control agreements, fear of nonsignatory countries may serve as a countervailing force. While the United States and the Soviet Union shared a nuclear monopoly, agreements between them would have been influenced and constrained only to a limited extent by the demands and military capabilities of other countries. But the day that Washington and Moscow could impose arms limitations on the rest of the world has long since passed—if, indeed, it ever existed. Moreover, as the diffusion of nuclear weapons accelerates, the problems of arms-control negotiations will become more complex. Identifying areas of mutual interest and converting these into acceptable arms-control formulas—difficult even in bilateral negotiations—is not apt to become easier as the number of governments directly involved increases and as the ability of alliance leaders to impose their wishes on junior members declines. China and France have long since indicated an unwillingness to follow the lead of their erstwhile allies on many issues involving weapons, and others (including Ukraine) may choose to follow their example. Indeed, it may be excessively optimistic to believe that the problem of nuclear proliferation is limited to states. Even if security arrangements for every existing nuclear weapon were absolutely foolproof—and there are reports that this is far from the case—the possibility cannot be written off as wholly implausible that criminal gangs, terrorist groups, self-appointed "liberation movements," and other subnational groups could gain access to fissionable materials and the knowledge to assemble a bomb of some kind for purposes of blackmail.

A traditional obstacle to substantial arms-control agreements is the problem of verification. As weapons become more powerful and as the perceived ability of adversaries to alter the existing military balance in a short span of time increases, the need for verification by inspection or other methods also increases. Atmospheric and underwater nuclear tests can be detected without on-site inspection, but control of production creates more difficult problems, which, despite some ingenious proposals, are still likely to require the presence of inspection teams. Owing to orbiting satellites and other advances in the technology of surveillance, the problem of monitoring has tended to become a less potent obstacle in recent arms-control negotiations. As noted earlier, the INF, START I, and START II Treaties established the principle that on-site verification is a standard feature of arms-control agreements. But as the case of Iraq makes clear, it is by no means impossible to circumvent verification procedures. Ironically, should future agreement result in significantly lower levels of armaments, concern over violations could be expected to increase; the smaller the arsenals, the greater the potential premium for cheating, and therefore the greater the fear that adversaries may be doing so.

A further obstacle to arms-control agreements is that of devising formulas that will not work to the disadvantage of any nation. Against a background of different perceived security requirements, *qualitatively* different weapons systems present a problem of comparability. How many bombers are equivalent to a battleship? How many infantry divisions are worth a missile-launching submarine or a squadron of jet aircraft? What is the deterrent value of an intermediate-range ballistic missile (IRBM) compared to that of an ICBM capable of reaching any spot on the globe? A piecemeal approach to disarmament—for example, starting first with nuclear weapons, then moving to conventional land forces—does not wholly resolve the problem.

Even a purely *quantitative* formula for reduction of a single type of weapon is likely to create controversy. Consider the case of countries A and B, which have stockpiles of 10,000 and 5,000 nuclear weapons, respectively. An across-the-board reduction of 50 percent, although requiring country A to scrap twice as many weapons, might be considered by country B's leaders a method of perpetuating their inferiority. To assert that even country B's smaller stockpiles may be enough to destroy any adversary's society several times over—in short, that when nuclear stockpiles become large enough, "superiority" ceases to have much significance—may not be persuasive to those responsible for national security. These two stockpiles might also be reduced to the same absolute level. Again, whatever its "mathematical equity," such a formula is unlikely to gain enthusiastic support from country A.

A final factor tending to inhibit arms-control agreements is that arms races and arms control may appear to involve different types of risks. Few foreign policy leaders are unaware that protracted arms races entail a danger of war, but this is at least a familiar risk. On the other hand, dangers associated with disarmament measures are much less familiar and may therefore appear more threatening. Thus, the acquisition of stable deterrent forces is probably a necessary, if not a sufficient, condition for significant reduction of arms. Only when finite deterrent forces are perceived capable of providing adequate security and when arms races and the proliferation of nuclear weapons are perceived to be a greater threat to security than the reduction of arms, are significant steps toward disarmament likely. But even at that point, disarmament efforts must proceed within the context of deterrence. Only arms control or disarmament measures that contribute to heightened confidence in deterrence are likely to gain much support among most countries. Conversely, only under conditions of stable deterrence and reduced political tensions are there likely to be genuine advances in reversing arms races. Vastly improved East-West relations during the late 1980s, followed by the end of the Cold War, and the political transformation of Eastern Europe created a window of opportunity for meaningful arms control; the former Cold War adversaries responded with a series of important arms reduction agreements. Conversely, there are far fewer indications that conditions in the Middle East provide a favorable setting for reversing the arms race in that region.

Summary

Weapons have traditionally been used for independent political units to help defend their interests and values when threatened from abroad or to achieve expansionist goals. By their conspicuous deployment or display, they are also used to make diplomatic threats credible in bargaining situations. Unlike conventional military forces, however, nuclear weapons are of no use in achieving such objectives as defeating a guerrilla movement, controlling strategic waterways, occupying territory, intervening to save a foreign government from internal rebellion, or ensuring supplies of foreign oil. Their main value lies in deterrence or the capacity to prevent major provocations or massive attack by enemies. Even in this limited area of influence between countries, weapons policies and deployment must be carefully planned, because effective deterrence depends upon credibility. Piling up weapons will not by itself establish credibility if the forces are vulnerable to destruction in a first strike. Various measures such as dispersal, concealment, or protection have been used to lower vulnerability, but none has been totally successful. Defense policy leaders must also consider the consequences of their actions on the policies of their adversaries. Actions that seemingly increase security may, in fact, appear provocative to potential enemies and lead to greater instability or uncontrolled arms races. Arms control and active defense policies have implications for the complex equations that create both stability and credibility.

Questions for Study, Analysis, and Discussion

1. Has the *para bellum* doctrine ("If you want peace, prepare for war") been rendered obsolete by the end of the Cold War? Why or why not?
2. Are military forces the symptoms or causes of international tensions? What examples can you cite in support of your answer? How strong is the evidence in support of the opposite position?
3. If, as some have argued, nuclear weapons contributed to the avoidance of war between the major powers during the Cold War, would nuclear proliferation similarly contribute to peace among smaller countries? Why or why not?
4. In what ways do the requirements of credibility and stability in deterrence policy reinforce or conflict with each other?
5. What are the major means of assuring the survivability of deterrence forces?
6. Do nuclear weapons strengthen or erode the motives for countries to join alliances? Why?
7. Which requirements for effective deterrence can impede arms-control agreements? Which can help to achieve such agreements?
8. If you had been a defense analyst in the government of Ukraine in 1993, would you have advised that it sign the START I Treaty? Why or why not?
9. At the Reykjavik Summit Conference in 1986, President Reagan and General Secretary Gorbachev proposed to eliminate all of their nuclear weapons within ten years. Had they been able to achieve such an agreement, would it have contributed to greater international stability? Why or why not?
10. During the 1980s, the American Catholic bishops criticized deterrence as being excessively and dangerously focused on credibility, thereby requiring states to enhance their reputations for standing firm rather than seeking to resolve conflicts through compromises. Do you agree with this criticism? Why or why not?

Selected Bibliography

Allison, Graham T., Essence of Decision: Explaining the Cuban Missile Crisis. Boston: Little, Brown, 1971.
Arms Control Today. Washington D.C. : Arms Control Association Bimonthly.

Aron, Raymond, The Century of Total War. Boston: Beacon, 1955.

Betts, Richard, Surprise Attack. Washington D.C.: The Brookings Institution, 1982.

Bracken, Paul, The Command and Control of Nuclear Forces. New Haven, Conn.: Yale University Press, 1983.

Brodie, Bernard, ed., The Absolute Weapon: Atomic Power and World Order. New York: Harcourt, Brace and Company, 1946.

———,*Strategy in the Missile Age.* Princeton, N.J.: Princeton University Press, 1959.

Buchan, Alastair F., War in Modern Society. London: Watts, 1966.

von Clausewitz, Karl, On War, ed. and trans. Michael Howard and Peter Paret. Princeton, N.J.: Princeton University Press, 1976.

"The Fate of Nuclear Weapons in the Former Soviet Union," *Carnegie Quarterly,* 37 (Winter/Spring 1992), 1–15.

Feaver, Peter D. Guarding the Guardians: Civilian Control of Nuclear Weapons in the United States. Ithaca, N.Y.: Cornell University Press, 1992.

Gaddis, John Lewis, Strategies of Containment. New York: Oxford University Press, 1982.

———,*The Long Peace.* New York: Oxford University Press, 1987.

George, Alexander L., and Richard Smoke, Deterrence in American Foreign Policy: Theory and Practice. New York: Columbia University Press, 1974.

———, *and William E. Simons, eds., The Limits of Coercive Diplomacy,* 2nd ed. Boulder, Colo.: Westview, 1993.

Gilpin, Robert, War and Change in World Politics. New York: Cambridge University Press, 1981.

Hoffmann, Stanley, The State of War. New York: Praeger, 1965.

Holsti, Ole R. "Crisis Decision Making," in *Behavior, Society and Nuclear War,* Vol. 1, Phillip E. Tetlock, et al. eds. New York: Oxford University Press, 1989.

Howard, Michael, War and the Liberal Conscience. New Brunswick, N.J.: Rutgers University Press, 1978.

Huntington, Samuel, The Common Defense. New York: Columbia University Press, 1961.

Huth, Paul, Extended Deterrence and the Prevention of Wars. New Haven, Conn.: Yale University Press, 1988.

International Institute for Strategic Studies, *Adelphi Papers.* London: I.I.S.S. Bimonthly.

———, *The Military Balance.* London: I.I.S.S. Annual.

———, *Strategic Survey.* London: I.I.S.S. Annual.

International Military and Defense Encyclopedia. McLean, Va.: Brassey's, 1993.

International Security. Cambridge, Mass.: M.I.T. Press. Quarterly.

Jervis, Robert, Richard Ned Lebow, and Janice Stein, eds., Psychology and Deterrence. Baltimore, Md.: Johns Hopkins University Press, 1985.

———, *The Meaning of the Nuclear Revolution.* Ithaca, N.Y.: Cornell University Press, 1989.

Keegan, John, A History of Warfare. New York: Alfred A. Knopf, 1993.

Lebow, Richard Ned, Between Peace and War. Baltimore: Johns Hopkins University Press, 1981.

Levi, Warner, The Coming End of War. Beverly Hills, Calif.: Sage, 1981.

Levy, Jack, "The Cause of War," in *Behavior, Society and Nuclear War,* Vol. 1, Phillip E. Tetlock, et al., eds., New York: Oxford University Press, 1989.

Mearsheimer, John J., Conventional Deterrence. Ithaca, N.Y.: Cornell University Press, 1983.

Morgan, Patrick, Deterrence: A Conceptual Analysis. Beverly Hills, Calif.: Sage, 1977.

Mueller, John. Retreat from Doomsday: The Obsolescence of Major War. New York: Basic Books, 1989.

Paret, Peter, editor. Makers of Modern Strategy from Machiavelli to the Nuclear Age. Princeton, N.J.: Princeton University Press, 1986.

Quester, George H., Deterrence before Hiroshima. New York: John Wiley, 1966.

Ropp, Theodore, War in the Modern World. Durham, N.C.: Duke University Press, 1959.

Schelling, Thomas C., The Strategy of Conflict. Cambridge, Mass.: Harvard University Press, 1960.

———, *Arms and Influence.* New Haven, Conn.: Yale University Press, 1966.

Shu Guang Zhang, Deterrence and Strategic Culture. Ithaca, N.Y.: Cornell University Press. 1993.

Singer, J. David, and Melvin Small, The Wages of War, 1816–1965. New York: John Wiley, 1972.

Smoke, Richard, War: Controlling Escalation. Cambridge Mass.: Harvard University Press, 1977.

Stein, Janice Gross, "Deterrence and Reassurance," in *Behavior, Society and Nuclear War,* Vol. 2, Phillip E. Tetlock, et al., eds. New York: Oxford University Press, 1991.

Stockholm International Peace Research Institute, SIPRI Yearbook of World Armaments and Disarmament. Stockholm, Sweden: Almqvist & Wiksell, annual.

Thompson, William R., On Global War. Columbia, S.C.: University of South Carolina Press, 1988.

Thucydides, The Peloponnesian War, trans. R. Warner. New York: Penguin, 1954 (431-411 B.C.).

Waltz, Kenneth, Man, the State and War: A Theoretical Analysis. New York: Columbia University Press, 1959.

Walzer, Michael, Just and Unjust War. New York: Basic Books, 1977.

Wiberg, Hakan, Ib Damgaard Peterson and Paul Smoker, Inadvertent Nuclear War. Tarrytown, N.Y.: Pergamon, 1993.

Wright, Quincy, A Study Of War, Vols. 1 and 2. Chicago: University of Chicago Press, 1942.

Chapter
11

Explanations
of Foreign Policy

Why in August 1990 did President Saddam Hussein of Iraq choose to invade and annex neighboring Kuwait? Why did Soviet President Mikhail Gorbachev jettison seventy years of Soviet foreign policy doctrine and practice, and instead accept major arms control proposals, the reunification of Germany, the integration of his country into the world capitalist system, and the dismantling of Soviet controls over the Eastern European countries? Why in contrast to neighboring Thailand, did Burma practice for thirty years a foreign policy strategy of strict isolationism? In the previous chapters we have described what states do to defend and pursue their purposes, whatever those might be. But it is not intellectually satisfying to stop there. We usually want to know *why* certain things happened, not just *how* they happened.

   Politics is a purposeful activity. Political parties and candidates seek office not just for the prestige and titles, but also to govern; that is, to preserve, change, or over-throw past practices and socioeconomic conditions in the country, province, city, or village. And so it is with foreign policy purposes and actions. They are designed to sustain or alter a current object, condition, or practice in the external environment. While some policies are designed to change conditions abroad for their own sake (e.g., various countries' efforts to help dismantle the apartheid system in South Africa), most are designed to promote some domestic purpose. The search for se-curity, welfare, autonomy, and prestige—the things that all governments pursue—arises primarily from domestic needs.

Whatever the purposes and the means employed to sustain, defend, or achieve them, those who define policies for the state have choices. Even though politicians often claim that they have "no choice" but to do something, in fact all policy making involves choosing among options. That is why we have policy debates. We as observers will defend or criticize those choices, using a variety of criteria for making judgments. Saddam Hussein chose to unleash his army against Kuwait for specific purposes, but he might have achieved them through other means as well. Gorbachev fundamentally altered many traditions of Soviet foreign policy. He was not compelled to do so. The Burmese military government after 1962 sealed off the country from the outside world; other leaders would have acted differently.

In searching for explanations, then, we must place ourselves in the positions of the policy makers and try to identify their intentions and purposes, and then understand why they chose various strategies and actions to sustain or achieve them. Few policies are chosen for a single reason; monocausal explanations are therefore seldom satisfactory. Nevertheless, they abound in journalistic and even academic foreign policy analyses. Examples of monocausal explanations would include the view, held by many people in the West during the height of the Cold War, that all Soviet foreign policy maneuvers were simply the playing out of some master plan for the communization of the world. This type of explanation emphasized the compelling importance of ideology as a source of foreign policy. Other monocausal theories have located personality characteristics (e.g., Stalin's paranoia) to explain a country's external relations, or the nature of its economic system (capitalism), or some conspiracy theory. Geographic determinism has always had popular appeal; country X is compelled to follow a particular policy line because of its location in relation to other countries, bodies of water, mountains, or other topographical features. While such explanations may contain germs of truth, they are not very satisfactory because they fail to account for variations in policy. For example, if geographic location, culture, religion, dominant personalities, or other factors are determining, why do two countries that share these characteristics have fundamentally different foreign policies? Libya and Tunisia have similar location, both are Muslim countries, and their ethnic composition is predominantly Arab. Thailand and Burma also share many common attributes and characteristics. Yet, in both examples, the two countries follow significantly different foreign policy lines and actions. Tunisia is a moderate, relatively passive actor that occasionally mediates conflicts between Arab States. Libya under Colonel Khadaffi is an aggressive, outward-looking actor that has involved itself in various forms of interventionary and subversive activities, has played a role in the domestic politics of countries as far away as the Philippines and some South Pacific island states, and has organized a variety of terrorist activities throughout the world. Burma has been an isolated state since 1962, sealing itself off from the outside world, shunning diplomatic contacts and involvement, and limiting its participation in regional and global economic processes to a minimum. Thailand, in contrast, linked its security during the Vietnam War to the United States, opened up its economy to foreign investment, has been an active player in the affairs of the Association of Southeast Asian Nations (ASEAN), and has allowed extensive ownership of its resources and some industries to foreigners.

Monocausal theories are inadequate because a major line or action of foreign policy is seldom chosen for a single reason or purpose. Governments operate in highly complex external and domestic environments. These contexts offer both opportunities and constraints, and policy makers have to respond to them constantly by making choices, all the time trying to protect or advance their nations' interests, however they define them. (We use the qualifying term because some leaders and regimes define those interests in narrow class or clique terms—"What is good for me and my friends is good for my country.") Very seldom is just a single condition compelling in the sense of vastly reducing the field of choice. Only in the case of a sudden military attack—the assault on Pearl Harbor on December 7, 1941, for example—do the choices narrow down to just one or two. In all other foreign policy situations, a variety of alternatives are always available.

For purposes of showing how foreign policy is made, we can distinguish between the external context—all those conditions and other countries' policies that impact on one's own choices—and the domestic environment. We list below how those two contexts relate to the purposes and actions of states. The list in Figure 11-1 is not exhaustive, but the individual items are often relevant to policy-making situations.

The External/Systemic Influences on Policy

The Structure of the System

As we have demonstrated in chapters 2 and 3, the overall structure of power in an international system expands or narrows the range of foreign policy strategies available to many members of the system. In a tight polar system, such as existed in Greece during the fifth century B.C., or during the height of the Cold War, most small states face strong pressures to become compliant alliance partners of the major powers. They ultimately choose to trade off a certain amount of autonomy for the sake of security. Alliance partners that defect to become neutrals, or in other ways fail to support their great power mentors, face compulsion. Athens' allies that withheld troop levies or payments of gold faced siege, occupation, and in some cases the slaying of the total adult male population. Similarly, Hungary's withdrawal from the Warsaw Pact in 1956 was met with the Soviet invasion of the country. In such system structures, the latitude of choice for security policies is restricted, particularly for smaller states. In a diffuse system, in contrast, alliance commitments tend to be transitory and the menu of choices for maximizing military security may range from isolation to neutrality to loose coalitions.

The distribution of power in a system also influences the nature of the international agenda. In a system distinguished by a great variety of states, ranging from superpowers to micro-states, the concerns of the midgets are not likely to command much attention, unless the small can band together to press their common concerns (e.g., the Group of 77). In a system with less pronounced hierarchical features, it is easier for all states to raise issues for debate and resolution.

FIGURE 11-1
Foreign Policy Sources, Constraints, and Opportunities

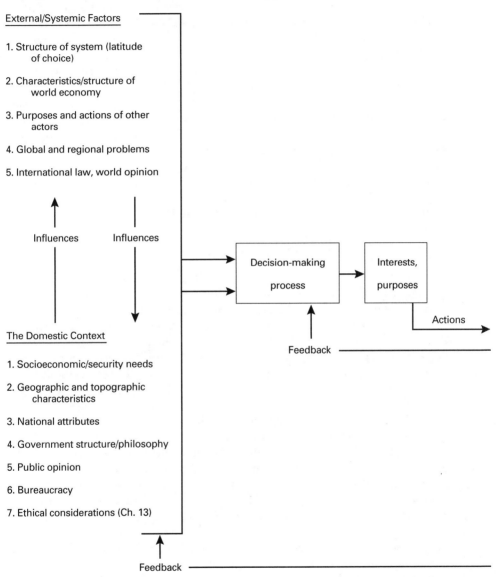

The Nature of the World Economy

Trends and developments in the world economy have both structural and more immediate impacts on the welfare policies of different countries. Consider the plight of a small, landlocked or island country that produces only several commodities—mostly raw materials—for export, and yet faces severe problems of overpopulation and high unemployment. What are its options? The system offers some opportunities. The government, for example, can obtain loans from international institutions such as the World Bank. The cost, of course, is indebtedness. The government can obtain technical assistance from a variety of external sources for developing new export commodities or for increasing yields and outputs of those that it already produces. The country can send its talented youth to foreign countries to obtain the highest levels of education. On the other hand, there are numerous systemic constraints. The foreign demand for the country's exports is limited, so expanding production will only have the effect of driving down prices. World price fluctuations can decimate the local economy, thus ruining all long-range government domestic programs and plans. It is almost impossible to develop new industries because of the commanding lead in technology held by the major industrial countries. Only if the government can locate a tiny niche of production—making specific components of computers, for example— might it possibly break into some industrial activity. Overall, for the small, developing country, the world economic system appears to have more built-in constraints than opportunities. This means that the area of practical or realistic choice is relatively small, compared with those available to major industrial countries.

The Policies and Actions of Other States

Most governments, most of the time, respond to the actions and policies of other governments; that is, to those that take initiatives that are perceived to have some impact on one's own interests, principles, and preferences. Over the past few years, NATO members have been struggling to define responses to the new problems facing Europe such as war in the Balkans. How should a security order for Europe be constructed? What should be the role of NATO in it? What should be an appropriate military strategy in a Europe no longer facing Cold War conditions? How many troops and what kind of equipment would be necessary for a new security order?

The response may not be just to the foreign policy initiatives of another government. They might arise from the domestic policies and events in a foreign country. How, for example, should India respond to the Tamil rebellion in Sri Lanka, given that there is a significant Tamil population in India? How should Pakistan respond to the Muslim separatist movement in Kashmir? How should the industrial countries respond to political and economic turmoil in Russia? Or how are Canada's economic policies going to be influenced by a significant increase in interest rates in Japan?

In some cases, governments can choose not to respond. Note that this is a choice in itself. What may be a foreign policy "occasion" for one country may be a matter of relative indifference to another. A great power is often identified as one whose interests are affected by domestic events and foreign policy initiatives almost anywhere in the world. Minor powers, in contrast, have only limited regional interests and may therefore afford the luxury of ignoring events and trends in faraway places.

Responses may be required not just for the decisions and actions, domestic or external, of other states. Nonstate actors may raise problems that require a policy.

International organizations, for example, may independently raise issues that impinge on a state's domestic policies or interests. So may drug cartels, environmental groups, and a host of other transnational private organizations.

The Global and Regional Problems Arising from Private Activities

In the course of conducting their ordinary lives, people create all sorts of problems that transcend national borders. The use of automobiles helps create a global pollution and earth-warming problem. Procreation creates a world population problem. Industrialization creates pollution and resource-depletion problems. Grazing goats and cattle cause deforestation and desertification, which in turn help to foster malnutrition. The list is almost endless. When more than 5 billion people indulge in everyday economic activities, they leave numerous residues that are harmful for future economic activities, for health, and for other aspects of welfare. When governments and numerous private groups become aware of the increasing dangers, they must respond in some manner. Because these problems are interconnected and transcend national boundaries, a purely national response is usually inadequate and ineffective. How other people live, produce, consume, and dispose thus can become an occasion for foreign policy decisions and actions, including the commitment of resources. We will take up this theme in the final chapter. Here it is sufficient to emphasize that increasingly the ordinary activities of individuals in pursuit of their private purposes eventually translate into a foreign policy problem for most governments. The whole ethos of modern production and mass consumption—which has now become global—has created a host of new difficulties and challenges for governments and private groups.

The Domestic Context

The standard purposes of security, welfare, autonomy, and prestige derive from a host of historical developments, ideologies, and assumptions about the good life. All countries face an actual or potential security problem because we assume or believe that communities should be organized into distinct and separate states. The idea of sovereignty is simply an acknowledgment that each community should govern itself, and that no other authority has the right to rule or legislate within its territorially defined confines. Similarly, the idea that governments should promote the economic and other dimensions of public welfare is relatively new. If we accepted the idea that man's material fate is divinely governed (e.g., if we are born poor we must remain poor), then we would not expect and demand that governments regulate and promote international trade and economic growth. And if we did not value our unique languages, cultures, and religions, we would not be concerned about questions of autonomy. All government is thus in large part concerned with promoting these kinds of social, economic, and symbolic values. Insofar as their realization depends upon the policies and actions of other states, then they become foreign policy problems. National economic welfare, for example, is strongly dependent upon foreign trade for many countries. And, as we have seen in Chapter 4, security strategies based on alliances or neutrality usually require the cooperation of other governments.

Geographical and Topographical Characteristics

Socioeconomic and security needs are clearly related to geographical and topographical characteristics. Natural endowments are not distributed evenly around the world. Some states are richly endowed with resources (think of the billions of dollars of oil wealth in some of the small Arab states); others are resource-poor. Some states are relatively isolated or distant from major centers of military power, and therefore relatively free of security threats. This was the case of the United States in the nineteenth century, and remains the case for some of the small South Pacific island states today. It is not difficult to expand at length on the opportunities, vulnerabilities, and constraints that geographic and topographic characteristics have on different countries' security, welfare, and autonomy problems.

But we must avoid forms of geographic determinism. Take the example of Japan. In the 1930s, the Japanese faced a severe mismatch between a growing population and the availability of resources. The depression created deep social misery, and restrictive practices by the major industrial countries prevented the Japanese from engaging in trade to obtain vital raw materials and energy resources. These were just some of the conditions that spawned the idea of the military conquest of Manchuria, starting in 1931, and ultimately of creating a Japanese-centered East Asia "Co-prosperity Sphere." Led by the military, the Japanese decided to resolve their acute welfare problem through military means. A monocausal explanation would emphasize Japan's island location, its rapidly growing population, and its lack of resources. The Japanese were therefore compelled to go to war.

As an explanation, there is some evidence to support the argument. Yet consider that faced with many similar conditions after World War II, the Japanese resolved the same sorts of problems through military dependence upon the United States, aggressive export-led growth, and the investment of significant public funds in research, development, and education. The problems were the same, but the solutions were fundamentally different. As in all policy, there were choices. Geographic and topographic features can substantially narrow and condition them, but they are rarely determining. Above all, technological innovations can alter their significance. The invention of long-range bombers and intercontinental missiles, for example, fundamentally changed the strategic isolation of North America after World War II and thus required Canada and the United States to develop entirely new strategies for coping with security problems. Similarly, the future development of alternative energy sources may fundamentally change the vulnerabilities and costs of industrialization in many developing countries. It would also reduce significantly the economic and diplomatic leverage of OPEC members.

National Attributes

By attributes we mean the main defining characteristics of states: their territorial size, population, economic system and performance, level of economic development, and the like. Does it make a difference what kinds of attributes states have? Researchers have been pondering this question for the last four decades, and there are many theories that go back several hundred years. We would ask, for example, Are there patterns of foreign policy behavior (purposes, goals, and actions) that are *unique* to small, developing countries, or to large, industrial countries? The research has uncovered either contradictory findings, or no significant findings. There is only one characteristic that holds through many years and across many states: Great powers are more likely than others to use military force as a means of defending their interests and pursing their purposes.[1] This is a valid generalization backed by voluminous empirical data. But is it size alone that accounts for it? An explanation might proceed as follows. Great powers have more purposes, interests, and objectives regarding the external environment than do lesser actors. They are able to do more things in international politics because they have superior capabilities; to put it another way, the larger the state, the more power, and the more power, the more diverse its goals. The more interests it has to extend or protect, the more likely it is to become involved in conflict. States with weak capabilities are less likely to formulate ambitious objectives, although the actions of Egypt under Nasser, Libya under Khadaffi, Iran under the clerics, and Iraq under Saddam Hussein show that lack of capabilities (compared with the great powers) does not necessarily inhibit a regime from pursuing broad revolutionary objectives at least on a regional level.

Another form of explanation is that traditionally great powers have arrogated for themselves special responsibilities for arranging the main contours of the international system and, in a metaphorical sense, of policing it. It was the great powers that refashioned the world after the Napoleonic wars, World War I, and World War II. In each case, they also assigned themselves the task of ensuring that the great peace settlements and the norms governing international conflicts would be observed. Under the charter of the United Nations, for example, the five great powers have a special responsibility for maintaining "international peace and security," and through the veto, hold special privileges of withholding consent from any great power-led police action. We have seen since the days of the Congress of Vienna (1815) repeated use of force by the "policemen" to enforce international norms. Recent examples would be the United States intervention into the Korean War (1950) under United Nations auspices; the formation of a multinational flotilla in the Persian Gulf to safeguard neutral shipping during the Iran-Iraq war (particularly from 1987 to 1988); and the creation of a multinational naval blockade, again in the Persian Gulf, as a means of applying United Nations economic sanctions against Iraq for its aggression against Kuwait in 1990. Leadership in upholding community purposes is one reason why the great powers have used force more than other types of states.

But we must not assume that this explanation is sufficient. The great powers have also been more war prone for purely national reasons; that is, for the advancement and protection of their narrower interests. They are more likely than other

---

[1]Quincy Wright, *A Study of War*, 2nd ed. (Chicago: University of Chicago Press, 1965), pp. 53, 58; George Modelski, "War and the Great Powers," *Peace Research Society (International) Papers*, Vol. 18 (1971), 45–60; Jack Levy, *War in the Modern Great Power System, 1495–1975* (Lexington: University of Kentucky Press, 1983).

states to be involved in the domestic affairs of a broad range of states, and to intervene militarily to support their friends and to try to topple their opponents. We have already seen in Chapter 9 the extent to which military interventions abroad have been a hallmark of the foreign policies of the great powers. Lesser states, particularly in recent years, have emulated them, but not with equal or greater frequency.

Other attributes do not relate to distinct foreign policy patterns, although in the area of economics and trade, there have been significant cleavages of interest and diplomatic styles between the developing and industrialized countries.

Government Structure and Philosophy

Governmental structures explain little about the substance of policies, but they do impose distinctly varying degrees of constraint. In systems of personalized authoritarian rule, where a single leader decides the main outlines of all policies, the constraints are few. We immediately think of Stalin, Hitler, Mussolini, Saddam Hussein, and many others. They command positions—often maintained in part through terror and suppression, and never subject to vote or specific term in office—which allow them to make commitments, change courses of action, and choose extreme policies, such as military force, without fear of domestic opposition, loss of office, or mass defection of loyal advisers. Other government structures have single groups (e.g., parties) in power, with substantial loyalty among party adherents. This is the case normally in parliamentary systems where a single party has a disciplined majority in the legislature. Great Britain under Margaret Thatcher's leadership provided one example. In this type of system, the latitude of choice remains fairly wide, although all policies eventually are judged through elections, and if too controversial, may lead to defections from the parliamentary majority, and possibly to the collapse of the government.

Yet another pattern is government through coalitions of groups, either within a single party (Japan) or between parties (the Likud-Labor coalition in Israel, from 1987 to 1989). Here all major policy initiatives and responses are subject to bargaining between groups and the constant need to develop majorities and a consensus. Policy paralysis is a frequent result of this kind of government structure. In Israel, for example, the Likud-Labor government could not develop a strategy for engaging in negotiations on the future of the Palestinians and the West Bank and Gaza areas because the parties' views were so different.

Finally, there are government structures where multiple autonomous groups vie with each other for influence, and where some may be in a position to veto policies decided upon by the ostensible centers of executive authority. Foreign policy making in the United States is difficult to manage not only because of multitudes of bureaucratic interests, but because an entirely independent body—Congress—has important controls over the executive. These include the authorization and withholding of funds, the approval of treaties and executive (including ambassadorial) appointments, and the right to investigate and inquire into almost any presidential policy. Throughout American history, Congress has been able to scuttle major presidential initiatives (failure to approve the peace treaty with Germany and the League of Nations covenant in 1919), to constrain or limit planned or anticipated executive policies (American policy in Vietnam, particularly after 1968), and to control the scope of other policies (establishing strict limits on the amount and types of American aid to the Nicaraguan *Contras* in the 1980s). Combined with limited terms of office and regular elections, the American presidency, despite all the resources it commands, faces constant challenges to its leadership in foreign policy.

The presence of multiple autonomous groups within a less structured situation than is found in the United States often leads to paralysis: No policy can be formulated because leading governmental groups cannot fashion any type of consensus. Plans are vetoed, scuttled, or sabotaged, sometimes even by nonofficial groups. During the Iranian-American hostage crisis from 1979 to 1980, there was no locus of authority in Teheran, despite the Ayatollah Khomeini's apparent authority. How to deal with the hostages became a matter of constant debate between moderates in the Iranian foreign ministry, members of the prime minister's office, the student militants, and the radical clergy. Several initiatives to resolve the crisis were blocked by the students, shifting majorities in the Revolutionary Council, and Khomeini himself.[2]

There are differences in regimes not only in terms of their composition but also in their philosophical and political programs. These have major consequences on the substance of their foreign policies. Following a distinction emphasized by Henry Kissinger,[3] charismatic-revolutionary and bureaucratic-pragmatic regimes not only make policy differently, but have fundamentally different objectives and purposes. The former often come into power not to adapt or adjust to regional and global circumstances, but to alter them in significant ways. Most revolutionary regimes go through a period when they want to export revolutionary principles and practices abroad. Such was the case for Soviet Russia after 1917, Hitler's Germany, China after 1949, Iran after the overthrow of the Shah's regime, and Nicaragua after the Sandinista revolution of 1979. For such regimes, foreign policy purposes are aimed at constructing entirely new international arrangements, and not just solving problems in piecemeal fashion. They are antagonistic not just to particular states, but to the norms, governing principles, and hierarchy of the entire system or within particular regions. Several examples will illustrate. The early Bolshevik leaders in their program and ideological pronouncements rejected the states system as they saw it at the turn of the last century and during World War I. Their plan was to pursue world revolution and to construct an entirely new system of relationships based on working class solidarity and socialist economic principles. They rejected all the norms and diplomatic practices of the "old" system as "bourgeois" and "reactionary." The revolutionary goals were, initially, nothing less than the reconstruction of the international system on fundamentally different principles.

---

[2]See Margaret C. Hermann, Charles F. Hermann, and Joe D. Hagan, "How Decision Units Shape Foreign Policy Behavior," in Charles F. Hermann, Charles W. Kegley, and James N. Rosenau, eds., *New Directions in the Study of Foreign Policy* (Boston: Allen & Unwin, 1987), pp. 322–23. For government structures and policy in general, see Joe Hagan, "Regimes, Political Opposition, and the Comparative Analysis of Foreign Policy," in the same volume.

[3]In *American Foreign Policy* (New York: W. W. Norton, 1969), pp. 17–43.

Adolph Hitler and his Nazi regime were similarly committed to revolutionary foreign policy purposes. Hitler considered the state an anachronism of the eighteenth and nineteenth centuries. He rejected all norms of international law, international institutions like the League of Nations, and traditional international economic arrangements. The state should be based on race, not on nationality or historical-legal grounds, and since the only way races could survive was through constant expansion and war, the German master race would have to expand throughout most of Europe and deep into Russia. There was to be a hierarchy of races, not of nations. Those at the top—the Aryans—would conquer the lesser races and use them as slave labor. Jews and Gypsies were to be exterminated. National frontiers were to be abolished and replaced with racial frontiers. All of the doctrines associated with the Westphalian system of sovereign states were to be abolished and replaced by looser norms appropriate to relations of racial domination and subordination.

At the regional level, some revolutionary governments have sought to achieve a wholesale restructuring of power relations, although few have emulated the bizarre dreams of a Lenin or Hitler. Colonel Nasser in the 1950s was committed to destroying the vestiges of British and French imperialism in the Middle East, and was largely successful in this endeavor. Although he spoke of Arab unity, he did not, like Hitler, seek to destroy the concepts and reality of sovereign states and the states system.

The bureaucratic-pragmatic style of policy making, in contrast, is characterized by (1) a generally reactive stance toward the external environment, in which policy is made up primarily of responses to situations abroad, rather than initiatives to alter established power relations; (2) a mode of thought that assumes that all events raise "problems" that can be solved by hard work and the give-and-take of diplomatic bargaining; and (3) a strong division of labor, emphasizing specialization. A "problem" is studied extensively by all sorts of bureaucratic experts; extensive data are gathered to illuminate the issue; and formal recommendations are made, reflecting the organizational traditions and biases of various government agencies. According to Kissinger, "outcomes depend more on the pressure or persuasiveness of contending [bureaucratic] advocates than on a concept of overall purpose."[4] This kind of government generally accepts the international status quo, the prevailing norms and procedures of international diplomacy, and prevailing relationships of domination and subordination, particularly within their own region.

Public Opinion

Probably no aspect of the study of foreign policy is more difficult to generalize about than the relationship of public opinion to a government's external objectives and diplomatic behavior. More research on this area, particularly in non-Western countries, needs to be completed before students of international relations can offer generalizations with much confidence. The characteristics of political systems in the world today vary so immensely—from primitive, patriarchal, or religious oligarchies to modern industrial democracies and totalitarian dictatorships—that any proposition would have to be qualified at least in terms of the type of society being consid-

[4]Ibid., p. 40.

ered. Our comments will refer, therefore, primarily to those societies in which the public has relatively free access to information from abroad, where there is a general awareness of the external environment, and where formal political institutions are maintained by widespread political support.

First, we should eliminate those hypotheses that suggest either that foreign policy goals and diplomatic behavior are merely a response to domestic opinions or that public attitudes are virtually ignored as important components of a definition of a situation. Some government officials have claimed frankly that their decisions could not be influenced by fickle public attitudes; it is also easy to cite examples where officials yielded to public pressures despite their own preferred policies. Instead of assuming a simple or direct relationship between public opinions on foreign affairs and government policies, we should distinguish (1) *who* is expressing opinions concerning (2) *what* issues in (3) *which* situations. The characteristics of these three qualifiers may have important effects on the ultimate influence of public opinion on the formulation of objectives and actions.

Studies of public attitudes conclude that the vast majority of people—even in highly literate societies—are unknowledgeable, uninterested, and apathetic with regard to most issues of world affairs.[5] They also reveal that public images and attitudes toward foreign countries are highly resistant to change even when dramatic events radically alter the main issues of international politics.[6] Other studies suggest that government, university, and private programs that have sought to create wider public knowledge and appreciation of the complexities of international politics have seldom met with success.[7] An investigation of opinions and actions on the Vietnam conflict, undertaken through a sample survey of American respondents during 1967, revealed that although a large proportion of the people were *concerned* about the war, only 13 percent reported that they had tried to convince someone to change his or her views on the war, and only 3 percent had done anything such as writing to officials or newspapers. Less than 1 percent of the 1,499 respondents had participated in marches or demonstrations.[8] Considering the very contentious nature of the war and the heated discussion it aroused, the figures are extremely low.

For purposes of analysis, any society has a small top layer of the "attentive" public[9] that is reasonably well informed, articulate, and interested, although not necessarily more prone to change basic attitudes when subjected to new information, propaganda, or dramatic events abroad. In most industrial countries, the attentive public

---

[5]For example, Gabriel Almond, *The American People and Foreign Policy* (New York: Harcourt Brace Jovanovich, 1950); Gabriel Almond and Sidney Verba, *The Civic Culture* (Princeton, N.J.: Princeton University Press, 1963), esp. Part II regarding knowledge of, and interest in, domestic policies; Warren E. Miller and Donald E. Stokes, "Constituency Influence in Congress," *American Political Science Review*, 57 (1963), 45–56; and Milton J. Rosenberg, "Images in Relation to the Policy Process: American Public Opinion on Cold-War Issues," in *International Behavior*, ed. Herbert C. Kelman (New York: Holt, Rinehart & Winston, 1965), pp. 277–334.

[6]Karl Deutsch and Richard Merritt, "Effects of Events on National and International Images," in *International Behavior*, ed. Kelman.

[7]Joseph Frankel, *The Making of Foreign Policy* (New York: Oxford University Press, 1963), p. 72.

[8]Sidney Verba and Richard A. Brody, "Participation, Policy Preferences, and the War in Vietnam," *Public Opinion Quarterly*, 34 (1970), 325–32.

[9]The concept is introduced by Almond in *The American People and Foreign Policy.*

is closely correlated with higher education, urban domicile, professional occupation, higher income, middle age, and male gender. Estimates of the size of the attentive public range from 1 to 15 percent, depending on how the category is defined. Next to the attentive public exists a layer of the population, normally comprising 30 to 50 percent of the total, that possesses established attitudes toward, and images of, foreign countries and their actions, some knowledge of a limited range of issues, and some capacity to express opinions if asked. Finally, the rest of a society, in some cases constituting 70 percent or more of the population, can be characterized on most issues as apathetic, uninformed, and nonexpressive, although in certain circumstances, these people can display considerable interest in some issue areas and, if properly mobilized, can express great hostility or loyalty to their leader's policies and to other countries.

On what kinds of issues are the opinions found in different layers or groups within society expressed as demands to establish certain foreign policy goals or to undertake certain actions vis-à-vis other states? The attentive public is likely to be concerned with a wide range of foreign policy problems and to express opinions on them either directly to policy makers or simply to friends and associates. They constitute probably the only segment of society that *introduces* ideas for the consideration of politicians and foreign policy officials.[10] They are also likely to have adequate information on a number of foreign countries, well-defined opinions, and preferred solutions to contemporary problems. Although the bottom layer may be generally apathetic, on certain issues it may become highly involved and express views through diverse channels. Consider one hypothetical example. Wheat farmers may not have much general interest in world affairs, may possess little knowledge about foreign countries and their problems, and may have unrefined attitudes and images based more on family or regional traditions than on a careful examination of contemporary information. But when foreign competition or subsidies hurt their export sales, they may become highly vocal and exert considerable pressure on their government for various forms of protection. In other words, apathy and ignorance end when a problem is perceived as having a *direct* impact on the life of the individual. The *scope* of public expression is thus related to the nature of the issue or problem under consideration.

It would still be an oversimplification to argue that those in the bottom layer of a society (in terms of interest and knowledge, not class) become involved only on issues of direct relevance to their private lives, whereas those of the attentive public are interested in a much broader scope of affairs. No matter what the level of interest or knowledge among people, they all hold some notions about appropriate and inappropriate foreign policy goals and actions. Gabriel Almond has used the term *foreign policy mood* to suggest those very *general* attitudes or predispositions that prevail in a nation at any given time. In the nineteenth and early twentieth centuries in the United States, the predominant public mood was isolation and indifference to European affairs. Until the late 1980s, it was a mood of pronounced fear of, and hostility toward, the Soviet Union. War weariness in Great Britain during the 1930s

---

[10]For further discussion and some empirical evidence, see Johan Galtung, "Foreign Policy Opinion as a Function of Social Position," in *International Politics and Foreign Policy: A Reader in Research and Theory*, rev. ed., ed. James N. Rosenau (New York: Free Press, 1969), pp. 55–72.

was an important basis for England's appeasement policy toward Hitler and Mussolini. Such moods, while not suggesting concrete foreign policy objectives, at least *set limits* around the theoretical policy alternatives of policy makers. On the major questions of a country's general orientation to the rest of the world, war and peace, and general style of diplomacy, everyone has opinions and is likely to express them when challenged. When the *scope* of public opinion is so broad, it is likely to have great influence on the alternatives that policy makers would regard seriously. The mood, in other words, has a constraining effect on policy alternatives, but not much direct impact on specific issues. The American public in the 1990s demands decreased defense spending and limited intervention abroad, but their mood does not specify which weapons should be developed or abandoned or exactly how many troops should join the UN humanitarian mission in Somalia. In Galtung's words, the public establishes a vast region of admissible policies surrounded by a belt of inadmissible policies. The vast majority of citizens or subjects thus figure in the definitions of situations by policy makers only in setting bounds to various alternatives. On most specific issues, they must be considered an insignificant element in policy making.

The impact of public attitudes and opinions on the selection of objectives and making decisions can be related, then, to the scope of the public, which in turn is related to the type of issue at stake. A third variable would be the general situation in which opinions are being expressed. Is the role of opinion in times of crisis the same as it is during a period of relative stability and noninvolvement in international affairs? We would expect the scope of the opinion-expressing public to vary directly with the degree of urgency or threat in a situation. More people are probably aroused to take interest in foreign affairs when a conflict develops than when diplomatic conditions are "normal," and there is much historical and experimental evidence suggesting that even societies strongly divided among themselves tend to become united in times of conflict. If a diplomatic-military confrontation creates a public consensus, this opinion is likely to restrict the number of options diplomatic officials would seriously consider. Public opinion in these critical situations, while it does not prescribe exact policies or responses, establishes limits beyond which few policy makers would normally dare to act.

In a *crisis* situation, however, public opinion probably constitutes only an insignificant factor in definitions of the situation. In contrast to a conflict, which may start slowly and drag on for years, a crisis is characterized by sudden unanticipated actions, high perceptions of threat, and feelings that something has to be done immediately (see Chapter 14 for further discussion). In these circumstances, decisions are almost always made by a few key policy makers; they believe that action of some sort is so necessary that there is little time to consult broadly among legislators or lower administrative officials, to say nothing of the public at large. Developments during a crisis may occur so fast, in any event, that the public seldom has the time to mobilize and express opinions through such institutionalized channels as political parties, legislatures, or interest groups. During the Cuban missile crisis, for instance, those who debated the various policy alternatives deliberately shielded themselves from public scrutiny and did their work mostly in secret. In President Kennedy's opinion, a "good" decision would be more likely if policy makers were immune from considerations of public pressure.

It would be omitting an important part of the relationship between opinion and foreign policy if we suggested that policy makers only *respond* to public pressures. In fact, the relationship in democratic societies involves complex interaction in which officials and the public or its component groups react to each other's behavior, values, and interests. If in some cases government officials feel constrained to choose policy goals and actions consistent with prevailing public moods, it is no less true that they spend considerable time advocating their own position and characterization of a situation to the population. Because of superior knowledge and access to information, governments occupy a position from which they can interpret events, purposes, and means to the population and actually create attitudes, opinions, and images where none existed before. Although independent communications media may express differing views, a prime minister or president can be very persuasive by virtue of his or her political prestige and expertise. It has often been observed that information or propaganda emanating from a reliable or prestigious source has more impact on opinions than has information dispersed by less credible sources.[11] Thus, what many people know of, or feel about, a critical situation abroad and their own government's actions and responses to it may originate from the government itself—from press conferences, parliamentary debates, or political speeches. Empirical studies demonstrate that changes in public attitudes *follow* government actions, which implies that governments are instrumental in creating the "mood" that also constrains them.[12]

In political systems where all information is controlled by the government, public opinion plays predominantly a supporting function. A person whose sources of information about the outside world are restricted to a government-controlled newspaper must have considerable initiative and access to unusual resources in order to develop attitudes and opinions contrary to those prescribed for one by one's government.[13] Since members of such societies normally have no independent sources of information and are not allowed channels of communication through which to express opposition to a government's foreign policies, the government is free to change its objectives, withdraw from untenable positions, or change allies without having to worry about domestic reactions. Domestic attitudes are not, therefore, a salient aspect of the definition of the situation. President Roosevelt, collaborating with members of Congress, executive officers, and many members of the press, labored many months to convince the American public that it should support an al-

---

[11]See C. I. Hovland, I. L. Janis, and H. H. Kelly, *Communication and Persuasion* (New Haven, Conn.: Yale University Press, 1953), pp. 19–55.

[12]James Rosenau, *National Leadership and Foreign Policy: A Case Study in the Mobilization of Public Support* (Princeton, N.J.: Princeton University Press, 1961); Barry B. Hughes and John E. Schwartz, "Dimensions of Political Integration and the Experience of the European Community," *International Studies Quarterly*, 16 (1972), 263–94; Martin Abravanel and Barry Hughes, "The Relationship Between Public Opinion and Governmental Foreign Policy: A Cross-National Study," in *Sage International Yearbook of Foreign Policy Studies*, Vol. I, ed. Patrick J. McGowan (Beverly Hills, Calif.: Sage, 1973), pp. 107–34.

[13]Irving L. Janis and M. Brewster Smith, "Effects of Education and Persuasion on National and International Images," in *International Behavior*, ed. Kelman, p. 193.

liance with the Soviet Union against Nazi Germany. But Joseph Stalin could easily switch from a policy and propaganda line that emphasized hostility toward Nazi Germany to one of collaboration with Hitler. Clearly, considerations about the state of public opinion in the Soviet Union played little role in Stalin's leadership; Stalin could never quite comprehend that governments in the Western democracies were not similarly free to alter policies with impunity.

Interest Groups and Political Parties

Public opinion is not usually an inchoate mass of millions of people. Opinions are *aggregated* and *mobilized* by interest groups and political parties. Their leaders are the ones that define a particular line on an issue and mobilize their members and adherents to share their views and sometimes to take actions. The farmers in France may organize vegetable-dumping demonstrations or block highways with tractors and trucks. These all make political points more poignantly than holding a town meeting. But the hard task of lobbying has to be undertaken by leaders of agricultural groups, or by a party which is broadly representative of agricultural interests. It is then up to the government of the day to decide whether to promote the farmers' interests, ignore them (and possibly face electoral retaliation), or work out some sort of compromise between the principles of free trade promoted by GATT and the practice of providing subsidies for the exports of France's farmers.

It is in these situations that such nonstate actors become involved in international politics, for many interest groups are not confined to single territorial jurisdictions. French farmers may make common cause with their German counterparts in an effort to prevent modification of the European Union's agricultural policies. Trade unions in the United States and Canada joined ranks, exchanged information, and promoted joint strategies in opposition to the NAFTA treaty. Environmental groups in many countries make tactical coalitions with each other to fight for or against particular government policies. Ethnic groups and diasporas (immigrant communities) frequently lobby governments on behalf of or in opposition to the politics and policies of their country of origin. Some examples: The Greek-American community strongly promoted an arms embargo against Turkey after the Turkish invasion of Cyprus in 1974. Chinese-Canadians actively urged the Canadian government to take a hard line against the regime in Beijing after the Tiananmen massacre of 1989. The Jewish lobby in the United States is well organized, funded, and led, and makes strong representations to American legislators on a variety of Middle East issues. It also has direct access to groups in Israel, including the Israeli government. Where there are high concentrations of Jewish voters, congressmen and senators must give sympathetic attention to their views. During the Reagan and Bush administrations in the United States, Cuban exiles organized the Cuban American National Foundation under the leadership of a multimillionaire contractor. This organization made generous donations to Republican presidential candidates and key members of Congress, and mobilized the Cubans in Florida. It reputedly had easy access to the White House and came to exercise a virtual veto over American policy toward

Cuba.[14] Wherever there are large immigrant communities, and particularly where they have not been fully assimilated, they will play or seek to play a role in defining their new home's foreign policies toward their countries of origin.

Bureaucracy

A full understanding of objectives, decisions, and actions must be based on a model of policy making that is more complicated than one that portrays policy makers as carefully fitting means to ends, gauging other states' intentions, and responding to certain conditions or events abroad. Choices in most nonrevolutionary and non–personal-authoritarian states are usually made in a bureaucratic-political context. Graham Allison reminds us that if we think of objectives, decisions, and actions as the result of bargaining between various government agencies, affected by organizational traditions and bureaucratic turf wars over jurisdiction, then important facts that may have been ignored in the "rational" model of decision making may emerge.[15] Policy makers, in other words, define the situation not only in terms of conditions abroad but also in terms of what is feasible bureaucratically. They receive information from various government agencies, and the alternatives they consider are often alternatives that have been drafted and debated by lower officials of various government departments. In part, then, how top-level policy makers see a problem, and the alternatives they contemplate, are an amalgam of how bureaucrats have characterized the situation and what positions they have come up with, taking into consideration organizational rivalries and bureaucratic traditions. Policy outputs, then, can be portrayed as the outcome of the pulling and hauling of bureaucratic politics.

The degree to which the bureaucratic characteristics affect the making of policy will vary from country to country, and in different circumstances. A policy developed over a period of time within the British government bureaucracy may differ significantly from a decision made by a few leaders of a small new state that barely has a foreign ministry.

Cases of policy that emerge only after long struggles within bureaucracies and with other government agencies, are numerous. In 1993, for example, President Clinton was unable to articulate a clear American policy on the Bosnian war because there were so many competing opinions within the State Department, in Congress, and among the European countries. Some wanted a NATO armed intervention to save the Bosnian Muslims from the Serbs' "ethnic cleansing" policies; many, including the Pentagon, warned that military intervention would be ineffective and probably escalate rather than end the war; many members of Congress were wary of the expenses, both human and monetary, of military action; some State Department officials despaired of American lack of leadership and resigned; and most European governments were unwilling to do more than provide some humanitarian relief

---

[14] *The New York Times*, October 6, 1993, p. A-13.

[15] Graham T. Allison, "Conceptual Models and the Cuban Missile Crisis," *American Political Science Review*, 63 (1969), 689–718. See also Allison and Morton H. Halperin, "Bureaucratic Politics: A Paradigm and Some Policy Implications," in *Theory and Policy in International Relations*, eds. Raymond Tanter and Richard H. Ullman (Princeton, N.J.: Princeton University Press, 1972), pp. 40–79.

through the United Nations. After many months of pulling and hauling by these disparate groups and interests, and after several policy changes in the White House, the Bosnian problems was resolved essentially by the military victory of the Serbs and Croatians. In the face of deep divisions, American policy was to refrain from military actions and to limit itself to providing humanitarian assistance.

Under what circumstances are administrative processes and organizational values, needs, and traditions likely to have an important role in the definition and implementation of foreign policy objectives? First, where political leadership at the top is weak or unstable, the main administrative organs of the state may have to make policy in the light of their own needs, values, and traditions. Second, most noncritical transactions between states are carried out by the lower echelons of policy-making organizations, often without the explicit direction of a foreign minister or head of government. For routine problems, traditional departmental policies and standard operating procedures, rather than direction from above, serve as the main guidelines for action. The American State Department on any day receives about 2,300 cables from American diplomatic and consular officials abroad providing information, requesting directions, or seeking permission to make certain decisions in the field. But of that large number of communications, the secretary of state will read only twenty to thirty—about 2 percent of the total. The State Department also sends out approximately 3,000 cables daily, many of which elucidate objectives and provide directions on policies designed to implement them; of these, the secretary of state may see only six, and the president will have only one or two of the most important communications referred to his office.[16] The implication of this type of communications system is clear: On routine and nonvital matters (even if a bad decision made on these may result in a diplomatic crisis), the experts and lower officials of policy-making organizations define specific objectives in the light of their own values, needs, and traditions, often through informal alliances with bureaucrats in other countries. High officials are generally concerned only with suggesting the main outlines of objectives, not with their specifics nor with the detailed means by which to implement them. High-ranking officials within policy-making hierarchies are far removed from information that describes the external environment in detail.

In a crisis, where decisions of great consequence have to be made rapidly, the effect of bureaucratic processes may be reduced considerably. In these circumstances a few key individuals at the highest level of responsibility and authority usually congregate to map strategy and responses to the problem or threat they are confronting. There is no time for detailed consultations, preparation of position papers, or thorough analysis of the situation and its background. Since urgency is the most salient aspect of the definition of the situation, decisions have to be made largely upon the basis of immediately available information, unverified rumors, and the views of upper-level advisers. Under such conditions, individual attitudes, values, beliefs, and images of the highest policy makers become particularly important in defining the situation, choosing responses and goals, and implementing policies.

[16]Testimony of Secretary of State Dean Rusk to a Senate subcommittee, reported in *Time* January 24, 1964, p. 19; "U.S. Foreign Policy: A Discussion with Former Secretaries of State," *International Studies Notes*, 11 (Fall 1984), 11.

The World of the Policy Maker: Purposes, Interests, and Choices

What happens when a foreign policy "occasion" arises (when a response is required) or when a government decides to take an important initiative? The exact process followed will depend on such variables as the degree of urgency (crisis or routine problem), the type of government structure (absence or presence of political-bureaucratic constraints), the significance of the issue (handled at the top level or among bureaucrats), and the time available for making decisions (impending deadline or open-ended). Whatever these characteristics, the mental processes are roughly similar, and they are not significantly different from those that you and I use whenever we make a decision that will be of some consequence in our lives. What do we do when we decide whether to attend university, choose which one, or select the specific program in which we will enroll? Procedurally, we might consult our friends and others who might know something about the problem. Some might discuss the choice with an astrologer (some foreign policy decisions in Thailand and other countries have been influenced by such consultations). Or we might just have a hunch, and act on it without seeking information or discussing the issue with others (some major world leaders have trusted their own intuition much more than the advice of politicians and bureaucratic experts). But aside from these procedural matters, what mental exercises are involved in making decisions? In foreign policy, as in most decisions, a number of steps are involved, something along the lines of the following.

We define the situation or problem that needs some response or initiative. This requires us to obtain information about it. It is a common assumption of "rational" decision making that the quality of our decisions (e.g., the probability that they will lead to desired results) will increase to the extent that we are well-informed about the problem[17] and that we understand the intentions of our friends and opponents.

Given the situation as we understand it—and sometimes we do not understand it well because our friends and opponents give mixed signals or the available information can lead to many different inferences—we then make some attempt to define how we would like to alter the situation (our purposes and goals), and how the situation affects our interests. If we decide that our interests are not engaged—threatened or enhanced—we may then just drop the matter.

If we do define purposes and engage in the issue, then we will look at alternatives. What should we *do* or *not* do? If there are alternatives, then we have to choose between them. How? We make some estimates of (1) costs; (2) risks; (3) advantages; and (4) predictions of results, including the estimated responses of our friends and adversaries. After consideration of the alternatives—and keep in mind that in foreign policy it might be a question of the least damaging or distasteful, not the best one—we will tend toward one favored course of action. We have made a decision.

---

[17]For an analysis of policy making under different assumptions, see Miriam Steiner, "The Search for Order in a Disorderly World: World Views and Prescriptive Decision Paradigms," *International Organization*, 37 (1983), 321–414.

But others who are involved in the problem may not agree with us. We may choose university A, but our parents might want us to go to their alma mater instead. At this point, we have to begin bargaining and facing advocates of other alternatives. And so it is within most governments. Advisers will have their pet alternatives and these have to be considered, if not always adopted. Justifications for our choice have to be developed and circulated to those whose opinions on the issue matter. In diplomacy, this would include many other governments, as well as fellow cabinet members, legislators, and important opinion leaders. If we enjoy considerable latitude of choice, maintain a strong political position, and have important allies where they are needed, we may prevail in our choice. More typically, perhaps, we will seek to alter the choice in such a manner as to meet the objections and interests of other policy makers and advisers. Ultimately, a statement of purposes and a course of action will emerge from all the discussions. A new foreign policy, a specific course of action, or a guide to future actions has been developed. But if, due to government structure as suggested above, there are too many players who can veto each other, then paralysis may be the result: No decision is made, or the favored choice is put away until some sort of winning coalition can be formed to support it.

In the post-decision phase, the policy makers justify their choice(s) to their publics, legislators, and those foreign governments whose cooperation will be necessary. They then watch and monitor the effects of their actions to see if they are bringing about the desired new state of affairs. Reevaluation and a possible change in policy will depend upon the consequences of the actions taken.

Of course we can make only more or less educated guesses about the short- and long-range consequences of our choices. Many policies have unintended—and often undesirable—results or side effects. Would Saddam Hussein have invaded Kuwait in 1990 if he had accurately predicted that he would face unanimous condemnation in the United Nations Security Council, mandatory international economic sanctions, a naval blockade of the Persian Gulf, and ultimately an overwhelming military defeat and civil war? Those were the immediate results of his choice. Long-run side effects would include extreme hardship for the Iraqi economy, an ecological disaster in the Persian Gulf, onerous war reparations, and total discredit among Arab leaders.

Diplomatic history is filled with well-laid plans going awry, resulting in harmful long-range effects and unanticipated consequences. Some governments alter their policies in response to the feedback mechanisms that indicate lack of success. Others stubbornly hew to a course of action, even at momentous personal and national cost. Hitler was willing to fight his war to the last German, including himself, rather than seek some alternative. Lyndon Johnson was willing to sacrifice his "Great Society" domestic programs and his political reputation for the sake of successfully coercing North Vietnam to stop its plan to unify Indochina by subversion and armed force, a project in which he failed. Saddam Hussein was willing to destroy his country in a gamble that the United Nations coalition would not use force to undo his aggression against Kuwait. He was more willing to suffer imminent military defeat than to change his policy. In other cases, policy is reasonably successful; that is, purposes are achieved and advantages gained at what is considered adequate cost.

We have suggested that the mental processes of making choices are similar if not identical in different decision-making contexts. As a type of activity, choosing a college or a major is not fundamentally different from choosing among alternative courses of foreign policy action. Yet, we feel that there *are* differences: The tasks are not similar in terms of complexity and long-range consequences. Choosing between two universities does not carry the same awesome responsibility and the potential consequences, as, for example, having to choose between war and surrender. As private individuals, we make decisions that may affect the lives and fortunes of few other than ourselves, whereas a foreign policy choice can vitally affect an entire society—including its survival. Choosing between two universities may be choosing between two potential winners. Formulating policy in a crisis situation that may turn into war may be to choose between two potential losers. Here ethical considerations enter. We will assess their impact on decision making in Chapter 13.

The model of rational choice outlined above vastly oversimplifies the world of the policy maker. He or she does not just calculate costs and advantages, easily identify the intentions of foreign governments, or glibly predict the outcomes of different policy options. Policy making is influenced by a host of informational, value, ideological, psychological, and perceptual problems, most of which lead to deviations from a model of perfect rationality. Some of them affect our *dispositions* toward certain alternatives; others affect the way we *define* problems and alternatives. These factors do not necessarily dictate or determine our choices, but they may in important ways influence how we approach a problem and how we tend to "tilt" toward certain solutions and preferences.

Policy making is based on the processing of information; the final decision will reflect not only how we do it but also what sorts of predispositions, values, likes and dislikes, stereotypes, and perceptions we have. As Yaacov Vertzberger has suggested, "Information processing is not primarily a rational-analytic process. It is wide open to irrational, non-rational intuitive, and affective influences, biases, and errors, especially in environments and issue-areas like international politics where uncertainty and complexity prevail."[18] The reader will have no difficulty citing examples of foreign policy failures, follies, and fiascoes. Some are attributable to poor judgment, unintended outcomes, and just poor luck. But others reflect poor decision-making procedures and the reigning influence of faulty historical analogies, misperceptions, unexamined assumptions, and an inability to adjust policy to feedback that shows errors are being made.

Perceptual and Attitudinal Influences on Policy Making

We turn, then, to consider all those perceptual and attitudinal elements of how we see and interpret the world, and how we are disposed initially toward certain kinds of responses to foreign policy situations.

---

[18] *The World in Their Minds: Information Processing, Cognition, and Perception in Foreign Policy Decision-making* (Stanford, Calif.: Stanford University Press, 1990), p. 343.

Images

Any delineation of objectives, choice among courses of action, or response to a situation in the environment may be explained partly in terms of policy makers' perceptions of reality. People act and react according to their *images* of the environment. In policy making, the state of the environment does not matter so much as what government officials believe that state to be. By image, we mean individuals' *perceptions* of an object, a fact, or a condition; their *evaluation* of that object, fact, or condition in terms of its goodness or badness, friendliness or hostility, or value; and the *meaning* ascribed to, or deduced from, that object, fact, or condition. Consider a trained fishing expert and the city-bred novice with no previous experience. The expert can deduce valid conclusions about fishing conditions from a variety of facts, conditions, or "clues," such as water temperature, depth, or color; weather; and time of day. The novice, in spite of seeing the water, feeling its temperature, and knowing it is late afternoon, is unable to draw any particular conclusions from these indicators because by themselves they have no meaning in terms of past experience. Because they see and interpret the same conditions or facts in different ways (in the case of the novice, hardly interpreted at all), the two fishermen will react and behave differently. Experts will go where the fish are and work their tackles in such a way as to catch them. Barring beginner's luck, novices will struggle up and down a stream, flail the water with an assortment of useless lures, scare the fish, and catch nothing. Similarly in foreign policy, different policy makers can read different meanings into a situation; and because they characterize a situation differently and deduce different conclusions from it, they will behave differently. In particular, complex situations involving many interests, historical, economic, or social factors, and value positions are likely to be perceived differently.

Even the most well-informed experts in a policy-making agency cannot know *all* the relevant factors in a situation; their images of reality will always be different from reality. The discrepancy between image and reality is partly a result of physical impediments to the flow of information owing to lack of time, faulty communications, censorship, or lack of competent advisers or intelligence sources. It is also a problem of the distortion of reality caused by attitudes, values, beliefs, or faulty expectations. Individuals are bombarded constantly by messages about the environment; but they select and interpret only a fraction of what they "see," because only a part of it may be relevant to a particular situation. Sometimes people also "see" only information that conforms to their values, beliefs, or expectations. There are both physical and psychological factors that can distort the information upon which policy makers' images of reality are based.

If policy makers rely on faulty information, misinterpret cues, twist the meaning of messages to fit their own preferences, or disregard information that contradicts their values and preferences, their psychological environment—upon which they will act—is quite different from the physical environment—in which their policies have be executed. The distinction between psychological environment, or definition of the situation, and physical environment, or "reality," must be kept in mind in all analyses of foreign policy. One can readily see the distinction in the case of the attack on Pearl

Harbor. In early December 1941, President Roosevelt and American diplomats were attempting to arrange high-level negotiations with the Japanese government to resolve some issues separating the two countries. At this time, American officials had predicted an impending military attack by the Japanese, but they expected it to occur somewhere in Southeast Asia. They could not imagine a direct attack on the American fleet at Pearl Harbor and so took no precautionary measures; they had facts about impending Japanese military actions but could not deduce or predict the correct "meaning" from those facts. The American definition of the situation was thus at odds with reality, and actions designed to cope with the expected Japanese moves were ineffective.

This example illustrates the problem of discrepancies between images and physical environment that arise from faulty or inadequate information and unwarranted expectations.[19] But how do we account for differing interpretations and characterizations of reality when easily verifiable facts are available? Here, the problem of attitudes, values, beliefs, doctrines, and analogies becomes important, for they help determine the meanings ascribed to a set of facts about internal and external conditions. Although distinctions among the concepts of attitude, value, belief, and doctrines are not always clear, they can be defined as follows for the analysis of foreign policy making.

Attitudes

Attitudes can be conceived as general evaluative propositions about some object, fact, or condition: more or less friendly, desirable, dangerous, trustworthy, or hostile. In any international relationship, policy makers operate—usually implicitly—within some framework of evaluative assumptions of hostility or friendship, trust or distrust, and fear or confidence toward other governments and peoples. These attitudes may have important effects on how policy makers react to the actions, signals, and demands of other states, perceive the intentions of other governments, and define their own objectives toward others. If a high-level policy maker receives a conciliatory message from the government of a state he perceives to be hostile, his attitudes of distrust and hostility may lead him to interpret the message in a different manner than if he had received even a less conciliatory message from the leader of a nonhostile state. Threats that are only potential may be viewed as actual because hostile attitudes predispose policy makers to distort the evidence. Particularly where evidence of intention is ambiguous, policy makers may fall back upon traditional attitudes of trust and friendship or of distrust and hostility. Intelligence agencies can learn a great deal about the capabilities of states, but policy makers also have to gauge *intentions*—and these may be badly misinterpreted because of hostile, distrustful, or excessively trustful attitudes.

Values

Our values are the result of upbringing, political socialization in various group contexts, indoctrination, and personal experience. They serve as standards against which

---

[19]See the careful analysis of this problem by Harold and Margaret Sprout, "Environmental Factors in the Study of International Politics," *Journal of Conflict Resolution*, 1 (1957), 309–28. The most elaborate analysis, with numerous examples, is Robert Jervis, *Perception and Misperception in International Politics* (Princeton, N.J.: Princeton University Press, 1976).

our own actions and those of others are judged and are thus the bases of many of our attitudes. Values point out the general direction toward which our actions should be directed (wealth, power, prestige, happiness, isolation), and for policy makers they also serve as reasons and justifications for goals, decisions, and actions. For example, in Western societies, the values of individual freedom, civil liberties, national self-determination, justice, independence, and economic progress are frequently cited as reasons behind certain policy objectives or as the objectives toward which actions are directed. To the policy maker and the public in general, actions that support these values are good; those that do not are to be avoided or resisted if undertaken by other states. In many developing countries, the values of rapid economic development, national unity, freedom from foreign control, and national prestige serve as the main criteria against which to judge one's own policies and those of other states. In socialist societies, the values of working-class solidarity, the struggle against "imperialism," and support for "national liberation movements" were observed frequently in policy statements. Such values as these do not necessarily prescribe specific responses for particular situations, but they do establish attitudes toward the situation and provide both justifications for, and guides to, the policies designed to cope with them.

Beliefs

Beliefs can be defined as propositions that policy makers hold to be true, even if they cannot be verified. They are the foundation of national "myths" and ideologies, and efforts to question or examine them systematically are often met with hostility or even persecution. Some beliefs that are widespread in societies and expressed in the behavior of policy makers include those claiming that a particular nation, "way of life," or ethnic group is superior to any other; that a particular political system or economic order is superior to others; that human progress and moral improvement are inevitable; that communism is inevitable; or that a particular country will always be a "threat." Some more specific Western beliefs (closely related to liberal values) claim that all conflicts can be resolved through negotiation; that the use or threat of force is unethical except for purposes of self-defense; that foreign aid will produce stability and democracy; and, as a corollary, that hunger and poverty create communism.

In foreign policy making, such beliefs are important, for they often become the unexamined assumptions upon which numerous policy choices are made—for instance, Woodrow Wilson's belief that secret diplomacy, autocracy, and the balance of power cause war; the common Western belief that communism represented basically a military threat; President Eisenhower's beliefs that all political leaders are essentially reasonable and that peace can be secured by frank discussion; and the long-held Soviet belief in the implacable hostility of all "imperialists."

Like most people, policy makers do not like to be told that their beliefs are wrong, or that the images upon which their actions are based are not consonant with reality. Social scientists have repeatedly observed human beings' resistance to "uncomfortable" facts, the stability of our images in the face of rapidly changing events in the environment, and our ability to distort or ignore facts and deny important aspects of reality.[20] When there is some inconsistency between policy makers' attitudes and beliefs on the one hand and incoming information on the other, they can react in one of three ways: (1) Ignore the inconsistency by withdrawing from the problem (that is, pretend the problem doesn't exist or isn't important); (2) reject the incoming information and somehow rationalize its lack of worth, thereby maintaining their initial attitudes and values; or (3) yield to the information by a change in values and attitudes. Of course, where the costs of changing attitudes are not very great, or where there are strong social supports or rewards for changing them, the third course may be easy to bring about. But in a highly institutionalized setting such as that in which policy makers work, there may be strong social pressures against changing attitudes and beliefs. Foreign ministers have to contend not only with information that challenges their pet beliefs and attitudes but also with bureaucratic roles and political restraints. They cannot easily change their views of the world if the important people they meet constantly reinforce their initial attitudes and beliefs, and if they find that by adhering to them they achieve more status and political efficacy. One can imagine, for instance, the difficulties faced by career deputy ministers in the Israeli or Syrian defense establishments if they received information indicating that the traditional adversary did not, in fact, constitute some sort of military menace. Even though they might undergo periods of uncertainty about their own attitudes and beliefs, the chances are only slight that they would easily adopt a "new line" and try to influence their colleagues to accept it.[21]

The story of diplomats in the field whose warnings and advice were shunted aside or ignored by a foreign minister because they contradicted the minister's pet beliefs is a recurring complaint in diplomatic memoirs. To take two examples, a study of President Eisenhower's secretary of state, John Foster Dulles, illustrated how he interpreted facts about, and incoming messages from, the Soviet Union to make them fit his own beliefs about that country, which always emphasized its aggressiveness and great hostility toward the West. In some instances, Dulles interpreted information—often ingeniously—in such a way as to reinforce a previously held belief.[22] Even more clear-cut was Hitler's sensitivity to all information that suggested the imminent defeat of Germany's armed forces. German intelligence sources provided Hitler with accurate statistics of American industrial and military production; but in the last two years of the war, the Führer became increasingly annoyed at these figures because they suggested pessimistic conclusions. Finally, Hitler ordered that no more statistics be quoted to him and forbade his officials to believe them or even to discuss them among themselves. Other officials who suggested that the morale of German citizenry was lagging by late 1944 were dismissed from their positions.[23]

[20]See Karl W. Deutsch and Richard L. Merritt, "Effects of Events on National and International Images," in *International Behavior: A Social-Psychological Analysis*, ed. Herbert C. Kelman, pp. 132–87; Charles A. Powell, Helen E. Purkitt, and James W. Dyson, "Opening the Black Box: Cognitive Processing and Optimal Choice in Foreign Policy Decision Making," in *New Directions in the Study of Foreign Policy*, eds. Hermann et al., pp. 203–20.

[21]For a summary of the problem of cognitive dissonance and inconsistency as it applies to international relations, see Milton J. Rosenberg, "Attitude Change and Foreign Policy in the Cold War Era," in *Domestic Sources of Foreign Policy*, ed. James N. Rosenau (New York: Free Press, 1967), pp. 111–59.

[22]Ole R. Holsti, "The Belief System and National Images: A Case Study," *Journal of Conflict Resolution*, 6 (1962), 244–52.

[23]John K. Galbraith, "Germany Was Badly Run," *Fortune* (December 1945), p. 200.

Policy makers who do change their views on important foreign policy programs, or who critically examine the assumptions upon which a policy is based, face all the pressures for conformity and loyalty commonly found in small groups or bureaucratic organizations. Sometimes they are welcomed as devil's advocates, but more frequently they are regarded as troublemakers and face considerable personal hostility and sometimes demotion or loss of office. The "Tuesday lunch group" composed of President Johnson and the highest foreign policy and military officials in his administration regularly made important decisions on the conduct of the war in Vietnam. Those officials who raised critical objections to American military involvement in Vietnam, who provided information that put the American military operations in an unfavorable light, or who asked for fundamental debates on the entire Vietnam policy were subject to sarcastic jibes from the president, appeals for loyalty and unanimity from the others, and eventual rejection from the group. Some were shifted to other government positions; others resigned.

Doctrines and Ideologies

A *doctrine* can be defined as any explicit set of beliefs that purports to explain reality and usually prescribes goals for political action. Foreign policy objectives that derive from political doctrines are often put into slogan forms, such as "extending freedom," "trade follows the flag," "he who holds the land will hold the sea," "the throne and the altar," "the white man's burden," "make the world safe for democracy," "the New Order," or "world revolution."

A coherent set of doctrines constitutes an *ideology*. Ideologies, as Carl Friedrich defines them, are reasonably coherent bodies of ideas concerning practical means of how to maintain, change, reform, or overthrow a socioeconomic-political order.[24] In the more restricted foreign policy context, ideology can be considered as those doctrines "intended to motivate actor(s) to pursue certain actions for the sake of the collective interest of the nation-state."[25] Doctrines and ideologies impinge on policy making in a number of ways. Some are fairly compelling, as we saw in the case of Soviet foreign policy behavior for more than seventy years after the Bolshevik revolution; others create only mild dispositions. Again, we must avoid simple determinist statements.

Doctrines and ideologies establish the intellectual framework through which policy makers observe reality. Messages and cues from the external environment are given meaning, or interpreted, within the categories, predictions, and definitions provided by doctrines comprising the ideology. Soviet policy makers interpreted a foreign civil war as a manifestation of a class struggle (as during the Spanish civil war); they saw conflicts among "capitalist" states as a fight between their ruling classes over markets (as in the official Soviet interpretation of World War I); and they regarded any recession in a free enterprise economy as evidence of Marx's predictions regarding the laws of economic development.

---

[24]As cited in Walter Carlsnaes, *Ideology and Foreign Policy: Problems of Comparative Conceptualization,* (Oxford: Basil Blackwell, 1986), p. 159.
[25]Ibid., p. 179.

Second, doctrines and ideologies prescribe for policy makers both national roles and an image of the future state of the world. They establish the long-range goals of a state's external behavior, to be promoted through diplomacy, propaganda, revolution, or force. Their relevance to day-to-day problem solving and to the development of specific actions in concrete situations, however, may be only very slight.

Third, they serve as rationalizations and justifications for the choice of more specific foreign policy decisions. As in Western countries, where foreign policies are often justified in terms of such popular values as "preserving freedom," so in the Soviet Union or China, foreign policy actions were justified as being consistent with the general values inherent in the Communist ideology.

Finally, doctrines and ideologies posit moral and ethical systems that help prescribe the correct attitudes and evaluative criteria for judging one's own actions and those of others. Communism was distinguished from other ideologies primarily because it claimed to be an objective and scientific ideology and moral system, rather than merely the preferred ideology of particular leaders. Communist theoreticians maintained that Marxism-Leninism is all-powerful because it is correct, and, since only Marxist-Leninists are "armed with the truth," only they have a legitimate claim to power in the world. They are on the side of history, they maintain, and all other doctrines or economic systems are retrograde. Good people are those who swim with the current of history, building communism and fighting imperialism and fascism, whereas bad people (or states) are those that are fighting history by clinging to outmoded (capitalist, feudal, and so on) economic systems and their colonies. Capitalism is immoral, according to the evaluative criteria of Marxist doctrines, because it is a barrier to human progress. Any technique used to fight capitalism or imperialism is *ipso facto* moral and justified, because it is in accord with the laws of historical development.

In the foreign policies of many democracies, the tenets of liberalism strongly influence the definition of policy purposes, the choice of means, and the justifications for action. Commitments to the liberal creed can be seen explicitly in these countries' relations with the former socialist states. They have made it clear that they would not recognize post-socialist governments unless they were committed to democratization and economies based on market principles. The 1990 Charter of Paris, signed by all of Europe's governments, the United States, and Canada, explicitly states that only democracies will be entitled to join the Conference on Security and Cooperation in Europe, and that all members must commit themselves to the observance of human rights, as well as the institutionalization of private market economies. Similarly the founding treaty of the European Community states that only democracies can become members.

Liberal democracies have granted immediate diplomatic recognition to fledgling democracies, and have frequently provided extra measures of financial support as well as technical assistance in teaching governments how to run elections, establish independent judicial systems, and organize labor unions and political parties. These governments have also occasionally intervened militarily to support beleaguered democracies. And they have frequently taken a variety of measures against regimes that systematically violate their citizens' human rights. A recent example is the Organization of American States' economic embargo against the military government in Haiti, a regime that had ousted the democratically elected president in a *coup* in 1991.

But while it is easy to cite numerous examples of the significance of liberalism in state's foreign policies, there are also many exceptions to the rule. Where strategic or significant commercial interests are at stake, such governments have been easily persuaded to support various authoritarian regimes. The record of the United States in Latin America and the Caribbean is illustrative of the inconsistent play of ideological principles in foreign policy. In Chapter 9, for example, we recounted how the American government helped bring about the military *coup* that brought down the popularly elected Allende regime in Chile. It had acted similarly in 1954 against a popular government in Guatemala, and in the 1970s it was essentially indifferent to the excesses of authoritarian governments in El Salvador, Brazil, Uruguay, and Argentina. In all these cases, the fear of communism—which was usually badly misperceived as a "threat"—underlay the support for authoritarianism and human rights abuses.

Ideologies, then, tend to shape policies in many circumstances, but they are seldom determinative when other values are at stake. Liberal principles can be and have been sacrificed when other values such as national security are at risk. Similarly, no Soviet leader failed to compromise Marxist-Leninist principles of socialist solidarity if critical Russian national interests were threatened.

Analogies

We have all experienced attempts to clarify and understand a phenomenon by making analogies. The physiology instructor may make an analogy between the heart and a pump, the eye and a camera, or the brain and a computer. In each case, the object under study is analyzed not in terms of its own properties or characteristics, but with reference to some other object. Similarly, in formulating policy goals and responses to conditions abroad, diplomats and government officials frequently characterize a situation and deduce appropriate actions to cope with it by reference to a different, but analogous, set of historical circumstances. The image of reality is based on, or compared to, a past situation, although of course current information must be available in order to suggest the comparison or analogy in the first place. For example, Prime Minister Eden of Great Britain found a close analogy between Hitler's foreign policy objectives and diplomacy in 1938 and President Nasser's behavior in the Middle East in 1956. As a British foreign secretary during the late 1930s, Eden had questioned his government's appeasement policy against the Nazis. Convinced that Nasser presented a threat similar to that posed by Hitler, Eden deduced that the only way to handle the analogous situation was through a show of force. Even though the decision to invade Egypt in 1956 was formulated in the light of careful intelligence estimates (which were faulty in many ways), Eden did not consult most members of his government to see if they thought his image of the situation and the assumptions of his decision were correct.

During the Vietnam conflict in the 1960s, American policy makers frequently justified their actions and helped characterize the situation by citing the appeasement analogy of the 1930s: If you let aggressors achieve their objectives, you only whet their appetite for more. Appeasement, they maintained, leads only to general war, usually fought at some disadvantage by the democracies; but a strong display of force and determination can discourage aggressors and save the peace in the long run. In what respects the situation in Southeast Asia in the 1960s was really analogous to Europe in the 1930s can be debated, but the analogy was an important part of the psychological environment in which policy makers formulated their goals and actions.

We all reason by analogy, often recalling lessons learned through previous experiences, whether good or bad. In policy-making situations, however, unexamined adherence to analogies may lead to poor policy. Analogies may act as a source of misperception, tending toward the choice of certain options while masking others.[26]

We can now see that the definition of the situation, identification of interests, calculation of costs and benefits, and prediction of results in foreign policy is not so simple as our "rational" model of policy making would suggest. There are many dispositional traits, assumed under attitudes, values, ideologies, and analogies, that bend us toward certain directions. Using again the analogy of choosing among universities, our decision may ultimately depend upon a "gut feeling" rather than on all the information and advice we have mustered to help us. Our choice may finally rest on something as irrelevant as our feeling of loyalty or admiration for the college's football team. Because of these feelings, we tended toward a specific choice initially, and even if we amassed a lot of information about other universities and their opportunities, we may have twisted it or played it down in order to be more comfortable with our original disposition.

Our images, values, and attitudes are all *learned* through experience, education, and a great variety of information sources. They affect the way we see things, define purposes, and choose among courses of action. But they are variable; for most people they change under a variety of circumstances. They influence policy but do not determine it. If it were otherwise, policies would seldom change. The vast revolution in Soviet foreign policy in the late 1980s was occasioned in part by the leadership's ultimate recognition that its images of the world, and previous policies, were inconsistent with reality, and were leading to costly errors and undesirable outcomes. Gorbachev and his associates slowly jettisoned the whole ideological underpinnings of seventy years of Soviet foreign policy, including major beliefs and doctrines such as the ultimate global triumph of communism and the implacable hostility of capitalist states, and undertook entirely new directions, redefined goals and purposes, and took bold policy initiatives.

Personality Factors

But aren't there more permanent aspects of personality that dispose policy makers toward certain kinds of initiatives and responses? Below we propose three different meanings for the term *personality*: (1) policy-making skills; (2) character traits that

---

[26]For further discussion, see Dwain Mefford, "Analogical Reasoning and the Definition of the Situation: Back to Snyder for Concepts and Forward to Artificial Intelligence for Method," in *New Directions in the Study of Foreign Policy*, eds. Hermann et al., pp. 221–44.

predispose individuals to behave in certain ways in given conditions; and (3) pathological traits. Each may have significant influences on types of actions chosen in policy-making situations.

That people have different skills or aptitudes for different kinds of jobs is obvious. In terms of foreign policy analysis, what may make a difference is traits such as tolerance/intolerance for diverging views, capacity to memorize, ability to weed out the essential information from trivia, capacity to think clearly in conditions of high stress, and the like. It would require a separate book to explore the links between such skills and policy choices. In situations fraught with danger, we are more likely to admire the policy makers who are known to look carefully at alternatives and who remain "cool" rather than those who have a reputation for impulsive behavior, arrogance, and indifference to advice which does not coincide with their hunches. The assumption, of course, is that more successful and safer policy will result from the deliberations of the former than the latter. Yet, some world-historical figures like Adolf Hitler were famous for their impulsive behavior while achieving phenomenal foreign policy successes—at least in the short run.

Recent research has suggested some intriguing relationships between certain personality traits and propensity to make certain types of decisions in foreign policy. Lloyd Etheredge's study of American government officials and former presidents and secretaries of state establishes reasonably well that *some* types of decisions reflect personality traits.[27] In the case of the top-level policy makers, he found that those with personalities defined as "high dominance" and "introvert" were significantly more likely to advocate "hard-line policies" in international crises than those characterized as "low dominance" and "extrovert."

Hard-liners are persons, whatever their images, attitudes, values, and sources of information, who have predispositions to deal with adversaries and certain kinds of general foreign policy problems by the advocacy of "tough" measures, including the use of military force; who find it difficult to compromise goals and purposes; and who generally are not empathetic to the perspectives of others. Their purpose is to win. While all societies contain such individuals, their political roles may be substantially enhanced when general social norms sustain the same kinds of policy predilections. There were important segments of the German population prior to World War I, for example, who strongly believed that war was an admirable way to weed out the weak from the strong, and to establish German supremacy in Europe.

Accommodationists, in contrast, find the use of force repugnant, place emphasis on avoiding conflicts, and should conflicts arise nevertheless, seek to find negotiated compromises. They also argue that policy should be channeled through international institutions, and in accordance with international norms and laws. Settlement of an issue is more important than winning. Such predispositions were strongly supported in Great Britain and the United States in the 1920s and 1930s. Throughout the Cold War, important segments of populations in West-

---

[27]Lloyd Etheredge, *A World of Men: The Private Sources of American Foreign Policy* (Cambridge, Mass.: M.I.T. Press, 1978).

ern countries argued in favor of more accommodationist strategies in dealing with the Soviet Union, and they had their counterparts in high foreign policy positions.[28]

Other personality characteristics that may influence the selection of choices include the propensity to take risks (or the reverse, to be extremely cautious), the willingness to pursue a policy line regardless of others' opinions (sensitivity/insensitivity), and amount of energy devoted to the analysis of a foreign policy situation.

Finally, writers of psychobiography have suggested that in certain circumstances, policy choices may reflect deep personal needs, which are then rationalized in terms of the national interest. Most experts agree that Stalin was afflicted by paranoia and pathological insecurity. Some of his foreign policy behavior—his unwillingness to countenance the possibility of a Nazi invasion of Russia in 1941 despite overwhelming information that it would happen—can perhaps best be understood as a manifestation of personality disorder. (Stalin's responsibility for the mass killings of the 1930s and his propensity to see plots everywhere were obviously related to pathological conditions.) Similarly, certain aspects of Hitler's behavior can be understood best in terms of psychopathological syndromes.[29]

But what of the prime minister of present-day Sweden, or the foreign minister of Japan, or the defense minister of Belgium? Can we best understand and explain the main patterns of those countries' foreign and defense policies today in terms of the personality characteristics of their key decision makers? Clearly the answer is no. The examples cited above are almost invariably taken from persons in unrestricted positions of authority over great powers in crisis situations. Where the policy problem relates to a less threat-laden issue, where it results from considerable bureaucratic discussion, and where it reflects the national needs of a relatively small country, then other types of explanations would be more powerful. We have discussed a variety of personality characteristics (including perceptual variables), because in certain situations, as hypothesized later, they provide a compelling explanation of foreign policy objectives or actions.

1. Idiosyncratic variables are most likely to provide a significant part of an explanation where (a) policy is made by one or a few key leaders; (b) bureaucracies are uninvolved; (c) public opinion traditionally plays an insignificant role in limiting the executive's options; (d) compelling national needs are not involved; and (e) there is a relatively diffuse international system.

2. "Aggressive" foreign policy decisions and actions are more likely to be taken and ordered by those with the following character traits: (a) introversion/dominance; (b) high propensity to take risks; (c) a tendency to dichotomize foreign policy actors as good/bad, trustworthy/untrustworthy, and the like; (d) personal insecurity combined with conditions such as sexual frustration; and (e) high need for esteem. Those with opposite characteristics are presumably more likely to be "doves."

[28]For further discussion, see John A. Vasquez, "Foreign Policy, Learning, and War," in *New Directions in the Study of Foreign Policy*, eds. Hermann et al., pp. 366–83.

[29]Among the prominent attempts at this kind of analysis are Alexander and Juliette George, *Woodrow Wilson and Colonel House: A Personality Study* (New York: Day, 1956); Arnold Rogow, *James Forrestal: A Study of Personality, Politics, and Policy* (New York: Macmillan, 1963); and Joseph de Rivera, *The Psychological Dimensions of Foreign Policy* (Columbus, Ohio: Merrill, 1968).

The reader may wish to develop further hypotheses. The important point to re-member is that no matter how satisfying it may be to attribute policy to a single per-son, other factors may be involved as well and may perhaps offer an even more com-prehensive explanation. We consider finally the *political* needs of key policy makers.

Press analysts and armchair observers often offer explanations of foreign pol-icy that emphasize the domestic political needs of a president, commissar, or prime minister. This is the case where a leader undertakes a particular foreign policy ven-ture for the sake of augmenting domestic popularity or increasing his or her influence with a legislature. In the United States, at least, studies suggest that *any* foreign pol-icy move—a new initiative, a foreign tour, a dramatic announcement—is likely to in-crease the number of those who say the president is doing a good job.[30] In the spring of 1981, the popularity of Menachem Begin's Likud coalition in Israel increased dra-matically after the prime minister took a hard line against the emplacement of Syr-ian SAM missiles in Lebanon, capable of shooting down Israeli reconnaissance flights. (This is not to argue that Begin's only concern was his domestic political problems— that would be another monocausal explanation.) While foreign policy issues seldom determine the outcome of a country's elections—issues closer to the pocketbook are usually more salient—there is little doubt that some key foreign policy decisions are timed to create maximum domestic impact and in some cases are taken primarily with a view to improving the leadership's sagging political fortunes.

Figure 11-2 summarizes the discussion on foreign policy decision making. Pol-icy makers perceive relevant conditions in the external and domestic environments. These offer both opportunities and constraints, as well as situations that require some sort of response or initiative. But their definitions of the situation are colored by im-ages, attitudes, values, doctrines, ideologies, and analogies. The availability and qual-ity of information is also important. Personality factors may affect the definition of the situation as well, but they are particularly relevant in disposing individuals to-ward particular kinds of responses; to the ways they calculate risks, advantages, and costs; and to their sensitivity—or lack of it—to the interests and perspectives of other players. Once choices have been made and implemented, there will be foreign and domestic responses that constitute feedback. Policy may or may not change. Again, personality and perceptual factors may enter into the explanation. Some policy mak-ers can make necessary adjustments; others will identify strongly with their previous purposes, commitments, and choices, and will hew to them even if the evidence is overwhelming that they are leading to policy disasters.

Relationships Among the Components

The analysis of policy makers' attitudes, values, beliefs, and personality needs implied that their relevance to a definition of a situation is related to factors of political role and various administrative procedures. In another section it was suggested that pub-lic opinion can impose restrictions on the options available to policy makers in a de-mocratic political system, whereas public opinion in authoritarian political systems,

---

[30]John E. Mueller, *War, Presidents and Public Opinion* (New York: John Wiley, 1973).

FIGURE 11-2
A Model of Foreign Policy Decision Making

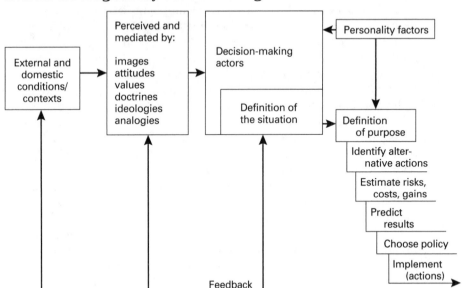

no matter what the situation, plays little or no role in helping to shape foreign policy objectives and actions. We also argued that organizational needs, values, and traditions are less important in influencing policy making during times of crisis than during consideration of routine problems. All these statements are really *hypotheses* about relationships among the various factors that may influence foreign policy behavior. It may be useful to know that the state of domestic opinion, the structure of the system, and traditional policies are important aspects, let us say, of the Danish foreign minister's view of a situation to which he must respond. But, ideally, we would also want to know *under what conditions* these are more important than organizational values or personality variables. Too often we assume that only one component of a definition of the situation can explain the behavior of states in their relations with other states.

In the absence of systematic, comparative analyses of foreign policies in different countries, it is difficult to make verified statements concerning which phenomena might be considered relevant or significant under different circumstances. Instead, we can suggest some hypotheses about which components are apt to constitute the most salient aspects of a definition of the situation, and under what conditions.

1. The more critical or urgent a situation is perceived to be, the fewer people will become directly involved in defining the situation, choosing responses, and selecting goals.
2. The fewer people making these decisions, the more likely that their actions will reflect personal idiosyncrasies, attitudes, beliefs, and personal political needs.[31]

---

[31]See Richard C. Snyder and Glenn D. Paige, "The United States' Decision to Resist Agreement in Korea.," in *Foreign Policy Decision Making,* eds. Richard C. Snyder, H. W. Bruck, and Burton Sapin (New York: Free Press, 1962).

3. The more people involved in defining a situation, formulating goals, or choosing alternatives, the more the decisions will reflect group and organizational values, needs, and traditions, and the less they will reveal the attitudes, beliefs, or images of any single person.[32]

4. The greater the threat perceived by the policy-making group, the more pressure for conformity and group consensus.[33]

5. The structure of the system is likely to be the most pervasive limitation on the selection of goals or actions when (a) it is polarized; (b) expressions of public opinion or nationalist sentiment are weak; (c) the state has few capabilities and perceives a common threat with the bloc leader; and (d) the situation is generally noncritical.

6. Conversely, a government's foreign policy objectives are *least* likely to be influenced by system structure when (a) the international system has a diffuse structure; (b) the situation is defined essentially by one person who can effectively control the domestic resources, including popular attitudes and opinions; (c) personal values, personality needs, or political needs can be achieved through foreign policies; (d) the state is neither a leader nor a member of an alliance or a coalition; and (e) the situation is deemed critical.

7. Domestic needs will be salient aspects of a definition of a situation when (a) the state is dependent upon external sources of food and supply; (b) policy makers are responsive to expressions of domestic opinion; and (c) a territory is perceived to be highly vulnerable to attack from abroad.

8. Capabilities establish limits on objectives for all states, no matter what other internal or external conditions prevail.

9. Capabilities are a less important consideration for governments that subscribe to long-range, revolutionary objectives.

10. The availability of capabilities may be a less important component of a definition of the situation in crisis situations.[34]

11. Doctrines and ideologies are more important in defining situations in political systems or governments (a) that subscribe to an official set of doctrines; (b) where the top leadership is not responsive to expressions of public opinion or domestic needs; (c) that are new or have undergone recent revolution; and (d) during noncritical situations. In conditions of crisis (such as attack or major threat), responses are seldom deduced from, or closely related to, doctrines or ideologies.

12. Bureaucratic influences will be important components of a definition of the situation (a) in long-established and stable states; (b) in noncritical circumstances; and (c) where the top leadership changes rapidly or is uninvolved in an issue area.

All of these statements are *probabilistic*. They are only more or less likely, and hypothetical. We would have to examine many foreign policy decision situations, across a number of states in different circumstances, before we could say that they are valid generalizations. At this stage in our knowledge, probabilities are better than just hunches.

[32]Sidney Verba, "Assumptions of Rationality and Non-Rationality in Models of the International System," *World Politics*, 14 (1961), 93–117.

[33]See Irving Janis, *Victims of Groupthink: A Psychological Study of Foreign-Policy Decisions and Fiascoes* (Boston: Houghton Mifflin, 1972), Chapter 1.

[34]Dina A. Zinnes, Robert C. North, and Howard E. Koch, Jr., "Capability, Threat, and the Outbreak of War," in *International Politics and Foreign Policy: A Reader in Research and Theory*, ed. James Rosenau (New York: Free Press, 1961), pp. 469–482.

If we look at single cases, we can try to estimate the relative importance of various sources of foreign policy purposes and actions. For illustrative purposes, Table 11-1 outlines the weighted considerations that went into Great Britain's joint decision with Israel and France in 1956 to invade the Suez Canal. The purpose of the operation from the British point of view was to wrest control of the canal from the Egyptians, who had previously nationalized it, contrary to stipulations in an 1888 treaty. The British were concerned primarily to ensure the freedom of navigation for shipping, given the importance of the waterway for the country's trade with the Middle East and Asia.

The story is long and complicated, but there are several critical points to consider if we look at this as a case study of foreign policy making. First, the decision was made by very few people. Prime Minister Anthony Eden's position was paramount, and he consulted only a few cabinet colleagues on his plans. His Conservative party enjoyed a significant majority in the House of Commons, so his government was not at risk. The bureaucracy was not involved in making decisions. In brief, his latitude of choice in terms of domestic politics was high.

Second, Eden's main sources of information were his government's intelligence units and military advisers. They provided information that confirmed the prime min-

TABLE 11-1

Estimated Significance of External, Domestic, and Decision Making Variables in Great Britain's Intervention, Suez Canal, 1956

EXTERNAL/SYSTEMIC FACTORS	SIGNIFICANCE/COMMENT
1. Structure of the system (latitude of choice)	– (no American support)
2. Characteristics and structure of world economy	0
3. Purposes and actions of other actors	+ + (threat perception)
4. International law, public opinion	+ (law governing control of canal; 1888 treaty)
5. Global values	0
The Domestic Context	
1. Britain's socioeconomic needs (economic security)	+ + (vulnerability to canal closure)
2. Geographic and topographic characteristics	0
3. National attributes	+ (trade dependence)
4. Public opinion	+ (anticipated favorable)
5. Government structure (latitude of choice)	+ + (decision made secretly)
6. Bureaucracy	0
As Mediated by:	
1. Images	+ + (hostile Egypt)
2. Attitudes/values	+ (distrust of Nasser)
3. Doctrines/ideologies	0
4. Analogies	+ + (Nasser and Hitler; "lessons of the 1930s")
5. Idiosyncratic personality factors	+ (personal dislike of Nasser)
6. Domestic political needs	0

Key: + + = strong influence on decision
    + = considered relevant, disposing toward intervention
    0 = not considered, or irrelevant
    – = considered relevant, disposing against intervention
    — = strong influence against decision

ister's estimation that Egyptian control of the canal could pose a very serious threat to Great Britain's economy. President Nasser was literally in a position, so they believed, to strangle the British. Military officials provided information showing that an airborne assault by British commandos, combined with Irsaeli and French military moves, could successfully gain control of the canal without a substantial cost in lives.

Third, historical analogies from Eden's past disposed him to resort to military force in this situation. He had been a foremost opponent of appeasement of Nazi Germany, and in the 1956 circumstances he drew parallels—incorrect ones—between President Nasser and Hitler. The lesson Eden had learned from the experience of the 1930s was never to let aggressors (as he perceived Nasser) make moves without some effort to deter or stop them. Inaction or diplomatic negotiations would only allow the aggressor to consolidate his position and to undertake new adventures.

Fourth, Eden anticipated some public opposition, but he estimated that the degree of threat justified extreme actions, and that the public would understand the need for them. He appears to have given little thought to the reaction of the United States and the Soviet Union, with whom he deliberately did not consult. This proved to be a major mistake in the execution of the policy: Vigorous opposition from the United States and other members of the United Nations Security Council, and threats of nuclear retaliation by the Soviet Union, helped put an end to the military intervention. Great Britain and its co-conspirators ultimately accepted a cease-fire, the establishment of a United Nations peacekeeping force in and around the Suez Canal, and a troop withdrawal. The policy failed because Egyptian control over the canal—the objective of the operation—was not removed. Because of lack of support from the United States and severe criticism by significant segments of the British public, Eden eventually resigned his prime ministership.

Summary

To summarize this chapter, external/systemic conditions and the nature of the domestic political context constitute the environments in which policy purposes and actions are formulated. Selected domestic and external characteristics provide the stimulus for foreign policy action, and establish varying latitudes of choice. How policy makers define situations abroad, and how they ultimately define their national interests and choose courses of action, are influenced by values, attitudes, ideologies, and a host of perceptual factors, including the use of analogies. Responses to situations may also be affected by personality characteristics and by the political needs of leading government officials. The relative importance of the variables changes from situation to situation. Degrees of threat, the urgency of a problem, the time available for making decisions, and a host of governmental characteristics will largely determine *how* decisions are made. But for the substance of policy, all the other variables have to be considered.

Questions for Study, Analysis, and Discussion

1. What is the distinction between poor judgment and misperception?
2. In what ways has the collapse of the Cold War bipolar system increased the latitude of choice of various governments and their foreign policies?

3. Some have argued that governments should not make important decisions, many of which will have long-term effects, under the influence of a fickle public opinion. Others insist that in a democracy opinion should both constrain and compel governments to act in certain ways. What is your opinion?

4. What would an ideal foreign policy decision-making procedure in your government look like? Using a recent case, do you think the actual procedures were reasonably consistent with the ideal model? If not, was the policy reasonably successful anyway?

5. Is it appropriate for immigrant communities to lobby on behalf of the country of their origin?

6. Cite a case where policy has become paralyzed, or where no policy could be developed due to bureaucratic pulling and hauling or to disagreements between various ministers involved in framing policy.

7. This chapter presents a historical example—the Suez invasion of 1956—to illustrate how various explanations can be used in foreign policy analysis. Use the scheme to explain a recent foreign policy decision of your government. In what ways could the scheme be amended to enhance its explanatory power?

Selected Bibliography

Allison, Graham T., and Morton H. Halperin, "Bureaucratic Politics: A Paradigm and Some Policy Implications," in *Theory and Policy in International Relations*, eds. Raymond Tanter and Richard H. Ullman. Princeton, N.J.: Princeton University Press, 1972.

Armstrong, David, *Revolution and World Order*. Oxford: Clarendon Press, 1993.

Barnett, A. Doak, *The Making of Foreign Policy in China: Structure and Process*. Boulder, Colo.: Westview Press, 1985.

Betts, Richard K., "Analysis, War, and Decision: Why Intelligence Failures Are Inevitable," *World Politics*, 31 (1978), 61–89.

Bloomfield, Lincoln P., *The Foreign Policy Process: A Modern Primer*. Englewood Cliffs, N.J.: Prentice Hall, 1982.

Brecher, Michael, *Decisions in Israel's Foreign Policy*. New Haven, Conn.: Yale University Press, 1975.

Carlsnaes, Walter, *Ideology and Foreign Policy: Problems of Comparative Conceptualization*. Oxford: Basil Blackwell, 1986.

Cassese, Antonia, ed., *Parliamentary Control Over Foreign Policy: The Foreign Policy Systems Approach*. Aldershot, Hants.: Elgar, 1989.

Cohen, Bernard C., *The Press and Foreign Policy*. Princeton, N.J.: Princeton University Press, 1963.

———, "The Influence of Special-Interest Groups and Mass Media on Security Policy in the United States," in *Perspectives on American Foreign Policy*, ed. Charles W. Kegley, Jr., and E. R. Wittkopf. New York: St. Martin's Press, 1983, pp. 105–30.

Cohen, Raymond, *Threat Perception in International Crisis*. Madison, Wisc.: University of Wisconsin Press, 1979.

Constas, Dimitri C., and Athanassios G. Platias, *Diasporas in World Politics*. London: Macmillan, 1993.

Dawisha, Adeed, ed., *Islam in Foreign Policy*. Cambridge: Cambridge University Press, 1983.

De Rivera, Joseph, *The Psychological Dimensions of Foreign Policy*. Columbus, Ohio: Merrill, 1968.

Etheredge, Lloyd S., *A World of Men: The Private Sources of American Foreign Policy*. Cambridge, Mass.: M.I.T. Press, 1978.

Falkowski, Lawrence S., ed., *Psychological Models in International Politics*. Boulder, Colo.: Westview Press, 1979.

George, Alexander, *Presidential Decisionmaking in Foreign Policy: The Effective Use of Information and Advice*. Boulder, Colo.: Westview Press, 1980.

Hagan, Joe D., *Political Opposition and Foreign Policy in Comparative Perspective*. Boulder, Colo.: Lynne Rienner, 1993.

Halliday, Fred, "The Sixth Great Power: On the Study of Revolution and International Relations," *Review of International Studies,* 16 (July 1990), 207–22.

Halperin, Morton, Bureaucratic Politics and Foreign Policy. Washington, D.C.: The Brookings Institute, 1974.

Hermann, Charles F., Charles W. Kegley, Jr., and James N. Rosenau, eds., New Directions in the Study of Foreign Policy. Boston: Allen & Unwin, 1987.

Hermann, Margaret G., "Personality and Foreign Policy Decision Making: A Study of 53 Heads of Government," in *Foreign Policy Decision Making: Perception, Cognition, and Artificial Intelligence,* eds. Donald A. Sylvan and Steve Chan. New York: Praeger, 1984.

——, *and Charles F. Hermann,* "Who Makes Foreign Policy Choices and How: An Empirical Enquiry," *International Studies Quarterly,* 33 (December 1989), 361–87.

Holmes, Jack E., The Mood/Interest Theory of American Foreign Policy. Lexington: University Press of Kentucky, 1985.

Holsti, K. J., Why Nations Realign: Foreign Policy Restructuring Since World War II. London: Allen & Unwin, 1982.

Holsti, Ole R., "Crisis Decision Making," in *Behavior, Society, and Nuclear War,* Vol. 1, eds. Philip E. Tetlock et al. New York: Oxford University Press, 1989.

——, "Public Opinion and Foreign Policy: Challenges to the Almond-Lippmann Consensus," *International Studies Quarterly,* 36 (December 1992), 439–66.

Hughes, Barry B., The Domestic Context of American Foreign Policy. San Francisco: Freeman, 1978.

Janis, Irving L., Victims of Groupthink: A Psychological Study of Foreign-Policy Decisions and Fiascoes. Boston: Houghton Mifflin, 1972.

——, *Crucial Decisions: Leadership in Policymaking and Crisis Mangement.* New York: Free Press, 1989.

Jensen, Lloyd, Explaining Foreign Policy. Englewood Cliffs, N.J.: Prentice Hall, 1982.

Jönsson, Christer, ed., Cognitive Dynamics and Foreign Policy. New York: St. Martin's Press, 1982.

Kelman, Herbert C., ed., International Behavior. New York: Holt, Rinehart and Winston, 1965.

Korany, Bahgat, How Foreign Policy Decisions Are Made in the Third World. Boulder Colo.: Westview Press, 1986.

——, *and Ali Hillal Dessouki, The Foreign Policies of Arab States,* 2nd ed. Boulder, Colo.: Westview Press, 1991.

Krasner, Stephen D., Defending the National Interest. Princeton, N.J.: Princeton University Press, 1978.

Laqueur, Walter, A World of Secrets: The Uses and Limits of Intelligence. New York: Basic Books, 1985.

Lippmann, Walter, Public Opinion. New York: Macmillan, 1922.

Maoz, Zeev, National Choices and International Processes. Cambridge: Cambridge University Press, 1990.

Maurer, Alfred C., Marion D. Tunstall, and James M. Keagle, eds., Intelligence: Policy and Process. Boulder, Colo.: Westview Press, 1985.

Merle, Marcel, La Politique Étrangère. Paris: Presses Universitaires de France, 1984.

Moon, Bruce, "The Foreign Policy of the Dependent State," *International Studies Quarterly,* 27 (1983), 315–40.

Risse-Kappen, Thomas, "Public Opinion, Domestic Structure, and Foreign Policy in Liberal Democracies," *World Politics,* 43 (1991), 479–512.

Sheffer, Gabriel, ed., Modern Diasporas in International Politics. New York: St. Martin's Press, 1986.

Snyder, Richard C., H. W. Bruck, and Burton Sapin, "Decision Making as an Approach to the Study of International Politics," in *Foreign Policy Decision Making,* eds. Richard C. Snyder, H. W. Bruck, and Burton Sapin. New York: Free Press, 1962.

——, *and Glenn D. Paige,* "The United States' Decision to Resist Aggression in Korea," in *Foreign Policy Decision Making,* eds. Richard C. Snyder, H. W. Bruck, and Burton Sapin. New York: Free Press, 1962.

Spanier, John W., and Eric M. Uslaner, American Foreign Policy Making and the Democratic Dilemma, 6th ed. New York: Macmillan, 1994.

Sprout, Harold, and Margaret Sprout, "Environmental Factors in the Study of International Politics," *Journal of Conflict Resolution,* 1 (1957), 309–28.

Spykman, Nicholas J., "Geography and Foreign Policy," *American Political Science Review,* 32 (1938), 28–50.

Stein, Janice Gross, "Can Decision-Makers Be Rational and Should They Be? Evaluating the Quality of Decisions," *Jerusalem Journal of International Relations,* 3 (1978), 316–39.

Steiner, Miriam, "The Search for Order in a Disorderly World: World Views and Prescriptive Decision Paradigms," *International Organization,* 37 (1983), 321–40

Tuchman, Barbara W., The March of Folly: From Troy to Vietnam. New York: Alfred A. Knopf, 1984.

Vasquez, John A., Explaining and Evaluating Foreign Policy: A New Agenda for Comparative Foreign Policy. New York: Praeger, 1986.

Verba, Sidney, "Assumptions of Rationality and Non-Rationality in Models of the International System," *World Politics,* 14 (1961), 93–117.

Vertzberger, Yaacov, Y. I., The World in Their Minds: Information Processing, Cognition, and Perception in Foreign Policy Decision-Making. Stanford Calif.: Stanford University Press, 1990.

Wallace, William, The Foreign Policy Process in Britain. London: Allen & Unwin, 1977.

Watanabe, A., "Foreign Policy Making Japanese Style," *International Affairs,* Vol. 54 (1978), pp. 75–88.

White, Ralph K., "Images in the Context of International Conflict: Soviet Perceptions of the U.S. and the U.S.S.R.," in *International Behavior: A Social-Psychological Analysis,* ed. Herbert C. Kelman. New York: Holt, Rinehart & Winston, 1965.

Zorgbibe, Charles, Les politiques étrangères des grandes puissances. Paris: Presses Universitaires de France, 1984.

Chapter
12

Law and World Opinion in Explanations of Foreign Policy

We often hear that a government in its diplomacy, use of force, or other actions has "violated international law." By this we mean that a government has done something that is inconsistent with codes and obligations contained in treaties and documents such as the charter of the United Nations, or with more abstract principles of justice. The question in this chapter is the role of legal norms and world opinion in the formulation of foreign policy. Do governments typically consult relevant treaties and other instruments of law before they decide what kinds of actions to take in a particular situation? In general, how do they respond to expressions of opinion toward their actions, particularly opinions articulated abroad? If a treaty obligation says one thing but a government wants to do something that is inconsistent with it, what usually happens?

Let us keep in mind the distinction between what generally happens and what *should* happen. The first is an empirical question, the second is normative. But they often blend. Policy critics often argue that a government must under all circumstances adhere to legal norms or the expressions of opinion and that in the case of the use of force, it can only be done if the cause is "just." Governments, in contrast, often argue that there is not always a choice between acting illegally and legally. They have to do what is necessary (what the circumstances require), and sometimes obligations have to be circumvented. The choices are not always easy. But what are these obligations? What kinds of constraints do they impose? Why accept such constraints in the first place? And if they act as constraints, what offsetting benefits do they provide?

Any obligation is a limitation on a government's freedom of action. Some parts of international law define what states *may* or *must* do; others point out what states *must not* do; still others attempt to define the *situation* in which positive or negative obligations become operational. If, in their foreign policy behavior, governments meet these obligations—even at the expense of their immediate interests or efficient conduct of diplomacy or war—we can infer that legal considerations at least in part explain their decisions. If, in other circumstances, governments interpret the rules in an arbitrary fashion or violate their permissive, positive, or negative obligations, we can conclude that other values, interests, or considerations were more important.

The main purpose of this chapter is to illustrate how international legal norms enter into the making of foreign policy, particularly in the realm of *decisions* and *actions*. To what extent can we explain any particular decision or action by reference to legal obligations? In decision-making situations, are legal obligations more or less important than policy makers' concern over public opinion, ideological preferences, the situation abroad, or organizational traditions? Are some states more "law-abiding" than others? Considering that there is a vast network of commercial, diplomatic, and military treaties between states, as well as customary rules of law and tradition, how often are actions consistent with the obligations that arise from these sources?

Before exploring the relationship between law and foreign policy—how governments use law—we should establish the extent to which a legal system, or comprehensive network of traditional and treaty law binding all states in the world, really exists. In looking at legal factors in foreign policy, then, our first problem is to establish the existence, nature, and shortcomings of the legal system, then inquire into the situations in which governments are more or less likely to fashion their objectives and actions to accord with legal obligations.

Legal Norms in Some Preindustrial International Systems

A review of preindustrial international systems reveals that legal or ethical norms, backed by religious sanctions, were often considered in organizing actions and transactions between independent political units existing *within a common civilization or culture*. In many civilizations, one can find legal or religious principles that established routines to handle (1) communications between the political units (various forms of diplomatic immunity, for example); (2) commercial transactions; (3) conduct of warfare; and (4) observance of treaties.[1] There is also evidence regarding the lack of legal or religious norms in ordering the relations *between political units of two distinct civilizations or cultures*. The laws existing among the political units of one culture were seldom applied in relations with "barbarians" beyond the geographical and cultural boundaries of the system. Until the twentieth century, Europeans and North Americans, much like the Hindus, Greeks, or Moslems of earlier ages, did not con-

---

[1]See, for example, Baron S. A. Korff, "An Introduction to the History of International Law," *American Journal of International Law*, 18 (1924), 246–59; Bronislaw Malinowski, "An Anthropological Analysis of War," *American Journal of Sociology*, 46 (1941), 521–50; Rudolf W. Holsti, *The Relation of War to the Origin of the State* (Helsingfors: Uusi Kirjapaino, 1913), pp. 60–70.

sider that the legal obligations observed in relations with each other could be applied equally in transactions with "savages" or tribal collectivities in entirely different cultures.

The second point is that there are many analogies between the rules found operating effectively in historical systems and those of modern international law. Both the reports of explorers and the more recent studies of anthropologists have noted the rather sophisticated rules and ceremonies that were associated with economic, diplomatic, and military transactions between tribes, lineage groups, city-states, and ancient empires. Almost all peoples used various forms of treaties—as we do—to secure peace, followed by some kind of ceremony, ritual, or sacrifice to seal obligations. The sanctions to these treaties were often religious beliefs that those who broke them would die or receive some violent punishment. Economic exchanges were normally consummated according to strict rules, and in many cases, tribes also possessed rules and customs regulating the outbreak and conduct of warfare. Regular observance of these religious restraints helps to explain why, despite frequent wars and violence, many tribes survived for centuries.[2]

In the ancient Hindu international system, the role of law in ordering transactions between independent units was much less in evidence, and few analogies with modern international law are to be found. Princes and kings recognized neither the concept of a family of sovereign states nor a well-defined body of law.[3] Although some vague understandings pertaining to diplomatic immunities and commercial transactions seemed to exist, sovereigns did not faithfully observe them except when they feared serious reprisals. There was so little faith in treaties that the signatories often exchanged hostages as a guarantee for compliance. Lack of the most basic rules for transactions in the Hindu system is revealed in a passage of Kautilya's *Arthasastra*, in which he recommends that a king threatened by a neighboring sovereign invite him to his realm on the pretext of attending a festival, wedding, or elephant hunt and then take him prisoner and even slay him.[4] War and use of force were accepted as normal activities of the state, whether undertaken for glory, plunder, territory, or creation of vassal states. There grew up later, with the fall of the Mauryan dynasties, a vague principle that certain forms of conquest ("demonaic conquest") involving indiscriminate annihilation and slaughter should be avoided. "Righteous" conquests to create vassal states were the ideal for which Hindu kings were expected to go to war. Other chronicles from the period claim that there were fairly strict rules governing conduct of warfare. These mention that warriors fighting from chariots could not strike those on foot; wounded enemies could not be slain; and, as a form of arms control, poisoned weapons could not be used.[5]

[2]Holsti, *The Relation of War to the Origin of the State*, p. 67.

[3]Adda Bozeman, "Representative Systems of Public Order Today," *American Society of International Law, Proceedings* (April 1959), p. 18.

[4]George Modelski, "Kautilya: Foreign Policy and International System in the Ancient Hindu World," *American Political Science Review*, 58 (1964), 556. There is other evidence, however, that the ancient Indians did, on the whole, observe treaties and develop some legal norms that were observed for reasons other than immediate gain. See Frank M. Russell, *Theories of International Relations* (New York: Appleton-Century-Crofts, 1936), pp. 41–46.

[5]A. L. Basham, *The Wonder That Was India* (London: Sidgwick and Jackson, 1954), pp. 122–24, 126.

The Growth of European International Law

Legal, religious, and ethical norms regulating transactions between diverse political units existed in many non-Western, preindustrial international systems and civilizations. However, it was in Greece, the Roman Empire, and particularly seventeenth-century Europe that the first coherent legal system, divorced from religion, developed. Among primitive tribes, and in India, China, and the Islamic empire, the norms observed in interunit transactions were inseparable from general precepts of morality or religion, or from ancient customs. The concepts of legal rights and obligations of sovereign governments, central to modern international law, did not come into existence until the appearance of the European state system in the fifteenth, sixteenth, and seventeeth centuries.[6]

What order existed in late medieval Europe grew out of the authority of the Church to prescribe general rules of conduct and from the customary rules of chivalry. In addition, medieval society incorporated the tradition of natural law and order from Rome, from which other principles relating to the transactions between political units were derived. Generally, however, it was the Church, with its notions of hierarchy, authority, and duty, and its ultimate sanction of excommunication, that had the largest impact in moderating the politics of the period. The Peace of God, declared by the Church in the tenth century, attempted to impose restrictions on war, violence, and plundering, but the results were negligible. The Truce of God (1041), established by the Bishop of Arles and the Abbot of Cluny, was more successful and did effectively limit the scope and degree of violence in certain parts of medieval Europe. There was to be, for example, no fighting between Wednesday evening and Monday morning. Such declaratory laws were never observed with any precision, nor did they gain acceptance as custom except in some localities. Later in the medieval period, the doctrine of "just war" arose and helped to deter some forms of violence. The Church considered war "illegal" and its perpetrators subject to ecclesiastical punishment if it was not properly declared by established authorities, with just causes and legitimate objectives.[7]

The basic premises and rules of modern international law—sovereignty, territorial integrity, legal equality, and noninterference in other states' internal affairs—developed simultaneously with the growth of centralized dynastic political units that no longer accepted the command of any authorities within or outside of their boundaries. Diplomats and dynasts might have acknowledged certain principles of justice deriving from the "law of nature," but generally their conduct in foreign relations was restrained, if at all, only by obligations undertaken with each other in treaties. Religious principles, the Church, and abstract notions of "natural law" no longer effectively limited what the new sovereigns or principalities could and could not do to their neighbors. Restraints were mostly self-imposed, voluntarily observed, and enforced primarily by the threat of counteraction and retaliation. Claims by dynasts

[6]Quincy Wright, *The Role of International Law in the Elimination of War* (Manchester, Eng.: Manchester University Press, 1961), pp. 18–19.

[7]See for details M. H. Keen, *The Laws of War in the Late Middle Ages* (Toronto: University of Toronto Press, 1965).

that certain customs were well established parts of international law were seldom met with agreement by other states.[8]

New European needs gave the impetus for rapid development of international law in the nineteenth century. In particular, the growing volume of intra-European trade and development of sources of raw materials and markets in non-European areas created similar types of transactions and hence similar outlooks toward the rules needed to place economic relations on a stable and predictable basis. Britain's dominant naval position enabled it to establish almost unilaterally the foundations for the modern law of the sea. The greatest expansion of legal doctrines covered matters pertaining to the obligations of debtor states, sanctity of money, protection of commercial property during civil strife, and expropriation of private property.[9] These aspects of international law expressed the contemporary European doctrines of laissez-faire economics and the mutual interests of European business owners in expanding markets and obtaining security for their foreign investments. Thus, nineteenth-century international law was the law of an expanding commercial civilization. But in regulating the use of force and tempering national and imperial rivalries, the law was much less effective.

The doctrine of "just war," which had placed some limitations on the use of force prior to the eighteenth century, was never carried through to the nineteenth century. On the contrary, governments viewed the threat and use of force as legitimate exercises of a sovereign's will. Some publicists fought for the cause of peace and disarmament, but the law of the period reflected the belief that war was a self-justifying instrument of inducement. The relative military stability of the nineteenth century and the restraints on the use of force flowed from the creation of deterrents and the operation of the Concert of Europe, not from the effectiveness of legal principles.

Nineteenth-century international law did incorporate limitations on the scope and degree of violence.[10] New laws of neutrality established definite rights and obligations for both belligerents and neutrals, helping prevent the extension of bilateral military confrontations into continental or regional holocausts, and certain areas or countries such as Switzerland (1815), Belgium (1831), and the Congo Basin (1885) were permanently neutralized by the great powers, thereby removing them from the arenas of conflict.[11] Series of multilateral conventions and codes were also drafted to prevent undue suffering among troops and civilians alike. In most cases, the laws of neutrality and warfare were observed until developments in military technology in the twentieth century made them more or less obsolete.

[8]See Percy Corbett, *Law in Diplomacy* (Princeton, N.J.: Princeton University Press, 1959), Chapter 1.

[9]See Richard A. Falk, "Historical Tendencies, Modernizing and Revolutionary Nations, and the International Legal Order," in *Legal and Political Problems of World Order*, prelim. ed., ed. Saul H. Mendlovitz (New York: The Fund for Education Concerning World Peace Through World Law, 1962), pp. 133–34; Charles De Visscher, *Theory and Reality in Public International Law*, trans. P. E. Corbett (Princeton, N.J.: Princeton University Press, 1957), p. 136; Morton A. Kaplan and Nicholas de B. Katzenbach, *The Political Foundations of International Law* (New York: John Wiley, 1961), p. 28.

[10]Richard A. Falk, "Revolutionary Nations and the Quality of International Legal Order," in *The Revolution in World Politics*, ed. Morton A. Kaplan (New York: John Wiley, 1962), p. 320.

[11]Belgium and the Congo (Zaire) are, of course, no longer neutral.

Contemporary International Law: The Sources and Existence of Legal Norms and Restraints

International law, based on its European origins, has continued to develop in scope and precision during the twentieth century despite the occurrence of two great world wars. An important part of contemporary international law has arisen from the *customary practices of states* over many decades and centuries. In many cases, governments have assembled to translate customary practices into multilateral *treaties* or *codes*, thus setting custom in a more precise framework of written rules. *International and domestic tribunals* have handled thousands of cases involving conflicts between citizens and governments of diverse states, and their decisions, although not strictly binding on subsequent cases, have established many important principles and precedents considered to be part of the modern law of nations. Finally, states have concluded thousands of *bilateral and multilateral treaties* establishing new rights and obligations as well as restrictions on what governments may or may not do in their external relations. Unlike the customary sources of international law, treaties can be drafted, changed, and adapted to particular needs and circumstances and can, therefore, establish immediately new principles, rights, and obligations to regulate the relations between states. For example, since there is no precedent or precise analogy to the problems presented by space exploration, the law covering this area must be *created* by governments through negotiated treaties. Treaties cannot establish new rights or obligations for those states that are not parties to them, whereas customary rules of law can be invoked by all states.

From these sources has grown a modern international law that displays, through custom and precedent, continuity with the past but is infinitely more complex than it was in the past. It seeks to regulate, stabilize, and make predictable types and quantities of commercial and political transactions that are largely unprecedented. In addition, the new law reflects contemporary ethical values that condemn the use of force as an instrument of inducement. The nineteenth-century attitude and doctrine toward war as an instrument of policy to be unleashed by any government solely at its own discretion has been replaced by prohibitions in the United Nations charter against recourse to force and even the threat to use force, except in cases of self-defense or in conformity with a collective decision. The old laws of neutrality have been superseded by the obligation of *all* states to assist victims of aggression. As an outcome of the Nuremberg trials of Nazi war criminals and the Genocide Convention, personal criminal liability can be imposed against those who launch wars of aggression. In short, under the new international law, war is no longer viewed as a duel between legally equal belligerents to be regulated only in its scope, but rather as a crime against all nations that must be prevented.[12]

It would be difficult to deny the existence of a comprehensive set of rules, rights, obligations, and legal doctrines in numerous treaties, in customs and codes, and in the thousands of decisions of national and international tribunals. These are designed to define rights, limit a state's freedom of action, and prescribe rules of con-

---

[12]Wright, *The Role of International Law in the Elimination of War*, pp. 27–28.

duct for all types of transactions—technical, commercial, diplomatic, and military. Before we investigate the extent to which these rules and customs influence decisions and actions, it is necessary to point out some of the shortcomings of modern international law, faults found in the body of norms rather than in the actions of governments.

In the first place, no legal norm is so precise as to convey absolutely clear meaning to all people. Although that part of international law based on custom may be more enduring because it reflects common usage and needs,[13] some aspects of it are also vague and imprecise, leaving each state to interpret the custom according to its own interests. Treaties can be formulated more precisely, but these, too, may contain phrases too vague to guide behavior in predictable fashion. Many provisions of the United Nations charter have been interpreted in different ways by governments. Until the day when all conflicts arising out of different interpretations of the law are submitted to impartial tribunals, governments—as do private citizens—will usually construe the meaning of treaties and conventions in such a way as to favor their own political objectives.

Second, legal norms, when they are not legislated by a central political body, tend to change very slowly, with the result that some rules of international law become obsolete before governments acknowledge their obsolescence. Although some governments may feel strong pressures to violate obsolete and unjust norms, their actions are violations nevertheless until a majority of states in the system agree, through practice or conventions, upon new norms. Can the killing of civilians be prevented, as required by the laws of land and naval warfare, when adversaries use nuclear-tipped missiles, long-range artillery, or conventional heavy bombs, or where military and civilian targets are inseparable? The tortuous debates in the Law of the Sea conferences during the 1970s illustrate the great difficulties involved in trying to fashion a consensus among more than 150 states. Every state agreed there is a problem—the inadequacy of old rules governing maritime matters—but a treaty outlining the extent of territorial jurisdiction, rights of access to fish stocks and research, passage rights through international straits, and many other matters required more than a decade of negotiations before an agreement emerged. Even so, a number of states, including the United States, have not ratified the treaty.

We should not place too much emphasis on these inadequacies of the body of legal norms, for it might lead us to conclude that the ineffectiveness of some legal restraints and limitations arises from deficiencies in the law itself. Nor should we assume that the behavior of governments in this respect will change simply because norms are brought up-to-date or made more precise. Despite the existence of hundreds of arbitration treaties between states, the League of Nations covenant, the Geneva Protocol of 1924, the Treaty for the Renunciation of War (The Kellogg-Briand Treaty, 1928), the Anti-War Treaty of Rio de Janeiro in 1933, and the United Nations charter, the use of force has not been effectively regulated yet. Some of these treaties and charters are not entirely clear in their details, but this should not suggest that more and better treaties or international institutions will solve the problem of war.

---

[13]De Visscher, *Theory and Reality in Public International Law*, p. 155.

More important is that relatively few disputes and conflicts of objectives arise out of differing interpretations of law. If international politics were defined only as the problems and processes of adjusting conflicts arising from differing conceptions of legal rights and duties, we should be concerned with studying ways to improve the content of the law. But since international politics involve the problems and processes of adjusting conflicts arising from more or less incompatible collective objectives, then no matter how clear, precise, and logical the law is, it would not be observed in all instances. The body of the law is far from perfect, but failure to observe legal norms does not necessarily result from imperfections of the law.

To this point, we have emphasized the body of law that exists in customary practice, charters of international organizations, and treaties. But there are also more subtle types of restraint systems operating between states. In Chapter 3, we noted that the collectivity of states, each pursuing its own interests, nevertheless constitutes a *society* of states. Like a club, this society has its norms, rites of entry, and forms of ostracism against those who habitually violate its unofficial and official rules. The fundamental rules of this society are sovereignty, legal equality, diplomatic immunities, and noninterference in internal affairs, but there are a number of less formal "rules" concerning how states ought to conduct their mutual relations. These include prohibitions against aggressive war, the fledgling norms dealing with international terrorism and airline hijackings, some aspects of human rights, the principle of self-determination, and perhaps some consensus that the grossest forms of inequality in the world should not be allowed to persist. Governments or regimes that consistently violate some or many of these norms are usually ostracized in the society of states. We thus have the concept of "pariah" states. Examples would include Communist China in the 1950s, Uganda in the 1960s (under the Idi Amin regime), and, in the contemporary setting, Iraq. States that have received regional, if not universal, ostracism include Israel and Libya.

The Use of Law in the Pursuit of Foreign Policy Objectives

In situations where governments perceive threats to vital collective, or core, objectives and interests, what role do legal principles play? In such crises strategic and other kinds of considerations tend to predominate. The records of history are filled with instances where governments knowingly violated international norms and treaty obligations in order to achieve or defend their purposes. Only a couple of examples are necessary to support the generalization. During the *contra* war against the Nicaraguan regime of Daniel Ortega during the 1980s, the United States undertook a variety of actions (such as mining Nicaraguan harbors) that were violations of international law. These actions were terminated only after they received wide publicity and a decision by the International Court of Justice condemned them. In the 1990 Persian Gulf crisis, Iraq's Saddam Hussein took thousands of foreigners hostage to use as a shield against any attack against his regime. After the United Nations forces began to employ military force to free Kuwait, Hussein again used hostages, this time captured prisoners of war—all in contravention of international treaties that prohibit such actions. It is precisely in periods of crisis and war when legal obligations and constraints are most often violated and therefore least relevant to the designing of policy.

The problem of measuring the influence of legal obligations in decision making is that such influence involves more than the observance or nonobservance of clearly defined rules of law. A government can take action that it *believes* is consistent with legal obligations or the permissive components of international law. Governments normally characterize conflicts in the legal and diplomatic terms *that are most advantageous to their interests and objectives.* This practice is not necessarily a capricious twisting of legal principle to fit facts; it arises out of different perceptions of reality. A government may claim in its attempt to punish or threaten a hostile neighbor that its own aggressive actions are legally justified as "self-defense." Hence, in 1956, when Israel invaded Egypt, it invoked the law of self-defense. A neutral observer may conclude that Israel used aggression, whereas Israeli policy makers may have been quite convinced that their attack on Egypt was a legitimate act of self-defense. In this situation, can it be determined precisely whether legal principles and obligations effectively restrained actions? The South African government consistently characterized its apartheid policies as purely a domestic affair, while those on the outside insisted that these policies were a threat to peace and a violation of the Declaration of Human Rights, hence subject to outside interference. When characterizations of one set of events vary so greatly, it becomes difficult to decide which actions are in accord with, or in violation of, the rules of international law. In either case, the policy makers may have believed sincerely that their actions were legally justified, given their understanding of the facts.

Governments thus may use the flexibility of the law to their advantage. Moreover, legal norms in crisis situations seem to be used not so much to determine actions as to build justifications for certain actions. Indeed, case studies of conflicts between states reveal that governments use law essentially to further their objectives; that is, as narratives of self-justification or as bases on which to condemn their adversaries. In this sense, legal norms enter into decision making less as criteria to determine what, substantively, governments should or should not do, than as sets of principles that can be put together into a case to *justify actions that have already been taken.* Legal norms thus become diplomatic capabilities; governments fabricate legal justifications for their decisions and actions in order to mobilize domestic and external support. The American experience in the 1962 Cuban missile crisis reveals, for example, that the legal argument justifying a U.S. "quarantine" against importation of Soviet missiles into Cuba was made *after* the quarantine was already established. There is little evidence showing that the decision, as it was being made, was seriously debated on legal grounds.[14] Similarly, during various Cold War crises over Berlin, the confrontation between Malaysia and Indonesia in the mid-1960s, and the American intervention in Panama in 1989,

---

[14]Lawrence Scheinman and David Wilkinson, eds., *International Law and Political Crisis: An Analytical Casebook* (Boston: Little, Brown, 1968), p. 201. However, one of the participants in the Cuban episode shows that legal considerations were more prominent in decision making than is commonly acknowledged in most memoirs. See Abraham Chayes, *The Cuban Missile Crisis* (New York: Oxford University Press, 1974).

law was used primarily to (1) establish the legitimacy of diplomatic positions; and (2) mobilize diplomatic and public support for each party's own position, while attempting to demonstrate that the opposition's policies or actions were illegitimate.[15]

Thus, we end with three hypotheses about the relevance of legal norms in explaining policy decisions and actions:

1. In (a) issue areas involving primarily private interests, commercial, technological, and cultural actions and transactions, and (b) between states that normally maintain friendly relations, legal norms are at least as important in policy making as are systemic conditions, capabilities, public opinion, organizational values (which probably include a strong commitment to the "legal" way of doing things), or the personal preferences, values, or political needs of individual decision makers. In "routine" matters between two governments, decisions almost always conform to both substantive and procedural norms.

2. In (a) issue areas involving the conflict of collective interests and core values, and (b) between states that ordinarily maintain friendly relations, governments will attempt to organize their actions to make them consistent with legal obligations. However, perceptions of threat (definition of the situation), the demands of public opinion, and the personal needs of decision makers may require that legal norms be violated, or at least interpreted arbitrarily.

3. In (a) issue areas involving the conflict of important collective interests and core values, and (b) between states that ordinarily do not maintain friendly relations, governments will always choose "effective action" against legal obligations, when the two are incompatible. Perceptions of threat, relative capabilities, demands of public opinion, and the political needs of decision makers will be much more important in explaining objectives and actions than will treaty obligations.

Two general conclusions about the place of law in international politics can be offered. First, as a vast proportion of transactions between states are not concerned with crises and conflicts, we can infer that the obligations and procedures established through custom, treaties, and general principles of law predominate in policy making. The fact that most governments respect each other's sovereignty, that they do not seize each other's vessels on the high seas, that they do not arbitrarily incarcerate travelers and tourists, that they do not imprison diplomats, and that they recognize each other's legal equality indicates the pervasiveness of the world's legal system in foreign policy. On the other hand, in crisis situations, law assumes different functions: It is used primarily for mobilizing support at home and abroad rather than for establishing limits on what can or should be done.

Law as Procedure

To this point, we have spoken of the substantive aspects of international law: the do's and don'ts of international politics. In addition, the international community has

[15]Henkin, in his own case studies, is less pessimistic about the influence of law in crisis decision-making situations. He sees that even where decisions contravene legal norms, policy makers often "soften" their actions, refrain from doing certain things they might otherwise do, because of their awareness of legal prohibitions. Louis Henkin, *How Nations Behave: Law and Foreign Policy*, 2nd ed. (New York: Columbia University Press, 1979), Chapters 13–16.

established hundreds of organizations and international institutions to help regulate transactions between states. The United Nations is of course the best known, but it is only one of many. Most of the organizations and institutions prescribe certain procedures that must be followed in cases where there are serious disagreements or conflicts between their members. In the United Nations, for example, parties to a conflict are supposed to employ a variety of conflict resolution procedures instead of threatening or using force. The GATT has procedures and quasi-judicial bodies for handling trade disputes between its members. The Conference on Security and Cooperation in Europe has a complicated dispute-settlement mechanism which members are supposed to use. In all these organizations and institutions, the presumption is that members will use the specified procedures for conflict resolution *rather than employing force or its economic equivalent.* When governments use these procedures—and most of them do most of the time—there is a presumption that some kind of third party can use some rule or standard to help settle the problem. This automatically undermines a government's ability to act arbitrarily, and it at least temporarily suspends a government's "right" to solve the issue through violence or some other form of coercion. To take a personal analogy: Would you be tempted to solve a problem by force if you had a case pending in a court?

The world is full of such procedures. To the extent that they are employed, they have a dampening effect on international conflicts. They are by no means perfect—sometimes governments withdraw from the procedures or do not accept them initially, preferring to act on their own—but their overall record in managing conflicts is impressive.

Nonlegal Obligations in Foreign Policy

It would be impossible for governments to regulate all their actions and transactions through legal instruments such as treaties. As Raymond Cohen has pointed out, international politics are too fluid, complicated, and rapidly changing "to permit prior legislation on all possible contingencies and developments."[16] The same is true in personal life: Rules and laws provide guidance for behavior, but it would be impossible to conduct our lives if every conceivable situation calling for action or decision were regulated. In fact, most of us conduct our relationships employing a variety of nonwritten agreements, understandings, and commitments.

Cohen has classified a number of these international "rules of the game" according to the degree of explicitness with which an agreement is communicated. At one end of the continuum are international treaties and covenants, explicit statements outlining behavioral obligations—the do's and don'ts of international politics. Less formal are *nonbinding written understandings.* They do not have the status of treaties but can be just as important in policy making. Cohen provides the example of the 1972 Shanghai Communiqué between the United States and China. After almost twenty-five years of deep hostility between the two governments, the authori-

---

[16]"Rules of the Game in International Politics," *International Studies Quarterly,* 24 (March 1980), 129–50.

ties of the two countries were able to hammer out a framework of rules that would guide the establishment of formal diplomatic relations, and a formula that would deal with the tricky problem of Taiwan's status. The communiqué outlined general principles but established no binding obligations; these were to be worked out in detail as the relationship developed. A less happy nonbinding agreement was former President Nixon's famous letter to President Thieu of South Vietnam to the effect that if the North Vietnamese violated the terms of the Paris Agreement (ending the Vietnam War), the United States would take "swift and severe retaliatory action." In the midst of the Watergate scandal in 1975, North Vietnam attacked. Facing a hostile Congress, President Nixon was unable to meet the commitments he had made to Thieu.

Gentlemen's agreements are also legally nonbinding. They differ from the previous category by not even being written; such agreements are only verbal exchanges of promises. That they are not engraved on paper does not necessarily reduce their effectiveness, however. As in private life, broken promises incur significant costs in a relationship. They are also useful in foreign policy because in some circumstances, particularly in a rapidly changing situation, formal treaties are inappropriate. Where leaders wish to avoid adverse publicity or to bind their successors, they may also rely on gentlemen's agreements.

Tacit understandings are never written, are certainly not binding, and result from hints, signals, and past behavior rather than from formal communication. They develop because they provide some net gain to each of the parties, but for a variety of reasons, they cannot be explicitly stated or put into a document. There are, for example, a variety of conventions and understandings between the intelligence agencies of the major powers. While their agents might indulge in all sorts of skullduggery, deception, and assassination and even turn traitor, some things simply "are not done." Almost all countries expel apprehended spies or hold them until they can obtain the release of their own agents. They do not, however, put them on trial. The few exceptions in the multitude of cases prove the rule.

These "rules of the game," while not resting on very secure foundations, are nevertheless important considerations in many decision-making situations. They provide flexibility; they can be denounced more easily than treaties; they have no legal status; governments can deny their existence (except the written ones). Despite their informalities, they may have as much importance in policy making as more formal instruments and, in some cases, even more. The important point is that they do guide behavior, and for much the same reasons as treaties: The costs of breaking or repudiating agreements are often very high. We turn, then, to a consideration of those costs, more commonly known as the sanctions of international law and "rules of the game."

Law in Foreign Policy: The Sanctions of International Norms

Why do governments, sometimes even in crisis situations, generally observe the obligations, constraints, and limitations of international laws and less formal agreements? If you observe your own behavior, you will probably find several answers. Consider your actions as a driver. Although it may be more convenient and perhaps save time to do otherwise, you normally drive on the right-hand side of the road (unless you live in Great Britain, Australia, Japan, and a few other countries). After you have learned to drive, it becomes habitual. You seldom make a decision to do it. But implicitly, you also understand that there are advantages to having everyone drive on the same side of the road. If you drive on the wrong side, you endanger your life. There is thus an immediate self-advantage to adhering to the law. If you are in an extreme hurry, you may try to skirt the traffic, but you understand that to do so incurs various risks. You then weigh the costs of being late against the costs of killing yourself (and perhaps others) or, at a minimum, getting a traffic ticket. If the latter is the consequence, your name may be published in the newspaper, something that most people do not relish under the circumstances. And finally, if you drive recklessly too often, you may find that someone will take exception and retaliate. In this simple situation you can see the bases of law observance.

In most legal systems, rules and customs are normally observed for four distinct, although similar, reasons: (1) self-advantage; (2) habit; (3) prestige; and (4) fear of reprisal. Legal norms are a suitable basis for conducting transactions, particularly where they can help advance the values and interests of one party and where the other party, by observing the rules, can also expect some benefit. Rules simplify procedures between governments and are consequently of advantage to all.

The expectation of *reciprocity* is also an important factor in the observance of legal norms and obligations. A government accepts the obligations and restrictions imposed by law because it expects, or hopes, that the partners with whom it is in a relationship will base their decisions and responses on similar legal criteria. Self-advantage is mutual. This does not mean that all other considerations are irrelevant to the making of foreign policy decisions; it means, rather, that governments in most situations recognize and acknowledge the long-run advantages—particularly reciprocity—of conforming their actions to legal norms. This realization tempers considerations of expediency, military "necessity," and short-run political advantages. When the advantages of law observation are clear and persistent, a habit or custom of conducting transactions according to certain principles and routines may also arise.

In addition to advantage, reciprocity, and habit, another reason for law observance is that a government may effectively raise its international prestige, and thus its diplomatic influence with other states, if it develops a reputation in the community as a "law-abiding" state. A reputation for meeting treaty obligations and observing well-established legal principles in many types of transactions may be an important asset in the daily dealings of diplomats. A government that persistently breaks treaties, defies resolutions of international organizations, and capriciously twists the accepted meaning of legal doctrines will lower its credibility in diplomatic negotiations and hence its influence. One need point only to the poor reputation of the Soviet Union until Stalin's death. For many years, Western governments were reluctant to enter into any trade or cultural negotiations with his regime on the ground that the Soviet government had violated the letter or spirit of many important political and commercial treaties to which it had been a signatory.

Negative sanctions, or fear of various forms of reprisal, may also prompt governments to observe their obligations. Development of norms relating to diplomatic immunities is a good example. It was common among new dynastic regimes in Europe not to accord immunities to foreign diplomats, with the result that sometimes foreign diplomats were abused, jailed, and even executed by the government to which they were accredited. But this situation did not prevail, because these governments quickly recognized that if they treated foreign diplomats in this manner, their own representatives abroad could be—and were—treated similarly.

In addition to self-interest, reciprocity, habit, prestige factors, and fear of reprisal, two other considerations must be mentioned as reasons why governments, when faced with alternative courses of action, often choose the one most closely in accord with legal obligations and established practice. First, all governments, whether they explicitly acknowledge it or not, desire at least some convenience, stability, and predictability in their external relations. The ordinary transactions between countries, which are necessary to maintain economic viability, communications, and even security, are based on routines protected by legal doctrines or treaties. If these transactions were made completely unpredictable by lack of law observance, chaos and the impossibility of orderly policy making would ensue. Even revolutionary regimes during their years of external aggressiveness willingly comply with many of the rules of law adhered to by their enemies simply in order to exist. For states with more modest external objectives, law observance for many types of transactions becomes so routine that policy makers would consider other alternatives only in great conflicts or emergencies. The desire for stability and predictability can also be seen when governments convene after great wars or periods of instability to make permanent the changes that had been achieved through political and military actions. The peace treaty—like many other types of treaty—creates a new order out of chaos, stability out of rapid change, and predictability out of uncertainty.

Governments may or may not accept the limitations on actions imposed by legal norms. Certainly, it is not difficult to cite obvious violations of international law. But diplomatic history also reveals abundant evidence that many statesmen do place high value on at least appearing to comply with written and unwritten rules, legal doctrines, and treaties and that in so doing they not only display concern over their prestige or possible retaliation, but demonstrate their belief in the ethical value of law observance. In selecting among alternative courses of action, policy makers do not always think, "This time I will observe the law because I fear retaliation, or a lowering of my prestige, if I do not; but perhaps next time, if I think I can get away with it, I will disregard legal prohibitions and seek to achieve my objectives the quickest way possible and at least material cost." Law is, after all, more than a set of arbitrary rules derived from custom and treaties. Insofar as legal norms and "rules of the game" prevent governments from doing certain things, punish others, or prescribe certain courses of action, they reflect values and moral judgments. The provisions of the United Nations charter prohibiting the threat or use of force and the principles of the Genocide Convention do not arise from custom, prior treaties, or court decisions. These rules—and many unwritten understandings—emanate directly from a widespread belief that the use of aggressive force or the systematic slaying of religious or ethnic groups is inherently immoral and ethically reprehensible.

The observance of these and many other types of rules thus derives from considerations other than convenience. Although policy makers often excuse certain illegal actions as being dictated by the demands of "national security" or "national interest," they do not consistently break rules and norms just because they are acting in the name of the state. People are usually anxious to do not only what is practical and convenient, but also what they believe is right. Policy makers, like private citizens, will frequently respect a rule or choose that course of action most consistent with legal norms, because they believe that the norms are intrinsically correct and ought to be observed regardless of some particular disadvantage derived from their observance. An eminent international jurist, Charles De Visscher, has written that the observance of international law is ultimately a problem of individual attitudes and morality and not a question of the existence of lack of perfection in legal doctrines.

> The problem of obligation in international law is part of the problem of obligation in general, and this in turn is a moral problem. The distinction between ethical and legal categories, reasonable in itself and in many ways necessary, must not be pushed to the point of completely separating law from the primary moral notions to which all the normative disciplines are attached as to a common stem. Between States as within the State, law belongs to morals insofar as the idea of the just, which forms its specific content, is inseparable from the idea of the good, which is a moral idea. What, then, in the international sphere, is the order of facts, interest, ideas, or sentiments that can provide the moral substratum of obligation? Merely to invoke the idea of an international community . . . is immediately to move into a vicious circle, for it is to postulate in men, shut in their national compartments, something that they will largely lack, namely the community spirit, the deliberate adherence to supranational values. No society has any legal foundation unless men believe in its necessity. The ultimate explanation of society as of law is found beyond society, in individual consciences.[17]

Foreign Expectations and "World Public Opinion" as Factors in Policy Making

To what extent do manifestations of opinion abroad influence foreign policy purposes and actions? Here it is difficult to generalize because there are so many types of policy-making situations, personalities, and regimes. There are also critical questions raised by the concept of "world public opinion." Let us look at these two problems separately.

For better or worse, governments are usually the creatures of the societies over which they rule, and in most cases whether or not those governments survive in office will be determined not by foreign audiences but by domestic groups. A general proposition would be that governments, while they hardly relish condemnation abroad, are not as sensitive to it as they are to expressions of opinion at home. Here we are speaking of relatively open political systems. In closed systems, or in totalitarian

---

[17]De Visscher, *Theory and Reality in Public International Law*, p. 98, trans. P. E. Corbett. Copyright © 1957 by Princeton University Press, revised ed. © 1968 by Princeton University Press.

regimes, governments consult neither domestic nor foreign opinions. As we have seen in the previous chapter, they manufacture opinion more than they are constrained by it. Apartheid, the Israeli occupation of the West Bank and other territories since 1967, or the lack of self-determination in the Kashmir—once promised by India—are all policies continuously protested or condemned in a variety of quarters. Until Mikhail Gorbachev became president of the Soviet Union, the Soviet regime was impervious to numerous and frequent criticisms in other countries of its violations of human rights treaties. It would appear, then, that many governments most of the time see external manifestations of public opinion as only a peripheral consideration in policy making. Totalitarian regimes, in any event, traditionally have had little to worry about since they control the means of communication. But with the increased availability of fax machines, satellite television, and other technological innovations, it has become increasingly difficult to seal off a society from outside influences. Publics eventually will come to learn what others know; whether they are in a position to do anything about it remains problematic, however.

But what is this world public opinion? What are we to make of vast public demonstrations when we know that in many cases they are created by governments in power, specifically for the benefit of television audiences abroad? Rent-a-crowds are readily available, and sometimes they seem genuinely concerned only when they know that the television cameras are focused upon them.

The concept of world public opinion also assumes that everyone in the world will have a common understanding of the events or conditions that are being criticized or supported. But this is seldom the case. People see the world differently, and even if they share similar values—justice being one of the most prominent—they will not agree on how to characterize a situation. Issues that arouse displays of public passion are generally characterized in very different terms by different people. To many people, dramatic foreign events are like theater: There are the good people, the bad people, the conflicting principles, the heroes and martyrs, the devils, and the victims. Foreign policy crises and wars, in particular, make good theater.

Consider the different characterizations of Saddam Hussein's invasion of Kuwait in August 1990, and the succeeding United Nations–sanctioned war to restore the sovereignty of that small Persian Gulf country. How was this narrative understood in different parts of the world? Vast publics in the industrial countries, some immediate neighbors of Kuwait, and many United Nations officials constructed a narrative of a brutal Iraqi dictator who invaded a small neighbor, brutalized its population, and plundered its wealth before it annexed the remains to Iraq. This was a clear-cut case of aggression. The members of the United Nations Security Council passed a dozen resolutions, most unanimously, demanding the Iraqis to stop their aggression and to withdraw from the country. At stake was the reputation of the United Nations, the norm against armed conquest, the bases of world order, the leadership of the United States, and the expressed will of dozens of governments from all areas of the world.

After defying this expression of world opinion, Saddam Hussein refused to negotiate seriously with anyone who attempted to undo the events of August 1990. He was committed to making permanent his conquest, regardless of the opinions of others, principles of the United Nations, or economic costs. Twenty-nine countries ultimately made troops available for an armed assault against the aggressor. Even Senegal, Morocco, Pakistan, and Bangladesh, all poor countries, helped out militarily. Another forty-eight countries provided financial support. Surely this was a strong indication of worldwide support.

Yet millions of others saw or heard a different narrative. Many in the Muslim world saw the United States, not Iraq, as the villain of the piece. Iraq's conquest of Kuwait, while perhaps precipitous, was not to be lamented because the Kuwaitis were ruled by a rich emir whose family lifestyle and political practices did not accord with Muslim precepts. The Kuwaitis were typical of the arrogant oil-rich. The real plot of the story was not Saddam Hussein's actions, but the desire of the United States to secure hegemony in the Middle East and to protect its client, Israel, against the demands of the Palestinian people. By the time the United Nations forces attacked in January 1991, for these people Hussein had become the hero or the victim of the drama, the United States was the devil, and the principle at stake was the autonomy and pride of the Arabs and Muslims and the fate of the Palestinians.

Yet another narrative developed among various peace groups in the industrial countries. While they acknowledged that Hussein had committed an unprovoked aggression against Kuwait and United Nations rules, the Americans in their haste to display military virtuosity did not exhaust all possibilities for the peaceful resolution of the conflict. Economic sanctions, given adequate time, would have imposed heavy costs on Iraq, resulting in an ultimate withdrawal from Kuwait. While the distinction between heroes and devils was blurred, the issue at stake was that the use of force would cost untold thousands of lives, produce long-range political instability in the Middle East, and, in the most pessimistic scenarios, dramatically increase the possibility of nuclear war. Many also agreed that the Americans and their allies were employing double standards: They did not use force to make Israel comply with many UN resolutions asking it to withdraw from the occupied territories; they looked the other way when Vietnam invaded Cambodia in 1978; they did nothing to prevent the violent incorporation of East Timor into Indonesia in the early 1980s; and several other cases. The conclusion was, then, that the seemingly high motives of the United States were really more crass. It led the coalition against Saddam Hussein not because of high principles but because it wanted to protect its access to the Gulf's oil resources. The moral of the tale was, for them, "beware of those who invoke legal and moral principles to justify the use of military force."

We see, then, three fundamentally different stories. There were others as well, but they were primarily variations on these three themes. The point to emphasize is that despite the existence of well-reported and verified facts, people do not draw the same conclusions from them. All the sympathies that appear in everyday life also appear in opinions about events abroad. We tend to root for the underdog; we sympathize with ethnic kin more than with strangers; we find it more comfortable to support those who are like-minded than those who are "different"; we tend to be selective in our perceptions, bending considerably to try to understand our friends and allies, but being much quicker to judge harshly those whom we do not know well or whose institutions we do not know or like. It seems to require absolutely outrageous actions, such as genocide, to create anything approaching a world consensus, but even in these cases there will be many who will argue that those events are far away and not worth our attention, much less the loss of life in war.

What, then, are we to conclude about the role of "world public opinion" and expectations of other governments in the conduct of a government's foreign relations? Because there are historical examples of both the effectiveness and the impotence of foreign opinion as influences on a government's behavior, it is difficult to generalize. However, some conclusions or hypotheses might be suggested. First, most governments *are* sensitive to the opinions expressed abroad about their policies and how they execute them. Otherwise they would not spend such large sums in trying, through diplomacy and propaganda programs, to create favorable impressions abroad. But they are not equally sensitive to all sources of opinion. Where, for example, perceptions of reality vary greatly, the government being condemned will probably not count hostile opinions as important. Also, governments are no doubt much more sensitive to opinions expressed by their closest friends and allies than those emanating from noninvolved or hostile countries. Similarly, they are more concerned with conforming their actions to their allies' expectations than to those of states with which they are not so directly involved.

Second, most governments are concerned with their prestige, an important, if intangible, aspect of their diplomatic effectiveness. No government could anticipate with pleasure a resolution in the General Assembly condemning its actions abroad. But in some crises, policy makers place such high value on achieving or defending their objectives that they are willing to break commitments, violate rules to which they normally adhere, and, in short, follow strictly national imperatives. In many other instances, policy makers *anticipate* the reactions of other governments and choose policy alternatives that are least likely to meet with hostile reactions. We can cite cases where resolutions in international organizations both failed and succeeded in persuading governments to observe legal and moral obligations; it is more difficult to know of all those cases where governments did *not* choose a particular course of action because their policy makers anticipated unfavorable responses abroad. If we conceive of world public opinion as being both the spontaneous and the organized expressions of attentive publics on particular situations, often communicated through propaganda channels, it can be an effective restraint on policy, provided that there is some agreement among the publics, that the attitudes are also expressed by friendly governments and are not merely the expected hostility of unfriendly states, and that defiance of those attitudes would lower a state's prestige and diplomatic influence.

Questions for Study, Analysis, and Discussion

1. Since there are so many different civilizations in the world, is it possible to have a single international law?
2. In what ways can it be argued that contemporary international law is "European law"?
3. Name the major sources of international law.
4. For what reasons do governments usually meet their international obligations? Under what circumstances are they likely to violate legal norms?

5. Under what circumstances, in your opinion, are violations of international legal obligations justified or excusable?
6. Can you cite examples where a government sacrificed its immediate interests for the sake of legal obligation?
7. In what ways can international institutions help promote legal behavior?
8. Why is it difficult to use the concept of world public opinion?
9. Can you cite cases where the expression of such opinion fundamentally altered the policies of a government? And cases where it failed to alter decisions and actions?

Selected Bibliography

Anand, R. P., *New States and International Law*. Delhi, India: Vikas Publishing House, 1972.

Bozeman, Adda, *The Future of Law in a Multicultural World*. Princeton, N.J.: Princeton University Press, 1971.

———, "Law, Culture and Foreign Policy: East Versus West," *Atlantic Community Quarterly*, 12 (1974), 219–32.

Chayes, Abram, and Antonia Handler Chayes, "On Compliance," *International Organization*, 47 (Spring 1993), 175–205.

Cohen, Raymond, *International Politics: The Rules of the Game*. New York and London: Longman, 1981.

Corbett, Percy E., *Law in Diplomacy*. Princeton, N.J.: Princeton University Press, 1959.

De Visscher, Charles, *Theory and Reality in Public International Law*, trans. Percy E. Corbett. Princeton, N.J.: Princeton University Press, 1957.

Falk, Richard A., "The Reality of International Law," *World Politics*, 14 (1962), 353–63.

———, *Law, Morality and War in the Contemporary World*. New York: Praeger, 1963.

———, *Legal Order in a Violent World*. Princeton, N.J.: Princeton University Press, 1968.

Forsythe, David P., *The Politics of International Law: U.S. Foreign Policy Reconsidered*. Boulder, Colo.: Lynn Rienner, 1990.

Henkin, Louis, *How Nations Behave: Law and Foreign Policy*, 2nd ed. New York: Columbia University Press, 1979.

Higgings, Rosalyn, *The Development of International Law Through the Political Organs of the United Nations*. London: Oxford University Press, 1963.

———, "Policy Considerations and the International Judicial Process," *International and Comparative Law Quarterly*, 17 (1968), 58–84.

———, "The Place of International Law in the Settlement of Disputes by the Security Council," *American Journal of International Law*, 64 (1970), 1–18.

Hoffmann, Stanley, et al., eds., *Right vs. Might: International Law and the Use of Force*, 2nd ed. New York: Council on Foreign Relations, 1991.

Johnson, James T., *Just War Tradition and the Restraint of War: A Moral and Historical Inquiry*. Princeton, N.J.: Princeton University Press, 1981.

Kaplan, Morton A., and Nicholas de B. Katzenbach, *The Political Foundations of International Law*. New York: John Wiley, 1961.

Korff, Baron S. A., "An Introduction to the History of International Law," *American Journal of International Law*, 18 (1924), 246–59.

Levi, Werner, "International Law in a Multicultural World," *International Studies Quarterly*, 18 (1974), 417–49.

———, *Law and Politics in the International Society*. Beverly Hills, Calif.: Sage, 1976.

McDougal, Myres S., and Florentino P. Feliciano, *Law and Minimum World Public Order: The Legal Regulation of International Coercion*. New Haven, Conn.: Yale University Press, 1961.

Nardin, Terry, *Law, Morality, and the Relations of States*. Princeton, N.J.: Princeton University Press, 1981.

Northedge, F. S., "Law and Politics Between Nations," *International Relations,* 1 (1957), 291–302.

Onuf, Nicholas Greenwood, ed., Law-Making in the Global Community. Durham, N.C.: Carolina Academic press, 1982.

Sanders, David, Lawmaking and Co-operation in International Politics: The Idealist Case Re-examined. London: Macmillan, 1986.

Schachter, Oscar, International Law in Theory and Practice. Boston: Martinus Nijhoff, 1991.

Scheinman, Lawrence, and David Wilkinson, eds., International Law and Political Crisis: An Analytic Casebook. Boston: Little, Brown, 1968.

Van Glahn, Gerhard, Law Among Nations, 6th ed. New York: Macmillan, 1992.

Chapter

13

Ethics in Explanations of Foreign Policy

We do not have to read too many newspaper headlines and editorial pages to come to the conclusion that international politics, like all politics, has to do with much more than power, goals, and the means of achieving them. Major questions of justice underlie the purposes and actions of states. At the instrumental level, we can say that governments act with "propriety," "dignity," "honor," "good faith," or their opposites. In making such judgments, we are implicitly or explicitly judging behavior according to certain normative standards. Like the person in the street, diplomats and government leaders make similar judgments. They, like us, are involved in defining rules and judging others according to the principles of fair play, equal treatment, reciprocity, and the like.

Beyond these judgments about how governments *behave* toward each other, we also bring principles of justice into play with regard to the *outcomes* of policy. Governments, like all people, are concerned about principles of distributive justice. At least since the early twentieth century, they have assumed or argued that economically advantaged societies have some responsibility or obligation to assist the less advantaged. Foreign aid policies are not built solely on short-term calculations of immediate advantage—although these are certainly not absent, as we saw in Chapter 8. Many of the debates within alliances are also concerned with questions of distributive justice or "fairness." Do all the members of NATO contribute proportionally? Or are there some "free riders," governments which obtain the collective good of security provided by the alliance, but which refuse to contribute adequately to alliance costs?

Certain types of actions which are prohibited by international norms—unprovoked aggression, for example—bring forth other kinds of debates both within governments and in broad publics. Was a case of aggression (difficult to define in any case) justified? Was it a case of preemptive war, with defense rather than conquest the main purpose? Should those who commit aggression be held responsible for compensation of victims (part of the debate after Iraq's conquest of Kuwait in 1990)? Should aggressors be "punished"—not just forced to give up their conquests, but face further military destruction of their homeland?

Cases of military intervention provoke lengthy debates about the justice of causes. Vietnam, Grenada, Panama, Nicaragua, Bosnia, and many other international problems were debated by many governments, condemned by some and upheld by others, all using a variety of notions of justice or international norms on which to base their claims.

There are also considerations of justice surrounding the whole area of human rights. No government that has taken actions to promote or protect human rights abroad—as in the case of South Africa—has failed to develop an argument that abuses of these rights justify economic and other forms of sanctions, even though in undertaking these sanctions countries technically violate one of the fundamental norms of the United Nations, namely that states cannot interfere in each others' internal affairs.

These and even other kinds of questions of justice are raised to the international agenda on almost a daily basis. Whether or not governments choose to act—by doing something more concrete than simply shaking a finger at a supposed evildoer (talk is cheap)—involves moral choices. Sometimes they choose to do nothing, to ignore issues, or simply to make pontifical pronouncements; other times they commit resources, time, diplomatic skills, and other scarce commodities to try to bring about solutions that improve the human condition either locally, regionally, or globally. And on other occasions, they commit the lives of their citizens to undo a perceived injustice. Thus, while understanding goals, power, and techniques of persuasion is critical to the understanding of international politics, so are notions of justice. They constitute one of the fundamental components of relations between states. The next time there is an international crisis, the reader should carefully review the statements of parties involved in the conflict and see to what extent, and how, they incorporate differing principles of justice to build a case of legitimacy. The reader should also be alert, however, to the use of the rhetoric of justice to hide or screen more self-serving purposes. How, then, are moral choices built into foreign policy decisions? How can they help us explain why governments behave in certain ways in the conduct of their relations with others?

Much of the public and scholarly debate on the place of ethics in a society's foreign relations assumes that policy makers have a choice between posing as "realists" or "moralists"—that ethical restraints are, in a sense, voluntary or optional. There is, in fact, an intellectual tradition in American diplomatic history reflecting the realists' and moralists' approaches to foreign policy. The moralists often list among their heroes Jefferson, Wilson, Hull, and some lesser figures; Hamilton, Calhoun, and Theodore Roosevelt are often cited as exponents of a realist's approach to foreign relations. Looking at the speeches—although not the actions—of these men, one can see the distinction between the two approaches. In the early 1790s, for instance, Jefferson and Hamilton conducted a debate over the young republic's obligations to revolutionary France. Jefferson claimed that the United States was committed to assist the French in their wars because the Franco-American alliance signed during the War of Independence was still in effect. He asserted that a country had to meet its commitments even if it was not in its direct interest to do so. Hamilton claimed the contrary, arguing that a nation's self-interest can be its only guide to policy. One cannot, he suggested, apply ethical principles to problems of foreign policy.

Regardless of historical context, commitments to self-interest or ethical principles have, to most observers, appeared incompatible. A clear expression of this supposed incompatibility can be found in one of Woodrow Wilson's campaign speeches, when he claimed that:

> It is a very perilous thing to determine the foreign policy of a nation in the terms of material interests. . . . We dare not turn from the principle that morality and not expediency is the thing that must guide us, and that we will never condone iniquity because it is most convenient to do so.[1]

The difficulty with this sort of view is that it oversimplifies reality. Both moralists and realists assert that there is a choice between following policies of self-interest and those of principle. The moralists imply that pursuit of self-interest at the expense of principle leads to immoral, or amoral, diplomatic and military behavior. The realists reply that self-interest, when prudently pursued, is ethically justifiable in itself, and that the pursuit of ideals only causes great ideological crusades that end in tragedy. Some would add, quoting Machiavelli, "A man who wishes to make a profession of goodness in everything must necessarily come to grief among so many who are not good."[2] A review of diplomatic history would not support such extreme views. It may be true that in Machiavelli's day, typical forms of diplomatic conduct were notoriously low when judged by today's standards. Diplomats commonly lied, and many took their own cooks abroad for fear that local servants would poison them. The record of assassination, intrigue, and duplicity in Renaissance diplomacy is well documented.

Continued progress in technical and economic development has made it possible for policy decisions to have ever-greater consequences, good and bad, on the lives of ordinary citizens. And as states become more interdependent, the decisions made by one government to protect its interests can have considerable negative impact on other societies. Ethical knowledge or moral norms, unlike technical knowledge, are not necessarily additive. By any standards, Hitler's policies were more evil than those of Prussian monarchs. All we can suggest is that the potential for doing harm to large numbers of people is greater today and that policy decisions may have greater impact on more people than in the past. But explanations of foreign policy that claim that all statesmen are immoral, concerned only with their own power and

---

[1]Quoted in Hans Morgenthau and Kenneth W. Thompson, *Principles and Problems of International Politics* (New York: Alfred A. Knopf, 1950), p. 24.

[2]N. Machiavelli, *The Prince*, trans. Luigi Ricci, rev. by E. R. P. Vincent (London: Oxford University Press, 1935), Chapter 15.

prestige, and indifferent to the consequences of their actions are surely not warranted. To condemn policy makers as a group overlooks the fact that in their values and moral predispositions, they are probably a fairly representative sample of the educated people in the world. We could not deny that often their calculations are wrong, that they frequently look only to the short run and fail to analyze the long-run impacts of their decisions, or that they often have a propensity to dismiss information that does not fit with their favorite theories or values. Yet are not all people guilty of these shortcomings? This is not to argue that publics should avoid criticism of their leaders. Rather, it is to suggest that policy makers are probably no better or worse, from an ethical point of view, than their compatriots. They are in a unique position, however, to make decisions that will have positive or adverse consequences on their own citizens and people all over the world.

The Sources of Ethical Constraints and Considerations

The influence of ethics in foreign policy making is substantially more subtle than moralists and realists suggest. The first problem is to locate the sources of the do's and don'ts, rights and wrongs, and goods and bads. Here we return to the levels of analysis problem introduced in Chapter 1.

Ethical imperatives and considerations come, in the first place, from transnational values in the society of states. They are the general mores and rules that are supposed to regulate the behavior of all states toward each other. In the contemporary international system, they are formalized in documents such as the United Nations charter, the UN Declaration of Human Rights, and the Charter of Paris (1990) of the Conference on Security and Cooperation in Europe (CSCE). Primary values in them include the obligation to respect the sovereignty and independence of states; the prohibition against the use of armed force except for self-defense or collectively in the name of the United Nations; the right of self-determination (though never specified exactly what that right means for whom); and prohibitions against systematic abuse of human rights through torture, deprivation of civil liberties, genocide, and the like. Values even more fundamental to the system include the legal prescription that treaties are binding (*pacta sunt servanda*), the notion of reciprocity (particularly in trade relations), and a rather vague idea, certainly implied in the United Nations charter, that all states have responsibilities to the international community that transcend their own particular interests.

Governments in their mutual relations generally adhere to these values, prescriptions, and prohibitions. If they did not, we would have a war of all against all, with life, security, and welfare constantly under siege from different sources. It is precisely because these types of norms are generally observed that their violation creates headlines and vigorous policy debates. Not all violations are clear-cut, and most are defensible according to other standards. Saddam Hussein's blatant armed conquest of Kuwait in the summer of 1990 was supported by many, particularly among disaffected groups in the Middle East who wanted to end Western influence in the area. In this case, aggression could be justified by the seemingly more important value of freedom from Western imperialism.

A second source of ethical values is the society in whose name governments act. The prevailing ideologies, social systems, and historical culture within societies mold the priorities, aspirations, and operating modes of governments and their personnel. As suggested in Chapter 4, Communist ideologies have their own ethical structures, and these have helped justify the foreign policies of Communist regimes. While the quotation by Woodrow Wilson may be an extreme statement of moralism, American foreign policy has often reflected Americans' open style of politics, the importance of consulting allies before making important decisions, and exhausting other means prior to the use of force. When American presidents conduct policy otherwise, they inaugurate intense national policy debates. The vigorous opposition to the war in Vietnam after 1968, and to the Reagan administration's subversion and intervention in Nicaragua during the 1980s, provide examples. In these cases, policy opponents justified their criticism on the grounds that the United States was violating the principle of self-determination in Vietnam and the prohibition against armed intervention in the case of Nicaragua. In addition, they argued that the policies violated American political norms. In Vietnam, Lyndon Johnson had duped the Congress to support his escalation of the war by fabricating the Tonkin Gulf incident (a supposed attack on an American naval vessel off the coast of North Vietnam). In Nicaragua, the Reagan administration funded and armed the *Contras* from profits made by secretly selling arms to Iran. This was done to circumvent a congressional prohibition against providing the *Contras* with American arms.

The importance of democratic ethical norms in the foreign policies of liberal states is underlined by the fact that almost every serious deviation from them has been planned and executed in secret. When uncovered, the governments and their leaders either suffer a serious political defeat or are forced to resign. The Suez invasion of 1956 ended Anthony Eden's political career; Lyndon Johnson's policies in Vietnam led to his decision not to run for re-election in 1968; and the Reagan administration's duplicity in Nicaragua resulted in contempt of Congress and perjury charges against several important officials. President Nixon's "secret" war against Kampuchea in the early 1970s would probably have led to his political demise had not the Watergate scandal done it earlier.

In totalitarian states, foreign policy goals and actions similarly reflect the political culture. In Nazi Germany, threats, duplicity, subversion, and armed aggression were only the external manifestation of domestic politics, where opposition elements were systematically liquidated, where factional strife within the Nazi party was settled by midnight roundups and subsequent executions, and where toadying to the leader was the only way to advance a political career. Domestic propaganda fabricated information in much the same way that Hitler fabricated cases of foreign "injustice" against Nazi Germany. Stalin's military conquests between 1939 and 1941, and subsequent relegation of his east European allies to mere satrapies similarly reflected the political culture in Moscow. Opposition was not tolerated, suspected opponents were liquidated, and uncritical loyalty became the prime political skill. The norms of the international system—except sovereignty—were to be subverted and dismissed as so much "bourgeois" rhetoric.

In between these democratic and totalitarian extremes, the diplomatic goals and methods of most states in one way or another reflect social mores, a nation's culture, and the main characteristics of its political system. The relationship may be subtle and the subject of debate between analysts, but it is always there.

Finally, ethical principles derive from the individual conscience of policy makers. While notions of right and wrong, the permissible and the impermissible, may derive largely from culture, society, and religion, they are sufficiently flexible and subtle that they do not always indicate what is to be done in particular circumstances. Diplomatic history is full of examples where a certain policy was not chosen because a key policy maker thought it inherently wrong, whether on moral or religious grounds. One example: During the Cuban missile crisis in 1962, when all the options for responding to the emplacement of Soviet medium-range missiles in Cuba were being contemplated in Washington, President Kennedy's brother, Attorney General Robert Kennedy, argued that the United States could not launch a secret attack on Cuba. Such a policy would be another Pearl Harbor, abhorrent both to the American public and to Kennedy's conscience.

The use of economic sanctions against regimes that systematically violate their citizens' human rights reflects not only the general interests of a society but also the conscience of individual decision makers. Leaders such as Margaret Thatcher and Ronald Reagan, who opposed such sanctions in the case of South Africa, did not personally approve of *apartheid* but argued that sanctions would be ineffective and would hurt South Africa's blacks more than the ruling white regime. In Thatcher's case, the opposition to sanctions was influenced more significantly by the calculation that loss of trade with South Africa would damage the British economy which was already suffering from a 12 percent unemployment rate. This is a good example of the conflict between one's conscience and the hardheaded calculation of economic gains and losses. In many cases, policy makers are not entirely free to follow their conscience.

Those who make and carry out foreign policies are "role" players. They are officials, which means that they conform more or less to the legal limitations of a particular office, as well as to the expectations of numerous constituents. Role tends to mediate individual attitudes and values to such an extent that policy makers are not always free to use their official position to institute their personal ethics, beliefs, or prejudices. As Louis Halle points out, the position of foreign policy officials is similar to that of corporate directors, who, however much they may believe in charity, cannot give away the stockholders' assets as if they were their own.[3] Policy makers are responsible for pursuing and protecting collective objectives, and in this capacity cannot always follow the dictates of their conscience. If they honestly disagree with a course of action, they can resign as one means of protest—although in totalitarian governments, such a course of action can lead to imprisonment or even execution. Despite the effect of role factors on policy making, it should not be assumed that "state" behavior is necessarily less ethical than private behavior. Given the difficult

[3]Louis J. Halle, "Morality and Contemporary Diplomacy," in *Diplomacy in a Changing World*, eds. Stephen Kertesz and M. A. Fitzsimmons (Notre Dame, Ind.: University of Notre Dame Press, 1959), p. 32.

situations with which officials have to deal, their behavior is frequently no less moral than that of private citizens.[4]

Ethics in Foreign Policy Ends and Means

Most governments' *main* foreign policy objectives are defined, promoted, justified, and publicly understood in terms of certain ethical ends or purposes. As noted in Chapter 4, all governments share core interests of political autonomy, status, welfare, and security. We may disagree on how these objectives should be achieved, maximized, or defended, but since the rise of the modern states system the objectives in themselves have been cast as the major purposes of most political associations. The charter of the United Nations, numerous international treaties, and customary practice raise these objectives to the level of fundamental principles of international political life. Thus, all states are accorded the right of sovereignty, self-defense, and disposition of national resources; and states are prohibited from undertaking actions that would compromise these fundamental rights. A maxim of the contemporary society of states is thus that a state cannot seek to maximize, achieve, or defend its objectives, whatever they may be, at the expense of the core interests of other states. We generally condemn governments that conquer neighboring states (Iraq's conquest of Kuwait in August 1990) or whose commercial policies have highly injurious effects on the welfare of other peoples.

Other types of objectives, particularly those that require changes in the external environment, raise a number of difficulties. Aside from their own security and welfare, many governments seek to achieve in a region or globally a future state of affairs that they perceive as more *just* or desirable than the present. For the Arab states, the creation of a homeland for the Palestinians is an objective consistent with the ethical principles inherent in the concept of national self-determination. For the Turks, the protection of their ethnic kin on the island of Cyprus is an objective that hardly needs debate on ethical grounds. There are many other examples of external objectives that reflect moral concerns. The problem is that often such objectives cannot be achieved except at the expense of the interests and values of other parties. One of the enduring dilemmas—and tragedies—of international politics is that the achievement of one state's "good" objectives may be contingent upon sacrificing another state's "good" interests or values. Hence, the pursuit of ethically justifiable ends may generate intense international conflict. War has been as often the clash of two "rights" as a conflict between right and wrong.

States that have held long-range objectives of transforming the international system or regions of it generally clothe those goals in ideological rhetoric that implies grand ethical purpose. The problem here is that such global visions are difficult to disconnect from the imperialist strivings of certain regimes. Was the objective of the French revolutionaries and Napoleon to "liberate" the rest of Europe from the yoke of autocracy, or to create a Paris-centered empire? The Soviet conception of a universal "socialist commonwealth," liberating people from capitalist exploitation, was

[4]Arnold Wolfers, "Statesmanship and Moral Choice," *World Politics*, 1 (1949), 178–80.

not entirely removed from a Soviet-dominated empire that destroys national independence and political/social pluralism. Some American visions of an acceptable world order are no more than the globalization of American political, social, and commercial practices. Regimes that deviate significantly from American practices—particularly those of a radical bent—are viewed with suspicion at best, and as the object of military intervention at worst. Long-range visions are perhaps inevitably parochial and, when pursued vigorously, constitute sources of international conflict. In the abstract, global "new orders" may have some ethical content, but in reality they can be achieved only by sacrificing the *essential* norms of the society of states, namely the sovereignty, independence, and autonomy of separate political communities.

The question, then, is not whether objectives contain ethical content; they all do in one way or another. It is, rather, whether the pursuit of objectives is consistent with, or antithetical to, the critical norms of the society of states. The charter of the United Nations summarizes those norms: sovereignty, legal equality, territorial integrity, the right to self-defense, observance of human rights, nonthreat or use of force in international relationships (except with the approval of the UN), and noninterference in other countries' internal affairs (except where those can constitute a threat to the peace, as in the case of apartheid).

The role of ethical considerations in foreign policy is perhaps most clearly revealed in the *actions*—the means to ends—governments take in pursuit of objectives, or how they seek to influence the behavior of other governments. The major rules of international law contain many do's and don'ts that reflect a broad consensus as to what types of behavior are acceptable and unacceptable in the relations between states. Some, of course, set very high standards that will never find universal compliance. Strictures against the threat of force, or against interference in internal affairs, are admirable but may not be very helpful in all diplomatic situations. But others are observed most of the time: These include the duties to observe treaties, to respect the immunity of ambassadors, to conduct hostilities in war in accordance with the laws of war, to respect the rights of neutrals, and to pay dues to international organizations.

Most debates about ethics and foreign policy do not revolve around these kinds of standards. They are assumed to incorporate ethical norms governing the ways governments deal with each other. It is, rather, when the requirements of *effective* action clash with generally accepted norms of conduct. In these instances, every observer and policy maker makes criticisms or offers defenses in terms of explicit or implicit moral criteria. Some examples: In the 1980s, the amount of terrorism increased dramatically, usually involving the loss of innocent civilian lives. In April 1986, the United States responded by directing a precision bombing attack against Libya, which, according to American intelligence estimates, had organized and funded a number of terrorist incidents previously. A strict interpretation of the United Nations charter would suggest that an armed attack by the forces of one state against the territorial integrity of another is an act of aggression, and hence the United States employed a technique of influence—punishment—that is unacceptable. In this instance, however, the United Nations charter remains mute about terrorism, and American attempts to deter terrorist acts by the imposition of economic sanctions against Libya and a demonstration of force in the Gulf of Sidra had proved ineffective. The American choice was clear: A limited act of aggression is justified as self-defense and, even if legally dubious, is a lesser evil than the continuation of terrorism.

In developing a response for Saddam Hussein's conquest of Kuwait in August 1990, members of the United Nations chose economic coercion rather than military sanctions as the preferred means of dealing with aggression. This may be seen as purely a logical or prudent choice. But it also revealed an ethical judgment that under the circumstances of August 1990, the longer and less certain imposition of economic sanctions was required before there could be any justification for employing armed force. Even on the eve of the anti-Hussein coalition's attack on Iraqi forces in Kuwait, there were many government officials in Paris, Moscow, Ottawa, Washington, and elsewhere who argued that the decision to go to war was incorrect because not enough time had been given for the economic sanctions to compel Hussein to retreat. The standard implicit in the critical and agonizing debates was that military force as a foreign policy means is justified only as a last resort.

Judgments about the means of foreign policy are not always justified after the event. It is one thing on the basis of hindsight to criticize policy makers for having acted immorally. It is another to make the claim before the decisions are made. We must keep in mind, also, that the best of intentions can lead to policy disasters. Perhaps there is no more apt illustration of the dilemmas of statesmanship and the conflicting values that come to play in policy making than the history of the 1930s. On hindsight, Great Britain's policy of appeasing Hitler seems to have been folly. But we must remember that at the time, Prime Minister Neville Chamberlain's strategy of conceding to Hilter's demands in exchange for Nazi commitments not to go to war was applauded and supported by vast segments of British opinion. Chamberlain's policies seemed to be consistent with the rules and norms of the League of Nations covenant. For two years they avoided war. The dismemberment of Czechoslovakia, demanded by Hitler and accepted by the British, French, and Italians, seemed to be a small price to pay for maintaining the peace of Europe and avoiding another military catastrophe of World War I dimensions. From an ethical point of view, Chamberlain's policies seemed infused with rectitude; here was a man who personally abhorred war, who believed in the League of Nations, and who thought that World War I had taught everyone the lesson that armed conflict in an age of modern technology represents the height of human folly. In 1938, Chamberlain was the most popular man in Europe and revered as a sincere peacemaker. His intentions were above reproach. But his diplomatic actions were partly responsible for the horror that became World War II. Moral intentions do not necessarily lead to moral outcomes. And the perhaps regrettable corollary of this observation is that ethically questionable means sometimes do lead to justifiable outcomes.

In these examples we can see the extent to which both moralists and realists oversimplify. The moralists fail to observe the necessities imposed on the policy maker by circumstances and conditions abroad over which he or she has no control; they also neglect the possibility that strict observance of rules and commitments might lead to catastrophic consequences. And they fail to realize that policy makers are often cast into a situation where *all* the alternatives are equally unpleasant. The realists, who say the policy makers' behavior is, or should be, dictated only by "reasons of state," also fail to observe the role of ethical limitations in ruling out what may be more expedient alternatives. Moreover, in focusing on behavior in crisis situations, the realists fail to acknowledge thousands of transactions between states in which diplomatic positions conform to the principles of international law and the charter of the United Nations. If in some situations all possible courses of action are ethically reprehensible, in many others, self-interest and ethical behavior are compatible.

Despite their rhetoric, policy makers have to choose constantly among courses of action that represent conflicting values and often feel compelled to accept not the "best" solution, but the one that requires the least sacrifice of direct interests and values. When governments are not deeply involved in a critical situation, they can afford to proclaim fidelity to ultimate purposes and commonly recognized rules; but when they are in the middle of conflict, general principles such as those in the United Nations charter may not help very much.

Policy makers thus confront difficult choices, and absolute fidelity to treaty obligations and other standards of diplomatic behavior may require sacrifices that few people would willingly condone. Fortunately, in most cases, the pursuit of interests and values does not conflict so obviously with the principles a government declares as guides to its external behavior.

Ethics as a Function of the Pattern of Relations Between States

It is still inadequate to argue that in some cases, commitment to ethical or legal principles may cause disaster or unethical consequences. We must also qualify the relationship of ethics to foreign policy by emphasizing that they combine in different ways depending upon the situation abroad or the nature of relations between any two states. We do not hear much criticism about the lack of morality in Swedish-Norwegian, Costa Rican–Panamanian, or British-American relations. In these types of relationships—which comprise a majority of all international relations—governments and their diplomatic representatives commonly observe the accepted forms of diplomatic etiquette, frankness, honesty, good faith, and tolerance. The techniques used to influence each other usually fall within the bounds of international law and the United Nations charter. Unfortunately, since these relationships seldom make headlines, we are seldom aware of the high standards to which they conform.

But when serious conflicts develop, when the objectives of two or more states are fundamentally incompatible, and where there is no tradition of responsiveness, characteristically government will be likely to use threats and military force. Observation of treaties, diplomatic niceties, and rules against interference give way to other forms of behavior. But does one instance of the use of violent power, even for unworthy objectives, mean that that state's policy makers are immoral in *all* their relationships? Or does it warrant the cynicism of some observers, who claim that in any case, power is always the final arbiter in international politics and that might makes right?

Perhaps the most fundamental norm of international relationships is that of reciprocity. It is often unstated, but it seems to influence a great deal of the behavior of governments, which tend to deal with others the way they are dealt with. While many international conflicts develop over incompatible purposes and objectives, they can also arise over questions of reciprocity. Reciprocity surely incorporates an ethical judgment about means: Means employed should be no more harmful, dishonest, costly in lives or other values than those that are being confronted. In international relationships, as in many interpersonal contexts, governments tend to follow tit-for-tat strategies, arguing that what one does in foreign policy is often justified as a commensurate response to what others are doing. If the others use tariffs or other devices to protect home producers, then it is often assumed that retaliation is justified; if others use spies, then we are justified in using them; if a government commits aggression, then others are justified in responding in kind. Reciprocity as a metric of ethics may not be one of the highest order, but it is for better or worse one of the most common.

The basis of all international relationships hinges on a notion of reciprocity. The concept of sovereignty cannot have any meaning unless it implies a reciprocal obligation of all states to respect the sovereignty and territorial integrity of one another. If this fundamental norm did not exist, the organization of the world would be very different. Perhaps it would be a universal empire run on Hitlerian lines; that is, a vast concentration camp. Or it could be something more benign, like a universal Roman Empire. Or it could be a world composed of multitudes of city-states. Whatever the case, mankind has chosen in this stage of history to organize on the basis of distinct states. And for a states system to survive, the notion of reciprocity is essential.

At times, foreign policies can demonstrate substantial charitable impulses, the commissioning of good works, and adherence to some notion of community goals and standards. Compared with previous eras, many governments in the late twentieth century have mobilized significant resources to assist poor countries and the victims of natural and other disasters. Humanitarian assistance to the Ethiopians, Somalis, Sudanese, and Kurds—to mention just some of the more prominent acts of international assistance in the 1980s and 1990s—have been borne of sensitivity to the plight of people far away and of no immediate foreign policy interest to the donors.

Other policies fall far short of such sentiments. International politics is made up of varying bundles of values, and policy makers constantly confront difficult choices between inconsistent and incompatible standards. Life for them would indeed be easy if all they had to do was to choose between morality and expediency. But the choices are seldom so simple.

Ethics and War

War is the ultimate means of achieving or defending state purposes. Unlike diplomacy, sanctions, and subversion, as a foreign policy instrument it is infused with uncertainties, immense risks, and high costs, including the intense scrutiny of the public. Thus, governments justify almost all decisions to use force in ethical terms, usually as a means of correcting some injustice.[5] Hitler justified his aggressions in terms of undoing the wrongs done to Germany in the Versailles Treaty. Saddam Hussein excused his attack on Kuwait on the grounds that the latter was poaching Iraqi oil fields and refusing to support Iraq's demands for an increase in oil prices. President Bush justified American armed intervention in Panama in 1989 on grounds that General Noriega was guilty of running drugs and preventing Panamanians from holding free elections. The reader will have no difficulty identifying other cases. They all reflect a near-universal consensus that no war can be just unless it is used to correct a grievous wrong.

Ethical considerations also affect the ways wars are fought. In most civilizations, political units have developed rules guiding war, even where armed combat has been glorified as virtuous and brave activity. The fury that is inherent in organized violence needs to be tempered. Modern laws of war, developed primarily in the late nineteenth and early twentieth centuries, distinguish between innocent civilians and legitimate military targets. They also prescribe rules for dealing with war prisoners and the wounded, and prohibit such actions as taking civilian hostages.

These efforts to sanitize war are sometimes effective, but their effect is seriously compromised by (1) modern arms technology, (2) the characteristics of "people's" wars, and (3) the inherent dynamic of war, in which escalation of violence leads to reprisals and revenge.

The Technology of War

In eras of hand-to-hand and close-range combat, war was fought primarily between the armed forces. In eighteenth-century Europe, there were strict rules of etiquette surrounding war. These guided decisions to surrender (for example, a surrender was honorable if a siege had succeeded in breaching a town's walls to a width of two meters), exchanges of prisoners, and care of the wounded. In general, there was a clear distinction between combatants and civilians. The latter were not legitimate targets of military action. Frederick the Great of Prussia, one of the eighteenth century's more successful military leaders, insisted that the preferred war was one in which civilians were not even aware that a war was taking place.

In an era of long-range artillery, high altitude bombing, submarine attacks, guerrilla tactics, and total economic mobilization for war, the civilian-combatant distinction has seriously eroded. To destroy a country's war-making potential, located mostly in cities, necessarily involves civilian casualties. Even "smart bombs," as the war against Iraq in 1991 demonstrated, cannot avoid civilian victims if their purpose is to destroy a country's war-making capacity (infrastructure, factories, government ministries, and the like). International controls over the development of chemical and biological weapons, and the nuclear non-proliferation treaty, all are manifestations of a recognition that modern arms technology brings with it the mass killing of innocent civilians. Technology itself is not the problem, however. It is people who decide to use it for the purposes of mass terror and destruction. Laws of war are de-

---

[5]For a full discussion of the role of justice in the origins of war, see David Welch, *Justice and the Genesis of War* (Cambridge: Cambridge University Press, 1993).

signed to inhibit the options, but the availability of the technology remains a strong temptation to anyone engaged in war.

People's Wars

Most wars since 1945 have been people's wars; that is, guerrilla-type combats in which the soldier-civilian distinction disappears. The strategy of this kind of war is to mobilize the population at large to support the combatants. Civilians become the safe havens, granaries, intelligence sources, and political motivators for the warriors. Mao Tse-tung's analogy of a revolutionary army was that of a fish in water. The fish is the combatant, but it cannot survive without the support of the water, the civilian population.

With this strategy, the adversary cannot ignore civilians since they play such a crucial role in sustaining the people's army. In Vietnam, American forces destroyed countless villages and killed hundreds of thousands of civilians in napalm and bombing raids against populations suspected of harboring Viet Cong troops. The French in Algeria and the Russians in Afghanistan did the same.

Since the people's army does not always receive enthusiastic support from the populace, it too resorts to terror. Unsympathetic village leaders are publicly executed, "traitors" are tortured, and innocent civilians are taken hostages. Whole towns may be destroyed as a means of "sending a message" to those whose loyalties to the revolutionary cause are in doubt. Systematic terror becomes an instrument of warfare on both sides. Rules designed to protect civilians negotiated by diplomats long ago in the Hague or at the United Nations lose relevance in this type or warfare.

The Dynamics of Violence

To borrow from Lord Acton's aphorism about power, we can argue that war tends to corrupt (ethical concerns), and absolute war tends to corrupt absolutely. Most wars tend to escalate in their levels of violence, and thus to destroy the sentiments that sustain the laws of war and the restraints of individual or social conscience. To sustain the fighting effort, the enemy has to be de-humanized. The just cause of the war excuses excesses. And most important, the attacks of the enemy justify reprisals at a similar level of destruction. Wars tend to develop a tit-for-tat psychology. What was inconceivable at the beginning of the war may become a preferred strategy or tactic by the end of the war.

In World War II, the Allies were outraged at German terror bombing of cities such as Rotterdam, Coventry, and Warsaw. But by 1944, British and American air raids on German cities no longer confined bombing to military or industrial targets. They favored, rather, the cities, on the grounds that mass bombings of civilians could undermine German morale. Evidence that the bombing raids had no such effect did not alter the policy. The massive killing of civilians then came to be justified as revenge for German attacks. Tit-for-tat psychology replaced military strategy. Similar descents into furies of attacks and parallel reprisals also characterized the Algerian, Vietnam, Afghanistan, and other wars. They are also commonly observed in civil wars.

This is not to say that there is "no choice" in these situations. Military leaders always have options, and even in conditions of total war, humanitarian considerations and ethical imperatives may play a role in decision making. The case of the decision to drop the atomic bomb on Hiroshima and Nagasaki, commonly condemned as illustrative of the revenge motive and American racism, looks somewhat different in the light of the details surrounding the decision to employ these weapons of mass destruction.

Three groups of people were involved in the decision. First were the scientists who had been working on perfecting the instrument. More than others, they were able to foresee both the frightening and the spectacular implications of the weapon. Many scientists were deeply concerned that such an instrument of destruction should be used at all, while others saw it as the most efficient way of ending the war quickly. The second group was composed of professional military men directly connected with the bomb project. They regarded the bomb project as just another administrative task, which had to be completed in the shortest time possible so that it could be used against the Japanese to force them to surrender. The third group, composed of high-level civilian policy makers, including the secretaries of war, state, and navy, as well as President Truman, also regarded the weapon as a means of forcing the Japanese to surrender, as well as a method of ending the war before the Soviet Union could become deeply involved in military actions against the Japanese. It was commonly anticipated that if the war dragged on and Soviet troops participated in an invasion of the Japanese islands, the Soviet government would insist upon being rewarded with a zone of occupation such as it had received in defeated Germany.

How did these three groups react to the situation in which they had to decide between employing or avoiding the use of this weapon of unprecedented destructiveness? Aside from some of the scientists working on the project, no one viewed the choice of using the bomb as essentially a moral or ethical problem. All the policy makers understood that a bomb dropped on a city would cause tens of thousands of deaths and as many injuries, to say nothing of the total devastation of the target cities. The army air force had already been conducting massive fire-bomb (napalm) raids on Japanese cities, causing a loss of life and level of destruction only slightly less than that resulting from some of the most dramatic strategic raids on German cities. In one raid on Tokyo fire bombs destroyed several square miles of the city and caused the death of 83,000 people—considerably more than were to die several months later at Hiroshima. Secretary of War Henry Stimson was the only high-level policy maker to question the morality of these raids. They were destroying Japan's capacity to wage the war, to be sure—but at a fantastically high cost in civilian lives.

When it came to making the decision to use atomic weapons, then, ample precedents for slaughter on a massive scale already existed. Both sides had fought World War II with widespread brutality, and there was no expectation that the atomic bomb would introduce any new dimension in suffering. Widespread death would just occur more rapidly. Neither the scientists, the armed-forces officials, nor the civilian policy makers argued against using the bomb on the grounds that it would involve a large loss of life.[6]

---

[6]Many interesting memoirs regarding Japan's surrender have been published. The facts discussed below are derived from Len Giovannitti and Fred Freed, *The Decision to Drop the Bomb* (New York: Coward-McCann, 1965). This study is based on written memoirs, diaries, and interviews of those who were involved in the decision to use atomic weapons against Japan.

In fact, very few of those participating in the bomb project ever questioned that the weapon would be used; this, it seems, was taken pretty much for granted. It was easily rationalized on the grounds that the Japanese would never surrender without some dramatic demonstration of force. An invasion of Japan had already been scheduled for the autumn of 1945, and it was anticipated that from one-half million to one million Allied casualties would result from such an operation, plus an even heavier toll of Japanese lives. The perceived alternatives were either to avoid using the bomb and accept an extremely high loss of life on *both* sides, or to use the weapon, at a *relatively* low cost in Japanese lives, hoping that the destruction of one or two cities would induce the Japanese government to surrender. A third alternative—a compromise negotiated peace—was never considered in Washington after the formula of "unconditional surrender" had been agreed upon by the Allied governments in 1943. It was also ignored probably because neither Congress nor the American people would have accepted less than total victory.

The main arguments concerning the bomb thus revolved around two subsidiary questions, and it is here that ethical considerations became more apparent in the making of decisions. Calculation of deaths occurring by atomic bombing as compared to an invasion of Japan was relatively easy to predict; even on hindsight, the decision to use the bomb seems to have been correct, provided that the alternative of a negotiated peace is left out. The first question flowing from the decision to use the weapon was whether the Japanese should be warned in some way about the destructiveness of the bomb. Among the civilian policy makers and the scientists, many argued that the United States should first demonstrate the bomb to the Japanese, either in a test in the United States or by exploding it over some unpopulated area in Japan. Those who argued along these lines felt that the United States was morally obligated to give the Japanese a clear warning and visual evidence of what fate should befall them if they did not surrender. In this way, the basic moral choice would pass from the Americans to the leaders of the Japanese government. If they did not surrender, it could not be argued that they had not been given clear warning.

This point of view was not accepted. The counterargument was based essentially on the American image of the decision-making process in Tokyo, an image that stressed the fanatic zeal of the military leaders in control of the Japanese government. This image was not far off the mark, for subsequent events in Tokyo revealed that even after the two atomic weapons had been dropped, the USSR had entered the war, and the United States had instituted an effective blockade of the Japanese islands, Japanese military leaders were willing to surrender only because the emperor ordered them to do so. Most of the Japanese military group had been trained in the view that the only honorable course of action was to fight to the last man. One officer had suggested that Japan might be willing to sacrifice 20 million lives to prevent an Allied occupation and destruction of the emperorship. Indeed, after the decision to surrender had been made, some military officials attempted a *coup d'état* in Tokyo, hoping to take over the government and continue the war. The American government did not know all these details, of course, but it had ample intelligence information indicating that the Japanese would continue to resist no matter how near defeat they were, and that the peace faction within the Japanese government could not overturn or overrule the military. It was argued in Washington, therefore, that in all probability, no demonstration of the bomb in a New Mexico desert or even in some relatively uninhabited area of Japan would adequately indicate to the Japanese the destructiveness of the weapon. This position was supported by the chief scientist on the project in New Mexico, Dr. Robert Oppenheimer.

A further consideration was that the United States possessed only two bombs, and, since it would take several weeks to produce others, the more that were used for purposes of demonstration and warning, the longer the war would continue, with a high Allied casualty rate in the Pacific islands and Southeast Asia campaigns.

Once the decision to drop one bomb had been made, a second choice remained: Which cities would be destroyed? The American military group selected cities that made important contributions to the Japanese war effort. One of these was Kyoto, from a military point of view the most desirable of targets. But this choice was vetoed by the secretary of war, on the ground that the city was a former capital of Japan and a great center of culture and historical tradition. Even though Stimson was well aware of the great loss of life involved in dropping the bomb on *any* city, he eliminated the most obvious choice. Clearly, the decision on this target was not made, then, purely on military grounds or reasons of expediency. Other considerations involving moral choices served to restrain action.

What does this story tell us about ethics and international politics? First, it demonstrates that for most military planners, the primary consideration is to win the war as quickly as possible. War is a technical problem, not a moral one. Its purpose is the enemy's surrender, at the least cost of soldiers' lives. Enemy civilians are a legitimate target if their death is necessary for military victory. Second, it demonstrates the meaning of "total war." War must result in victory and defeat. There can be no compromise short of unconditional surrender. War is total in its purposes and total in its means. Third, given the uncompromising purposes, there is still room for concern about human life. Note that the relevant calculation in Washington was not confined to Allied casualties. The argument included a concern for Japanese as well: A land invasion of the Japanese islands, it was estimated, would result in significantly more Japanese civilian casualties than those lives that were ultimately destroyed in Hiroshima and Nagasaki. This consideration was hardly an encouraging compensation for the overwhelming loss of life in the total war. But it demonstrates that even in such circumstances, humanitarian concerns may play a role, albeit a secondary one.

Summary

Foreign policy making seldom involves simple choices between self-interest and morality. Circumstances constrain choices; good and noble intentions may lead to disastrous policy; often the choice is between the least worst, not between good and evil; and general principles seldom provide a sure recipe for action, if for no other reason than adhering to one principle may compromise another one.

Ethical standards come from international norms and standards, from sociocultural, political, religious, and historical norms within the state, and from individual conscience. However, policy makers are role players and are not always in a situation to "let their conscience be their guide." Their first responsibility is to the citizens of their state.

Ethical values are implicit and explicit in the purposes of foreign policy, as well as in the means that are employed to defend or achieve them. In war—which in a sense is the ultimate failure of policy—ethical standards are seriously compromised because of technology, the nature of modern people's war, and by the inherent dynamics of organized violence.

We turn next to the sources of international conflict, the situation where ethical considerations seem to play a secondary role.

Questions for Study, Analysis, and Discussion

1. Are there any absolute moral guides to foreign policy? If so, where do they come from? Are there any circumstances where they could or should be compromised?
2. What should the major powers have done to terminate the policy of "ethnic cleansing" during the war in Bosnia in 1992–1994? Why were actions limited to United Nations humanitarian assistance to civilians and economic sanctions against Serbia? Given the costs and risks involved in military intervention, what would you have counseled?
3. What should a policy maker do if the dictates of his or her conscience/religion are inconsistent with the desires of the electorate?
4. One of the basic rules of the contemporary international system is the prohibition against interference in internal affairs of a state (see article 2, paragraph 4 of the United Nations charter). If a regime abuses the human rights or civil liberties of its population, can/should other states intervene, including by military means, to prevent further abuses? Would you support foreign intervention in *your* country's domestic affairs if such abuses occurred?
5. What are the essential differences between realist and moralist views on the role of ethics in foreign policy?
6. Are there any religious precepts that bear directly on the conduct of foreign policy?
7. Identify the moral rhetoric, if any, of a recent foreign policy decision by your government.
8. Can it be argued that in any serious international conflict, the issue is not two conflicting interests but two conflicting versions of justice?

Selected Bibliography

Acheson, Dean, "Morality, Moralism, and Diplomacy," *Yale Review,* 47 (1958), 481–93.

Brilmayer, L., Justifying International Acts. Ithaca, N.Y., and London: Cornell University Press, 1989.

———, "The Problem of Relativism in International Ethics," *Millenium,* 18 (Summer 1989), 149–62.

Cohen, Marshall, Thomas Nagel, and Thomas Scanlon, eds., War and Moral Responsibility. Princeton, N.J.: Princeton University Press, 1974.

George, Alexander L., and Richard Smoke, Deterrence in American Foreign Policy: Theory and Practice, Appendix, entitled "Theory for Policy in International Relations," New York: Columbia University Press, 1974.

Halle, Louise J., "Morality and Contemporary Diplomacy," in *Diplomacy in a Changing World,* eds. Stephen Kertesz and M. A. Fitzsimmons. Notre Dame, Ind.: University of Notre Dame Press, 1959.

Hoffmann, Stanley, Duties Beyond Borders: On the Limits and Possibilities of Ethical International Politics. Syracuse, N.Y.: Syracuse University Press, 1981.

Johnson, James T., Just War Tradition and the Restraint of War: A Moral and Historical Inquiry. Princeton, N.J.: Princeton University Press, 1981.

Jones, Dorothy, Code of Peace: Ethics and Security in the World of Warlord States. Chicago: University of Chicago Press, 1973.

Kaplan, Morton A., ed., Strategic Thinking and Its Moral Implications. Chicago: University of Chicago Press, 1973.

Keal, Paul, ed., Ethics and Foreign Policy. St. Leonards, New South Wales: Allen and Unwin Pty., 1992.

Kennan, George, "Morality and Foreign Policy," *Foreign Affairs,* 64 (Winter 1985–1986), 205–18.

Lefever, Ernest S., Ethics and World Politics: Four Perspectives. Baltimore: Johns Hopkins University Press, 1972.

Maxwell, Mary, Morality Among Nations: An Evolutionary View. Albany, N.Y.: State University of New York Press, 1990.

Morgenthau, Hans J., "The Twilight of International Morality," *Ethics,* 58 (1948), 77–99.

Nardin, Terry, Law, Morality and the Relations of States. Princeton, N.J.: Princeton University Press, 1983.

———, *and David R. Mapel, Traditions of International Ethics.* Cambridge: Cambridge University Press, 1992.

Pettmann, Ralph, ed., Moral Claims in World Affairs. London: Croom Helm, 1979.

Thompson, Kenneth W., Morality and Foreign Policy. Baton Rouge and London: Louisiana State University Press, 1980.

Walzer, Michael, Just and Unjust Wars. New York: Basic Books, 1977.

Warner, Daniel, An Ethic of Responsibility in International Relations. Boulder, Colo.: Lynne Rienner, 1991.

Welch, David, Justice and the Genesis of War. Cambridge: Cambridge University Press, 1993.

Wolfers, Arnold, "Statesmanship and Moral Choice," *World Politics,* 1 (1949), 175–95.

Chapter

14

The Interaction of States: Conflict and Conflict Resolution

We now turn from the *actions* of states to the *interactions* of two or more states—to relationships, not foreign policy. Interactions between states in the contemporary system are numerous and diverse. We often classify them according to issue areas, such as trade, international security, tourism, technical cooperation, cultural exchanges, control of nuclear weapons, and the like. Another method of classification focuses on *types* of interaction that predominate in the relations between any given pair of states, no matter what issues are involved. Sociologists similarly classify relationships within families. They can be characterized as harmonious, dominant-dependent, or conflictual, regardless of the issues. In this and the next chapter, we will outline the basic conditions and behavioral characteristics of two common types of relationships between states: conflict and collaboration.

This chapter examines conflict relationships in which there is the likelihood of violence or its organized use. Virtually all relationships contain characteristics of conflict. Even in the most collaborative enterprise between governments, some areas of disagreement will arise. In the next chapter, we will examine specifically how conflict is handled in these collaborative relationships. What concerns us here is the type of conflict that can lead to organized violence.

The Characteristics of Conflict, Crisis, and Competition

Conflict leading to organized violence emerges from a particular combination of parties, incompatible positions over an issue, hostile attitudes, and certain types of diplomatic and military actions. The *parties* to an international conflict are normally, but not necessarily, the governments of states (obvious exceptions would include the various Palestinian guerrilla bands and the secretary-general of the United Nations). Parties seek to achieve certain objectives, such as additional or more secure territory, security, control of valuable resources, access to markets, prestige, unification with neighboring ethnic groups, world revolution, the overthrow of an unfriendly government, and many other things. In efforts to achieve or defend these objectives, their demands, actions, or both will run counter to the interests, ideals, and objectives of other parties.

An *issue field* or stake is the subject of contention between the parties and includes the positions they are attempting to achieve. Conflict behavior (attitudes and actions) is likely to result when party A occupies a position that is incompatible with the wishes, ideas, or interests of party B and perhaps others. The critical condition is thus one of scarcity, where a move in an issue field by one party is seen to be at the expense of the other party's position. This is often called a *zero-sum* situation: One's gain is the other's loss.

The term *tensions* refers to the set of attitudes and predispositions—such as distrust and suspicion—that populations and policy makers hold toward other parties. Tensions do not by themselves cause conflict but only predispose parties to employ or manifest conflict behavior should they seek to achieve incompatible objectives. The Israeli and Syrian governments display distrust, fear, and suspicion toward each other, but incompatible positions on an issue, such as control of Jerusalem and the Golan Heights, must arise before these predispositions or attitudes lead to diplomatic or military actions. In other words, antagonism, distrust, suspicion, and the like are not sufficient conditions for the occurrence of conflict or crisis.[1]

Finally, conflict includes the *actions*—the diplomatic, propagandist, commercial, or military threats and punishments discussed in Part III—that the contending parties take toward each other. We thus distinguish the issues created out of incompatible collective objectives, the attitudes of policy makers that predispose them to make threats and carry out punishments, and the actions taken. Tensions are only a part of conflict, the underlying psychological dimension. What, then, is a crisis?

A crisis is one stage of conflict; its distinguishing features include a sudden eruption of unexpected events caused by previous conflict. A conflict, such as the fate of the Palestinians or sovereignty over Taiwan, may continue for decades, but occasionally, sudden and unexpected hostile actions by one party will raise tensions and perceived threat to such a point that policy makers of the respond-

---

[1]C. R. Mitchell, *The Structure of International Conflict* (London: Macmillan, 1981), Chapter 1.

ing state feel compelled to choose between extreme alternatives, including making war or surrendering. From the policy makers' point of view, the hallmarks of crisis are (1) unanticipated (surprise) actions by the opponent; (2) perception of great threat; (3) perception of limited time to make a decision or response; and (4) perception of disastrous consequences from inaction.[2] None of these events or perceptions is likely to occur unless there has been a preceding conflict.

If we adhere to these definitions of conflict and crisis, we can eliminate some situations that are frequently classified as conflict. First, situations in which private citizens become involved with another government or with citizens of another country over some contentious issue and subsequently call upon their own government to provide them with protection or redress can be called "disputes." We will exclude them from most of the ensuing discussion because, in most cases, they do not involve the collective objectives of governments. To cite some examples: the accidental shooting of farm animals near the frontier by the border police of a neighboring state; the violation of an international frontier by a group of armed bandits; and frontier guards shooting at each other, where such an incident was not organized and commanded by a government. Such incidents and the ensuing disputes may lead to conflict and even war if there are tensions and other conflicts between the two states. In most cases, however, they are dealt with through legal or administrative procedures and have little bearing on relations between governments.

Second, our definition of conflict and crisis excludes what may be termed international competition. Recall that the perception of scarcity is a central ingredient of conflict, where a move of position by one state in an issue field is considered a loss or threat by the other party. In a conflict, the issue field, like a pie, is usually of a fixed size. If state A obtains a larger piece, state B perceives it will necessarily receive a smaller one. In competition, however, the size of the pie varies. State A may try to achieve some objective or increase some value, but this effort means neither that state B's share of the value will decrease nor that it will be totally excluded from sharing in that value. In the heyday of European and American imperialism during the latter part of the nineteenth century, the Western states could compete with each other for colonies and markets as long as the territory available for colonization and commercial exploitation kept expanding. However, once all the non-Western areas of the world had been carved up between the imperial nations, none could gain more except at the expense of some other imperial power. Thus, competition changed to conflict.

We can now examine international conflict in the twentieth century according to the four components: parties, issue fields, attitudes, and actions. This will provide us with a basis for assessing the relative effectiveness of means of resolving international conflicts.

[2]See Charles F. Hermann, "International Crisis as a Situational Variable," in *International Politics and Foreign Policy: A Reader in Research and Theory*, rev. ed., ed. James N. Rosenau (New York: Free Press, 1969), p. 414. For a model of stages in a conflict, see Lincoln P. Bloomfield and Amelia C. Leiss, *Controlling Small Wars: A Strategy for the 1970s* (New York: Knopf, 1969), Chapter 2; and an alternative formulation in Michael Brecher, "A Theoretical Approach to International Crisis Behavior," *The Jerusalem Journal of International Relations*, 3 (Winter–Spring 1978), 5–24.

The Incidence of International Conflict

Thanks to major research projects investigating the characteristics and correlates of international conflicts since 1815, we are today in a better position to understand not only the sources of international conflict but also the nature of those that are more or less likely to end in war. In a major study of "serious interstate disputes" (what we have called conflicts), Zeev Maoz has identified the incidence of such conflicts, all involving the threat, display and/or use of military force, their location, participants, and outcomes.[3] In the period from 1815 to 1976, he identified 827 conflicts, 210 of which occurred in the nineteenth century, with the remaining 617 in the twentieth century. For the entire period, there was an annual average of 5.2 war-threatening or war-producing conflicts. The most peaceful period followed the Napoleonic wars, while the period since 1945 has seen the highest number of conflicts. In an absolute sense, the world today is significantly more "war-prone" than it was in previous eras. However, when we consider that in the 1820s and 1830s there were only about 23 states, and that today there are more than 180, the incidence of conflicts, when divided by the number of actors, has not actually increased. Maoz' figures indicate, on the contrary, that the most conflict-prone era was between 1910 and 1920 (an artifact of World War I), while the period since 1950 has been comparable to the 1850s and 1860s. Put in statistical terms, in an average for five-year periods, there have been about 1.2 conflicts per state in the system between 1950 and 1976, while the figure for the relatively peaceful 1830s and 1840s is about 0.8. Overall, the twentieth century has been somewhat more conflict-prone than the preceding eras, but not startlingly more so.

Parties

Maoz' findings support a conclusion from a number of other studies: The great powers account for a significant number of conflicts. Although their number has fluctuated between four and eight in the two centuries studied, they have participated in about 41 percent of all conflicts, either as initiators of the conflicts, as targets, or as parties eventually embroiled in quarrels started by others. Table 14-1 lists the eleven leading states ranked according to participation in international conflicts.

These figures underline the predominance of the great powers as initiators, targets, and involved parties in international conflicts. While they emphasize the conflict-proneness of these kinds of states, the bulk of conflicts—about 58 percent—are between minor states. However, since the data do not include the number of years a state has been in the system, they do not serve as an entirely satisfactory measure of the propensities of various kinds of states to become involved in international conflicts. Maoz has thus divided the raw numbers of state participation by the years of statehood, giving an annual frequency of conflict involvement (see Table 14-2).

---

[3]Zeev Maoz, *Paths to Conflict: International Dispute Initiation, 1818–1976* (Boulder, Colo.: Westview Press, 1982).

TABLE 14-1
Conflict Participation by States, by Rank, 1815–1976

STATE	AS INITIATOR	AS TARGET	TOTAL INVOLVEMENTS
United States	51	28	120
Great Britain	56	18	119
Russia/USSR	47	31	117
France	26	16	99
Prussia/Germany	27	28	76
Turkey	12	40	70
Italy	20	11	58
China	21	19	52
Japan	25	16	50
Peru	29	18	47
Israel	14	16	45

Source: Data from Zeev Maoz, *Paths to Conflict,* p. 55.

Again, the great powers predominate, although medium or small states almost perpetually involved in conflicts since 1945 head the list. Note also that among the major powers, England and the United States are the countries most likely to initiate a war-threatening or actually violent conflict.

The figures establish the predominance of the great powers in the world's map of international conflicts for 160 years. Yet, various research projects suggest a possible reversal of the pattern: The incidence of major power confrontations has declined slightly (2.16 annually from 1945 to 1976 compared with 2.60 prior to World War I), while the incidence of minor power conflicts has grown dramatically—from 2.47 annually from 1900 to 1914, to 10.10 annually in the post-1945 period.[4] Most of the minor power conflicts since 1945 have occurred in the Third World. Many in-

TABLE 14-2
Annual Frequency of Country Conflict Involvement, 1815–1976

STATE	ANNUAL FREQ. INITIATE	ANNUAL FREQ. TARGET	FREQ. OF INVOLVEMENT
Israel	.50	.52	1.61
India	.52	.41	1.10
North Vietnam	.50	.36	.86
Uganda	.57	.29	.86
United States	.32	.18	.75
Great Britain	.35	.11	.74
Russia/USSR	.29	.19	.73
France	.16	.10	.63
Prussia/Germany	.21	.22	.59
Peru	.17	.13	.54
Japan	.23	.15	.46
China	.18	.16	.45
Italy	.13	.07	.36

Source: Data from Zeev Maoz, *Paths to Conflict,* p. 57.

[4]Wolf-Dieter Eberwein and Thomas Cusack, "International Disputes: A Look at Some New Data" (Berlin: International Institute for Comparative Social Research, March 1980, mimeo). Data provided by J. David Singer, University of Michigan.

volve attempts of the newer states to develop secure borders and to unify ethnic/language and religious groups divided by colonial frontiers. Secessionist movements have also generated a number of conflicts between Third World countries. Meanwhile, the traditional arena of international conflict—Europe—has become a zone of peace, where there has been an absence of armed conflict between states for a half century.

Table 14-3 supports the observation that most wars since 1945 have occurred in what was known as the Third World. When we investigate the genesis of those wars, moreover, we find that most began as civil disturbances, rebellions, secessionist movements, and civil wars. The pattern that emerges indicates that the prime locale for wars has been "weak states," a point we emphasized in Chapter 3. If the eighteenth, nineteenth, and first half of the twentieth century were the eras of wars *between* European states, and imperial wars *by* European states, the last half of the twentieth century has been the era of wars *within* weak states. These have often escalated to interstate wars when one or more outside powers—usually the traditional great powers—intervened. Typical examples would include the civil wars in Vietnam, Afghanistan, and Sri Lanka (all weak states as defined in Chapter 3), which escalated through outside armed intervention by the United States, Russia, and India, respectively. More recently, the weak successor states of the former Soviet Union and Yugoslavia have been the locales for war, warlordism, and ethnic hatreds. The main problem facing the world at the end of the millenium is less classical-type wars between states, but wars arising from rebellions, ethnic secession movements, and the birth of new states and the collapse of old states. The figures on *issues* that led to these wars support the generalization.

The Issue Fields in International Conflict

What were the parties quarreling about? Over what kinds of issues were they making threats and occasionally going to war? If we go back far enough in the history of the modern states system, we can see dynasts warring over questions that strike us as bizarre by today's standards. They fought over claims to thrones, dynastic inheritances, and religious questions. But they also went to war to expand their domains, to control strategic waterways and mountain passes (thus giving them increments of security), over colonies, and to control fishing resources—things that still give rise to international conflicts today.

The figures in Table 14-4 indicate that most armed conflicts have multiple issues underlying them. This is why the columns add up to more than 100. The Gulf War of 1991, for example, involved a valuable resource—oil—but the issue of Kuwait's sovereignty—its survival—was perhaps even more important. Territory was also an issue. The Vietnam War involved the survival of South Vietnam as an independent state (not recognized by Communist states), government composition, and ideology, and from the North Vietnamese perspective, national unification.

Problems of state-creation, ethnicity, secession, and national unification have been the major issues underlying wars since 1945. All of these are associated with

TABLE 14-3
Armed Contests by Type and Region, 1945–1993

				Region					
TYPE	AFRICA	CENTRAL AM./CARIB	EAST EUROPE	EUROPE	SOUTH AMERICA	MIDEAST	SOUTH ASIA	S.E. ASIA	TOTALS
State vs. state, external intervention	5	3	2	—	1	8	5	3	27
Ethnic/secession wars	5	—	2	1	—	4	4	7	23
Ideological civil wars	3	4	1	2	6	5	1	8	30
TOTAL	13	7	5	3	7	17	10	18	80
Of which internal	8	4	3	3	6	9	5	15	53
Percent internal	62	57	60	100	86	53	50	83	66

TABLE 14-4
Issues Underlying Fifty-Nine Armed Conflicts Since 1945

ISSUE	FREQUENCY	APPEARS IN PERCENT OF CONFLICTS
State-creation/ethnic unification/irredenta/ protect ethnic kin abroad	42	73
Territory or boundary disputes	31	53
Ideology/government composition	16	28
State or regime survival	12	21
Defend/support ally	9	16
Resources/trade/and/or navigation	8	13

Source: K. J. Holsti, *Peace and War: Armed Conflicts and International Order, 1648–1989* (Cambridge: Cambridge University Press, 1991), Chapter 11.

the problems of weak states, government legitimacy, and the status and rights of minorities. The search for statehood and the struggle of weak states to survive have spread in the 1990s to the former Yugoslavia and to many of the former Soviet republics. As of the mid-1990s there were major nationalist-inspired armed conflicts taking place in locations as diverse as Georgia, Bosnia, Croatia, Sri Lanka, Myanmar, Sudan, and Rwanda. In each case, there is a minority movement seeking statehood, on one side, and a weak state seeking to survive in its original format, on the other.

Control over territory constitutes the second most important issue underlying armed conflicts. This category refers to outright land grabs, as has been seen in the wars in the former Yugoslavia, as well as disputes over the exact location of boundaries.

Wars have also arisen over the composition of governments. These reflect ideological issues where, for example, a major power will intervene militarily to prop up a beleaguered ally or to topple a regime it considers a threat to its own security or to the security of its allies. The United States has intervened militarily on numerous occasions as a means of overthrowing regimes it could not, for whatever reason, tolerate, or of supporting those that requested military assistance. Included in the long list of such interventions are Lebanon (1958), Vietnam (starting in the late 1950s), Grenada (1982), Nicaragua in the 1980s, and Panama (1989). The Soviet Union intervened militarily in Hungary (1956), Czechoslovakia (1968), and Afghanistan (1979) to quell reformist or anti-Soviet revolutionary regimes.

The reader may wish to speculate on the kinds of issues that will generate conflicts in the future. Now that the Cold War has passed into history, will ideological divisions continue to drive wars? If the world's resources diminish, while demand continues to increase, will we see more uses of force to maintain access to or control over them? Will population pressures compel some states to search for more territory? Or, if the value of territory in general has declined, given that national strength today is based more on science, technology, and economic performance than on control of geographical space, will scrambles for territory cease to be a major source of war? Will the collapse of weak states become more frequent?

Attitudes

We can say little regarding the unique configuration of attitudes that underlay the action taken in each of these international conflicts. Our comments will refer, therefore, primarily to the general conclusions that can be drawn from the diplomatic-historical literature on crisis behavior, as well as the studies of social scientists who have concerned themselves with foreign policy decision making in conditions of great stress. These studies show that certain attitudes and psychological predispositions typically surround any serious conflict or crisis. These frames of mind help to explain the propensity to use violence in attempts to achieve or defend collective objectives. The following are some of the most typical attitudes; in each case, we can illustrate how the attitude affects the decisions policy makers ultimately take in a crisis.

1. *Suspicion* is directed toward opponents, their intentions, and the motives underlying their actions. Intentions and actions of friendly states not in conflict are largely predictable. In a conflict or crisis, however, a sudden change in relationships is likely,[5] as well as a high degree of uncertainty and unpredictability—as indicated by the great lengths hostile governments will go to engage in espionage against each other, and to deduce intentions from capabilities ("Why should they have such large military forces if they don't plan to use them against us?"). Suspicion colors (usually pessimistically) speculation as to the other side's intentions. Peace gestures, for example, will probably be rejected as a trick.

2. *A feeling of urgency* surrounds the policy makers, at least during the crisis stage of an international conflict. They commonly feel that only a little time is available for making critical decisions and correspondingly believe that unless decisions and actions are taken rapidly, disastrous consequences, ensuing from the enemy's hostile actions, may result.[6]

3. Under the feeling of urgency and the uncertainties surrounding the adversary's motives and actions, policy makers *perceive fewer alternative courses of action* open to themselves than to the enemy. In the typical crisis situation, a government will announce that it has "no choice" but to respond by some military means, yet asserts that it is in the hands of the enemy to decide whether peace or war will result.[7] One's own options appear to be closed, while it is perceived that those of the enemy remain open.

4. Policy makers *perceive the crisis, if not all conflicts, as a turning point* in the relationship between the parties and sometimes in the history of the world.[8] A corollary is the common opinion that a war will somehow "solve" the problems between the conflicting parties.

---

[5]Dean G. Pruitt, "Stability and Sudden Change in Interpersonal and International Affairs," *Journal of Conflict Resolution*, 13 (1969), 18–38.

[6]Robert F. Kennedy, *Thirteen Days* (New York: W. W. Norton, 1969); Charles F. Hermann, *Crises in Foreign Policy Making: A Simulation of International Politics* (China Lake, Calif.: Project Michelson Report, U.S. Naval Ordnance Test Station, April 1965), p. 29; Ole R. Holsti, "The 1914 Case," *American Political Science Review*, 59 (1965), 370.

[7]Karl W. Deutsch, "Mass Communication and the Loss of Freedom in National Decision-Making: A Possible Research Approach to Interstate Conflict," *Journal of Conflict Resolution*, 1 (1957), 200–11; Holsti, "The 1914 Case," pp. 365–78.

[8]Oran R. Young, *The Intermediaries* (Princeton, N.J.: Princeton University Press, 1967), p. 18.

5. In a crisis, *perceptions of threat are more salient than perceptions of the opponent's relative capabilities.*[9] The practical consequence of this common response is that if a government perceives a great threat to a fundamental value, it will be willing to resist with armed force even though the odds of staving off the enemy's military actions are perceived as slight.

Underlying these situational attitudes are two more fundamental predispositions. In longstanding conflicts, policy makers tend to become captives of their own propaganda and stereotypes. Adversaries are often "constructed" through the media and other means. While in any conflict there are conflicting issues and stakes, it is also the case that our attitudes toward adversaries are deeply influenced by our images of them. In crisis situations, these images are often little more than gross stereotypes and caricatures.

Consider American perceptions toward Japan. In the 1960s and 1970s, the media charaterized Japan as an industrious, pacifist, well-ordered society making great headway in overcoming the ravages of World War II. By the 1990s, a spate of American books and films appeared characterizing Japan and the Japanese in highly stereotypic and malevolent terms. These emphasized Japanese plans to conquer the world through financial and industrial manipulation, evil designs against American consumers and producers, cunning, economic cheating, and Japanese racism. Now that the Cold War is over, we can see the processes by which a new enemy is being created in the popular imagination.

The same processes have been repeatedly observed as the level of conflict between countries increases. Policy makers who generally have more sophisticated views of adversaries are nevertheless prone to rely on such stereotypes; and when they have little or no firsthand knowledge of their adversaries, they may demonstrate images as crude as those in the popular media. Hostile attitudes are also amplified by conceptions of justice.

Many serious international conflicts are based on notions of right and wrong, conceptions of injury, lack of fair play or reciprocity: Together, they can be considered questions of justice, and not just of "interest." Take the difficult problem of Israel and the Palestinians as one example. For more than forty years territorial, resource, security, and statehood issues, as well as stereotypes, underlay the conflict. Many of these were fairly concrete. But all of these arose because two peoples had fundamentally incompatible goals, the achievement of which constituted an injustice for the other. For the Israelis, the founding of a state in the biblical lands to protect Jews who had faced systematic persecution and genocide in Europe was an eminently moral goal. Unfortunately, the creation of a Jewish state meant the dispossession of a land inhabited for centuries by Palestinians. The creation of the Jewish state, in other words, resulted in a major injustice to the Palestinian people. What the Jews desired—a state—was denied to the original inhabitants of the territory. This was an almost perfect zero-sum situation: The gain of one was at the expense of the other. The entire conflict, then, was fundamentally about two opposing

---

[9]Dina A. Zinnes, Robert C. North, and Howard E. Koch, Jr., "Capability, Threat, and the Outbreak of War," in *International Politics and Foreign Policy: A Reader in Research and Theory,* ed. James N. Rosenau (New York: Free Press, 1961).

conceptions of justice—two rights. To resolve this conflict requires some sort of compromise that subtracts from important principles of justice. The more one feels that a great injustice has been done, the more difficult it is to negotiate a compromise. It is easier to compromise over something tangible like the terms of a trade treaty or access to resources than it is to compromise fundamental principles. It is for this reason that many wars begin.

Empirical studies show that an injured sense of justice clouds judgment, diminishes risk-aversion, and reduces fear of loss. It also "closes" the mind—"don't bother me with the facts"—and renders policy makers less open to persuasion through argument, offers of rewards, or threats.[10] In general, compromise is difficult to achieve because fundamental principles of right and wrong are at stake. One cannot compromise principle without appearing to be unrighteous. This is the foundation of conflicts that are likely to escalate to war.

Actions

Various research projects have demonstrated that the presence of these and other attitudes—hostility, lack of trust, stereotypes, and sense of justice—are directly linked to the *propensity of people to overreact to provocations*. The studies help to explain why armed force is frequently the action that is ultimately taken in crisis, although other action may precede the use of force. In the early stages of conflict or crisis, protest, rejections, denials, accusations, demands, warnings, threats, and symbolic actions are likely to occur, whereas formal negotiation is more likely in the settlement stage of the conflict or crisis.[11] Some common forms of action include:

1. Protest notes
2. Denials and accusations
3. Calling ambassadors home for "consultations"
4. Withdrawal of ambassador assigned to the opponent's capital
5. Threat of "serious consequences" if certain actions by the opponent do not cease
6. Threat of limited or total economic boycott or embargo
7. Extensive official denunciation of the opponent; propaganda at home and abroad
8. Application of limited or total economic boycott or embargo
9. Formal break in diplomatic relations
10. Exemplary nonviolent military actions—alerts, cancelling leaves, partial or full mobilization
11. Harassment or closing of travel and communication between the antagonists' citizens
12. Formal blockades
13. Exemplary limited use of force; reprisals
14. War—of which there may be a great variety according to the nature of the objectives, level of force, geographic scope, and so forth.

[10]For case studies and further discussion of the role of justice in precipitating wars, see David A. Welch, *Justice and the Genesis of War* (Cambridge: Cambridge University Press, 1993).
[11]Charles A. McClelland, "Access to Berlin: The Quantity and Variety of Events, 1948–1963," in *Quantitative International Politics*, ed. J. David Singer (New York: Free Press, 1968), pp. 159–86.

Note that a conflict or crisis may involve any of these actions and that many may be taken simultaneously. Also, it should not be assumed that all conflicts and crises necessarily "escalate" from one step to the next; policy makers may decide to go from denunciation and warnings to use of military force rather than proceed step by step to war. Maoz' data set includes seven wars that erupted suddenly, without a preceding crisis. Notice also that many of the actions in the list involve symbolic communication. A decision to call home an ambassador for consultation commonly indicates a government's serious concern with a situation or constitutes a limited form of reprisal. A partial mobilization involves more than just effecting some military plan; its main purpose may be to impress the opponent with one's own resolve to fight.

A review of conflicts and crises reveals a common sequence of actions and counteractions that may end in the use of force. One government (the "offensive" party) presents demands or takes actions to change the status quo or its position in an issue field. In almost all cases, it makes its position on some principle of justice. The present situation, in other words, is regarded as violating some standard of justice, whether ethnic unity, "historical rights," rule by a repressive and corrupt government, or the like.[12] The "defensive" party communicates to the initiator that these actions or demands are a violation of a treaty or are a threat to its security or "vital interests." The offensive party responds by claiming that its actions or demands are fully justified according to various historical, legal, moral, or ideological criteria and that it has no intention of withdrawing from them, although it is certainly willing to negotiate. The defensive party thereupon begins to consider various responses to protect its interests, to block (deter) the fulfillment of the offensive state's demands, or to repel the latter's actions if they have already been taken. Moreover, the defensive party usually refuses to negotiate until the initiator has first withdrawn its demands or physical presence from the field or area under contention. The offensive government, however, is publicly committed to its demands or course of action and refuses to withdraw, although it still offers to negotiate. At this point, the defensive party, after indulging in the usual protests and denunciations, begins to take various reprisals and symbolic actions by withdrawing diplomats or ordering mobilizations. If these actions have no effect—and they usually don't—the crisis stage may follow; the decision then has to be made whether to reply with force or to seek some avenue of peaceful settlement. Overall, tit-for-tat patterns are often observable, but many crises are also characterized by escalation strategies.[13]

One study provides some clues about the incidence of various levels of coercion and violence in international conflict. It classified 638 twentieth-century conflicts according to the *highest* level of threat, coercion, or force used in each. The possibilities were (1) verbal threat to use force; (2) demonstrations of force (e.g.,

---

[12]See F. S. Northedge and M. D. Donelan, *International Disputes: The Political Aspects* (London: Europa Publications, 1971), Chapter 4.

[13]For full elaboration of bargaining strategies in crisis situations, see Glenn H. Snyder and Paul Diesing, *Conflict Among Nations* (Princeton, N.J.: Princeton University Press, 1977). For theory and case studies, see Michael Brecher, ed., "Studies in Crisis Behavior," special issue of *The Jerusalem Journal of International Relations*, 3 (Winter–Spring 1978); Russell J. Leng and Charles S. Gochman, "Dangerous Disputes: A Study of Conflict Behavior and War," *American Journal of Political Science*, 26 (1982), 669–87; Russell J. Leng, *Interstate Crisis Behavior* (Cambridge: Cambridge University Press, 1993).

alerts, mobilizations); (3) use of force with no casualties (e.g., blockades); (4) use of force involving fewer than 1,000 fatalities; and (5) war, involving more than 1,000 fatalities. Only 4 percent of the confrontations ended at the level of *verbal threats*; 22 percent ended with the parties involved in *displays of force*; 27 percent involved forms of *nonviolent coercion* such as blockades and commercial embargoes and boycotts; and 31 percent reached the level of *force*, but with relatively few fatalities. The remainder, 16 percent, resulted in *war*.[14]

What were the outcomes of the 827 conflicts spanning the years 1815 to 1976, as identified by Zeev Maoz? Sixty-three ended in wars; that is, there was less than a 10 percent probability that a "serious international dispute" involving military threats of various kinds escalated to actual combat involving the loss of 1,000 or more lives. Temporally, the rates of escalation to war have been declining since a peak of 20 percent was reached in the late 1940s and early 1950s. For the period 1955 to 1976, the probabilities have fallen to about 6 percent, but the time period is probably too brief to establish this as a definite trend. Maoz' figures reveal that conflicts between major powers are more likely to escalate to war (23 percent for the entire 160-year period) than those between minor powers (6 percent). These figures are badly skewed by the history of war until 1945, however. Since that time there has been no war (with the possible exception of the Chinese "volunteers" fighting American troops in Korea) between the major powers. Finally, Maoz' study reveals clearly the pattern of outcomes defined by wins, losses, and ties. Regrettably, the conclusion is that aggression, or at least conflict-initiation, tends to pay. Of the 827 conflicts, initiators won 59 percent and lost only 13 percent. Ties constituted the remaining 28 percent. And, as we would expect, major powers tend to prevail when confronting the smaller parties. In major power versus minor power confrontations, where the former were initiators, the great powers won 68 percent of the conflicts, lost only 8 percent, and the remaining 24 percent ended as ties.[15]

The Possible Outcomes of International Conflict

We will distinguish the *outcomes* or *settlements* from the *procedures* of formal diplomatic bargaining. In our discussion, then, a conflict may be "settled" through conquest—with virtually no "diplomacy" except perhaps in drafting the terms of surrender—or it may be resolved through some official compromise arrived at after extended negotiations and mediation. In other words, we will use the term *outcome* or *settlement* to mean *any sort of final result of the conflict*, no matter how it was achieved. The term *procedures*, on the other hand, refers only to the formal diplomatic means of arranging some sort of settlement. There are at least six possible outcomes: avoidance or voluntary withdrawal, violent conquest, forced submission or effective deterrence, compromise, award, and passive settlement.[16]

---

[14]Eberwein and Cusack, "International Disputes: A Look at Some New Data."
[15]Maoz, *Paths to Conflict*, pp. 62, 68.
[16]Kenneth E. Boulding, *Conflict and Defense* (New York: Harper & Row, 1962).

Avoidance

When the incompatibility of goals, values, interests, or positions is perceived by both sides, one possible solution is for one or both parties to withdraw from a physical or bargaining position or to cease the actions that originally caused hostile responses. Although this may not seem very likely, it is probably the most common behavior among governments that normally maintain friendly relations.[17] When, for instance, a government initiates a proposal with its neighbor to make certain frontier adjustments in its favor and the neighbor insists that the status quo must be maintained, the initiator may, not wishing to create bad relations, withdraw the request or demand.

Conquest

A second outcome, conquest, requires overwhelming the opponent through the use of force. Even the termination of violent conquest involves some agreement and bargaining between the antagonists, however. One side must be made to realize that peace, even under terms of unconditional surrender, is more desirable than the continuation of the conflict. One side may achieve this goal by forcing the other to realize that the possibilities of achieving even reduced objectives or successfully defending itself have disappeared. This realization may come only after one side has achieved a symbolic or important military confrontation, such as the defeat of the Spanish Armada, the Battle of Waterloo, the Nazi occupation of Paris, or the fall of Dien Bien Phu. The conflict may also be terminated, however, if the winning side offers lenient peace terms. The policy makers of the losing side may thus be induced to believe that they can still salvage something—their military forces, an intact economy, or the avoidance of foreign occupation—by suing for peace. In 1940, the French surrendered quickly to Germany, expecting that an early capitulation would lead to softer peace terms. This decision, although considered by many a blot on French honor, succeeded in part because it enabled the French to keep their navy—an important bargaining instrument against Nazi Germany later—and to keep the southern portion of the country free of German occupation.[18] In 1991 Saddam Hussein avoided a probable occupation of Iraq by a UN coalition by agreeing to stiff armistice terms, but terms that allowed him to keep all but his offensive military forces intact.

Submission or Deterrence

The criterion used to distinguish submission or deterrence from conquest is whether a threat to employ force is implemented. In submission or deterrence, one side withdraws from a previously held value, position, or interest because the opponent makes effective threats to "push" him out by the use of force (in a voluntary withdrawal, or course, no such threats are made). Even though no violence may occur, we will consider any submission resulting from military threats a nonpeaceful mode of conflict resolution. One of the parties accomplishes deterrence or forced submission (deterrence if the initiator of change in the status quo is forced to withdraw the offen-

---

[17]Ibid., p. 398.
[18]Paul Kecskemeti, *Strategic Surrender* (Stanford, Calif.: Stanford University Press, 1958).

sive demand, submission if the initiator of new demands accomplishes them at the expense of the status quo) by demonstrating to another party that the probable risk of pursuing its actions or maintaining its position outweighs the costs of retreating and withdrawing. For instance, most observers believe that the Allied military buildup in Berlin and West Germany in 1961 forced the Soviet government to withdraw its plan to sign a separate peace treaty with East Germany. The Soviets apparently concluded that the risks of nuclear war were not worth the possible gain in East German prestige resulting from a peace treaty.

Compromise

The fourth outcome of an international conflict or crisis is some compromise in which both sides agree to a partial withdrawal of their initial objectives, positions, demands, or actions. The withdrawal need not be of the same magnitude to both parties (symmetrical). Any settlement that entails some sacrifice of initial position by both sides can be considered a compromise, even if one side seems to get the better of the bargain.

The main problem in arranging a compromise settlement is to get both sides to realize that the price of continued conflict is higher than the costs and consequences of reducing demands or withdrawing from a diplomatic or military position. An important prerequisite for achieving a compromise thus may be a military stalemate, a condition wherein both parties have neither the resources nor the will to conquer or force submission of the opponent. Unfortunately, many governments do not raise international issues to compromise them and are convinced at the beginning that no goal short of total "victory" is consistent with national honor, some ideological principle, or "sacred trust." Stalemate may thus come only after a protracted and tragic military encounter, as in Korea, Vietnam, and Bosnia. In each case, neither side was willing to discuss a settlement seriously until a military stalemate had developed. As long as any party believed it could achieve its objectives, even if slightly altered because of strong resistance, settlement was not likely. The anticipation of possible victory is thus a serious impediment to compromise, as are suspicion and distrust, the constriction of communication, and a sense of justice.

Award

A complicated outcome based on a previous compromise is the award, wherein the opponents agree to a settlement achieved through nonbargaining procedures. An award is any binding decision effected by an independent third party (such as a court) or criterion (such as majority rule), which sets out the substantive terms of settlement. Most conflicts are not, of course, resolved through awards, because procedurally they involve a surrender of bargaining and require a willingness to resolve the issue on the basis of some impartial criterion, such as law, under which *there can be only a winner and a loser.* If one side has only a weak chance of gaining a favorable decision, it is not likely to accept such a criterion, especially when it sees a possibility of obtaining more favorable terms through a bargained compromise. On the other hand, if a stalemate develops in a conflict and if both sides trust the third party and expect a fair award, they may be induced to accept the impartial determination of certain issues by means of formal judicial proceedings.

An award settlement need not, however, be made through litigation. As long as some external and impartial criterion for settlement is accepted by both sides, the outcome may be termed an award, even though it is administered by a nonjudicial institution. A plebiscite to determine the allocation of contested territory and population is an impartial device used occasionally to settle both international disputes and conflicts.

Passive Settlement

Often, international conflicts have no formal outcome (deterrence, avoidance, compromise, conquest, or award), but persist for a long period until the parties implicitly accept a new status quo as partially legitimate. Quincy Wright has suggested that most international conflicts are resolved by becoming obsolete.[19] That is, both sides learn to live with a situation over a period of time, even though their formal positions are incompatible. The involved governments have quietly reduced commitments to their respective objectives to the point where no overt military actions are deemed worth the costs. It is almost impossible, however, to determine when a conflict reaches obsolescence. Some conflicts—India-Pakistan and perhaps Cyprus, for example—have been shelved, if not resolved, through the slow acceptance of new positions rather than through formal agreements or settlements. These outcomes may never be very secure, of course, but since many recent conflicts have been handled in this fashion, it suggests that sometimes the least violent method of settlement is the one in which both sides learn to live with their common problem until neither is tempted to impose a solution by force.

Any conflict will culminate in one of these six outcomes. Some, such as compromise and award, are usually achieved through negotiations, mediation or adjudication, and formal agreements, whereas others, such as avoidance and passive settlement, result from unilateral self-abnegation or bilateral nonaction. The latter do not require formal negotiations or treaties, yet they are just as much a way of settling conflicts and crises as are surrenders or formal agreements.

Outcomes of International Conflicts, 1919–1994

Table 14-5 lists the outcomes of ninety-eight armed conflicts for the period 1919 to 1994. For purposes of comparison, we can divide the conflicts into the interwar (1919–1939) and postwar (1945–1994) periods. The interwar period, culminating in the rush for territorial expansion and empire-building by Nazi Germany, Fascist Italy, the Soviet Union, and Japan, featured a large percentage (42) of armed conquests. The figure for the postwar period is significantly lower, at 26 percent. In the past twenty-five years, however, there have been some significant conquests, including Turkey's successful invasion of Cyprus in 1974, North Vietnam's military con-

---

[19]Quincy Wright, *A Study of War* (Chicago: University of Chicago Press, 1942), pp 1256–57.

TABLE 14-5
Outcomes of International Conflict, 1919–1993

OUTCOME	1919–1939 (% OF 38 CONFLICTS)	1945–1994 (% OF 60 CONFLICTS)	% OF 98 CONFLICTS
Conquest	42	26	31
Forced submission, deterrence	21	17	19
Compromise	13	25	20
Award	21	8	13
Passive settlement	—	8	5
Withdrawal—avoidance	3	17	12
Total	100	101	100

quest of South Vietnam in 1975, Vietnam's invasion of Cambodia in 1979, Iraq's forceful annexation of Kuwait in 1990, and the Bosnian Serbs' territorial expansion in 1992–1994. The difference between the two periods, however, is that with only the exceptions of the Iraqi invasion, Israel's annexation of the Golan Heights in 1981, and Bosnia, none of the conquests has led to the formal annexation of territory and the destruction of a preexisting state. Vietnam represents a dubious exception because it can be argued that this was a case of national unification, not of one state destroying another.

Also of interest is the 21 percent of conflicts that had award outcomes in the interwar period. The figure reflects the extensive use of plebiscites to settle territorial issues in Eastern Europe. Aside from the lower number of conquests since 1945, the figures to note in the postwar period are the percentages of conflicts solved (at least temporarily) by passive settlements and voluntary withdrawals. These have never resulted in formal agreements or peace treaties.

The Categories of Conflicts and Conflict Resolution

Table 14-6 establishes links between conflict characteristics and outcomes. We can classify conflicts as class I, II, III, and IV, reflecting the likelihood that they will escalate to war, the relative difficulties of resolving them short of armed violence, and the types of outcomes that are typical in each class. Class I conflicts have the following characteristics:

1. The parties recognize each other as legitimate and are therefore willing to negotiate with and generally to "respect" each other, as states and governments with whom they can deal in a civilized fashion.

2. The issues generally refer to concrete interests and are relatively easy to identify. The situation is often characterized as one that, if a compromise is reached, both (or more) parties will gain. Many trade agreements are of this type. There may be serious differences on some issues (e.g., American irritation with certain Japanese trade policies), but both sides recognize that if these irritants can be resolved, they will gain through the otherwise mutually profitable trade.

3. The attitudes of the participants are "open." That is, they are willing to listen to factual arguments, they search for data and information to get an accurate picture of a situation before taking steps, and implicitly at least, they acknowledge that their poli-

TABLE 14-6
Conflict Characteristics by Type

CLASS	MUTUAL LEGITIMACY?	ISSUE TYPE	ATTITUDE	THIRD PARTY ACCEPTANCE	JUSTICE AT ISSUE	COST/BENEFIT	MEANS	OUTCOME(S)
I	Yes	Joint gains possible	Open (search for data)	Not necessary	No	Prefer solution to "win"	Argument	Agree to disagree Withdraw Compromise
II	Yes	Zero-sum	Open	Yes	Yes/no	Prefer "solution" to "win"	Argument Rewards Threats	Compromise
III	Yes/no	Zero-sum	Closed	Perhaps, but only to reduce costs (e.g., accept cease-fire)	Yes	"Win" > "solution," "solution" > "lose"	Threats Punishments	Armed stalemate
IV	No	Zero-sum	Closed	Reject	Yes	"Win" > "solution," "lose" > "solution"	Punishments	"Holy war" to last man; unconditional surrender

cies might be wrong or amendable, in which case they indicate to the adversary, "Show me why your position is better."
4. The parties might accept an outside mediator, but often since the motivation to resolve the conflict is high, they do not need outside help.
5. While some norms such as reciprocity may be in play, class I conflicts are seldom based on serious challenges to one or both parties' conceptions of justice and integrity. Overall, then, the parties prefer a "solution" to the problem rather than a mighty victory for one side at the expense of the other.
6. The means of handling the conflict have primarily the character of debate and argument.
7. And the possible outcomes of such conflicts are usually some sort of compromise, an agreement to disagree—let the issue ride—or one or both parties withdrawing from their initial demands.

Class II and III conflicts move up the scale of intensity, with compromise the likely outcome of the former and armed stalemate of the latter. In class IV conflicts, the parties refuse to recognize each other's legitimacy. (Israel refused to recognize the Palestine Liberation Organization as anything but a terrorist organization between its inception in 1964 and 1993; the PLO refused to recognize Israel's right to exist as a sovereign state until 1988.) Therefore, negotiation is out of the question. The issues, usually based on mutually incompatible notions of justice, are structured in such a way that any gain by one party will be perceived as a loss by the other. Minds are closed: There is no search for information, there is absolutely no acknowledgment that the other party might be right, and all facts are interpreted to verify initial stereotypes and suspicions. Peace offers are usually rejected as stratagems and deceit. Third parties are not wanted because they are suspect of being "soft" toward the adversary. They are also rejected because the purpose of the conflict is to win, not to compromise. As suggested, fundamental principles are difficult to compromise. The conflict is carried out primarily through threats and punishments. These are likely to lead to armed violence which takes on the characteristic of a "holy war" in the sense that nothing short of total victory is acceptable. Only in the case of an actual defeat or a wearying war of attrition associated with extremely high costs will an armistice become an acceptable option. In recent history, the war between Iraq and Iran in the 1980s, the Israel-Arab conflict throughout most of the 1940s, 1950s, and 1960s, the Vietnam War, and the thirty-year war between the province of Eritrea and Ethiopia took on these characteristics. The reader can classify other conflicts and perhaps recognize that the lines between the classes are not fast and firm. Some conflicts waver between classes (the Cold War), and many will escalate or de-escalate over a long period of time. The interesting question to ponder is why they move from one category to the other.

This categorization of conflicts helps raise important questions about conflict resolution and the problems and prospects of peacekeeping and peacemaking by organizations such as the United Nations. What kinds of conflicts are amenable to third-party intervention? What are organizations such as the United Nations supposed to do to prevent war outcomes, or if war should occur, to help terminate them?

The Institutions and Procedures
for Resolving International Conflicts

Conquest, forced submission, and deterrence are outcomes usually achieved by manipulation of the instruments of violence. Diplomats may meet to avert crises or to draft peace treaties at the end of a war, but the ultimate results of these conflicts are usually determined by the threat or actual use of force, not by formal negotiations. Voluntary withdrawals, avoidance, and passive settlements are also usually achieved through unilateral policies and means other than formal negotiations. Consequently, when we discuss conflict resolution in the remainder of the chapter, we will be looking at procedures associated primarily with compromises and awards.

There are three basic procedures for arranging compromises and awards: (1) bilateral or multilateral negotiations among the parties directly involved; (2) mediation, wherein a third party with no direct interest in the issue areas under contention intervenes in the bargaining processes; and (3) adjudication, wherein an independent third party determines a settlement through some type of award.

Negotiations Among Parties

Direct negotiations among opponents are as old as conflicts between organized societies. Whereas the character of war and other aspects of international relationships have changed greatly over the centuries, the techniques of diplomatic bargaining have remained essentially the same. Bilateral discussions between special emissaries or professional diplomats have been the historical rule, but since many conflicts involve more than two parties, multilateral conferences have been used extensively as well. The bargaining ploys and gambits used by diplomats or heads of state in direct negotiations are many and varied, so it is not possible to single out any that are particularly effective as means of achieving settlements.

The essence of the bargaining process involves the establishment of commitments to essential positions, determination of areas where concessions can be made, commissioning of credible threats and promises (even if only bluffs), and maintaining patience. The necessary, although not sufficient, condition for the success of any negotiation, however, is a common interest on the part of the opponents to avoid violence, or if that has already occurred, to put an end to it. Without this minimal common interest, there can be no compromise. If negotiations are undertaken when such a common interest does not exist, the purpose can only be to deceive the opponent, to play for time, or to make propaganda. It should not be assumed, therefore, that all negotiations have the purpose of reaching some agreement.

Much has been written on the theory, assumptions, and practices of bilateral or multilateral diplomatic bargaining. Bargaining strategies and tactics are varied and complicated, but case studies and controlled experiments suggest some conditions that are conducive to the arrangement of compromises. These findings suggest, for example, that compromises or successful negotiations are more likely to result if:

1. The issues or objectives under contention are specific and carefully defined rather than vague or symbolic.

2. The parties avoid use of threats.
3. In their general relationships, the states in conflict have many other common interests.
4. The issues are defined in such a way that payoffs can be arranged for both sides, or that the rewards for both parties will increase through cooperation.
5. In disarmament negotiations, at least, the parties are equal militarily.
6. Similar negotiations have led to compromise outcomes previously.[20]

Mediation

One of the potential consequences of international conflict is the "spillover" of violence between two or more parties into the territory or issue fields of third parties. We can imagine that several thousand years ago, the distribution of human population was so sparse that violent conflict between two tribes, rural communities, or city-states had little impact on surrounding areas. Anthropological and historical evidence indicates, however, that even in primitive political systems, mediation by third parties was often practiced as a means of preventing involvement of additional parties in the conflict. In ancient China, India, Greece, and elsewhere, governments commonly recognized that they had an interest in limiting the violent excesses of warring communities. Some societies coped with the problem by formulating rules of neutrality; others, such as the Greeks, developed procedures for mediation and arbitration, whereby an eminent citizen of a noninvolved city-state would bring representatives of the warring communities together and bargain with them until some sort of settlement could be fashioned.[21]

Efforts to institutionalize mechanisms for interjecting third parties into crises and conflicts have been, in the European historical setting, sporadic. Prior to the development of the nation-state, when Europe was carved into a patchwork of duchies, free cities, city-states, aspiring monarchies, and semi-independent provinces, mediation services were often available and occasionally involved the pope. By the end of the seventeenth century, the states of the European international system had achieved some measure of independence and, through the legal doctrines of sovereignty, recognized no higher authority over their internal affairs or external relations. The international law of the period regarded force as a legitimate instrument for achieving or defending state objectives, and no sovereign would admit that a third party had any right to intervene diplomatically in a crisis or war. The only protection against drawing more parties in was the specific rights and duties ascribed to neutral states.

During the nineteenth century, a number of states concluded treaties that called for arbitration of disputes, and almost 300 unimportant international disputes were resolved through ad hoc arbitral proceedings. In the latter part of the century, owing partly to the influence of the successful arbitration of a dispute verging on conflict between the United States and Great Britain (the Alabama Claims case, 1871), a num-

---

[20]Many of these findings are summarized in Jack Sawyer and Harold Guetzkow, "Bargaining and Negotiations in International Relations," in *International Behavior: A Social-Psychological Analysis*, ed. Herbert C. Kelman (New York: Holt, Rinehart & Winston, 1965), pp. 464–520. See also Louis Kriesburg, *International Conflict Resolution: The U.S.–USSR and Middle East Cases* (New Haven: Yale University Press, 1992).

[21]Coleman Phillipson, *The International Law and Custom of Ancient Greece* (London: Macmillan, 1911).

ber of private groups began to agitate for creation of permanent international institutions for handling conflicts and disputes. They argued that establishment of a permanent international tribunal, armed with enforcement powers and supported by limitations on armaments, would give rise to a new era of peace. These sentiments eventually influenced some governments, and in 1899 and 1907, they reluctantly convened international conferences at The Hague to discuss plans for such institutions. The only important result of the first meeting was the "General Act for the Pacific Settlement of International Disputes" (amended in 1907), to which almost fifty states eventually adhered. The delegates also drafted a convention establishing the Permanent Court of Arbitration, which was neither permanent nor a court, but a list of arbitrators (nominated by members of the convention) who could be selected by disputing states to decide a particular case. The convention also delineated common rules of procedure for all arbitral cases. Even though Article 38 of the General Act urged the signatories to use arbitral procedures for "questions of a legal nature, . . . especially in the interpretation or application of international conventions," the same document exempted states from submitting disputes or conflicts involving questions of "national honor" or "vital" national interests. It was left to the states themselves to decide which situations involved national honor. These arrangements thus gave only a weak basis for the court's jurisdiction and failed to provide it with means for enforcing those few decisions referred to it. As today, submission of cases to arbitral procedures was based on the principle of voluntarism.

The most far-reaching innovation in establishing procedures for peaceful resolution of international conflicts, as well as disputes, came with the creation of the League of Nations in 1919. The major new principle of the League's covenant was that the international community had not only a right but a duty to intervene in international conflicts and, correspondingly, that the parties to a conflict or dispute also had the obligation to submit their differences to some procedure for pacific settlement, ranging from bilateral negotiations to submission of the case to the Permanent Court of International Justice. Primary responsibility for recommending solutions to disputes and conflicts was lodged in the League Council, made up of some of the major powers plus other elected countries, whose number ranged from six in 1922 to eleven in 1936. Under Article 13 of the covenant, which provided for judicial or arbitral procedures, the members accepted the obligation not to resort to force to challenge the decisions or awards of international tribunals. To help prevent noncompliance with such decisions, Article 16 empowered the Council to order economic or military sanctions. Under Article 15, the Council was authorized to consider any matter brought before it, even if one party did not accept the "jurisdiction" of the League. Once the case came before the Council, it could attempt to effect a settlement through any means it wished. In practice, the Council used a variety of procedures, including mediation (often performed by the president of the Council), commissions of inquiry, and conciliation commissions. In one case (the conflict between Poland and Lithuania in 1921 over the city of Vilna), it planned to send an international force to the scene of hostilities to separate the combatants and organize a cease-fire. In other instances, the League supervised plebiscites to determine the outcome of territorial claims. If the Council could not achieve a settlement through these methods, it was authorized to submit a report recommending the terms of settlement. If the report was adopted unanimously by the Council (parties to the conflict or dispute had no vote), no member of the League could use force against the party that complied with the report, upon penalty of having economic or military sanctions imposed upon it. But if the Council could not agree unanimously on the report and its recommendations, the parties to the conflict were free to do as they wished, provided they did not go to war for a period of three months following the vote on the report.

Article 16 of the covenant provided for automatic sanctions if any member should "resort to war in disregard of its covenants under Articles 12, 13, or 15." All members of the League were to consider the use of force in violation of these articles as an attack on themselves. While the provisions for economic and military sanctions were designed to deter aggression and assure compliance with all decisions or plans of settlement reached through the various settlement procedures, the history of the League in fulfilling these commitments was disappointing. In 1921, three Scandinavian states introduced a resolution proposing that each member of the League, rather than the Council, should decide for itself when a breach of the covenant had occurred; in 1923, the Canadian government sponsored a resolution that further reserved for each member the decision as to whether aggression had occurred and whether each should apply sanctions. Although the resolution did not pass, it had only one vote (Persia) against it, indicating clearly that the vast majority of governments were not ready to delegate to the Council the authority to order sanctions— or even to determine that an act of aggression had occurred. Thus, the League Council was stripped of whatever authority it had under the covenant to undertake action on its own authority. From 1923 to 1939, European governments displayed repeatedly that they, rather than the League Council, would make all final decisions relating to implementation of the League's efforts in the pacific settlement of disputes and collective security. The League of Nations was notable for introducing flexible procedures to help reach accommodations in disputes and conflicts involving small nations; but when action had to be taken against the aggressions of the major powers, it was powerless.

Under the charter of the United Nations, provision is again made for use of diverse procedures for handling disputes and conflicts. Chapter VI, entitled "The Pacific Settlement of Disputes" (Articles 33 through 38), obligates the parties to a conflict or dispute "likely to endanger . . . international peace and security" to submit it to some procedure for pacific settlement, whether negotiation, enquiry, mediation, conciliation, arbitration, judicial settlement, resort to some regional agency, or any other method the parties can devise. Under Article 2, the members are prohibited from using force, even if these procedures should fail. There is no assumption in the charter that the United Nations should, or would, become involved in most threats or breaches of the peace, although Article 37 stipulates that conflicts or disputes *not* resolved outside the United Nations must be referred ultimately to the Security Council. Any party, whether or not a member of the United Nations, can submit an issue to the organization; the General Assembly may notify the Security Council of any dangerous situation; and under Article 99, the secretary-general may also bring to the attention of the Security Council any matters that in his or her opinion threaten the maintenance of peace. On its own authority, the Security Council may, if the five permanent members agree, investigate any situation (Article 34) and may recommend at any time "appropriate procedures or methods of adjustment" (Article 36). Any action taken under Chapter VI, including dispatch of mediators or peacekeeping forces, is of a recommending nature only, however, and can be carried out only with the consent of the states directly involved in the conflict or dispute.

In Chapter VII, however, the Security Council is provided with enforcement powers if it has previously determined that there exists a threat to the peace, a breach of the peace, or an act of aggression. If it comes to such a conclusion, as in the Kuwait crisis of 1990, it can order the parties to a conflict and all member states to accept "provisional measures" (Article 40), such as a cease-fire or an order prohibiting intervention by outside powers. Under Article 41, the Security Council may "decide what measures not involving the use of armed force are to be employed to give effect to its decisions" and may call upon the members of the United Nations to apply such measures. These may include complete or partial interruption of economic relations; that is, boycotts and embargoes. If these measures are considered inadequate as a means of halting aggression or obtaining implementation of provisional measures taken under Article 40, the Security Council can use force. Under Article 43, the members of the United Nations are to make available to the Security Council "on its call . . . armed forces, assistance, and facilities, including the right of passage, necessary for the purpose of maintaining international peace and security."

In 1990, the Security Council voted to authorize member states to use "any means," including force, to compel Iraq to withdraw its troops from occupied Kuwait. Eventually twenty-nine countries contributed armed forces in the Persian Gulf War, and many more supported the effort with financial and logistical assistance. The coalition forces were comprised of voluntary contributions, and the military leadership of the coalition remained under American direction. This was not, then, a United Nations operation, but the application of military sanctions by individual states mandated by a vote of the UN Security Council.

These forces are not to be confused with the international peacekeeping groups. The latter are formed primarily to effect cease-fires, separate combatants, supervise withdrawal of forces, provide humanitarian assistance, and patrol frontiers. They are not fighting forces in the sense that their function is to halt aggression. Most have been organized under Chapter VI of the charter, which deals with pacific settlement of disputes. The forces, made up of contingents from many countries, have no directives to engage in hostilities except in self-defense and function only because the parties directly involved in the conflicts have accepted their presence. Without this consent, which is the basis of all action and decisions taken under Chapter VI, peacekeeping forces could not operate. It remains, however, for the United Nations to organize an international army that could be used as an instrument of collective security to repeal aggression through force of arms.

The charter gives to the General Assembly only a secondary role in handling international conflicts. Although the Assembly may *discuss* any situation, it can recommend procedures or terms of settlement only if the Security Council is *not* considering the situation. Under the Uniting for Peace resolution of 1950, however, the General Assembly has given itself the authority to determine the existence of a threat to the peace or an act of aggression; and it may recommend appropriate action to its members in case the Security Council, on account of the veto, fails to act. It was under this resolution that the General Assembly organized the United Nations Emergency Force (UNEF) for the Suez crisis to supervise cessation of hostilities and secure a line dividing the combatants. The Hungarian question (1956) was also considered in the General Assembly, although its recommendations were never accepted by the Soviet Union. In 1960, the General Assembly played a key role in the Congo crisis after the agreement of the major powers in the Security Council had broken down.

Although the United Nations charter has covered some of the gaps found in the League covenant, the procedures for pacific settlement are restricted by the necessary agreement among the five permanent members of the Security Council and by the principle that any actions taken under Chapter VI need the consent of the parties to a conflict. In effect, two agreements normally have to be achieved before the Security Council can deal effectively with a dangerous situation or a breach of the peace: The antagonists, with some exceptions, should agree to submit their conflict to this body, and then the five permanent members of the Council have to agree on the procedures to be used in attempting to effect reconciliation. The Security Council can discuss any situation brought to its attention, but any recommendations or actions, such as establishing commissions of inquiry or sending peacekeeping forces, are subject to the veto.

We will see below to what extent the United Nations has worked effectively in the fields of conflict prevention, crisis management, and conflict resolution. Before we do so, however, let us review in more detail some of the services and functions that third-party mediators may provide in helping arrange compromise outcomes.

It is generally recognized that in any social conflict, whether between husband and wife, trade union and industrial firm, or two states, the attitudes and patterns of behavior commonly exhibited during the "crisis stage" are precisely those most likely to lead to violence and destruction. We have already noted how, in the international crisis, communications are constricted, symbolic actions replace explicit discussions, and certain attitudes predispose the opponents to overreact to each other's actions. Thus, the most important functions of the third party—a party outside the "emotional field" of the conflict[22]—are to restore communications between the disputants, impose cooling-off periods, investigate conditions in the area of conflict, and provide, if necessary, a variety of services to the parties in conflict. From a bargaining point of view, third-party intervention into a conflict or crisis may provide a feasible avenue of retreat for governments that wish to withdraw gracefully without appearing to back down before threats from the main opponent. As in all conflict relationships, a compromise yielded to a third party may be easier to arrange than withdrawing in the face of the adversary. Finally, a mutually acceptable third party whose

[22]Boulding, *Conflict and Defense*, p. 316.

sole objective is to achieve a compromise settlement will probably be perceived as a more trustworthy bargaining agent than will a traditional rival.

The role and tasks of the mediator are extremely complex, and the initiatives and bargaining strategies the mediator adopts vary greatly from case to case. Intervention ranges from passing messages between the parties to active engagement in the bargaining and attempts to place pressure on the antagonists to accept peace proposals that the mediator himself has formulated.

The extent to which third parties "penetrate" a conflict depends upon many variables, none of which alone could explain success or failure. Since pacific settlement procedures in contemporary international organizations are based on the principle of voluntarism—both parties to a conflict must accept the role and functions of the third party—it is the protagonists themselves, through their responsiveness and willingness to be influenced, who will ultimately determine the third party's success. Power does not seem to be particularly relevant in mediation efforts. Small states as well as large have rejected the initiatives of third parties, a notable example being the unwillingness of Israel and Syria to accept certain formulas proposed by an American mediator during the crisis over Syrian anti-aircraft missiles placed in Lebanon in 1981. Also, a weak state may be inclined to continue the conflict rather than agree to mediation if it can generate support for its position among allies and supporters. Impartiality, as perceived by the protagonists, is of course one critical element in creating responsiveness toward mediating efforts. Few parties to a conflict would be likely to accept intervention by an outsider if they perceived that party to hold views on the nature and sources of the conflict greatly at variance with their own, or if that party is not disinterested.

Adjudication and Arbitration

The final procedure for resolving international conflicts is adjudication and arbitration, whereby the parties, by prior agreement, submit the issues under contention to an independent legal tribunal. The court is supposed to decide the case on the basis of international law, and jurisdiction usually extends only to legal issues.[23] According to the optional clause of the Statute of the International Court of Justice, a legal issue is defined loosely as: (1) the interpretation of a treaty; (2) any question of international law; (3) the existence of any fact that, if established, would constitute a breach of an international obligation; and (4) the nature or extent of the reparation to be made for the breach of an international obligation.

International tribunals can take a case only if both parties agree to its jurisdiction. This means that there must be considerable common interest between the opponents before the procedure can be used. Not only must they both agree that settlement of the conflict is preferable to its continuation, but they must also agree that the settlement should be based on rules of international law and that it should be an award outcome, whereby one party wins and one loses, rather than a compromise. The prerequisites of successful adjudication and arbitration—the existence of legal

[23]One major difference between adjudication and arbitration is that in the latter, the parties, by previous agreement, may have the issue settled according to other than legal criteria.

issues, voluntary submission of the case by both parties, agreement that settlement is preferable to continued conflict, and willingness to accept an award rather than bargain for a compromise outcome—are seldom found simultaneously in conflicts and crises. Hence, as the next section will reveal, this procedure is seldom used except to handle disputes and minor issues between normally friendly states.

The United Nations, Regional Organizations, and Conflict Resolution: Successes, Failures, and Tasks

Most international and civil conflicts and wars are resolved unilaterally by conquest (for example, Indonesia's conquest of East Timor in 1976) or through direct bilateral negotiations between the conflict parties. But the United Nations and regional organizations such as the Organization for African Unity (OAU), the Arab League, and the Organization of American States (OAS) were created to act as mechanisms and procedures for the resolution of conflicts that present a threat to peace. Since 1945, about one quarter of all international and many civil conflicts have been submitted to the United Nations or regional organizations. A few have be submitted to both.[24] The absolute numbers are impressive, however: Between 1945 and 1990, these organizations have handled 291 cases, of which 68 (23 percent) were classified as high-intensity conflicts (involving a high level of armed force), usually class III and IV as defined above. Since 1990, they have added significant cases such as the Gulf War, and operations in the former Yugoslavia, in Somalia, and in Kampuchea.

Until the end of the Cold War in 1989, most successes were in the field of decolonization. Here, the UN and several regional organizations provided a range of services to the conflict parties, including writing constitutions, organizing and monitoring elections, and establishing administrative and financial organs for the new states. Most of these conflicts were class II because the former imperial powers had more or less agreed to grant independece to their colonies. Disputes were primarily over timing and modalities, not whether there would be independence. Where the imperial powers resisted, as in Kenya, Algeria, Cyprus, Vietnam, and elsewhere, war was the usual result. The organizations were also reasonably successful in handling armed conflicts between small states, but in two arenas their record was one of almost total failure.

Cold War conflicts pitting the United States, its allies, or its clients against the Soviet Union and its clients were rarely managed or resolved by international organizations. Indeed, during these years the United Nations became less a mechanism for resolving international conflicts than an arena in which the great powers could conduct the Cold War. The organization was frequently paralyzed because of Soviet vetoes in the Security Council. And, in the few instances when it passed resolutions recommending withdrawals, mediation, or other means of conflict resolution, these measures were ignored or bypassed by one or both of the superpowers.

[24]These and all the figures in the discussion below have been derived from the very useful analysis of international conflict resolution in Ernst B. Haas, "Collective Conflict Management: Evidence for a New World Order?" in *Collective Security in a Changing World*, ed. Thomas G. Weiss (Boulder, Colo.: Lynne Rienner, 1993), pp. 63–120.

The UN was similarly ineffective in the Middle East. It helped to police cease-fires, but its efforts to bring the various parties to the bargaining table led to no results. In the Cold War conflict, the Soviet Union was the object of most complaints and was the primary wielder of the veto during consideration of its cases. Yet, on the Middle East issue the United States and Israel have been the main targets of complaints, and the United States was the most prolific wielder of the veto. Note that both of these conflicts had class III and IV characteristics.

During the Cold War era, these organizations had some impact on conflict prevention or conflict resolution (defined as the successful implementation of resolutions, not necessarily a final settlement of the conflict) in about 25 percent of the conflicts they considered.

Between 1985 and 1990, the success rate increased to 36 percent, and since 1990 the implementation of important resolutions such as those invoking sanctions against Iraq, Serbia, and Haiti, as well as the dramatic success of the Kampuchean settlement have increased this figure. Since 1988, in fact, the United Nations has played an instrumental role in bringing about settlements to long-running civil wars and foreign armed interventions such as those in Afghanistan, Mozambique, El Salvador, Namibia, and Kampuchea. It has done this in part by some innovative forms of peacekeeping.

From Peacekeeping to Peacemaking

The United Nations has launched more than thirty armed "missions" into international and intrastate conflicts since 1945. They are known by bizarre acronyms such as UNIKOM (UN Iraq-Kuwait Observer Mission); UNPROFOR I and II (UN observation patrols and mine clearance in Croatia and humanitarian assistance in Bosnia); UNOSOM (distribution of relief supplies in Somalia); UNYOM (truce observation and reporting in the Yemen civil war, 1963–1964); and UNGOMAP (confirm withdrawal of Soviet troops from Afghanistan).

The task of the first international peacekeeping force, sent to the Middle East in 1956, was to monitor the cease-fire between Israel, England, and France, and Egypt. This type of activity earned the name "peacekeeping," although in a sense it is a misnomer because there was no peace to keep. Instead, the forces or observer missions had the task of *implementing cease-fire or armistice agreements.* It was expected that these activities would then allow diplomacy to lead to a final peace treaty. But these expectations were rarely fulfilled. Cease-fires have not often led to peace. Wars have stopped, but they have not been followed by formal settlements between the parties. Instead, the conflicts remain frozen without a final outcome. The agenda of the United Nations is littered with cases which under certain circumstances could reignite into war. An observer group has been stationed in Kashmir since 1948; a United Nations force has been in Cyprus since 1964; cease-fire observer forces have been in the Golan Heights since 1967, and in Lebanon since 1982. The cease-fire patrol in Croatia—sent there to help terminate a war between Serbia and Croatia in 1991—will likely remain in the field for a decade or more. All of these and several other operations have helped terminate armed conflict, but they have not led to peace.

One of the reasons these conflicts have been intractable is that most are conflicts between communities *within* states. They involve ethnic hatreds, religious cleavages, attempts to secede from pre-existing states, irredentist movements, ideological civil wars, and the collapse of states into chaos. Most have been of the class III and IV types, meaning that there is little prospect of negotiated compromises. It is relatively easy to re-draw frontiers between states or to devise schemes for sharing resources or to negotiate power-sharing agreements between political parties. It is much more difficult to create tolerance between warring communities, or to build confidence and security among minorities which have been systematically persecuted or excluded from political influence by majorities. Ethnic hatreds are not necessarily constant, but once they have been heightened to the point of mass violence, it is difficult to create the bases for mutual harmony and tolerance. International organizations can provide an essential service in helping to put an end to the killing, but that is not sufficient to create peace through a compromise settlement.

Nevertheless, since the first peacekeeping operations, the UN and some regional organizations have greatly expanded their menu of services to conflict parties. Taken together, these are really efforts to move from the minimal cease-fire monitoring functions to actual *peacemaking*. Operations have included diverse tasks. Those at the bottom of the list are innovations put into effect since the end of the Cold War.

1. Separate warring parties (most peacekeeping missions)
2. Create buffer zones (Croatia, Iran-Iraq, Namibia)
3. Observe compliance with cease-fires (most operations)
4. Deter potential use of force (UN forces in Kosovo)
5. Observe withdrawal of forces (Afghanistan)
6. Disarm parties (Kampuchea, Kuwait)
7. Provide humanitarian assistance and civilian relief (Bosnia, Somalia)
8. Help organize and supervise elections (Namibia, Kampuchea, El Salvador)
9. Restore civilian economy and infrastructure (Kampuchea)
10. Train police forces to take over from military (Haiti in 1993, but unsuccessful)

The Kampuchea operation by the UN is a particularly significant success. It is perhaps the first instance where the organization, in an operation costing almost $2 billion, has been instrumental in creating peace, not just policing a cease-fire. It has done it through assisting the conflict parties in their negotiations, by disarming the civil war factions, repatriating refugees, providing humanitarian relief, rebuilding roads and communications facilities, organizing a national election, and monitoring the flow of arms into the country. If Kampuchea is able to reconstruct an economy and build a government that enjoys reasonable popular legitimacy, much of the credit will go to UN efforts. Whether or not this operation can be duplicated in chronic and latent wars such as in Kashmir, Cyprus, Bosnia, Croatia, Somalia, and elsewhere remains to be seen. But it is an important precedent—one that has brought considerable prestige to the organization.

Note, finally, that in the 1990s the United Nations has been involved more in the problems caused by weak states than in classical state-to-state conflicts. In Bosnia, Somalia, and Kampuchea, the fundamental issues have involved state collapse, ethnic hatreds, civil war, and local warlordism. This creates serious problems since the

UN was designed to help manage interstate wars; instead, it is confronted today primarily with intrastate wars.

The International Court of Justice and Conflict Resolution

What about the successes and failures of the International Court of Justice? The record indicates that governments are rarely willing to submit important problems to the Court. Even in those rare instances when they are so inclined, they often do not abide by Court decisions. Between 1945 and 1990, the Court heard thirty-one cases that involved state political, territorial, military, or resource interests. The remainder of the cases involved private economic concerns and are therefore not classified as conflicts. Of the thirty-one, seven were not settled for procedural reasons; in eight cases, one party refused to participate or refused to implement the Court's decision; and in nine advisory opinions, one or both parties to the proceedings ignored the outcome. In a classic case of security interests overriding legal obligations, the United States in 1984 refused to accept the Court's jurisdiction or its decision in a complaint by Nicaragua that American mining of Nicaraguan ports constituted a breach of international law since the two countries were not formally in a state of war.

The general pattern has been that when two countries are in a state of high hostility, they will ignore the Court as a mechanism for conflict resolution, or they will refuse to implement its decisions. Between friendly countries, on the other hand, the Court has helped resolve some minor frontier and fisheries disputes, or its actions have prompted the parties to resolve issues through bilateral and multilateral diplomacy. Compared to the flexible conflict resolution procedures and services improvised by the UN and regional organizations, the Court has not been a major player in the roster on international conflicts since 1945.

Making Peace

We have now examined the various ways that conflicts of interests between states are resolved. Most are compromises, but significant numbers of conflicts, often involving high costs in lives, are not resolved short of the use of force. Wars often result in negotiated peace, but sometimes a conquest is made final through state annexation. Since 1945, a large number of conflicts have had no formal outcome. They remain in limbo, with no formal settlement in sight. Yet in other cases, parties to a conflict resolve the issue through negotiations, plebiscites, or other conflict-resolving techniques, and the outcomes are registered through treaties and other formal instruments. A new situation has been created, and it has achieved legitimacy. Peacemaking can have a grand scope, as in 1815, 1919, and 1945, when after pan-European or world wars, the parties—usually the victors—came together to plan the postwar order. Wars are important learning experiences, and those who plan the peace usually take steps to build institutions and elaborate procedures so that the past great war will not be repeated. The Congress of Vienna, whatever its other faults, built an international order for Europe that significantly helped reduce the incidence of war in the succeeding decades. In contrast, the League of Nations and the peace it represented was a failure in the sense that the incidence of war and conflict was significantly higher in the postwar period than it had been in the previous century. Those who drafted the charter of the United Nations wanted to prevent a repeat of the serial aggressions of Japan, Germany, Italy, and the Soviet Union in the 1930s. As we have seen, the post-1945 record has been somewhat more impressive in this regard.

Planning for peace is an extremely difficult undertaking. Those who are responsible must try to anticipate the issues of the future as well as prevent a recurrence of the past. They must deal with the defeated countries. Is it better to exact revenge, as the Treaty of Versailles did against Germany in 1919? Or should the defeated be re-assimilated into the society of states as quickly as possible? How should the peace be crafted so that the defeated parties will not seek wars of revenge or, when opportunities are more favorable, seek to undo the peace? What provisions should be included so that the security of all parties is enhanced rather than endangered? What mechanisms and procedures should be established to deal with conflicting interpretations of peace treaties and other conflict-resolving instruments? There are no hard and fast answers to these questions, but the questions must be asked as guides to policy. Otherwise, an outcome achieved through military means and a subsequent *diktat* is likely to constitute the breeding ground for a new war.

Building a stable peace is a much more exacting task than going to war. Yet scholars, state leaders, and politicians give these questions much less thought than they do to the development of defense policies, military doctrines, and war plans. It is unfortunate that we do not have any proven recipes. The methods, institutions, and procedures of crisis management and conflict resolution outlined in this chapter tell us something about how conflicts can be abated and sometimes successfully resolved. But there is the next crucial step, which is to elaborate the conditions and arrangements that are necessary to create enduring peace within states and between a pair of states, regionally, or globally. While the following list is hardly exhaustive, it does suggest some of the necessary conditions. You may wish to add other items, and as an exercise of statesmanship, you might speculate how the principles could be applied to an ongoing and difficult conflict, such as that in Bosnia or between Israel and its Palestinian and Arab neighbors.

1. Justice
2. Assimilation of the defeated party into the international system and its organizations and institutions
3. No reparations except in cases of clear-cut aggression involving willful destruction of lives and property beyond those associated with military campaigns (as was applied to Iraq in 1991)
4. Creation of a system to monitor implementation of the terms and conditions of a peace treaty
5. Guarantees for the security of the conflict parties, usually provided by an outside power or an international organization
6. Programs to enhance economic interdependence and contacts between the conflict parties or within a region as a whole
7. Building procedures and institutions to resolve conflicts over interpretations of peace treaties and other peace arrangements

8. Arms-control regimes between the parties, with international monitoring, inspection, and sanctions
9. Periodic reviews of peace treaties and other post-conflict arrangements, to make necessary adjustments, given changing domestic and international circumstances.

Conclusion

Most conflicts arise over incompatible positions in various issue areas. If the incompatible values and positions of both parties are perceived as fundamental, the parties' behavior, buttressed by hostile, stereotypic, distrustful, and suspicious attitudes, may well be violent. Unless stalemate, obsolescence, or effective third-party intervention occurs, the outcome is likely to be physical conquest or forced withdrawal. The critical point in the conflict occurs when the actions of one state lead the government of another to consider the possibility of using force. Mild threats, pressures, and reprisals can often be controlled, but if tensions are high enough, actions perceived as extremely threatening and stakes involving fundamental questions of justice, a crisis situation—where a decision to use organized force may be required—results. In a crisis, symbolic communication often increases while overt bargaining and negotiation decrease; and the behavior of policy makers may well be vitally affected by the pressures of time, perceptions of threat, and the need to act quickly. Violence often results. It is in this situation that the fact-finding, mediation, interposition, and supervisory tasks developed in international organizations become important. Both the League of Nations and its successor have in fact dealt primarily with crises rather than conflicts. In this field, they have been reasonably successful. In the most difficult task, mediation, the United Nations has achieved desired results in about 40 percent of the attempts, while in reporting, interposition, and supervision, rates of success have been higher. However, in resolving conflicts or promoting peaceful change—that is, arranging some sort of new legal or political situation that is accepted by all the parties directly involved—the record is not nearly so impressive. Indeed, one of the most discouraging facts about international organizations has been their inability or unwillingness to cope with conflicts *before* they reach the crisis stage. Yet it is probably in the crisis stage that formal settlements are least likely to be attained. Only in the area of transition from colonialism has the organization proved truly effective as an instrument of peaceful change. Yet, recent involvement and successes such as Kampuchea, where innovative tasks leading to peacemaking were employed, provide strength and prestige for the UN.

Questions for Study, Analysis, and Discussion

1. What are the main differences between *disputes, competition,* and *conflict?*
2. Provide some examples where nonstate actors have helped generate interstate conflict.
3. What sorts of issues or problems have generated armed conflicts most frequently since the end of World War II?
4. Are there similarities in the ways individuals and states manage their conflicts? What are they? Are there significant differences?

5. What is the role of justice in the origins of wars?
6. What are some of the most frequent *outcomes* of international conflicts?
7. Is the U.S.-Japan debate over trade issues likely to escalate to a class III conflict? Why or why not?
8. Under Chapters VI and VII of the UN charter, what authority does the United Nations have to manage/control international conflicts? What are the limits of its authority?
9. List some of the tasks undertaken by the United Nations in its various peacekeeping operations. Is peacekeeping a misnomer?
10. Why has the International Court of Justice been used so infrequently to resolve international conflicts?
11. Given that (a) the UN was designed to maintain *international* peace and security, and that (b) most conflicts today begin as *domestic* quarrels, should the charter of the organization be amended? How and why?

Selected Bibliography

Bell, Coral, The Conventions of Crisis. New York: Oxford University Press, 1971.

Bercovitch, Jacob, "Third Parties in Conflict Management: The Structure and Conditions of Effective Mediation in International Relations," *International Journal,* 40 (Autumn 1985), 736–52.

Boulding, Kenneth E., Conflict and Defense: A General Theory. New York: Harper & Row, 1962.

Brecher, Michael, Crises in World Politics: Theory and Reality. Oxford: Pergamon Press, 1993.

Canada, Standing Senate Committee on Foreign Affairs, Meeting New Challenges: Canada's Response to a New Generation of Peacekeeping. Ottawa, 1993.

Cioffi-Revilla, Claudio, The Scientific Measurement of International Conflict: Handbook of Datasets on Crises and Wars, 1495–1988 A.D. Boulder, Colo.: Westview Press, 1990.

Claude, Inis L., Jr., Swords into Plowshares: The Problems and Prospects of International Organization, 4th ed. New York: Random House, 1971.

Coser, Lewis A., "The Termination of Conflict," *Journal of Conflict Resolution,* 5 (1961), 347–53.

Diehl, Paul, International Peacekeeping. Baltimore: Johns Hopkins University Press, 1993.

Donelan, M. D., and M. J. Grieve, International Disputes: Case Histories 1945–1970. London: Europa Publications, 1973.

Falk, Richard A., Samuel S. Kim, and Saul H. Mendlovitz, eds., The United Nations and a Just World Order. Boulder, Colo.: Westview Press, 1991.

Fisher, Roger, International Conflict for Beginners. New York: Harper & Row, 1970.

George, Alexander, ed., Avoiding War: Problems of Crisis Management. Boulder, Colo.: Westview Press, 1991.

Goldstein, Erik, Wars and Peace Treaties 1816–Present. London: Routledge, 1992.

Haas, Ernst B., "Regime Decay: Conflict Management and International Organizations, 1945–1981," *International Organization,* 37 (Spring 1983), 189–256.

Hermann, Charles F., ed., International Crises: Insights from Behavioral Research. New York: Free Press, 1972.

Holsti, Kalevi J., Peace and War: Armed Conflicts and International Order, 1648–1989. Cambridge: Cambridge University Press, 1991.

Hopmann, P. Terrence, Resolving International Conflicts: The Negotiation Process. Columbia, S.C.: University of South Carolina Press, 1994.

James, Alan, Peacekeeping in International Politics. New York: St. Martin's Press, 1990.

Katz, Milton, The Relevance of International Adjudication. Cambridge, Mass.: Harvard University Press, 1968.

Kecskemeti, Paul, Strategic Surrender. Stanford, Calif.: Stanford University Press, 1958.

Kriesberg, Louis, International Conflict Resolution: The U.S.–USSR and Middle East Cases. New Haven, Conn.: Yale University Press, 1992.

Leng, Russell J., Interstate Crisis Behavior: Realism Versus Reciprocity. Cambridge: Cambridge University Press, 1993.

————, *and Charles S. Gochman,* "Dangerous Disputes: A Study of Conflict Behavior and War," *American Journal of Political Science,* 26(1982), 664–87.

Liu, F. T., United Nations Peacekeeping and the Non-Use of Force. Boulder, Colo.: Lynne Rienner, 1992.

Lockhard, Charles, Bargaining in International Conflicts. New York: Columbia University Press, 1979.

Luard, Evan, ed., The International Regulation of Frontier Disputes. London: Thames & Hudson, 1970.

Maoz, Zeev, Paths to Conflict: International Dispute Initiation, 1816–1976. Boulder, Colo.: Westview Press, 1982.

Mitchell, C. R., The Structure of International Conflict. London: Macmillan, 1981.

Northedge, Fred S., and Michael Donelan, International Disputes: The Political Aspects. London: Europa Publications, 1971.

Patchen, Martin, Resolving Disputes Between Nations. Durham, N.C.: Duke University Press, 1988.

Princen, Thomas, Intermediaries in International Conflict. Princeton: Princeton University Press, 1992.

Randle, Robert F., A Study of Peacemaking and the Structure of Peace Settlements. New York: Free Press, 1973.

Rikhye, Indar Jit, and Kjell Skjelsbaek, The United Nations and Peacekeeping: Results, Limitations, and Prospects: The Lessons of 40 Years of Experience. New York: St. Martin's Press, 1990.

Rosenau, James N., The United Nations in a Turbulent World. Boulder, Colo.: Lynne Rienner, 1992.

Schelling, Thomas C., The Strategy of Conflict. Cambridge, Mass.: Harvard University Press, 1960.

Singh, Narendra, The Role and Record of the International Court of Justice. Dordrecht, the Netherlands: Martinus Nijhoff, 1989.

Skjelsbaek, Kjell, "The U.N. Secretary-General and the Mediation of International Disputes," *Journal of Peace Research,* 28 (February 1991), 285–306.

Small, Melvin, and J. David Singer, Resort to Arms. Beverly Hills, Calif.: Sage Publications, 1982.

Snyder, Glenn H., and Paul Diesing, Conflict Among Nations. Princeton, N.J.: Princeton University Press, 1977.

Stein, Janice, "Detection and Defection: Security 'Regimes' and the Management of International Conflict," *International Journal,* 40 (Autumn 1985), 599–627.

Thakur, Ramesh, ed., International Conflict Resolution. Otago, New Zealand, and Boulder, Colo.: University of Otago Press and Westview Press, 1988.

Touval, Saadia, and I. William Zartman, eds., International Mediation in Theory and Practice. Boulder, Colo.: Westview Press, 1985.

United Nations, The Blue Helmets: A Review of United Nations Peacekeeping. New York: United Nations Department of Public Information, 1990.

————, *Report of the Secretary-General on the Work of the Organization: An Agenda for Peace: Preventive Diplomacy, Peacemaking, and Peacekeeping.* Document A\47\277, June 17, 1992. New York: United Nations, 1992.

Wall, James A., Jr., and Ann Lynn, "Mediation: A Current Review," *Journal of Conflict Resolution,* 37 (March 1993), 160–94.

Wallensteen, Peter, and Karin Axell, "Armed Conflict at the End of the Cold War," *Journal of Peace Research,* 30 (August 1993), 331–46.

Weiss, Thomas G., ed., Collective Security in a Changing World. Boulder, Colo.: Lynne Rienner, 1993.

Winham, Gilbert R., ed., New Issues in International Crisis Management. Boulder, Colo.: Westview Press, 1988.

Young Oran, The Intermediaries. Princeton, N.J.: Princeton University Press, 1967.

Chapter
15

The Politics
of International Cooperation

Each day millions of transactions between individuals, organizations, and the governments of states are routinely conducted. Most do not involve threats, and the possibility of organized violence does not lie in the background. Crises and wars are not the prime datum of international relations. As in families, there may be occasional quarrels, but most life is fairly routine, predictable, and undramatic. While the study of international politics has traditionally focused upon the causes of war, we must not ignore the routine forms of collaboration just because conflict and war seem more interesting. International cooperation and collaboration make our lives easier, more comfortable, and more efficient. We often take them for granted because they rarely make the headlines.

Consider some of the conveniences we enjoy because at some previous time several or many governments got together to draft treaties governing the conduct of certain kinds of transactions. When we travel to many countries, we are required to have a card that verifies immunization against cholera, hepatitis, and other diseases. One set of immunizations will gain us entry into many different countries. We do not need to be reimmunized every time we travel, say, from Algeria to Morocco. The card has equal authority wherever we travel. It does so only because many years ago governments, through the World Health Organization, set international standards of immunization and means of verification. Not only did these standards make travel more efficient, but they also helped to reduce the worldwide incidence of certain communicable diseases.

Our lives are made easier because of thousands of such agreements. But at one time they did not exist and the problems of communicable diseases and inefficiencies in business, travel, government, and many other areas were much greater. Here, then, is one paradox of international politics: While wars and crises recur, the processes of collaboration and cooperation go on, often unhindered by political, ideological, and military divisions. The question underlying our last chapter is why and how governments manage to make our lives easier, more efficient, and more comfortable despite crises and wars. Why do they resolve or manage so many problems without threatening to use force? In the high politics of security, incompatible purposes, and clashing ideologies, war always lurks in the background. But it is seldom within sight or sound when governments get together to solve their common problems. Why is this the case?

The Sources of Cooperation

In Chapter 3 we argued that most governments are committed in some way or other to advancing the welfare interests of their populations, when we define welfare in broad economic, social, artistic, and lifestyle terms. But few societies are endowed sufficiently to meet public aspirations through their own devices. Few societies are, in other words, self-reliant. They cannot generate the goods, services, and protection (security) which their populations demand and expect without the assistance of other societies.

We have already demonstrated how the law of comparative advantage is supposed to maximize economic welfare for all. The car you drive or ride in has raw materials and components produced or made in perhaps thirty different countries. The vast majority of countries could not produce a car unless they imported a large proportion of the raw materials and components; or, if they did, the cost would be extremely high. Consider what it would cost Americans, for example, to produce their own rubber for tires, or Japanese to produce the oil necessary to make plastic components. Governments cooperate for the primary and essential reason of *reducing costs.*

They also cooperate in order to *increase efficiency,* which of course is another way of reducing costs. In the 1930s, if a traveler wanted to fly from Stockholm to Rome, he or she had to change planes in Denmark, Germany, and Switzerland. In those days, airlines were truly national. Today, in contrast, civilian airplanes are allowed to overfly many different countries to reach a distant destination. This is an obvious advantage to passengers. In the eighteenth century, if you wanted to send a letter from London to St. Petersburg, you had to buy stamps for every different country, dukedom, or principality through which the letter would have to travel. Today, one stamp will get the same results. Everybody benefits through lower costs and faster service.

Cooperation also develops from *common threats or problems.* Today, most people agree that unregulated production and consumption of goods creates serious common problems of pollution, resource depletion, and environmental degradation. Their source is not the nefarious schemes of a few greedy corporations. They result, rather, from every consumer's day-to-day activities. Every time you consume an item, think of the consequences if you multiply that consumption by a factor of many millions. You may not think that consuming a tank of gasoline creates a problem. But when over a billion people do that every week for many years, we create a problem called the "greenhouse effect" that may have immense consequences on our welfare, or that of our children. The process of multiplication of individual acts is called *aggregation*.[1] But it does not stop there. Problems also *combine*. The warming of the earth may cause increased desertification in some areas, thus driving populations to migrate to other countries. That population movement might cause severe social tension within the host country, leading to riots, civil war, and ultimately to outside military intervention. A pollution problem is thus coupled to, or is transformed into an international security problem. As individuals, we may not see how our actions, taken for purely personal reasons, may help bring about the unintended consequence of war. But as the societies of the world become increasingly intermeshed, the ripple effects of aggregated and combined individual actions extend to increasingly distant locations.

Governments are compelled to cooperate in these situations because individual action would be ineffective. A government may agree to reduce the quantity of carbon dioxide emissions from its citizens' cars, but if no other country joins in establishing lower emission levels, the impact of a single national standard will be slight, globally speaking. The threats created by modern life are, at a minimum, regional, and most have become global in recent decades. National solutions would be mostly tilting at windmills.

Finally, governments cooperate in order to *reduce the negative costs their individual actions may have on others*. Frequently, societies and their governments would rather pass off the costs of their activities to others, but the latter protest or take retaliatory actions to persuade or coerce the former to change their ways.

Consider a common situation: Industrial activities in country A cause airborne or waterborn pollution that migrates to country B. Country A passes off the costs to the citizens of country B. The government of B, in this case, then tries to convince A to adopt pollution regulations to reduce or stop the migration. To the extent that A complies, some form of collaboration is necessary. This was the scenario in the acid rain controversy between Canada and the United States. It took more than a decade of persuasion from Ottawa to convince American authorities that the unregulated burning of coal for power in the United States was killing hundreds of lakes in Canada. The terms of the deal were that the Canadian government had to commit itself to reducing locally produced sulphur emissions. We thus come again to the importance of *reciprocity* as a basis for cooperation and policy harmonization. It is the expectation of *joint gains* that drives most international cooperation. Where only one side benefits, the party that creates the problem is not going to change its policies enthusiastically. In some cases, it may change only under threat and compulsion. But if all parties stand to gain, the foundations for policy change and harmonization are dramatically enhanced.

---

[1]For an excellent study that identifies the sources and processes of global problem-creation, see Andrew Scott, *The Dynamics of Interdependence* (Chapel Hill: University of North Carolina Press, 1982).

The Political Processes of Cooperation

The sources that drive various forms of cooperation are often highly political, and thus may involve conflict. We can think of the collaborative enterprise as going through four overlapping but distinct stages.

Stage I: The Genesis of Problems

In the first stage, the processes of aggregation and combination carry on to the point where they begin to create a *problem*. We can define a problem as a significant change in an environment, political, or social condition. But the significant change often does not reach the point of mass awareness until long after some damage has been done. We can say today that, for example, the global population problem became acute in the 1950s, but few people were aware of it at that time. Similarly, deforestation in North America was probably well beyond safe limits by the 1960s, but it did not become a public issue demanding government action until the 1980s. In brief, the identification of a problem is seldom immediate or based on a consensus.

Stage II: Identifying Problems

At some point, the warnings of citizens, scientists, nongovernmental groups, and perhaps governments will bring the "problem" to wide public awareness. It is at this stage, in particular, that nongovernmental organizations play such a pivotal role in international relations. They are the ones, often sustained by the individual work of scientists, who issue the first warning calls and who demand some form of international regulation. Their work may take decades before publics acknowledge the existence of the "problem," and perhaps even longer before governments agree to act. Rarely, however, is there a consensus among those who provide the necessary scientific evidence to sustain belief in the existence of the problem. Today, for example, there are many eminent scientists who claim that there is not sufficient evidence about global warming to justify rigorous international standards to reduce carbon dioxide emissions.

Stage III: Negotiating Solutions

Assuming that there is a reasonable consensus surrounding the identification of a problem, stage III involves governmental efforts to create international regulations to control the processes of aggregation and combination. This is an eminently political process because serious costs and sacrifices may be involved. In any system or regulation, there will be costs and often significant economic losses to certain groups. How will the costs be shared? Should everyone contribute according to ability or according to how much he, she, or the society contributes to the problem?

Stage IV: Establishing Regulation

Controls and regulations over the consequences of aggregation and combination are numerous. Some are little more than bilateral "gentlemen's agreements"; others end with multilateral treaties and international organizations. Most take the form of international regimes, which we consider next.

The Forms and Formats of Cooperation

Some problems are unique to bilateral relationships and are therefore handled exclusively between two governments. There are thousands of bilateral treaties between states that regulate behavior, provide rules or procedures for regulating conflicts over an issue area (e.g., establishing arbitral procedures for resolving trade disputes between governments), and allocate costs and responsibilities in joint undertakings. The management of the St. Lawrence Seaway, for example, is a joint Canadian-American responsibility. Shipping rules and regulations governing transit and costs of vessels are worked out bilaterally. Many governments negotiate reciprocal airline routes, double taxation agreements, rules relating to extradition of each other's citizens in case of serious crimes, and the like. In almost all of these cases, reciprocity is the underlying principle of agreements.

International Regimes

We give the term *regime* to those rules, regulations, norms, and principles that guide and govern transactions and the solutions of problems or issue areas that affect two or more states. Some regimes are institutionalized in the sense that they include special multinational monitoring and enforcement agencies, but many are embodied only in treaties and even in less formal undertakings. A regime is not an organization, but many regimes have organizations to help decision making, monitoring, and enforcement. To list some examples:

1. Since the mid-nineteenth century there have been various rules (often contested and changed) regulating the transit of commercial and naval vessels through the Turkish Straits.
2. There have been rules regulating the charge of tolls (outlawed) and other navigation matters on Rhine traffic, basically making this an international waterway.
3. Since the early 1920s the International Labor Organization has drafted rules to protect workers against occupational hazards.
4. Transboundary agreements for protecting migratory birds and managing shared water resources (particularly in Canada and the United States) have existed since the early twentieth century.
5. In 1987, a majority of the world's governments met in Montreal to negotiate a *Protocol on Substances That Deplete the Ozone Layer*, under which each signatory is provided with a target emission maximum for release of chlorofluorocarbons. The targets were lowered two years later at a conference in London.
6. One of the most prominent security regimes is addressed to the problem of nuclear proliferation. The 1968 *Treaty on the Non-Proliferation of Nuclear Weapons* commits the signatories to use nuclear fuels only for peaceful purposes and establishes a monitoring agency (the International Atomic Energy Agency) to examine all nuclear facilities to see that fuels are not diverted to the construction of weapons of mass destruction

The list could be extended at length; just to enumerate the international agreements covering the environmental area would require several pages. Some examples include regulation of trade in endangered species, limits on transborder air pollution, a moratorium on certain kinds of whaling, the conservation of Antarctic living resources, control of emissions of nitrogen oxides, a European agreement restricting the use of certain detergents in washing and cleaning products, and the development of thousands of "ecostandards" in bilateral, regional, and universal treaties dealing with specific products.

In addition, there are regimes that regulate international trade (GATT), allocate radio waves to countries (International Telecommunication Union), develop international shipping regulations (International Maritime Organization), standardize weights and measures (consider the consequences if each country had its own system and stuck to it), and develop airline safety rules (International Civil Aviation Organization), just to mention a few. We seldom hear of their activities, but their work is essential in lubricating the channels of international trade, communication, finance, health, and many other areas.

The means of regulating activities through regimes are numerous, but four are most common and need emphasis.

Setting Standards.   Many bilateral, regional, and multilateral treaties establish levels or targets for reduction of pollution-creating activities. One example of international cooperation for the purpose of standard-setting will show to what extent regimes have become dependent upon collaboration and scientific research.

In the 1980s a team of French and Soviet paleo-glaciologists excavated a 2,000-meter-deep core of ice from the Antarctic. The core exposed successive layers of ice containing bubbles of air going back as far as 160,000 years. French scientists were then able to identify atmospheric conditions and temperature changes on the surface of Antarctica for that extended period of time. The data from this research were then compared with other available information from different earth environments, and correlated. In the last 30,000 years, approximately, methane levels have almost doubled, carbon dioxide has increased about 80 percent, and temperatures in Antarctica have increased on average almost 10 degrees Celsius in the same period. A string of research projects started by Soviets and continued by French, Swiss, and American scientists provided the data base upon which the Intergovernmental Panel on Climate Change (IPCC) reported to the World Climate Conference in Geneva in November 1990. The attempt to create a universal standard and to establish national targets for reducing carbon dioxide emissions failed, in part because the United States delegation argued that "more study" of the problem was required before that country would agree to any targets. But on regional levels, particularly in Europe, there are comprehensive standards, many of which have been revised even further downward than originally planned. For example, in the Helsinki Protocol, eighteen countries, including the former Soviet Union and Canada, committed themselves to reduce sulphur emissions by 30 percent by 1993 and, on average, about 55 percent by 1995.[2]

International standard-setting is beginning to cover many areas of human activity: production of medicines and drugs, foods, automobile safety features (mostly at the regional level to this point), health, nuclear plant safety facilities, and fishing quotas.

---

[2]For a review of these and other standard-setting activities, see Peter H. Sand, *Lessons Learned in Global Environmental Governance* (Washington, D.C.: World Resources Institute, 1990).

Numerous multilateral treaties, both universal and regional, set standards for human rights and attempt to prevent their systematic violation. These include the Universal Declaration of Human Rights, the Covenant on Civil and Political Rights, and the Convention on the Elimination of All Forms of Discrimination against Women. The standards enunciated in these and other documents are reasonably specific but hardly beyond debate. Human rights issues become entangled in the foreign policies of governments. Governments tend to be myopic over human rights violations. They denounce those of their adversaries but often overlook, ignore, or even support those of their allies and friends. It is not difficult to cite cases of double standards (African countries' denunciation of *apartheid*, while remaining silent on the mass killings of Idi Amin in Uganda in the 1970s; the United States' focus on human rights violations in Communist countries, while being complicit to similar violations by the Pinochet regime in Chile during the 1970s). Voluntary organizations such as Amnesty International can monitor and report, but they lack means of enforcement beyond the capacity to embarrass through publicity.

Obligations.   Many regimes specify what governments must do or not do under specified circumstances. Under the non-proliferation treaty, for example, signatories must open their nuclear facilities to international inspection. During times of war, combatants must allow the International Red Cross or Red Crescent to visit prisoners of war to ensure that their treatment is consistent with the obligations of the Geneva Conventions on Treatment of War Prisoners. Under the General Agreement on Tariffs and Trade (GATT), states are obligated to reduce trade barriers on a basis of reciprocity, and to avoid—except in emergency situations—the imposition of new trade-restricting devices.

Allocations.   Most resources are finite. If their exploitation is not limited, species will become extinct, or access to physical space, such as radio frequencies or "parking spaces" for geo-stationary satellites, will become filled up. Hence, many treaties and some institutions are designed to allocate shares of resources, usually on an annual basis, or to assign radio waves and "parking spaces" to particular countries. While these matters may seem noncontentious, in fact bargaining over shares and access may become very difficult and sometimes acrimonious. There have been several "fish wars" between countries that have to exploit limited resources in specific waters. Canada and Spain, France, and Portugal have had numerous disputes about fish quotas in Canada's territorial waters, problems of over-fishing, and declining resources. Canada and the United States have had similar altercations over halibut and salmon stocks in waters off British Columbia.

Who should have access to limited resources? Those who get there first, or equal access to all? Countries that develop technology to exploit those resources generally argue that the first come–first served principle should prevail. They would, for example, take up all the "parking spaces" for geo-stationary satellites. Developing countries take the opposing position: Places must be guaranteed for all. Those without the necessary technology cannot be excluded.

Prohibitions.   Prohibitions are a kind of standard-setting, but rather than setting quotas, they totally ban a particular type of activity. There is, for example, a complete moratorium on whaling of certain species (except for "research" purposes), and there is now considerable public agitation for a similar moratorium on the use of driftnets for open ocean fishing. In the security field, there are prohibitions against the placement of weapons of mass destruction on celestial bodies, under the sea, and in outer space. There is also a moratorium on all atmospheric nuclear explosions and tests.

We need not extend the list to establish the point that many types of international activities are regulated by norms, standards, and institutions. There are literally hundreds of international regimes that effectively govern what governments, private organizations, and individuals can and cannot do, and how they can go about their business. Taken together, they provide considerable predictability in international transactions and, in varying degrees, help to tackle pressing international and regional problems. Most of the rules and regulations are contained in treaties and other formal undertakings, but in some areas the treaty-making process takes a great deal of time (on average, it takes about five years from the time an international treaty is negotiated to the time that it comes into effect after enough states have ratified it).[3]

What happens to all of these rules, standards, and regulations when one or more countries decide not to observe them? Recall that international law is in part enforced through the principle of reciprocity. A country that systematically refuses to observe standards may face powerful sanctions from other states. For example, it will not be able to export products that fail to meet national and international standards. It can fail to take steps to reduce environment-damaging emissions from its industrial plants, but if it does so, it may have to face grass-roots or official boycotts of its exports. There is also the power of publicity. Environmental groups can publicize the activities that contravene established international standards and lobby for punitive sanctions (how else would the trade in rare species and ivory have become regulated?).

In addition, the regimes themselves may incorporate monitoring and enforcement powers, although there is a conspicuous absence of international regulatory institutions for human rights and environmental issues. In fact, most enforcement in the latter comes through licenses, investigations, and certifications made by national bureaucracies. For example, the 1973 Washington Convention on International Trade in Endangered Species of Wild Fauna and Flora establishes worldwide trade controls effected through a set of national permits and certificates. In human rights the major sanction is the power of publicity. The United Nations, for example, has rarely gone beyond passing resolutions or issuing reports in cases of documented human rights abuses.

Enforcement through international tribunals has been slow, cumbersome, and generally hedged by the unwillingness of parties to accept the jurisdiction of such courts. In the 1980s, the United States led the way in refusing to accept the automatic jurisdiction of third-party dispute mechanisms, reserving for itself the right to veto any automatic referral of a case to an international tribunal. Compulsory in-

---

[3]Ibid., p. 15.

ternational adjudication is, at least in human rights and environmental matters, an exceptional rather than a usual way of enforcing rules and norms.[4]

Rules and norms can also be enforced through international audits. While few international organizations have full enforcement powers, many can monitor and inspect facilities and practices to locate violations. The International Labor Organization, for example, requires its members to report annually or biennially on labor conditions within the country, and there is an independent technical committee of experts to investigate any complaints. The biennial conference of the parties to the endangered species convention reviews compliance; noncompliance brings forth condemnation by the conference and strong action by nongovernmental organizations. There are, in short, many ways that regimes can be made effective.

This is not to say that most have 100 percent compliance. In many fields there are laggards, cheaters, and "free riders" (those who get the benefits of others' sacrifices and contributions, but who do not pay their fair share). On international environmental law and rule-making, the United States has been a major laggard, pleading frequently for "more studies" and watering down or refusing to accept compulsory dispute-settlement procedures. The Japanese have developed ingenious ways of violating the moratorium on whaling. The French persisted in nuclear testing on their South Pacific atolls. Many developing countries refuse to accept lower emission standards on the grounds that it is the industrial countries, and not them, that cause most of the world's atmospheric pollution. During the Gulf War in 1991, Saddam Hussein's Iraq refused to allow the International Red Cross or Red Crescent to visit coalition prisoners of war, and in fact in some ways violated the Geneva Conventions. And the list of governments that systematically violate the human rights of their citizens is depressing. So backsliders and miscreants do exist.

The behavior involved in the construction and maintenance of international regimes differs from that observed in international conflict in two major ways:

1. In the bargaining and implementation of regimes, force or its threat are seldom, if ever, in the background. We would be greatly puzzled were some European countries, for example, to issue threats of armed action against the United States in order to compel the latter to reduce emissions of carbon dioxide.
2. Most of the bargaining in the creation and maintenance of regimes deals with *means* rather than ends.[5] Compare the conflict between Iraq and Kuwait in 1990, one that led to aggression, conquest, and war. The security goals of the two parties were diametrically opposed; Iraq could not make a "gain" except at the expense of Kuwait. In building international regimes, in contrast, the parties roughly agree on ends or purposes. What they bargain about is the kinds of measures that should be devised to cope with the problem, who is going to pay what share of the costs, what principles should underlie the main regulations, and what the targets should be. In a setting where goals or purposes are held in common, discussion of means rarely leads to the kinds of threats that are employed in international conflicts. Note also that most regimes deal with problems connected to welfare values, rather than security. It may be—but for reasons that are not yet understood—that questions of wealth,

---

[4]Ibid., p. 22.

[5]Cf., Donald Puchala and Stuart Fagan, "International Politics in the 1970s: The Search for a Perspective," *International Organization*, 28 (Spring 1974).

health, efficiency, and the like do not generate the kinds of fears that threats to security do. Responses are therefore less likely to provoke military responses. No one threatened to go to war against the Soviet Union after the Chernobyl disaster, even though radiation dispersion to some countries in Europe created costly threat-reduction programs.

Although war is not in the background of most negotiations to create international regimes, it does not follow that governments remain oblivious to the costs and consequences of war. Indeed, one of the areas in international relations that has spawned more agreements than most involving prohibitions, the setting of standards, and monitoring is in the security field. The institution of war itself is surrounded by certain formalities. These refer to procedures for beginning and terminating wars (although declarations of war have not been used since World War II), laws regulating treatment of prisoners of war, the injunction in the charter of the United Nations against the use of force except in self-defense or when undertaken by authorization of the United Nations itself, the prohibition against use of certain kinds of weapons (chemical and bacteriological), and the like. Table 15-1 lists the major regional and universal arms control and disarmament agreements that today constitute the regime on the use of force and the limitation of weapons. While we have a long way to go to ensure a safer world, over the past three decades governments have negotiated a fairly impressive roster of regulations, prohibitions, and restraints, many of them including strict verification systems.

Weak Regimes and Strong Regimes

While global and regional transactions and problems are regulated by a great web of understandings, norms, agreements, treaties, and monitoring devices, it is clear that their effectiveness in preventing the worsening of problems varies a great deal. We have, in fact, a continuum of regimes, ranging from the very weak—and therefore largely ineffective—to the very strong. Weak regimes have the following characteristics:

1. No consensus on the existence or severity of the problem to be regulated
2. Vague standards, commitments, or prohibitions that can lead to debates as to what, exactly, is allowed or prohibited
3. No monitoring capacity to identify abuses, violations, or avoidance of payments
4. No sanctions to punish rogue governments, companies, or individuals that are violating norms, regulations, or standards

Strong regimes, in contrast, are built around a reasonable consensus on the nature of the problem and how to resolve it. Violations can be easily identified, and there are mechanisms available for sanctions against those who are so identified. The human rights regime tends toward the weak end of the spectrum because there is no global consensus on what, exactly, human rights are, because there is no formal and effective international monitoring mechanism and because the sanctions are relatively weak. While the General Assembly of the United Nations may pass resolutions condemning governments for systematic violations of human rights, most of the burden of punishing rogues resides in individual governments. The past fifty

TABLE 15-1

The Arms-Control and Disarmament Regime

TREATY/AGREEMENT	DATE	MAJOR PROVISIONS	NUMBER OF SIGNATORIES, 1992
Geneva Protocol	1925	Bans use of chemical and bacteriological weapons	130
Antarctic Treaty	1959	Demilitarizes the Antarctic	40
Limited Test Ban	1963	Bans nuclear tests in atmosphere, space, and underwater	119
Outer Space Treaty	1967	Demilitarizes space and all celestial bodies	93
Latin America Nuclear-Free Zone	1967	Bans stationing or transfer of nuclear weapons in the region	23
Non-Proliferation Treaty	1968	Bans selling, giving, or receiving nuclear weapons, technology, or materials for weapons; includes inspection	146
Seabed Arms Treaty	1971	Bans placement of nuclear weapons in or under seabed	85
Biological Weapons Treaty	1972	Bans production or possession of biological weapons	115
ABM Treaty	1972	Limits U.S. and USSR to two ABM sites each and bans further development of ABM systems	2
Threshold Test Ban Treaty	1974	Limits U.S. and USSR underground testing to 150 kilotons	2
Environmental Modification	1977	Bans environmental modification as a form of warfare	55
SALT II	1977	Limits number and types of strategic weapons for U.S. and USSR	2
Rarotonga Treaty	1985	Bans manufacture, acquisition, or transit of nuclear weapons in South Pacific	11
Intermediate-Range Nuclear Forces	1987	Disarmament of all U.S. and USSR intermediate-range missiles in Europe plus inspection	2
Conventional Forces in Europe	1990	Conventional forces in Europe reduced to specified limits by type of weapons	23
START	1991	U.S. and USSR limits on numbers and types of strategic launchers and warheads	2
Chemical Weapons Convention	1992	Prohibits production, acquisition, stockpiling, transfer, or use of chemical weapons	—

Source: Stockholm International Peace Research Institute, *SIPRI Annual*, 1992 (Oxford: Oxford University Press), p. 598.

years of human rights actions indicates that governments are highly selective in identifying the worse miscreants and doing something effective about systematic abuses. In contrast, the non-proliferation regime is located toward the strong end of the continuum. There is a specific treaty, obligations are not the subject of intense debate, the monitoring function is well organized and financed (though not foolproof), and while there are no automatic sanctions, the global consensus against proliferation suggests that those who violate the treaty obligations can expect various forms of punishment, including economic sanctions and the cut-off of all aid for the development of peaceful nuclear capacities. As North Korea has learned in the 1990s, the costs of violating the non-proliferation treaty are very high.

Collaboration in Security Communities

Just over a half-century ago, the countries of Europe were arrayed against each other in one of the most murderous wars of history. War was by no means unusual on the continent; it was rather a characteristic feature of the European diplomatic landscape for centuries. Yet today the possibilities of war between, let us say, Italy and France seem more than remote. Why is this the case?

Karl Deutsch, one of this generation's leading political scientists, devoted years of research to an examination of the sources and nature of what he called "pluralistic security communities." He defined these as a condition between two or more states where the likelihood of the use of force has virtually disappeared. The main indicator of this state of affairs is the absence of any military plans or deployments targeted toward the other members of the "community."[6] There has been no expectation of war, for example, between the United States and Canada for almost a century, and the last contingency plans developed for such a war go back to 1931. A similar state of affairs exists today throughout most of Western Europe, and in a few other areas of the world. A third indicator of the existence of security communities could be mutual acceptance and regular observance of certain rules of international law. These would include, as well as avoidance of military threats, meeting treaty obligations, avoidance of interference in each other's internal affairs, and observance of normal diplomatic protocol and etiquette in all transactions and negotiations. If behavior conforms to these three indicators—no targeted military forces, no expectations of war, and observance of treaties—we can say that a pluralistic security community exists between the two or more states.

In such relationships there are, of course, conflicts. But as in international regimes, they tend to focus on means rather than ends. Bargaining involves issues of costs, distribution of gains, the development of rules for resolving conflicts, and other matters, but within an overall context of consensus. The lengthy negotiations between Canada, Mexico, and the United States over the North American Free Trade Agreement (NAFTA) were difficult and sometimes acrimonious. But since all parties were committed to the proposition that some type of free trade arrangement would bring benefits to all, the discussions focused on specifics. There was no question of the legitimacy of the partners (compare the parties to the Middle East conflict where for more than forty years they refused even to discuss issues), there was no possibility of linking issues (coercing the opponent by threatening to cut off defense

---

[6]The main ideas, and supporting evidence, are in Karl Deutsch et al., *Political Community and the North Atlantic Area* (Princeton, N.J.: Princeton University Press, 1957).

relations in order to get a concession on trade), and certainly no one in Ottawa, Mexico City, or Washington contemplated an act of armed force as a means of breaking a stalemate on an issue of access to markets.

Collaboration and Bargaining in Brussels

The fifteen states that make up the European Union undoubtedly constitute a pluralistic security community. The main indicators of such a security community, the lack of targeted military capabilities or military plans, are to be found in these states as well as in North America. But whereas Canada, Mexico, and the United States are in no process of economic or political integration, and possess no institutions with supranational powers, France, Germany, Italy, and the Benelux countries created an organization that does possess such powers. In 1967, the three main institutions of European economic integration—the Common Market, the Coal and Steel Community, and Euratom—were combined into one organization, the European Community (EC). In 1993 it became the European Union. Although the members still conduct most of their foreign and defense policies independently or within NATO, commercial life proceeds under regulations and policies developed by the EU.

The main institutions of the EU combine features of both ordinary intergovernmental organizations such as NATO or the United Nations, where the members negotiate and bargain with each other until they can reach some kind of settlement or common policy, and a type of supranational organization, where international civil servants, not responsible to any one government, possess some authority to make binding decisions over member states and their citizens. In the EU, some decisions made by the member governments are reached through majority votes; policies resulting from these votes are binding on all members, including those who oppose them. In the United Nations, on the other hand, no state is compelled to accept or implement decisions reached in the organization relating to pacific settlement of disputes and conflicts. The European Union possesses institutions that themselves administer a common policy; to implement these policies, they are not dependent, in many cases, on national administrative structures, although these necessarily have to cooperate. It has some direct authority over citizens and corporations within the member states and may enforce its policies by bringing suit or levying fines against individuals or corporations that do not conform to the policies established by the organization.

The institutions of the EU that possess these mixed characteristics of intergovernmental and supranational powers include the following:

1. The executive Commission is made up of technical experts appointed by common agreement among the member governments, and responsible only to the organization. They initiate policy recommendations and administer those policies that have been approved by the member governments. Members of the Commission also sit in on all meetings of the Council of Ministers, and represent the viewpoint of the Union.
2. The Council of Ministers, attended by national representatives, has the final authority to formulate and approve common policies, and to bargain with other member states. It is analogous to a national legislature.

3. The European Council, meeting three times yearly, is attended by the heads of government of members. These are informal meetings, but often important decisions are taken, and it often serves as a useful device for resolving impasses in the Council of Ministers.
4. The Assembly, made up of representatives elected by popular vote, has the authority to discuss and review the policies and actions of the Commission and the Council of Ministers.
5. The Court of Justice of the communities reviews the legality of Commission and Council decisions and disposes of legal cases arising under the founding treaties. It considers conflicts brought by governments against each other, by governments against the Commission, and by individuals or business enterprises against the Commission. By 1990, the Court had disposed of more than 6,000 cases involving individual, intergovernmental, and organizational matters.

The pattern of decision making and collaboration within the Commission and the Council of Ministers is complex and involves work by hundreds of bureaucrats, both national and international. Typically, the Commission will begin planning rules, regulations, and directives that give effect to the goal of economic integration. In making up the multitude of proposals, members of the Commission consult with the Permanent Representatives of the member states, who are all located in Brussels. The Permanent Representatives report to their own governments and naturally consult extensively with their own bureaucrats in the national capital. The Permanent Representatives defend national points of view, but, as they are intimately connected with all the affairs of the Union, they often urge their own governments to support the Commission's point of view as well. When the long process of consultation has been completed and a coherent set of proposals emerges, the Commission presents them to the Council of Ministers, comprising the foreign, economics, agriculture, finance, or trade ministers of the member states. The Commission sits in the Council as a sort of thirteenth member, except that it represents the viewpoint of the Union, not that of any member state. It can argue in favor of its proposals, make new proposals, or act as a mediator should some of the ministers find themselves in a deadlock.

Voting in the Council of Ministers is complicated. Most decisions are based on qualified majorities, based on a system of weighted voting (for example, France has more votes than Luxembourg or Belgium). In other cases, unanimity is required. The important point is that theoretically most decisions of the Council can be taken against the will of one or more of the governments—although, as we will see, the informal "code" of operation in the Council requires the ministers to reach an agreement acceptable to all. De Gaulle's vetoes on Britain's entry to the Common Market in 1963 and 1967, his threat to withdraw from the institutions of the EC in 1966, and Prime Minister Thatcher's showdown over British fees to the Community in 1980 were serious breaches of the normal pattern of decision making. Most policy for the Union is made through the slow and difficult process of fashioning an overall consensus through persuasion, presentation of evidence, and documentation of need.

Certain assumptions, traditions, and unwritten rules govern the settlement of problems, the pattern of collaboration, or the fashioning of new policies. Most proposals reaching the Council of Ministers involve losses and gains for the member states. Each minister will naturally attempt to see that the final outcome reflects the interests of his or her government to the maximum extent possible. But unlike negotiations in a violent conflict, where the basic issue is a settlement or the continuation of conflict, the negotiators in the Council of Ministers start with an implicit agreement that a final decision must be the end result; they assume that mutual concessions must be made, since the normal practice is to exclude the possibility of not reaching an agreement at all. Moreover, in the lengthy discussions, a built-in mediator is always present. The Commission constantly represents the views of the Union, and because it is armed with technical expertise and an aura of legitimacy, it is in a position to influence the bargaining positions of the member states. Ministers are more apt to make concessions and to justify those concessions to their home governments, if they are made in the name of the Union rather than, for example, of another state such as Germany or Luxembourg. The Commission, in sum, is in a strong position to overcome strictly national imperatives.

Moreover, most issues are dealt with as "problems." That is, solutions can be based on data, the elucidation of needs, and the application of technology. Ideological principles seldom color the bargaining that takes place within the European Council, Council of Ministers, or between the Commission and the Permanent Representatives. Thus, decisions and settlements are based less on the power, prestige, capabilities, or reputation of member states than on the objectives of the organization and the most convincing needs of its members. On many issues before the Council, French ministers have reduced their demands to accommodate the Netherlands, and on other issues, the Germans or Italians have retreated from their bargaining positions in order to placate the Belgians. In other words, no government consistently gains or withdraws from its objectives because it is economically or militarily weak or strong.

The bargaining that goes on within the Council of Ministers offers a dramatic contrast to the formality, coldness, and vituperation that goes on in negotiations between hostile states. According to Lindberg, the ministers generally display considerable sensitivity toward the needs of other member states. The atmosphere is informal, in part because the ministers know each other well and are, in some cases, personal friends. Long, formal speeches are rare; banter and jokes are often in evidence. There seems to be an awareness that the ministers are working on a common problem, one in which compromise is expected from all sides in order to obtain a Union solution.[7] If agreement cannot be fashioned, the proposals or projects are normally returned to the Commission for reworking. The Commission then reestablishes contact with the Permanent Representatives, or with national bureaucrats, and irons out the remaining problems.

The European Union, then, features a complex mixture of traditional interstate policies, an established pluralistic security community, and in some policy sectors such as agriculture, an integrated political organism that effectively shares pol-

---

[7]Leon Lindberg, *Political Dynamics of European Economic Integration* (Stanford, Calif.: Stanford University Press, 1963), pp. 76–77.

icy making and administering authority with the member states. The Union, on its own authority, administers some policies across all members, issues regulations (such as standardization of safety features on automobiles), and monitors their compliance. Its executive role includes management of internal policies (the common agricultural policy) and the operation of policies on behalf of the EU vis-à-vis third countries on questions of trade.

What are all these negotiations about? What are the costs and benefits to individual countries? The ultimate purpose of the European Union remains contested. For some, it is to create a United States of Europe; that is, a federal structure in which there would be a single European policy in a number of areas such as trade, defense, foreign relations, currency, citizenship, and the like. Each member country would retain its separate identity for some policy areas (local taxes, immigration, sports fishing) but would delegate authority to the Union in most other areas. Others see ultimately a more confederative structure, in which separate states delegate to the Union authority in specified areas, mostly agriculture and commerce, but reserve for themselves the ultimate authority in all Union legislation and regulation. There would be a "pooling" of sovereignty in specified areas, but not a formal delegation of authority in the sense that any particular government would lose its ultimate right to stay out of various Union arrangements.

While long-term goals of the Union remain under debate, there is a consensus going back to the original Treaty of Rome (1957) that Europe must create a single economic market. This means that for all practical purposes, all the barriers to trade within the Union (frontiers, customs, different laws on banking, currency, health and welfare regulations) must be removed. In a 1988 report, the EC estimated that the various barriers to free trade among the twelve countries cost about $200 billion annually, or about 5 percent of the EC's gross domestic product. Such costs drastically reduce the efficiency of commerce.

Again, we encounter the logic of *reducing costs and increasing efficiencies.* Various treaties, including Maastricht (1991), are designed to eliminate these barriers and to promote further standardization and harmonization of national policies and practices. Among the thousands of acts, regulations, and agreements are those eliminating frontier customs posts (a major headache for truckers and airline travelers); instituting harmonization of health standards, product components, minimum wages, and holidays for workers, and such things as classification of restaurants and hotels. As an example, a car produced in Germany will no longer have different kinds of headlights or seat belts for exports to France, England, or Italy. There is now a single "Euro-headlight" and "Euro-seat belt"; obviously, the cost of car production will decline to the extent that there is no longer a need to differentiate components according to different markets.

For individuals, mobility increases dramatically. Now Italian lawyers and doctors can practice in Belgium. Spanish factory workers can move to wherever job opportunities exist. Indeed, even in theory a Greek civil servant can apply for a job in the Dutch agricultural ministry.

The European Union thus seeks to maximize the free flow of goods, people, ideas, money (investment), all in the name of dramatically increasing economic efficiency. But beyond the unified market, there is not yet a common currency, nor common defense and foreign policies. In these realms, policy coordination rather than integration is the rule.

While we can speak only in a very limited sense of a "Community Foreign Policy," in some areas, the members of the EU have come to expect that they will not individually take major foreign policy initiatives or stake out final positions without consultations. The efforts at harmonization have been impressive. At the Conference on Security and Cooperation in Europe (CSCE), the delegations of the EC countries met regularly and developed common policies in the negotiations. In 1980, the EC members developed a "European Initiative" on the Middle East to demonstrate to the Arab world the difference between European and American approaches to the Arab-Israel conflict. In 1986, the foreign ministers of the EC countries hammered out a common set of limited economic sanctions against Syria, in response to the latter's involvement in terrorist activities. On questions of foreign aid to Africa, trade agreements with third parties, and economic relations with Eastern Europe, policy harmonization has become the rule rather than the exception. On other issues, however, the members have been unable to develop a common policy. Nowhere was this more evident than in 1992–1994 during the Bosnian war. While the Community was attempting to work out a common policy whereby individual members would extend diplomatic recognition to Croatia and Bosnia only if those governments would agree to respect human rights and guarantee the rights of minorities, Germany acted on its own and granted unconditional recognition. This step helped to lead to the disastrous war in Bosnia, the factions there anticipating that they could go to war and follow "ethnic cleansing" policies without general European condemnation. Once the war began, the European countries could not agree on steps to take beyond supporting United Nations relief operations and an economic embargo of Serbia, the main sanctuary and supporter of the Bosnian Serbs.

While the negotiations between members to establish new policies for the Union are extremely complicated and feature many of the characteristics of traditional bargaining and distributive politics, there are also a number of characteristics of the Union that distinguish it from ordinary bilateral relationships. Among these is the legitimacy and influence accorded to the Commission, the guardian of the Union ethos, the extent to which technical information is brought to bear on negotiations, the disinclination to use the veto (contentious matters are often put on the back burner rather than vetoed), the extension of the Union administrative capacity, and the successful harmonization of the members' foreign policies on some key world issues.

The European Union is a unique format for international collaboration. It is at once an intergovernmental organization, a supranational institution with direct monitoring and enforcement powers over the citizens and commercial firms of member states, and an organic agency that charts and oversees the creation of a single economic market throughout Western Europe.

Does this mean the end of national governments? By no means. They will continue to develop and enforce national policies; but increasingly, there will be strong forces compelling them to harmonize those policies according to Union standards.

Social welfare and taxation policies will either have to become similar, or there will be large population migrations to take advantage of those members who, for example, provide the highest unemployment insurance rates, or whose income tax rates are the lowest. Since the Treaty of Rome that established the Common Market, we have seen the gradual emergence not of a superstate, nor the demise of the traditional European states, but some entirely new entity that almost defies categorization. But from the point of view of international collaboration, the important point is that within a historically short period of time, Western Europe has evolved from a scene of frequent warfare to a zone of peace, where armed forces no longer play a role in adjusting the mutual relations of fifteen countries.

Conclusion

On certain kinds of issues governments effectively collaborate to increase economic, communications, and transportation efficiency; to regulate or control problems that pose common threats to states and societies; and to develop means of conducting predictably peaceful relationships. In some regions the habits of cooperation have become deeply engrained, resulting in pluralistic security communities. But pluralistic security communities are not yet a global phenomenon. They exist in North America, Western Europe, Scandinavia, and a few other regions of the world. Regrettably, there is scant evidence that regions such as the Middle East, the Balkans, or Africa are moving in the same direction. In those areas of the world, security problems will continue to be a source of international instability, war, mass refugee movements, and domestic turmoil. Many of the states remain weak in the sense of being fractured by communal and ethnic conflicts, government repression, secessionist movements, and the like. It is primarily these internal problems that will fuel future armed conflicts.

But we must remember that most of the states in these areas of the world are very young; many are states mostly in name, and not in the fact of social cohesiveness. When the states of Europe were being formed in the seventeenth to nineteenth centuries, they too suffered from chronic instability, rebellion, revolution, and war. It has taken hundreds of wars in Europe since 1648 to come to the point where, as in the European Union, the member countries have learned to live in peace with one another. We may hope that some day the characteristics that remain unique to the few pluralistic security communities in the world will become universal. It would seem that the building or evolution of strong states (again, not in the military sense) is one of the prerequisites for such a development.

While these long historical processes are taking place, governments still have to face the immediate problems posed by population and economic growth and their resulting costs: global pollution, overpopulation, economic refugees, desertification, resource depletion, and the like. Governments have made great headway in fashioning international regimes to cope with some of them. But the processes of aggregation and combination seem to move ahead faster than the capacity of governments to deal with them. Through the construction of international regimes, we have been able to make great strides in increasing efficiency and generating wealth. But the paradox that we all face in the future is that in the process of making our lives filled with greater opportunities and well-being, we create new kinds of problems that seriously degrade the accomplishments.

The subject of this book—how and why states act in certain ways—is not likely to be overtaken by events. The processes of establishing goals, conducting diplomacy and bargaining, formulating policies, and engaging in conflict and collaboration will look much the same as they have for generations. What will change is the nature of the international agenda. While old kinds of issues—war and peace, for example—will not go away, we are constantly adding new kinds of issues. Thirty years ago, no one had heard of AIDS. Today, it is a universal problem. Deforestation goes back as far as the ancient Mediterranean civilizations, but because of simple technology and primitive transportation modes, its consequences were limited primarily to the immediately affected regions. Today, the scale and speed at which these problems multiply or expand are alarming. Governments are compelled to take action, and increasingly it will have to be on a collaborative basis. It remains to be seen whether the lengthy processes of diplomatic negotiations, regime construction, and international monitoring will be adequate.

Questions for Study, Analysis, and Discussion

1. List some of the ways that your life or lifestyle is enhanced as a result of collaborative arrangements between governments.
2. What are the main sources of international collaboration?
3. In what ways do the processes of aggregation and combination create global problems? How do your daily activities contribute to these problems?
4. Define an international regime and provide examples.
5. Distinguish between strong and weak international regimes, and provide examples of each kind.
6. What are the indicators of a "pluralistic security community"?
7. Describe the typical policy-making process in the European Union.
8. Should the EU become a superstate based on the American model, or a confederation of sovereign states that delegates power to Brussels only to create a common market?

Selected Bibliography

Axelrod, Robert, *The Evolution of Cooperation.* New York: Basic Books, 1984.

Caldwell, Lynton K., *International Environmental Policy: Emergence and Dimensions.* 2nd ed. Durham, N.C.: Duke University Press, 1990.

Carroll, John E., *International Environmental Diplomacy.* New York: Cambridge University Press, 1988.

Deutsch, Karl W., *Political Community at the International Level: Problems of Definition and Measurement.* Garden City, N.Y.: Doubleday, 1954.

———, *et al., Political Community and the North Atlantic Area.* Princeton N.J.: Princeton University Press, 1957.

Dinan, Desmond, *Ever Closer Union? An Introduction to the European Community.* Boulder, Colo.: Lynne Rienner, 1994.

Donnelly, Jack, Universal Human Rights in Theory and Practice. Ithaca, N.Y.: Cornell University Press, 1989.

Fox, W. T. R., A Continent Apart: The United States and Canada in World Politics. Toronto: University of Toronto Press, 1985.

George, Stephen, Politics and Policy in the European Community, 2nd ed. London: Oxford University Press, 1991.

Groom, A. J. R., and Paul Taylor, eds., International Institutions at Work. London: Pinter, 1988.

Haas, Peter, ed., "Knowledge, Power, and International Policy Coordination," special issue of *International Organization,* 46 (Winter 1992).

Keohane, Robert O., After Hegemony; Cooperation and Discord in the World Political Economy, Princeton, N.J.: Princeton University Press, 1984.

———, *and Stanley Hoffmann, eds., The New European Community: Decision Making and Institutional Change.* Boulder, Colo.: Westview Press, 1991.

Krasner, Stephen D., ed., International Regimes, Ithaca, N.Y.: Cornell University Press, 1983.

Laffan, Brigid, Integration and Cooperation in Europe. London: Routledge, 1992.

Matthews, Jessica Tuchman, ed., Preserving the Global Environment. New York: W. W. Norton, 1991.

Miller, Lynn H., Global Order: Values and Power in International Politics. Boulder, Colo.: Westview Press, 1985.

Milner, Helen, "International Theories of Cooperation Among Nations: Strengths and Weaknesses," *World Politics,* 44 (April 1992), 466–96.

Nugent, Neill, The Government and Politics of the European Community, 2nd ed. London: Macmillan, 1991.

Olson, Mancur, The Logic of Collective Action. Cambridge, Mass.: Harvard University Press, 1965.

Ostrom, Elinor, Governing the Commons: The Evolution of Institutions for Collective Action. Cambridge: Cambridge University Press, 1990.

Oye, Kenneth, ed., Cooperation under Anarchy. Princeton, N.J.: Princeton University Press, 1985.

Pinder, John, European Community: The Building of a Union. London: Oxford University Press, 1991.

Porter, Gareth, and Janet Welsh Brown, Global Environmental Politics. Boulder, Colo.: Westview Press, 1991.

Rosenau, James N., and Ernst-Otto Czempiel, eds., Governance without Government: Order and Change in World Politics. Cambridge: Cambridge University Press, 1992.

Scott, Andrew, The Dynamics of Interdependence. Chapel Hill: University of North Carolina Press, 1982.

Sidjanski, Dusan, L'Avenir Fédéraliste de l'Europe: La Communauté Européenne des Origines au Traité de Maastricht. Paris: Presses Universitaires de France, 1992.

Young, Oran, International Cooperation: Building Regimes for Natural Resources and the Environment. Ithaca, N.Y.: Cornell University Press, 1989.

Index